Persistence Pays

NATURAL RESOURCE MANAGEMENT AND POLICY

EDITORIAL STATEMENT

There is a growing awareness of the role that natural resources such as water, land, forests and environmental amenities play in our lives. There are many competing uses for natural resources, and society is challenged to manage them to improve social well being. Furthermore, there may be dire consequences to natural resources mismanagement. Renewable resources such as water, land and the environment are linked, and decisions made with regard to one may affect the others. Policy and management of natural resources now require an interdisciplinary approach including natural and social sciences to correctly address our societal preferences.

This series provides a collection of works containing the most recent findings on economics, management and policy of renewable biological resources such as water, land, crop protection, sustainable agriculture, technology, and environmental health. It incorporates modern thinking and techniques of economics and management, Books in this series will combine knowledge and models of natural phenomena with economics and managerial decision frameworks to assess alternative options for managing natural resources and the environment.

The Series Editors

For other titles published in this series, go to
www.springer.com/series/6360

Julian M. Alston • Matthew A. Andersen
Jennifer S. James • Philip G. Pardey

Persistence Pays

U.S. Agricultural Productivity Growth and the Benefits from Public R&D Spending

Springer

Julian M. Alston
Department of Agricultural
and Resource Economics
University of California, Davis
1 Shields Avenue
Davis, CA 95616-8512
USA
julian@primal.ucdavis.edu

Matthew A. Andersen
Department of Agricultural and Applied Economics
University of Wyoming
1000 E. University Avenue
Laramie, WY 82071
USA
mander60@uwyo.edu

Jennifer S. James
Department of Agribusiness
California Polytechnic State University
San Luis Obispo, CA 93407
USA
jsjames@calpoly.edu

Philip G. Pardey
Department of Applied Economics
University of Minnesota
1994 Buford Avenue
St. Paul, MN 55108
USA
ppardey@umn.edu

ISBN 978-1-4419-0657-1 e-ISBN 978-1-4419-0658-8
DOI 10.1007/978-1-4419-0658-8
Springer New York Dordrecht Heidelberg London

Library of Congress Control Number: 2009941307

Printed on acid-free paper

Springer is part of Springer Science+Business Media (www.springer.com)

This book was many years in the making. In different ways and at different times along the way we received advice, inspiration, and encouragement from many friends and colleagues. We owe a particular intellectual debt and personal thanks to Zvi Griliches (1930–1999), Bruce Gardner (1942–2008) and Vernon Ruttan (1924–2008). This book is dedicated to their memory.

Advance Praise for *Persistence Pays*

Persistence Pays is a definitive source book on the economics of agricultural R&D in the United States. The topical coverage is impressively comprehensive, ranging from discussion of the historical development of U.S. agriculture and U.S. agricultural research policy, through a quantification of the patterns of production and input use, to econometric models of R&D and productivity and their implications. The treatment of particular themes is careful and instructive. The authors provide new, detailed, state-level data on both agricultural R&D investments and productivity, along with a critical survey and review of relevant measures, methods, and models, before presenting brand-new econometric results. These new results refine and extend past work in the area, reinforcing many of the past findings about the high social returns to agricultural research and the persistent patterns of underinvestment. The book has significant technical content that will be primarily of interest to other economists both in the classroom and in research applications, but it is also readily accessible to research administrators and policy makers, well beyond the United States, who wish to understand the links between public research policy, agriculture, and the economy.

—Jock R. Anderson. Emeritus Professor of Agricultural Economics at the University of New England, Armidale, Australia, and Adviser, Agriculture and Rural Development, World Bank, Washington, DC.

This is a sophisticated book on a critically important subject. Many people have talked about the importance of public R&D in propelling the growth in American agricultural productivity but there has been scant hard evidence on the issue. Alston, Andersen, James, and Pardey rectify this deficiency with a brilliant book that represents a major contribution to our understanding of technological change—this is the new gold standard in the field. Their achievement is multidimensional—they carefully construct new state-level data series on the quantity and quality of agricultural inputs and outputs, they offer a wealth of information on the institutions and functioning of the public agricultural research system, and they employ well-conceived models and state-of-the-art econometrics to tease out the effects of R&D expenditures on productivity growth. In the process they provide entirely new insights into myriad issues such as the extent of research spillovers, the nature of the lags in R&D investments, and the extent of the policy failures since the 1970s giving rise to a slowdown in farm productivity in the past 10–20 years.

—Alan L. Olmstead. Distinguished Research Professor, Department of Economics, University of California, Davis and co-author of *Creating Abundance: Biological Innovation and American Agricultural Development*, Cambridge University Press, 2008

This book presents new solid empirical evidence about the past, current and required future role of research and innovations to prepare U.S. agriculture to meet future domestic and international food demand in a sustainable manner. The economic rates of return are high and spillovers across states are large. The authors make a strong and well-supported case for expanding federal funding for agricultural research. Global food demand is likely to double over the next 50 years. Given the long time lag between research investments and productivity gains, documented in this book, and the recent global food crisis, expanded investments are long overdue. Policy-makers, advisors and analysts should pay attention to the findings reported in this book and take appropriate action now to stop the current trend of decreasing rates of productivity growth.

—Per Pinstrup-Andersen. H. E. Babcock Professor of Food, Nutrition and Public Policy, J. Thomas Clark Professor of Entrepreneurship, and Professor of Applied Economics at Cornell University; and Professor of Agricultural Economics at Copenhagen University. World Food Prize Laureate, 2001

Foreword by Norman Borlaug

The invention of agriculture heralded the dawn of civilization. Through the domestication of plant and animal species, and subsequent productivity improvements which began with irrigation, humankind has moved from a hand-to-mouth existence to one in which surplus food supplies permitted the establishment of permanent settlements and urban societies which, in turn, engendered culture, science, and technology. The rise and fall of ancient civilizations in the Middle East and Meso-America were closely tied to successes and failures in agriculture. It behooves us to remember that this axiom remains valid today. Indeed, without abundant and stable food supplies we cannot hope to achieve and sustain global peace and prosperity.

The United States today is the world's second-largest producer of agricultural products and the world's largest agricultural exporter. The success story of American agriculture is not accidental, nor is it exclusively due to natural resource endowments. Rather, it is the result of investments in agricultural education, research, and extension; mechanization and transport; fertilizers; irrigation; energy; credit; stimulatory agricultural policies; and lastly, but certainly not least, extremely productive farmers and ranchers.

The success of American agriculture owes much to the agricultural institutions and policies first established nearly one century and a half ago. In 1862 President Lincoln signed into law three bills that played a vital role in raising the U.S. to its preeminent position: The Homestead Act, which made relatively large (at the time) tracts of land on the frontier available to persons who committed themselves to living on the property and developing it; a law establishing the U.S. Department of Agriculture; and the Morrill Act, which established publicly supported land-grant colleges of agriculture and mechanical arts in every state. These laws later were supplemented in 1887 by the Hatch Act, which provided for the establishment of agricultural experiment stations, as well as closer collaboration between the agricultural colleges and USDA, by the Smith-Lever Act in 1914, which established the cooperative extension service, charged with introducing new technology to farm and ranch families; and by the Smith-Hughes Action in 1917, which established vocational agriculture programs in high schools.

The significance of these institutional developments cannot be over-emphasized. They truly revolutionized agricultural production in the United States, and had many positive spillover effects around the world. Indeed, few industries have been as productive and innovative as agriculture during much of the 20th Century. The quantity, quality, and availability of food have increased manyfold, and real food prices have steadily declined. Today, less than 1 percent of the U.S. population is directly engaged in primary agricultural production, yet American farmers are able to provide consumers with an abundant, high-quality and safe food supply at a low cost while still maintaining a strong position in world markets.

American farmers and ranchers not only have been able to increase agricultural production many-fold through the application of science and technology, I contend that they have also been able to achieve these production feats in ways that have helped conserve the environment, not destroy it. For example, had the U.S. agricultural technology of 1940—when relatively little chemical fertilizer and agricultural chemicals were used—still persisted today we would have needed an additional 675 million acres of agricultural lands—of the same quality—to equal the 2006–07 output of roughly 800 million tons for the 17 main food and fiber crops produced in the United States.

Put another way, thanks to the agricultural productivity increases made possible through research and new technology development since 1990, an area greater than all the land in the 26 states east of the Mississippi River, has been spared for other uses. Imagine the environmental disaster that would have occurred if hundreds of millions of environmentally fragile acres, not suited to farming, had been ploughed up and brought into production. Think of the soil erosion, loss of forests and grasslands, and biodiversity, and extinction of wildlife species that would have ensued!

During the past two decades, U.S. public agricultural research funding, in real terms, has stagnated, as has support to international agricultural research. U.S. private sector agricultural research funding has followed a similar pattern. If these trends continue, we risk losing the broad continuum of agricultural research, from the more basic to the more applied and practical, needed to keep agriculture moving forward.

In an earlier day, public sector institutions—mainly the U.S. Land Grant Universities and the USDA's Agricultural Research Service, were concerned with this full gamut. But with the advent of hybrids and modern varieties, and crop protection chemicals, private companies became more and more involved in applied research activities in which the marketplace will enable them to capture a return on their investments. As the scope and quantity of private sector agricultural research has expanded, publicly funded research has tended to shift away from farm productivity oriented R&D, with longer payback periods to society, and where the private sector cannot easily capture directly the benefits from the investments.

Private sector research, which tends to be more narrow and short term, and public sector research, which can be broader and longer term, complement each other, and should not be seen as competitive. It is important to maintain a healthy balance between the two and strong and growing support for both.

Science-based agriculture is really a 20th Century invention. Until the 19th Century, crop improvement was in the hands of farmers and food production and was largely increased by expanding the cultivated land areas. Improvements in farm machinery expanded the size of a farm that could be cultivated by one family. Machinery also made possible better seedbed preparation, conservation and utilization of moisture, and improved planting practices and weed control, resulting in modest increases in yield per hectare.

By the mid-1930s, much of the scientific knowledge needed for high-yield agriculture was available in the United States. However, its utilization was delayed due to the Great Economic Depression. It was not until WWII brought a great demand for food that the new research findings began to be applied widely. In no crop has this modernization process been more evident than in maize (corn). In 1940, U.S. farmers produced 56 million tons of maize on roughly 31 million hectares, with an average yield of 1.8 tons per hectare. In 2007, U.S. farmers produced 331 million tons of maize on roughly 35 million hectares, with an average yield of 9.5 tons per hectare. This more than five-fold yield increase—which continues to grow—is the impact of modern seed-fertilizer-weed-pest control technology!

Most agricultural increases over the next several decades will have to come from lands already in production through yield improvements. Fortunately, productivity improvements in crop management can be made all along the line—in plant breeding, crop management, tillage, water use, fertilization, weed and pest control, and harvesting.

By 2050, we will likely need to double current crop production again. This cannot be done unless farmers across the world have access to high-yielding crop production methods and new biotechnological breakthroughs that can increase the crop yields, dependability, and nutritional quality.

To meet projected food, feed, and fiber demands will require breakthroughs in both conventional and transgenic breeding to raise the maximum genetic yield potential of the major food crop species. Without increased investments in agricultural research and technology development it is unlikely that we will achieve adequate growth in agricultural production, and certainly not in environmentally sustainable ways.

While we must continue to push the frontiers of science forward, we also must be mindful of the need to protect the gains already made. Agriculture is a continuing struggle against mutating pathogens and insects. A clear example is the new race of stem rust that has emerged in East Africa, which is capable of devastating most of the world's commercial bread wheat varieties.

I commend the authors of this path-breaking book. It is an extraordinarily comprehensive analytical review of the benefits from public research and development spending on U.S. agricultural productivity growth. The story looking back is of remarkable returns to investment. The story going forward is one of faltering agricultural productivity gains, almost surely due to a slowdown in the growth of farm productivity oriented agricultural R&D in America. Unless these disturbing trends change, the future adequacy of U.S. and global food supplies is in jeopardy.

July 4, 2009

Norman E. Borlaug (1914–2009)
Founder, the World Food Prize
1970 Nobel Peace Prize Laureate

Acknowledgments

The series of projects that evolved into this book began at least fifteen years ago, possibly twenty. It had its initial genesis in the IR-6 regional research project, led by W. Burt Sunquist, funded by the USDA. Over time the group of participants evolved along with the focus, which was initially U.S. agriculture in aggregate. Barbara Craig and W. Burt Sundquist participated in early elements of that work which helped set the scene for the work in the past decade. The data for the analysis has also been revised and updated several times including two major revisions to incorporate results from censuses in 1996 and 2002, and a number of other revisions. The current form of the project, with its current participants and use of state-level data ending in 2002, took shape in the early 2000s as we faced up to yet one more major revision of the data to bring it up to 2002 (and at the time of writing we are engaged in further updating to 2007). In the course of a project of such long duration we have benefited from discussions with many colleagues in formal and informal settings, we have been supported by funding from a variety of sources, we have received help with data and other resources, and we have employed a large number of research assistants. We are grateful for all of this help and we do our best here to remember and acknowledge all of those who contributed significantly, one way or another, to the elements of the work that ended up in this book.

Much of the work has entailed data grubbing and we have employed many graduate students at Davis and Minnesota, some postdoctoral fellows, and others along the way to assist with these aspects. We are grateful for research assistance provided by Jason Beddow, Connie Chan-Kang, Steve Dehmer, Klaus Deininger, Michelle Hallaway, Lousie Letnes, Sydney Pardey, and Sue Pohlod, all at the University of Minnesota as well as Albert Acquaye, Theresa Bauer, Jason Christian, Kate Fuller, Joanna Parks, Nick Piggott, T J Wyatt, Bin Zhang, and Mingxia Zhang all at the University of California, Davis. Some assistance was also provided by staff at the International Service for National Agricultural Research (ISNAR) and the International Food Policy Research Institute (IFPRI), including Nienke Beintema and Patricia Zambrano. Some people who assisted must be singled out for individual recognition. Chief among these is Connie

Chan-Kang, who contributed hundreds of hours to the data development and analysis behind Chapters 2 through 7. Steve Dehmer contributed significantly to the development of parts of Chapters 6, especially in relation to general funding for R&D and private agricultural R&D, and Jason Beddow helped compile some of the historical evidence presented in Chapters 2 and 3. A team of Cal Poly Agribusiness students, led by Samantha Stokman, ran the simulations for the meta-analysis in Chapter 12. Sue Pohlod provided general secretarial support and assisted in particular with documentation of the references. Michelle Hallaway carefully proofread and checked the entire manuscript to make sure the details of cited references were complete and accurate and matched the list of references.

Several people helped us obtain access to various sources of unpublished data and other information. Dennis Unglesbee, Allen Moore, and Ed Kane from the USDA furnished access to CRIS data files. They were also generous with their knowledge about the details of these data sets that proved especially helpful for developing measures of research spending and intensities in Chapters 6 and 7, and stocks of knowledge used throughout Part IV of the book. Erich Sachs of Monsanto and Nicholas Kalaitzandonakes of the University of Missouri provided advice and information about the release and adoption of biotech crop varieties. John Smylie and the Association of Equipment Manufacturers provided us with sales data on tractors and combines, which we used to estimate capital service flows.

The work here is inspired by and seeks to build on prior work by Zvi Griliches, Vernon Ruttan, and Robert Evenson, in particular, among a long list of others. As well as drawing on their written work, we have benefited from their comments and advice about how to improve the work. In the context of presentations of elements of the ongoing work at various conferences and seminars, and in less-formal settings, we have also benefited from discussions with many other colleagues including (in alphabetical order): Jock Anderson, Kym Anderson, John Antle, Walt Armbruster, Eldon Ball, Nicole Ballenger, Ron Bewley, Mary Bohman, John Brennan, Steven Buccola, Derek Byerlee, Jim Chalfant, Jean-Paul Chavas, Tom Cox, Jeff Davis, Dana Dalrymple, John Dillon, Robert Dixon, Ruben Echeverría, Geoff Edwards, Shenggen Fan, Brian Fisher, John Freebairn, Lilyan Fulginiti, Keith Fuglie, Murray Fulton, George Frisvold, Bruce Gardner, Dinos Giannakas, Richard Gray, Terry Hurley, Wally Huffman, Frank Jarrett, Richard Just, Nicholas Kalaitzandonakes, Bruce Kefford, John Kerin, Yoav Kislev, Bonwoo Koo, Frikkie Liebenberg, Bob Lindner, Alan Lloyd, Michele Marra, Will Martin, Alex McCalla, Ian McLean, Catherine Morrison-Paul, John Mullen, Bob Myers, George Norton, John O'Connor, Chris O'Donnell, Alan Olmstead, Richard Perrin, Willis Peterson, Roley Piggott, Prabhu Pingali, Carl Pray, Per Pinstrup-Andersen, Gordon Rausser, Paul Rhode, Bob Richardson, Rick Roush, Scott Rozelle, Jim Ryan, David Schimmelpfennig, Andy Schmitz, Ed Schuh, Grant Scobie, Robbin Shoemaker, Vince Smith, Daniel Sumner, Michael Taylor, Colin Thirtle, Wally Thurman, Kien Tran, Greg Traxler, Alistair Watson, Mike

Wohlgenant, Stan Wood, Brian Wright, and David Zilberman. We thank these friends and colleagues for their advice and assistance, and do not absolve them entirely from responsibility for some of what we have done and written.

This project required significant institutional and financial support. Primary sources of partial support were the University of California, the University of Minnesota, and the U.S. Department of Agriculture. Additional support came from the Farm Foundation, the University of Wyoming, California Polytechnic and State University, and the Department of Primary Industries in Victoria, Australia. Elements of support from the University of California came through the Department of Agricultural and Resource Economics, the College of Agriculture and Environmental Sciences, and the Institute for Governmental Affairs, all at UC Davis, as well as the University of California Agricultural Issues Center, the Division of Agriculture and Natural Resources, and specific grants from the Giannini Foundation of Agricultural Economics, the UC Pacific Rim Research Program, and the UC President's Industry-University Cooperative Research Initiative. Particular individuals who were involved in facilitating that support include Colin Carter, Dan Dooley, Alan Olmstead, Rick Standiford, Daniel Sumner, and Neal van Alfen. Elements of support from the University of Minnesota came through the Department of Applied Economics, the Minnesota Agricultural Experiment Station, the College of Food, Agricultural and Natural Resource Sciences, the Office of the Vice President for Research, and the International Science and Technology Practice and Policy (InSTePP) center. Particular individuals who were involved in facilitating that support include Chuck Muscoplat, Al Levine, Bev Durgan, and Tim Mulcahy. Over the years parts of the work have been funded with grants from various elements of the USDA, including the Economic Research Service, the Agricultural Research Service, and the CSREES National Research Initiative. Several economists at USDA facilitated these grants and provided advice and feedback, including Nicole Ballenger, Mary Bohman, Keith Fuglie, Paul Heisey, Robbin Shoemaker, Susan Offutt, and Kitty Reichelderfer-Smith. It has taken a long time to realize a return on some of these investments of support, and we thank our supporters in California, Minnesota, and elsewhere for their continuing faith and patience.

We undertook to develop camera-ready copy in-house at InSTePP. This would not have been feasible without Amy Praught. Amy took hundreds of pages of manuscript, including dozens of complex figures and tables, and turned them into (slightly fewer) hundreds of book pages, with attention to placement of items, format, fonts, and so on, all of which is meant not to be noticed by the reader. This work requires creativity and precision, which in turn requires painstaking care. Amy combines these qualities with patience and good humor. We also thank our Springer editor, Jon Gurstelle, for his gracious guidance as we brought this work to fruition.

Contents

Tables

Figures

Boxes

PART I

Context

CHAPTER 1

Introduction

Agricultural science policy in the United States has profoundly affected the growth and development of agriculture worldwide, not just in the United States. Over the past 150 years, and especially over the second half of the 20th Century, public investments in agricultural R&D in the United States grew faster than the value of agricultural production. Public spending on agricultural science grew similarly in other more-developed countries, and collectively these efforts, along with private spending, spurred agricultural productivity growth in rich and poor nations alike.

The value of this investment is seldom fully appreciated. The resulting productivity improvements have released labor and other resources for alternative uses—in 1900, 29.2 million Americans (39 percent of the population) were directly engaged in farming compared with just 2.9 million (1.1 percent) today—while making food and fiber more abundant and cheaper. The benefits are not confined to Americans. U.S. agricultural science has contributed with others to growth in agricultural productivity in many other countries as well as the United States. The world's population more than doubled from around 3 billion in 1961 to 6.54 billion in 2006 (U.S. Census Bureau 2009). Over the same period, production of important grain crops (including maize, wheat and rice) almost trebled, such that global per capita grain production was 18 percent higher in 2006. This increase in production came largely from unprecedented increases in yields.[1] Notwithstanding the persistence of chronic hunger for hundreds of millions of people around the world, the absence of a Malthusian nightmare is in significant measure attributable to historically unprecedented improvements in agricultural productivity achieved largely through technological change enabled by investments in agricultural R&D.

1 Pardey et al. (2007, p. 12) noted that "Since 1961, around 78 percent of the increase in [global cereal] production has come from increases in yields, except in Africa where about 60 percent of the gains have come from expanding the area of cultivation."

J.M. Alston et al., *Persistence Pays: U.S. Agricultural Productivity Growth and the Benefits from Public R&D Spending*, Natural Resource Management and Policy 34,
DOI 10.1007/978-1-4419-0658-8_1,

Over the past 20 years or so, several patterns have emerged suggesting that public policymakers around the world may have begun to take continuing agricultural productivity growth for granted, to have decided that it is no longer an important priority, or to have determined that it has become the responsibility of the private sector. With a few notable exceptions, the rate of growth in public agricultural research investments has slowed worldwide (Pardey et al. 2006), and research resources have been progressively diverted away from farm productivity enhancement, with an increased focus on newer, seemingly more-pressing issues related to human health, the environment, food safety, and so on.[2] Agricultural science takes a long time to generate benefits, many of which are broadly distributed and not easy to observe directly. In a world where people, and particularly policymakers, seem increasingly impatient (and, perhaps, short-sighted) and demanding immediate outcomes, it is easy to understand why investing in agricultural science has lost some of its political appeal.

Perhaps reflecting the past redirection of research resources, in the 1990s some early warning signs of a slowdown of agricultural productivity growth became visible in the United States (and also in some other countries, including Australia, Canada and the United Kingdom).[3] If such a slowdown were to be sustained and widespread, the long-term consequences for the world's poor could be tragic. As in the case of other global public goods such as the mitigation of air and water pollution, the full social costs of today's agricultural R&D policies could take many years to become apparent but the effects will last for decades and might be difficult to reverse.

More recently, the global commodity market boom of 2006–2008 has drawn attention to agricultural productivity and resource scarcity, but perhaps in a way that may not lead to the right agricultural R&D policy solution. The boom in grain prices—associated with high oil prices, exacerbated by the U.S. government's biofuels policy—may have reminded people in rich and poor countries alike that resources for producing agricultural commodities are scarce and agricultural productivity is valuable. But the discussion of the Research Title of the U.S. Farm Bill in late 2007 and early 2008 did not promise a significant reinforcement of the national investment in farm productivity enhancement. Instead, the emphasis has shifted to biofuels research.

This book is predicated on the notions that (a) public investments in agricultural science by the U.S. government have been important for the United States and the world, (b) notwithstanding a significant body of prior scholarly work by economists and others, the payoffs to investment in agricultural research are still poorly understood and little appreciated, and (c) providing information

2 See Pardey, Alston and Piggott (2006) for more discussion of these trends.

3 For instance, see Thirtle et al. (2004), Kokic, Davidson and Boero Rodriguez (2006), Veeman, Unterschultz and Stewart (2007), Zhao et al. (2008) and Alston, Babcock and Pardey (2009).

about these issues can facilitate better decisions by policymakers about agricultural research investments for the future. To achieve this purpose we have sought to provide a clear, contemporary, convincing and empirically comprehensive assessment of the links between public investments in agricultural science in the United States and agricultural productivity, and the value of the productivity gains relative to the costs of the research that allowed them.

The focus here is on the role of public agricultural R&D, including both state and federal investments. We aim to shed new light on the role of spatial spillovers among states in moderating incentives of individual state governments to invest in public agricultural R&D, and the implications both for the generally observed tendency towards an underinvestment in agricultural R&D and for appropriate roles to be undertaken by the federal government to correct the underinvestment problem or to modify the incentives of the states.[4] With this aim in view, we measure the impacts of federal and state-government investments in agricultural research and extension (1900–2002) on productivity and estimated rates of return using state-specific data on U.S. agricultural productivity (1949–2002). We pay particular attention to the specification of the research lag structure (i.e., the temporal aspects of the relationship between knowledge stocks and productivity) and interstate spillovers (i.e., the spatial aspects), and the roles of these and other aspects of the model specification in influencing the findings.

To complete Part I of the book, which sets the scene for the chapters that follow, Chapter 2 presents an overview of the changing structure of farms and farming and the patterns of agricultural input, output and productivity growth in the United States for the past 150 years. This long-run perspective provides context for the more detailed and original data we present in Chapters 3, 4, and 5, respectively concerning agricultural input, output, and productivity patterns over the period 1949–2002 across the 48 contiguous U.S. states. These three chapters comprise Part II of the book. The emphasis is on describing and interpreting the broad trends, although important details of the data and methods used to construct these indexes, and the underlying trends in disaggregated inputs and outputs, are also presented. These indexes reveal important differences among states in the shifting pattern of input use and production over time, but with a consistent pattern among the states indicating a pronounced and widespread slowdown in the rate of productivity growth in the most recent period of our data, which ends in 2002. The productivity slowdown may reflect past shifts in public support for agricultural R&D, and raises concerns about the prospects for coming years.

4 See Ruttan (1980 and 1982) and Pasour and Johnson (1982) for an exchange on the veracity of the underinvestment hypothesis. Much of the Pasour and Johnson critique centers on the accuracy of the evidence of high measured rates of return to agricultural research. Alston et al. (2000a and 2000b) provide a comprehensive cataloging of the literature and undertake a formal meta-analysis of the sources of variation in the measured rates of return. See also Chapters 8 and 9 of this volume.

Part III is devoted to describing agricultural research investments and institutions. Chapter 6 provides an overview of the trends in U.S. agricultural R&D investments, including new, state-specific data on expenditure by the State Agricultural Experiment Stations (SAESs), state-specific expenditure on extension, and intramural research expenditure by the USDA, as well as some details on the sources of the funds. These long-run historical trends for U.S. agricultural R&D are couched in the context of overall R&D spending in the United States and more contemporary trends in agricultural R&D around the world. Entirely new information is also presented on total (including private) funding for agricultural R&D, the changing balance among sources of funding, and changes in the allocation of those funds among different types of research—in particular the shifts of research focus away from farm-level productivity enhancement and towards off-farm aspects of agricultural production, to environmental issues, and to other non-agricultural concerns such as obesity, bio-security, and food safety. Chapter 7 describes the federal role in public agricultural R&D in the United States. It provides a summary history of the changing regulatory (especially intellectual property), institutional and legislative realities that underpinned the trends described in Chapter 6, along with some further detail on the evolving forms of federal funding for research undertaken in the SAESs.

Part IV of the book relates the research investments described in Part III to the productivity patterns documented in Part II. The first two chapters in this part are concerned with modeling issues. Chapter 8 lays out some issues that arise in modeling agricultural R&D lags and agricultural technology spillovers, and ways to address them, and discusses previous work applied to nonagricultural as well as agricultural technologies. Chapter 9 lays out the general theoretical framework for our models of U.S. state-level agricultural productivity. The primary questions revolve around how to represent the multi-dimensional impacts of particular research expenditures on productivity over time (across many years) and space (across 48 contiguous U.S. states); i.e., the specification of the lag structure and the spillover relationships. Our relatively large and rich data base allows us to examine alternative hypotheses about R&D lags. Unlike previous studies that either ignored spillovers or represented them with measures based primarily on spatial proximity, in our model state-to-state spillover effects are represented by an index of output-mix similarity.

Chapter 10 reports the results from estimation of the productivity model developed in Chapter 9, evaluates the implications of alternative specifications, and discusses the interpretation of the estimates. We find in favor of a model that includes longer R&D lags (i.e., up to 50 years) than most previous studies have allowed, with an important role played by R&D spillovers. The main effects are robust across alternative specification choices although particular findings are somewhat sensitive to some of the details of the specification; in particular the functional form of the model matters, and our results support the use of a model with the variables in logarithms rather than in their natural units. The logarithmic specification is predominant in previous work.

In Chapter 11 we use the econometric estimates from Chapter 10 to derive implications and draw inferences for estimates of returns to R&D. First, we report an accounting of the contributions of different elements of research investments to state-level productivity growth. The results indicate that spillover effects are very important. In most states, interstate spillins account for about as much agricultural productivity growth as own-SAES research. This means that estimates can be significantly biased if we omit interstate spillovers from the model of own-SAES effects. It also means that the national social benefits from (or rates of return to) SAES research are much higher than the own-state benefits from (or rates of return to) SAES research that do not count the spillover benefits to other states. Next, we evaluate the state-specific and national benefits from the alternative forms of public investments, which we report as marginal benefit-cost ratios (and, to allow comparisons with other studies, as internal rates of return), and discuss the sensitivity of our findings to model specification choices. Like most previous studies, we find evidence of very large returns to public agricultural research and extension, albeit at the lower end of the range reported in previous work; an outcome that may be attributable to our careful attention to model specification, lag length, spillovers, and the accurate attribution of productivity growth among causes. Finally, we project future productivity growth to 2050 under alternative assumptions about the likely time path of state and federal research and extension spending over the coming decades. The results show that the slowdown in productivity of the 1990s is likely to extend well into the 21st Century, even if we return to much faster spending growth rates.

Part V summarizes, interprets the findings, and concludes the work. In Chapter 12 we interpret and assess the results documented in detail in Chapter 11. First, we summarize and interpret our main findings from the benefit-cost analysis. Then, we evaluate the roles of different factors in influencing those results, including some model characteristics and specification choices as well as patterns across the states in research spending, productivity, and size of the agricultural sector. This evaluation combines some analytical results and a regression analysis in which the dependent variable is the benefit-cost ratio and the explanatory variables are potential determinants of the results. Next, we confront some natural skepticism about high measured benefit-cost ratios for research. To do this we document the annual value of agricultural productivity growth, which is very large compared with the annual flow of research expenditures (such that, as shown in Chapter 11, if not for our use of relatively long research lags our estimates of benefit-cost ratios might be even larger). We show that the benefit-cost ratios will be well greater than 1.0, even if only a small share of the benefits from productivity growth is attributed to public agricultural R&D.

Chapter 13 briefly summarizes the main findings and concludes the book. The message is mixed. The great success story of American agriculture has involved a significant partnership of private enterprise with public research and extension facilitating extraordinary agricultural productivity growth, especially during the second half of the 20th Century. But the agricultural science and productivity tides seem to be turning. Past successes may have contributed to a complacent confidence among some policymakers that has allowed research resources to be diverted away from enhancing farm productivity to issues that are currently more pressing. The recent slowdown in agricultural productivity growth may have been caused—at least in part—by the slowdown in growth of research spending that began to become evident in the late 1970s. Regardless, a return to past productivity performance is likely to require an acceleration in research spending; and even if research spending accelerates today, it will take many years to take full effect. But it will be worth the wait: persistence pays. Our benefit-cost analysis indicates that even though we have to wait a long time to realize the benefits, an enhanced investment in farm-productivity-oriented agricultural R&D would pay very handsome dividends to the U.S. economy while potentially averting future food scarcity and relieving pressure on the natural resource base.

CHAPTER 2

A Brief History of U.S. Agriculture

Almost 150 years have passed since U.S. public-sector agricultural research and development (R&D) began in earnest with the establishment of the U.S. Department of Agriculture and the passage of the Morrill Land Grant College Act in 1862, to be followed 25 years later by the passage of the Hatch Experiment Station Act in 1887. During that time, and especially in the more recent decades, U.S. agriculture changed dramatically. Public and private agricultural R&D played a major role in bringing about those changes, and the R&D systems and institutions evolved alongside and as part of agriculture.

To provide some context for our econometric assessment of the impacts of agricultural R&D, which is presented in later chapters, this chapter provides an overview of some important structural changes in the role of agriculture in the economy, in the spatial location of production within the United States, and in the number of farms and their size distribution. The following chapters in Part II describe some of the more pertinent developments regarding agricultural inputs, outputs and productivity in the United States.

In this part of the book in particular we take a long-run perspective, emphasizing developments since the beginning of the 20th Century.[1] In later parts of the book, while the analysis focuses on agriculture during the period since World War II, we emphasize the point that the long R&D lags mean that the postwar changes in U.S. agriculture were much influenced by agricultural R&D and related policies during the first half of the 20th Century.

2.1 Trends in Agricultural Output

Over the past 150 years, the share of U.S. gross domestic product (GDP) accounted for by farm value-added declined significantly—from 37.5 percent of

1 See Cochrane (1958 and 1993), Olmstead and Rhode (2000 and 2006), Gardner (2002) and Dimitri, Effland and Conklin (2005) for additional details on these developments.

J.M. Alston et al., *Persistence Pays: U.S. Agricultural Productivity Growth and the Benefits from Public R&D Spending*, Natural Resource Management and Policy 34, DOI 10.1007/978-1-4419-0658-8_2,

GDP in 1869 to 0.8 percent of GDP in 2006 (Figure 2-1, Panel a). This decline in the farm share of GDP was not the result of a shrinking farm sector. Indeed, farm value-added increased rapidly over the period but the U.S. economy expanded even more rapidly. Over the period 1929–2006, U.S. farm value-added grew nearly six fold, from $17 billion to $98 billion (2000 prices), while U.S. GDP increased thirteen fold, from $866 billion to $11.3 trillion. As agriculture declined as a share of the economy and became increasingly more productive, substantial labor was released from the sector, helping to fuel growth elsewhere in the economy.

Data on the share of national income by sector are available since 1929 and summarized in Figure 2-1, Panel b. The graph shows that the share of national income attributable to agriculture (here, including forestry and fisheries) held steady through to the end of the World War II, averaging about 9 percent over the period 1929–1948, but since then it declined to around 0.8 percent of national income during the period 2000–2007. Agriculture now represents a much smaller share of the industrial sector which itself shrank as a share of the economy. During the period from the 1930s through to the mid-1950s, the share of national income generated by industry increased generally (although with a temporary dip after the cessation of war in 1945) to a peak of 48 percent in 1953. Since then, the share of national income generated by industry declined to around 23 percent in 2007, while the share generated by the service sector increased inexorably, up to almost two-thirds of national income by 2007.

Geography of U.S. Production

During the second half of the 20th Century, U.S. agricultural production shifted generally south and west and became much more spatially concentrated (Figure 2-2). In the mid-1920s, Texas and Iowa were the largest states in terms of agricultural production (with an average of 6.9 and 6.7 percent of the 1924–1926 value of U.S. production, respectively). The Central region produced around one-third of the entire U.S. agricultural output at this time. This region includes Iowa and Illinois, then the third-largest producer with a state share of 5.5 percent, along with the rest of the generally fertile, well-watered heartland of the United States. California was the fourth-ranked state in the mid-1920s, producing 5.4 percent of national production. The Northeast region produced 11.2 percent of U.S. agricultural output at that time.

While the value of agricultural output grew overall, regional and state shares had not changed much by the middle of the 20th Century. Thereafter agriculture was on the move. Changes in domestic and export demand as well as changes in off-farm technology contributed to changes in the composition of demand for U.S. agricultural output, which in turn contributed to the changes in the

Figure 2-1 U.S. Output Trends

Panel a. Farm value-added and share of GDP, 1869–2006

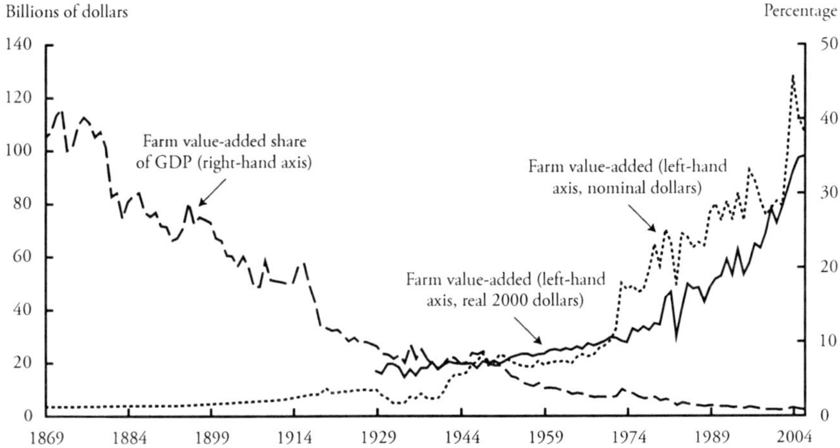

Panel b. National income share by sector, 1929–2007

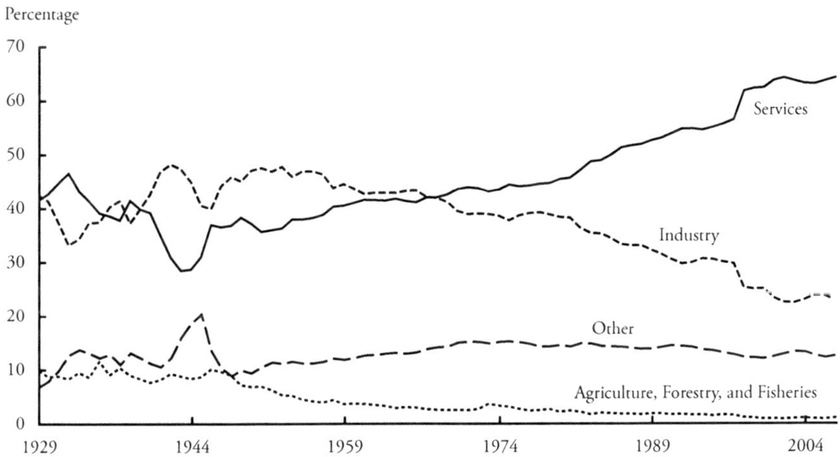

Sources: Panel a. Data on farm value-added for 1869–1928 are from U.S. Bureau of the Census (1975, series F-127); 1929–2006 are from BEA (2007a, NIPA Table 1.3.5). Nominal GDP for 1869–2002 data are from Sutch (2006); values for 2003–2006 are from BEA (2007a, NIPA Table 1.3.5). Real series expressed in 2000 prices using "Price Indexes for Gross Value Added by Sector (series: Farm Business)" taken from BEA (2007a, NIPA Table 1.3.4). Panel b. Data were taken from national income disaggregates in the National Income and Product Accounts (NIPA) compiled by the BEA (2008b).

Notes: Panel a. Farm value-added for 1869–1928 was estimated by applying the annual rate of change in series F-127 to the 1929 value for gross farm business value added from BEA (2007a, NIPA Table 1.3.5). Panel b. While measures such as Gross Domestic Product represent the value of what is produced, national income measures denote the net incomes resulting from that production (net of the consumption of fixed capital). In theory, these measures should be equivalent, but in practice, however, they vary to some degree. See Gutierrez et al. (2007) and BEA (2008a).

Figure 2-2 Shares of the Value of Agricultural Production Among States

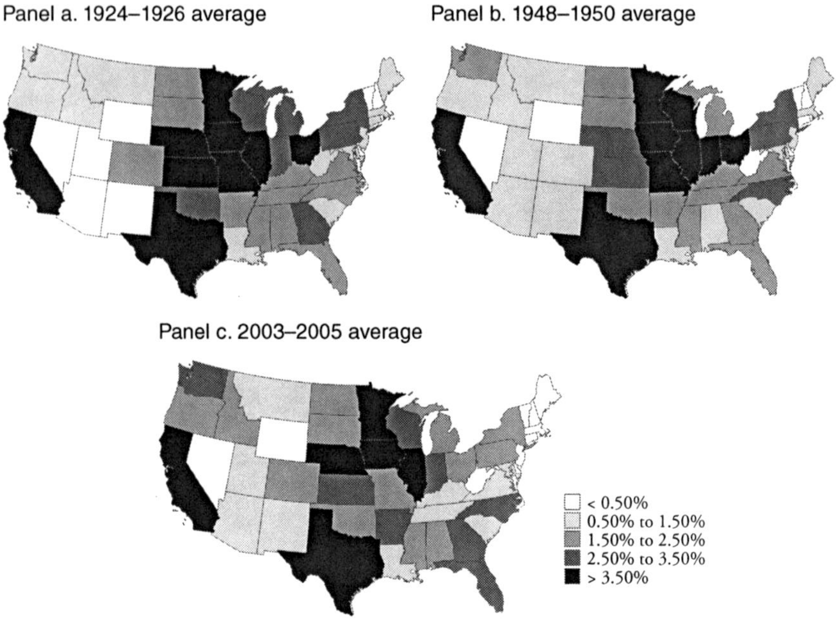

Sources: Compiled by authors from data in InSTePP data files along with USDA (various years) *Agricultural Statistics*, USDA ERS (2007), U.S. Bureau of the Census (1956-1991), USDA NASS (2000-2009) and Johnson (1990).

Notes: The value of production dataset covers 194 commodities for the period 1924–2005. For 73 commodities we used price and quantity data from the cited USDA sources. Most of the quantity data are reported quantities produced per state, and the price data are state-specific prices received on farms. For 139 commodities that are almost wholly sold off farm, we used cash receipts (i.e., sales) data to represent value of production, where the implied price data represent farm-gate or first-point-of-sale measures and the implied quantity data are marketings. Data for the greenhouse nursery and marketing category constitute cash receipts for the period 1924–1948, and for 2005. For all other years, InSTePP data assembled from multiple other USDA sources were used.

composition and location of production.[2] The shifting geography of population (as well as a substantial migration off farms)—combined with improved infrastructure for communication, electrification, transportation, and logistics, which meant that perishables and pre-prepared foods could be moved efficiently over much longer distances—also contributed to this changing spatial pattern of production in the second half of the 20th Century. Substantial on- and off-farm technological innovation underpinned much of these changes.

The regional shifts were substantial. The Central region lost some ground (averaging 27.0 percent of the total value of output in the 2003–2005 period

2 Changes in diets and food consumption habits from increasing per capita incomes and an increasing share of women working outside the home explain some of the changes in the composition of demand for food and fiber commodities, especially during the latter half of the 20th Century (e.g., Senauer, Asp and Kinsey 1991).

compared with 32.4 percent in 1924–1926), while the Northeast region's share of national agricultural output fell markedly from 11.2 percent in 1924–1926 to 6.2 percent in 2003–2005. The big increase was in the Pacific region, whose share more than doubled over the almost 80 years since 1924–1926 to average 18.3 percent of U.S. agricultural output in 2003–2005.

Part of the shift south and west in the value of production was a quantity effect, but part was a move to a larger share of higher-valued output nationally, combined with a massive increase in the share of that higher-valued output being produced in the Pacific region. In the mid 1920s, the Pacific region produced 29 percent of the country's specialty crops (including fruits, vegetables and ornamental crops); by the beginning of the 21st Century that share had grown to more than 50 percent (Table 2-1).[3] Over the almost 80-year period from the mid-1920s to the early 2000s, for all the output categories in Table 2-1, the share of national output from the Northeast region declined, and by 2003–2005 this region produced just 6.2 percent of the total U.S. value of agricultural production. The Central region captured a much larger share of U.S. output of "other crops" (including field crops such as corn, soybeans, and wheat), up from 24.3 percent in the mid 1920s to almost 44 percent by 2003–2005, such that "other crops" accounted for nearly 55 percent of the region's total agricultural output. Livestock production moved heavily out of the Central and Northeast regions to become increasingly concentrated in the Southern Plains and Southeast.

Input versus Output Trends

The long-run aggregate output and input indexes plotted in Figure 2-3 show a remarkable pattern. Over the period 1912–2002, the aggregate quantity of U.S. agricultural output increased by a factor of 4.95 (equivalent to an annual rate of growth of 1.73 percent) whereas aggregate input use grew only 1.11 fold (or 0.14 percent per year). Clearly, output was growing faster than inputs and productivity was growing throughout the entire 90 year period, though not necessarily at a constant rate.

The comparative patterns of input and output growth varied between the first and second halves of the 20th Century. While output grew at similar rates during both halves of the century (1.61 percent per year for 1912–1948 and 1.81 for 1949–2002) the growth rate in input use contracted (from 0.47 percent per year for 1912–1948 to -0.08 percent per year for 1949–2002). In other words, the relationship between measured growth in aggregate inputs and measured growth in aggregate outputs changed, implying a faster rate of measured productivity growth in the second half of the century.

3 In 2003–2005 specialty crops also constituted almost two-thirds of the total value of agricultural production of the Pacific region.

Table 2-1 Regional Production Shares: Three-Year Averages Centered on 1925, 1949, and 2004

	Regional Shares of National Commodity Group Production Value				Commodity Group Shares of Region Production Value		
	Total	Specialty Crops	Other Crops	Livestock	Specialty Crops	Other Crops	Livestock
United States				*percentage*			
1924–1926	100.0	100.0	100.0	100.0	12.8	44.3	42.9
1948–1950	100.0	100.0	100.0	100.0	11.9	40.3	47.8
2003–2005	100.0	100.0	100.0	100.0	22.3	31.5	46.1
Pacific							
1924–1926	7.8	28.8	2.9	6.7	47.0	16.3	36.7
1948–1950	9.8	36.1	5.7	6.8	43.8	23.4	32.8
2003–2005	18.3	51.8	6.7	10.0	63.3	11.6	25.1
Mountain							
1924–1926	5.6	5.5	4.5	6.8	12.5	35.3	52.2
1948–1950	6.2	7.9	5.7	6.2	15.1	36.8	48.1
2003–2005	7.8	6.4	5.8	10.0	18.2	23.1	58.7
Northern Plains							
1924–1926	12.1	1.3	12.5	15.0	1.4	45.7	52.9
1948–1950	10.7	1.7	14.0	10.2	1.9	52.8	45.3
2003–2005	11.4	1.2	18.4	11.5	2.4	50.9	46.7
Southern Plains							
1924–1926	14.8	6.4	25.2	6.6	5.5	75.4	19.1
1948–1950	13.2	6.0	18.6	10.4	5.4	56.8	37.8
2003–2005	14.0	5.3	13.3	18.6	8.5	30.0	61.4
Central							
1924–1926	32.4	18.3	24.3	45.1	7.2	33.2	59.6
1948–1950	35.8	14.4	34.6	42.2	4.8	38.9	56.3
2003–2005	27.0	8.8	43.7	24.3	7.3	51.1	41.6
Southeast							
1924–1926	15.9	16.1	25.0	6.5	12.9	69.6	17.5
1948–1950	14.4	15.5	18.2	11.0	12.8	50.8	36.3
2003–2005	15.4	18.0	9.8	17.9	26.2	20.1	53.7
Northeast							
1924–1926	11.2	23.7	5.7	13.3	27.0	22.3	50.7
1948–1950	9.9	18.5	3.3	13.3	22.4	13.3	64.3
2003–2005	6.2	8.5	2.3	7.7	30.8	11.5	57.7

Sources: See Figure 2-2.

Several factors could account for these patterns. First, different indexing procedures were used for the two sub-periods, 1912–1948 and 1949–2002. These differences, in conjunction with differences in the nature of the data being indexed, may have resulted in false findings of differences in the relative rates of growth of aggregate output and input between the two periods. Second, unmeasured changes in the quantity and composition of the inputs (and out-

Figure 2-3 Aggregate Agricultural Output and Input Quantity Trends, 1880–2004

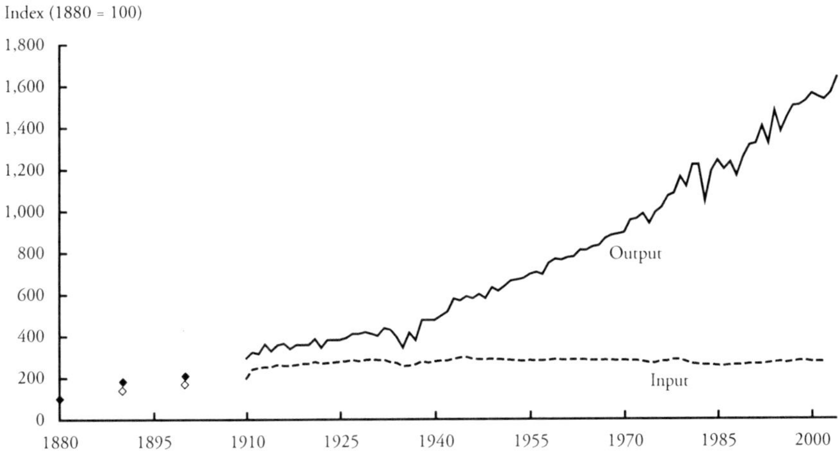

Sources: Indexes of the quantity of output and input are from USDA ERS (1984) for 1880–1938; from USDA ERS (1986) for 1939–1948; and from InSTePP for 1949–2004 (for output), 1949–2002 (for input).

Notes: Additional details concerning the 1880–1949 data can be found in Olmstead and Rhode (2006, series Da 1117 for outputs and Da 1118 for inputs). The InSTePP Fisher indexes of inputs and outputs for 1949–2002 were backcast using the annual growth in the corresponding Laspeyres index for the period 1880–1949 from the aforementioned USDA publications.

puts) between the two periods might be a source of some differences.[4] Chapters 3 and 4 in Part II address the use of indexing procedures to correct for index number problems and changes in composition and quality of input and output aggregates. A third possibility is that actual as well as measured productivity growth accelerated in the second half of the 20th Century as a result of research investments in earlier years or other factors. Chapter 5 explores this aspect using data corrected to address some of the potential input and output measurement pitfalls.

4 The pre-1949 aggregates were formed using a fixed-weight (Laspeyres) indexing procedure, whereas the measures for 1949 and later were formed using chain-linked Fisher indexes. If the relative prices of the components of the aggregates changed markedly over time and the components grew at different rates, then the use of fixed- versus variable-weight aggregation procedures would have measurable consequences for the quantity aggregates so formed (see, for example, Star 1974). Changes in the relationship between inputs and outputs may reflect either changes in the technical relationship between inputs and outputs (attributable to R&D and other influences) or economies of scale or scope effects attributable to gains from specialization as the structure of farms changed over time (for example, the shift to larger farms with, generally, less heterogeneous production processes and output mixes).

Figure 2-4 U.S. Population Trends, 1869–2006

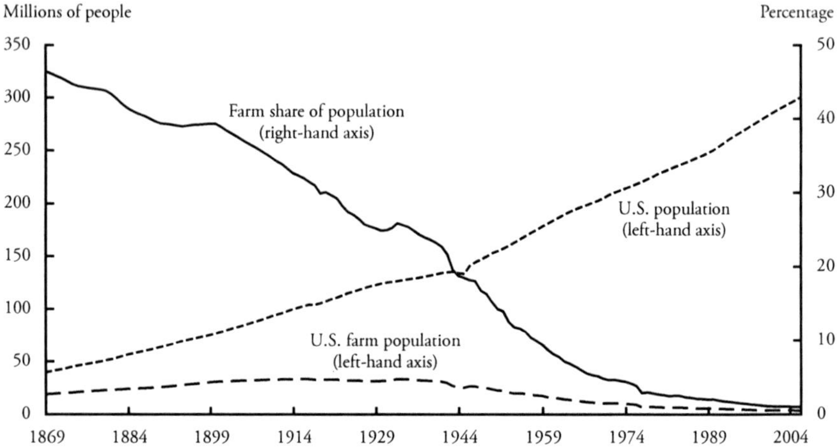

Sources: General population data for 1869–1999 are from Haines and Sutch (2006, series Aa7); values for 2000–2006 are from U.S. Bureau of the Census (2007). Farm population data for 1860–1970 are from U.S. Bureau of the Census (1975, series K-1) and Wells (1937); 1971–1991 data are from Olmstead and Rhode (2006, series Da 1).

Notes: Farm population intercensal values from 1869 through 1889 are a linear interpolation and extension of values from series K-1 and those presented by Wells (1937); 1992–1999 were derived using a linear interpolation of the 1991 and 2000 values. Values for 2000–2006 were derived assuming that population per farm remained constant over that period.

2.2 Farms and Farmers

The structure of agriculture changed markedly, along with the amount, composition and spatial location of production. In 1869, the U.S. farm population constituted 46.3 percent (18 million people) of the total U.S. population of 38.9 million. The farm population increased at an average annual rate of 1.26 percent to 32.5 million people in 1916; 31.9 percent of the total population of 102.0 million in 1916. Thereafter, the U.S. population continued growing while the farm population steadily declined to 2.9 million in 2006; just 1.0 percent of the total population of 299.4 million (Figure 2-4).

Average farm size changed markedly over time as well.[5] The number of acres per farm, calculated as the total land area in U.S. farms divided by the number of farms, is one indicator of farm size.[6] The 1.4 million U.S. farms in 1850 averaged

5 The statistical notion of a farm has changed over time. For example, the 1890 Census of Agriculture definition used both acreage and sales criteria (at least 3 acres or annual agricultural sales of at least $500) while the censuses beginning in 1974 required only that agricultural product sales be at least $1,000. See Olmstead and Rhode (2006, pp. 4.41) for other examples.

6 As discussed by Sumner (1985 and 1986), for example, acres per farm can be a useful measure of size for comparing similar types of mid-western cropping farms, but other measures of farm size, such as value of sales, herd size, or number of employees may be more appropriate for comparing

Figure 2-5 U.S. Farm Acres, Farm Numbers and Average Farm Size, 1850–2006

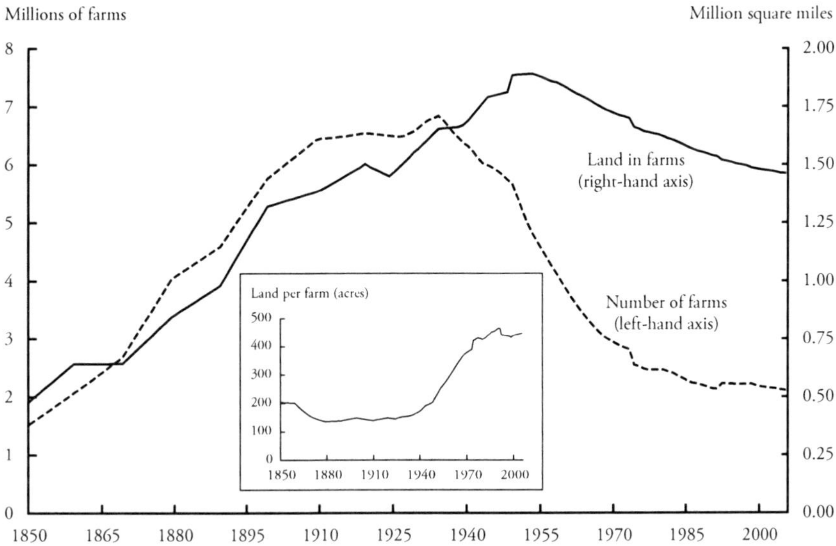

Sources: Number of farms (1910–1999) and Land in farms (1911–1999) are from Olmstead and Rhode (2006, series Da 4 and Da 5, respectively). For both variables, values for 2000–2006 are from USDA ERS (2007); 1900 and 1890 values for farm numbers are from the U.S. Bureau of the Census (1975, series K-4 and K-5); 1910, 1900, and 1890 values for land in farms are from series K-5 of the same resource.

Notes: For farm numbers, intercensal values were estimated using a linear interpolation wherever no value was provided.

203 acres per farm (Figure 2-5, Inset).[7] For about the next 85 years, the number of farms increased (roughly in line with the growth in the farm population) to 6.8 million in 1935, while the area in farms also expanded with new settlement, such that average farm size crept up to 162.1 acres per farm in 1938 (Figure 2-5, Inset). Thereafter, and again in parallel with farm population trends, the number of farms in the United States declined at a rapid rate (by 2.33 percent per year) through to 1980 and thereafter at the much slower rate of 0.60 percent per year (through to 2006).[8] The obverse of these trends in total farm area and

among specialty crops producers, among intensive livestock producers, or across different types of farms.

7 According to USDA (2004, p. 1) "Land in farms is all land operated by farms and ranches during the year. It includes crop and livestock acreage, wasteland, woodland, pasture, land in summer fallow, idle cropland, and land enrolled in the Conservation Reserve Program (CRP), Wetland Reserve Program (WRP), and other set aside or commodity acreage programs. It excludes public, industrial and grazing association land and nonagricultural land."

8 Hoppe and Korb (2006, p. i) noted that " . . . the rate at which U.S. farms go out of business, or exit farming, is about 9 or 10 percent per year, comparable to exit rates for nonfarm small businesses in the United States. The relatively stable farm count since the 1970s reflects exits and entries essentially in balance. The probability of exit is higher for recent entrants than for older, more established farms. Farms operated by Blacks are more likely to exit than those operated by

Figure 2-6 Distribution of Total U.S. Farm Acreage by Farm Size, 1900–2002

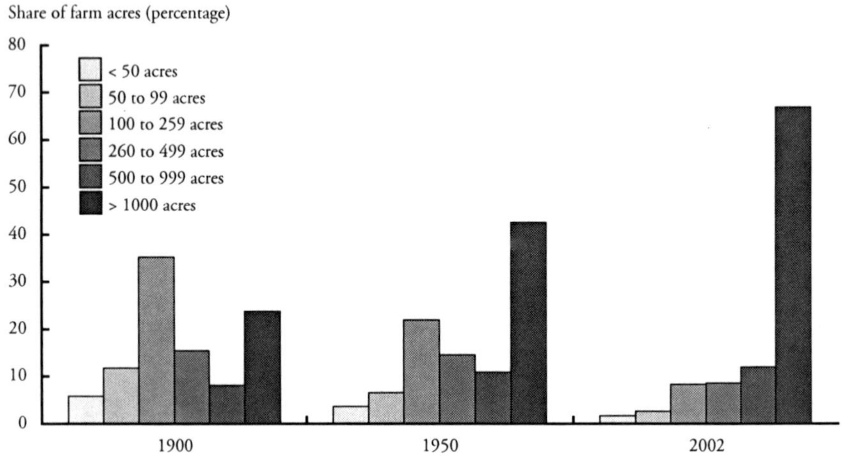

Sources: Authors' calculations based on Olmstead and Rhode (2006, Table Da 597-611) for the period 1900–1950; USDA (2004, Table 55) for 2002.

farm numbers is that average farm size grew rapidly from 162.1 acres per farm in 1938 to 464.2 acres per farm in 1992. Since then average farm size shrank a little, down to 431.8 acres per farm by 1999, and then inched up again to 446.1 acres per farm by 2006.

Other aspects of the distribution of farm size changed along with the average (Figure 2-6). In 1900, 17.5 percent of U.S. farm acreage was in holdings less than 100 acres; by 2002, just 4.3 percent. At the other end of the spectrum, the share of acreage in large farms (i.e., farms of 1,000 acres or more) grew from just under 24 percent of the total in 1900 to nearly 67 percent of the total in 2002. The comparative stability of average acres per farm in recent years masks a good deal of continuing structural change, including some further concentration of agricultural land in larger operations. Key and Roberts (2007) report that the number of farms with more than 1,000 acres increased by 14 percent between 1982 and 2002, while the number with 50 to 1,000 acres declined by about 17 percent, and the number with fewer than 50 acres increased by about 17 percent.

Some writers have attributed the consolidation of farms into larger units mostly, if not entirely, to the adoption of new technology, particularly embodied in machinery that directly reduced labor requirements and involved economies

---

Whites, but the gap between Black and White exit probabilities has declined substantially since the 1980s. Exit probabilities differ by specialization, with beef farms less likely to exit than cash grain or hog farms."

of size.[9] Such innovations imply a less labor-intensive and larger minimum efficient scale in farming operations. But rising nonfarm wages, drawing labor away from agriculture, played a role in stimulating the development and adoption of these innovations.[10] The relative importance of on-farm technology, pushing labor off the farm, versus off-farm technology, pulling it, remains a matter for conjecture, but clearly both forces were at work along with other economy-wide changes.

Notwithstanding the growth in the share of U.S. agricultural output produced on "nonfamily" (sometimes described as "industrial" or "corporate") farms, family operated farms continue to account for the bulk of U.S. agricultural production; around 86 percent in 2003 (MacDonald, Hoppe and Banker 2006).[11] Most striking, however, has been the rapid growth in agricultural output coming from very large family operations with sales of at least $500,000 per farm per year (in 2003 prices). They accounted for 45 percent of U.S. agricultural output in 2003, up from 32 percent in 1989 (Figure 2-7, Panel a). Correspondingly, the share of production coming from smaller family farms ($10,000 to $250,000 per farm per year in sales) fell from 40 to 26 percent.

Over recent decades the distribution of farm numbers stratified by farms of differing sales classes has changed markedly. The number of very large family farms (sales greater than $500,000 per year) grew from 39,000 in 1989 to 66,700 in 2003; the number of farms with sales between $250,000 and $500,000 per year totaled 85,300 in 2003. Collectively, the 152,000 farm operations with sales in excess of $250,000 per year represented just 7 percent of all commercial farms in the United States in 2003 but accounted for 70 percent of the value of farm sales (Jones, El-Osta and Green 2006).[12] The 1.77 million farms—85 percent of total farms—with sales of less than $100,000 per year accounted for only 12.9 percent of U.S. farm sales. Jones, El-Osta and Green (2006) also report that operators of these small farms derived almost all of their household income from

9 In contrast, Kislev and Peterson (1982, p. 578) found that they could explain "...virtually all of the growth in the machine-labor ratio and in farm size [in the United States] over the 1930–1970 period by changes in relative factor prices without reference to 'technological change' or 'economies of scale'."

10 Hayami and Ruttan (1970 and 1971) were the first to extensively examine the factor-biased direction of technical change in U.S. agriculture induced by changes in relative factor prices.

11 The USDA Economic Research Service has developed a typology for different categories of farms, as described in Hoppe (2001), including various kinds of non-commercial farms, and several different sizes of family farms, as well as "nonfamily farms," which are farms organized as nonfamily corporations or cooperatives, as well as farms operated by hired managers. See, also, Hoppe et al. (2007).

12 The concentration of production in very large farms (farms with sales greater than $500,000 per year) spans all agricultural sectors. MacDonald, Hoppe and Banker (2006) report that in 2003, these types of farms accounted for 61 percent of U.S. hog production and 75 percent of poultry and egg production, and also produced rapidly growing shares of cash grains, soybeans, tobacco, cotton and peanut production.

Figure 2-7 Distribution of Agricultural Production and Household Income Sources by Farm Size

Panel a. Share of agricultural value of production by sales class of farms, 1989 and 2003

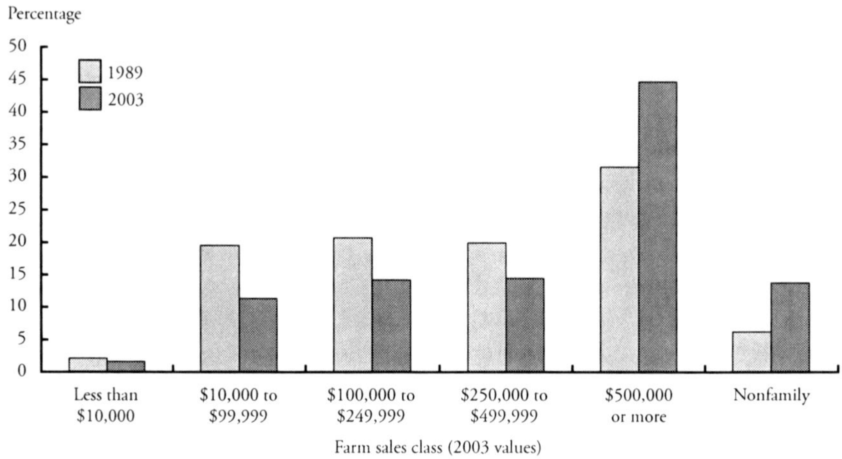

Panel b. Agricultural household income by sales class of farm, 2003

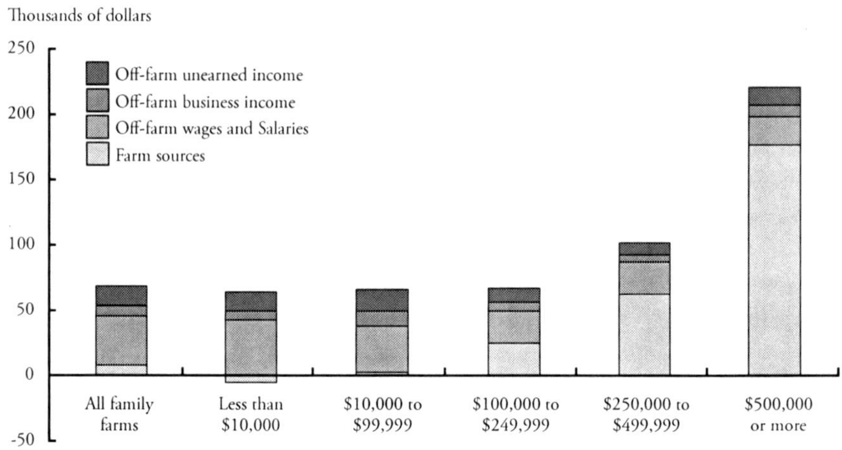

Sources: Panel a. MacDonald, Hoppe and Banker (2006, Figure 1). Panel b. Reconstruction of Jones, El-Osta and Green (2006, Figure 2) based on extraction from USDA ERS (2008a).

off-farm work and from unearned income such as social security, pensions and investments (Figure 2-7, Panel b). Meanwhile, those households operating farms with sales in excess of $250,000 per year derived 74 percent of their household incomes from farm sources in 2003.

2.3 Conclusion

In spite of the evident, seismic shifts in the structure of American agriculture, some elements are little changed. The agricultural production sector is still composed of comparatively small, mainly family-owned and -operated farming units. Natural inputs such as rainfall, sunlight, and temperature are still paramount. As a consequence, the vagaries of weather and site-specific differences in climate, topography, soil and other agroecological attributes still shape crop and livestock production choices. In turn, variations in these natural factors influence the management and technological options designed to deal with them.

Variable production conditions confer advantages on a decentralized (perhaps family) form of farm management (Olmstead and Rhode 2000, p. 740). Sectors of agriculture where capital and other knowhow have substituted for, or ameliorated the effects of, these natural variations (such as confinement poultry and pork production) have muted but by no means eliminated the need for on-the-spot management protocols. They have also meant these natural elements have less impact on choices regarding the location of production, with consequences for the scale and concentration (and perhaps ownership) of the means of production.[13]

These enduring natural elements are influenced by, or have influences on, the nature and pace of the technical changes designed to affect agricultural production, as well as production choices more generally. Changes in inputs, outputs, and productivity are reviewed in the next three chapters with some additional attention given to the locational aspects of these production indicators.

13 Key and McBride (2007, p. i) noted that "During the past 15 years… the number of farms with hogs has declined by over 70 percent, as hog enterprises have grown larger. Large operations that specialize in a single phase of production have replaced farrow-to-finish operations that performed all phases of production. The use of production contracts has increased. Operations producing under contract are larger than independent operations and are more likely to specialize in a single phase of production. These structural changes have coincided with substantial gains in efficiency for hog farms and lower production costs. Most of these productivity gains are attributable to increases in the scale of production and technological innovation. Productivity gains likely contributed to a 30-percent reduction in the price of hogs at the farm gate." MacDonald (2008) documents parallel developments in the U.S. broiler industry.

PART II

Inputs, Outputs and Productivity

The aggregate quantity of inputs used in U.S. agriculture grew slowly throughout the 20th Century, with most of that growth occurring in the first half of the century. However, there was a substantial change in the composition and quality of inputs used on farms: labor use declined markedly, land and capital use grew a little, and the use of materials inputs grew at quite a rapid rate. Aggregate output grew at a much faster pace than the growth of inputs and the composition and spatial location of that production also changed considerably. States tended to specialize in producing a narrower range of outputs. One consequence of these changing patterns of inputs and outputs is that U.S. agricultural productivity grew quite rapidly, especially during the second half of the century. This part of the book documents in detail these changes in inputs, outputs, and productivity in U.S. agriculture. Chapter 3 quantifies and discusses the changing amount, composition, and quality of U.S. agricultural inputs, Chapter 4 quantifies and reviews the changing structure and amount of agricultural output, and Chapter 5 provides estimates of productivity indexes and discusses the changing productivity patterns. Broad measures of input, output and productivity are provided for the whole century, with more detailed data and discussion for the period spanning the past 50 years. These more detailed data are used in Part IV to analyze the consequences of public spending on agricultural research and extension for state-level U.S. agricultural productivity patterns.

CHAPTER 3

Agricultural Inputs

The structure of U.S. agriculture changed dramatically over the past 100 years, and these changes coincided with large increases in agricultural productivity. Revolutionary technological advancements transformed inputs such as seed, fertilizers, and agricultural chemicals, and the quality of agricultural inputs—notably capital, labor and land—increased generally, especially during the latter half of the 20th Century. The apparent decline in the use of conventional agricultural inputs, particularly over recent decades and especially labor, is offset somewhat when we account properly for the changing composition and quality of inputs over time. For example, farmers are much better educated and more experienced on average compared with 50 years ago, and a higher proportion of cropland is irrigated. Identifying these important structural changes in the nature of inputs helps in constructing an informative picture of U.S. agricultural production and the sources of output growth during the 20th Century; particularly developments during the post-1948 period, which is the subject of more detailed analysis in this volume.

3.1 Overview

General Developments

The indexes of aggregate U.S. agricultural input and output in Figure 2-3 of Chapter 2 reveal a remarkable development. While the quantity of U.S. agricultural output increased by an average of 2.23 percent per year from 1880 to 2002, the measured use of aggregate inputs grew by only 0.81 percent per year. Moreover, most of the growth in input use took place in the 1880s and 1890s, a period of eventually improving prosperity in U.S agriculture after the harsh economic conditions that took hold in the early-1870s and persisted until the

J.M. Alston et al., *Persistence Pays: U.S. Agricultural Productivity Growth and the Benefits from Public R&D Spending*, Natural Resource Management and Policy 34,
DOI 10.1007/978-1-4419-0658-8_3, © Springer Science + Business Media, LLC 2010

Table 3-1 Shares of Operating Costs, 1910–2007

	Inputs of Farm Origin			Inputs Purchased Off Farm					
Year	Feed	Seed	Total	Hired Labor	Fertilizer	Pesticide	Energy	Other	Total
	percentage			percentage					
1910	20.2	2.7	32.3	35.8	7.2	0.3	0.6	23.9	67.7
1920	23.4	3.3	34.6	33.4	7.3	0.3	3.5	21.1	65.4
1930	19.6	3.1	31.7	29.2	7.4	0.8	8.0	22.9	68.3
1940	22.1	4.4	37.9	22.8	6.8	1.0	8.4	23.3	62.1
1950	23.8	3.8	42.1	20.4	7.1	1.3	9.2	20.0	57.9
1960	24.4	2.8	40.5	16.4	7.2	1.6	8.9	25.5	59.5
1970	27.5	3.2	45.5	14.8	8.3	3.3	6.9	21.2	54.5
1980	24.9	3.8	41.3	11.0	11.3	4.2	11.1	21.1	58.7
1990	19.6	4.3	38.0	13.5	7.9	5.2	8.1	27.5	62.0
2000	17.6	5.4	34.5	14.9	7.2	6.1	7.3	29.9	65.5
2007	19.9	6.2	35.9	13.4	8.7	5.2	8.8	28.0	64.1

Sources: USDA ERS (2008b).

Notes: All entries refer to costs of the category of inputs as a share of total operating costs.

mid-1890s, during which substantial additional labor was still being drawn into agriculture (Wells 1937; Cochrane 1993, pp. 93-103).

The measured patterns of aggregate U.S. input use are not necessarily representative of input use for any particular region or state within the United States and they also hide marked changes in the composition of the aggregate input as a result of changes in the relative use of particular inputs in U.S. agriculture. The disaggregated details reveal important differences across input categories and among states, although sources of information on these details are incomplete, especially for earlier years.

Data on the cost of various categories of inputs are reported by USDA ERS (2008b) for the period 1910–2007. A primary distinction is between (a) the annual use and costs of inputs supplied by farmers, including operator labor, capital and land, which are typically not observed in market transactions and must be imputed from other information, and (b) operating cost, which reflects purchased inputs and is observable in farm accounts. Table 3-1 summarizes the changing costs of various inputs as a share of total operating cost. Hired labor (including contract labor) accounted for a share of total operating expenses that fell from 36 percent in 1910 to 13 percent by 2007. As a share of total operating costs, energy grew rapidly from 1910 to 1932, and after 1948 was little changed, averaging around 9 percent for the period through to 2002. Purchased feed now accounts for around 20 percent of all operating expenses. In 2007, fertilizer, seed, and pesticide expenses accounted for around 9, 6 and 5 percent, respectively, of operating expenses (combined, about 20 percent of total operating costs, compared with 10 percent in 1910, with pesticides having accounted for much of

> **Box 3-1 Agricultural Mechanization Controversies**
>
> The mechanization of U.S. agriculture has been much studied, and is also controversial. For example, the mechanical tomato harvester developed at the University of California, Davis in the early 1960s gained notoriety for ostensibly displacing much labor from the sector. Schmitz and Seckler (1970) estimated that the rate of return to the resources invested in developing the harvester was 929 to 1,282 percent per annum, but this fell to between minus 8 and 345 percent after adjustments were made to compensate those who lost employment as a result of the harvester being adopted. Brandt and French (1981) claimed there were fewer jobs lost than Schmitz and Seckler determined. Alston, Pardey and Carter (1994, pp. 91-92) argued that the lower (adjusted) rates of return are less appropriate than the unadjusted ones for four reasons: (a) such compensation is rarely paid, and the conventional welfare measures ignore the distribution of benefits, (b) the amount of compensation was too high, at 100 percent of wages forgone (the compensation should at most cover the net benefits of being employed harvesting tomatoes), (c) in a sense, double counting is involved since the cost of producing tomatoes already included the opportunity costs of harvest labor, and (d) the labor was less likely forced out by the harvester as much as drawn out by the withdrawal of labor (as a result of the termination of the Bracero program). Martin and Olmstead (1985) developed these arguments. The notion of labor displacement attributable to mechanization is of enduring interest in U.S. agriculture (see, for example, Kislev and Peterson 1982 and Olmstead and Rhode 1994).

this growth). Since the 1970s, the cost of purchased inputs of farm origin (including feed, seed, livestock and poultry) has generally declined as a share of total operating costs, while the shares of inputs from other sectors such as agricultural chemicals and energy have increased.

These trends in cost of purchased inputs provide a useful but only partial picture of the changing structure of input use in U.S. agriculture. Most importantly they ignore the important cost categories of operator labor, capital, and land. In addition, they refer to input expenses rather than quantities of inputs, as used to form primal measures of productivity. Finally, they conceal important changes in the quantity versus quality (or composition) of certain categories of inputs. Information on these aspects is necessary for assessing the respective roles of changes in relative prices versus technical changes (some embodied as quality changes in inputs) when accounting for the sources of change in agricultural output.

Simple quantity counts of each input category are not useful metrics of input use when the quality of particular inputs is changing or the composition within the category is changing. For example, machines are much more productive than they were fifty or even five years ago, and the mix of types of machines used on farms has changed as well. Similarly, the composition of the labor force

Box 3-2 Land Requirements to Feed Horses and Mules

Barton and Cooper (1948, p. 121) observed that "... the man-hours used to grow horse and mule feed and to care for farm horses and mules accounted for 17 percent of the total man-hours used in agriculture at the time of World War I and this proportion has now been reduced to 7 percent." Similarly, Olmstead and Rhode (2001, pp. 664-665) wrote "Given the crop yields prevailing over the late nineteenth and early twentieth centuries, a mature farm horse required about 3 acres of cropland for feed each year. In aggregate, farm draft animals consumed the output of roughly 22 percent of all cropland harvested over the 1880 to 1920 period; draft animals in cities and mines consumed the output of another 5 percent. The cropland used to feed horses and mules peaked in 1915 at about 93 million acres; 79 million acres for maintaining work animals on farms and 14 million acres for those off farms. From 1915 on, there was a steady decline. In 1930, 65 million acres of cropland were used to feed horses and mules, with all but 2 million acres devoted to farm stock. By 1960 only 5 million acres were needed."

in agriculture has changed to include a larger proportion of more-experienced and better-educated farmers, and this means that "hours of work" in agriculture means something quite different today compared with 1910.

Labor-saving machinery contributed very substantially to the growth in farm productivity. Important innovations in cropping were made when tractors began replacing horses in the early part of the 20th Century—after an almost uninterrupted threefold increase in the equine stock on farms over the previous half century to a peak of 27.2 million horses and mules in 1917—and self-propelled grain combines replaced tractor-drawn combines (Figure 3-1). In addition to increasing labor productivity by mechanizing operations like preparing and harvesting cropped land, the uptake of tractors also meant that much manhandling of bagged grain, along with fertilizer, seed and other inputs could be replaced with bulk handling processes (see, for example, Schillinger and Papendick 2008).[1] In addition, substituting tractor for animal power released the large areas of agriculture (plus the associated labor, seed and other inputs) that had been required to feed and house draft animals. In earlier periods, of course, the mechanical reaper and binder replaced the sickle and manual shocking (David 1966; Olmstead 1975).

More Detailed Developments

To add to the available evidence on these long-run trends in U.S. agriculture, more-refined measures of aggregate outputs and input use were developed by the

1 We thank Philip Raup for emphasizing the importance of this particular, and often overlooked, aspect of mechanization.

Figure 3-1 Stock of "Working" Equines, Tractors and Combines on U.S. Farms, 1867–2002

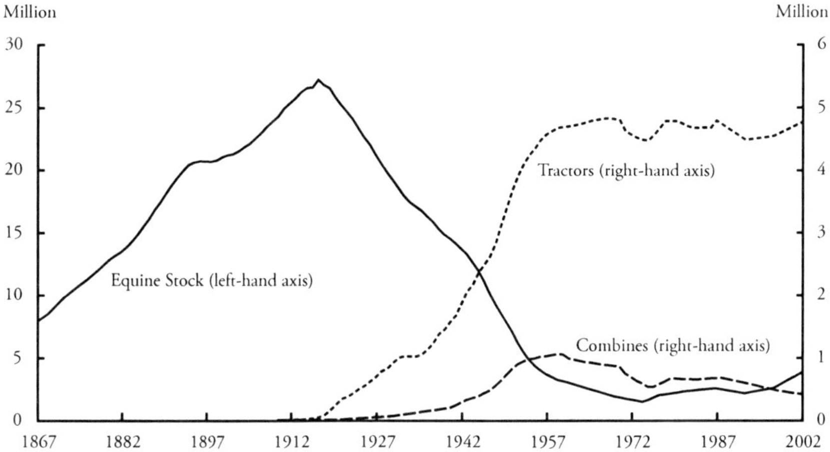

Sources: Horses and mules: 1867–1919 from Olmstead and Rhode (2006, Series Da 983-987); 1920–1960 from USDA (1962, p. 432); 1969 from U.S. Bureau of the Census (1975, Table K570); 1978, 1982, 1987, 1992, and 1997 from U.S. Bureau of the Census (various years); and 2002 estimated, including ponies, from USDA NASS (2004). Other values are linearly interpolated. Tractors: 1910–1990 from Olmstead and Rhode (2006, Series Da 623-634); 1991–2003 are "agricultural tractors, total in use" from FAO (2008). Other values are linearly interpolated. Combines: 1910, 1920, 1930, 1940–1988, 1993, and 1998 from Olmstead and Rhode (2006, Series Da 629; 2002) from USDA NASS (2004). Other values are linearly interpolated.

Notes: Horses and mules: These data are an estimate of the "work stock" of horses and mules on farm. We opted for the work stock criteria used by USDA (1962, p. 432), which includes only horses and mules aged 2 or more years. Olmstead and Rhode (2001) used a criteria of 3 or more years, while Olmstead and Rhode (2006, Series Da 983-987) report work stock as animals aged 2 or more years. For 1969 and 1974 the number of "horses and ponies" was available for all farms, while horses and ponies were reported separately for larger farms and the number of mules, burros and donkeys were only reported for large farms. To estimate the total number of horses on farms, we assumed the ratio of horses to ponies on large and all farms was the same. Similarly, we assumed that the horse to donkey ratio was the same on large and all farms. Tractors: These data represent a count of tractors on farm. Notably, the 1920 U.S. Census of Agriculture (U.S. Bureau of the Census 1922, Table 8, p. 512) states that only 3.6 percent of farms reported using tractors.

International Science and Technology Practice and Policy (InSTePP) Center at the University of Minnesota (hereafter called the InSTePP series) for the period after 1948.[2] In constructing the InSTePP series, considerable effort went into accounting for changes in the composition and quality of inputs (and outputs, as discussed in Chapter 4) over time and space.[3] During the period 1949–2002,

2 A brief overview of the data source and construction details for this series are provided in Appendix II, and more particulars are included in the detailed documentation prepared by Pardey et al. (2009a).

3 The "quality" or compositional adjustments made here update and extend the approaches developed by Craig and Pardey (1996b).

Figure 3-2 Quantity of Capital and Land Services, Labor, and Materials Inputs Used in U.S. Agriculture, 1949–2002

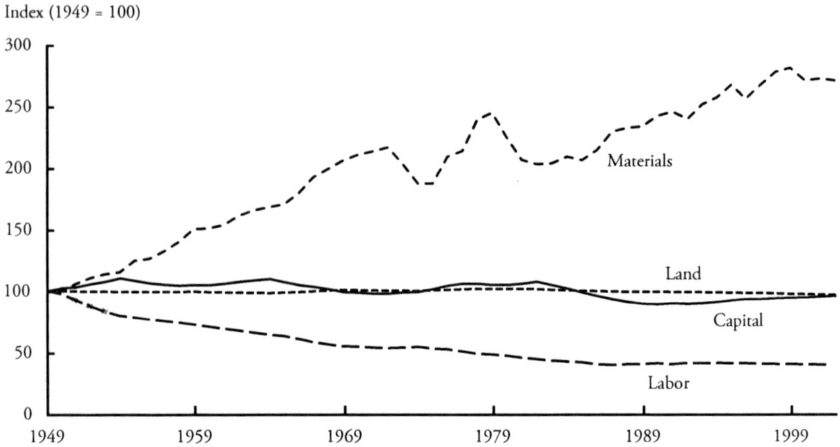

Sources: Authors' calculations based on InSTePP series.

Notes: Fisher index of input quantity aggregates indexed at 1949 = 100.

while the quantity of U.S. agricultural output grew by nearly 250 percent, the aggregate input quantity declined marginally (Figure 2-3, Chapter 2).[4] This aggregate trend was the net effect of a large increase in the quantity of materials inputs, a decrease in labor inputs, and little or no trend in inputs of services from land and services from capital stocks (Figure 3-2).

Over the period 1949–2002, the aggregate quantity of input fell at an average rate of 0.11 percent per year for the United States as a whole, but there was a large dispersion around this average. In fact, as Figure 3-3 reveals, states were fairly evenly distributed around the mean of this distribution: 22 (46 percent) of the states had an input growth rate above this national average rate; and of these states, 15 (31 percent) experienced an overall increase in input use during this period. However, the dispersion among states in the rate of growth of aggregate input use is not at all representative of the dispersion among states in growth rates for specific categories of inputs. Relative to the distribution of growth rates of total inputs, the distribution of growth rates for labor is positioned to the left (with all of the states experiencing a decline in aggregate labor use) and the distribution for materials is to the right (with 90 percent of the states increasing their use of materials inputs), while the capital and land distributions indicate

---

4 Over the entire period 1880–2002 the quantity of aggregate output grew at an average rate of 2.23 percent per year—2.57 percent per year for the period 1880–1948 and 1.68 percent per year for the period 1949–2002. The corresponding input growth was 0.81 percent per year for the entire period, with growth of 1.52 percent per year for the period 1880–1948 and -0.11 percent per year for the period 1949–2002.

Figure 3-3 Distribution Among States in the Growth of Input Use, 1949–2002

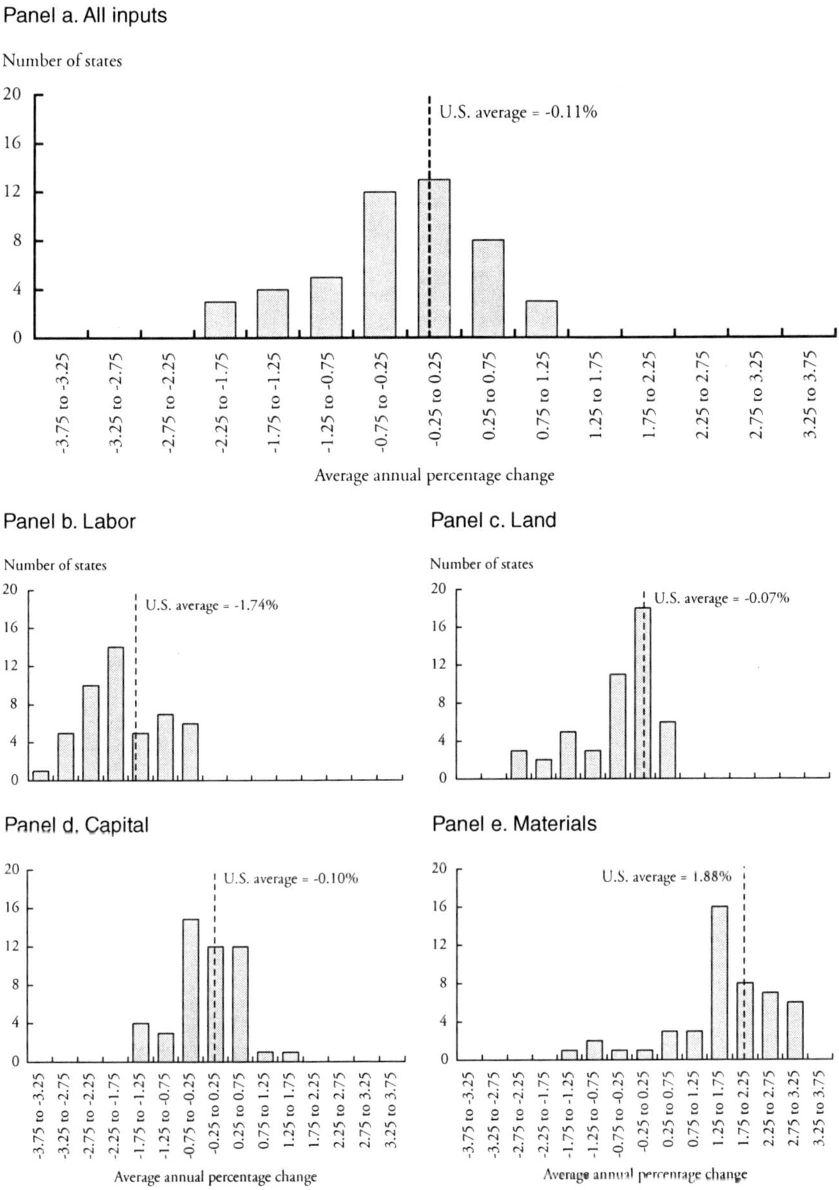

Sources: Authors' calculations based on InSTePP series.

Figure 3-4 State and Regional Patterns of Input Use, 1949–2002

Panel a. Trends in aggregate input use in selected states

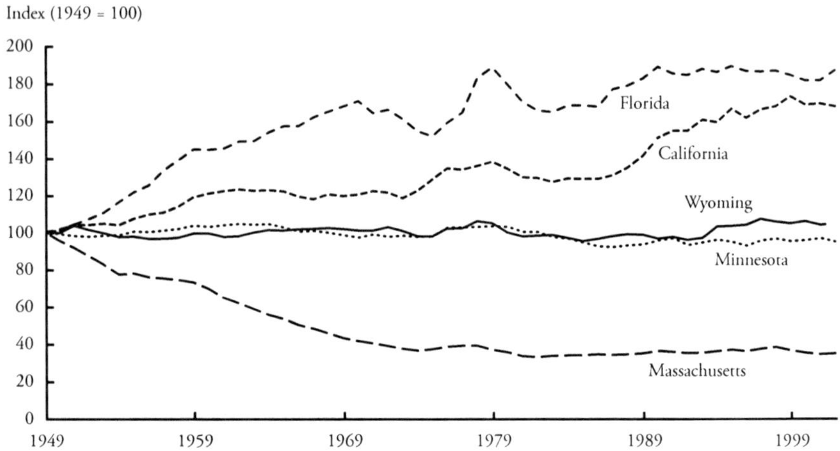

Panel b. Regional rates of change

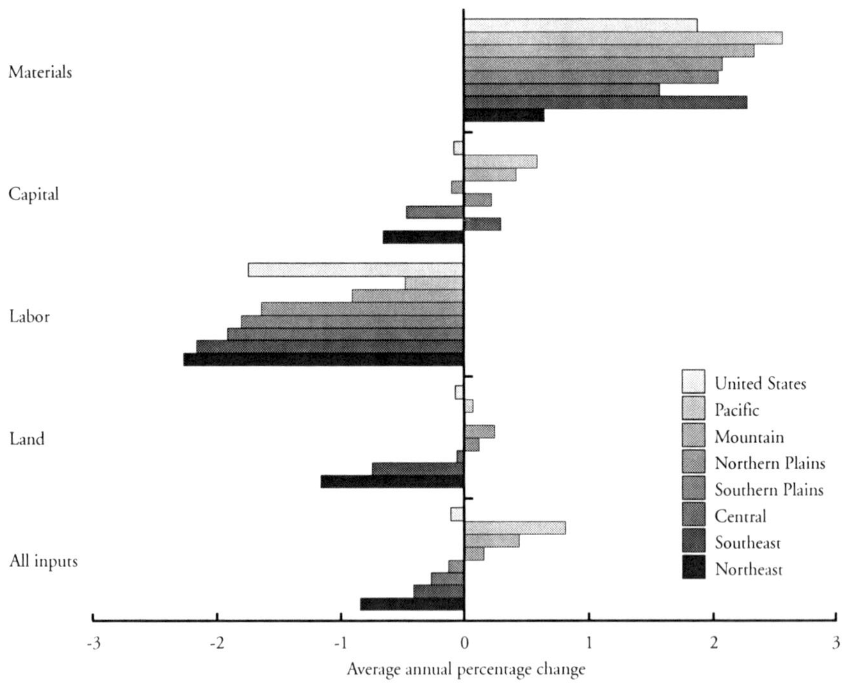

Sources: Authors' calculations based on InSTePP series.

Notes: Regional rates of change represent the average annual rates of growth of regional input quantity indexes, 1949–2002.

that 63 and 50 percent of the states reduced their use of land and capital services inputs respectively.

Figure 3-4, Panel a shows the input-use paths of selected states. Aggregate input use grew fastest in Florida (1.18 percent per year during 1949–2002) and declined the most in Massachusetts (shrinking by 1.99 percent per year, such that aggregate input use in 2002 was just 35 percent of the 1949 amount). Minnesota's pattern was characteristic of the Midwestern states, tracking the national trend fairly closely. The Northeast region experienced the slowest growth in materials inputs and the fastest decline in the use of land, labor, and capital of all the regions in the United States (Figure 3-4, Panel b). The rates of decline in labor use were also pronounced in the Southeast and Northeast regions. The Pacific region, dominated by developments in California, increased its use of materials and capital inputs the fastest and had the smallest rate of decline in the aggregate use of labor. After adjusting for quality-cum-compositional changes, notably those brought about by the growth in irrigated acreage, measured land use grew by 0.25 percent per year in the Northern Plains and 0.02 percent per year in the Mountain region, but declined across the 48 states. Likewise, even after adjusting for the changing composition of capital services used in U.S. agriculture (in particular factoring in the changing vintage, durability and quality of the machines used on farms), aggregate capital use declined by 0.65 and 0.47 percent per year in the Northeast and Central regions respectively.

The detailed compositional changes in the main categories of inputs are interesting in their own right as well as important for understanding changes in agricultural production and productivity. The remainder of this chapter provides some more details of the changes in quality of inputs and composition of input aggregates over the period 1949–2002.

3.2 The Composition of Capital

The composition of agricultural capital changed substantially over time. Figure 3-5 shows the real dollar value of the annual flows of services from the three broad categories of assets that comprise the InSTePP capital aggregate. This aggregate measures the flows of services from machinery, buildings, and the stock of biological capital—which includes breeding stock such as sows, ewes, and cattle along with milking cows.[5] Andersen, Alston and Pardey (2009) discuss the implications of the more-important assumptions used to estimate capital service flows from data on capital stocks or purchases. They also compare the InSTePP series to one developed by Ball, Butault and Nehring (2001) for the USDA.

5 Pardey et al. (2009a) give more detail on the underlying data and methods used to construct the capital service flows reported here.

Figure 3-5 Real Value of Capital Services Used on U.S. Farms, 1949–2002

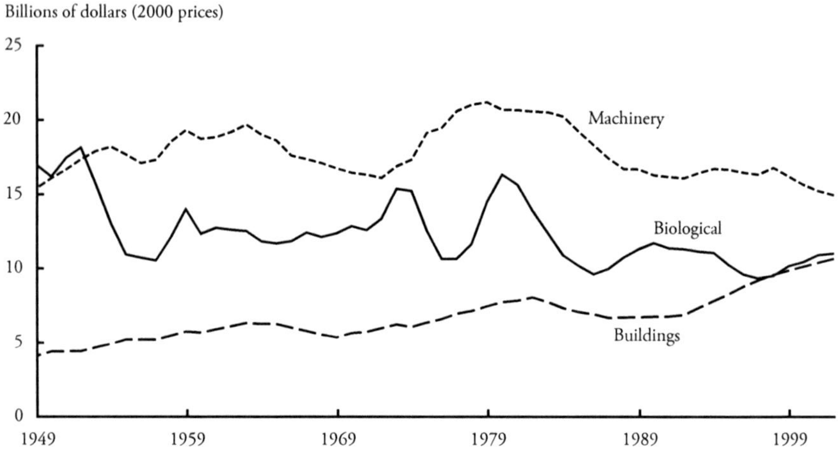

Sources: Authors' calculations based on InSTePP series.

Notes: Annual imputed rental value of capital deflated using the GDP implicit price deflator with base year 2000.

The estimation of capital stocks and service flows requires decisions about the nature and degree of disaggregation of the basic data to be compiled on capital stocks (or purchases if the perpetual inventory approach is to be used), as well as assumptions about the nature, form, and length of the depreciation profiles associated with each class of capital. Table 3-2 summarizes the parameter choices used to construct the InSTePP capital series, compared with the corresponding assumptions used to construct the USDA series. The InSTePP series distinguishes among different *classes* of capital that differ in their service lives (and implied rates of depreciation) and different *types* of capital within each class that differ in their productive attributes (which ideally get revealed as differences in per unit rental rates).[6]

The values reported in Figure 3-5 represent the annual cost to rent the services from the different assets in the given year. The rental costs of buildings increased relative to the rental cost of biological capital and machinery over the sample period. By 2002, the annual rental costs of biological capital and buildings were roughly equal at $11 billion apiece, and the rental cost of machines was approximately $15 billion.

6 Thus, the InSTePP capital index includes five separate classes of biological capital, whereas the USDA series reported by Ball, Butault and Nehring (2001) includes all livestock and crop inventories in a single class. Furthermore, the InSTePP series identifies different types of tractors, and treats mowers, combines, and pickers/balers as separate classes of machinery, whereas in the USDA series Ball, Butault and Nehring (2001) include these in a single class labeled "other machinery," though they do not provide details of the exact content of this class.

Table 3-2 Composition of Capital Aggregate and Service-Life Assumption

InSTePP			USDA		
Category and Class	**L**	**δ**	**Category and Class**	**L**	**β**
Machinery			*Machinery*		
Automobiles*	9	0.23	Automobiles*	na	0.50
Trucks*	12	0.18	Trucks*	9	0.50
Tractors*	15	0.14	Tractors*	9	0.50
Combines*	15	0.14	Other machinery*	14	0.50
Mowers*	15	0.14			
Picker/balers*	15	0.14			
Biological capital					
Breeding cows*	5	0.00	*Inventories of crops/livestock**	1	1.00
Chickens*	1	0.00			
Ewes*	6	0.00			
Milking cows*	5	0.00			
Sows*	3	0.00			
*Service structures**	45	0.05	*Service structures**	38	0.75

Sources: Pardey et al. (2009b) and Ball, Butault and Nehring (2001).

Notes: Asterisks denote categories (e.g., service structures) or classes within categories (e.g., automobiles) with asset-specific estimates of stocks and rental rates. L denotes service life in years; δ is the annual rate of depreciation; and β is a decay factor. Capital class indicates capital with a specific depreciation profile and service life. Capital type indicates distinct items within each class. Combines are distinguished by width of combine head. For 1964–1989 the types of combines include 6 widths ranging from less than 12 feet to 30 or more feet; for 1994–2002 the types include widths or less than 24 feet, 24–30 feet, and 30 or more feet. Tractors types are distinguished according to horsepower. For 1964–1989 there are 16 types of 2WD tractors ranging from less than 20 horsepower to 180 horsepower or more as well as 3 types of 4WD tractors up to 250 horsepower. Data for the same 16 types of 2WD tractors were available for the 1994–2002 period, and for 4 types of 4WD tractors to 350 horsepower or more in capacity.

The composition of machinery services was more stable than the composition of the capital aggregate over the sample period. Figure 3-6 shows estimates of the annual value of capital services from (or, equivalently, rental costs of) combines, tractors, and trucks on U.S. farms in constant (2000) dollars during the period 1949–2002. Perhaps, in part, as a consequence of the spike in commodity prices in the early 1970s (e.g., see Alston, Beddow and Pardey 2009), the rate of capital investment increased throughout the 1970s and early 1980s—thereby increasing the stock of relatively new and larger tractors and thus causing a surge in the use of tractor services. The quantity of tractor services then declined dramatically in the second half of the 1980s, reflecting responses to the boom and bust cycle in agriculture during those years.

The real value of services from combines peaked in 1986 at $3.2 billion, declining thereafter to $1.2 billion in 2002. Thus, during 1986–2002 an 11 percent increase in the production of field crops was achieved in spite of a 61 percent reduction in the real value of combine harvester services.[7] Combine technology changed significantly during the 1960s and 1970s, with a dramatic shift

7 See Appendix Table II-1 for a list of crops included in the field crops index.

Figure 3-6 Real Cost of Services from Combines, Tractors, and Trucks on U.S. Farms, 1949–2002

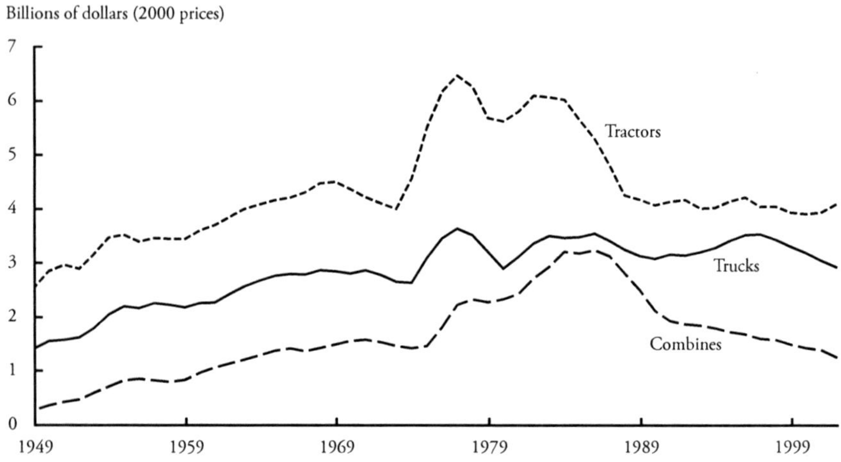

Sources: Authors' calculations based on InSTePP series.

Notes: Annual imputed rental value of capital deflated using the GDP implicit price deflator with base year 2000.

from pull-type to self-propelled combines. In the early years of our sample, virtually all of the combines on farms were pull-type machines hitched to tractors when in use. Unpublished figures on sales of pull-type combines were available only through to 1973, by which time sales had dropped to negligible amounts, and so the stock of combines now on farms consists almost entirely of self-propelled machines.[8] Unlike tractors, the capacity of these combines (as indexed by the width of the combine head) increased fairly steadily, but unit sales decreased dramatically, falling from 33,048 units in 1975 to 8,411 units in 1985. In the period 1985–2002, annual sales of combines averaged less than 10,000 units per year, with 5,052 units sold in 2002.[9]

According to our estimates, the real value of tractor services in U.S. agriculture peaked at approximately $6.4 billion in 1977, after which it declined to $4.1 billion by 2002. These estimates of the aggregate value of tractor services mask substantial structural changes over time in the use of tractor-related capital in U.S. agriculture, and substantial spatial differences in the stock of tractors.

8 For an economic assessment of the adoption processes in play during the initial wave of mechanization of crop harvesting in the United States following the first commercialization of reapers in 1833 see David (1966), Olmstead (1975), Manuelli and Seshadri (2003) and Martini and Silberberg (2006). Cooper, Barton and Brodell (1947, p. 38) describe the subsequent technological transition that began in the 1940s from horse-drawn and tractor-drawn grain binders to combine harvester-thresher machines.

9 The source of sales data is the Association of Equipment Manufacturers.

In turn, these patterns reflect differences in the composition of agricultural output within a state, over time and among states, as well as changes in the size and structure of farms and farming operations.[10] Figure 3-7 depicts various indicators of the changing number and attributes of tractors in U.S. agriculture since 1917.

The number of tractors on U.S. farms rose steadily during the first half of the 20th Century, then more-or-less plateaued after 1958 (Figure 3-1). Unit sales of tractors collapsed during the Great Depression, after which they increased dramatically until around 1950 (Figure 3-7, Panel a). Tractor sales declined from 1950 to 1990 but since then they have increased again. While both the annual sales and stock of tractors on farms, as measured by the simple count, increased a little since the early 1990s, the real value of services from tractors continued to decline. This reflects a reduction in the average horsepower of tractors purchased during the period 1990–2005. The average size of tractors sold in the United States peaked at 96 horsepower in 1976 (with total horsepower purchases peaking a few years earlier in 1973, Figure 3-7, Panel a), and generally declined thereafter to an average of 59 horsepower in 2005 (Figure 3-7, Panel b). Figure 3-7, Panel c shows fluctuations in the average age (or vintage) of tractors on farms.

Figure 3-8 depicts the spatial variation in the average horsepower of tractors purchased in U.S. agriculture since 1964. The Northeast region consistently purchased the smallest tractors in the country, as might be expected given the region's very limited production of field crops and its emphasis on specialty crops (see Chapter 2). The Northern Plains, where field crops constitute more than half the agricultural output, purchased the largest tractors—in 2005 averaging 134 horsepower, compared with a national average of 59 horsepower. The Central region, likewise heavily oriented to field crop production, also purchased comparatively large tractors.

Figure 3-8 also shows that the disparities in tractor size among regions widened over time. Tractors purchased in the Northern Plains region in 2005 were over 80 percent larger than those purchased in 1964, whereas tractors purchased in the Northeast region in 2005 were 30 percent smaller than in 1964. Reflecting these two trends, in 2005, on average tractors in the Northern Plains had 4.2 times as much horsepower as tractors in the Northeast; whereas in 1964 tractors in the Northern Plains had only 1.6 times as much horsepower as tractors in the Northeast. Adjusting for these large differences over time and space in the implied composition of the tractor stock has measurable consequences for estimates of the capital services derived from these machines.

10 Tractor use in U.S agriculture has been much studied by economists. In addition to the studies cited in footnote 8, see also Hurst (1933), Jasny (1935), Brodell and Kendell (1950), Griliches (1960c), Fox (1966), and Olmstead and Rhode (1994).

Figure 3-7 Tractor Attributes, 1917–2005

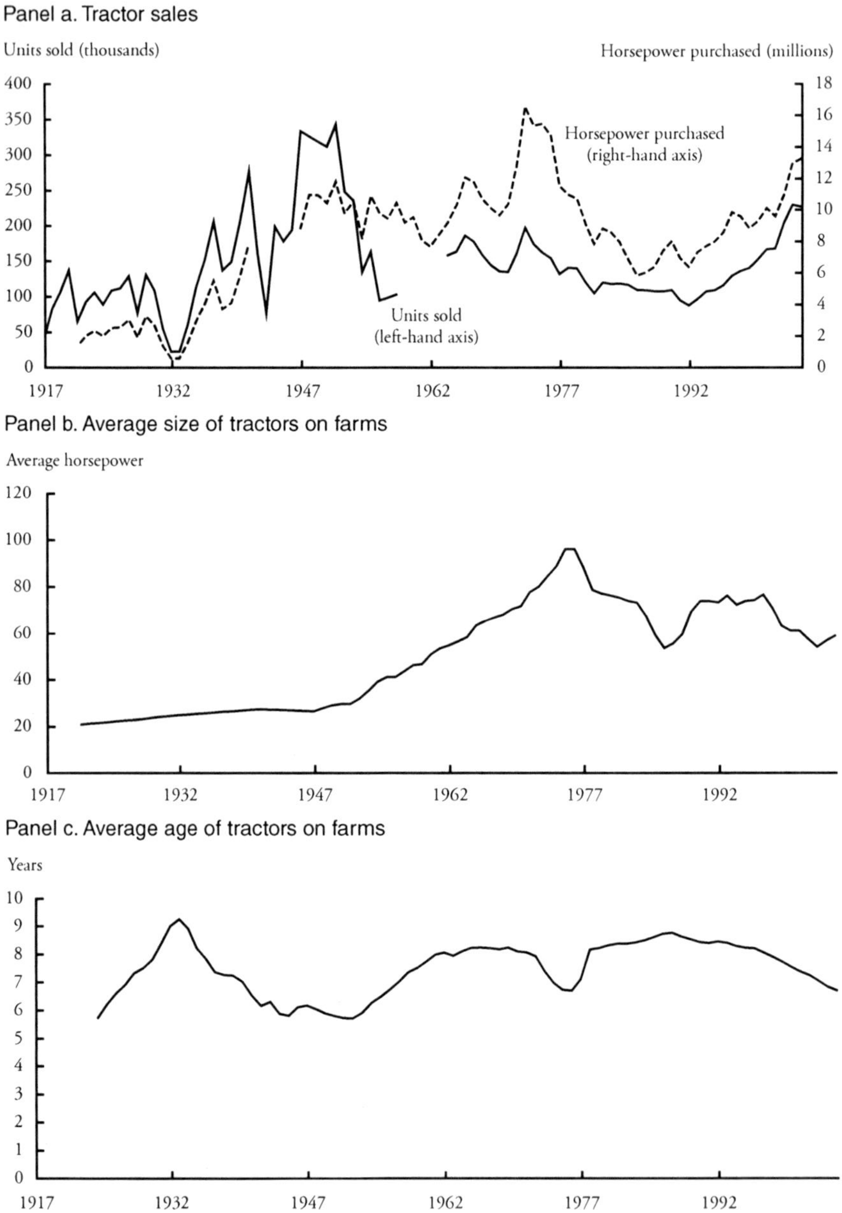

Sources: Panel a. Tractor sales represent purchase data from Brodell and Kendall (1950) for the period 1917–1947, extrapolated to 1958 using manufacturers' shipment data from Strickler and Hines (1960, Table 16), then spliced to unpublished Association of Equipment Manufacturers (AEM) sales data for the period 1964–2005 that were used to develop the InSTePP capital series. Panel b average size and Panel c average age for 1921–1962 from Fox (1966, Table 5). Average size for 1964–2005 from AEM, and average age 1963–2005 compiled by authors using data from various Census of Agriculture.

Notes: Sales data are interpolated for the period 1959–1963, and average size data are interpolated for the year 1963.

Figure 3-8 Average Horsepower of Tractors on Farms, Regional Averages, 1964–2005

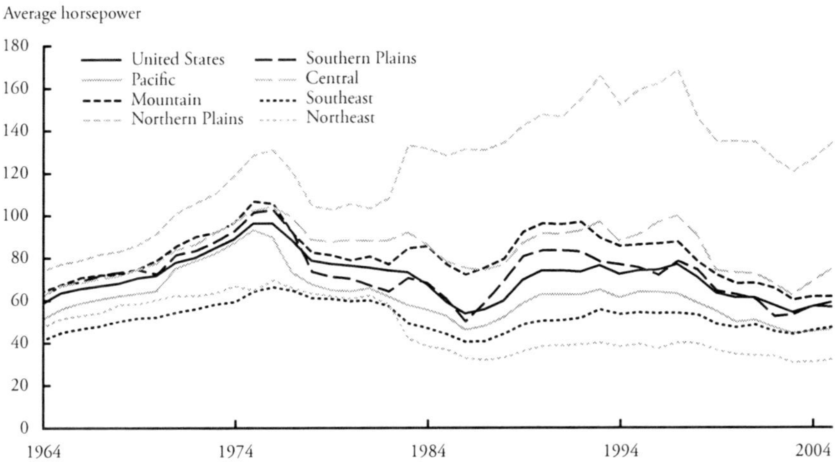

Sources: Authors' calculations using unpublished data provided by the Association of Equipment Manufacturers (AEM).

3.3 The Composition of Labor

In 2002, U.S. agriculture used only 40 percent of the quantity of labor used in 1949. This estimate reflects our accounting for the (state-specific) changes in the age, education, and off-farm work status of farm operators, along with changes in the mix of operator, family and hired labor. Using a Fisher index of aggregate labor use, total annual hours of quality-adjusted labor on U.S. farms fell from approximately 20 billion in 1950 to 7 billion in 2002, an average rate of decline of 1.74 percent per year. If 1949 (i.e., initial period) prices were used instead of annual sets of price weights to estimate the aggregate quantity of quality-adjusted agricultural labor (i.e., if a Laspeyres rather than a Fisher indexing procedure were used), the estimated rate of decline would have been marginally lower: around 1.67 percent per year (Figure 3-9, Panel a). If no attempt had been made to account for the changing composition of labor, and we had simply counted unweighted hours in agriculture (while still adjusting for the substantial increase in part-time farming) the measured rate of decline would have been more pronounced (2.15 percent per year).

Our labor input measures are based on estimates of the hired, family and operator hours in agriculture in each state, not a head count of persons engaged in agriculture as reported by agencies such as the United Nations Food and Agriculture Organization.[11] An hours-in-agriculture metric enabled us, among other things, to account for the significant shift towards part-time farming by U.S.

11 See the FAOSTAT on-line database at http://faostat.fao.org for more information.

Figure 3-9 Aggregate Labor Use, 1949–2002

Panel a. Alternative measures of aggregate labor use

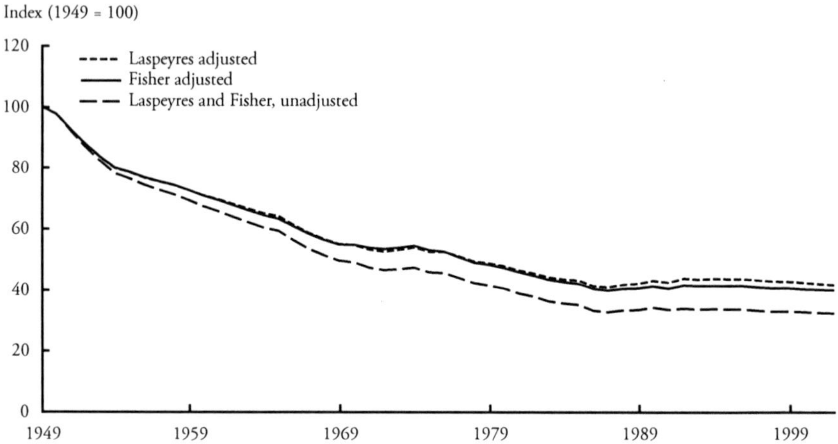

Panel b. Alternative measures of operator hours in U.S. agriculture

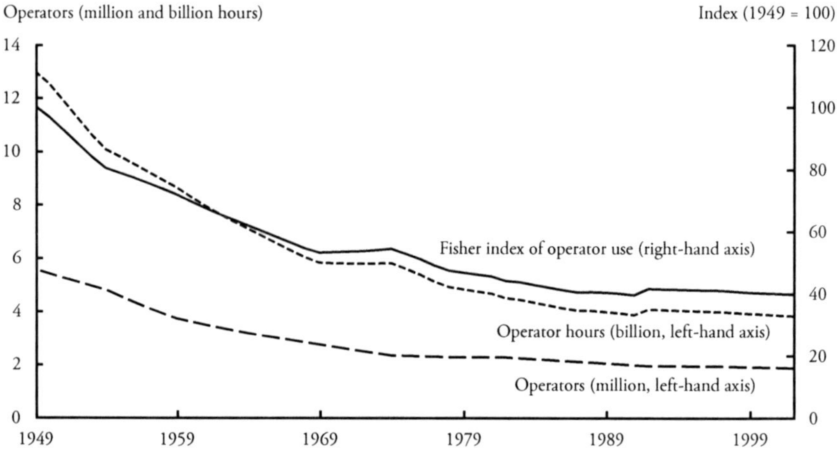

Sources: Calculated by the authors based on InSTePP data.

Notes: Appendix II provides some additional details about the InSTePP labor series reported here. Unadjusted Laspeyres and Fisher indexes were calculated using a national average wage for all states and categories of labor. The adjusted indexes use state- and category-specific estimates of wages. Number of operators and operator hours include full- and part-time operators.

farm operators, especially after World War II. For example, according to our estimates, in 1930 around 6 percent of all operators worked more than 200 days per year off-farm. A little more than fifty years later, in 1982, this off-farm share was 35 percent (the 2002 figure was also 35 percent). To account for the general shift toward more days spent off farm, we formed an estimate of the average number of hours operators worked off farm relative to the hours in a full-time farm year. In 2002, part-time farmers worked 61 percent of their total work hours off-farm, compared with 31 percent in 1930.[12] As a consequence, the total number of operator hours in agriculture declined at an average annual rate of 1.75 percent per year after 1949 compared with a more modest rate of decline (2.08 percent per year) in the number of farm operators (Figure 3-9, Panel b).

Most of the reduction in total and operator hours in agriculture during the latter half of the 20th Century occurred prior to the mid-1980s (Figure 3-10, Panel a). Since then, the quantity of labor inputs has been comparatively constant. While the quantity of labor trended downward, the wages of farm workers increased substantially. In 1975 the average nominal wage of a farm operator was $5.10 per hour, and by 2002 the nominal wage rate had almost trebled to $14.90 per hour.[13] This is one possible reason why labor stopped moving out of agriculture around the mid-1980s; that is, farm wages had equilibrated with wages in other sectors of the economy.[14] The composition of labor hours changed as well—in 1950 operator hours represented 63 percent of the total hours in U.S. agriculture, family hours 17 percent, and hired labor hours 20 percent. By 2002 the share of operator hours had dropped to 52 percent, hired labor hours increased to 33 percent, and family labor hours dropped to 15 percent of the total.

Once again, the U.S. averages hide a good deal of variation among regions and states. Reflecting in part the labor-intensive cropping and handling practices associated with perishable crops, the Pacific region (including and dominated by California, which accounted for 73 percent of all the hired labor in the region in 2002) consistently used more hired labor relative to other labor than any other

12 After some experimentation and calibration of our estimates of hours against data reported in the 1980 and 1990 U.S. Department of Commerce "Earnings by Occupation and Education" supplemental reports that were issued in conjunction with the corresponding population censuses, we assumed that a full-time farm year consists of 50 weeks per year, 7 days per week, at an average of 8 hours per day, or 2,800 hours per year. Agricultural Census reports classify farmers by various cohorts in terms of days-worked-off-farm. For instance in 2002 they identified five categories of number of days off-farm: 1–49, 50–99, 100–149, 150–199, and 200 days or more.

13 These are the authors' calculations based on InSTePP data. Estimates are a weighted average of separate wage rates for each of 30 age-cum-education cohorts, where the weights are the shares of total hours provided by each cohort.

14 In an investigation of the forces affecting the increase of (low) incomes in U.S. agriculture Gardner (2000) stressed the gradual integration of agricultural and non-agricultural labor markets. Analyzing data for the 1950–1990 period he observed that "...the growth of income in low-income farm households appears almost entirely attributable to increased earnings as labor markets adjusted to the disequilibrium (as indicated by initial earnings disparities) that existed in 1960, but which appear to have largely disappeared by the 1990s (as indicated by approximate equality of U.S. average farm and non-farm incomes after that date (p. 1071)." He also noted that "... these [hired farm worker] wage rates showed almost complete convergence of farm wage rates across states (p. 1072)." This same phenomenon is evident in the InSTePP data, the coefficient of variation of farm wage rates across states in 1949 was 0.112 narrowing to 0.006 by 2002.

Figure 3-10 Composition of Labor Use in U.S. Agriculture, 1949–2002

Panel a. Operator, family, and hired labor hours in U.S. agriculture

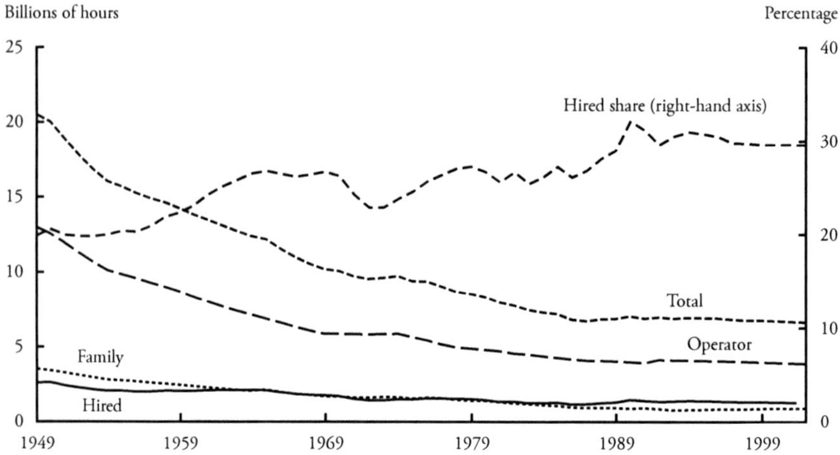

Panel b. Share of hired labor in total labor hours

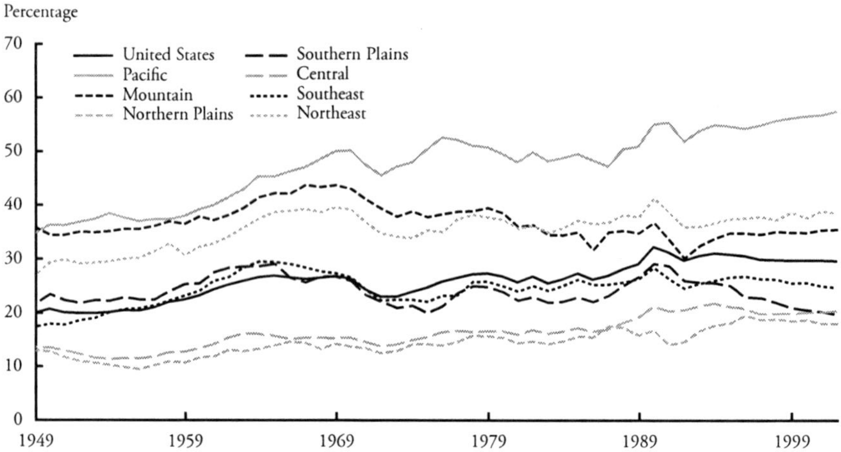

Sources: Calculated by the authors based on InSTePP data.

Notes: Appendix II provides some additional details about the InSTePP labor series reported here. U.S. hired share represents the share of hired labor hours in total labor hours in U.S. agriculture. Regional estimates are the simple average of the shares of the states within each region.

region of the country. Hired labor accounted for 50 percent of all the hours in agriculture in the Pacific region over the period 1949–2002, trending up from 35 percent in 1949 to 57 percent in 2002 (Figure 3-10, Panel b). The Central region, with its generally larger farm acreages and greater concentration of production in non-perishable field crops such as corn, soybeans and wheat, obtained 14 percent of its labor from hired workers over the 1949–2002 period. But even

Table 3-3 Farm Operator Age and Education Attributes

Education			Age		
Grade	1950	2002	Years	1950	2002
	percentage of operator hours			*percentage of operator hours*	
0 to 7th grade	43.5	3.1	25 to 34	16.4	5.3
8th grade	27.7	3.3	35 to 44	25.4	16.3
Some high school	13.0	6.2	45 to 54	25.1	23.5
Completed high school	10.7	42.8	55 to 64	21.4	23.1
Some college	3.2	23.4	65 and over	11.7	31.8
4 years college or more	1.8	21.2			

Sources: U.S. Department of Commerce (1950) and USDA ERS (2006).

Notes: The 1950 estimates are the number of rural males 25 years and older stratified by age-education cohorts.

here the tendency has been toward an increasing share of hired labor as the total hours of labor used in agriculture has declined, such that the share of hired labor in total hours in agriculture in the Central region grew from 13 percent in 1949 to 20 percent in 2002, whereas the total amount of hired labor shrunk from 448 million to 199 million hours for this region over the same period.

While the quantity of labor decreased in absolute terms and the composition changed, the average quality of farm operators improved substantially. Farm operators with no more than eight years of schooling provided 71 percent of the total hours worked by operators in 1950 compared with only 6 percent in 2002 (Table 3-3). Conversely, operators with any college education provided only 5 percent of operator hours in 1950, but 45 percent in 2002. Farmers 25–34 years old accounted for 16.4 percent of farm operator hours in 1950, but only 5.3 percent in 2002. Conversely, farmers older than 65 years provided 11.7 percent of operator hours in 1950 and 31.8 percent in 2002. The shift to more-experienced and better-educated farm operators represents an increase in the quality-constant hours in agriculture. These compositional changes have offset the reduction in the (unadjusted) hours in agriculture to some degree, thereby slowing the rate of decline in the index of quality-adjusted agricultural hours versus the index of unadjusted counts of hours plotted in Figure 3-9, Panel b.

Figure 3-11 juxtaposes trends in the average age (upper bars) and estimated education levels (lower bars) of U.S. farm operators differenced against similar trends for men in the general U.S. population. They indicate that in the post-World War II era at least, farmers have been older on average than U.S. men generally. Moreover they are aging at a faster rate. In 1949, the average age of U.S. farmers was 48.5 years, 3 years (6.5 percent) older than the average adult U.S. male; in 1997, the average age of U.S. farmers was 54.2 years, 7 years (15.5 percent) older than the average adult U.S. male. In contrast, the education gap between farm operators and the U.S. male population generally has narrowed.

Figure 3-11 Age and Education Differences between Farmers and U.S. Males

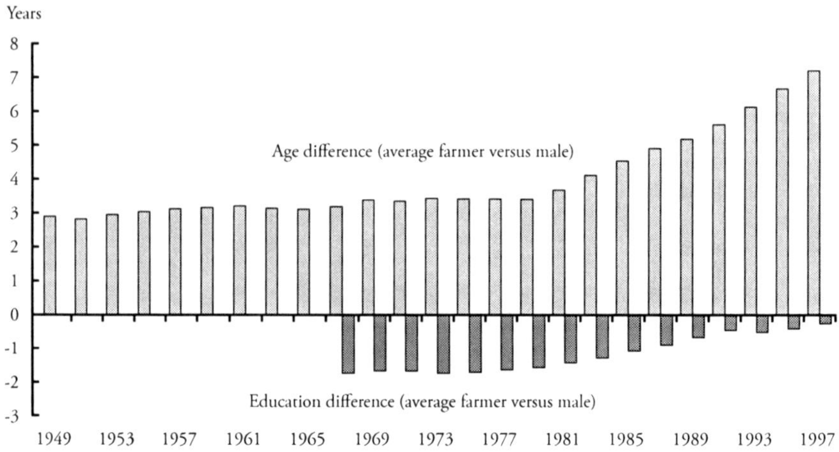

Sources: General male population education estimates were calculated using Goldin (2006). General male population age estimates were calculated using Haines (2006). Farmer age and education estimates derived from InSTePP data files.

Notes: The top bars represent the average number of years older the U.S. farmer population was compared with the general U.S. male population. The bottom bars represent the average fewer years of education attained by U.S. farmers compared with the general U.S. male population.

In 1966, U.S. farmers averaged 8.8 years of schooling, 1.8 years less than the average for U.S. males (10.6 years), but by 1997 the gap had shrunk to 0.3 years: 12.8 years of schooling for farm operators versus 13.0 years for adult males.

3.4 The Composition of Land

In the second half of the 20th Century the quantity of land in U.S. agriculture declined slightly. According to the InSTePP measures (see Appendix II for details), total acreage in U.S. agriculture—i.e., simply counting acres, irrespective of what type of acres they are—fell by 0.15 percent per year over 1949–2002. However, offsetting the decline in agricultural acreage was an increase in the average quality of those acres over the same period; the share of irrigated cropland acres increased and the share of marginal land decreased. In the period 1949–2002, acres of non-irrigated cropland fell by 15 percent, and acres of grassland fell by 7 percent, while irrigated acreage grew by 114 percent. Irrigated cropland represented approximately 12.5 percent of all U.S. cropland (irrigated plus non-irrigated) in 2002 compared with 5.4 percent in 1949. Consequently, the rate of contraction in counts of acres (0.15 percent per year) was substantially faster than the rate

Figure 3-12 Aggregate Land Use, 1949–2002

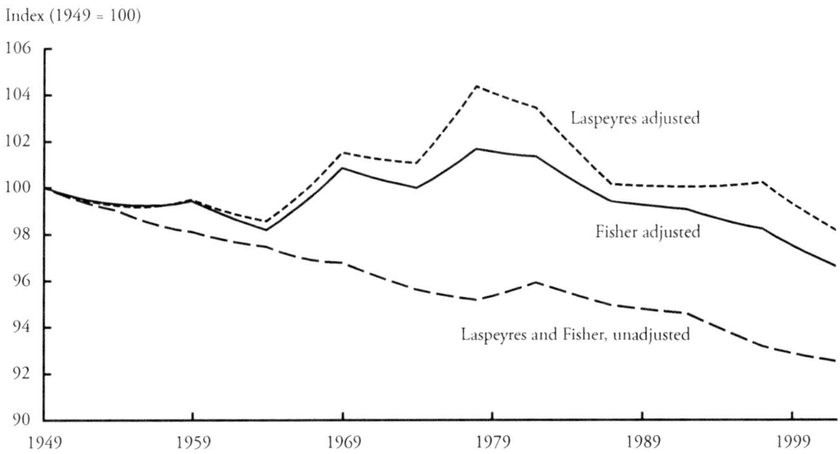

Sources: Authors' calculations based on InSTePP series.

Notes: The adjusted Laspeyres and Fisher indexes include different rental price and acreage estimates for each state, as well as the three categories of land input—rainfed cropland, irrigated cropland, and pastureland. The unadjusted series use a single national annual average price series for all states and categories. When the different categories of an index all have the same price, the Fisher index collapses to the Laspeyres index, and thus they are equal for the unadjusted series.

of decline in the quality-adjusted Fisher index of aggregate land use (just 0.07 percent per year), as shown in Figure 3-12.[15]

As one might expect, much of the irrigated cropland is concentrated in the drier southern states, and, especially, in the western half of the country, although an increasing share of the cropland in many states is now irrigated (Figure 3-13, Panel a). By 2002 all of the Pacific and Mountain states (except for Montana) irrigated more than 20 percent of their cropland, with Arizona and California irrigating more than 75 percent of their land in crops. In 1949, California, Colorado and Texas each accounted for more than 10 percent of the total irrigated cropland in the United States (Figure 3-13, Panel b). The total number of irrigated acres throughout the country increased markedly during the second half of the 20th Century, from 25.8 million acres in 1949 to 55.2 million acres in 2002. In addition, irrigated acres became more disbursed among the states, such that,

15 The InSTePP series includes set-aside acres and CRP acreage as part of the land used in U.S. agriculture. Farmers earn a return to the land either by actively farming that land or participating in the Conservation Reserve Program (CRP). By the same token, the returns to CRP acres are deemed an output in the InSTePP series (see Chapter 4 for more discussion). The CRP program was initiated in 1986. CRP acreage as a share of total cropped acreage peaked in 1993 at 7.93 percent; in 2002 it was 7.68 percent. Sullivan et al. (2004) provide a good description of the history and an assessment of some of the economic implications of this program.

Figure 3-13 Distribution of Irrigated Cropland, 1949 and 2002

1949 2002

Panel a. Share of cropland that is irrigated, by state

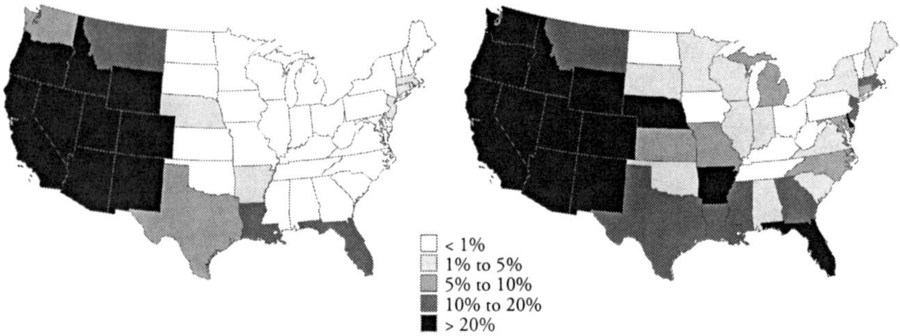

Panel b. State share of total U.S. irrigated cropland

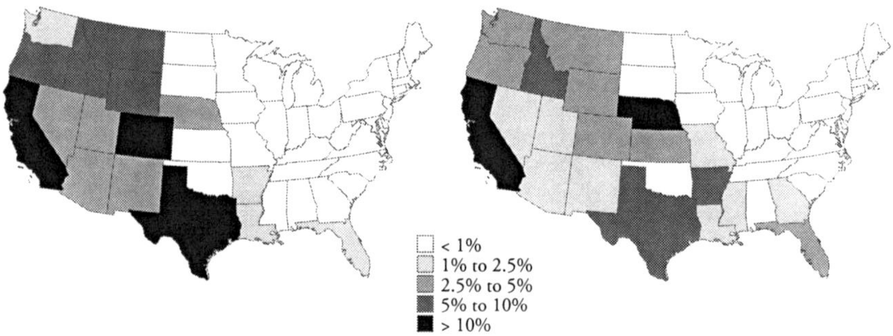

Sources: Authors' calculations based on InSTePP series.

by 2002, California and Nebraska were the only two states to account for more than 10 percent of the country's total irrigated cropland.[16]

3.5 Other Inputs

Materials

A notable feature of U.S. agriculture, especially during the second half of the 20th Century, was the rise in the cost share of materials, which includes livestock feed, crop seeds, breeding stock, chemicals (including fertilizer, herbicides and pesti-

16 Irrigated acres include a heterogeneous set of irrigation technologies and management methods. In gravity flow systems, water is conveyed to the field by means of open ditches, above-ground pipe (including gated pipe and flexible tubing), or underground pipe, and released along the upper end of the field through siphon tubes, ditch gates, pipe valves, or pipe orifices. Alternatively, pressurized systems use a variety of sprinkler and low-flow irrigation techniques to distribute water across a fielded system (Schaible and Aillery 2006).

cides), electricity and other forms of energy, and myriad other items and services. In 1949, purchased materials accounted for 23 percent of the total cost of inputs used in the InSTePP series; by 2002 this share had grown to 38 percent, exceeding that of all other input classes, including labor (Appendix Table 3-1).

The composition of materials has also changed markedly. In 1950, feed (40 percent of all materials expenses), repairs (19 percent), and energy (15 percent) were the most important categories of materials (Table 3-4). Furthermore, 93 percent of energy costs were from fuel and only 7 percent from electricity. None of the other categories in Table 3-4 represented more than 10 percent of materials costs. By 2001, the share of materials cost attributable to feed inputs had dropped substantially (to 26 percent), as had repairs (to 11 percent) and energy (to 11 percent, although electricity now accounted for 36 percent of these energy costs compared with just 7 percent in 1949). Pesticides and seeds had increased their respective cost shares, but they each still accounted for less than 10 percent of materials costs. The biggest increase came in the miscellaneous category, which includes a diverse set of inputs.[17] By 2002 this category rivaled feed as the largest single cost category in this particular class of inputs. The structure of materials costs varied substantially among regions within the United States, although the trends over time within each region tended to follow the U.S. pattern.

R&D contributed to changes in the composition or quality of many of these purchased inputs, and for some of these inputs the private sector played a pivotal role, especially in the early part of the 20th Century. Notable is the improved quality and expanded range of chemical inputs that changed the composition and formulation of fuels, synthetic fertilizers, pesticides, and growth promotants, which had their biggest impacts in the second half of the 20th Century.[18] Inputs that embody information technologies—such as those involving computers, electronics, robotics, remote sensing, and geographic information systems (GIS)—are mainly a relatively recent phenomenon, though the telephone and telegraph (see Chapter 8) can be seen as earlier examples.

---

17 Prior to 1978 this series included estimates of insurance, binding materials, dairy supplies, unidentified greenhouse and nursery expenses, grazing fees, harness, saddlery and blacksmithing, hardware and hand tools, telephone, vet fees and supplies. After 1978 it included health and breeding supplies, grazing fees, custom feeding fees, irrigated water fees, farm supplies, tools, non-capital equipment, net insurance, motor vehicle registration and licensing, telephone and water, other farm business management expenses and production expenses. The miscellaneous expense data and additional documentation are available from USDA ERS (2009b).

18 Baum and Clement (1958) give a descriptive history of the changing U.S. fertilizer sector in the first half of the 20th Century. Griliches (1958) studied the short- and long-run aggregate demand for fertilizer in the United States from 1911 to 1956. Daberkow and Huang (2006) review more recent developments.

Table 3-4 Material Costs, Three-Year Averages Centered on 1950 and 2001

	Feed	Seed	Fertilizer	Pesticide	Energy	Machine Hire	Repairs	Misc.
				percentage of materials cost				
Panel a. 1949–1951 average								
United States	40	6	8	2	15	1	19	9
48 state								
Average	41	6	9	2	14	1	18	9
Minimum	11	2	0	0	4	0	6	4
Maximum	77	9	36	9	33	1	30	19
Selected states								
California	47	4	7	5	13	1	14	9
Minnesota	35	8	3	1	19	1	23	10
Wyoming	48	4	1	1	16	1	19	12
Regions								
Pacific	45	5	6	4	13	1	16	9
Mountain	37	5	3	2	18	1	21	13
Northern Plains	31	7	2	1	23	1	25	11
Southern Plains	35	7	9	3	17	0	20	8
Central	40	7	6	1	15	1	21	9
Southeast	30	7	24	3	12	0	17	7
Northeast	57	5	7	2	8	0	14	7
Panel b. 2000–2002 average								
United States	26	9	8	9	11	4	11	23
48 state								
Average	27	9	7	8	12	4	12	23
Minimum	5	3	2	2	6	1	4	15
Maximum	50	22	19	19	22	10	19	30
Selected states								
California	26	8	3	10	13	8	8	26
Minnesota	24	12	9	9	10	5	10	21
Wyoming	26	3	5	3	14	3	16	30
Regions								
Pacific	24	8	3	10	12	7	10	25
Mountain	28	6	5	6	13	5	11	26
Northern Plains	20	10	8	10	12	5	12	23
Southern Plains	27	6	7	9	12	4	10	25
Central	22	12	12	11	9	4	11	19
Southeast	37	7	7	7	9	2	8	23
Northeast	33	9	4	5	11	4	12	22

Sources: Authors' calculations based on InSTePP series.

Notes: Figures represent the percentage cost shares of each category in total materials cost.

Biological Inputs

One distinguishing feature of agricultural production processes is their reliance on biological inputs. Some of these constitute materials such as seed and plant cuttings for vegetatively propagated crops, or calves, lambs, and piglets for fattening, layer hens and other animals; some constitute biological capital inputs such as animal breeding stock, cows for milking, and perennials like orange trees, almond trees, and grape vines. Table 3-4 gives an indication of the changing cost implications for some of these biological inputs (specifically feed and seed); Figure 3-5 shows the trends in the livestock component of biological capital reflected in the InSTePP series.

The attributes of biological inputs have changed dramatically, often as a result of private or public R&D. For example, a considerable amount of purposeful genetic change has created new crop varieties and animal breeds, even pre-dating the scientific approaches to genetic change that picked up pace during the early part of the 20th Century (Olmstead and Rhode 1993 and 2008). These changes have led to improved disease resistance; quality improvements such as more uniform grain and fruit, among others; better tolerance for drought, waterlogging, or shorter growing seasons; introduction of "dwarfing" genes in the seeds of crops like wheat and rice, increasing their harvest indexes; better crop adaptation to particular climates or soil conditions; or greater suitability for mechanical harvesting (including more uniform ripening and the ability of the plant or its fruit to withstand mechanical processes).[19] For certain crops such as corn, soybeans, and certain high-value specialty crops, an increasing share of the genetic improvement embodied in seed inputs was attributable to private research.[20] However, for other crops such as wheat, rice, and strawberries, the bulk of the work was conducted by breeding programs in public agencies.

Important innovations have also been embodied in animals as biological inputs into agricultural production with beneficial consequences for stocking rates, disease control, reproductive efficiency, and feed conversion efficiency.[21] Such changes have enabled the development, for instance, of intensive large-scale, highly cost-efficient hog and poultry operations. To do so has meant combining elements of improvements in genetics, animal housing, feed, veterinary knowledge and medicines, and, importantly, livestock husbandry. Many of these

---

19 Dwarfing refers to a characteristic of the wheat (and other grain) plant, where the growth of the plant's stalk is limited. Not only is more of the plant's energy directed to the production of the edible wheat grain, rather than inedible straw, but the plant is mechanically stronger (Syme 1970). Thus plants with larger wheat heads arising from the use of fertilizer (and irrigation) no longer lodge (or tip over), making them easier to harvest, reducing grain loss and increasing crop yields.

20 Chapter 6 provides some discussion of the long history of informal innovation as well as the more recent phenomenon of organized research; it also includes some data on research spending trends of private corporate entities. See, also, Pardey, Alston and Ruttan (2010).

21 For details on developments affecting livestock breeding and animal management, see Leavitt (1933), Johnson and Ruttan (1997) and Orland (2004).

changes have been somewhat controversial. People concerned with animal welfare have questioned the intensive livestock systems; people concerned about food safety have questioned the use of growth hormones (for example, rBST used to increase milk yield in dairy cattle was very controversial) and transgenic forms of biotechnology in animals.

Natural Inputs

Another distinguishing feature of agriculture is its reliance on natural inputs. Some are embodied in measured inputs like land that carries with it certain quality attributes including soil structure, depth, organic matter, slope and aspect. Others, principally weather- or climate-related variables, are rarely or less directly captured as measured inputs into agriculture. This includes inputs such as precipitation (including its amount, timing, frequency, and intensity) day length, sunlight, and wind duration, timing and speed. All of these natural inputs have site-specific characteristics, which means that some of their attributes may be reflected in the price or rental rates used to aggregate land inputs that have been spatially segmented (in our case down to the state level). But in practice, many of these types of inputs are rarely included—by economists at least—among the set of measured inputs that affect agricultural output, even though they have significant implications for production and productivity.[22]

3.6 Factor Proportions, Relative Prices and Cost Shares

Factor proportions in U.S. agriculture changed markedly over the past 50 years at least.[23] Figure 3-14 tracks the changes in relative factor use for four broad input categories, namely land, labor, capital services, and materials. Indexes of factor proportions were computed as ratios of the indexes of the quantities of individual inputs, all of which were normalized to a value of 100 in 1949 (i.e., all of the ratios start at 1.0 in 1949). Since then, the materials:labor and materials: land ratios increased the fastest by 3.62 and 1.94 percent per year respectively, on average. By 2002 the quantity of materials input per unit of labor was almost

---

22 See Chapter 9 for a more complete discussion of the treatment and effects of weather variables in economic assessments of agricultural production and productivity.

23 Hayami (1969) and Hayami and Ruttan (1970 and 1971) were the first to document and extensively examine the influences of changes in relative prices on the long-run pattern of factor proportions in U.S. (and Japanese) agriculture. In addition to direct input substitution effects, they also suggested that the changes in relative prices would induce factor-biased changes in technology. Binswanger (1974a, 1974b and 1974c) laid out the microeconomic formulation of the induced-innovation model in a dual framework and developed additional empirical methods for assessing the conformity of empirical data with the notion that changes in relative (factor) prices may influence the factor bias of technical changes. More recently, Olmstead and Rhode (1993 and 1998) presented criticisms that related to specific elements of the U.S. empirical evidence presented by Hayami and Ruttan (1970 and 1971). Pardey, Alston and Ruttan (2010) provide a succinct review of this literature.

Figure 3-14 Factor Proportions for U.S. Agriculture, 1949–2002

Panel a. Land, labor, and materials ratios

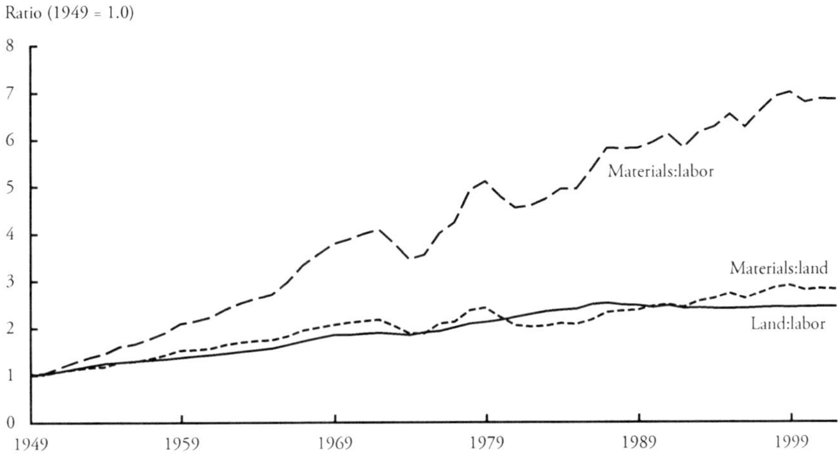

Panel b. Land, labor, and materials relative to capital

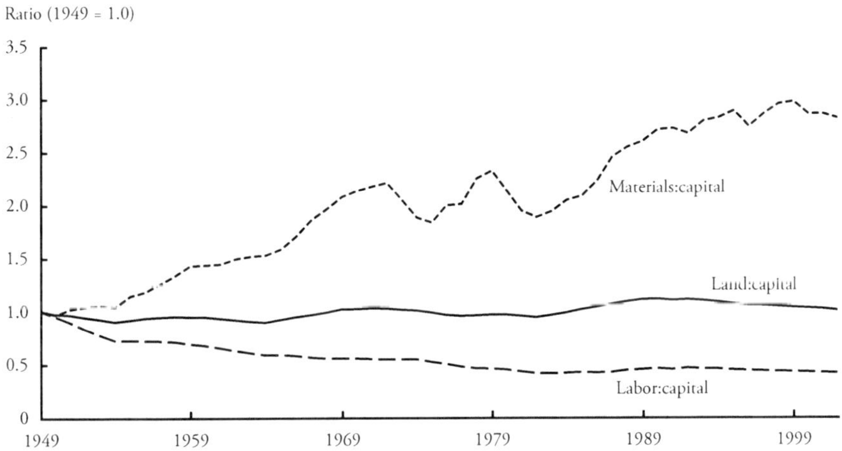

Sources: Authors' calculations based on InSTePP series.

Notes: Annual factor proportions are the ratios of the Fisher indexes of the quantities of the given inputs in U.S. agriculture for the period 1949–2002.

seven times what it had been in 1949, and the quantity of materials input per unit of land used in 2002 was around three times what it had been in 1949. Land:labor ratios experienced less dramatic but still substantial increases, as did both the capital:labor and capital:land ratios.

The general trends in U.S. factor proportions were emblematic of the trends among many, but not all regions and states, and the rates of change varied mark-

Table 3-5 Factor Proportions, Average Annual Growth Rates, 1949–2002

	Materials to			Land to		Labor to
	Labor	Land	Capital	Labor	Capital	Capital
			average annual percentage change			
United States	3.62	1.94	1.95	1.68	0.01	-1.67
48 state						
Average	3.40	2.11	1.70	1.28	-0.41	-1.69
Minimum	1.21	0.73	0.01	0.18	-1.80	-3.35
Maximum	5.72	3.95	2.88	2.71	0.82	-0.62
Selected states						
California	3.16	2.68	1.92	0.48	-0.76	-1.24
Minnesota	3.89	1.97	2.43	1.93	0.46	-1.47
Wyoming	2.25	1.32	1.07	0.93	-0.25	-1.18
Regions						
Pacific	3.05	2.50	1.98	0.55	-0.52	-1.07
Mountain	3.25	2.33	1.92	0.92	-0.41	-1.33
Northern Plains	3.72	1.83	2.18	1.89	0.35	-1.54
Southern Plains	3.85	1.92	1.82	1.93	-0.10	-2.03
Central	3.49	1.63	2.04	1.86	0.41	-1.45
Southeast	4.44	3.03	1.99	1.41	-1.05	-2.46
Northeast	2.91	1.81	1.30	1.11	-0.51	-1.61

Sources: Authors' calculations based on InSTePP series.

Notes: Factor proportions used in calculating growth rates are the ratios of the Fisher indexes of the quantities of the given inputs and are all normalized to equal 1.0 in 1949.

edly among regions (Table 3-5). For example, the materials:labor ratio increased for all regions, but it grew on average by 4.44 percent per year for the Southeast region compared with just 2.91 percent per year for the Northeast region. While the land:capital ratio decreased for most regions, it increased marginally for the United States overall given significant increases in the Central and Northern Plains regions that saw average annual growth in the ratio of 0.41 and 0.35 percent, respectively, over the period 1949–2002.

Changes in the factor ratios reflect changes in production practices and technologies. For example, irrigated cropland as a share of total acres increased dramatically in the Northern Plains region from 1949 to 2002; from 3.7 to 33.5 percent of total cropped area in Nebraska and from less than 1 percent to 8.8 percent in Kansas. Furthermore, total acres in agriculture decreased only slightly in Kansas between 1949 and 2002; but the composition of agricultural land changed, including a 13.2 percent decrease in pastureland and a 3.5 percent increase in cropland. Consequently, from 1949 to 2002, quality-adjusted land in Northern Plains agriculture increased by an average of 0.25 percent per year, while capital use decreased by 0.09 percent per year. Similar processes were at work in the Central region, land use decreased by 0.06 percent per year and

Figure 3-15 Aggregate Prices and Cost Shares of Inputs Used in U.S. Agriculture, 1949–2002

Panel a. Prices

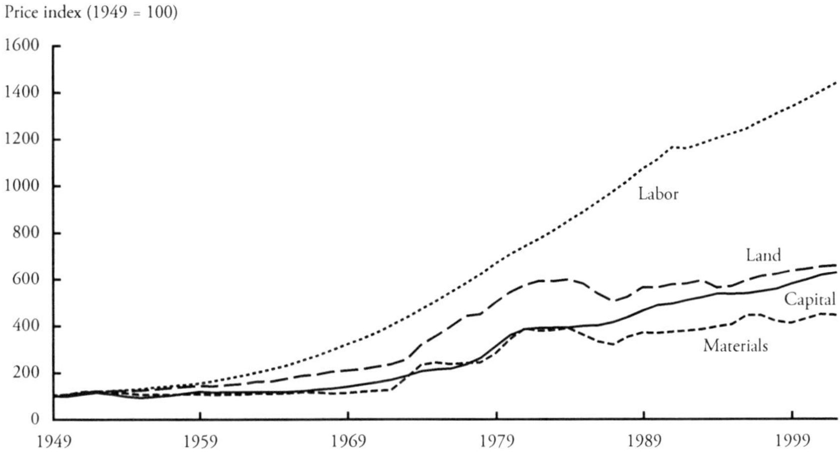

Panel b. Cost shares

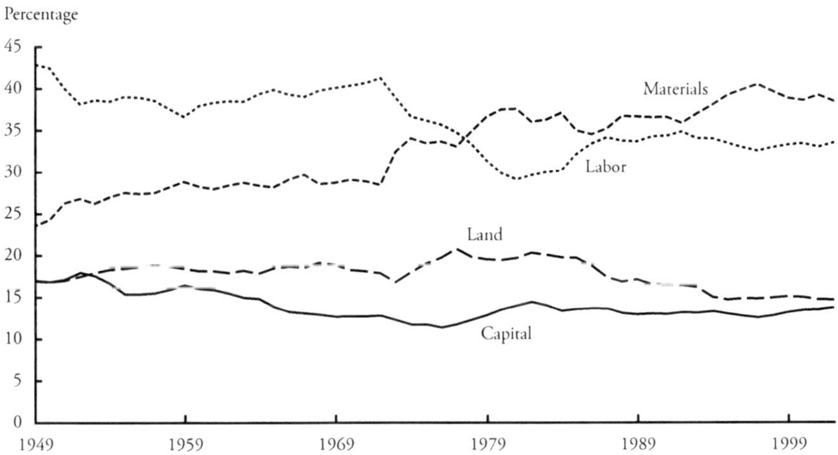

Sources: Authors' calculations based on InSTePP series.

Notes: See Appendix Table 3-1 for input price indexes, quantity indexes, and cost shares.

capital use decreased by a much larger 0.47 percent, such that the land-to-capital ratios rose.

Panel a in Figure 3-15 is the price index counterpart to the aggregate input quantity indexes plotted in Panel a of Figure 3-2. Notably, but perhaps not surprisingly, while the quantity of materials (or purchased inputs) grew faster than the quantity of all other input classes, the aggregate (nominal) price of materials grew the slowest (by an average of 2.80 percent per year since 1949). Conversely, among all measured inputs, labor use declined fastest while the aggregate price of labor grew fastest (5.02 percent per year since 1949). As a consequence of these offsetting price and quantity effects, the decline in the share of total costs attributable to labor is much more muted than the decline in the quantity of labor (Figure 3-15, Panel b). Similarly, the increase in the share of total costs attributable to purchased inputs is much more modest than the increase in the quantity of purchased inputs used in U.S. agriculture.

3.7 Conclusion

Aggregating all measured inputs, the quantity of total input use in United States agriculture changed little in well over half a century. In contrast, the composition of input use changed dramatically, with U.S. agriculture now much more reliant on materials inputs purchased off farm and less reliant on labor. Total use of land and capital inputs was about the same in 2002 as it was in 1949. However, the lack of change at the national level in total inputs or in some broad factor classes masks important variation at finer scales of inputs and spatial resolutions. For example, the composition of land used in agriculture is now much different than it was half a century ago, with irrigated cropland constituting 12.5 percent of cropped acres in 2002 compared with 5.4 percent in 1949. So, too, has the composition of capital changed. While aggregate labor use has declined substantially, the labor used in agriculture is now very different. A much greater proportion of the labor consists of hired workers with much less operator and family labor. Moreover, those farm operators remaining in agriculture are generally older and much more educated than they were decades ago.

The spatial structure of aggregate input use in U.S. agriculture changed markedly during the past 50 years. The spatial composition of individual inputs changed even more dramatically. Chapter 4 explores counterpart changes in the amount, composition and spatial patterns of U.S. agricultural outputs during the past 50 to 100 years.

Appendix Table 3-1 U.S. Agricultural Input Prices, Quantities and Cost Shares, 1949–2002

	Price Indexes					Quantity Indexes					Input Cost Shares			
Year	Capital	Labor	Land	Materials	Total	Capital	Labor	Land	Materials	Total	Capital	Labor	Land	Materials
	index, 1949 = 100					index, 1949 = 100					percentage share			
1949	100	100	100	100	100	100	100	100	100	100	17	43	17	23
1950	98	103	101	105	102	103	97	100	100	99	17	42	17	24
1951	108	111	111	117	112	103	92	100	106	99	17	40	17	26
1952	114	116	119	118	117	106	88	99	110	98	18	38	17	27
1953	107	121	119	110	115	108	83	99	113	97	18	39	18	26
1954	98	124	120	110	115	111	80	99	115	96	17	38	18	27
1955	92	128	121	104	113	109	78	99	124	97	15	39	18	27
1956	96	134	126	105	117	107	77	99	126	97	15	39	19	27
1957	101	140	132	104	121	105	75	99	132	97	15	38	19	27
1958	110	145	137	105	125	105	74	99	140	98	16	37	19	28
1959	118	151	141	105	130	105	73	99	150	99	16	37	18	29
1960	116	162	140	103	132	105	71	99	151	98	16	38	18	28
1961	118	173	145	104	136	106	69	99	153	98	16	38	18	28
1962	117	185	150	104	141	108	68	99	161	99	15	38	18	28
1963	117	198	160	108	148	109	66	98	165	99	15	38	18	29
1964	117	212	160	107	151	110	64	98	168	98	15	39	18	28
1965	117	228	171	109	158	107	63	99	170	98	14	40	18	28
1966	121	248	183	113	168	105	61	99	179	97	13	39	19	29
1967	127	268	189	113	176	104	58	100	192	98	13	39	18	30
1968	132	292	200	108	182	102	56	100	199	97	13	40	19	28
1969	139	317	206	110	191	99	55	101	206	97	13	40	19	29
1970	149	339	211	115	202	99	55	101	211	97	13	40	18	29
1971	158	367	222	120	214	98	54	100	213	97	13	41	18	29
1972	168	397	232	123	227	98	53	100	217	97	13	41	18	28
1973	185	431	253	174	267	99	54	100	203	96	12	39	17	32
1974	205	467	315	230	318	99	54	100	187	93	12	37	18	34
1975	212	501	353	239	339	102	53	100	187	93	12	36	19	33
1976	216	540	394	233	353	105	52	101	209	96	11	36	20	34
1977	233	576	438	237	374	106	51	101	213	96	12	35	21	33
1978	262	616	445	239	390	106	49	102	239	99	12	33	20	35
1979	312	663	496	278	440	105	48	102	245	99	13	31	19	37

(continued)

Appendix Table 3-1 (continued)

	Price Indexes					Quantity Indexes					Input Cost Shares			
Year	Capital	Labor	Land	Materials	Total	Capital	Labor	Land	Materials	Total	Capital	Labor	Land	Materials
	index, 1949 = 100					*index, 1949 = 100*					*percentage share*			
1980	359	702	539	338	499	105	47	101	224	95	13	30	19	37
1981	383	737	569	384	541	106	46	101	206	92	14	29	20	37
1982	389	769	587	374	547	108	44	101	203	90	14	30	20	36
1983	390	806	587	378	557	105	43	101	204	89	14	30	20	36
1984	392	846	594	386	571	102	42	100	209	89	13	30	20	37
1985	398	884	576	357	561	99	42	100	206	88	13	32	20	35
1986	399	928	532	328	546	96	40	100	214	88	14	33	19	34
1987	413	971	499	316	543	93	40	99	229	89	14	34	17	35
1988	436	1,016	520	349	579	91	40	99	232	89	13	34	17	37
1989	463	1,067	560	366	612	90	40	99	233	90	13	34	17	37
1990	486	1,106	559	364	622	89	41	99	242	91	13	34	16	36
1991	492	1,159	572	370	639	90	40	99	245	91	13	34	16	36
1992	507	1,155	576	374	644	90	41	99	239	91	13	35	16	36
1993	519	1,176	589	381	657	90	41	99	251	93	13	34	16	37
1994	533	1,199	559	393	665	91	41	99	257	93	13	34	15	38
1995	530	1,219	565	401	675	92	41	98	267	95	13	33	15	39
1996	531	1,239	590	440	709	93	41	98	256	93	13	33	15	40
1997	540	1,273	607	440	720	93	41	98	267	95	12	32	15	40
1998	550	1,303	616	416	712	93	40	98	278	96	13	33	15	40
1999	572	1,332	631	408	718	94	40	97	281	96	13	33	15	39
2000	587	1,364	638	426	739	94	40	97	271	95	13	33	15	38
2001	607	1,398	649	444	763	94	40	97	272	95	13	33	15	39
2002	617	1,433	653	441	770	95	40	97	271	95	14	33	15	38
Average annual growth rates (percentage)														
1949–1960	1.35	4.37	3.07	0.29	2.49	0.44	-3.15	-0.08	3.73	-0.15	-0.55	-1.12	0.64	1.67
1960–1970	2.47	7.40	4.10	1.12	4.28	-0.60	-2.60	0.15	3.36	-0.09	-2.33	0.61	0.06	0.29
1970–1980	8.84	7.29	9.37	10.75	9.05	0.62	-1.48	0.08	0.62	-0.23	0.64	-3.01	0.64	2.55
1980–1990	3.01	4.54	0.36	0.75	2.20	-1.63	-1.40	-0.23	0.76	-0.43	-0.38	1.37	-1.63	-0.26
1990–2002	1.99	2.16	1.30	1.59	1.78	0.50	-0.26	-0.22	0.93	0.31	0.40	-0.18	-1.00	0.44
1949–2002	3.43	5.02	3.54	2.80	3.85	-0.10	-1.74	-0.07	1.88	-0.11	-0.41	-0.47	-0.27	0.93

Sources: Authors' calculations based on InSTePP series.

CHAPTER 4

Agricultural Outputs

Over the past 100 years and more, U.S. agricultural production grew rapidly and the composition and location of production changed markedly, too. Different measures of agricultural output give different perspectives on these changes. This chapter provides a detailed assessment of the temporal and spatial patterns in the quantity and value of U.S. agricultural production and its composition. The chapter concludes with a presentation of Fisher indexes of output quantities. These indexes are used with the corresponding indexes of input quantities from Chapter 3 to compute the productivity indexes for 1949–2002 that are presented in Chapter 5 and used in the econometric models in subsequent chapters.

4.1 Value, Composition and Location of Production

The value of U.S. agricultural production has varied over space and time, reflecting the impacts of changes in prices and quantities of inputs and outputs, changes in technologies, and a host of other factors that directly or indirectly affect these variables. In this section we present a brief summary of the long-term trends, followed by a closer look at developments in the period for which we have more detailed data, beginning in the middle of the 20th Century. The analysis includes a consideration of the changing mix of outputs among states and over time, as well as changes in the value of the output.

Longer-Term Trends

Chapter 2 provides a long-term perspective on the value of U.S. agricultural production using new comprehensive data on commodity values for the period 1924–2005.[1] The total nominal value of U.S. agricultural production grew from

1 Appendix II provides an overview of the nature and sources of this compilation of data on the value of production. For 2005, this comprehensive series includes data on value for production for

J.M. Alston et al., *Persistence Pays: U.S. Agricultural Productivity Growth and the Benefits from Public R&D Spending*, Natural Resource Management and Policy 34,
DOI 10.1007/978-1-4419-0658-8_4,

$12.3 billion dollars in 1924 to $229.8 billion dollars in 2005 (equivalent to compound growth of 3.68 percent per year). In comparison, national GDP grew at a compound annual rate of 6.32 percent per year over the same period. As agricultural output grew, its composition changed, reflecting changes in the composition of demand for food and fiber products, as well as changes on the supply side driven by a host of technological innovations (Figure 4-1).

The changing share of output value accounted for by specialty crops (fruits, nuts, vegetables, and ornamentals) illustrates the phenomenon. From the beginning of this value-of-production series in 1924 until 1980, on average specialty crops accounted for about 13 percent of the total value of production (ranging between 10 and 17 percent). After 1980, the specialty crops share of production value increased fairly steadily, and it exceeded 20 percent for the 9 years ending in 2005. Within specialty crops, nursery and greenhouse products accounted for 7.1 percent of the value of output in 2005, well above their 1.3 percent share in 1924. Other crops (i.e., the category comprising all crops other than specialty crops) declined in importance as a group, but field crops (including oilseeds, grains, fiber crops, sugar, and tobacco) still accounted for 26.5 percent of crop production in 2005. In the mid-1920s, oil crops accounted for just 1.9 percent of the value of production, but by 2005 their share had grown to 8.5 percent.[2] The replacement of the horse with the tractor, especially during the first half of the 20th Century, accounts for a significant shift to reduce production of oats (used to feed horses) and to increase both the production of other crops and the cattle herd.

Composition and Value of Agricultural Production, 1949–2006

The analysis of research benefits described in Chapters 11 and 12 uses U.S. state-specific data on the quantity and value of agricultural output for the period 1949–2002, taken from the InSTePP dataset. In addition to estimates of the value of output, these data include indexes of quantities and prices for a set of 74 outputs, including 16 field crops, 9 livestock commodities, 22 fruits and nuts, 22 vegetables, implicit quantities of nursery and greenhouse products, implicit quantities of machines rented out by farmers, Conservation Reserve Program (CRP) acreage, and two other miscellaneous outputs (see Table II-1 in Appendix II for details on the grouping of outputs). Here we report on the output value component of that same InSTePP series, extended for four years to run from 1949 to 2006.

---

1 34 distinct commodities.

2 Here, oil crops include canola, cottonseed, flax, peanuts, rapeseed (canola), safflower, sesame, soybeans, and sunflower seeds, along with several other minor crops. See Appendix II for details on commodity categories.

Figure 4-1 Output Value Trends, 1924–2005

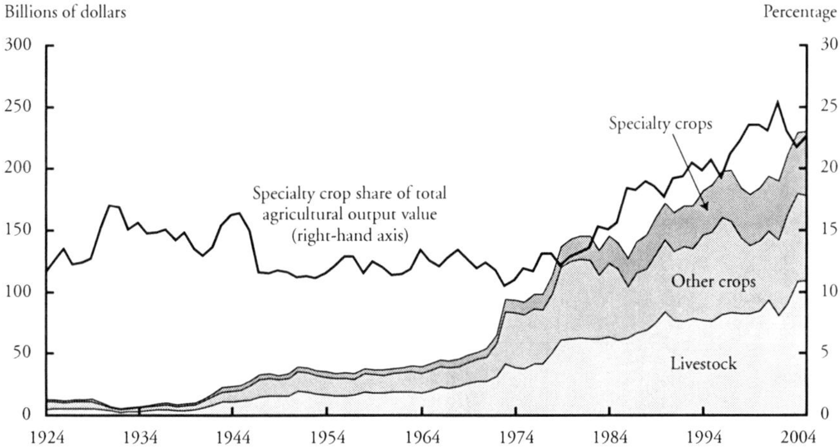

Sources: Compiled by the authors. See Appendix II for details.

Notes: Data represent a comprehensive compiliation of a value-of-production series for U.S. agriculture. As the number of commodities explicitly reported in the underlying data increase over time, so to do the number of commodities included in this constructed value of production series (99 commodities listed in 1924 and 134 commodities in 2005). The production value of commodities not explicitly reported is ostensibly captured in various "other" sub-totals which are also included in the respective totals reported here.

Table 4-1 shows summary information for the outputs included in the data set. Along with the average of annual values over the period of the data set (1949–2006), for each of the variables the average annual percentage change is included (in parentheses). Column 1 shows the average annual value of production of each aggregated output category and the three individual outputs in that category with the highest value of production, measured in billions of real 2000 dollars (i.e., nominal prices adjusted for inflation by dividing the nominal values by the implicit price deflator for Gross Domestic Product; in short, the implicit GDP deflator). Column 2 shows the same value of production, expressed as a percentage of the national total. For instance, field crops accounted for approximately $72 billion in annual production value, averaged across the time period. On average over the period 1949–2006, field crops accounted for 37.2 percent and livestock outputs accounted for 48.0 percent of the U.S. value of production of all agricultural outputs included in the data set. Fruits and nuts accounted for 5.0 percent of U.S. production value, and vegetables accounted for about the same share of value (5.0 percent).

The next two columns in Table 4-1 indicate the degree to which the production of each output was spread among states. Column 3 indicates the average number of states with some measured production of the output indicated over the time period. Column 4 indicates the number of states that accounted

Table 4-1 Summary of Production, Average Annual Value with Annual Average Percent Change in Parentheses, 1949–2006

Output	Value (1)	Share of Total Value (2)	Number of States with: Value > 0 (3)	Number of States with: Value > 1% (4)	Share of Production from: Top 4 States (5)	Share of Production from: Top 10 States (6)
	billions of dollars (2000)	*percentage*	*number of states*		*percentage*	
Livestock (9 outputs)	*91.5*	*48.0*	*48.0*	*30.8*	*26.6*	*51.3*
	(-0.19)	*(-0.27)*	*(0.00)*	*(0.06)*	*(0.07)*	*(-0.01)*
Cattle	32.7	17.0	48.0	29.9	35.5	60.9
	(0.47)	(0.39)	(0.00)	(-0.18)	(0.67)	(0.33)
Milk	25.0	13.1	48.0	26.1	40.0	63.7
	(-0.55)	(-0.63)	(0.00)	(-0.54)	(0.72)	(0.42)
Hogs	15.4	8.0	48.0	17.4	53.5	79.7
	(-1.23)	(-1.31)	(0.00)	(-0.59)	(0.46)	(0.28)
Field crops (16 outputs)	*72.0*	*37.2*	*46.0*	*27.8*	*33.0*	*59.2*
	(-0.28)	*(-0.36)*	*(-0.11)*	*(-0.35)*	*(0.45)*	*(0.37)*
Corn (grain)	24.6	12.7	42.6	16.9	54.8	80.9
	(0.12)	(0.04)	(-0.28)	(-0.39)	(0.39)	(0.25)
Soybeans	13.5	6.8	29.8	16.1	54.9	84.1
	(3.06)	(2.98)	(0.12)	(0.93)	(-0.67)	(-0.25)
Wheat	10.4	5.4	41.6	19.0	45.1	73.0
	(-1.20)	(-1.28)	(0.09)	(0.00)	(0.30)	(0.11)
Fruits and nuts (22 outputs)	*9.4*	*5.0*	*43.0*	*10.7*	*79.1*	*89.5*
	(1.41)	*(1.33)*	*(-0.08)*	*(-1.10)*	*(0.39)*	*(0.21)*
Oranges	1.8	1.0	4.2	3.1	100.0	100.0
	(0.11)	(0.03)	(-0.39)	(-0.71)	(0.01)	(0.00)
Grapes	1.7	0.9	14.0	5.0	96.3	99.7
	(2.80)	(2.72)	(-0.63)	(-0.98)	(0.07)	(0.02)
Apples, all varieties	1.4	0.7	34.8	16.9	64.1	82.5
	(0.92)	(0.84)	(-0.16)	(-1.40)	(0.71)	(0.28)
Vegetables (22 outputs)	*9.5*	*5.0*	*46.2*	*18.6*	*56.0*	*76.7*
	(1.01)	*(0.93)*	*(-0.23)*	*(-0.53)*	*(0.63)*	*(0.35)*
Potatoes	2.8	1.4	40.1	17.1	50.5	77.1
	(-0.20)	(-0.28)	(-0.69)	(-0.59)	(0.52)	(0.37)
Lettuce	1.1	0.6	13.3	5.7	93.4	98.7
	(1.44)	(1.36)	(-2.32)	(-1.93)	(0.11)	(0.02)
Tomatoes, fresh	1.0	0.5	23.3	13.2	78.5	90.9
	(1.54)	(1.46)	(-0.98)	(-0.14)	(0.09)	(0.11)
Nursery and greenhouse	*6.9*	*3.7*	*47.8*	*23.7*	*45.3*	*67.6*
	(3.14)	*(3.06)*	*(-0.04)*	*(0.00)*	*(0.47)*	*(0.15)*

Sources: Calculated by the authors using InSTePP data.

for more than one percent of the national value of production, on average. For instance, on average, 46.0 states reported some production of field crops, but only 27.8 states accounted for more than one percent of the total U.S. value of production of field crops. For livestock, 48 states reported some production and 30.8 states accounted for more than one percent. Production of fruits, nuts, and vegetables was much more spatially concentrated. Only 10.7 states accounted for

Figure 4-2 Value Shares of Output Categories, 1949–2006

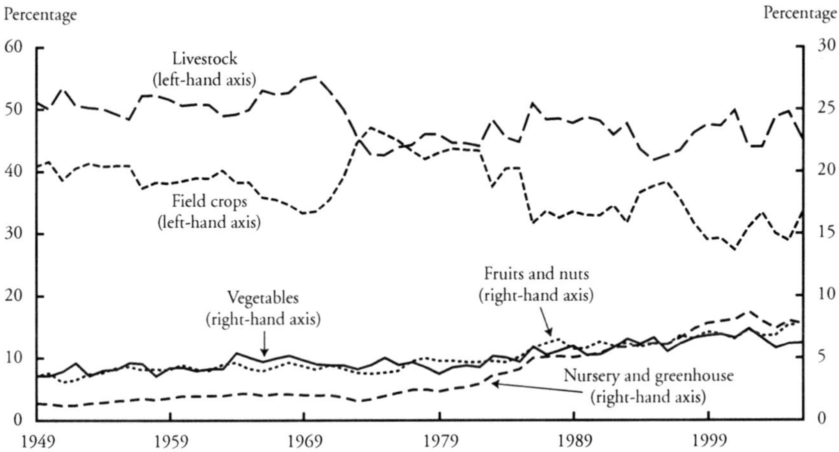

Sources: Developed by the authors using InSTePP data.

more than one percent of the value of production of fruits and nuts, and only 18.6 states accounted for more than one percent of the value of production of vegetables.

The last two columns of Table 4-1 provide another measure of the degree of concentration of production of a particular output among states—the average share of production value from the four (column 5) and 10 (column 6) states with the greatest production of that output. For instance, the top four states accounted for only 33.0 percent of the total value of field crop production (on average), whereas the top four states accounted for over 79 percent of total production of fruits and nuts.

While some of the aggregate measures reveal interesting differences (e.g., between livestock versus fruits and nuts), the aggregate measures mask variation among outputs. Data presented in Table 4-1 also indicate the relative importance and concentration of selected individual outputs within aggregates. For instance, while the top four states accounted for only 26.6 percent of total U.S. production of livestock, production of hogs was much more concentrated, with the top four states accounting for roughly half of the value of production. Appendix Table 4-1 includes the same information for all 74 outputs.

Figure 4-2 shows how the value shares of the output categories changed since 1949. The value share of field crops jumped to more than 40 percent in the 1970s and 1980s when commodity prices were high (Figure 4-2). Aside from that period of time, the share of agricultural output value coming from field crops fluctuated around a generally downwards trend, declining from approximately 40 percent of the total value of agricultural output in this data set in

1949 to around 30 percent in more recent years. The value of livestock as a share of agricultural production value also trended down, declining from about half the value of production in the 1950s to around 45 percent in more recent years. Mirroring the declining shares of output value contributed by livestock and field crops was an increase in the value shares for fruits and nuts, vegetables, and nursery and greenhouse products (Figure 4-2). The value shares for vegetables and the fruits and nuts group followed very similar paths over latter half of the 20th Century—they both increased from about 3.5 percent in 1949 to 6 or 7 percent in recent years. The value share of nursery and greenhouse products increased much more quickly, from less than 1.5 percent in 1949 to around 8 percent in the 2000s.

The Changing Location of Production

The spatial concentration of production also varied over time. Figure 4-3 shows the share of the value of production generated in the top four states for each output category. While the concentration ratios for the aggregates probably understate the concentration of any individual output, even at the aggregate level they show clear differences and time trends. Production is more dispersed for livestock than any other output category. The four-state concentration ratio for livestock is the lowest of the five aggregates, starting at around 26 percent in 1949 and increasing only slightly over time (Figure 4-3). The concentration ratio for field crops started around 30 percent, slightly higher than for livestock, and increased more noticeably, to about 40 percent in more recent years.

Specialty crops accounted for a comparatively smaller but increasing share of U.S. production, as discussed above, and their production was also much more spatially concentrated (Figure 4-3). The four-state concentration ratio for production of fruits and nuts was about 70 percent in 1949, and increased to 85 percent in 2006. Production of nursery and greenhouse outputs also became more concentrated over time: the top four states accounted for less than 40 of production value in the 1950s but nearly half of production value in more recent years. Vegetable production was less concentrated, but became increasingly concentrated with a four-state concentration ratio of around 43 percent in the 1950s that grew to about 65 percent in 2006.

Table 4-2 summarizes several measures of agricultural production across regions in the United States, expressed as averages of annual values over the period 1949–2006 (data for all states are included in Appendix Table 4-2). Column 1 shows the average total annual value of production (in billions of real 2000 dollars), along with the average annual percentage change in the value of production (in parentheses). After adjusting for inflation, the total annual value of agricultural production averaged $189.8 billion (2000 prices) between 1949 and 2006 and grew only slightly—at an average rate of 0.05 percent per year (in real terms). Across the 48 states and over the period 1949–2006, the average value of

Figure 4-3 Shares of U.S. Value of Production from the Top Four Producing States, by Output Category, 1949–2006

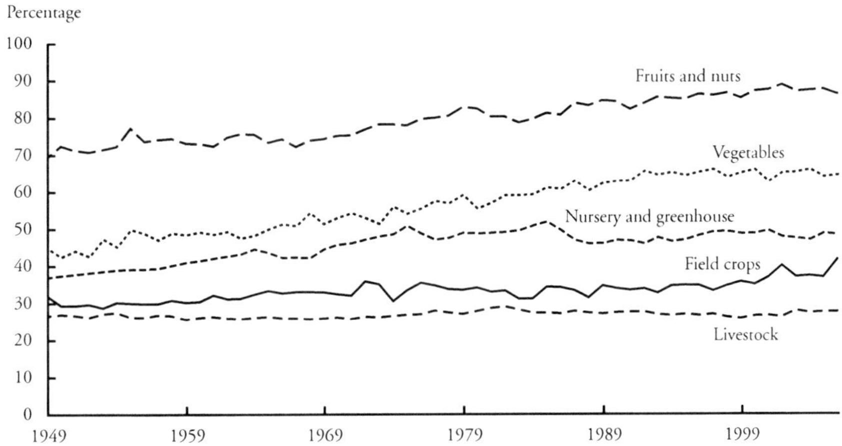

Sources: Developed by the authors using InSTePP data.

agricultural production was approximately $4 billion per state per year. Rhode Island had the lowest average value of output, with $75.5 million, while California had the highest, with $17.7 billion on average.

Regional patterns in the value of agricultural production are evident in the lower portion of Table 4-2 and in Figure 4-4. Column 2 of Table 4-2 shows the shares of the value of U.S. agricultural production contributed by particular states and regions, averaged over 1949–2006. If agricultural production had been distributed uniformly across the 48 states, each state would have accounted for 2.08 percent of the U.S. total. Clearly, the distribution is far from uniform. California accounted for an average of 9.4 percent of the U.S. total, while the eleven states in the Northeast region combined accounted for only 7.4 percent of the U.S. total (or just 3 percent if we omit New York and Pennsylvania). Figure 4-4 shows the spatial distribution of the value of production, with California, Iowa, Texas, and Illinois each accounting for more than 5 percent of the total. Most states in the Central region individually accounted for more than 3 percent of the total, despite the fact that the real value of their output had been decreasing over time. Several states in the Northeast and Mountain regions individually accounted for less than 0.5 percent of the U.S. total.

The spatial patterns of the expansion and contraction of agricultural production throughout the second half of the 20th Century are of interest. The lower portion of Table 4-2 and Figure 4-5 show the shifting regional patterns in the value of agricultural production over the period 1949–2006. The shading in Figure 4-5 reflects the average annual percentage growth in the real value of agricultural production for each state. States shaded medium gray (e.g., Nevada

Table 4-2 Summary of Agricultural Production by State, Averages of Annual Values with Annual Average Percent Change in Parentheses, 1949–2006

Output	Value (1)	Share of Total Value (2)	Number of States with: Value > 0 (3)	Number of States with: Value > 1% (4)	Share of Production from: Top 4 States (5)	Share of Production from: Top 10 States (6)
	billions of dollars (2000)	*percentage*	*number of states*		*percentage*	
United States	*189.8*	*100.0*	*69.5*	*14.9*	*52.6*	*80.2*
	(0.05)	*(0.00)*	*(0.32)*	*(0.13)*	*(-0.10)*	*(-0.07)*
48 State						
Average	4.0	2.1	25.0	11.0	74.0	93.8
	(0.05)	(0.00)	(-0.40)	(-0.23)	(0.18)	(0.04)
Minimum	0.1	0.0	11.6	4.5	42.8	65.6
	(-2.18)	(-2.22)	(-1.45)	(-1.22)	(-0.22)	(-0.08)
Maximum	17.7	9.4	56.5	24.3	97.1	99.8
	(1.39)	(1.35)	(0.30)	(0.71)	(0.73)	(0.22)
Selected states						
California	17.7	9.4	56.5	24.3	42.8	65.6
	(1.39)	(1.35)	(0.30)	(-0.55)	(0.29)	(0.14)
Minnesota	8.9	4.7	25.3	11.7	68.4	94.2
	(0.13)	(0.08)	(-0.14)	(-0.32)	(0.14)	(0.03)
Wyoming	0.7	0.4	15.8	10.3	81.8	97.3
	(-0.40)	(-0.44)	(-0.44)	(-0.65)	(0.47)	(0.10)
Regions						
Pacific	23.4	12.4	62.1	23.4	41.8	64.2
	(1.24)	(1.19)	(0.34)	(-0.15)	(0.21)	(0.11)
Mountain	12.5	6.6	46.4	14.5	68.0	87.6
	(0.42)	(0.38)	(0.04)	(-0.61)	(0.35)	(0.15)
Northern Plains	21.7	11.4	25.6	10.3	76.8	95.6
	(0.42)	(0.37)	(-0.47)	(-0.56)	(0.20)	(0.02)
Southern Plains	25.1	13.2	46.0	12.7	63.1	89.8
	(-0.14)	(-0.18)	(0.00)	(0.14)	(0.01)	(0.00)
Central	63.6	33.4	47.7	9.3	74.4	94.9
	(-0.29)	(-0.34)	(0.24)	(0.18)	(0.11)	(0.03)
Southeast	29.6	15.7	43.7	15.0	49.9	82.9
	(0.05)	(0.00)	(-0.12)	(0.00)	(0.04)	(-0.16)
Northeast	13.8	7.4	43.8	12.5	67.1	88.7
	(-0.87)	(-0.91)	(0.13)	(0.13)	(0.10)	(-0.02)

Sources: Calculated by the authors using InSTePP data.

Notes: Figures include 72 agricultural outputs (i.e., Conservation Reserve Program and machinery hired out are excluded).

and both Dakotas) had average growth rates between -0.25 and 0.25 (i.e., very close to the growth rate for the United States as a whole and close to zero). States with no or light shading had negative growth, on average, while darkly shaded states had positive growth, with darker colors reflecting average growth rates of larger magnitudes. Regional totals for value of production are in the lower part of Table 4-2, along with the regional growth rates.

Figure 4-4 Average Share of U.S. Value of Agricultural Production, 1949–2006

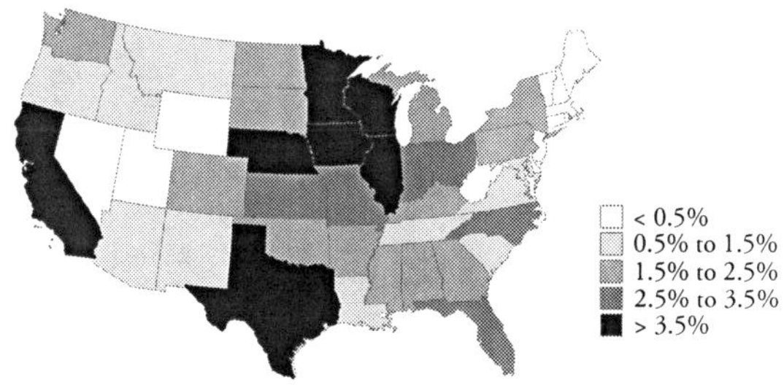

Sources: Developed by the authors based on InSTePP data.

Notes: Figures include 72 agricultural outputs (i.e., Conservation Reserve Program and machinery hired out are excluded).

On average, the Pacific region produced agricultural output that was worth \$23.4 billion per year, and grew by 1.23 percent per year, over the period 1949–2006. California alone contributed \$17.7 billion per year, on average, and its real value of agricultural production grew by an average of 1.39 percent per year. The Mountain region was comparatively small, with an average of \$12.5 billion per year of agricultural output, and slower growing, with growth of 0.42 percent per year. The Northern and Southern Plains regions each accounted for a similar value of production to the Pacific region (\$21.7 and \$25.1 billion per year, respectively), with the Northern Plains growing at a much slower rate. The Central region, which includes the Corn Belt and Lake states, produced \$63.6 billion per year worth of agricultural production, but the real annual value of agricultural output in this region decreased over the period 1949–2006, particularly in Missouri and Ohio. The patterns were mixed among states in the Southeast region, which produced an average of \$29.6 billion worth of agricultural production per year. The real value of agricultural production increased on average by nearly one percent per year in Florida and Arkansas, and decreased by more than one percent per year in West Virginia. Other states in the Southeast region showed more moderate rates of growth or contraction, with the value for the region as a whole increasing by 0.05 percent per year. Finally, the most noticeable regional pattern is the contraction of agricultural production in the Northeast region, with the real value of production decreasing in ten of the eleven states, and by more than one percent per year in seven of them.

Specialization of States in Agricultural Production

The concentration of production of particular outputs discussed above is a likely result of states specializing in producing more of the outputs for which their resources are better suited. One way of examining the degree of specialization over time is to look at the number of agricultural outputs produced in each state. We

Figure 4-5 Average Annual Growth in Real Value of Agricultural Production by State, 1949–2006 (Percent per Year)

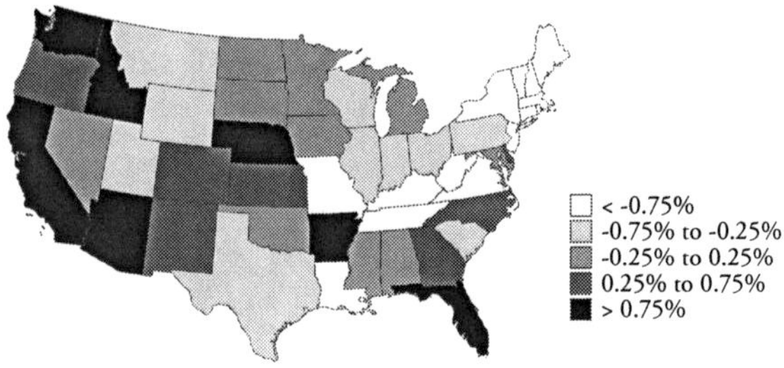

Sources: Developed by the authors using InSTePP data.

Notes: Figures include 72 agricultural outputs (i.e., Conservation Reserve Program and machinery hired out are excluded).

calculated the number of outputs produced in each state and the average of these annual values. Two counts are provided in Table 4-2: column 3 has the average number of outputs produced for selected states as well as the average number of outputs produced within the seven regions; column 4 includes similar counts, but excludes those outputs that accounted for less than one percent of the value of agricultural output for the state or region. On average, each state produced approximately 25 outputs, but once relatively "small" outputs are excluded, the average is much smaller—only 11. The average number of outputs per state varies quite a bit—from 11.6 in Rhode Island to 56.5 in California. Excluding outputs that accounted for less than one percent of a state's value of production, the range is narrower, from 4.5 outputs in Vermont to 24.3 in California. Appendix Table 4-2 includes equivalent data for all 48 states in the data set.

Figure 4-6 shows two measures of change in the number of outputs produced. For each panel, the average number of outputs was calculated for the first five years of data (1949–1953) and for the last five years of data (2002–2006), and the shading indicates the change in the two averages. In Panel a, the averages include all outputs produced, with darker shading indicating an increase in the number of outputs produced and lighter shades indicating decreases. Only three states had increases in the number of outputs produced, with seven states producing at least ten fewer outputs in recent years compared with the 1950s. Panel b of Figure 4-6 reflects the same calculations, but excludes outputs that accounted for less than one percent of the state-specific value of production. While the shading in Panel a indicates most states becoming more specialized over time, when relatively small outputs are excluded (in Panel b), many states actually increased the diversity of their agricultural output. Notably, however, states with the number of outputs increasing over time had fairly modest increases. Arizona had the largest increase of 3.4 outputs. The majority of states produced fewer

Figure 4-6 Change in the Average Number of Outputs by State, 1949–1953 to 2002–2006

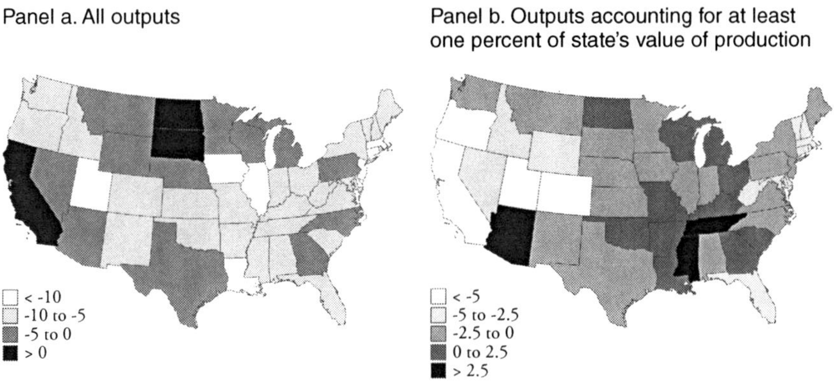

Sources: Developed by the authors using InSTePP data.

outputs in more recent years, particularly in the Northeast and in the Pacific and Mountain regions.

A final measure of the degree of specialization of agricultural production is provided in column 5 of Table 4-2 and used to shade states in Figure 4-7. The numbers in column 5 of Table 4-2 are based on state-specific measures of the value of the top four outputs, as a percentage of the total value of agricultural output, averaged across time (column 6 includes a similar measure, but includes the top 10 outputs). For the United States as a whole, the top four outputs accounted for over half of the value of production, and the top 10 outputs accounted for over 80 percent, on average. Individual states tend to be relatively specialized, with an average of 74 percent of the value of production in each state coming from its top four outputs, and 94 percent coming from the top 10 outputs. In addition, each of these shares increased over time (as reflected in the positive average percentage change in parentheses). The extent of specialization tends to be relatively high in the Mountain, Central, Northern Plains, and Northeast regions, as seen in the regional average concentration ratios in Table 4-2 and in Figure 4-7. Only seven states had less than 60 percent of their value coming from the top four outputs, with the top four outputs in Nevada and Vermont accounting for more than 90 percent of the respective state totals.

Shifting focus to particular commodity categories, states in the Central, Northern and Southern Plains regions produced about 69 percent of the total value of U.S. field crop production in 1949; 82 percent in 2006. The Northeastern states were generally getting out of field crop production and by 1960 New Hampshire and Rhode Island no longer reported production of any field crops. In 1949, soybeans accounted for only 4.1 percent of the value of U.S. field crop production, but in 2006 it was the second-most valuable field crop (behind

Figure 4-7 Average Share of Value of Production from Top Four Outputs, by State, 1949–2006

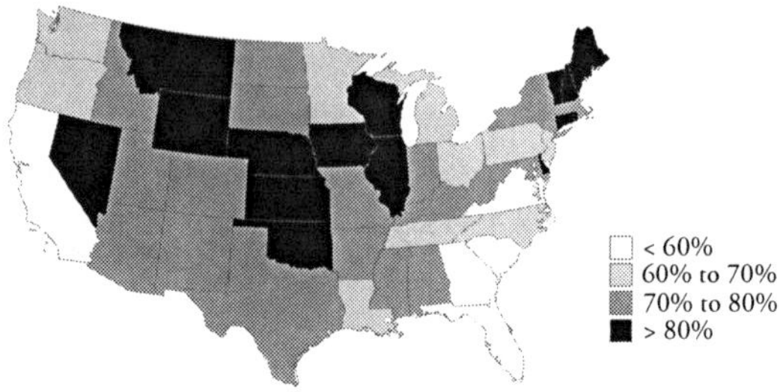

Sources: Developed by the authors using InSTePP data.

corn) and accounted for 28 percent of the value of field crop production. Production of soybeans increased predominantly in the Lake States and Corn Belt sub-regions.

Wheat production stayed predominantly in the Northern Plains, which accounted for 33 percent of national wheat production in 1949 and 40 percent in 2006. Two regions (Central and Northern Plains) were responsible for most of the field corn production. In 2006 these two regions accounted for 70 percent and 18 percent of the value of field corn production, respectively. Tobacco production stayed mainly in the Southeast region, with 89 percent and 93 percent of total production in 1949 and 2006, respectively, a consequence of the farm program for tobacco that restricted where tobacco could be grown. In 1949, the Southern Plains produced 64 percent of the total cotton crop, but in 2006 this share had fallen to 53 percent and the Southeast region produced 28 percent.

Fruits and nuts are mainly produced in the Pacific and Southeast regions; together they accounted for about 74 percent of the value of national production of fruits and nuts in 1949, and 88 percent in 2006. The Pacific and Southeast regions also accounted for the bulk of production of vegetables, with the Pacific region accounting for 29 percent of the total value of production of vegetables in 1949 and 52 percent in 2006. The real value of national production of nursery and greenhouse products in 2006 was about six times as much as in 1949. California and Florida accounted for about 33 percent of the national value of nursery and greenhouse products in 2006, compared with 16 percent in 1949.

Besides broilers, every category of livestock production was present in all 48 contiguous states in 1949. In 1949, eight states (Idaho, Montana, Nevada, New Mexico, North Dakota, South Dakota, Utah, and Wyoming) did not produce broilers, and in 2006, 28 states did not. By 2006, only 33 states produced sheep and wool, and only 21 states produced turkeys.

4.2 Indexes of the Quantity and Price of Output

The econometric analysis in this book uses indexes of multi-factor productivity (as documented in Chapter 5), which combine indexes of aggregate quantities of agricultural inputs (as documented in Chapter 3), and corresponding indexes of aggregate quantities of agricultural outputs for the period 1949–2006. Output quantity indexes will show similar patterns to those exhibited by measures of the value of production, deflated by the GDP deflator, but will also show some differences, reflecting both (a) various forms of index number problems that index number methods have been developed to correct, and (b) movements in prices of agricultural commodities relative to the GDP deflator. Here, the indexes of aggregate output quantities and output prices are formed using state-specific commodity prices and quantities and a Fisher indexing procedure (see Appendix II for more details).

Trends over Space and Time

Figure 4-8 reports trends in national indexes of aggregate quantities and prices for five categories of commodities (livestock, field crops, fruits and nuts, vegetables and nursery and greenhouse products) all set to a base value of 100 in 1949. The aggregate quantities produced moved roughly together for all five categories until the early 1970s (Figure 4-8, Panel a). The growth in livestock slowed (averaging just 1.16 percent per year during the period 1973–2006 versus 1.69 percent per year for 1949–1973). The growth rate of field-crop production accelerated briefly during the early 1970s—reflecting an above-trend rate of increase in the prices received by farmers for this group of commodities (Figure 4-8, Panel b). The rate of growth in field-crop production began to slow beginning in the early 1990s, such that this category grew by only 1.00 percent per year on average during the period 1990–2006 compared with 1.90 percent per year for the period 1949–1990. The category of nursery and greenhouse products stands out: its quantity in 2006 was nearly eight times the corresponding quantity in 1949 (Figure 4-8, Panel a, Inset). During the period 1949–1975 the quantity of nursery and greenhouse products grew by 2.22 percent per year; roughly in line with the other crop categories in Figure 4-8. Since then, output of nursery and greenhouse products grew by 4.75 percent per year, while the growth rates of quantities of the other four categories of crops were much lower, in the range of 1.30 to 1.69 percent per year. In fact, the nursery and greenhouse products was the fastest-growing category of agricultural outputs for all but five of the 48 contiguous U.S. states during second half of the 20th Century.

Figure 4-9 reveals the pattern of dispersion among states in the average rate of growth of output for our five commodity categories and for output overall during the period 1949–2006. Aggregate output grew in all but five states. Likewise, during the latter half of the 20th Century production of each commodity

Figure 4-8 National Output Quantity and Price Indexes for Commodity Categories, 1949–2006

Panel a. Quantity indexes

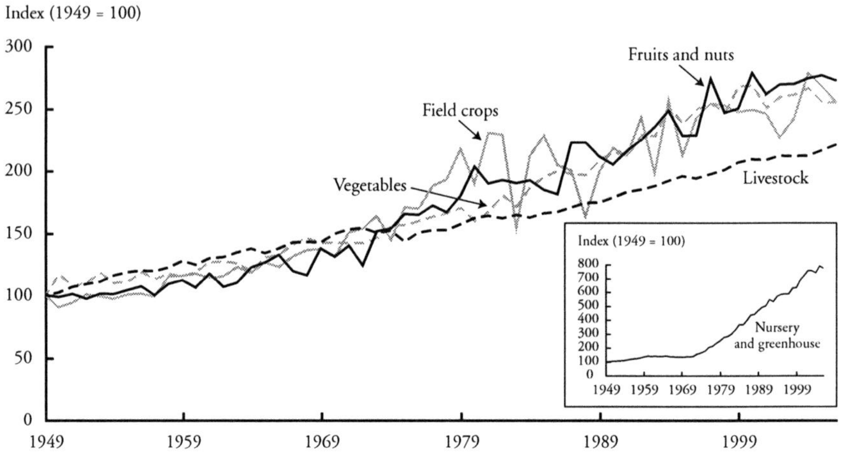

Panel b. Price indexes

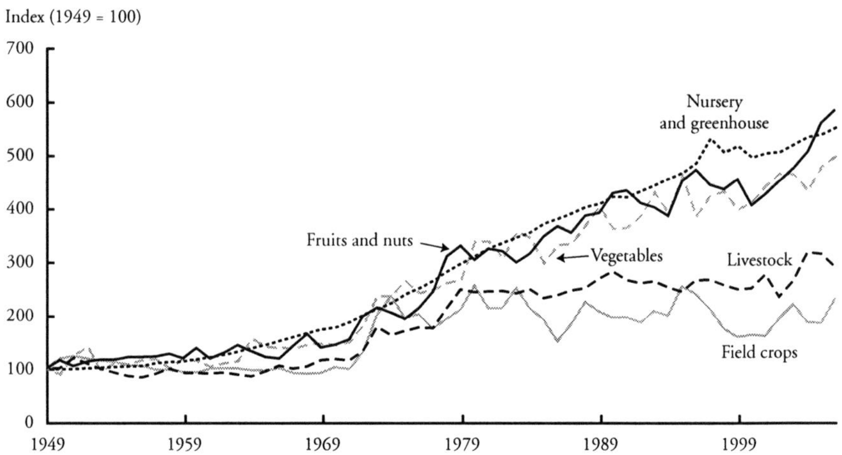

Sources: Developed by the authors using InSTePP data.

Notes: See Appendix II for details on indexing procedure.

category contracted in a number of states. A notable exception is nursery and greenhouse products, for which only one state (West Virginia) reduced its output during this period, and 19 states reported output in this category growing by more than 3.75 percent per year over the period 1949–2006.

Figure 4-8, Panel b shows that that the nominal price index for each of the categories of specialty crops—fruits and nuts, vegetables, and nursery and

Figure 4-9 Distribution of State-Specific Growth of Production, by Output Category, Average Annual Percentage Changes, 1949–2006

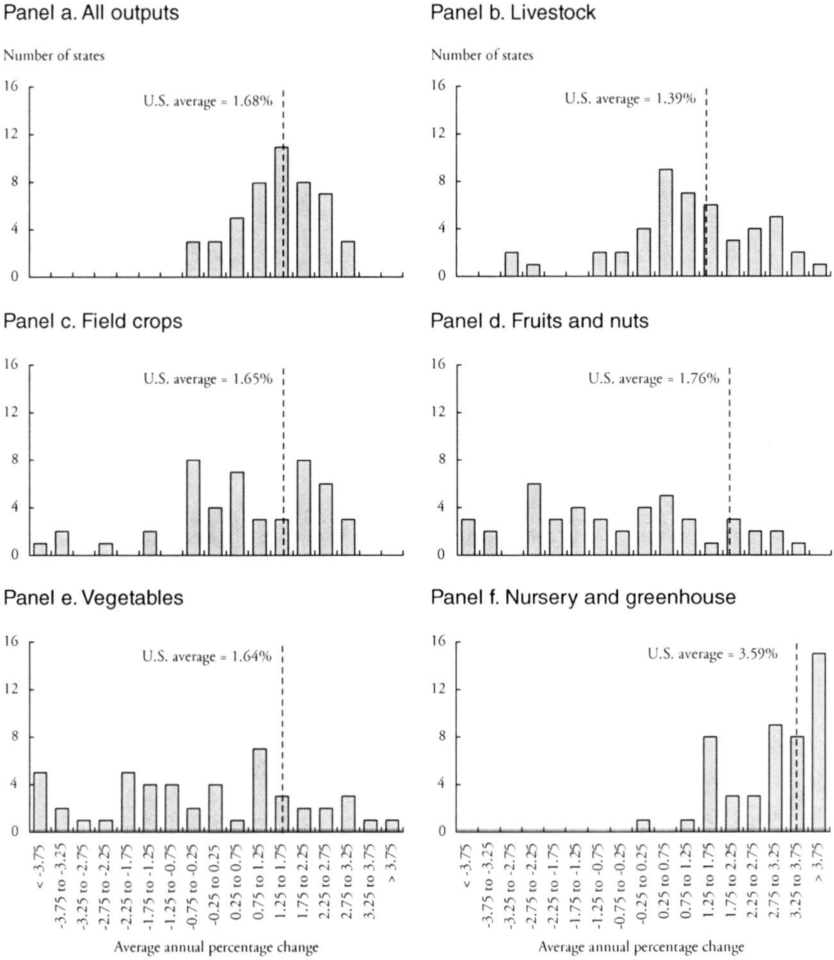

Sources: Developed by the authors using InSTePP data.

greenhouse—grew at a steady pace for the entire period 1949–2006. The growth in relative importance of these categories (measured in terms of value of production) reflects an increase in both the quantities produced and the prices received by farmers. In contrast, aggregate nominal prices for livestock and field crops stagnated after 1980, such that by 2006 these prices were only two to three times higher than they were in 1949 (compared with prices five to six times higher for each of the specialty crops categories, and with evident variation among sub-categories and commodities in this grouping).

Figure 4-10 Regional Output Quanitity and Price Indexes, 1949–2006

Panel a. Quantity indexes

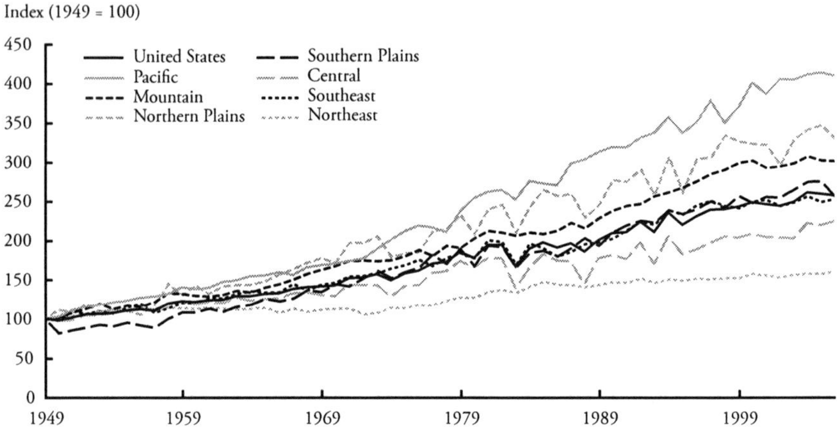

Panel b. Price indexes

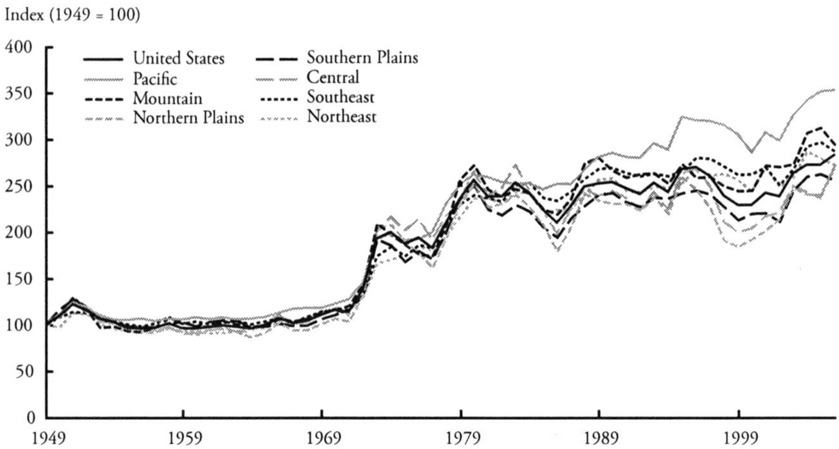

Sources: Developed by the authors using InSTePP data.
Notes: See Appendix II for details on indexing procedure.

Shifting to a regional perspective, average agricultural output quantities increased at different rates in the different regions (Figure 4-10, Panel a). Table 4-3 summarizes the region-by-commodity group rates of growth for the period 1949–2006 and Appendix Table 4-3 provides U.S. figures. In 2006, the aggregate output quantity produced in the Pacific region was over four times its corresponding 1949 value, whereas output in the Northeast region increased by a factor of a little more than 1.5. Aggregate agricultural output prices moved in a similar pattern among regions until the mid-1970s, and then began diverging,

Table 4-3 Average Annual Percentage Change in Indexes of Output Quantity and Price, 1949–2006

	All Outputs	Livestock	Field Crops	Fruits and Nuts	Vegetables	Nursery and Greenhouse
			average annual percentage change			
Panel a. Quantity index						
United States	*1.68*	*1.39*	*1.65*	*1.76*	*1.64*	*3.59*
48 state						
Average	1.37	1.08	0.39	-0.57	-0.70	3.21
Minimum	-0.65	-3.19	-16.29	-5.57	-11.11	-0.14
Maximum	2.85	4.00	2.95	3.60	4.03	6.95
Selected states						
California	2.59	2.70	0.36	2.27	2.80	4.63
Minnesota	1.86	0.88	2.77	0.52	1.54	2.69
Wyoming	0.76	0.76	0.19		-3.66	2.99
Regions						
Pacific	2.50	2.32	0.76	2.23	2.92	4.60
Mountain	1.97	2.03	1.00	0.75	2.50	4.28
Northern Plains	2.12	1.44	2.60	-5.01	1.14	1.95
Southern Plains	1.66	2.16	0.95	-0.21	-0.48	4.63
Central	1.44	0.44	2.29	0.59	1.05	2.36
Southeast	1.63	2.34	0.27	1.22	1.36	4.81
Northeast	0.84	0.78	0.60	0.55	-1.37	2.09
Panel b. Price index						
United States	*1.85*	*1.87*	*1.52*	*3.10*	*2.82*	*3.00*
48 state						
Average	1.84	1.75	1.40	3.32	3.10	3.05
Minimum	1.18	0.31	-2.13	1.95	-0.18	2.57
Maximum	2.37	2.64	3.52	5.27	12.22	3.77
Selected states						
California	2.29	1.23	1.84	3.47	2.71	3.08
Minnesota	1.76	2.02	1.43	5.27	2.00	2.95
Wyoming	2.34	2.58	1.84		1.12	2.70
Regions						
Pacific	2.23	1.39	1.72	3.43	2.54	3.11
Mountain	1.95	2.20	1.56	3.52	2.13	2.82
Northern Plains	1.78	2.32	1.37	4.67	2.22	3.12
Southern Plains	1.68	2.00	1.03	2.54	4.56	3.31
Central	1.75	1.89	1.54	3.07	2.47	2.95
Southeast	1.87	1.66	1.59	2.39	3.45	3.05
Northeast	1.76	1.42	1.67	3.09	3.20	2.92

Sources: Calculated by the authors using InSTePP data.

Notes: See Appendix II for details on grouping states into regions and commodities into commodity groups.

with prices increasing fastest in the Pacific region, and slowest in the Northern Plains (Figure 4-10, Panel b). These trends in regional price indexes reflect the pattern of relative price movements among categories, combined with the spatial pattern of commodity production noted earlier. In particular, the category with the fastest rate of price increase, specialty crops, was already concentrated in the Pacific region (and specifically California) but became more so, whereas the Northern and Southern Plains regions were relatively specialized in production of field crops for which prices increased comparatively slowly.

4.3 Conclusion

During the 20th Century, U.S. agricultural production increased dramatically. Between 1924 and 2005, the value of production increased by a factor of 18.7, from $12.3 billion to $229.8 billion. Much of this growth occurred in the second half of the century: between 1949 and 2006, the value of production increased by a factor of 7.5, from $29.9 billion to $223.5 billion while the quantity increased by a factor of 2.6. However, prices of agricultural outputs fell relative to prices in the economy more generally, such that in real terms (after deflating nominal prices by the GDP deflator), the value of production increased by a factor of only 1.05, from $183.0 billion to $191.5 billion over the period 1949–2006.[3] This relatively modest increase in real value reflected an increase in quantity that was offset significantly by decreases in real prices, because U.S. agriculture faces a downward sloping demand for much of what it produces.[4] Such measures of real value are misleading as indicators of the quantity of production. A better indication is given by the Fisher indexes of output quantities, described in the latter half of this chapter, which are to be used in measuring increases in productivity and their value. By this measure, the real quantity of U.S. agricultural output increased by a factor of more than 2.5 over the period 1949–2006, while the real monetary value of that production barely increased.

These aggregate measures of the changing price, value, and quantity of production mask very significant differences among categories of output and among states and regions of the United States. As discussed in Chapter 3, some U.S.

3 A notable exception to the general trend of stagnant or declining prices is the nursery and greenhouse sector. Here the story is one of the growth in demand generally outpacing the considerable growth in supply, causing both nominal (and real) average prices along with the quantities produced to continue trending up for the past 50 years.

4 The long-run elasticity of demand for aggregate U.S. output is currently probably in the range of -1.5, but might be less elastic and could even be inelastic (see, for instance, Alston 2007 for estimates and discussion of previous work, evidence, and interpretation). Johnson (1977, p. 736), suggested an elasticity of -1.15, very close to the earlier estimate from Tweeten (1967) of -1.11 (see also Tweeten 1977). Given increases in the share of U.S. agricultural output traded, and reductions in trade barriers, these estimates are consistent with a long-run elasticity of -1.5 for the more recent period.

states increased their use of agricultural inputs over the period 1949–2002 while others were contracting input use, some to the point where their total agricultural production contracted against the national trend of rapidly increasing production. Combining the changing patterns of input use with differences among states in the established and evolving mixture of outputs produced, a diverse story of production change among the states emerges. As a consequence of these enduring and on-going changes, the structure of U.S. agricultural production is now much different than it was decades ago. Some states (such as California and Florida) gained significantly larger shares of the value of U.S. agricultural production during the 20th Century and other states (such as Massachusetts and New Hampshire) lost ground in absolute terms as well as relatively.

Technical changes spurred by public and private investments in agricultural R&D have reshaped the relationship between agricultural inputs (discussed in the previous chapter) and outputs (discussed in this chapter). The next chapter addresses these changing input-output relationships and measures of productivity that reflect them.

Appendix Table 4-1 Production by Output Category, Average of Annual Values with Annual Average Percent Change in Parentheses, 1949–2006

			Number of States with		Share of Production from	
Output	Value (1)	Share of Total Value (2)	Value > 0 (3)	Value > 1% (4)	Top 4 States (5)	Top 10 States (6)
	billions of dollars (2000)	*percentage*	*number of states*		*percentage*	
Livestock (9 outputs)	*91.5*	*48.0*	*48.0*	*30.8*	*26.6*	*51.3*
	(-0.19)	*(-0.27)*	*(0.00)*	*(0.06)*	*(0.07)*	*(-0.01)*
Cattle	32.7	17.0	48.0	29.9	35.5	60.9
	(0.47)	(0.39)	(0.00)	(-0.18)	(0.67)	(0.33)
Milk	25.0	13.1	48.0	26.1	40.0	63.7
	(-0.55)	(-0.63)	(0.00)	(-0.54)	(0.72)	(0.42)
Hogs	15.4	8.0	48.0	17.4	53.5	79.7
	(-1.23)	(-1.31)	(0.00)	(-0.59)	(0.46)	(0.28)
Broilers	8.2	4.3	31.9	17.3	49.0	80.5
	(3.01)	(2.93)	(-1.22)	(-0.82)	(0.61)	(0.45)
Eggs	6.9	3.7	46.9	27.7	29.8	58.0
	(-2.20)	(-2.28)	(-0.28)	(-0.20)	(0.44)	(0.42)
Turkey	2.1	1.1	35.7	18.7	48.6	77.9
	(0.83)	(0.75)	(-1.45)	(-0.90)	(0.44)	(0.59)
Sheep	0.8	0.4	42.7	23.4	37.9	67.8
	(-2.90)	(-2.98)	(-0.66)	(-0.59)	(0.57)	(0.39)
Wool	0.3	0.1	42.7	18.9	48.5	77.9
	(-6.03)	(-6.11)	(-0.66)	(-0.87)	(0.09)	(0.24)
Honey	0.2	0.1	46.4	26.9	36.2	60.6
	(-0.76)	(-0.84)	(-0.32)	(-0.36)	(0.82)	(0.44)
Field crops (16 outputs)	*72.0*	*37.2*	*46.0*	*27.8*	*33.0*	*59.2*
	(-0.28)	*(-0.36)*	*(-0.11)*	*(-0.35)*	*(0.45)*	*(0.37)*
Corn (grain)	24.6	12.7	42.6	16.9	54.8	80.9
	(0.12)	(0.04)	(-0.28)	(-0.39)	(0.39)	(0.25)
Soybeans	13.5	6.8	29.8	16.1	54.9	84.1
	(3.06)	(2.98)	(0.12)	(0.93)	(-0.67)	(-0.25)
Wheat	10.4	5.4	41.6	19.0	45.1	73.0
	(-1.20)	(-1.28)	(0.09)	(0.00)	(0.30)	(0.11)
Cotton	7.4	3.9	17.6	13.0	66.3	92.7
	(-2.03)	(-2.11)	(0.11)	(-0.27)	(-0.16)	(0.05)
Tobacco	4.4	2.3	17.4	9.6	79.3	97.0
	(-2.96)	(-3.04)	(-0.98)	(-0.50)	(0.17)	(0.07)
Sorghum	2.2	1.1	21.3	10.2	84.5	96.8
	(-0.59)	(-0.67)	(0.37)	(0.39)	(-0.07)	(-0.05)
Oats	2.0	1.1	38.4	18.2	48.9	76.8
	(-6.22)	(-6.30)	(-0.82)	(0.32)	(-0.32)	(-0.09)
Rice	1.7	0.9	6.0	5.5	93.0	100.0
	(0.88)	(0.80)	(0.00)	(0.71)	(-0.21)	(0.00)
Barley	1.5	0.8	33.2	14.3	62.5	86.5
	(-2.21)	(-2.29)	(-0.84)	(-0.71)	(0.66)	(0.29)
Peanuts	1.2	0.6	10.1	7.5	79.6	99.9
	(-1.44)	(-1.52)	(-0.46)	(0.63)	(0.06)	(0.01)
Sugarbeets	1.2	0.6	15.4	12.5	65.9	94.1
	(1.44)	(1.36)	(0.35)	(0.18)	(0.20)	(0.00)

(continued)

Appendix Table 4-1 (continued)

Output	Value (1)	Share of Total Value (2)	Number of States with: Value > 0 (3)	Number of States with: Value > 1% (4)	Share of Production from: Top 4 States (5)	Share of Production from: Top 10 States (6)
	billions of dollars (2000)	*percentage*	*number of states*		*percentage*	
Field beans	0.7	0.3	14.0	10.2	71.5	97.4
	(-0.90)	(-0.98)	(0.71)	(0.50)	(-0.32)	(-0.11)
Sugarcane	0.6	0.3	2.6	2.6	100.0	100.0
	(2.02)	(1.93)	(0.71)	(0.71)	(0.00)	(0.00)
Sunflower seeds	0.3	0.1	3.2	3.1	97.2	100.0
	(8.56)	(8.02)	(4.23)	(4.23)	(-0.20)	(0.00)
Flax	0.2	0.1	5.9	3.8	98.6	100.0
	(-5.05)	(-5.13)	(-2.54)	(-0.98)	(0.22)	(0.01)
Rye	0.1	0.0	25.5	18.7	58.5	79.5
	(-5.55)	(-5.63)	(-5.02)	(-4.43)	(1.31)	(0.56)
Fruits and nuts (22 outputs)	*9.4*	*5.0*	*43.0*	*10.7*	*79.1*	*89.5*
	(1.41)	*(1.33)*	*(-0.08)*	*(-1.10)*	*(0.39)*	*(0.21)*
Oranges	1.8	1.0	4.2	3.1	100.0	100.0
	(0.11)	(0.03)	(-0.39)	(-0.71)	(0.01)	(0.00)
Grapes	1.7	0.9	14.0	5.0	96.3	99.7
	(2.80)	(2.72)	(-0.63)	(-0.98)	(0.07)	(0.02)
Apples, all varieties	1.4	0.7	34.8	16.9	64.1	82.5
	(0.92)	(0.84)	(-0.16)	(-1.40)	(0.71)	(0.28)
Strawberries	0.6	0.3	19.2	10.3	81.3	93.1
	(2.12)	(2.04)	(-1.81)	(-2.99)	(1.44)	(0.62)
Peaches	0.6	0.3	31.9	13.6	71.7	86.8
	(-0.71)	(-0.79)	(-0.44)	(-1.08)	(0.63)	(0.38)
Almonds	0.6	0.3	1.0	1.0	100.0	100.0
	(5.17)	(5.09)	(0.00)	(0.00)	(0.00)	(0.00)
Grapefruit	0.4	0.2	3.9	3.8	100.0	100.0
	(-0.55)	(-0.63)	(0.00)	(-0.50)	(0.00)	(0.00)
Pears	0.3	0.2	13.2	4.9	95.2	99.2
	(0.09)	(0.01)	(-2.11)	(-0.98)	(0.30)	(0.16)
Cherry (sweet and tart)	0.3	0.1	11.3	8.4	84.9	99.4
	(0.96)	(0.88)	(-0.32)	(-1.38)	(0.50)	(0.04)
Walnuts	0.3	0.1	1.5	1.4	100.0	100.0
	(1.62)	(1.54)	(-1.22)	(-1.22)	(0.00)	(0.00)
Lemons	0.3	0.1	1.8	1.8	100.0	100.0
	(0.60)	(0.52)	(1.22)	(1.22)	(0.00)	(0.00)
Pecans	0.2	0.1	11.7	9.6	79.7	98.9
	(1.10)	(1.02)	(0.71)	(-0.39)	(0.23)	(-0.04)
Prunes	0.2	0.1	1.0	1.0	100.0	100.0
	(0.69)	(0.61)	(0.00)	(0.00)	(0.00)	(0.00)
Avocados	0.2	0.1	2.0	2.0	100.0	100.0
	(2.83)	(2.75)	(0.00)	(0.00)	(0.00)	(0.00)
Cranberries	0.1	0.1	5.0	5.0	96.9	100.0
	(2.73)	(2.65)	(0.00)	(0.00)	(-0.01)	(0.00)
Plums	0.1	0.0	1.0	1.0	100.0	100.0
	(1.52)	(1.44)	(0.00)	(0.00)	(0.00)	(0.00)

(continued)

Appendix Table 4-1 (continued)

Output	Value (1)	Share of Total Value (2)	Number of States with: Value > 0 (3)	Value > 1% (4)	Share of Production from: Top 4 States (5)	Top 10 States (6)
	billions of dollars (2000)	*percentage*	*number of states*		*percentage*	
Pistachios	0.1	0.0	0.5	0.5	100.0	100.0
	(12.32)	(12.75)	(0.00)	(0.00)	(0.00)	(0.00)
Tangerines	0.1	0.0	2.4	2.4	100.0	100.0
	(1.28)	(1.20)	(1.93)	(1.93)	(0.00)	(0.00)
Blueberries	0.1	0.0	4.3	3.7	80.5	99.3
	(6.37)	(7.41)	(3.26)	(1.96)	(-1.53)	(-0.08)
Apricots	0.1	0.0	2.9	2.4	100.0	100.0
	(-2.14)	(-2.22)	(0.00)	(-0.71)	(0.00)	(0.00)
Nectarines	0.1	0.0	1.0	1.0	100.0	100.0
	(4.20)	(4.12)	(0.00)	(0.00)	(0.00)	(0.00)
Raspberries	0.0	0.0	1.2	1.2	100.0	100.0
	(10.77)	(11.81)	(1.56)	(1.56)	(0.00)	(0.00)
Vegetables (22 outputs)	*9.5*	*5.0*	*46.2*	*18.6*	*56.0*	*76.7*
	(1.01)	*(0.93)*	*(-0.23)*	*(-0.53)*	*(0.63)*	*(0.35)*
Potatoes	2.8	1.4	40.1	17.1	50.5	77.1
	(-0.20)	(-0.28)	(-0.69)	(-0.59)	(0.52)	(0.37)
Lettuce	1.1	0.6	13.3	5.7	93.4	98.7
	(1.44)	(1.36)	(-2.32)	(-1.93)	(0.11)	(0.02)
Tomatoes, fresh	1.0	0.5	23.3	13.2	78.5	90.9
	(1.54)	(1.46)	(-0.98)	(-0.14)	(0.09)	(0.11)
Tomatoes, processed	0.7	0.4	12.4	7.3	89.8	97.9
	(0.82)	(0.74)	(-3.07)	(-2.07)	(0.79)	(0.17)
Onions	0.6	0.3	17.9	12.6	62.2	93.6
	(1.36)	(1.28)	(-1.15)	(-0.93)	(0.16)	(0.22)
Carrots	0.3	0.2	12.8	10.0	85.9	97.7
	(1.06)	(0.98)	(-1.83)	(-1.68)	(0.39)	(0.11)
Sweet corn, fresh	0.3	0.2	21.9	16.7	61.1	85.7
	(4.24)	(4.16)	(3.79)	(3.14)	(-0.92)	(-0.36)
Celery	0.3	0.2	6.9	4.9	96.8	99.7
	(-0.18)	(-0.26)	(-3.14)	(-2.64)	(0.22)	(0.02)
Cantaloupe	0.3	0.2	8.3	6.3	94.8	100.0
	(0.38)	(0.38)	(0.00)	(0.28)	(0.00)	(0.00)
Broccoli	0.3	0.1	5.2	4.7	96.5	100.0
	(3.33)	(3.32)	(-2.48)	(-2.48)	(0.19)	(0.00)
Sweet potatoes	0.3	0.1	10.4	9.6	72.4	98.9
	(-1.01)	(-1.01)	(-0.19)	(-0.91)	(0.97)	(0.00)
Watermelon	0.2	0.1	17.5	14.0	70.7	91.4
	(1.24)	(1.23)	(-0.49)	(-0.28)	(0.06)	(0.07)
Bell peppers	0.2	0.1	9.8	8.3	88.3	99.5
	(2.90)	(2.82)	(0.00)	(-0.23)	(0.11)	(0.00)
Sweet corn, processed	0.2	0.1	11.5	9.7	75.1	97.9
	(-0.09)	(-0.17)	(-1.61)	(-1.49)	(0.72)	(0.20)
Peas	0.2	0.1	9.7	8.5	84.3	98.3
	(-1.46)	(-1.54)	(-2.11)	(-1.61)	(0.47)	(0.19)

(continued)

Appendix Table 4-1 (continued)

Output	Value (1)	Share of Total Value (2)	Number of States with: Value > 0 (3)	Number of States with: Value > 1% (4)	Share of Production from: Top 4 States (5)	Share of Production from: Top 10 States (6)
	billions of dollars (2000)	*percentage*	*number of states*		*percentage*	
Cauliflower	0.2	0.1	7.0	6.4	93.3	99.8
	(1.28)	(1.20)	(-2.11)	(-2.82)	(0.31)	(0.00)
Snap beans, processed	0.1	0.1	6.9	6.8	87.5	100.0
	(0.73)	(0.65)	(0.50)	(0.50)	(-0.16)	(0.00)
Cucumber	0.1	0.1	13.3	12.1	67.4	94.8
	(-0.04)	(-0.12)	(-1.57)	(-1.12)	(0.38)	(0.25)
Asparagus	0.1	0.1	3.3	2.9	98.4	100.0
	(-2.13)	(-2.37)	(-1.31)	(-1.31)	(0.12)	(0.00)
Garlic	0.1	0.0	1.2	1.2	100.0	100.0
	(5.06)	(4.98)	(1.93)	(1.22)	(0.00)	(0.00)
Honeydew melons	0.1	0.0	2.9	2.9	100.0	100.0
	(1.78)	(1.78)	(0.72)	(0.72)	(0.00)	(0.00)
Spinach	0.0	0.0	4.0	3.9	100.0	100.0
	(2.40)	(2.39)	(0.00)	(0.00)	(0.00)	(0.00)
Nursery and greenhouse	*6.9*	*3.7*	*47.8*	*23.7*	*45.3*	*67.6*
	(3.14)	*(3.06)*	*(-0.04)*	*(0.00)*	*(0.47)*	*(0.15)*
Miscellaneous (4 outputs)	*2.4*	*1.3*	*47.1*	*27.3*	*33.6*	*57.4*
	(4.90)	*(4.89)*	*(0.08)*	*(-2.38)*	*(-0.91)*	*(-0.33)*
Machine hire out	1.4	0.8	47.1	30.1	31.1	54.3
	(5.23)	(5.23)	(0.08)	(-0.28)	(0.80)	(0.37)
CRP	0.6	0.3	16.1	8.7	34.8	66.6
	(12.52)	(11.86)	(0.34)	(0.00)	(-0.30)	(0.22)
Mushrooms	0.3	0.2	4.9	3.7	96.0	100.0
	(2.66)	(2.42)	(-3.21)	(-2.35)	(0.05)	(0.00)
Hops	0.1	0.1	2.9	2.9	100.0	100.0
	(-0.80)	(-0.80)	(0.00)	(0.00)	(0.00)	(0.00)

Sources: Developed by the authors using InSTePP data.

Appendix Table 4-2 Agricultural Production by State, Averages of Annual Values with Annual Average Percent Change in Parentheses, 1949–2006

Output	Value (1)	Share of Total Value (2)	Number of States with: Value > 0 (3)	Number of States with: Value > 1% (4)	Share of Production from: Top 4 States (5)	Share of Production from: Top 10 States (6)
	billions of dollars (2000)	*percentage*	*number of states*		*percentage*	
Pacific	*23.4*	*12.4*	*62.1*	*23.4*	*41.8*	*64.2*
	(1.24)	*(1.19)*	*(0.34)*	*(-0.15)*	*(0.21)*	*(0.11)*
California	17.7	9.4	56.5	24.3	42.8	65.6
	(1.39)	(1.35)	(0.30)	(-0.55)	(0.29)	(0.14)
Oregon	2.1	1.1	34.9	17.2	61.0	82.2
	(0.40)	(0.36)	(-0.21)	(-0.61)	(0.43)	(0.18)
Washington	3.6	1.9	35.8	15.8	62.9	85.9
	(1.05)	(1.01)	(-0.16)	(-0.27)	(-0.21)	(0.05)
Mountain	*12.5*	*6.6*	*46.4*	*14.5*	*68.0*	*87.6*
	(0.42)	*(0.38)*	*(0.04)*	*(-0.61)*	*(0.35)*	*(0.15)*
Arizona	1.9	1.0	28.4	12.7	74.7	90.2
	(0.78)	(0.74)	(0.13)	(0.42)	(-0.16)	(-0.04)
Colorado	3.1	1.6	30.8	13.9	71.8	90.3
	(0.41)	(0.36)	(-0.50)	(-0.93)	(0.48)	(0.20)
Idaho	2.6	1.4	22.9	10.6	73.2	94.7
	(1.17)	(1.12)	(-0.39)	(-0.32)	(0.40)	(0.12)
Montana	2.1	1.1	17.5	8.9	88.0	98.1
	(-0.30)	(-0.35)	(-0.29)	(-0.35)	(0.18)	(0.04)
Nevada	0.2	0.1	12.9	7.2	91.2	99.2
	(-0.14)	(-0.19)	(-0.39)	(-0.71)	(0.22)	(0.03)
New Mexico	1.1	0.6	21.2	11.3	79.7	94.3
	(0.63)	(0.59)	(-0.71)	(-0.71)	(0.41)	(0.11)
Utah	0.8	0.4	23.2	12.2	72.6	92.9
	(-0.28)	(-0.32)	(-0.90)	(-0.98)	(0.73)	(0.22)
Wyoming	0.7	0.4	15.8	10.3	81.8	97.3
	(-0.40)	(-0.44)	(-0.44)	(-0.65)	(0.47)	(0.10)
Northern Plains	*21.7*	*11.4*	*25.6*	*10.3*	*76.8*	*95.6*
	(0.42)	*(0.37)*	*(-0.47)*	*(-0.56)*	*(0.20)*	*(0.02)*
Kansas	6.5	3.4	21.9	7.6	81.7	98.9
	(0.34)	(0.29)	(-0.58)	(-0.23)	(0.16)	(0.03)
Nebraska	7.8	4.1	20.3	8.0	84.1	98.2
	(0.80)	(0.75)	(-0.35)	(-0.50)	(0.25)	(0.03)
North Dakota	3.5	1.9	19.4	11.4	72.7	95.2
	(0.09)	(0.05)	(-0.09)	(0.17)	(0.05)	(-0.02)
South Dakota	3.9	2.1	18.7	9.8	75.8	96.7
	(0.07)	(0.02)	(0.00)	(-0.39)	(0.21)	(0.01)
Southern Plains	*25.1*	*13.2*	*46.0*	*12.7*	*63.1*	*89.8*
	(-0.14)	*(-0.18)*	*(0.00)*	*(0.14)*	*(0.01)*	*(0.00)*
Arkansas	4.6	2.4	24.4	10.3	70.6	96.9
	(0.80)	(0.75)	(-0.59)	(0.00)	(0.15)	(0.03)
Louisiana	2.1	1.1	24.4	11.4	65.9	95.3
	(-0.84)	(-0.88)	(-1.10)	(0.65)	(-0.03)	(-0.01)
Mississippi	3.2	1.7	20.9	9.7	76.7	97.6
	(-0.03)	(-0.07)	(-0.50)	(0.56)	(-0.04)	(-0.01)

(continued)

Appendix Table 4-2 (continued)

Output	Value (1)	Share of Total Value (2)	Number of States with: Value > 0 (3)	Number of States with: Value > 1% (4)	Share of Production from: Top 4 States (5)	Share of Production from: Top 10 States (6)
	billions of dollars (2000)	*percentage*	*number of states*		*percentage*	
Oklahoma	3.5	1.8	23.2	10.4	80.6	96.0
	(-0.21)	(-0.26)	(-0.62)	(-0.18)	(0.28)	(0.02)
Texas	11.8	6.2	41.5	12.0	70.4	90.4
	(-0.35)	(-0.40)	(0.10)	(-0.50)	(0.13)	(0.05)
Central	*63.6*	*33.4*	*47.7*	*9.3*	*74.4*	*94.9*
	(-0.29)	*(-0.34)*	*(0.24)*	*(0.18)*	*(0.11)*	*(0.03)*
Illinois	11.2	5.9	25.5	7.6	85.9	98.9
	(-0.42)	(-0.47)	(-0.80)	(-0.44)	(0.39)	(0.03)
Indiana	6.5	3.4	27.6	8.9	78.1	97.4
	(-0.37)	(-0.41)	(-0.54)	(-0.18)	(0.28)	(0.05)
Iowa	14.4	7.5	20.3	6.3	88.8	99.5
	(-0.09)	(-0.13)	(-1.22)	(-0.27)	(0.22)	(0.02)
Michigan	4.0	2.1	37.9	14.3	60.1	84.9
	(-0.25)	(-0.29)	(-0.10)	(0.25)	(0.15)	(-0.03)
Minnesota	8.9	4.7	25.3	11.7	68.4	94.2
	(0.13)	(0.08)	(-0.14)	(-0.32)	(0.14)	(0.03)
Missouri	6.0	3.1	25.5	10.7	71.8	96.2
	(-0.77)	(-0.82)	(-0.47)	(0.17)	(0.12)	(0.02)
Ohio	5.7	3.0	32.7	9.8	68.4	94.5
	(-0.60)	(-0.64)	(-0.42)	(0.35)	(0.07)	(0.02)
Wisconsin	6.8	3.6	29.1	8.1	83.8	95.7
	(-0.38)	(-0.43)	(-0.13)	(0.23)	(0.14)	(0.01)
Southeast	*29.6*	*15.7*	*43.7*	*15.0*	*49.9*	*82.9*
	(0.05)	*(0.00)*	*(-0.12)*	*(0.00)*	*(0.04)*	*(-0.16)*
Alabama	3.1	1.6	23.9	10.3	70.6	95.8
	(0.10)	(0.12)	(-0.22)	(-0.90)	(0.37)	(0.04)
Florida	5.1	2.7	30.0	16.8	58.2	85.1
	(1.11)	(1.07)	(-0.23)	(-0.22)	(0.10)	(0.08)
Georgia	4.6	2.4	28.1	12.3	59.5	92.2
	(0.58)	(0.53)	(-0.06)	(0.27)	(0.48)	(-0.08)
Kentucky	3.4	1.8	20.8	8.6	76.3	98.8
	(-0.77)	(-0.82)	(-0.53)	(0.39)	(-0.06)	(0.03)
North Carolina	6.1	3.3	32.9	12.4	65.9	92.0
	(0.48)	(0.44)	(0.06)	(0.14)	(-0.11)	(-0.04)
South Carolina	1.7	0.9	27.6	13.2	57.5	89.0
	(-0.50)	(-0.55)	(-0.41)	(0.39)	(-0.14)	(-0.08)
Tennessee	2.7	1.4	22.3	10.9	61.4	96.4
	(-0.89)	(-0.94)	(-0.71)	(0.71)	(-0.07)	(0.02)
Virginia	2.5	1.3	29.1	14.2	57.5	88.1
	(-0.76)	(-0.81)	(-0.36)	(0.00)	(0.18)	(0.03)
West Virginia	0.5	0.3	17.3	11.4	70.9	95.1
	(-1.87)	(-1.91)	(-0.79)	(-0.85)	(0.46)	(0.12)

(continued)

Appendix Table 4-2 (continued)

Output	Value (1)	Share of Total Value (2)	Number of States with: Value > 0 (3)	Number of States with: Value > 1% (4)	Share of Production from: Top 4 States (5)	Share of Production from: Top 10 States (6)
	billions of dollars (2000)	*percentage*	*number of states*		*percentage*	
Northeast	*13.8*	*7.4*	*43.8*	*12.5*	*67.1*	*88.7*
	(-0.87)	*(-0.91)*	*(0.13)*	*(0.13)*	*(0.10)*	*(-0.02)*
Connecticut	0.5	0.3	16.8	8.5	86.3	98.3
	(-1.65)	(-1.70)	(-0.93)	(-0.79)	(0.27)	(0.03)
Delaware	0.6	0.3	20.9	9.6	83.6	96.1
	(0.58)	(0.53)	(-1.02)	(-0.44)	(0.17)	(0.06)
Maine	0.7	0.4	14.2	7.4	88.5	99.4
	(-1.76)	(-1.80)	(-0.61)	(-0.21)	(-0.15)	(0.02)
Maryland	1.5	0.8	27.0	10.7	72.2	94.3
	(-0.24)	(-0.28)	(-0.37)	(-0.56)	(0.50)	(0.10)
Massachusetts	0.6	0.3	18.8	11.4	77.6	95.7
	(-2.13)	(-2.18)	(-0.90)	(-0.50)	(0.21)	(0.05)
New Hampshire	0.2	0.1	12.5	7.6	85.4	99.7
	(-2.18)	(-2.22)	(-1.45)	(-0.71)	(0.22)	(0.01)
New Jersey	0.9	0.5	29.8	15.4	65.4	85.9
	(-1.51)	(-1.56)	(-0.66)	(0.00)	(-0.05)	(0.04)
New York	3.8	2.0	34.5	10.9	76.9	92.3
	(-1.13)	(-1.18)	(-0.37)	(0.00)	(0.21)	(0.07)
Pennsylvania	4.3	2.3	31.6	12.1	68.9	92.3
	(-0.48)	(-0.53)	(-0.17)	(-0.29)	(-0.22)	(0.01)
Rhode Island	0.1	0.0	11.6	8.3	89.3	99.3
	(-1.92)	(-1.97)	(-1.34)	(-0.90)	(0.18)	(0.01)
Vermont	0.5	0.3	11.6	4.5	97.1	99.8
	(-0.89)	(-0.94)	(-1.01)	(-1.22)	(0.13)	(0.01)

Sources: Developed by the authors using InSTePP data.

Notes: Figures include 72 agricultural outputs (i.e., Conservation Reserve Program and machinery hired out are excluded).

Appendix Table 4-3 U.S. Agricultural Output Prices, Quantities and Value Shares, 1949–2006

	Price Indexes					Quantity Indexes					Output Value Shares			
Year	Livestock	Field Crops	Specialty Crops	Misc.	Total	Livestock	Field Crops	Specialty Crops	Misc.	Total	Livestock	Field Crops	Specialty Crops	Misc.
	index, 1949 = 100					*index, 1949 = 100*					*percentage share*			
1949	100	100	100	100	100	100	100	100	100	100	51	41	8	0
1950	101	119	103	100	109	102	90	106	100	97	50	41	9	0
1951	120	124	115	100	122	107	94	103	147	101	53	38	8	0
1952	110	119	125	97	115	109	101	104	200	105	51	40	9	0
1953	100	115	106	86	106	111	99	109	226	106	50	41	8	0
1954	93	113	114	84	103	116	97	106	268	107	50	41	9	0
1955	86	106	114	83	96	119	100	108	319	110	49	41	10	0
1956	84	106	118	84	95	120	101	114	365	112	48	41	10	0
1957	90	98	120	87	96	119	99	109	423	110	52	37	10	1
1958	100	98	115	90	101	122	115	115	537	119	52	38	9	1
1959	92	94	119	89	96	127	116	117	550	122	51	38	10	1
1960	92	93	126	88	96	124	117	117	576	121	50	38	10	1
1961	91	100	114	88	97	130	114	124	563	123	51	39	10	1
1962	93	101	122	90	99	131	115	120	595	124	51	39	10	1
1963	89	100	130	91	97	134	123	121	656	129	49	40	10	1
1964	86	97	145	90	95	137	118	123	688	128	49	38	12	1
1965	95	97	135	92	100	134	126	131	782	131	50	38	11	1
1966	106	101	134	95	107	138	123	133	815	132	53	36	10	1
1967	100	92	144	99	101	142	131	131	980	138	52	35	11	1
1968	104	91	157	100	104	143	136	131	1,044	140	52	35	12	1
1969	116	92	149	105	110	142	137	139	1,078	141	55	33	11	1
1970	118	103	151	109	116	149	131	137	1,022	142	55	33	10	1
1971	116	99	158	116	113	153	150	140	1,107	151	53	35	11	1
1972	133	130	192	124	137	154	154	134	1,067	152	50	39	10	1
1973	178	201	224	144	193	150	164	150	1,098	156	45	44	9	1

(continued)

Appendix Table 4-3 (continued)

Year	Price Indexes					Quantity Indexes					Output Value Shares			
	Livestock	Field Crops	Specialty Crops	Misc.	Total	Livestock	Field Crops	Specialty Crops	Misc.	Total	Livestock	Field Crops	Specialty Crops	Misc.
	index, 1949 = 100					*index, 1949 = 100*					*percentage share*			
1974	163	236	222	160	199	152	144	157	907	149	43	47	10	1
1975	171	195	232	176	187	143	170	163	972	157	42	46	11	1
1976	177	202	233	180	193	150	170	169	990	161	44	45	10	1
1977	176	175	251	185	182	152	188	174	1,074	170	44	43	12	1
1978	214	193	286	191	211	152	193	177	888	172	46	42	12	1
1979	249	211	299	206	236	157	217	187	913	185	46	43	11	1
1980	244	256	317	228	256	162	190	197	762	177	44	44	11	1
1981	245	213	330	260	238	164	230	195	805	194	44	43	12	1
1982	246	214	318	267	238	162	229	205	1,238	194	44	43	12	1
1983	241	252	331	271	253	164	154	205	925	166	48	37	13	1
1984	249	213	336	268	241	162	212	219	1,085	189	45	40	13	1
1985	233	192	334	257	224	166	228	219	1,427	197	45	40	14	1
1986	238	151	356	266	210	167	204	224	1,206	190	51	31	17	1
1987	247	183	355	274	227	170	200	248	1,927	196	48	33	16	2
1988	251	225	382	279	249	174	163	249	2,227	185	48	32	17	2
1989	269	207	398	290	252	174	199	254	2,561	200	48	33	17	3
1990	283	196	400	296	253	178	218	257	2,757	209	49	33	16	3
1991	266	197	402	291	247	183	212	262	2,677	210	48	33	17	3
1992	260	187	405	300	241	185	243	281	2,563	223	46	34	18	2
1993	264	208	420	304	253	187	198	282	2,551	210	48	32	18	2
1994	253	199	405	308	243	192	257	304	2,460	235	43	36	18	2
1995	244	255	454	310	267	196	212	292	2,393	219	42	37	19	2
1996	266	240	440	312	270	194	242	298	2,314	230	42	38	17	2
1997	267	213	458	317	260	197	254	319	2,254	239	43	35	19	2
1998	257	175	450	319	239	200	252	313	2,226	239	46	31	20	2
1999	249	160	448	320	229	206	247	323	2,240	242	47	29	22	2

2000	251	163	430	321	229	209	249	345	2,239	248	47	29	22	2
2001	277	162	449	321	242	208	246	337	2,221	245	50	27	21	2
2002	235	194	465	330	238	212	226	350	2,222	243	44	31	23	2
2003	265	221	477	331	263	211	242	350	2,222	249	44	33	21	2
2004	318	187	482	337	272	212	278	352	2,236	260	49	30	20	2
2005	315	185	516	339	274	216	268	357	2,992	262	48	28	21	2
2006	290	238	534	346	287	220	256	352	2,894	260	44	33	21	2
Average annual growth rates (percentage)														
1949-1960	-0.78	-0.67	2.07	-1.12	-0.42	1.98	1.46	1.40	15.92	1.73	-0.12	-0.53	2.15	16.29
1960-1970	2.54	1.04	1.83	2.08	1.90	1.83	1.08	1.58	5.73	1.60	0.88	-1.37	-0.10	4.30
1970-1980	7.22	9.09	7.45	7.40	7.94	0.80	3.72	3.65	-2.94	2.22	-2.14	2.64	0.94	-5.71
1980-1990	1.48	-2.69	2.30	2.61	-0.09	0.96	1.39	2.67	12.86	1.63	0.89	-2.84	3.43	13.93
1990-2002	-1.55	-0.08	1.26	0.90	-0.53	1.44	0.31	2.57	-1.80	1.28	-0.86	-0.51	3.09	-1.65
1990-2006	0.17	1.22	1.81	0.97	0.78	1.33	1.00	1.97	0.30	1.38	-0.65	0.07	1.63	-0.88
1949-2002	1.61	1.25	2.90	2.25	1.63	1.41	1.54	2.36	5.85	1.68	-0.29	-0.52	1.95	5.16
1949-2006	1.87	1.52	2.94	2.18	1.85	1.39	1.65	2.21	5.90	1.68	-0.27	-0.36	1.62	4.89

Sources: Authors' calculations based on InSTePP data.

Notes: A list of outputs included in each category is provided in Part II Appendix Table II-1. Specialty crops consist of nursery and greenhouse as well as all commodities grouped under vegetables and fruits and nuts in Appendix Table II-1.

CHAPTER 5

Agricultural Productivity Patterns

At the center of our empirical work is a model of state-specific productivity growth as a function of investments in agricultural research. While the notions of productivity and changes in productivity are intuitive, it is not easy to develop meaningful measures of productivity or to identify the productivity consequences of investments in agricultural R&D. Schultz (1953) argued that the root reason for an interest in the sources of productivity growth is an interest in the sources of output growth. And, expressing an idea he attributed to Zvi Griliches, Schultz (1956, p. 758) wrote:

> The analytical task, as I see it, is to re-establish a strong and satisfactory linkage between input and output over time. In our efforts to do this, we would do well to place before us and keep in mind the characteristics of an *ideal input-output formula* for this purpose. It would be one where *output over inputs . . .* stayed at or close to one. The closer we come to a one-to-one relationship in our formulation, the more complete would be our (economic) explanation.

In other words, a complete accounting of output growth would incorporate all inputs and outputs, and all other factors that affect the relationship between inputs and outputs—including the scale of production and shifts in the technical relationship between inputs and outputs typically referred to as technological changes. To the extent that our measures are less than complete and accurate, we are left with some ignorance about the sources of the measured residual output growth that is typically called productivity.[1]

1 It was Abramovitz (1956, p. 11) who wrote "Since we know little about the causes of productivity increase, the indicated importance of this element may be taken to be some sort of measure of our ignorance about the causes of economic growth in the United States." See also Griliches (1960a, 1960b and 1963).

J.M. Alston et al., *Persistence Pays: U.S. Agricultural Productivity Growth and the Benefits from Public R&D Spending*, Natural Resource Management and Policy 34,
DOI 10.1007/978-1-4419-0658-8_5,

Griliches (1961, p. 446) echoed these ideas when he wrote:

> As I understand it, we are interested in 'productivity' because we are interested in understanding . . . the forces that affect 'output' because we hope, ultimately, to be able to affect them for the better. We approach this task first by trying to take into account the 'obvious' factors: changes in labor and capital (and other materials if our output measures are gross). We measure these inputs as best we can, aggregate them using some sensible weighting procedure and get a 'total input' index. We compare this index with our output index and call any discrepancy 'productivity.' Crudely speaking then, the 'productivity' indexes measure the changes in output that have not been accounted for by the analyst's input measures. It is a measure of our ignorance, of the unknown, and of the magnitude of the task that is still ahead of us.... The task is to open this box, whose dimensions we know, and see what is inside of it. Is it returns to scale, the size of the market, changing market structure, changing quality of inputs, 'pure' technological change, or something else besides all that?

In this chapter we briefly describe how economists commonly define, measure, and interpret productivity, building on the related measures of aggregate input and output presented in the previous two chapters. Then we provide an empirical assessment of agricultural productivity developments in U.S. agriculture, drawing on our own measures and others. This assessment includes a brief description of the labor-use-requirements measures once reported by USDA. We also tabulate and discuss the prior literature on multi-factor productivity measurement that deals with U.S. agriculture.

Our review of the empirical evidence involves a discussion of structural changes in measures of productivity over time. Additionally, we compare regional and state-specific estimates to further highlight important spatial aspects of U.S. agricultural production. The examination of productivity patterns over time and among regions and states suggests a general slowdown of productivity growth toward the end of the period, and we present some graphical and statistical analysis of the hypothesis that U.S. agricultural productivity growth has slowed.

5.1 Partial Factor Productivity Measures

The most widely used productivity measures express a single output per unit of a particular input such as land or labor. Commonly used *partial* factor productivity (PFP) indexes divide an index of the aggregate quantity of output (Q) by an index of the quantity of a particular input, or input aggregate, X_i: that is, $PFP_i = Q/X_i$.

Familiar PFP measures are crop yields (a land productivity measure, where output for a particular crop is expressed relative to a measure of land used to produce that crop) and labor productivity.

Changes in PFP may arise from changes in technology—i.e., changes in the relationship between measured inputs and outputs—or changes in the use of other (unmeasured) inputs. Changes in a PFP measure are sometimes, and erroneously, interpreted as an indication of the direction and extent of technological changes. However, an increase in crop yields, for example, could simply reflect an increased use of fertilizer, while an increase in labor productivity may have resulted from increased use of machinery and other capital items. Thus, partial factor productivity indexes cannot be used by themselves to distinguish between the effects of changes in the state of technology and changes in the input mix induced by shifts in relative prices.[2] Still, PFP measures are widely reported, and they are of intrinsic interest and analytical value, so long as they are interpreted with care.

Crop Yields

Figure 5-1 shows partial productivity indexes for corn, rice, tobacco, wheat, and cotton for the period 1866–2007. U.S. corn yields grew at a long-run average rate of 1.30 percent per year from 1866–2006. Yields grew faster for corn, cotton, and rice than they did for wheat and tobacco. The average rates of growth of yields for these crops ranged from 0.71 percent per year for tobacco to 1.55 percent per year for rice.[3] Yield growth took off in the second half of the 20th Century. For example, the average yield of wheat in 1866 was 11 bushels per acre. It took 92 years (i.e., from 1866 until 1957) for wheat yields to double, but it took only 47 years (i.e., from 1957 to 2003) for U.S. wheat yields to double again and reach 44 bushels per acre. Many other crops in the United States experienced similar yield accelerations, beginning in the mid-1930s.

Olmstead and Rhode (2002 and 2008) stressed the importance of adaptive and maintenance research as elements of biological innovation in American agriculture.[4] They pointed out that it would be a mistake to interpret the comparatively slow rate of growth in average U.S. wheat yields, for example, during the 19th Century (and in fact for the period prior to 1935 for most crops) as indicat-

2 For example, if the price of purchased inputs such as fertilizer fell relative to land rent, then farmers would lower their costs of production by substituting fertilizer for land and thereby raise land productivity even in the absence of any research-induced changes in technology, such as crop varietal change.

3 For additional insights on crop-yield growth in the United States and elsewhere in the world, see Evans (1993), Naylor, Falcon and Zavaleta (1997), and Calderini and Slafer (1998).

4 Attempts to assess the overall importance of "maintenance" research in the United States include Heim and Blakeslee (1986), Adusei and Norton (1990) and Sparger (2009). See also Ruttan (1982, p. 60) who was an early commentator on the prospect that sustained productivity growth would require committing a rising share of agricultural R&D to maintaining past productivity gains.

Figure 5-1 National Average Yields for Selected Crops, 1866–2007

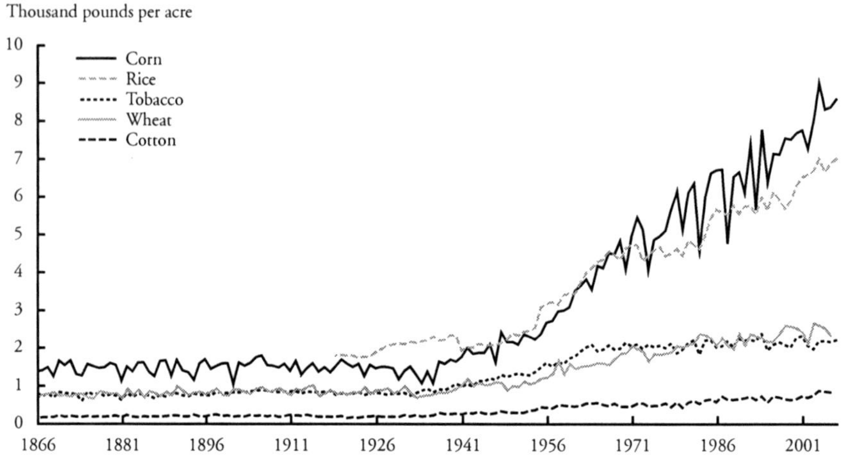

Sources: Data for 1866–1998 for wheat and tobacco are from Acquaye, Alston and Pardey (2006, Table Da 1095-1107). Maize and cotton yields for 1866–1997 and rice yields for 1919–1997 are from the same source. Other data to fill in the remaining portions of the 1866–2007 periods for each crop are from USDA NASS (2009).

Notes: National average yields represent total annual U.S. crop production divided by corresponding harvested area.

ing an absence of innovation or productivity growth. One form of innovation was to adapt varieties to deal with co-evolving pests and diseases; another was to adapt varieties as the industry moved west. In both cases, the impact may have been mainly to prevent observed average yields from falling in a world where the relevant counterfactual alternative was not one of constant average yields in the absence of innovation.

In the early 1800s, U.S. wheat production was confined almost exclusively to the eastern part of the country, mainly Ohio and upstate New York. Areas west of the Appalachian Mountains accounted for 92 percent of U.S. wheat production by 1909, compared with less than one-half of the output in 1839 (Olmstead and Rhode 2002). Massive changes in varietal use facilitated this spatial shift of U.S. wheat production into new locations—specifically the Northern Prairies and the Great Plains—and new agroecologies, where the varieties suitable for the eastern seaboard states faltered or failed (Chan-Kang and Pardey 2009). Moreover, reported average yields would have been much lower if not for changes in the biological basis of U.S. wheat production that staved off the effects of ever-evolving pests and diseases through the use of resistant varieties and improved management practices.

Similar spatial and temporal effects have been evident for other crops in the United States and elsewhere in the world (see, for example, Chapter 4 and

Table 5-1 National Average "Yields" for Selected Livestock Commodities

Year	Liveweight per Animal				Eggs per Layer	Milk per Cow
	Cattle	Hogs	Turkeys	Broilers		
	pounds per animal					*pounds*
1930	956.3		13.4		124.0	4,515.3
1940	948.0	237.7	15.3	2.9	135.7	4,651.7
1950	985.7	244.3	18.4	3.1	172.0	5,296.7
1960	1,039.7	240.7	19.0	3.6	220.3	9,386.7
1970	1,039.7	240.7	19.0	3.6	220.3	9,386.7
1980	1,077.0	242.3	18.9	3.9	241.7	11,542.0
1990	1,148.3	250.3	21.3	4.4	251.0	14,712.0
2000	1,219.3	262.0	25.7	5.0	256.7	18,040.7
2007	1,278.7	268.7	28.5	5.5	263.0	20,165.0

Sources: For the period prior to 1999, all data obtained from Acquaye, Alston and Pardey (2006, Table Da 1108-1116). Data for cattle, hogs, turkeys and broilers for the period after 1998 from USDA NASS (2009); from USDA (2008, *Agricultural Statistics*, Table 8-62) for eggs; and from USDA (2008, *Agricultural Statistics*, Table 8-10) for butterfat.

Notes: Numbers are three-year averages centered on the year noted. Series for cattle, hogs, turkeys, and broilers are average live weight per animal at slaughter. Eggs are number of eggs per year per layer, and milk is pounds of butterfat per cow. The entries for eggs per layer and milk per cow for 2007 are based on preliminary data.

Beddow, Pardey and Hurley 2009). Consequently, reported changes in average national crop yields alone may be a misleading indicator of the rate and extent of the technological change in agriculture attributable to the innovative efforts of farmers or more formal forms of R&D. The same possibilities should be kept in mind when considering changes over time in any measure of productivity, and attempting to draw inferences about the underlying rate of innovation, since the counterfactual alternative might not be simple or easy to define.

Livestock "Yields"

Output per acre (usually per year, and, perhaps, by season) is an obvious and reasonably accessible partial productivity metric for crops. Comparable productivity measures for livestock are less obvious and less accessible. One measure is animal output (say, milk, meat or egg production) per unit of input such as a standardized unit of feed rations used by Peterson (1969) in his classic study of the returns to U.S. poultry research. Others could be constructed, such as the annual yield of milk, meat, or wool per acre for grazing-based livestock production. Several yield-like metrics are presented in Table 5-1. Some, such as eggs per layer per year and milk per cow per year, approximate a type of partial productivity measure. Like crop yields, these and similar measures can provide some indication of the effects of technical improvements such as better feed efficiencies, enhanced animal management methods, or streamlined slaughtering practices. Others such as the average live-weight (at slaughter) of cattle, hogs, broilers and turkeys are potentially informative but do not constitute partial productivity measures in that they do not represent a ratio of output to a particular input. Such measures are also affected by the confounding influence of other factors, including policies such as the World War II price premiums paid to farmers for delivery of larger hogs (specifically, 240-270 pound hogs) which caused the average slaughter weight of hogs to spike in 1945 (see, for example, Wilcox 1947 and Benedict 1953).[5]

Similar to the crops sector, within the livestock sector rates of "yield" growth vary substantially among outputs and over time. Some of this variation is attributable to differences in the rate of uptake and effectiveness of innovations affecting stocking rates, disease control, reproductive efficiency, and feed conversion efficiency. Such changes enabled the development, for instance, of intensive large-scale, highly cost-efficient hog and poultry operations—enterprises that combined innovations in genetics, animal housing, feed, veterinary knowledge and medicines, and livestock husbandry.

Land, Labor, Capital, and Materials Productivity

Another partial perspective on productivity can be gleaned from the long-run indexes of *aggregate* output per acre and output per hour of work for U.S. agriculture, as plotted in Figure 5-2, Panel a. Land productivity more than quadrupled between 1911 and 2002, but this was dwarfed by the more than fifteen-fold increase in labor productivity over the same period. This comparison reflects a more than five-fold increase in the quantity of output against a comparatively unchanging land base (with corresponding large increases in yields of important crops like corn, wheat, and soybeans) along with a rapidly declining labor force in agriculture.

The increases in land and labor productivity occurred mainly after the 1940s, and the growth rates of both productivity indexes slowed starting in the 1980s. Increases in the quantities of other, mainly purchased, inputs, such as fertilizers, herbicides, electricity, fuels, and irrigation (see Chapter 3), account for some of the growth in output per hour or per acre, but much of the measured growth in productivity reflects changes in technology (some of which is embodied in the purchased inputs).

Figure 5-2, Panel b presents the same land and labor productivity paths as in Panel a but this time for the period 1949–2002 and now using data from the InSTePP series; it also includes corresponding capital and materials input productivities. Once again the rapid growth in labor productivity (which increased on average by 3.42 percent per year during the period shown) dominates the

5 Predictably, these price premiums skewed market deliveries towards larger hogs. However, they also resulted in a substantial expansion of the breeding stock that was not sustainable owing to wartime limitations on the availability of livestock feed. Consequently, the average weight of hogs at slaughter jumped from 234 pounds in 1939 to 261 pounds in 1945. It then fell to 235 pounds by 1955, after which it resumed its long-term upward trend.

Figure 5-2 Partial Factor Productivities

Panel a. Land and labor productivity, 1911–2002

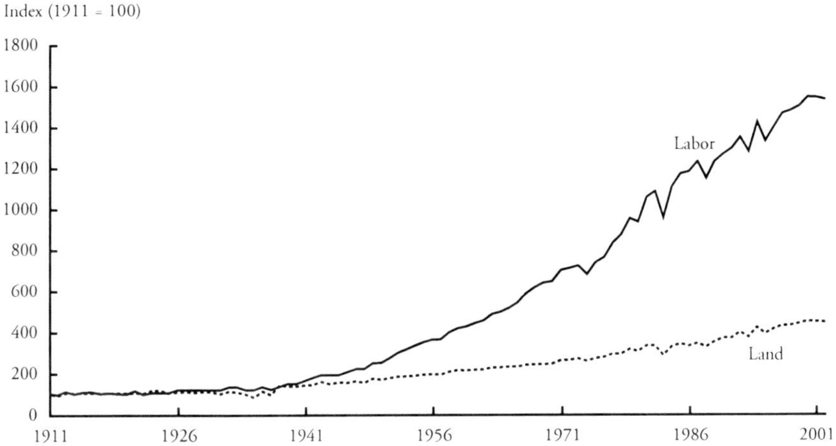

Panel b. Land, labor, capital and materials productivity, 1949–2002

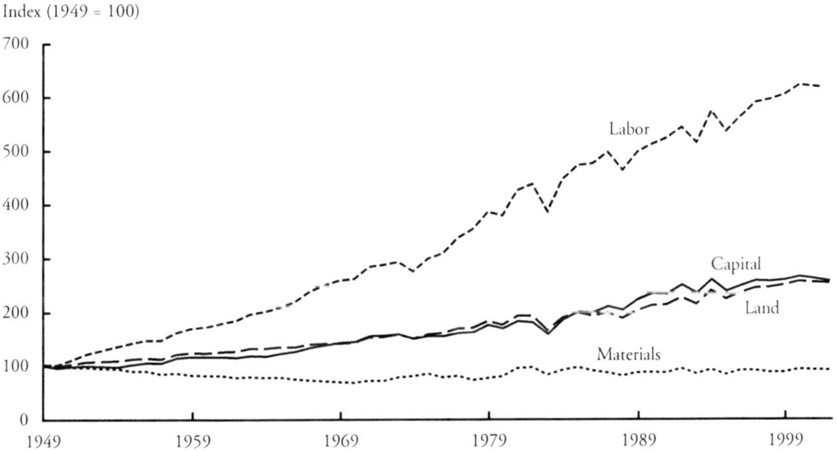

Sources: Panel a. 1910–1938 from USDA ERS (1984, Table 13); 1939–1946 from USDA ERS (1984, Table 13); 1947–1948 from USDA ERS (1992), and the USDA (1998); 1949–2002 from InSTePP data series. Panel b. InSTePP data series.

Notes: The partial productivity indexes were calculated as the index of aggregate output divided by the index of aggregate input use. For Panel a, the InSTePP Fisher indexes available for the 1949 to 2002 period were backcast to 1910 using the growth in a corresponding Laspeyres index for the 1910 to 1949 period.

picture. At the other end of the growth spectrum is a small contraction in materials productivity (which shrank by 0.20 percent per year from 1949 to 2002); a reflection of the rapid growth in the use of materials inputs by U.S. agriculture during the second half of the 20th Century. Output per unit of capital services grew by 1.78 percent per year during this period, about the same as the rate of growth of land productivity (1.74 percent per year). Appendix Table 5-1 provides region- and decade-specific rates of growth in partial productivity measures.

Measures of the pace and pattern of growth of partial productivities are sensitive to data and aggregation issues. For example, Figure 5-3, Panel a shows a range of land productivity measures that use the InSTePP series in conjunction with fixed-weight (Laspeyres) and variable-weight (Fisher) aggregation methods. Panel b shows the same set of productivity measures for labor.[6] Both panels also include corresponding measures based on data compiled and published online by the USDA Economic Research Service (2008c). Taking the adjusted Fisher series as our point of reference, both the unadjusted Laspeyres and unadjusted Fisher indexes substantially overstate the rates of increase in land and labor productivity, while the adjusted Laspeyres index understates the partial productivity gains for both land and labor. These discrepancies reflect a combination of several factors that give rise to biases in the indexes of input and output. These index number biases can be reduced by making quality adjustments, using state-specific rather than national prices, and using variable weight (Fisher) rather than fixed weight (Laspeyres) indexes (see Acquaye, Alston and Pardey 2003, for instance, as well as Chapter 3 and Chapter 4).[7]

Notably, the discrepancies among alternative estimates of rates of change in aggregate output are much smaller than the discrepancies among alternative measures of rates of change of aggregate land and labor inputs.[8] Two factors account for this observation. First, changes in quality and composition of the aggregate were more important for inputs than outputs, whether they reflected responses to relative price changes or other changes (e.g., in technology). Second,

---

6 The partial productivity indexes were calculated in two ways. The first set of "unadjusted" indexes was calculated using a national average rental price for land, a national average hourly wage for labor, and a national average price for outputs as weights in the indexing procedure. The national average price weights were then combined with estimates of total acres and total annual hours in U.S agriculture to calculate "unadjusted" indexes of land and labor input in the sense that they do not account for the changing composition of the aggregate over the sample (a single input category and a single average price), and they do not account for spatial variation among states (national as opposed to state-specific prices). A second set of "adjusted" partial productivity indexes was calculated using the disaggregated data and state-specific prices for comparison with the unadjusted measures.

7 Ostensibly the state-specific average prices as used here refer to prices received by farmers, and measured at point of first sale (Brinkman, personal communication, 2009), that reflect distance from market as well as differences in the composition of output among states. For example, in 2007, 97 percent of the wheat grown in Minnesota was spring wheat, whereas in California winter wheat accounted for the majority (70 percent) of wheat produced.

8 For the period 1949–2002, the unadjusted Fisher index of output grew at an average rate of 1.73 percent per year and the adjusted index grew by 1.68 percent per year. Considering the alternative land and labor aggregates, unadjusted labor inputs shrank at an average rate of 2.15 percent per year and adjusted labor inputs shrank at an average rate of 1.74 percent per year; unadjusted land inputs shrank at an average rate of 0.15 percent per year and adjusted land inputs shrank at an average rate of 0.07 percent per year.

Figure 5-3 Alternative Measures of Land and Labor Productivity, 1949–2002

Panel a. Land productivity

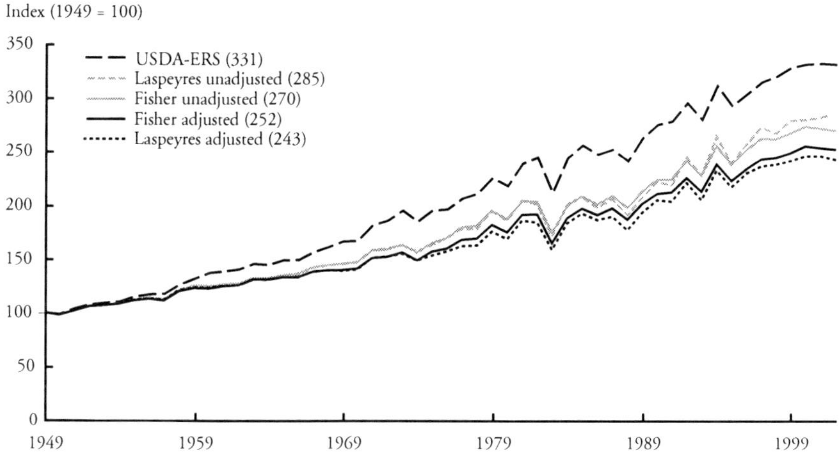

Panel b. Labor productivity

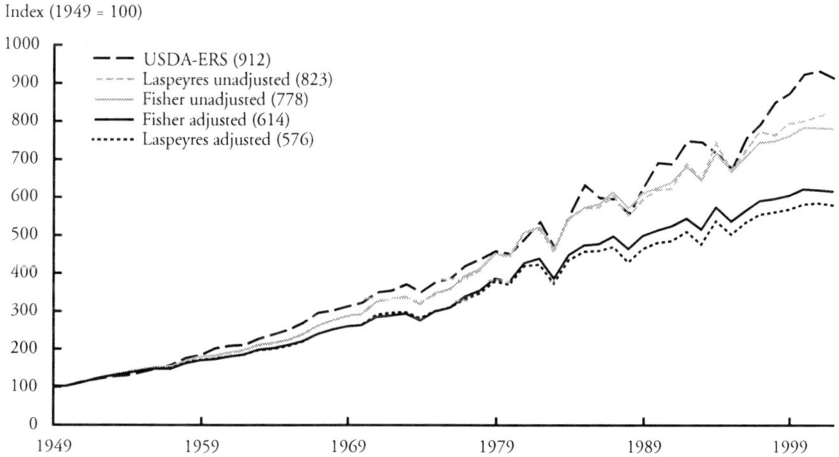

Sources: Compiled by the authors using InSTePP data and data from USDA ERS (2008c).

Notes: The adjusted series use state- and commodity-specific prices as weights in the indexing procedure, and the unadjusted series use a national average price for all states and categories in the indexing procedure. Numbers in parentheses represent the value of the index in 2002.

relative prices and cost shares of major input categories changed much more than their counterparts on the output side.[9]

9 For more details on the issue of changing relative prices and the index number problem more generally see Richter (1966) and Star (1974). The term "index number problem" refers to a situation when quantity changes in response to relative price changes are not properly distinguished

Substantial regional differences in partial productive developments are revealed in Figure 5-4. Here we used the graphical technique developed by Hayami and Ruttan (1971), where the horizontal axis measures labor productivity (in logarithms) and the vertical axis measures land productivity (in logarithms). Productivity loci for seven regions and the U.S. total are included in Figure 5-4. The productivity measures were formed by taking a ratio of the Fisher indexes of the quantities of output and the relevant input, and multiplying those ratios by the ratio of the value of output to the value of the corresponding input in the base year 1949, then taking the natural logarithms of the scaled ratios.[10] Since both axes are measured in natural logarithms a unit increase in either direction is interpreted as a proportional increase in land or labor productivity, and the length of the productivity locus is an indication of the average annual rate of change in productivity. All of the productivity paths move in a northeasterly direction, starting in 1949 and ending in 2002, indicating productivity growth. The diagonals indicate constant labor-to-land ratios. As the productivity locus for a particular region crosses a diagonal from left to right, it indicates a decrease in the number of quality-adjusted hours of labor per quality-adjusted acre in that region.The graphs show increases in the productivity of both land and labor but with a decrease in the labor-land ratio, implying pronounced growth in the productivity of labor versus land—i.e., the horizontal spans of the productivity loci are greater than their vertical spans. These general patterns are common across regions, but vary in the details among regions.

Output per hour was much lower than the national average in the southern states (notably the Southeast and Southern Plains regions) in the period immediately following the Second World War, yet labor productivity was very similar among regions in the more-recent years. The Central region had the highest labor productivity at the beginning of the period 1949–2002, but by 2002, the Northern Plains region had the highest. On average, labor productivity was 26 percent higher in the Central region compared with the national average in 1949, and 37 percent higher in the Northern Plains compared with the national average in 2002. Labor productivity was substantially and persistently lower in the Southern Plains, Northeast and Southeast regions.

A relatively low (or high) ranking in terms of labor productivity does not necessarily translate into a correspondingly low (or high) ranking in terms of land productivity. In the Mountain region, labor productivity was close to the national average for most of the time period, but land productivity was the lowest among all of the regions throughout the latter half of the 20th Century. The

from other types of changes. This problem is also discussed in detail in relation to productivity measurement by Alston, Norton and Pardey (1995, chapter 3).

10 The output and input indexes are all normalized to a value of 100 in base year 1949, which means the productivity paths for each region and the United States would begin from the same value if they were not scaled by the respective base-year value ratios.

Figure 5-4 Regional Land and Labor Productivity Measures

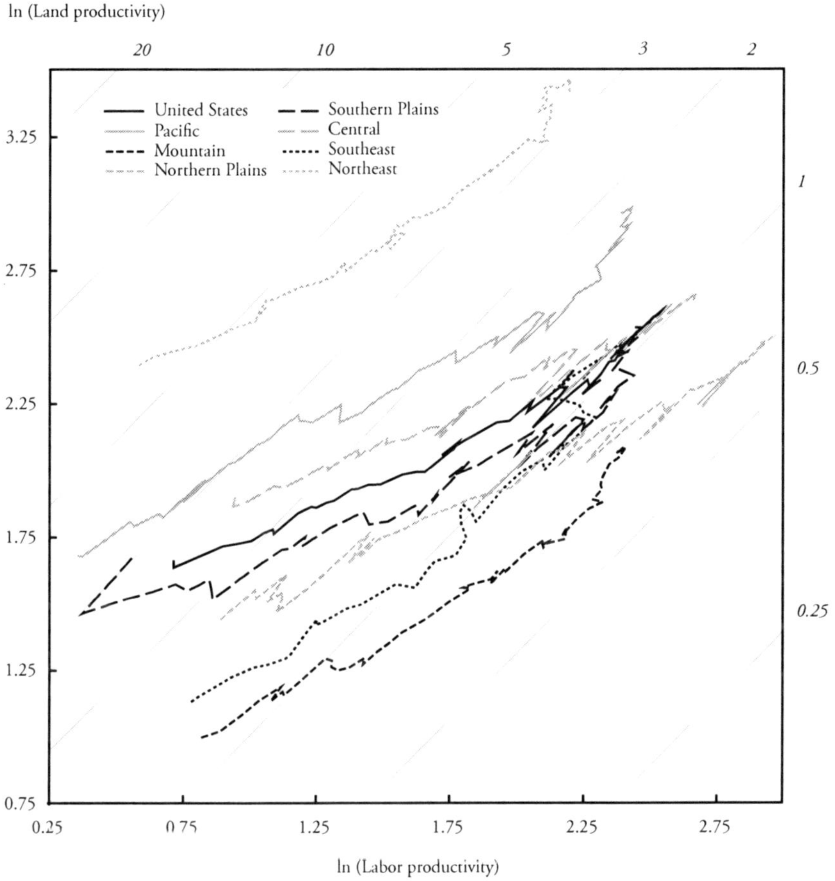

Sources: Calculated by the authors using InSTePP data.

Notes: Diagonal lines reflect constant labor-to-land ratios (measured as quality-adjusted hours over quality-adjusted acres), as labeled with numbers in italics. See Appendix Table II-2 for the grouping of states into regions. Land and labor productivity are expressed in natural logarithms.

Mountain region emphasizes livestock production (accounting for 59 percent of the value of agricultural output in 2003–2005, as shown in Table 2-1), which ostensibly could be a source of the lower land productivity in this region. Although it is also heavily focused on livestock production, the Northeast region sustained the highest land productivity ratio for the entire post-1948 period, but livestock production in the Northeast is mainly confinement turkey and broiler production operations, with very different land, labor, and productivity implications compared with cattle ranches in the Mountain region.

Regional differences in land and labor productivity paths reflect the interplay between changes in the quantity and composition (or quality) of inputs—these

Table 5-2 Regional Indexes of Land-to-Labor Price Ratios, 1949–2002

Region	Price Ratio 1949	2002	Average 1949–2002	Average Growth 1949–2002
		ratio		*percent per year*
United States	1.00	0.46	0.70	-1.48
Pacific	1.00	0.48	0.64	-1.37
Mountain	1.00	0.55	0.83	-1.13
Northern Plains	1.00	0.54	0.78	-1.17
Southern Plains	1.00	0.28	0.57	-2.40
Central	1.00	0.59	0.83	-0.98
Southeast	1.00	0.31	0.55	-2.23
Northeast	1.00	0.35	0.61	-1.98

Sources: Calculated by the authors using InSTePP data.

land and labor indexes are developed from three and 32 different input subclasses, respectively—and changes in the amount and composition of outputs.[11] While land inputs generally declined, they increased in quality-adjusted terms in some of the drier western states, like Nebraska, reflecting a faster increase in higher-quality irrigated cropland in those states. The reduction in total hours worked was more dramatic in the Southern states than in the rest of the 48 states, while in both the Mountain and Pacific regions the quantity of quality-adjusted labor used in agriculture actually increased over the 1970s, 1980s, and the 1990s against a national trend of decreasing labor use.

In addition to (and as part of) these compositional changes, the regional productivity differentials also reflect factor substitution (and, perhaps, induced innovation) effects stemming from spatial differences in the relative price of (quality-adjusted) land and (quality-adjusted) labor. Table 5-2 shows regional indexes of the land-to-labor price ratios for 1949 and 2002, as well as the average for the period 1949–2002, and the average annual growth in the ratio for the period 1949–2002. The general decline in these regional indexes of the input price ratio since 1949 is consistent with the pervasive increase in land-to-labor input quantity ratios noted in Table 3-5 (Chapter 3). Notably, the Southern Plains region had the fastest rate of decline in the price of land relative to labor and the fastest increase in the use of land relative to labor inputs. Land-to-labor prices declined slowest in the Central region but the Pacific region experienced the slowest rate of increase in land relative to labor use of all the regions in Table 3-5. Clearly the simple substitution of land for labor (in response to an increase

11 As Star (1974, p. 129) observed "The great advantage of using disaggregated data is that *quality changes are transformed into quantity changes*" [emphasis in original]. In the same article he also observed that "In order to be able to add together different units of items, the items must be homogenous: each unit must be a perfect substitute for any other unit, i.e., the marginal rate of substitution is constant and the units of measurement are chosen so that the marginal products of every unit are equal (p. 125)."

Table 5-3 Labor-Use Requirements for Various Commodities, 1800–1980s

	Crops										Livestock		
	Hours per Unit of Output					Hours per Acre					Hours per Unit of Output		
	Corn	Wheat	Hay	Potato	Cotton	Corn	Wheat	Hay	Potato	Cotton	Milk	Chicken	Eggs
	per 100 bushels		*per ton*		*per bale*						*per cwt*	*per 100 broilers*	*per 100 eggs*
1800	344	373			601	86	56			185			
1840	276	233			438	69	35			135			
1880	180	152			303	46	20			119			
1900	147	108			284	38	15			112			
1910s	134	102	10	26	288	35	14	12	75	111	3.8		
1920s	119	82	10	22	282	32	11	12	74	96	3.5		1.9
1930s	116	69	9	21	231	28	9	11	69	98	3.4	25.0	1.8
1940s	66	39	7	15	164	22	7	10	69	91	2.9	19.5	1.6
1950s	27	22	4	7	91	12	4	6	58	66	2.0	6.0	1.1
1960s	9	12	2	5	39	6	3	4	47	39	1.1	2.5	0.5
1970s	4	9	2	3	8	4	3	3	38	8	0.4	0.6	0.3
1980s	3	7	1	2	5	3	3	3	33	5	0.2	0.4	0.2

Sources: Data details reported by Acquaye, Alston and Pardey (2006, Table Da 1143-1171).

Notes: Values for decades are averages of reported values during that decade. These represent data for the full decade except the 1920s for egg values that are based on 1925–1929; the 1930s for broiler chicken values that are based on 1935–1939; and the 1980s when all values are based on 1982–1986.

in the price of land relative to labor) is confounded by changes in the relative prices of other inputs and shifts in the underlying production function attributable to technical changes. Over the period 1949–2002, the indexes of land-to-labor price ratios were highest (0.83) for the Mountain and Central regions and lowest (just 0.55) in the Southeast region, consistent with the relatively slow rates of decline in the Mountain and Central regions.

Labor Requirements

The figures on "labor requirements" for various farming operations are among the most cited historical agricultural statistics. Table 5-3 includes a summary of these labor-requirement figures, which were compiled from 1800 (for some agricultural activities) through to 1986, after which they were discontinued. Some of these labor requirements measures are a type of inverse partial productivity measure (reflecting hours per unit of output produced); others are measures of factor intensity or factor proportions (in this case hours per acre). Like partial productivity measures generally, changes in labor requirements reflect the effects of changes in technology and myriad other factors, including the scale of production. For example, for corn production the number of reported hours worked per acre fell from 35 in the 1910s to 3 in the 1980s, and the number of hours required to produce one hundred bushels fell from 134 to 3 over the same time period. The much greater saving in hours per bushel, compared with hours per acre, reflects an implied increase in yields from an average of 26 bushels per acre in the period 1910–1914 to 103 in the period 1982–1986, broadly consistent with the average yield trends in Figure 5-1. In chicken production, the figures on the number of hours worked per hundred broilers produced fell from 25 in the 1930s to 0.4 in the 1980s, a much greater improvement in labor productivity compared with corn, reflecting great changes in input combinations as well as technological improvements.

The labor requirements series were discontinued in 1986 because of concerns over their accuracy and interpretation. It is not known how the figures were derived in the past, but it seems that they were based on expert opinions about best or average practice.[12] The main virtue in these figures is that the series extend back for a long time, into periods where little or no alternative data are available on input-output relationships. They are more useful as indicators of longer-term changes rather than as specific measures of average productivity at any particular time, and they illustrate the dramatic changes that have taken place, but they must be used with care.

5.2 Multi-Factor Productivity Measures

A more meaningful measure of changes in productivity attributable to R&D-induced changes in technology is given when ideal index number procedures are used that account properly for all inputs, and index number problems are minimized. A *total* factor productivity (TFP) index is comprehensive in that all of the relevant outputs are included in the output quantity index, Q, and all of the relevant inputs are included in the input quantity, X^N: $TFP = MFP^N = Q/X^N$. In practice the available data make it impossible to get a truly comprehensive accounting of all of the inputs used in production, and notably so in agriculture which uses significant amounts of (unmeasured or unpriced) natural inputs such as heat, light, rainfall and so forth. Consequently, a TFP index is really a conceptual construct rather than a practical reality. Instead, what is usually reported are *multi-factor* productivity (MFP) indexes that account for a measured subset, M, of the N inputs, and divide the output index by the input index, X^M: i.e., $MFP^M = Q/X^M$. Since some inputs are omitted from this index of input quantities (i.e., X^M versus X^N), the MFP index is only an approximation of the TFP index. Further, some outputs may be omitted (e.g., nonmarketed outputs from agriculture, including positive and negative environmental externalities). Fewer inputs are omitted in the MFP index than in the PFP measure, but this only changes the degree of the problem of interpreting productivity measures where some inputs are omitted; it does not eliminate the problem of omitted inputs or omitted outputs.

12 See Short (1987).

Measures of multi-factor productivity growth may be greater or less than the total factor productivity growth being approximated, depending on what was left out and how the left-out variables changed over time. Typical MFP growth measures do not account fully for changes in the quality of inputs (e.g., the size and power of machinery and other capital inputs, or the schooling of workers and other human capital attributes), inputs represented by infrastructure (e.g., roads, telecommunications, rail facilities, irrigation systems) and other rural public goods (e.g., agricultural R&D or education investments), or inputs that are otherwise difficult to measure (including natural resource stocks of soil fertility and other exhaustible resources); likewise, some outputs may be mismeasured because of unmeasured variation in quality or other compositional changes, and certain types of outputs (e.g., environmental amenities from rural landscape) are typically omitted. Such omissions cloud the interpretation of the measures.

Different MFP indexes may be appropriate for different purposes, and in using indexes it is important to be clear about what is left out of the input index (hence, what is included in the set of things that account for growth in measured productivity). When the aim is to measure the contribution of public-sector agricultural R&D, it is desirable to account for all other influences in the index. Otherwise the productivity growth attributable to R&D will be confounded with productivity growth attributable to other omitted variables.[13]

Earlier Productivity Evidence for the United States

A number of statistical databases of inputs, outputs, and productivity in U.S. agriculture have been constructed over the past half century or so, no two of which used exactly the same methods. Acquaye, Alston and Pardey (2003) and Andersen (2005) reviewed previous studies of U.S. agricultural productivity patterns, and documented the evolution of approaches and results. Significant refinements in methods have increased the accuracy and clarified the interpretation of measures of inputs and outputs in U.S. agriculture. Some of these improvements include refinements to indexing procedures, the incorporation of quality changes, utilization adjustments, and the use of disaggregated data.

Barton and Cooper (1948), Barton and Durost (1960), Durost and Barton (1960), and Loomis and Barton (1961) were the first researchers to compile national indexes of aggregate inputs, outputs, and productivity in U.S. agriculture. These authors calculated fixed-weight indexes, where the weights applied to quantities were equal to the average price of each sub-aggregate over a few selected years (see also Griliches 1960b). The U.S. Department of Agriculture (USDA) published fixed-weight (Laspeyres) indexes of inputs, outputs, and pro-

13 On the other hand, for instance, if the objective is to measure the productivity effects of both R&D and investments in education, it would be inappropriate to "remove" the effects of investments in education by adjusting the labor variable.

ductivity annually in reports on *Changes in Farm Production and Efficiency* until the early 1990s. According to Capalbo and Vo (1988, p. 101), Brown (1978) was the first researcher to compile (approximate) Divisia indexes of inputs and outputs in U.S. agriculture. These and more-recent studies of U.S. agricultural productivity are listed in Table 5-4. The studies are divided into those that used index number (or growth accounting) methods to estimate productivity and those that used parametric methods (in the context of econometrically estimated production functions, cost functions and the like).

Across all of the 32 studies listed in the table, estimates of the average annual rate of productivity growth range from 0.21 to 3.50 percent per year; the simple average of these estimates is 1.75 percent per year. The wide range of the estimates of productivity growth reflects differences in time-periods, databases, and estimation procedures among the listed studies. Two of the estimates of rates of productivity growth are very small (i.e., less than 1.0 percent per year) and three are very large (i.e., greater than or equal to 3 percent per year), and these are probably outliers, which we can discount for one reason or another—for example, because they apply to a particular time period. Excluding these five outliers, the remaining 27 studies reported estimates ranging between 1.00 and 2.00 percent per year. Among these, the more-recent estimates, especially for the more-recent period spanning the second half of the 20th Century, are probably more reliable as a result of their use of better data and better methods; these estimates are more typically in the range of 1.50 to 2.00 percent per year. Although the sample of studies is too small to allow clear inferences to be drawn about methods, it appears as though the parametric studies based on production functions tend to yield smaller estimates of productivity growth rates compared with other types of parametric studies (using cost or profit function methods) and index number methods. Finally, most of the estimates of productivity growth rates for U.S. agriculture in Table 5-4 are larger than their counterparts for other sectors of the economy (Jorgenson and Gollop 1992).

Studies using a growth accounting approach switched noticeably from the use of Törnqvist-Theil indexes to Fisher Ideal indexes in more recent studies. The numerical difference between these indexes is typically small in practice. However, the Törnqvist-Theil index requires taking logarithms of quantity variables and, if any of the quantity variables contain any observations equal to zero, it is impossible to calculate the index unless ad-hoc adjustments are made.[14] Quantity variables with zero values are not a problem with the Fisher Ideal indexing procedure, and this is one reason why this procedure has become popular, especially when working with disaggregated panel data.

---

14 This is a significant problem in finely differentiated panel data sets that often contain variables with zero values for some observations. The problem becomes worse the more the data are disaggregated. See Craig and Pardey (1996a and 1996b) for more on calculating the Törnqvist-Theil index using data sets containing variables with observations equal to zero.

Table 5-4 Estimates of Multi-Factor Productivity Growth in U.S. Agriculture

Study				
Authors	**Date**	**Method**	**Sample Period**	**Average Annual Growth Rate**
Index number approaches				*percent per year*
Barton and Cooper	1948	Fixed-weight	1910–1945	1.65[a]
Loomis and Barton	1961	Fixed-weight	1870–1958	0.80
Brown	1978	Tornqvist-Theil	1947–1974	1.42
Kendrick	1983	Tornqvist-Theil	1948–1979	3.50
Ball	1984 & 1985	Tornqvist-Theil	1948–1979	1.75
Capalbo and Vo	1988	Tornqvist-Theil	1948–1983	1.22
Cox and Chavas	1990	Tornqvist-Theil	1950–1983	1.89
USDA ERS	1991	Tornqvist-Theil	1948–1989	1.58[b]
BLS	1992	Tornqvist-Theil/Fisher Ideal	1948–1990	3.06[b]
Jorgenson and Gollop	1992	Tornqvist-Theil	1947–1985	1.58
Huffman and Evenson	1993	Tornqvist-Theil	1950–1982	1.84
Craig and Pardey	1996a	Tornqvist-Theil	1949–1991	1.76[c]
Ball et al.	1997	Fisher Ideal	1948–1994	1.94[c]
Ball et al.	1999	Tornqvist-Theil	1960–1990	2.00
Schimmelphennig and Thirtle	1999	Fisher Ideal	1973–1993	3.00
McCunn and Huffman	2000	Tornqvist-Theil	1950–1982	2.00
Ball, Butault and Nehring	2001	Fisher Ideal	1960–1996	1.94[c]
Acquaye, Alston and Pardey	2003	Fisher Ideal	1949–1991	1.90[c]
Ball et al.	2004	Malmquist	1960–1996	1.54
USDA ERS	2008c	Fisher Ideal	1960–2004	1.70[c]
USDA ERS	2008c	Fisher Ideal	1948–2004	1.77
Parametric approaches				
Ruttan	1956	Cobb-Douglas production	1919–1950	1.23
Ray	1982	Translog cost	1939–1977	1.80
Capalbo and Denny	1986	Translog production	1962–1978	1.41
Capalbo	1988	Translog cost	1950–1983	1.4–1.6[d]
Jorgenson	1990	Translog production	1948–1979	1.61
Dorfman and Foster	1991	Translog production	1948–1983	0.21
Luh and Stefanou	1991	Generalized Leontief value	1948–1982	1.50
Karagiannis and Mergos	2000	Profit function	1948–1994	1.91 & 1.99[e]
Acquaye	2000	Translog cost	1949–1991	1.99
Andersen	2005	Translog production	1949–1991	1.31
Andersen, Alston and Pardey	2007	Translog production	1949–2002	1.55

Sources: Compiled by the authors.

[a] Calculated as the growth in output minus the growth in inputs from 1910 to 1945, divided by the number of periods.

[b] Calculated from multi-factor productivity indexes using the regression formula, $\ln(Z) = \beta_0 + \beta_1(T)$, where Z = productivity index and T = year.

[c] Represents average of 50 states.

[d] Data range spans a 95 percent confidence interval.

[e] Estimates represent an input-based and an output-based measure, respectively.

Table 5-5 State-Specific Input, Output and Productivity Growth, 1949–2002

	Growth, 1949–2002			MFP Growth				
	Input	Output	MFP	1949–1960	1960–1970	1970–1980	1980–1990	1990–2002
				average annual percentage change				
United States	*-0.11*	*1.68*	*1.78*	*1.89*	*1.69*	*2.46*	*2.07*	*0.97*
Pacific	*0.82*	*2.64*	*1.82*	*1.60*	*2.31*	*2.99*	*1.21*	*1.15*
California	0.97	2.74	1.77	1.66	2.22	2.84	1.01	1.24
Oregon	0.37	2.03	1.65	1.41	1.90	2.68	1.28	1.13
Washington	0.62	2.55	1.93	0.71	2.76	3.79	2.11	0.64
Mountain	*0.45*	*2.04*	*1.59*	*1.73*	*2.10*	*1.89*	*1.85*	*0.57*
Arizona	0.94	2.43	1.48	1.45	0.70	3.17	0.67	1.44
Colorado	0.54	1.90	1.35	1.54	1.98	1.81	2.31	-0.53
Idaho	0.68	2.82	2.14	1.70	2.92	2.64	2.80	0.94
Montana	0.26	1.31	1.04	1.81	2.00	0.94	1.54	-0.78
Nevada	0.21	1.09	0.88	0.89	0.94	1.48	-0.14	1.16
New Mexico	0.59	2.36	1.77	1.05	2.15	1.45	1.62	2.51
Utah	-0.08	1.43	1.51	1.89	2.38	0.06	2.61	0.72
Wyoming	0.09	0.93	0.84	2.06	0.71	1.21	0.21	0.04
Northern Plains	*0.16*	*2.05*	*1.89*	*2.84*	*1.22*	*1.76*	*3.39*	*0.43*
Kansas	0.23	1.90	1.67	3.48	0.44	1.22	2.54	0.67
Nebraska	0.42	2.35	1.94	2.41	1.41	2.06	3.42	0.60
North Dakota	-0.18	1.94	2.12	2.19	1.63	2.00	4.99	0.19
South Dakota	-0.07	1.70	1.77	2.96	1.59	1.33	3.39	-0.15
Southern Plains	*-0.12*	*1.76*	*1.88*	*1.53*	*2.06*	*1.99*	*2.49*	*1.47*
Arkansas	-0.02	2.87	2.89	3.12	3.59	2.81	3.12	2.00
Louisiana	-0.78	1.26	2.04	1.05	4.32	1.96	1.67	1.42
Mississippi	-0.97	1.99	2.95	3.86	3.90	1.42	2.57	2.93
Oklahoma	-0.04	1.29	1.33	2.01	0.33	2.90	1.42	0.15
Texas	0.20	1.53	1.32	0.39	1.01	1.39	2.61	1.32
Central	*-0.27*	*1.34*	*1.61*	*1.46*	*0.97*	*2.74*	*1.66*	*1.30*
Illinois	-0.27	1.27	1.54	1.47	0.08	2.61	2.61	1.03
Indiana	-0.34	1.21	1.56	1.48	0.55	2.87	2.13	0.89
Iowa	-0.03	1.65	1.68	1.10	0.97	2.80	1.10	2.37
Michigan	-0.59	1.20	1.79	0.94	2.34	3.69	1.50	0.76
Minnesota	-0.10	1.89	1.99	1.88	1.41	2.67	2.09	1.91
Missouri	-0.23	0.96	1.19	1.64	0.58	1.96	0.74	1.02
Ohio	-0.58	0.83	1.40	1.22	0.92	3.57	1.57	0.02
Wisconsin	-0.40	1.00	1.40	1.49	1.37	1.97	1.46	0.82
Southeast	*-0.41*	*1.68*	*2.09*	*2.33*	*2.39*	*2.96*	*2.30*	*0.72*
Alabama	-0.59	1.86	2.45	3.37	2.29	2.58	3.38	0.85
Florida	1.18	2.90	1.72	0.97	2.12	4.07	-0.38	1.87
Georgia	-0.09	2.63	2.71	4.02	2.65	2.17	2.99	1.80
Kentucky	-0.46	0.41	0.87	1.32	1.55	1.95	1.66	-1.69
North Carolina	-0.44	2.04	2.48	2.34	2.67	3.14	3.88	0.74
South Carolina	-1.38	0.94	2.32	1.82	3.10	3.03	3.04	0.93
Tennessee	-0.63	0.65	1.28	1.55	1.26	3.17	1.05	-0.32
Virginia	-0.58	0.78	1.36	1.33	1.51	1.86	3.54	-0.97
West Virginia	-1.60	-0.15	1.44	1.95	0.83	2.68	2.44	-0.38

(continued)

Table 5-5 (continued)

	Growth, 1949–2002			MFP Growth				
	Input	Output	MFP	1949–1960	1960–1970	1970–1980	1980–1990	1990–2002
				average annual percentage change				
Northeast	*-0.84*	*0.80*	*1.64*	*2.34*	*2.36*	*1.72*	*2.18*	*-0.14*
Connecticut	-1.39	0.00	1.39	2.54	2.09	0.77	2.14	-0.36
Delaware	0.45	2.78	2.33	3.83	2.66	1.02	3.02	1.20
Maine	-1.37	0.31	1.67	3.47	4.73	-1.38	2.04	-0.28
Maryland	-0.30	1.69	1.99	2.71	2.82	1.30	2.69	0.62
Massachusetts	-1.99	-0.62	1.37	2.97	3.18	1.99	-0.41	-0.62
New Hampshire	-1.88	-0.42	1.46	3.31	3.66	-0.54	0.91	0.06
New Jersey	-1.25	-0.22	1.03	2.22	1.00	0.89	2.07	-0.81
New York	-0.99	0.31	1.30	1.81	1.92	1.88	1.76	-0.54
Pennsylvania	-0.53	1.30	1.83	2.04	2.20	2.80	2.53	-0.05
Rhode Island	-1.84	-0.39	1.45	2.68	2.79	1.01	4.20	-2.70
Vermont	-0.87	0.57	1.44	2.71	3.08	0.62	1.04	-0.07

Sources: Developed by the authors using InSTePP data.

Notes: The estimates in this table are the averages of year-to-year percentage changes in the index. Corresponding estimates obtained by fitting regressions to the data are reported in Appendix Table 5-3. Box 5-1 provides details on the alternative methods.

InSTePP Estimates

In 1949, agriculture accounted for 6.99 percent of U.S. national gross domestic product (GDP). Since then the agricultural sector has shrunk in relative terms to 0.76 percent of GDP in 2002, while continuing to grow in absolute terms. Table 5-5 shows the average annual growth rates of output, input, and MFP indexes for each state and region over the full period, 1949–2002, as well as for different sub-periods. The MFP growth measures used here were calculated using Fisher Ideal indexes by subtracting the input growth rate from the corresponding output growth rate. In 2002, the quantity of output produced in U.S. agriculture was approximately 2.6 times the 1949 quantity. During the same period, aggregate measured inputs declined slightly, causing our index of MFP to grow faster than our index of output. In annual rate-of-change terms, over the period 1949–2002, output increased by 1.68 percent per year, inputs used in agriculture declined by 0.11 percent per year, and measured MFP grew by 1.78 percent per year. The overall growth in output is (more than) entirely attributable to productivity growth, since the aggregate index of measured inputs fell slightly.

Higher-than-average rates of output growth in some states (e.g., Florida and Idaho) and some regions (e.g., the Pacific, Mountain, and Northern Plains regions), were associated with correspondingly higher-than-average growth rates of input use. The Southeast, Northern Plains, and Southern Plains regions recorded the highest regional productivity growth rates; the Central, Mountain, and Northeast regions, the lowest. However, each region experienced solid pro-

Figure 5-5 Input versus Output Growth Rates, by State, 1949–2002

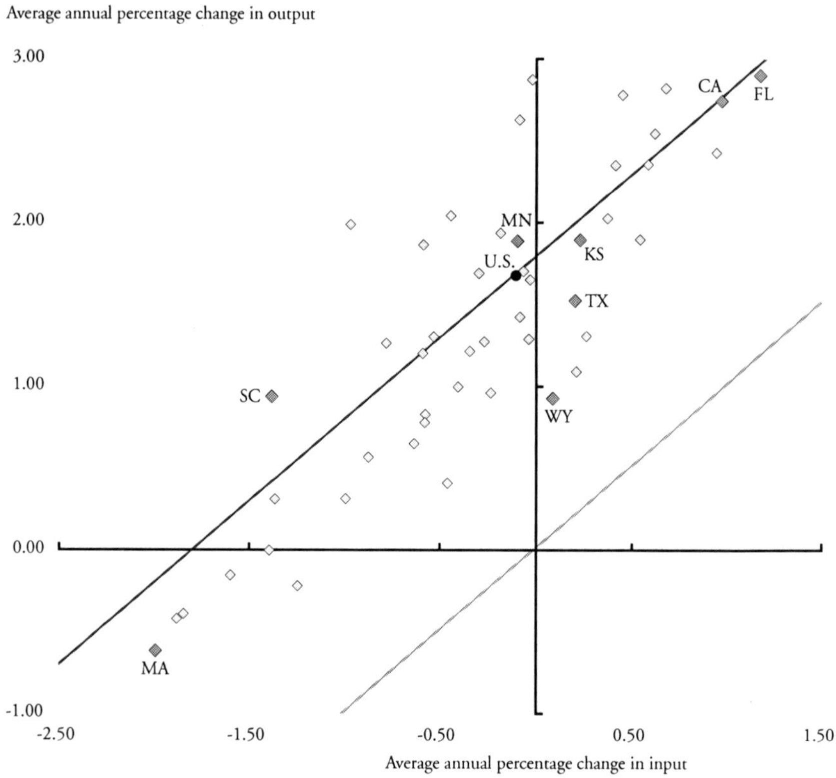

Sources: Calculated by the authors using InSTePP data.

ductivity growth on average during the period 1949–2002—average annual productivity growth ranged between 1.59 percent and 2.09 percent among regions.

Figure 5-5 plots the average annual growth rate of agricultural output against the corresponding annual average growth rate of agricultural input, state by state and for the nation as a whole over the 54 years, 1949 to 2002. Points on the 45-degree line that passes through the origin have output growing at the same rate as input, and thus zero productivity growth. Input-output-growth coordinates above and to the left of the 45-degree line through the origin indicate output growth exceeding input growth, and thus increases in productivity. Some states had both inputs and outputs growing, some had both falling, but all states had productivity growth, and the majority had output growing against a declining input quantity. In a few (mostly Northeastern) states productivity growth reflected input use contracting faster than aggregate output. The 45-degree line in Figure 5-5 that passes through the observation for the national aggregate cuts the vertical axis at 1.78 percent per annum, the national annual average productivity

Figure 5-6 The Geography of Input, Output and Productivity Growth, 1949–2002

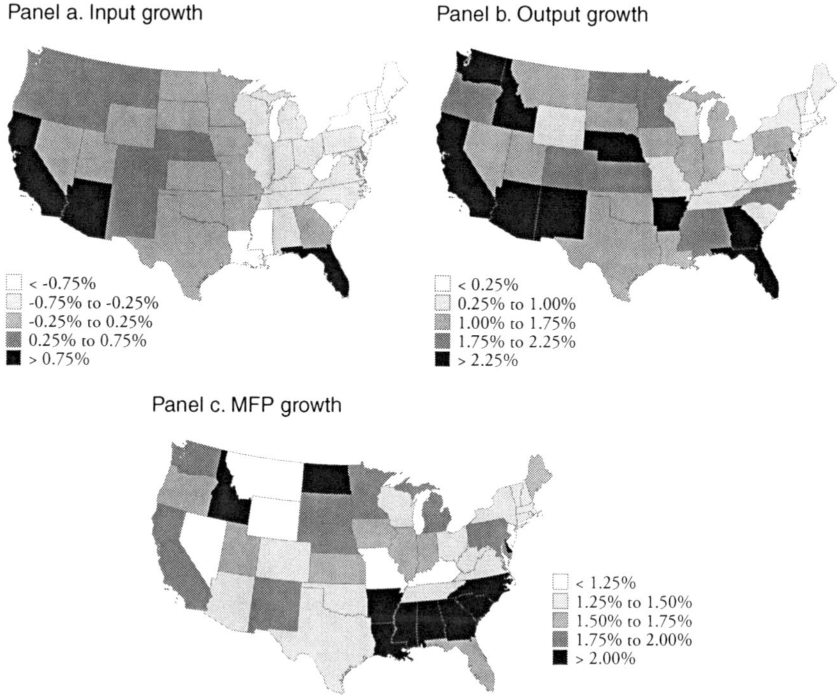

Sources: Calculated by the authors using InSTePP data.

Notes: Shading denotes designated range of average annual growth rates for the period 1949–2002.

growth rate. A point above that line indicates a relatively fast output growth rate for the given input growth rate (or a relatively fast reduction in inputs for a given rate of output growth), and a point below the line, the converse. In turn, we can think of the points above the line as reflecting states with faster-than-average productivity growth.

Figure 5-6 represents these same input, output and MFP growth rates on maps, to further clarify the geographical structure of the rates of change in these variables during the latter half of the 20th Century. The input growth rates, in Panel a, tend to increase from east to west, with states east of the Mississippi river generally exhibiting smaller rates of growth in input use than those to the west. Output growth was also generally higher in the west, but the spatial pattern is less pronounced since some southern states also had relatively high output growth (Panel b). However, the northeastern states had generally slow growth in outputs and inputs. The multi-factor productivity growth rates exhibit a different pattern, not clearly tied to the growth rate of inputs or outputs. In particular the contiguous group of southern states that had comparatively high productiv-

Figure 5-7 Sensitivity of MFP to Aggregation Method, 1949–2002

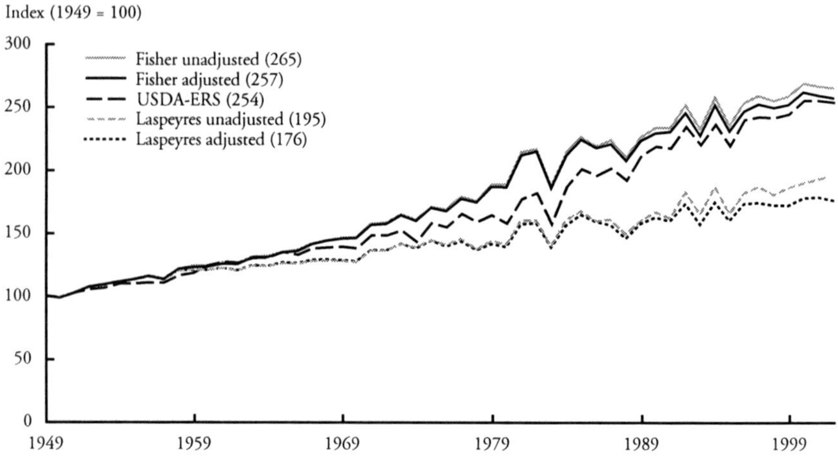

Sources: Calculated by the authors using InSTePP data and data from USDA ERS (2008c).
Notes: Numbers in parentheses represent the value of the index in 2002.

ity growth did so through various combinations of comparatively fast growth in output, contraction in input use, or both.

This depiction of U.S., regional, and state-specific productivity developments for the period 1949–2002 is based on the use of Fisher indexes, with adjustments for quality and composition of the aggregates, as discussed previously in this chapter. To explore the sensitivity of these results to the use of alternative aggregation procedures, we used the InSTePP data to compile adjusted and unadjusted Fisher and Laspeyres indexes of MFP. In both the Laspeyres and Fisher indexes, the adjusted series use disaggregated state- and category-specific prices of inputs and outputs as weights in the indexing procedure, and the unadjusted series use a national average price for all states and categories in the indexing procedure. All four series, along with the USDA Economic Research Service (2008c) series, are included in Figure 5-7.

For the national MFP series in Figure 5-7, the choice of indexing procedure matters more than choices about whether to use state- and category-specific prices. Both forms of the Fisher index indicate much faster rates of growth in MFP over the period 1949–2002 (1.84 percent per year for the unadjusted measure and 1.78 percent per year for the adjusted measure) compared with the Laspeyres index (1.26 percent per year for the unadjusted measure and 1.06 percent per year for the adjusted measure). These differences are driven largely by differences in measured rates of growth in aggregate inputs rather than differences in measured growth in aggregate output (see Figure 5-8, Panel a versus Panel b). For example, the Laspeyres input aggregate (for quality-adjusted inputs) indicates a

Figure 5-8 Sensitivity of Indexes of Inputs and Outputs to Aggregation Method, 1949–2002

Panel a. Input quantity indexes

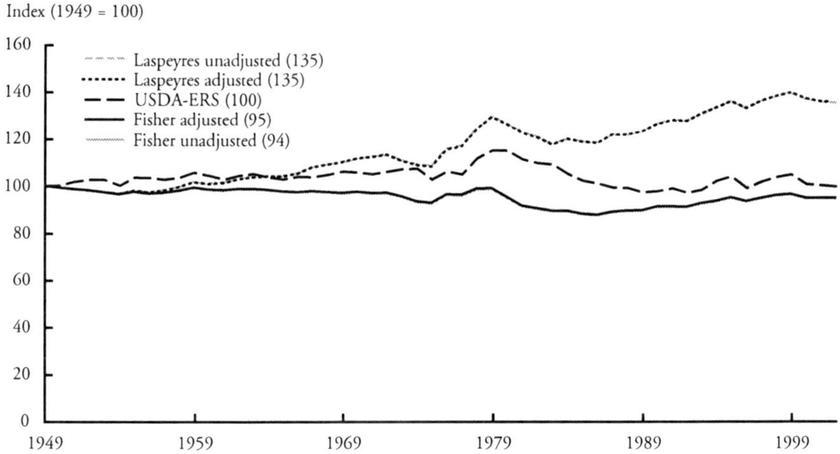

Panel b. Output quantity indexes

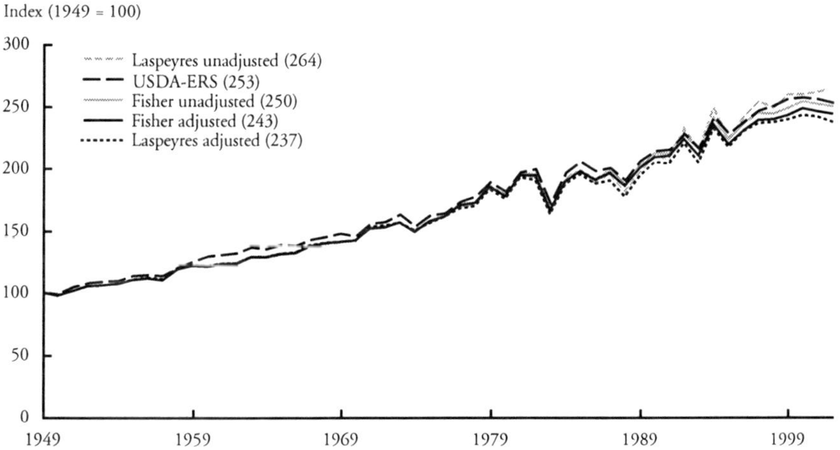

Sources: Compiled by the authors using InSTePP data and data from USDA ERS (2008c).

Notes: Numbers in parentheses represent the value of the index in 2002.

positive rate of growth in aggregate input use (0.57 percent per year for 1949–2002), while the corresponding adjusted Fisher index indicates a negative rate of growth (-0.11 percent per year). This translates into the much higher measured rates of growth in Fisher versus Laspeyres MFP measures plotted in Figure 5-7.

Over the full period 1949–2002, the annual rate of growth in the USDA MFP series (1.76 percent per year) falls closest to that of the Fisher index based on the quality-adjusted InSTePP series (1.78 percent per year). However, these two series do not track so closely for certain sub-periods. The InSTePP series implies a faster rate of growth in the period 1965–1985 (2.56 percent per year versus 1.99 percent per year for the USDA series) and a slower rate of growth in the period 1985–2002 (0.82 percent per year versus 1.37 percent per year for the USDA series). We suspect the difference can be traced to the USDA capital series.[15] Along with differences among sub-periods at the national aggregate level, more pronounced differences between the InSTePP and USDA series are revealed in comparing series for the individual states and regions whether for the entire period or sub-periods (for instance, see Andersen, Alston and Pardey 2009).

5.3 A Systematic Slowdown in Productivity Growth?

In this chapter we have presented a variety of partial and multi-factor measures of U.S. agricultural productivity. At times in the process we have noted the possibility of a slowdown in the rate of U.S. agricultural productivity growth towards the end of our dataset—perhaps as a reflection of an earlier slowdown in the growth of support for productivity-enhancing agricultural R&D, starting in the late 1970s, as quantified in Chapter 6 and discussed further by Alston, Beddow and Pardey (2009).[16] In this section of the chapter we address the issue of a productivity slowdown more formally, paying attention to the sensitivity of the findings to a range of measurement issues.

Measuring and interpreting changes in productivity growth rates is difficult to do given the substantial year-to-year movements and spatial differences. Substantial year-to-year variation in multi-factor productivity, and the associated year-to-year variation in aggregate output (and to a much lesser extent aggregate input use) make it difficult to discern the onset, magnitude and duration of a productivity slowdown (e.g., see Figure 5-9). Year-to-year variations in measured productivity growth might reflect the influences of short-term, transient factors such as weather impacts or policy changes; they might also be the result of measurement errors such as those associated with variable capital utilization rates (e.g., see Andersen 2005; Andersen, Alston and Pardey 2009).

15 Acquaye, Alston and Pardey (2003) compared earlier versions of the USDA and InSTePP data, and suggested that differences between the capital measures may have been a substantial source of differences between the USDA and InSTePP MFP series. Andersen, Alston and Pardey (2009) examined the more recent versions of the USDA and InSTePP capital series in detail and identified important sources of differences.

16 Here we focus exclusively on the U.S. evidence. Alston, Beddow and Pardey (2009) present this U.S. evidence in the context of the changing pattern of agricultural productivity growth in other countries, and give indications of a much more pervasive slowdown worldwide.

Figure 5-9 Year-on-Year Input, Output and MFP Growth Rates, 1911–2002

Panel a. Input quantity index

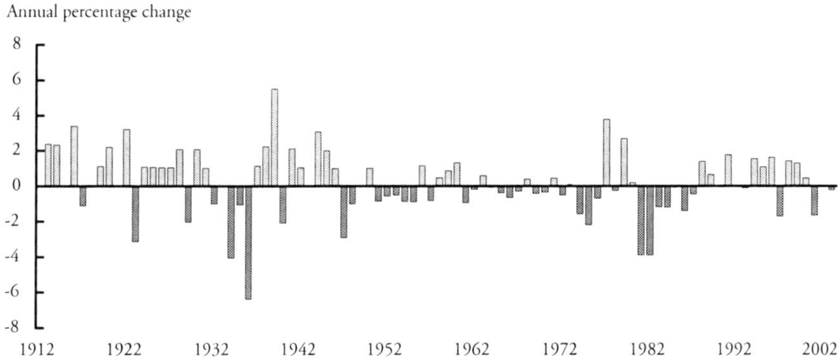

Panel b. Output quantity index

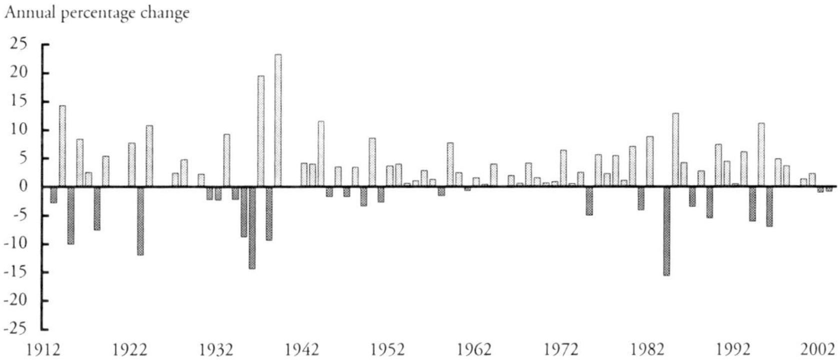

Panel c. Multi-factor productivity index

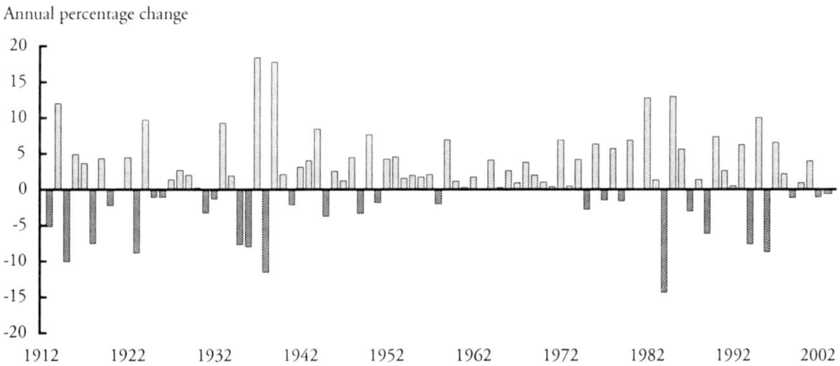

Sources: 1911–1938 from USDA ERS (1984, Table 13); 1939–1946 from USDA ERS (1986, Table 13); 1947–1948 from USDA ERS (1992), and the USDA (1998); 1949-2002 from InSTePP data series.

Notes: See Figure 5-2. Bars represent year-on-year percentage changes.

Box 5-1 Calculating Growth Rates

Growth rates can summarize and reveal important time patterns in data. Different methods that may be used for calculating growth rates can yield different results, with potentially important implications. This box describes two methods that are commonly used for calculating growth rates, and compares them for several key measures.

All growth rates are derived from the basic relationship between a measure and its past values:

(B5.1) $$x_t = x_s \left(1+\frac{r}{c}\right)^{(t-s)*c}$$

Where *t* and *s* index time periods (*s* occurs earlier than *t*), and *r* is the growth rate per time period. The variable *c* indicates how frequently growth is compounded. Differences among methods of calculating growth rates are driven by assumptions made about the length of the relevant interval and the frequency of compounding.

The method for calculating all growth rates in this book (unless noted otherwise) assumes that growth is continuously compounded (i.e., *c* is very close to infinity). Under this assumption, the growth rate (*r*) can be found by solving equation (B5.1) for *r* and taking the limit as *c* approaches infinity, yielding

(B5.2) $$r = \frac{\ln\left(\frac{x_t}{x_s}\right)}{(t-s)}$$

Hence, a period-average growth rate can be calculated using only the first and last year of data for the period, and consequently these measures can be sensitive to the choice of endpoints. An identical result would be obtained by computing the simple average of the year-to-year proportional changes, which is a common approach for computing annual growth rates, and hence they too are sensitive to endpoints.[1]

Some alternative methods for calculating growth rates assume that growth is compounded in discrete time periods (i.e., *c* is finite). Under this assumption, the implied growth rate could be found by solving equation (B5.1) for *r*. An alternative, explored below, is to estimate *r* by fitting a trend line to the logarithms of the underlying data. First, set *c* = 1 and take logarithms of equation (B5.1):

(B5.3) $$\ln(x_t) = \ln(x_s) + (t-s)\ln(1+r)$$

To estimate $\ln(1+r)$, regress $\ln(x_j)$ on an intercept and a time trend using ordinary least squares:

(B5.4) $$\ln(x_j) = \hat{\alpha} + \hat{\beta} * j$$

where *j* indexes years. The estimated growth rate is then:

(B5.5) $$r = e^{\hat{\beta}} - 1$$

1 The authors thank Jason Beddow for pointing out this property of annual average growth rates.

(continued)

Box 5-1 (continued)

An advantage of this approach is that it uses all of the data points to calculate the growth rate. However, the method suffers from the general shortcomings of regression analysis. A single outlier may unduly influence the growth-rate estimate, and estimates may be imprecise (particularly with small numbers of observations). Because it implicitly smoothes data throughout the time period, patterns revealed at the beginning and ending of the interval may not be reflected in the growth-rate estimate.

Box Table 5-1 compares growth rates for inputs, outputs, and productivity, and for research and extension expenditures, computed using the alternative approaches (See Appendix Table 5-2 for more complete details). It can be seen that the different approaches yield different results, more so when the period is shorter because the role of idiosyncratic factors is less muted. Throughout this book, unless stated otherwise, we use the growth rates computed as the average of annual proportional changes, or logarithmic differences.

Box Table 5-1 Summary of Growth Rates, 1949–2002

State or Region and Measure	Annual Percentage Change, 1949–2002				Average Annual Percentage Change 1949–1960	1960–1970	1970–1980	1980–1990	1990–2002
Input, output and productivity indexes									
	Input	*Output*	*MFP*				*MFP*		
Diff. in logs	-0.11	1.68	1.78		1.89	1.69	2.46	2.07	0.97
Regression	-0.15	1.82	1.97		2.09	1.87	2.26	1.38	1.06
Difference	-0.04	0.14	0.18		0.20	0.18	-0.20	-0.69	0.09
R&D and extension spending									
	SAES	*IM*	*Ext.*	*Total*	*Total (SAES+USDA-IM+Extension)*				
Diff. in logs	2.64	1.32	1.36	1.89	3.30	2.64	2.78	0.38	0.51
Regression	2.66	1.28	1.46	1.92	3.75	2.53	2.82	0.17	0.27
Difference	0.00	-0.04	0.10	0.03	0.46	-0.11	0.04	-0.21	0.24

Sources: Estimated by the authors using data described in Appendices II and III.

Notes: Input, output and multi-factor productivity data are from the InSTePP series. SAES represents the 48-state total spending on agricultural research by the state agricultural experiment stations, excluding forestry, IM represents intramural research conducted by the USDA, and Ext. represents extension expenditures, all expressed in real (2000 dollar) values.

As discussed in Box 5-1, findings regarding productivity growth over subperiods may depend on the choice of where to divide data (measures may be sensitive to starting and ending points), as well as choices about how to measure growth rates and whether to measure them in absolute or percentage changes, in yields per acre or in partial- or multi-factor productivity indexes. Our richly detailed data make it possible to test for structural changes and to examine the sensitivity of the findings to choices we make as analysts.

Crop Yields

While the mid-1930s break point in the rate of growth in U.S. crop yields is obvious from Figure 5-1, it is less obvious that rates of growth in crop yields declined in recent decades. The upper half of Table 5-6 quantifies the annual percentage rates of growth in U.S. wheat, corn, cotton, tobacco and rice yields. For all five crops, the annual rate of growth in yields was much higher for the period after 1935 than during the previous decades. Between 1866 and 1935, wheat, corn, and cotton yields grew at annual average rates of 0.1, -0.4, and 0.5 percent per year, respectively, and between 1936 and 2006 the growth rates were 1.6, 2.9, and 2.2 percent per year, respectively. However, the rates of growth over the period 1990–2006 were markedly slower for all five crops. In particular, corn and wheat yields grew at annual rates of 2.6 and 1.6 percent per year over the period 1936–1990, and 1.4 and -0.1 percent per year over the period 1990–2006, respectively.[17]

A more nuanced perspective on the changing pattern of crop yield growth is obtained by comparing the upper and lower halves of Table 5-6. The lower half of Table 5-6 reports the annual average *absolute* change in yields for the corresponding crops and periods for which the average annual *proportional* changes in yields are recorded in the upper half. For each of the five crops, the upper half of the table shows that the annual rate of proportional yield gain for 1990–2006 was lower than for the preceding decades (specifically 1936–1990). In contrast, the average annual absolute increases in crop yields for corn, cotton, and rice during the period 1990–2006 exceeded the average annual absolute yield gains achieved in the earlier period. In many policy contexts, the relevant measure is proportional growth in yields, and sustaining proportional growth requires ever-increasing absolute growth. Hence, a slowdown in proportional growth could be associated with a constant (or even increasing) rate of absolute growth in yield—i.e., gains measured in, say, pounds per acre per year rather than as a percentage.

Other Partial- and Multi-Factor Productivity Measures

Evidence of a recent productivity slowdown can be seen in Figure 5-10, which shows distributions of average annual state-specific multi-factor productivity

---

17 Reporting yields on the basis of harvested area would understate the rate of growth in crop yields compared with crop yields measured on the basis of arable area if the intensity of crop plantings per year had increased over time. As Alston, Beddow and Pardey (2009, p. 12) observed, "...if rice yields [for example] averaged 2 tons per harvested hectare in 1961 and doubled to 4 tons per harvested hectare by 2007, that would be equivalent to an average annual yield growth of 1.5 percent per harvested hectare per year. In contrast, if yields per harvested area doubled from 2 to 4 tons per hectare from 1961 to 2007 while the cropping intensity also increased from one to two crops per calendar year, yields reported on the basis of arable area would have grown from 2 to 8 tons per arable hectare, or 3.1 percent per year."

Table 5-6 Yield Growth for Various Commodities, 1866–2006

	Commodity				
Measure and Period[a]	**Wheat**	**Corn**	**Cotton**	**Tobacco**	**Rice**
Average rate of change			*average annual percentage change*		
Entire period	0.9	1.3	1.4	0.7	1.6
Through 1935	0.1	-0.4	0.5	0.1	1.3
1936–2006	1.6	2.9	2.2	1.3	1.6
1936–1990	1.6	2.6	2.1	1.2	1.6
1990–2006	-0.1	1.4	1.6	-0.2	1.4
1980s	1.6	2.6	4.5	1.3	2.3
1990s	0.6	1.4	0.0	0.1	1.3
2000s	-1.4	1.4	4.2	-0.8	1.5
Average yield gain			*pounds per acre per year*		
Entire period	11.9	49.9	4.9	9.6	58.4
Through 1935	1.0	-4.6	0.7	0.7	25.4
1936–2006	22.2	101.4	8.9	17.9	65.3
1936–1990	22.4	98.5	8.9	17.5	66.1
1990–2006	-3.0	107.1	11.3	-4.6	83.7
1980s	36.0	154.0	23.0	27.9	111.6
1990s	15.0	103.0	-0.2	2.6	75.2
2000s	-33.0	113.9	30.3	-16.7	97.8

Sources: See Figure 5-1.

[a] Rice values are for 1919–2006, other values are for 1866–2006.

growth rates over ten-year periods since 1949.[18] Each of the distributions refers to a particular period, and the data are the number of states with average annual multi-factor productivity growth rates for the period falling in the range specified. By inspection, it can be seen that the general shape and position of the distribution of state-specific multi-factor productivity growth rates seems reasonably constant across periods until the last time period, 1990–2002, when it shifts substantially to the left, indicating a widespread slowdown in productivity growth. In what follows, we present various measures as evidence of a substantial slowdown of productivity growth in the period 1990–2002 compared with the prior period 1949–1990.[19]

18 The periods are decades beginning in the year ending in zero except for the first period, which includes one extra year, and the last which is extended by two years to 2002.

19 Some other work questions the case for a productivity slowdown (e.g., Fuglie, MacDonald and Ball 2007). Definitive answers are difficult, and the acid test will take some time (including time required to access additional years of data and for additional countries), but the issue is likely to be more nearly resolved within the next year or two, and we suspect it will be resolved in favor of the slowdown conjecture. Notably, recently released data from USDA ERS obtained as this volume neared completion, supports our notion of a productivity slowdown. These issues are discussed in Alston, Babcock and Pardey (2009). One reason for expecting a structural slowdown in the rate of productivity growth in U.S. agriculture is the evidence on R&D patterns described and discussed in Chapter 6.

Figure 5-10 Distributions of Average Annual MFP Growth Rates across States

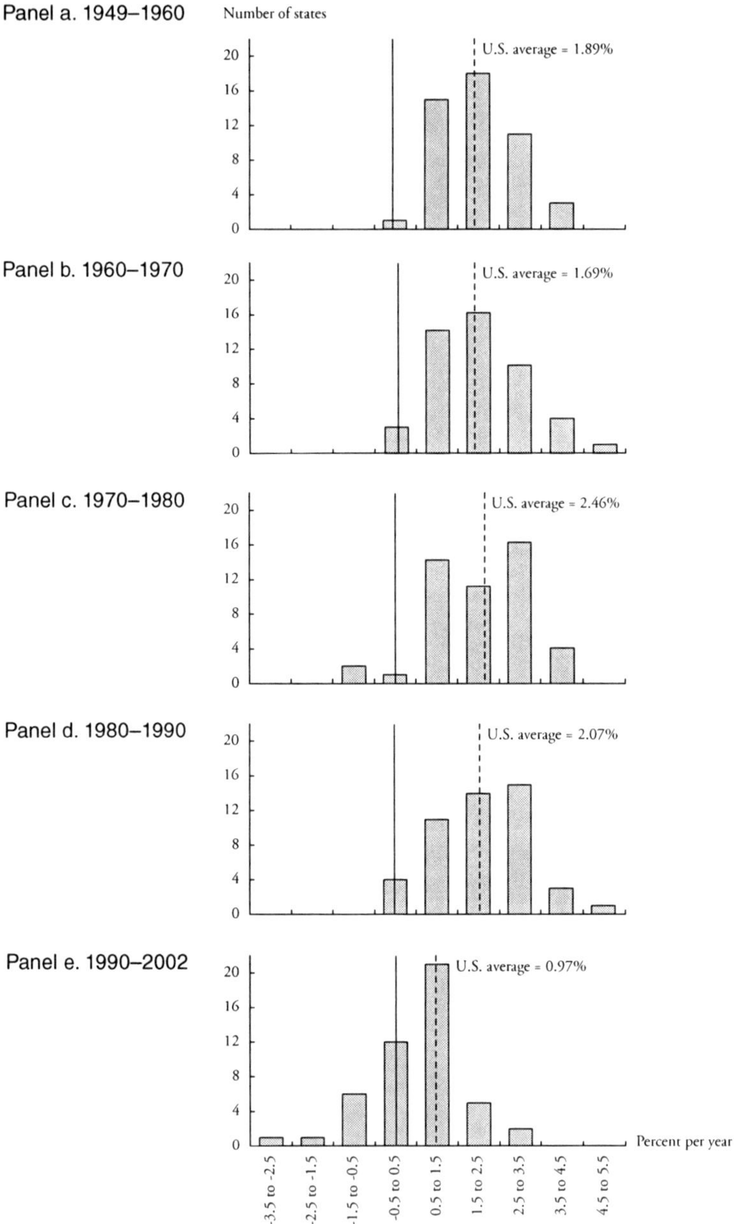

Sources: Calculated by the authors using InSTePP data.

Notes: Solid vertical line in each panel indicates zero growth.

Figure 5-11 plots state-specific MFP growth rates for two periods: 1949–1990 and 1990–2002. As shown in Panel b, during the period 1949–1990, multi-factor productivity grew positively in all 48 states, whereas during the period 1990–2002, for 15 states multi-factor productivity growth was negative. Multi-factor productivity grew faster in the more-recent period compared with the earlier period in only four states (8 percent of the total); 44 states had statistically slower rates of productivity growth. U.S. agricultural productivity grew on average by just 0.97 percent per year over 1990–2002 compared with 2.02 percent per year over 1949–1990. The average of the state-specific MFP growth rates fell even farther, to just 0.54 percent per year over 1990–2002 compared with 2.02 percent per year over 1949–1990.

Figure 5-11, Panel a plots linearized distributions (showing the minimum, maximum, and mean) of state-specific MFP growth rates grouped by region. These linearized distributions reveal a comprehensive and significant slowing in the rate of growth in multi-factor productivity in 1990–2002 compared with 1949–1990. The regional means all moved leftwards (indicating a contraction in the average rate of multi-factor productivity growth), as did the mass of most of the regional distributions. The slowdown was most pronounced in the Pacific, Northern Plains, Southeast and Northeast regions.

Figure 5-12 gives a geographical perspective on the same story. Maps on the left depict the state-specific average annual growth rates of input, output and multi-factor productivity for 1949–1990; maps on the right depict the same information for 1990–2002. Aggregate input growth was generally higher in the period 1990–2002 (and notably so for most western states), whereas output growth generally slowed in the later period. The combination of these reinforcing input and output trends resulted in the pervasive slowdown in multi-factor productivity growth that is especially evident in comparing the lowest two maps.

The slowdown in multi-factor productivity is also reflected in measures of partial factor productivities. In Table 5-7, the average U.S. productivity of capital, labor, land, and materials grew by 1.78 percent per year, 3.42 percent per year, 1.74 percent per year, and -0.20 percent per year over the period 1949–2002; the materials outlier reflects the very substantial substitution of materials inputs for other inputs, especially labor. Over the period 1990–2002 the corresponding partial productivity growth rates for capital, labor, land, and materials were 0.78 percent per year, 1.54 percent per year, 1.50 percent per year, and 0.35 percent per year. A substantial slowdown is evident in the growth rate of productivity of both capital and labor. Only materials productivity grew more rapidly over 1990–2002, reflecting a slower rate of increase in the use of materials input in this period compared with the several decades immediately following the Second World War. Appendix Table 5-1 provides region-specific growth rates that echo these findings in the national data. The crop yield evidence in Table 5-6 reinforc-

Figure 5-11 Distributions of MFP Growth, 1949–1990 and 1990–2002

Panel a. Linearized distributions, states grouped by region

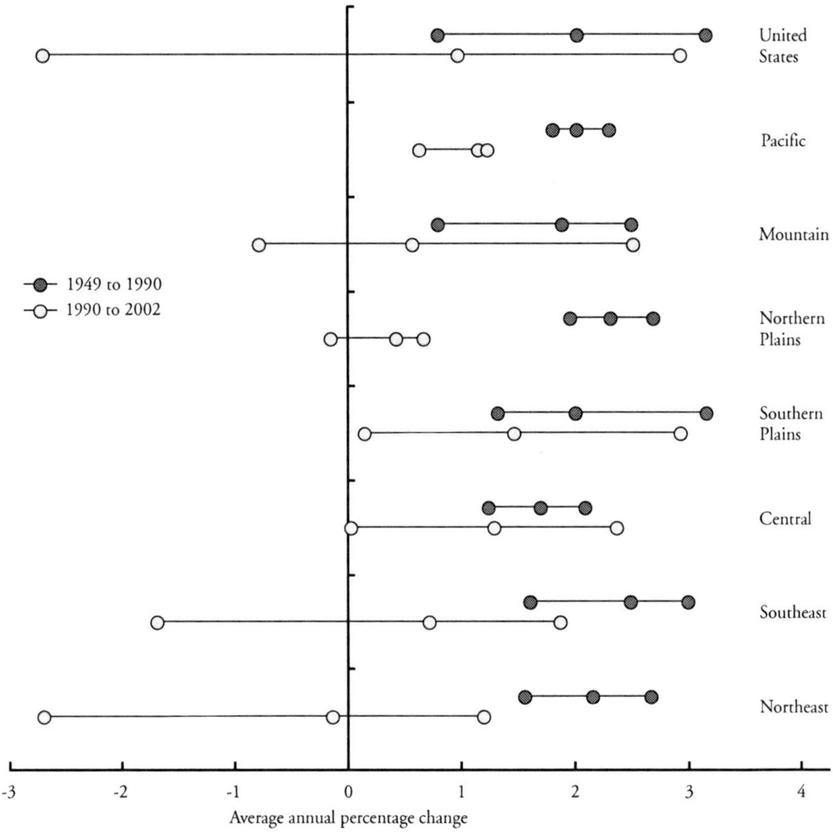

Panel b. Full distributions, individual states

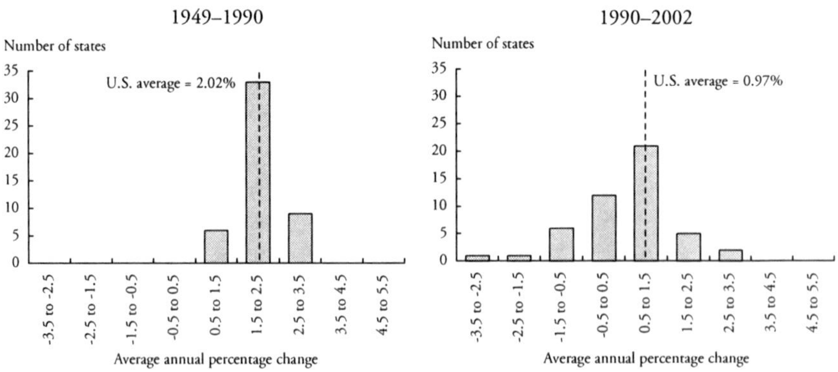

Sources: Calculated by the authors using InSTePP data.

Notes: In Panel a, the three dots represent the minimum, mean and maximum growth rates among states in the respective regions.

Figure 5-12 Input, Output and Productivity Growth Rates, 1949–1990 versus 1990–2002

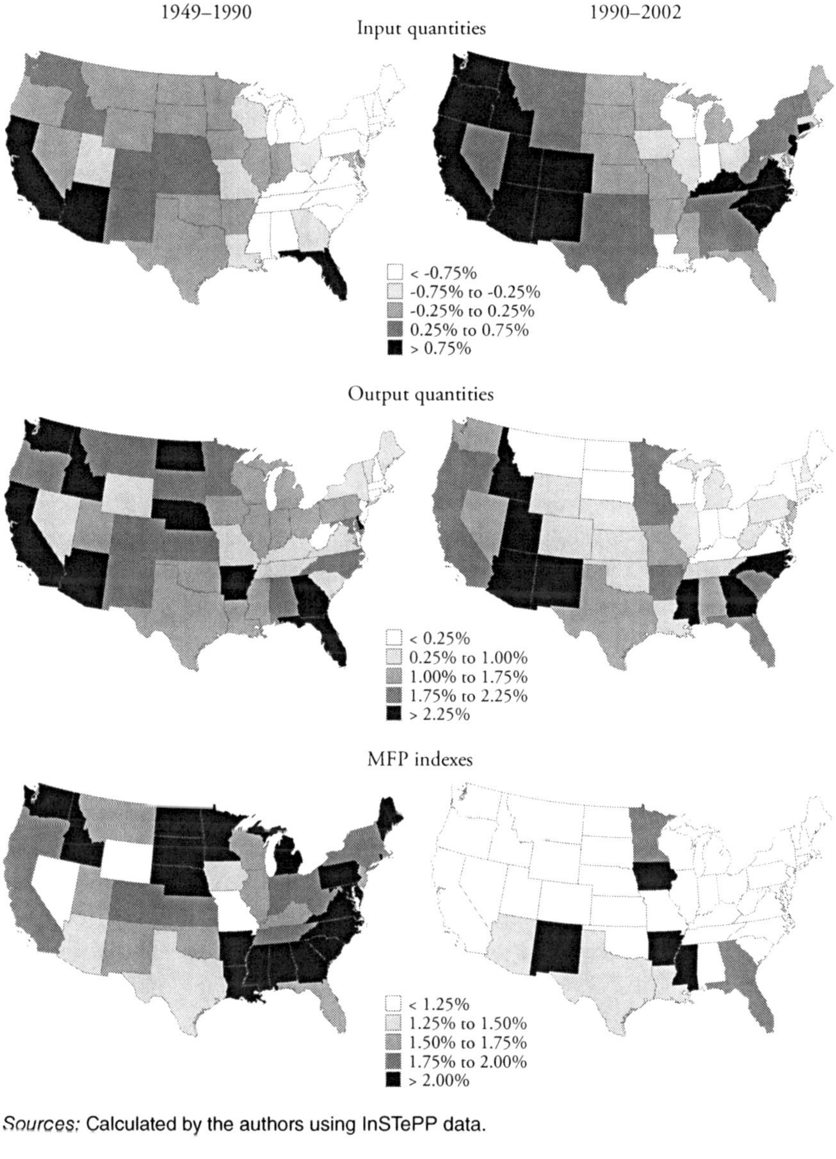

Sources: Calculated by the authors using InSTePP data.

es the slowdown in growth evident in the measures of multi- and partial-factor productivity. For the four major crops shown in this table, yields grew at a much slower rate over the period 1990–2006 than they did in the period 1936–1990 (and, not shown, 1949–1990).

Table 5-7 Annual Growth Rates in Partial Productivity Measures, Various Sub-Periods

	Capital	Labor	Land	Materials
		average annual percentage change		
1949–1960	1.30	4.88	1.82	-1.99
1960–1970	2.20	4.19	1.44	-1.76
1970–1980	1.61	3.71	2.14	1.60
1980–1990	3.26	3.03	1.86	0.87
1990–2002	0.78	1.54	1.50	0.35
1949–1990	2.07	3.98	1.82	-0.36
1949–2002	1.78	3.42	1.74	-0.20

Sources: Calculated by the authors using InSTePP data.

Returning to the most meaningful measures pertinent to the issue of a slowdown, we conducted some formal statistical tests using the state-specific multifactor productivity data for 1949–2002, comparing various sub-periods. Conscious of the possibility that different measures may imply different findings, we tried two measures of growth—either linear (the annual change in the level of the index), or proportional (the annual change in the logarithm of the index)—combined with two methods for estimating the growth rate—either the average of the annual changes in the index (in levels or logarithms), or the coefficient from the regression of the index (in levels or logarithms) against a time trend. We computed these four alternative measures for various time periods, and tested for statistically significant differences for each measure, before and after the split point of the data. The results are reported in Table 5-8.

The upper half of Table 5-8 refers to the measures related to proportional growth in MFP, measured either as the average of year-to-year growth rates or from a regression of the logarithm of the index against a trend. In every case with either measure the tests indicate a substantial and statistically significant (at the 10 percent level in every case, and in most cases at a significance level well less than 1 percent) slowing of productivity growth for any period that includes the years 1990–2002 compared with any prior period. The slowdown is most pronounced for 1990–2002 compared with 1949–1990. As noted earlier, an absolute increase in productivity is necessary but not sufficient to sustain proportional productivity growth. The lower half of Table 5-8 indicates a slowdown in absolute productivity growth in 1990–2002 compared with 1949–1990, but the evidence is more mixed for the earlier breakpoints.

5.4 Conclusion

There can be little doubt that the InSTePP multi-factor productivity data exhibit evidence of a slowdown in multi-factor productivity growth in the period

Table 5-8 Statistical Tests for a Slowdown in MFP Growth

Time Period	During Period	After Period	Difference	P-Value
Using differences in logarithms[a]		*average annual percentage change*		
1949–1960	2.04	1.59	-0.45	0.00
1949–1970	2.01	1.47	-0.54	0.00
1949–1980	2.01	1.23	-0.78	0.00
1949–1990	2.02	0.54	-1.48	0.00
Using regression of logarithms[b]				
1949–1960	2.06	1.77	-0.29	0.06
1949–1970	1.90	1.53	-0.37	0.02
1949–1980	1.99	1.00	-0.99	0.00
1949–1990	2.06	0.57	-1.49	0.00
Using differences in levels[c]		*average annual change in index*		
1949–1960	2.34	3.03	0.69	0.00
1949–1970	2.62	3.07	0.45	0.13
1949–1980	2.87	2.93	0.06	0.82
1949–1990	3.28	1.56	-1.72	0.00
Using regression of levels[d]				
1949–1960	2.33	3.45	1.12	0.00
1949–1970	2.46	3.29	0.83	0.01
1949–1980	2.86	2.43	-0.43	0.16
1949–1990	3.36	1.54	-1.83	0.00

Sources: Calculated by the authors using InSTePP data.

[a] Calculated as described in equation (B5.2) over the period specified.

[b] Calculated as described in equations (B5.4) and (B5.5), using data from the period specified.

[c] Calculated by applying equation (B5.2), but using data in levels rather than logarithms.

[d] Calculated by fitting a trendline to MFP over the period specified.

1990–2002 compared with the previous period. We have not sought to establish whether 1990 is the ideal breakpoint; different breakpoints may provide stronger or weaker evidence of a slowdown, and different states may have had different experiences. Questions remain concerning the extent to which the measured slowdown may reflect measurement error or chance. Other questions concern whether the effects may be temporary (such as would follow from measurement errors or weather cycles that balance out over time) or enduring, such as would follow from more-enduring changes in weather or technology.

Our particular emphasis in the work that follows is on the role of knowledge stocks created as a result of public investments in agricultural research and extension. In Chapter 6 we present evidence of a slowing down of total growth in spending on agricultural R&D and a shifting balance of research spending away from farm-productivity enhancement. In subsequent chapters we examine the links between those changes in spending patterns and the growth in productivity that they are meant to foster. In all of that work, the main emphasis is not on the recent slowdown in productivity growth but rather on the benefits from the remarkable growth in productivity that was sustained over 50 years and more.

Appendix Table 5-1 Average Annual Growth Rates of Partial Productivity Measures

	1949–2002	1949–1960	1960–1970	1970–1980	1980–1990	1990–2002
Capital productivity			*average annual percentage change*			
United States	1.78	1.30	2.20	1.61	3.26	0.78
Pacific	2.05	1.82	3.52	2.55	1.83	0.83
Mountain	1.62	1.24	2.49	1.36	2.17	1.02
Northern Plains	2.18	2.32	1.89	1.24	4.87	0.82
Southern Plains	1.55	0.20	2.06	1.05	3.68	1.02
Central	1.84	1.24	2.00	1.85	3.67	0.73
Southeast	1.39	0.70	1.83	1.19	2.69	0.74
Northeast	1.47	1.98	2.45	1.63	1.91	-0.34
Labor productivity						
United States	3.42	4.88	4.19	3.71	3.03	1.54
Pacific	3.11	4.24	4.49	3.26	1.26	2.35
Mountain	2.94	4.43	4.38	2.85	2.39	0.90
Northern Plains	3.68	5.26	3.87	3.15	4.78	1.62
Southern Plains	3.56	5.47	5.42	3.42	3.35	0.56
Central	3.25	4.19	3.08	3.92	3.01	2.19
Southeast	3.83	5.36	5.05	4.64	3.03	1.42
Northeast	3.06	4.95	4.26	2.34	3.33	0.69
Land productivity						
United States	1.74	1.82	1.44	2.14	1.86	1.50
Pacific	2.56	2.59	2.40	3.38	2.70	1.88
Mountain	2.02	2.39	2.42	1.81	1.69	1.79
Northern Plains	1.80	2.75	1.27	1.60	2.69	0.77
Southern Plains	1.64	0.35	1.98	1.47	2.60	1.87
Central	1.40	1.39	0.74	2.57	1.13	1.18
Southeast	2.42	3.21	2.10	2.23	1.93	2.52
Northeast	1.95	2.43	2.29	1.57	2.66	0.96
Materials productivity						
United States	-0.20	-1.99	-1.76	1.60	0.87	0.35
Pacific	0.06	-2.11	-0.26	2.62	0.33	-0.03
Mountain	-0.31	-2.08	-1.01	1.19	1.42	-0.81
Northern Plains	-0.04	0.03	-2.57	0.73	2.37	-0.65
Southern Plains	-0.29	-3.80	-2.47	1.00	1.17	2.45
Central	-0.24	-1.90	-2.27	2.05	0.08	0.82
Southeast	-0.61	-3.32	-1.94	1.52	1.33	-0.42
Northeast	0.14	-0.33	0.01	1.23	1.03	-0.96

Sources: Calculated by the authors using InSTePP data.

Appendix Table 5-2 Average Growth Rates of Input and Output Quantities, and MFP, 1949–2002

	Average Growth Rate (Diff. in Logs)			Average Growth Rate (Regression)			Difference (Regression – Diff. in Logs)		
	Input	Output	MFP	Input	Output	MFP	Input	Output	MFP
				average annual percentage change					
United States	*-0.11*	*1.68*	*1.78*	*-0.15*	*1.82*	*1.97*	*-0.04*	*0.14*	*0.18*
Pacific	*0.82*	*2.64*	*1.82*	*0.81*	*2.69*	*1.87*	*-0.01*	*0.05*	*0.04*
California	0.97	2.74	1.77	0.92	2.71	1.77	-0.05	-0.03	0.00
Oregon	0.37	2.03	1.65	0.38	2.06	1.67	0.01	0.03	0.02
Washington	0.62	2.55	1.93	0.74	3.00	2.24	0.12	0.45	0.32
Mountain	*0.45*	*2.04*	*1.59*	*0.31*	*2.07*	*1.75*	*-0.14*	*0.03*	*0.16*
Arizona	0.94	2.43	1.48	0.55	2.09	1.53	-0.39	-0.34	0.04
Colorado	0.54	1.90	1.35	0.47	2.39	1.91	-0.07	0.50	0.56
Idaho	0.68	2.82	2.14	0.46	2.74	2.27	-0.22	-0.08	0.13
Montana	0.26	1.31	1.04	0.17	1.23	1.05	-0.09	-0.08	0.01
Nevada	0.21	1.09	0.88	0.23	1.07	0.84	0.02	-0.02	-0.03
New Mexico	0.59	2.36	1.77	0.44	2.59	2.14	-0.15	0.23	0.37
Utah	-0.08	1.43	1.51	-0.16	1.23	1.40	-0.08	-0.19	-0.11
Wyoming	0.09	0.93	0.84	0.06	0.86	0.80	-0.03	-0.07	-0.04
Northern Plains	*0.16*	*2.05*	*1.89*	*0.11*	*2.27*	*2.16*	*-0.05*	*0.22*	*0.27*
Kansas	0.23	1.90	1.67	0.24	2.18	1.94	0.01	0.29	0.27
Nebraska	0.42	2.35	1.94	0.37	2.62	2.24	-0.04	0.27	0.30
North Dakota	-0.18	1.94	2.12	-0.27	2.15	2.42	-0.08	0.21	0.30
South Dakota	-0.07	1.70	1.77	-0.21	1.73	1.94	-0.14	0.03	0.17
Southern Plains	*-0.12*	*1.76*	*1.88*	*-0.03*	*2.22*	*2.26*	*0.09*	*0.46*	*0.37*
Arkansas	-0.02	2.87	2.89	0.17	3.35	3.17	0.20	0.47	0.27
Louisiana	-0.78	1.26	2.04	-0.77	1.55	2.34	0.01	0.29	0.30
Mississippi	-0.97	1.99	2.95	-1.10	1.71	2.84	-0.13	-0.28	-0.11
Oklahoma	-0.04	1.29	1.33	0.10	1.81	1.72	0.13	0.53	0.39
Texas	0.20	1.53	1.32	0.32	2.15	1.83	0.12	0.63	0.50
Central	*-0.27*	*1.34*	*1.61*	*-0.30*	*1.41*	*1.71*	*-0.02*	*0.08*	*0.10*
Illinois	-0.27	1.27	1.54	-0.30	1.37	1.68	-0.04	0.10	0.14
Indiana	-0.34	1.21	1.56	-0.32	1.40	1.73	0.02	0.19	0.18
Iowa	-0.03	1.65	1.68	-0.11	1.51	1.62	-0.07	-0.14	-0.06
Michigan	-0.59	1.20	1.79	-0.67	1.45	2.13	-0.08	0.25	0.34
Minnesota	-0.10	1.89	1.99	-0.14	1.86	2.01	-0.05	-0.02	0.03
Missouri	-0.23	0.96	1.19	-0.26	1.08	1.34	-0.03	0.12	0.15
Ohio	-0.58	0.83	1.40	-0.57	1.27	1.84	0.01	0.44	0.44
Wisconsin	-0.40	1.00	1.40	-0.30	1.10	1.41	0.10	0.10	0.01
Southeast	*-0.41*	*1.68*	*2.09*	*-0.58*	*1.81*	*2.40*	*-0.17*	*0.13*	*0.31*
Alabama	-0.59	1.86	2.45	-0.60	2.04	2.66	-0.02	0.18	0.21
Florida	1.18	2.90	1.72	0.99	2.72	1.71	-0.19	-0.18	-0.01
Georgia	-0.09	2.63	2.71	-0.15	2.68	2.84	-0.07	0.05	0.12
Kentucky	-0.46	0.41	0.87	-0.56	0.83	1.40	-0.10	0.42	0.53
North Carolina	-0.44	2.04	2.48	-0.92	2.06	3.01	-0.48	0.02	0.52
South Carolina	-1.38	0.94	2.32	-1.76	0.96	2.77	-0.38	0.02	0.45
Tennessee	-0.63	0.65	1.28	-0.75	0.88	1.65	-0.12	0.23	0.36
Virginia	-0.58	0.78	1.36	-0.71	1.03	1.76	-0.13	0.25	0.40
West Virginia	-1.60	-0.15	1.44	-1.65	-0.07	1.61	-0.06	0.09	0.17

(continued)

Appendix Table 5-2 (continued)

	Average Growth Rate (Diff. in Logs)			Average Growth Rate (Regression)			Difference (Regression – Diff. in Logs)		
	Input	Output	MFP	Input	Output	MFP	Input	Output	MFP
				average annual percentage change					
Northeast	*-0.84*	*0.80*	*1.64*	*-0.91*	*0.84*	*1.77*	*-0.07*	*0.05*	*0.13*
Connecticut	-1.39	0.00	1.39	-1.57	-0.48	1.11	-0.18	-0.48	-0.29
Delaware	0.45	2.78	2.33	0.77	2.96	2.18	0.32	0.18	-0.15
Maine	-1.37	0.31	1.67	-1.60	-0.01	1.61	-0.23	-0.32	-0.06
Maryland	-0.30	1.69	1.99	-0.17	1.97	2.15	0.12	0.28	0.16
Massachusetts	-1.99	-0.62	1.37	-1.93	-0.69	1.26	0.06	-0.07	-0.11
New Hampshire	-1.88	-0.42	1.46	-1.88	-0.89	1.01	0.00	-0.46	-0.45
New Jersey	-1.25	-0.22	1.03	-1.87	-0.79	1.10	-0.62	-0.57	0.07
New York	-0.99	0.31	1.30	-1.16	0.33	1.51	-0.17	0.02	0.21
Pennsylvania	-0.53	1.30	1.83	-0.54	1.58	2.13	0.00	0.28	0.29
Rhode Island	-1.84	-0.39	1.45	-1.94	-0.28	1.70	-0.10	0.11	0.24
Vermont	-0.87	0.57	1.44	-0.87	0.57	1.45	0.00	0.00	0.01

Sources: Calculated by the authors using InSTePP data.

Appendix Table 5-3 Fitted Annual Growth Rates in Input, Output, and MFP

	Growth, 1949–2002			MFP Growth				
	Input	Output	MFP	1949–1960	1960–1970	1970–1980	1980–1990	1990–2002
				average annual percentage change				
United States	*-0.15*	*1.82*	*1.97*	*2.09*	*1.87*	*2.26*	*1.38*	*1.06*
Pacific	*0.81*	*2.69*	*1.87*	*1.65*	*2.48*	*2.36*	*1.39*	*1.04*
California	0.92	2.71	1.77	1.61	2.36	2.22	1.36	1.01
Oregon	0.38	2.06	1.67	1.91	2.11	2.28	1.04	1.03
Washington	0.74	3.00	2.24	1.05	3.09	2.90	1.78	1.01
Mountain	*0.31*	*2.07*	*1.75*	*1.79*	*2.31*	*1.36*	*1.20*	*0.78*
Arizona	0.55	2.09	1.53	0.61	0.58	2.37	0.69	1.51
Colorado	0.47	2.39	1.91	1.84	2.05	1.54	2.17	0.19
Idaho	0.46	2.74	2.27	2.08	2.91	1.88	2.08	1.25
Montana	0.17	1.23	1.05	1.52	3.17	0.71	-0.90	-1.44
Nevada	0.23	1.07	0.84	1.22	1.32	0.64	-0.87	1.59
New Mexico	0.44	2.59	2.14	1.94	1.62	1.23	1.66	2.56
Utah	-0.16	1.23	1.40	2.03	2.51	-0.49	2.00	1.23
Wyoming	0.06	0.86	0.80	1.93	1.30	-0.09	-0.33	-0.05
Northern Plains	*0.11*	*2.27*	*2.16*	*2.15*	*2.18*	*1.44*	*1.97*	*1.01*
Kansas	0.24	2.18	1.94	2.33	1.26	0.30	1.54	1.53
Nebraska	0.37	2.62	2.24	1.67	2.30	2.13	2.90	0.86
North Dakota	-0.27	2.15	2.42	2.39	3.36	2.07	0.44	0.10
South Dakota	-0.21	1.73	1.94	2.26	2.42	0.80	2.02	1.22
Southern Plains	*-0.03*	*2.22*	*2.26*	*2.62*	*2.08*	*2.76*	*1.40*	*1.27*
Arkansas	0.17	3.35	3.17	4.08	3.63	3.60	2.10	1.67
Louisiana	-0.77	1.55	2.34	0.78	4.62	2.78	0.73	1.43
Mississippi	-1.10	1.71	2.84	3.65	3.50	2.45	1.08	2.55
Oklahoma	0.10	1.81	1.72	2.42	1.17	2.97	0.98	0.51
Texas	0.32	2.15	1.83	2.26	0.85	2.29	1.35	1.04
Central	*-0.30*	*1.41*	*1.71*	*1.90*	*1.18*	*2.32*	*1.09*	*1.57*
Illinois	-0.30	1.37	1.68	2.07	0.70	2.40	1.43	1.24
Indiana	-0.32	1.40	1.73	1.36	0.65	2.39	1.40	1.56
Iowa	-0.11	1.51	1.62	1.29	1.20	1.99	0.74	2.32
Michigan	-0.67	1.45	2.13	1.59	1.84	3.42	0.71	0.67
Minnesota	-0.14	1.86	2.01	2.44	1.58	2.41	1.42	2.37
Missouri	-0.26	1.08	1.34	2.48	0.89	1.94	0.33	1.28
Ohio	-0.57	1.27	1.84	1.40	1.21	3.39	1.34	1.04
Wisconsin	-0.30	1.10	1.41	2.26	1.16	1.33	1.33	1.16
Southeast	*-0.58*	*1.81*	*2.40*	*2.14*	*2.20*	*2.86*	*1.30*	*0.55*
Alabama	-0.60	2.04	2.66	3.98	2.16	2.87	1.30	0.20
Florida	0.99	2.72	1.71	0.01	2.34	3.02	0.00	2.09
Georgia	-0.15	2.68	2.84	4.08	2.47	2.19	1.45	1.30
Kentucky	-0.56	0.83	1.40	1.70	1.33	1.97	0.03	-1.36
North Carolina	-0.92	2.06	3.01	1.32	2.11	3.16	2.80	0.39
South Carolina	-1.76	0.96	2.77	1.08	2.77	2.96	2.10	0.82
Tennessee	-0.75	0.88	1.65	2.03	1.05	3.57	-0.15	-0.98
Virginia	-0.71	1.03	1.76	1.10	1.33	1.87	2.48	-0.87
West Virginia	-1.65	-0.07	1.61	2.17	0.83	3.04	0.95	-0.78

(continued)

Appendix Table 5-3 (continued)

	Growth, 1949–2002			MFP Growth				
	Input	Output	MFP	1949–1960	1960–1970	1970–1980	1980–1990	1990–2002
				average annual percentage change				
Northeast	*-0.91*	*0.84*	*1.77*	*2.18*	*2.34*	*1.68*	*1.85*	*-0.08*
Connecticut	-1.57	-0.48	1.11	1.89	2.09	0.42	2.23	0.04
Delaware	0.77	2.96	2.18	3.64	2.88	1.46	1.98	0.62
Maine	-1.60	-0.01	1.61	3.36	4.39	-1.27	1.44	-0.19
Maryland	-0.17	1.97	2.15	2.53	3.13	1.58	1.75	0.61
Massachusetts	-1.93	-0.69	1.26	2.18	2.72	1.58	-0.14	-1.22
New Hampshire	-1.88	-0.89	1.01	3.16	3.85	-0.80	0.58	-0.03
New Jersey	-1.87	-0.79	1.10	1.48	1.25	0.48	2.18	-0.60
New York	-1.16	0.33	1.51	1.74	1.84	1.61	1.57	-0.36
Pennsylvania	-0.54	1.58	2.13	2.16	2.21	3.01	2.16	0.10
Rhode Island	-1.94	-0.28	1.70	1.95	2.11	0.83	3.44	-4.16
Vermont	-0.87	0.57	1.45	2.88	2.56	-0.12	1.19	-0.66

Sources: Calculated by the authors using InSTePP data.

Notes: The estimates in this table are obtained by fitting regressions to the index data. Corresponding estimates calculated as the averages of year-to-year percentage changes in the index are reported in Table 5-5. Box 5-1 provides details on the alternative methods.

APPENDIX II

The InSTePP Production Accounts

Version 4 of the InSTePP production accounts is the latest in a series of accounts all developed under the leadership of Philip Pardey at the University of Minnesota's International Science and Technology Practice and Policy (InSTePP) center as a joint effort with colleagues now at Oberlin College (Barbara Craig), the University of Wyoming (Matthew Andersen), and the University of California, Davis (Julian Alston). Jason Beddow, Connie Chan-Kang and Michelle Hallaway, all from InSTePP, and Louise Letnes, from the Department of Applied Economics, University of Minnesota, also gave generously of their time and creativity in the development of this data set, as did numerous individuals at the USDA's Economic Research Service (notably Eldon Ball) and the National Agricultural Statistical Service.[1]

Version 4 consists of state-specific measures of the prices and quantities of 74 categories of outputs (including two non-commodity outputs) and 58 categories of inputs for the 48 contiguous U.S. states. The input dataset covers the period 1949–2002 while the output dataset runs from 1949 to 2006. This version of these data (see Andersen 2005) represents a revised, expanded and updated version of the dataset published by Acquaye, Alston and Pardey (2002 and 2003), which ran from 1949 to 1991. The original version of the dataset, which ran from 1949 to 1985, was first described and used by Craig and Pardey (1990) and then used (with updates and revisions) more formally by Craig and Pardey (1996a and 1996b) and Alston, Craig and Pardey (1998). Here we provide a brief overview of the InSTePP production accounts, emphasizing some of the more important data construction choices used to assemble the data. More complete descriptions of the data sources and development details can be found in Pardey et al. (2009a).

The primary motivation for constructing these production accounts was to enrich our understanding of the national and state-specific economic history of inputs, outputs, and

1 These production accounts were first developed during the period 1986–1989 and subsequently reworked and expanded through three significant rounds of revisions with the generous financial and institutional support of the Minnesota agricultural experiment station (MAES), the Dean's office of the University of Minnesota's College of Food, Agriculture and Natural Sciences (CFANS), InSTePP, the USDA Economic Research Service, the USDA National Research Initiative, the Farm Foundation, the University of California (UC) Pacific-Rim Research Program, the UC Division of Agriculture and Natural Resources, the UC Davis College of Agriculture and Environmental Sciences, and the Giannini Foundation of Agricultural Economics.

productivity in American agriculture, and to gain a better understanding of the relationship between investments in R&D and agricultural output and productivity. To that end, special attention was given to accounting for variation in the composition of input and output aggregates, with particular reference to the quality of inputs and outputs and the spatial dimension. The work of Star (1974) motivated a decision to disaggregate the data as finely as possible to serve the analytical objectives of this research. Star showed that one is safe in using pre-aggregated data only if all of the inputs (or outputs) in the class are growing at the same rate or are perfect substitutes for one another. If, for example, the rate of growth of the higher-priced inputs (outputs) exceeds the rate of growth of the lower-priced inputs (outputs), the estimated rate of growth of the group will be biased downwards when pre-aggregated data are used. Hence, growth rates of agricultural productivity will tend to be overstated if the quantities of higher-priced (i.e., higher-quality) inputs are growing relatively quickly. Using earlier versions of these data, Craig and Pardey (1996b) and Acquaye, Alston and Pardey (2002 and 2003) investigated the implications of carefully accounting for price variation across qualities or U.S. states for measures of aggregate national and regional output and input growth, and that assessment is pushed further in this book.

Variable Description

For much of the analysis in this volume, the 58 categories of inputs are grouped into four broad categories: land, labor, capital, and materials inputs. The land input is subdivided into service flows from three basic types of land, namely pasture and rangeland, non-irrigated cropland, and irrigated cropland. This measure of the quantity of land in agriculture differs from the more-traditional measures of land in farms in that it excludes non-grazed forest and woodlands (areas which, although in farms, are not in agriculture), and includes federally owned land rented or leased for rangeland grazing purposes. Also included in the cropland measures are land acres idled for whatever reason.[2] The price weights used for aggregation of the land input are annual, state- or region-specific, cash rents for each of the three land types.

Annual data for a total of thirty-two categories of labor—comprising thirty categories of farm operators, as well as hired labor and family labor—were used to form the labor aggregate. Data on days worked off-farm by farm operators were used to adjust the measure of operator labor, and to account for the substantial but uneven shift towards part-time farming. State-specific wages were obtained for the hired and family labor, whereas implicit wages for operators were developed using national income earned by farm, ranch, and other agricultural managers categorized by age and educational attainment.

The twelve different capital inputs in this data set include seven classes of physical capital and five classes of biological capital. A physical inventory method, based on counts of assets purchased or in place was used to compile the data as described in some detail

2 At times under U.S. farm commodity programs (e.g., as they operated under the 1985 Farm Bill), farmers who opted to participate in crop programs were obliged to set aside some land as a condition for receiving farm program loans or subsidy payments. Under these policies, the decision to participate in the program involved the choice to take a support price instead of a market price and, jointly, to commit some additional land as set aside. In this way a program crop can be seen as higher-priced but effectively lower-yielding in terms of the acreage that must be committed to produce a bushel that is eligible for the high price. Having used distorted prices to value program crops, on the grounds that they are the decision prices and represent the "opportunity cost for the producer," it is logically consistent also to treat the set-aside acres as an input, because they are also part of the producer's decision calculus. Footnote 3 in this section provides additional justification for this decision.

in Andersen, Alston and Pardey (2009) and Pardey et al. (2009b). In addition, we adjusted inventories of the physical capital classes to reflect quality change over time, depending on the nature of the data available and the service-flow profile of each capital type. For all farm machinery, automobiles, and trucks, inventories on farm were converted to equivalent head counts of a new machine, using information on the average age of machines. For tractors and combines, additional information on the productive characteristics of machines on farms was used to adjust for quality as well, which led to inventories measured in equivalent numbers of new, numeraire tractors (two-wheel drive, 55 horsepower) or combines (medium capacity). Biological capital, here consisting of breeding, milking, and egg-laying livestock assets, were also included. For only one capital class, buildings, the quantities were implicit quantities derived by dividing the total rental value of buildings on farms by a price index developed for the purpose. Rents for capital items were taken to be specific fractions of the purchase price, fractions that varied among capital types. Purchase prices were assumed to reflect the expected present value of real capital services over the lifetime of the specific type of capital.

Eleven types of materials inputs are included in this data set. Apart from fertilizers, measured as quantities of elemental nitrogen, phosphorous, and potash, the purchased input quantities were implicit quantities derived from state-specific expenditure totals. The miscellaneous category was preaggregated, and included a list of disparate inputs, such as fencing, irrigation fees, hand tools, veterinary services, and insurance costs, among others. In the materials input category, state-specific prices were available only for electricity; all other input prices were national prices or price indices based on national prices paid by farmers.

In the disaggregated form, the output data cover 74 output categories, including 16 field crops, 22 fruits and nuts, 22 vegetables, implicit quantities of nursery and greenhouse products, nine livestock commodities, and four miscellaneous items including implicit quantities of machines rented out by farmers, and CRP acreage.[3] Because data were not available, horses and mules are not included in this data set either as biological capital inputs or as outputs even though they have been important, particularly in some states.

The prices used as weights to form various output aggregates are state-specific prices received by farmers for all commodities, except machines for hire and nursery and greenhouse products. For these composite commodities a price index based on national prices for their subcomponents was constructed and used to deflate reported current dollar values. A standard (but somewhat questionable) choice was to use the (policy-distorted) prices paid and received by farmers as the relevant prices for aggregating inputs and outputs (see footnotes 2 and 3 in this appendix for some related discussion). Table II-1 summarizes the input and output variables and their groupings into various categories. Table II-2 summarizes the groupings of states into the regions used throughout this book.

Aggregating Inputs and Outputs

Index number theory provides insight into how to minimize bias from the procedure used to aggregate inputs and outputs by choosing an appropriate index procedure, carefully

3 As a departure from Craig and Pardey (1996a and 1996b) and other studies, in this version of the production accounts CRP acreage is treated as an output for which producers receive revenue equal to the CRP payments from the government. This is consistent with treating idled acres under the Acreage Reduction Program as an input.

Table II-1 InSTePP Input and Output Categories

Input and Output Categories	Details
Inputs	
Land (3)	
Cropland	
Irrigated cropland	
Pasture and grassland	
Labor (32)	
Family labor	
Hired labor	
Operator labor (30)	Thirty classes characterized by: Education: 0–7 years, 8 years, 1–3 years of high school, 4 years of high school, 1–3 years of college, 4 years or more of college Age: 25–34, 35–44, 45–54, 55–64, or 65 or more years of age
Capital (12)	
Machinery (6)	Automobiles, combines, mowers and conditioners, pickers and balers, tractors, trucks
Biological capital (5)	Breeding cows, chickens, ewes, milking cows, sows
Buildings	
Materials (11)	Electricity, purchased feed, fuel, hired machines, pesticides, nitrogen, phosphorous, potash, repairs, seeds, miscellaneous purchases
Outputs	
Crops (61)	
Field crops (16)	Barley, corn, cotton, flax, field beans, oats, peanuts, rice, rye, sugar beets, sugarcane, sorghum, soybeans, sunflowers, tobacco, wheat
Fruits and Nuts (22)	Almonds, apples, apricots, avocados, blueberries, cherries, cranberries, grapefruit, grapes, lemons, nectarines, oranges, pears, peaches, pecans, pistachios, plums, prunes, raspberries, strawberries, tangerines, walnuts
Vegetables (22)	Asparagus, bell peppers, broccoli, carrots, cantaloupes, cauliflower, celery, cucumbers, garlic, honeydews, lettuce, onions, peas, potatoes, snap beans for processing, spinach (processed), sweet corn (fresh and for processing), sweet potatoes, tomatoes (fresh and for processing), watermelons
Nursery and greenhouse products	Aggregate of nursery and greenhouse products
Livestock (9)	Broilers, cattle, eggs, hogs, honey, milk, sheep, turkeys, and wool
Miscellaneous (4)	Hops, mushrooms, machines rented out, Conservation Reserve Program acreage

Notes: Numbers in parentheses indicate the number of items in each category.

selecting value weights for all inputs and outputs, and disaggregating inputs and outputs as finely as possible. Throughout most of this volume, we use indexes of the quantities and prices of aggregate output and input that were formed using a Fisher discrete approximation to a Divisia index.[4] To illustrate the nature and magnitude of the biases involved in using a

4 The Fisher indexes of multi-factor productivity reported and used throughout this volume are not adjusted for procyclical changes in capital asset utilization in U.S. agriculture, although such changes have been studied in some detail by Andersen (2005) and Andersen, Alston and Pardey (2007).

Table II-2 Regional Groupings of States

Region	States in region
Pacific	California, Oregon, Washington
Mountain	Arizona, Colorado, Idaho, Montana, Nevada, New Mexico, Utah, Wyoming
Northern Plains	Kansas, Nebraska, North Dakota, South Dakota
Southern Plains	Arkansas, Louisiana, Mississippi, Oklahoma, Texas
Central	Illinois, Indiana, Iowa, Michigan, Minnesota, Missouri, Ohio, Wisconsin
Southeast	Alabama, Florida, Georgia, Kentucky, North Carolina, South Carolina, Tennessee, Virginia, West Virginia
Northeast	Connecticut, Delaware, Maine, Maryland, Massachusetts, New Hampshire, New Jersey, New York, Pennsylvania, Rhode Island, Vermont

fixed-weight index, in some instances Laspeyres indexes are also presented for comparison. Using the formation of an output quantity aggregate to illustrate the development of these indexes, let $q_{i,t}$ = quantity of output item $i = 1,2,\ldots,N$, in year t, $p_{i,t}$ = the price of item i in year t, and $p_{i,0}$ = price of item i in the base year = 0. A Laspeyres quantity index, using base-period prices as weights, is defined as:

$$\text{(II.1)} \qquad Q_L = \frac{\sum_{i=1}^{N} q_{i,t} p_{i,0}}{\sum_{i=1}^{N} q_{i,0} p_{i,0}}$$

and a chained Fisher quantity index is defined as:

$$\text{(II.2)} \qquad Q_F = \left(\frac{\sum_{i=1}^{N} q_{i,t} p_{i,t}}{\sum_{i=1}^{N} q_{i,t-1} p_{i,t}} \right)^{1/2} \left(\frac{\sum_{i=1}^{N} q_{i,t} p_{i,t-1}}{\sum_{i=1}^{N} q_{i,t-1} p_{i,t-1}} \right)^{1/2}.$$

Price indexes are constructed similarly by switching the roles of prices and quantities.

The detailed InSTePP database of state- and commodity-specific prices and quantities of goods also enabled an examination of the sensitivity of the aggregation procedure to two types of errors (a) using an identical average price for each distinct item included in a particular sub-aggregate (such as using an average price for all 32 types of labor included in the aggregate of labor versus a price specific to each of the 32 classes of labor), and (b) using a national average price for each item (such as using the national average price of wheat versus a state-specific price of wheat). For example, the use of national prices ignores variation in the quality and varietal composition of the wheat crop among states that is captured by using state-specific prices.

Major Sources of Data

The price and quantity data for agricultural outputs are annual estimates from the U.S. Department of Agriculture (USDA) Economic Research Service (ERS) and National

Agricultural Statistics Service (NASS). The estimates come principally from two publications, *Agricultural Statistics* and *Statistical Bulletins*, supplemented with NASS and USDA occasional commodity reports.[5] The output price and quantity data are all state- and commodity-specific except for the machines hired out category, for which we used a national average price.

The agricultural input data come from a host of sources, most importantly various issues of the *U.S. Census of Agriculture* (since 1997 conducted under the auspices of the USDA, and the U.S. Census Bureau for earlier years). For almost all of the input data, quinquennial *Census of Agriculture* estimates were also used to benchmark each of the time series.

To compile the data on land, state-specific estimates of acres devoted to agricultural production were obtained primarily from an ERS publication titled, *Major Land Uses*.[6] Rental rates for agricultural land include estimates of average cash rent per acre for irrigated and non-irrigated cropland, and pastureland, for USDA regions and selected states. For more recent years, estimates of cropland and pastureland rental rates were drawn from the *Agricultural Land Values and Cash Rents* series included online as part of the USDA's Economics, Statistics, and Market Information System.[7] Hard copies of this and related reports were used to compile data for earlier years.

Estimates of operator labor differentiated into 30 classes consisting of five age and six education cohorts were developed using NASS data from the Census of Agriculture and the Agricultural Resource Management Survey (ARMS), as well as data on earnings by occupation and education data from the U.S. Department of Commerce, *Census of Population*. Estimates of days worked off farm taken from various issues of the *Census of Agriculture* were used to calculate the extent of part-time farming by farm operators. Data on hired and family labor were taken from various *Farm Labor* reports published for many years by the USDA Crop Reporting Board and now available online.[8]

U.S. Census of Agriculture reports were the primary source for the data on stocks of machinery on farms as used to estimate the series of capital service flows. For the period after 1963, the *Census of Agriculture* data were supplemented with unpublished information purchased from the Association of Equipment Manufactures (AEM) on annual, state-specific sales of tractors and combines (differentiated by machine type and size). *U.S. Census of Agriculture* reports, supplemented with information from a range of other sources (including *Agricultural Statistics*) were used to compile the data used to construct estimates of the capital service flows derived from service structures (including buildings on farm net of farm dwellings) and biological capital.

---

5 Data for the initial years were compiled by hand from the respective reports. For the more-recent years (1992 and thereafter) these publications, and associated data files, are available online at http://www.nass.usda.gov/Publications/Ag_Statistics/index.asp and http://www.nass.usda.gov/Publications/Statistical_Bulletins/index.asp.

6 The ERS land-use data are online at http://www.ers.usda.gov/Data/MajorLandUses/.

7 For the years 1997 and after, the USDA estimates of land values and cash rents for irrigated and non-irrigated cropland and pastureland are available online at: http://usda.mannlib.cornell.edu/MannUsda/viewDocumentInfo.do?documentID=1446.

8 See http://usda.mannlib.cornell.edu/MannUsda/viewDocumentInfo.do?documentID=1063.

Implicit quantities of most of the materials inputs were developed using state-specific expenditure data from the Economic Research Service (ERS) and a national average price.[9] Price indexes for most of the materials inputs were obtained from the Bureau of Labor Statistics and the Bureau of Economic Analysis. Notable exceptions are the fertilizer and electricity inputs. Fertilizer data consist of state-specific quantities (tons of plant nutrient content) of nitrogen, potash, and phosphate and national average prices (dollars per ton) specific to each of these components. The electricity data include state-specific prices (dollars per kilowatt) and implicit quantities developed using electricity expenditures in each state.

Satellite InSTePP Value-of-Production Accounts

To support an assessment of the long-run change in the composition of U.S. agricultural output (Chapter 4) and the intensity of state-specific investments in agricultural R&D (Chapter 6) we developed a satellite set of accounts representing state- and commodity-specific value-of-production (VOP) estimates for the period 1924–2005. The VOP accounts span 89 agricultural commodities in 1924 growing to 128 agricultural commodities in 2005—compared with 72 commodities (excluding CRP acreage and machines hired out) in the InSTePP production accounts—as the availability of commodity data improved.[10] The VOP series ostensibly spans all agricultural outputs (including horticultural and ornamental and nursery production, but excluding aquaculture and forestry outputs); commodities not explicitly listed were included in respective "other" output sub-totals.

The VOP accounts constitute a blending of derived value-of-production estimates using the specific price and corresponding quantity data for 72 agricultural commodities from the InSTePP production accounts for the period 1949–2005 supplemented with farm cash receipt data from http://www.ers.usda.gov/data/FarmIncome/finfidmu.htm and various occasional publications for nursery and greenhouse products, including the NASS *Census of Horticulture*. For some commodities (for example, cotton, field and sweet corn, mushrooms, onions, peaches, rice, sugarbeets, tomatoes and wool) we detected a significant discrepancy between the value of production and the farm cash receipts data (representing the value of commodities produced that were sold off farm) in the period 1949–2005. In these cases, state- and commodity-specific prices-received and quantities-produced data were compiled by hand for the period extending back to 1924, mainly from USDA *Agricultural Statistics* publications. In addition, some data were missing for some commodities in some states in some years, and were estimated by linear interpolation, but these observations never exceeded 0.1 percent of the total value of production in any year.

9 The ERS data on purchased inputs are now available on line at: http://www.ers.usda.gov/Data/FarmIncome/finfidmu.htm.

10 The 128 commodities in the VOP accounts for 2005 consist of 74 specialty crops (including fruits, vegetables, and a nursery and greenhouse marketing category), 40 other crops (including various field crops), and 14 livestock products. The InSTePP series treats fresh and processed tomatoes and fresh and processed sweet corn as separate items, while data limitations allowed for the inclusion of only one tomato (fresh and processed combined) category and one (fresh and processed sweet corn, combined) category in the VOP series. The additional commodities in the VOP versus the InSTePP series were mainly niche specialty crops and various turf and pasture grasses that individually constituted a small share of the national total and were typically produced in just a handful of states. The value of production totals in the InSTePP production accounts ranged between 91 and 97 percent of the 48-state value of production total in the VOP satellite accounts.

PART III

Agricultural R&D Funding and Policies

As described and documented in Chapter 5, productivity growth has been a striking feature of the development of U.S. agriculture during the past 50 years but with important differences in the rate, timing, and the nature of productivity gains among states within states. The fundamental sources of these gains may have varied, too, including such diverse factors as public infrastructure investment, education of farmers, and economies of size and scale, as well as innovations in agricultural production processes and technological improvements embodied in inputs used on and off farms, some of which are attributable to R&D. The focus here is on the role of public agricultural R&D, including both state and federal investments. In this Part of the book we provide a brief institutional and legislative history of agricultural R&D in the United States. We also document data on the patterns of intellectual property rights sought, along with R&D investments made by the state and federal governments and private firms operating in the United States, and place U.S. agricultural R&D spending within the context of changing national research realities and the shifting structure of agricultural R&D worldwide. Chapter 6 documents the funding and performance of research for agriculture and Chapter 7 explores the evolving federal role.

CHAPTER 6

Research Funding and Performance

How has public and private sector participation in agricultural R&D in the United States changed over the decades, and how has research spending on agriculture fared relative to research spending in all areas of science? Given the international interdependencies in agricultural R&D, how has research spending in the United States evolved relative to spending elsewhere in the world? This chapter describes public and private investments in R&D directed to agriculture in the United States, placing them in the context of both the overall spending on all sciences, and global spending on agricultural R&D. Then, we explore patterns of public spending on agricultural R&D within the United States, both in aggregate and among the states, with attention to the separate and joint roles of the federal government through its USDA intramural labs and the State Agricultural Experiment Stations. We consider the evolving sources of funding as well as the evolving patterns of spending. In Chapter 7, these trends in the funding and performance of agricultural R&D are linked to legislative and other policy changes.

6.1 Overall Spending on the Sciences

Agricultural research and technological changes in agriculture have, since their inception, been inextricably intertwined with research in other areas of science. Darwin's theory of evolution, the pure-line theory of Johannson, the mutation theory of de Vries, and the "rediscovery" of Mendel's laws of heredity all contributed to the rise of plant and animal breeding in the beginning of the 20th Century.[1] The mid-19th Century work of organic chemists like von Leibig led to

1 In 1900, the Dutch botanist Hugo de Vries, the German botanist Correns, and the Austrian agronomist Tschermark independently published studies on the laws of heredity that had been anticipated in the 1866 paper by the Austrian monk Gregor Mendel. When Mendel's paper was published in the *Proceedings of the Natural History Society of Brünn*, it had little impact, and was cited very few times over the subsequent thirty-five years. Pardey, Alston and Ruttan (2010) offer additional perspective on the changing role of science and innovation in agriculture.

J.M. Alston et al., *Persistence Pays: U.S. Agricultural Productivity Growth and the Benefits from Public R&D Spending*, Natural Resource Management and Policy 34,
DOI 10.1007/978-1-4419-0658-8_6,

substantive improvements in our understanding of the role that soil fertility plays in plant growth.[2] Pasteur's germ theory of disease and other fundamental insights gained from bacteriology, virology and related microbiological sciences spurred the development of animal vaccines, and more broadly promoted the development of methods to manage and mitigate production losses associated with crop and livestock diseases. Similarly, the more-recent applications of biotechnology to agriculture stand firmly on the findings and genetic transformation techniques rooted in the more basic biological sciences, genetics, genomics, proteomics and information sciences. Consequently, an appreciation of investment trends in the sciences generally is essential for properly understanding the implications of the shifting structure of investments in agricultural science.

International Developments

In 2006, about $887 billion (2000 international dollars), or 1.7 percent of global GDP, was spent on all the sciences worldwide (Pardey and Dehmer 2010).[3] Patterns of R&D spending changed significantly in the past two decades. Global spending on R&D more than doubled in real (2000 international dollar) terms between 1980 ($374 billion) and 2006 ($887 billion).

The United States accounted for 31 percent of the world's science spending in 1980, and 33 percent in 2006. Collectively, the high-income countries (those with per capita incomes in excess of $10,726) accounted for 80 percent of the world's R&D in 2006.[4] The developing-country share of the world total has grown over time from 5 percent in 1980 to 15 percent in 2006. Notably, China, India and Brazil account for a growing and now dominant share of this developing-country total—61 percent of the developing world's total R&D spending in 1980, increasing to 83 percent in 2006. China now ranks third, behind the United States and Japan, in terms of total science spending worldwide (denominated in international dollars), South Korea ranks sixth, Brazil eighth and India twelfth.

---

2 Von Liebig's book *Organic Chemistry in Its Application to Agriculture and Physiology* published in 1840 in both Germany and Great Britain triggered widespread demand for the application of science to agriculture. Within eight years of its publication, von Liebig's book had gone through 17 different editions, translations and revisions, mostly in Germany, England, France, and the United States, but also in Denmark, Italy, the Netherlands, Poland, and Russia (Salmon and Hanson 1964; Russell 1966; and Rossiter 1975). Like others, Ruttan (1982) considered von Liebig's book to represent the critical dividing line in the evolution of modern agricultural research.

3 This figure includes the total spending by public and private entities across all areas of science (i.e., including agricultural, medical, and engineering R&D, information technology, social sciences, and so on).

4 The per capita income classes used here come from World Bank (2007). Countries classified by the World Bank as either Low or Lower-Middle income countries were here considered as "developing countries."

Domestic R&D Developments

In 2007, the United States invested $368.1 billion current U.S. dollars in all areas of R&D, substantially up on the $5.2 billion it invested in 1953 when these data were first collected. About 85.2 percent ($313.5 billion) of total science spending in 2007 was non-defense related, compared with 67.4 percent in 1967 (Figure 6-1, Panel a).[5] About 78 percent of the total R&D in the United States was done by private entities in 2007; about 73 percent by industry and 5 percent by non-profit organizations. The industry share of R&D has varied somewhat over time (Figure 6-1, Panel b, Inset): it averaged 77 percent in the late 1950s (1956–1959) but fell to just below 68 percent of the total by 1975 after which it grew, somewhat erratically, to peak at 80 percent in 2000. Many firms curtailed their investments in R&D following the dotcom bust and subsequent economic slowdown of 2001 and 2002, such that business R&D declined (in real, inflation-adjusted terms) by 1.87 percent per year from 2000 to 2003 and the industry share of total R&D spending fell to 70 percent. A more recent rebound in business R&D spending pushed the industry share back to its 2007 share of 73 percent. Research performed by federal government labs has fallen over time to 7 percent of the total in 2007, less than half the corresponding university and college share of 15 percent, which is substantially up from its 8 percent share in 1953 (Figure 6-1, Panel b).

While it performed only 7 percent of total U.S. R&D, the federal government funded 27 percent of R&D in 2007. Half of all federal government funding for R&D ($50.5 billion in 2007) was obligated through the Department of Defense (DOD). Most of this DOD spending (90.5 percent) went into development—predominantly encompassing the costs of developing, testing and evaluating defense systems, technologies and components (DOD 2008, p. 96-98). Moreover, most DOD-funded research (74 percent) was carried out by industrial firms (NSB 2008, pp. 4-23). Only 7.3 percent of the DOD research budget went to applied research, and just 2.2 percent to basic R&D. In stark contrast, the remaining half of federally funded R&D oriented to civilian research was directed to applied research (39 percent of this non-DOD share) and basic research (48 percent), with only 14 percent classified as development (NSB 2008, pp. 4-25).[6]

The orientation of R&D performed in the United States has shifted markedly over the years, along with the R&D spending priorities of the federal government. Federal outlays on all forms of R&D grew nominally from $16.1 bil-

---

5 Pardey and Dehmer's (2010) non-defense share estimate approximately tracks the U.S. "civil research" share reported by OECD (2008) since 1981.

6 These federal funds were obligated through agencies in the Departments of Health and Human Services, Energy, and Agriculture along with the National Aeronautics and Space Administration, National Science Foundation, National Institute of Standards and Technology and several other government entities.

Figure 6-1 Structure of Science Spending in the United States, 1953–2007

Panel a. Spending trends, 1953–2007

Panel b. Sector shares of science spending by performer, 1953 and 2007

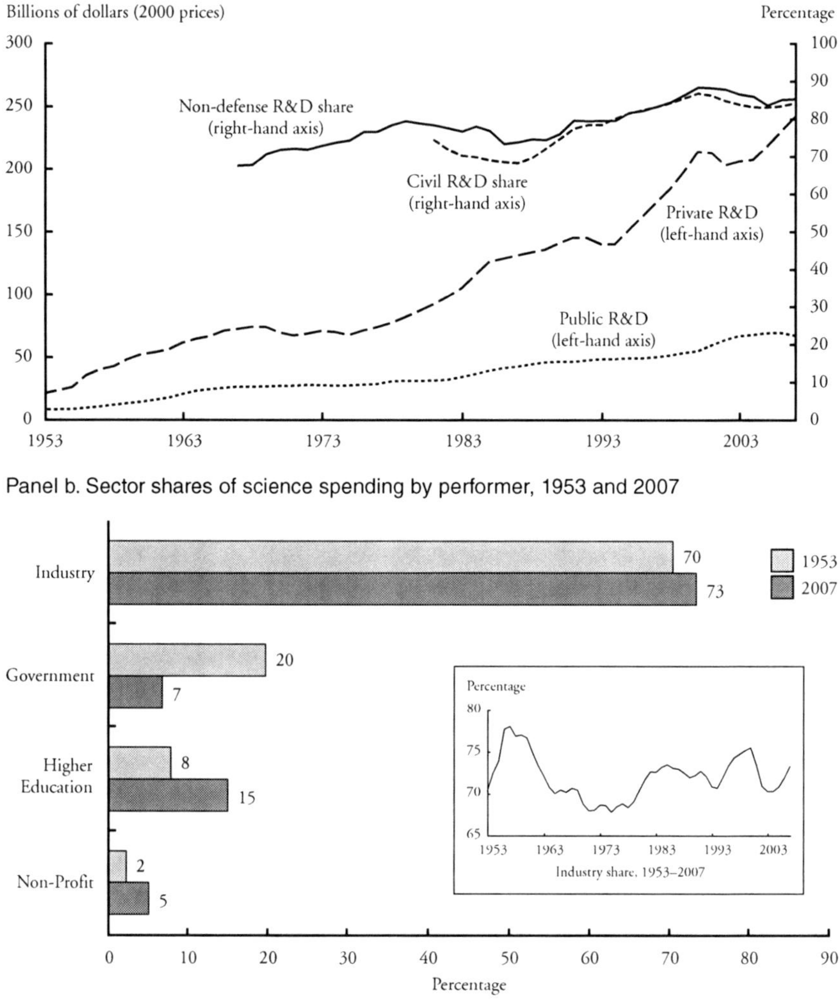

Sources: Adapted from Dehmer and Pardey (2010). Panel a. Public and private R&D totals are from NSF (2008a). The Department of Defense R&D expenditures used to construct the non-defense share of R&D are from NSF (2009b). Civil R&D is from OECD (2008). Panel b. NSF (2008a). Implicit GDP deflator used to express R&D in 2000 prices is from BEA (2008b).

Notes: Panel a. Public totals are the sum of research performed by the federal government agencies and universities and colleges (including Federally Funded Research and Development Centers). Research and development performed by state agencies is not explicitly considered. Private total is the sum of R&D performed by industry and non-profit agencies (including Federally Funded Research and Development Centers). Non-defense share of R&D is calculated by subtracting the Department of Defense R&D expenditures from the domestic total. Civil R&D is another estimate of non-defense R&D produced by the OECD.

Figure 6-2 U.S. Federal Government R&D Spending by Department, 1967–2007

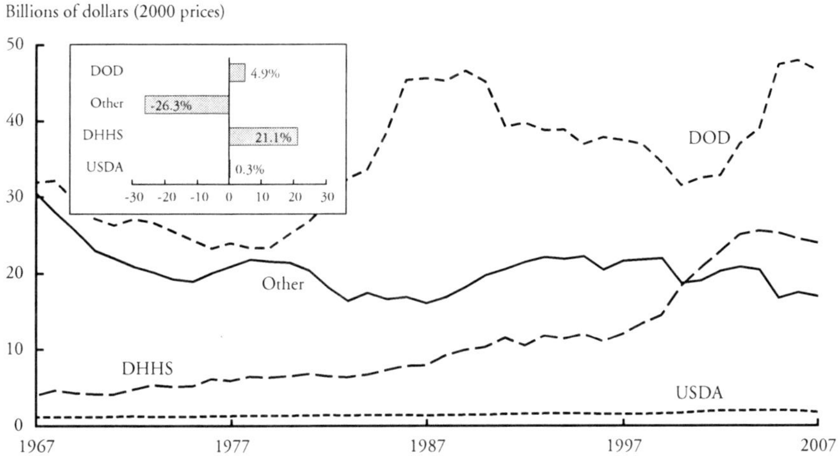

Sources: NSF (2008c). Implicit GDP deflator from BEA (2008b) was used to express R&D in 2000 prices.

Notes: DOD indicates Department of Defense, DHHS indicates Department of Health and Human Services, and USDA indicates U.S. Department of Agriculture. The inset represents the change in the share of federal spending (already expressed as a percentage) by the respective federal department from 1967 to 2007.

lion in 1967 (1.9 percent of GDP in that year) to $106.3 billion (0.8 percent of GDP) in 2007; a nominal rate of growth of 4.7 percent per year (or 0.70 percent per year once inflation is taken into account using an implicit GDP deflator). Federal research disbursements to the Department of Defense (DOD) were $7.6 billion (or 47 percent of total federal outlays on R&D) in 1967 and $55.5 billion in 2007 (52 percent of the total). In inflation-adjusted terms, DOD research expenditures grew by an average of 0.94 percent per year since 1967. But the growth was erratic, with periods such as the early to mid-1980s and the post-2000 period experiencing relatively rapid growth, and other periods, including most of the 1990s, in which DOD research spending was drawn down as part of the post Cold War "peace dividend" that saw a scaling back of DOD spending generally (OMB 2008, pp. 59-60) (Figure 6-2). The major growth area was research spending by the Department of Health and Human Services (DHHS), which includes spending directed to the National Institutes of Health (NIH) where much of the growth occurred (Figure 6-2, Inset). Inflation-adjusted, federal government R&D spending by the United States Department of Agriculture (USDA) grew 1.10 percent per year during the 40 year period after 1967 compared with 4.56 percent per year for DHHS, and 0.94 percent per year for DOD. The combined R&D expenditures by all other federal government

Figure 6-3 Agricultural Share of R&D in the Life Sciences, 1973–2005

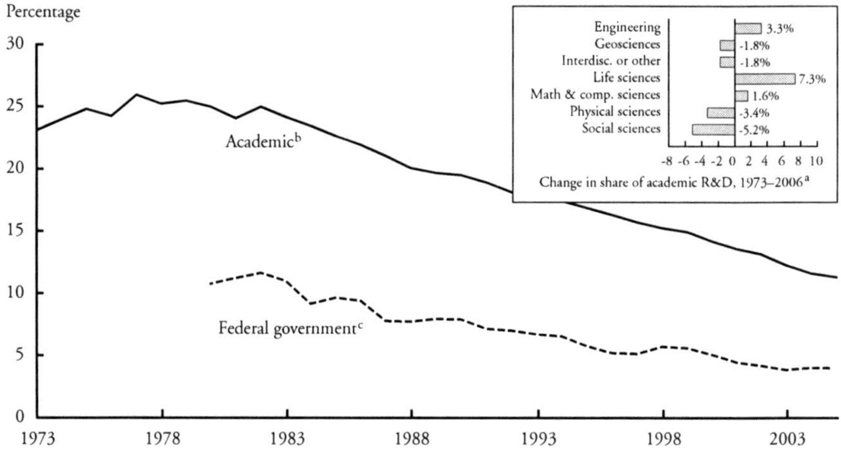

Sources: Academic agricultural R&D expenditures used in constructing the agricultural share of the academic life sciences are the SAES series exclusive of forestry from Appendix Table 6-1. Total academic life sciences data are from NSF (2007). The federal government shares were constructed from NSB (1993, Appendix Tables 4-15 and 4-16) and NSB (2008, Appendix Table 4.32).

[a] The inset figure shows the changes in shares of federal academic R&D spending (already expressed as a percentage), by field of science, from 1973 to 2006.

[b] Represents federal agricultural R&D spending by the SAESs exclusive of forestry from Appendix Table 6-1 as a share of all federal outlays on academic life sciences research.

[c] Represents all federal agricultural R&D obligations by the USDA and other government agencies and the SAESs exclusive of forestry from Appendix Table 6-1 as a share of all federal obligations on life sciences research.

departments (including the Department of Energy) decreased by 1.47 percent per year.

Although both federal government funding and the emphasis of academic R&D swung heavily towards life sciences R&D in the past several decades (Figure 6-2, Inset), this additional funding largely by-passed the agricultural sciences, a branch of the biological-cum-life sciences. Agricultural research as a share of federal government funds directed to the life sciences declined precipitously, from 10.7 percent in 1980 to just 3.9 percent in 2005, (Figure 6-3).[7] Likewise, in 1980 about 23.0 percent of academic life sciences research was oriented to agriculture; but by 2005, that share had dropped to 11.2 percent. The share of life-science research funding devoted to agriculture has decreased by an average of 4.0 percent per year for federal funding over the period 1980–2005, compared to a slightly slower decline of 3.2 percent annual decrease for academic funding.

7 The federal government spending shares here relate only to research (i.e., excluding development).

Figure 6-4 Global Public Agricultural R&D Spending, 1981 and 2000

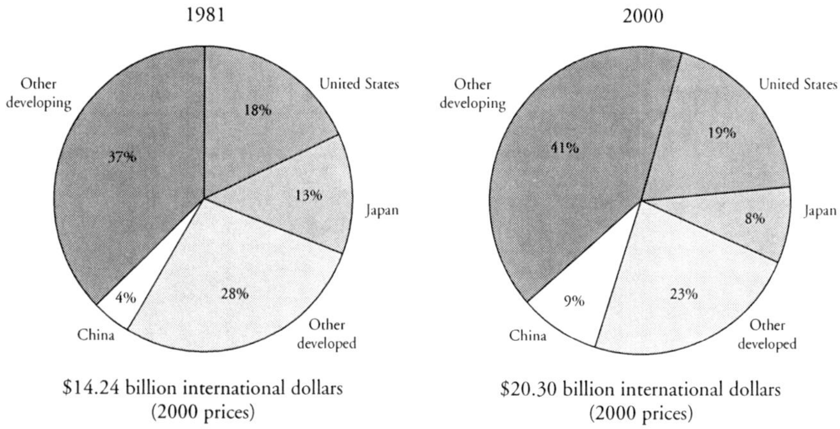

Sources: From James, Pardey and Alston (2008) based on ASTI data (www.asti.cgiar.org) reported in Pardey et al. (2006).

Notes: Data in nominal local currency units were first deflated with an implicit GDP deflator to 2000 prices then converted to international dollars using the World Bank's (2008) 2000 purchasing power parity index.

6.2 Global Agricultural R&D Spending

Agriculture's share of total R&D is generally modest. In 2000 (the latest year for which comparable global agriculture R&D and all-of-science data are available), only 1.8 percent of total R&D spending by rich countries was oriented towards agriculture. The corresponding developing-country share was 6.0 percent.[8] As a share of public R&D spending, agricultural R&D has remained steady among the developed countries at around 7 percent in both 1981 and 2000. In contrast, among developing countries the share of public research spending directed to agriculture declined from 22 percent in 1981 to 15 percent in 2000; albeit still more than double the corresponding rich-country share.

Worldwide, public investment in agricultural R&D increased by 43 percent in inflation-adjusted terms between 1981 and 2000, from an estimated $14.2 billion to $20.3 billion in 2000 international dollars (Figure 6-4). The developing world now accounts for about half of global public-sector spending—up from an estimated 41 percent share in 1981 (Table 6-1).[9] However, developing coun-

8 In 2000 high-income countries spent $574.6 billion (international dollars) on R&D in total, of which $22.5 billion was spent on public and private agricultural research. In the same year, developing countries spent $138.8 billion on R&D in total of which $10.7 billion was spent on public and private agricultural R&D. These shares are likely to understate the agricultural share of R&D since reported "agricultural R&D" figures typically omit research in basic biology, health, (bio-) informatics and other disciplines that have relevance for agriculture.

9 As Pardey, Roseboom and Craig (1992) described, these country and regional estimates of spending totals, shares, and rates of change are sensitive to the underlying national spending estimates as

Table 6-1 Public and Private Spending on Agricultural R&D, 1981 and 2000

Country or Region	Public Spending	Private Spending	Private Share Total	Share of World Public Total	Rank by Total Public Spending	Public Agricultural R&D Spending: Per $100 Ag GDP	Public Agricultural R&D Spending: Per Capita
	millions of international dollars (2000 prices)		*percentage*		*rank score*	*international dollars (2000 prices)*	
1981							
United States	2,568.7	2,495.0	49	18	1	1.68	10.99
Japan	1,821.3	1,048.5	37	13	2	2.64	15.47
Germany	547.4	701.1	56	4	5	1.85	7.01
Australia	522.0	32.6	6	4	7	3.36	35.41
United Kingdom	533.4	676.5	56	4	6	3.08	9.56
Canada	520.7	109.2	17	4	8	2.54	21.02
France	478.5	377.7	44	3	10	1.17	8.84
Total OECD	*8,339.8*	*6,478.4*	*44*	*59*		*1.62*	*10.97*
Brazil	628.0			4	3	0.91	5.05
China	586.9			4	4	0.41	0.58
India	332.4			2	12	0.18	0.47
Total developing	*5,903.2*			*41*		*0.49*	*1.81*
World total	**14,243.0**			**100**		**0.84**	**3.55**
2000							
United States	3,882.2	4,118.8	51	19	1	2.65	13.62
Japan	1,646.2	2,331.8	59	8	3	3.62	12.96
Germany	758.2	877.6	54	4	6	3.22	9.21
Australia	588.6	193.9	25	3	7	3.38	30.73
United Kingdom	495.5	1,244.6	72	2	9	3.57	8.41
Canada	474.3	244.5	34	2	10	2.54	15.41
France	341.9	1,009.2	75	2	15	0.91	5.77
Total OECD	*10,267.6*	*12,184.5*	*54*	*51*		*2.36*	*12.01*
Brazil	928.8	36.8	4	5	5	1.43	5.41
China	1,762.8	73.5	4	9	2	0.40	1.37
India	1,159.5	128.8	10	6	4	0.34	1.14
Total developing	*10,030.7*	*686.5*	*6*	*49*		*0.50*	*2.13*
World total	**20,298.3**	**12,871.1**	**39**	**100**		**0.84**	**3.65**

Sources: See Figure 6-4.

tries account for about one third of the world's total agricultural R&D spending when private investments are included. Public spending on agricultural R&D is highly concentrated among countries, with the top 5 percent of countries in the data set (i.e., 6 countries in a total of 129 underlying Table 6-1) accounting for

well as the procedures used to deflate and convert national spending estimates from the nominal local currency units in which they are typically compiled into the common currency unit reported here, 2000 international dollars. Aside from a revision to the public-sector series for Japan, the series used in this chapter are the same as those reported in Pardey et al. (2006) except that the currency conversions were done using a recently revised purchasing power parity (PPP) series obtained from World Bank (2008). As a consequence of these revisions, the estimate of the OECD share of the total global agricultural R&D spending increased from 44.3 percent as reported in Pardey et al. (2006) to 50.6 percent as reported here.

Figure 6-5 Average Annual Rates of Growth in Public Agricultural R&D Spending

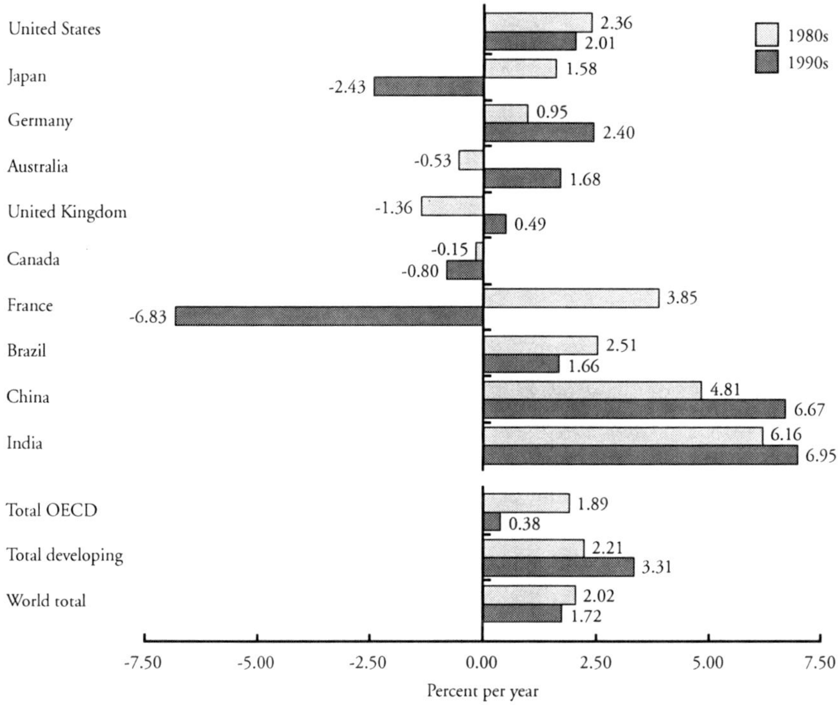

Sources: See Figure 6-4.

approximately half of the spending, and the top 20 percent of countries accounting for over 80 percent of spending.

Figure 6-5 shows annual average rates of growth in public agricultural R&D spending during the 1980s and 1990s for the United States, a selection of other rich countries, and several large developing countries. Notably, agricultural research spending grew faster in the developing countries than in the OECD (Organization for Economic Cooperation and Development) countries as a group during both the 1980s and the 1990s. Moreover, driven largely by trends in large developing countries, the overall annual rate of increase in the developing world was faster during the 1990s (3.31 percent per year on average) than the 1980s (2.21 percent per year on average). In contrast, the rate of growth in the OECD countries slowed considerably during the 1990s, sufficient to cause the global annual rate of growth in public agricultural R&D spending to be slower in the 1990s (1.72 percent per year) than the 1980s (2.02 percent per year).

Among the regions of the world, the Asia and Pacific region gained considerable ground, accounting for an ever-larger share of the world and developing country total since 1981 (25.1 percent of the world total in 2000, up from 15.7

percent in 1981). In 2000, just two countries from this region, China and India, accounted for 29.1 percent of *all* expenditure on public agricultural R&D by developing countries, a substantial increase from their 15.6 percent combined share in 1981.

The OECD countries as a group spent $2.36 on public agricultural R&D for every $100 of agricultural output in 2000 (in this case, agricultural output measured in terms of gross domestic product). This represents a sizable increase over the $1.62 spent per $100 of output in 1981, but is about the same as the estimate of $2.33 per $100 of output in 1991 (Table 6-1). In contrast, the overall agricultural R&D intensity was static in developing countries. In 2000, developing countries spent just $0.50 on agricultural R&D for every $100 of agricultural output compared with $0.49 in 1981.

Since everyone consumes agricultural outputs, agricultural R&D spending per capita is potentially interesting. Per capita spending rates were much lower among developing compared with developed countries: developing countries (especially those in sub-Saharan Africa) typically spent less than $2.50 per capita whereas more than half of the developed countries invested more than $10 per capita in 2000. For developed countries, spending per capita rose substantially from 1981 to 1991 (a continuation of earlier trends documented by Pardey and Beintema 2001) but then fell between 1991 and 2000. This developed-country reversal was driven mainly by developments in Japan, although only half the developed countries continued to increase their per capita spending on agricultural R&D throughout the 1990s. Spending per capita for developing countries increased from $1.81 in 1981 to $2.13 in 2000. The outliers from this general trend are Latin America and sub-Saharan Africa, where spending per capita decreased between 1981 and 2000.

Private Agricultural R&D Investments

The private sector has continued to emphasize inventions that are amenable to various intellectual property (IP) protection options such as hybrid crops, patents, and more recently, plant breeders' rights, along with other (sometimes technological) forms of protection. The private sector has a large presence in agricultural R&D, but with dramatic differences among countries. In 2000, the global total spending on agricultural R&D (including pre-, on-, and post-farm oriented R&D) was estimated to be $33.7 billion. Approximately 40 percent was conducted by private firms and the remaining 60 percent by public agencies (Table 6-1). Notably, 95 percent of that private R&D was performed in developed counties, where some 54 percent of total agricultural R&D was private, a sizeable increase from the 44 percent private share in 1981.

As the science of agriculture increasingly looks like the sciences more generally, one might expect this rich-country trend towards an increasing private agricultural R&D share to continue, reflecting increasing industry R&D by the farm-input supply and the food processing sectors. Around the general trend was much country-specific variation. In 2000, 59 percent of food and agricultural R&D in Japan was conducted in the private sector, compared with 51 percent in the United States. In contrast, in Australia and Canada—both reliant on privately developed, technology-intensive imports of farm machinery, chemicals and other agricultural inputs—the private-sector conducted less than 35 percent of food and agricultural R&D spending in 2000.[10] In developing countries, only 6.4 percent of the food and agricultural R&D was private, and the private share varied widely among regions of the developing world. In the Asia and Pacific region, 9.8 percent of the agricultural R&D was private, compared with only 1.7 percent throughout sub-Saharan Africa.

6.3 U.S. Public and Private Agricultural Research

In the United States, the private sector and public sector nowadays spend similar amounts on agricultural research, but it has not always been so. Further, the emphasis of that spending is different, reflecting different incentives and opportunities available to the private sector.[11]

U.S. Private Agricultural Research Spending

According to Dehmer and Pardey (2010), in 2006 $4.6 billion of privately performed research in the United States was directed towards food and agriculture, compared with a total in 1953 of just $90.5 million ($929 million in 2000 prices) (Figure 6-6, Panel a).[12] This implies an annual average rate of growth in private food and agricultural R&D of 7.40 percent per year over the period 1953–2006 (or 2.63 percent per year after deflating by the Pardey, Andersen and Alston (2009) agricultural R&D price index). The highest sustained real rate of growth (4.56 percent per year) was realized in the period 1953–1980, a period of correspondingly rapid growth in public investment in agricultural R&D. Real growth slowed during the 1980s and early 1990s (0.19 percent per year for 1986–1992), but picked up pace during the latter part of the 1990s (5.96 percent per year during the period 1993–1998) as large agricultural chemical, machinery, and food companies ramped up their investments in agricultural research in the United States, along with a substantial number of smaller, new entrants (King 2001; King and Schimmelpfennig 2005). Private food and agricultural R&D spending declined immediately thereafter—from $4.2 billion (nominal dollars) in 1998 to

10 Details reported here are based on Pardey et al. (2006) and the underlying more-detailed data.

11 For prior compilations and interpretations of U.S. agricultural R&D spending data see Huffman and Evenson (1993 and 2006a), Alston and Pardey (1996 and 2006a and 2006b), Fuglie et al. (1996) and Schimmelpfennig and Heisey (2009).

12 The Dehmer and Pardey (2010) series is an entirely new compilation of U.S. private food and agricultural R&D spending. Prior compilations can be found in Pray and Neumeyer (1989), updated by Klotz, Fuglie and Pray (1995), and Huffman and Evenson (2000, pp. 105-106).

Figure 6-6 U.S. Private and Public Agricultural R&D, 1950–2007

Panel a. Public, private and total U.S. agricultural R&D, 1950–2007

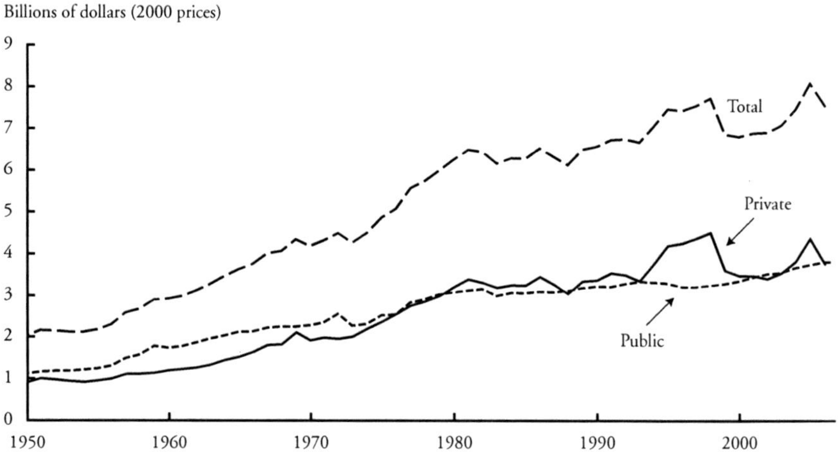

Panel b. Private percentage shares of R&D, 1950s and 2000s

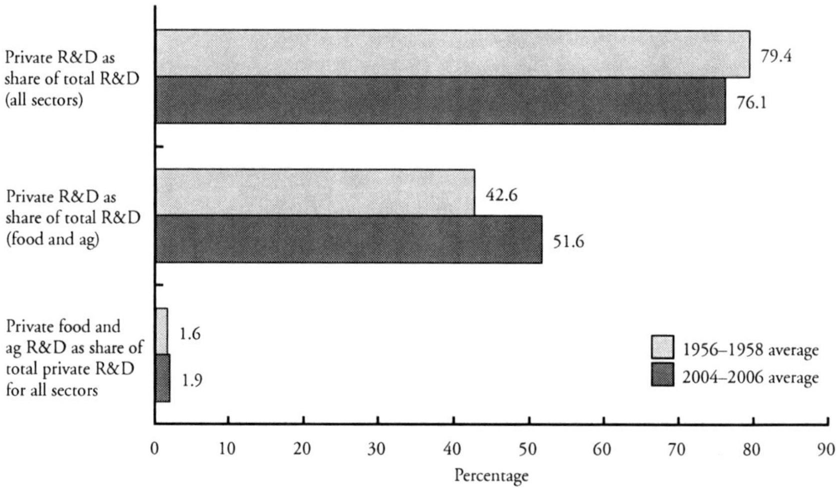

Sources: Public agricultural research series (exclusive of forestry) from Appendix Table 6-1. Private food and agricultural research series (also exclusive of forestry) from Dehmer and Pardey (2010). For private science spending see Figure 6-1. Implicit GDP deflator from BEA (2008b) used to deflate all R&D spending series.

Notes: Private agricultural R&D series ends in 2006.

$3.5 billion in 1999—a prelude to the more general reduction in private research spending noted above. It then recovered (even after adjusting for inflation) for a few years beginning in 2001, only to falter again in 2006.

The public and private agricultural R&D sectors grew hand in hand over the past 50 years. During the twenty-five year period after 1950 (the first year of data reported in Figure 6-6, Panel a), public spending exceeded private spending on agricultural R&D. Thereafter, private spending marginally exceeded public spending in most but not all years.

Figure 6-6, Panel b reports various private R&D spending shares, comparing a three-year average for 1956–1958 with the recent three-year period 2004–2006. About 76 percent of all U.S. R&D was performed by private firms in the more-recent period, compared with just under 80 percent in the earlier period.[13] Agriculture appears to have slightly increased its share of total private R&D in the United States—from an estimated 1.6 percent in the mid-1950s to 1.9 percent now. This growth in agriculture's share of private R&D may reflect the increased research and, especially, technological opportunities arising in the past several decades from fundamental advances in the genetic manipulation of crops and animals combined with an expansion in the scope of patentable, and thus appropriable, innovations described in Chapter 7. It contrasts with the major reduction in the share of federal government R&D spending directed towards agriculture over the past three to four decades, and might be related (to the extent that public and private research spending may be causally connected).

U.S. Public Agricultural Research Spending

In 2007, an estimated $9.4 billion was spent on food and agricultural R&D performed in the United States—including intramural research undertaken by the USDA and the State Agricultural Experiment Stations (SAESs) plus the private-sector totals discussed immediately above. This total represented just 2.6 percent of the total spending on all areas of R&D in the United States in 2007 (Figure 6-7). The public sector performed just over 51 percent of agricultural R&D compared with only 21.7 percent of the total for all areas of R&D. Almost 35 percent of total agricultural R&D in 2007 was performed by universities and colleges compared with 14.9 percent for R&D generally; similarly, 16.7 percent of agricultural R&D was performed in federal government research labs, compared with 6.7 percent for R&D overall.

These contemporary differences in shares no doubt reflect, at least in part, the institutional and legislative histories of government involvement in agricultural R&D versus other forms of research. They might also reflect differences in the nature of the science and the economic sectors being served by that science.

---

13 The private share of agricultural R&D is substantially less; averaging around 52 percent over 2004–2006 compared with 43 percent over 1956–1958.

Figure 6-7 U.S. R&D Spending by Performing Sectors, 2007

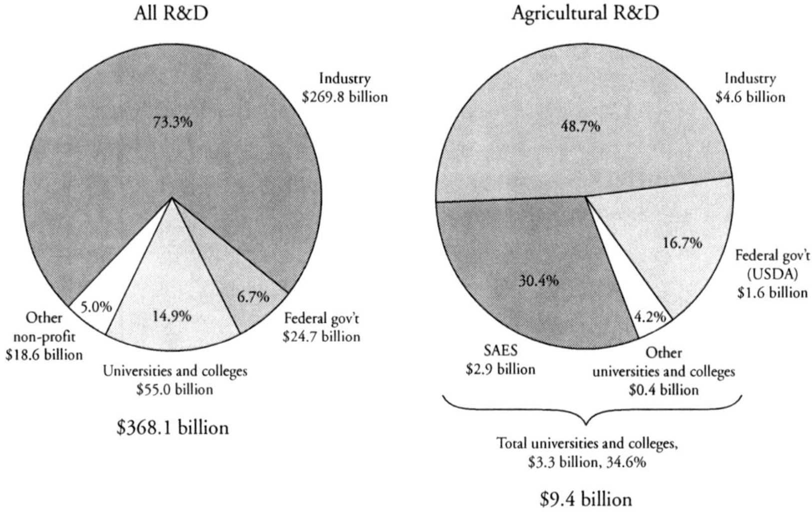

Sources: All R&D spending figures are from NSF (2008b). For public agricultural research series see Appendix Table 6-1 (SAES excludes forestry). Private food and agricultural research series are from Dehmer and Pardey (2010).

Notes: All figures are in nominal U.S. dollars. The "Other Univ & Colleges" category of agricultural R&D spending includes 1890 Colleges and Veterinary Schools. The agricultural R&D series includes spending in all 50 U.S. states (plus Washington, D.C.), and excludes research expenditures by Forestry Schools, which are reported by USDA CRIS to total $168.8 million in 2007. The private or industry food and agricultural R&D estimate is for the year 2006.

Agricultural production takes up a lot of physical space—almost 55 percent of the contiguous U.S. land mass is devoted to agriculture (Lubowski et al. 2002; Homer et al. 2007).[14] Moreover, the biological basis of most agricultural production processes and their interaction with characteristics of land and climate, mean that location plays a critical role. Matching agricultural innovations (like new crop varieties or pest- and disease-control methods) to the context in which these new ideas and technologies are to be used is an important determinant of the success of most agricultural innovations. Locating agricultural R&D facilities (be they the central or satellite campuses of the SAESs, or the regional research labs and personnel employed by the USDA) in the agroecologies being served by that science helps orient the research to those site-specific realities. However, the optimal location of particular research activities may involve trading off the advantages of specific locations against economies of size, scale, and scope, giv-

14 Lubowski et al. (2002) estimated that the 2002 agricultural share would increase from 54.7 percent to 61.8 percent for the 48-contiguous state total if grazed forestland was also included. Foley et al. (2005) estimated that around 40 percent of the world's land mass was devoted to agriculture (crops and pastureland) in the 1990s.

ing rise to more-centralized or spatially concentrated modes of conducting the research.[15]

6.4 Trends in U.S. Public Agricultural Research and Extension Spending

In 1889, shortly after the Hatch Act was passed, federal and state spending appropriations for agricultural R&D totaled $1.12 million. Over a century later, in 2007 the public agricultural R&D enterprise had grown to $4.82 billion, an annual rate of growth of 7.09 percent per year in nominal terms and 3.72 percent per year in real (i.e., inflation adjusted) terms.[16] For much of the first half of the 20th Century (specifically, 1903–1942), intramural USDA and SAES research accounted for roughly equal shares of public research spending, after which the SAES share grew to a peak of 75 percent of total public spending on agricultural R&D in 2002 (Figure 6-8). Thereafter, nominal SAES spending (excluding forestry) grew by 3.01 percent per year while corresponding intramural USDA spending grew by 10.29 percent per year, such that the USDA share of U.S. public agricultural R&D increased from its recent low of 25.1 percent in 2002 to 32.6 percent in 2007.

Beginning in the middle of the 20th Century, U.S. agricultural R&D spending experienced several distinct growth phases. Building on the science successes during the Second World War and spurred by a widespread, post-war consensus about the benefits that science could bring—as reflected to great political effect in the Vannevar Bush report *Science: The Endless Frontier*, commissioned by President Roosevelt and presented to President Truman in July 1945—public and private spending on all science, including agricultural R&D, surged during

15 In considering the diseconomies of distance associated with many agricultural innovations, Alston and Pardey (1999, p. 18) observed, "One way to think of this is in terms of the unit costs of making local research results applicable to other locations (say, by adaptive research), which must be added to the local research costs. Such costs grow with the size of the market. A close analogy can be drawn with spatial market models of food processing in which processing costs fall with throughput but input and output transportation costs rise with throughput so that when the two elements of costs are combined a U-shaped average cost function is derived (e.g., Sexton 1990). Economies of size, scale, and scope in research mean that unit costs fall with size of the R&D enterprise, but these economies must be traded off against the diseconomies of distance and adapting site-specific results (the costs of 'transporting' the research results to economically "more distant" locations). Thus, as the size of the research enterprise increases, unit costs are likely to decline at first (because economies of size are relatively important) but will eventually rise (as the costs of economic distance become ever-more important)." See, also, Jin et al. (2005).

16 These figures are net of forestry research; including it would increase total public agricultural R&D spending to $4.99 billion in 2007. To convert research spending from nominal values to real terms reflecting the purchasing power of the spending, in this book we divide nominal spending by an index of the unit costs of agricultural research, a price index for agricultural R&D, documented by Pardey, Andersen and Alston (2009). To reflect the opportunity cost of that spending we might alternatively deflate by a general price index such as the price deflator for GDP.

Figure 6-8 U.S. Public-Sector Agricultural R&D Spending by Performing Agencies, 1890–2007

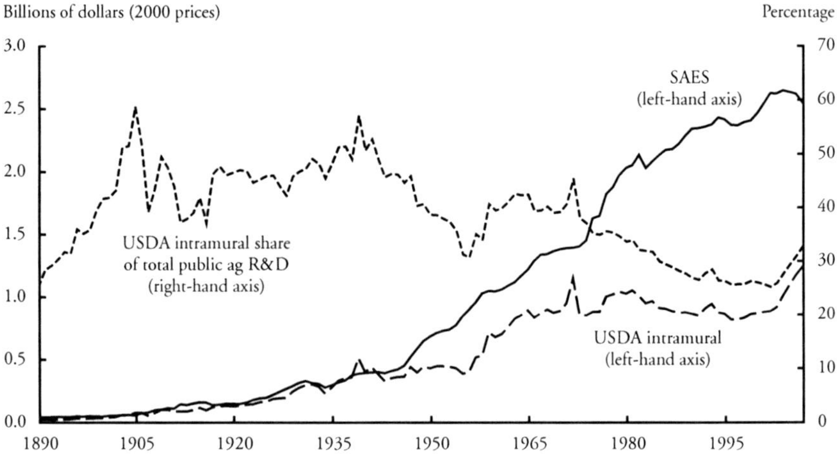

Sources: SAES research series (total excluding forestry research) and USDA intramural series from Appendix Table 6-1. Nominal research expenditure data were deflated by a U.S. agricultural research price index reported in Pardey, Andersen and Alston (2009).

Notes: SAES total includes 48 contiguous states, excluding Alaska and Hawaii which totaled $34.3 million in 2007 (or $26.9 million in 2000 prices)—just 1 percent of the 50 state total. These data are inclusive of all but the forestry R&D performed by the SAESs, other cooperating institutions and the USDA.

the 1950s and 1960s (Figure 6-9, Panel a).[17] Thereafter the real rate of growth of U.S. science spending progressively slowed to 3.16 percent per year during 1970–2006 and 2.94 percent per year for 1990–2006. The slowdown in total agricultural R&D spending growth has been even more dramatic: from 4.03 percent per year during the years 1953–1970, to 1.65 percent per year for 1970–2006, and 0.88 percent per year for 1990–2006 (Figure 6-9, Panel c). The slowdown has affected public and private agricultural R&D spending alike.

Figure 6-9, Panel b, which uses an implicit GDP deflator to account for inflation (compared with the specific agricultural R&D deflator used to deflate the same nominal spending series in Figure 6-9, Panel c), indicates that the magnitude of the slowdown in real agricultural R&D spending growth is sensitive to the price deflator deployed, but reinforces the finding that the rate of growth

17 Barfield (1997, pp. 2-3) observed that "By all contemporary accounts, the [Bush] report became an instant success, enjoying widespread editorial support and commendation that transcended party, geography, and ideology. Because the principles set forth in the Bush report subsequently became the foundation stone of postwar U.S. science policy, they now have 'achieved a kind of timeless, abstract quality,' notes science historian Daniel J. Kevles (1990, reprinted 1992). The reality … is that the Bush Report was not the product of 'above-the-fray' philosopher-kings but rather the conscious attempt by wartime science administrators such as Bush … not only to create a new federal responsibility but also to set the terms and rules by which that responsibility would be carried out."

Figure 6-9 Research Spending Slowdown

Panel a. Average annual percentage change in overall science spending (deflated using implicit GDP deflator)

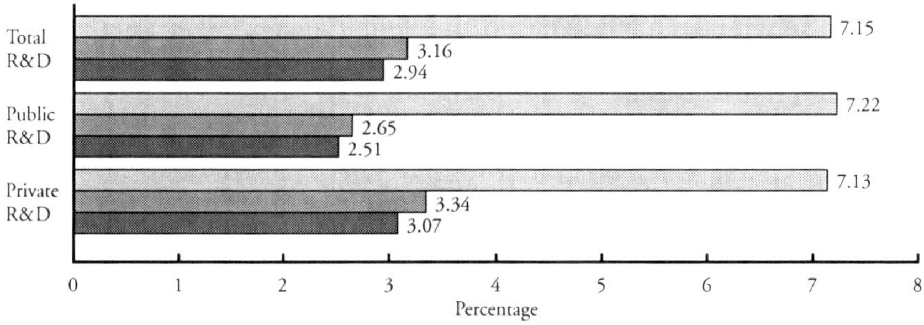

Panel b. Average annual percentage change in agricultural R&D spending (deflated using implicit GDP deflator)

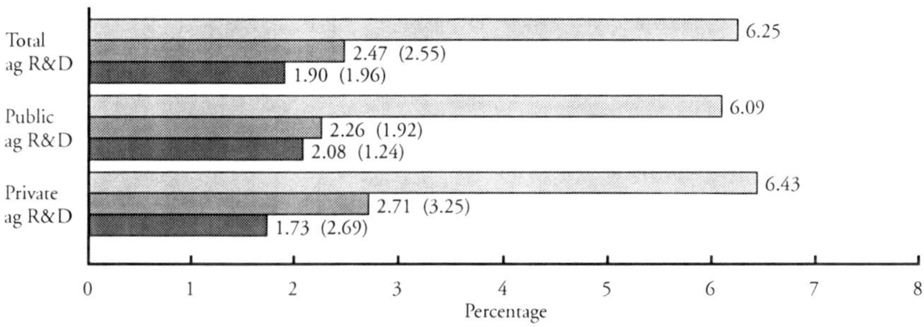

Panel c. Average annual percentage change in agricultural R&D spending (deflated using agricultural R&D deflator)

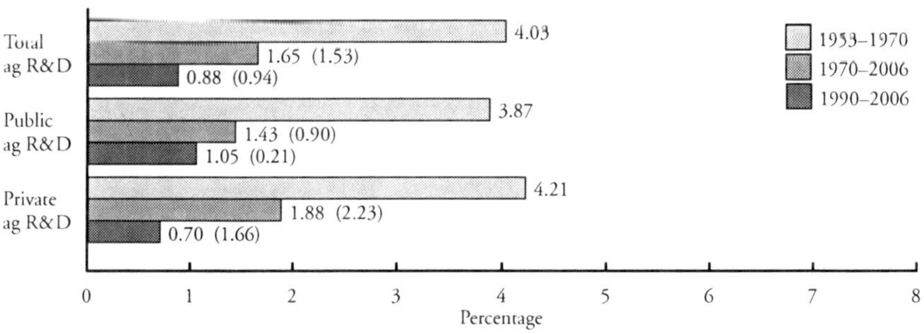

Sources: Figures are adapted from Dehmer and Pardey (2010). Public agricultural R&D series (excluding forestry) are from Appendix Table 0-1. Private agricultural R&D series (also excluding forestry) are from Dehmer and Pardey (2010). Total R&D is from NSF (2008a). Numbers in parentheses are rates of growth of productivity-oriented research based on extractions from unpublished USDA CRIS data tapes (see Figure 6-11). The agricultural R&D deflator is from Pardey, Andersen and Alston (2009) and the implicit GDP deflator is from BEA (2008b).

Notes: Average annual growth rates are calculated using the exponential growth rate (which assumes continuous growth), as described, for example, by World Bank (2009) and Box 5-1, Chapter 5. Growth rates of productivity-oriented research for post-1970 are for 1975–2006.

Figure 6-10 Commodity Orientation of Public Agricultural Research Spending, 1975 and 2007

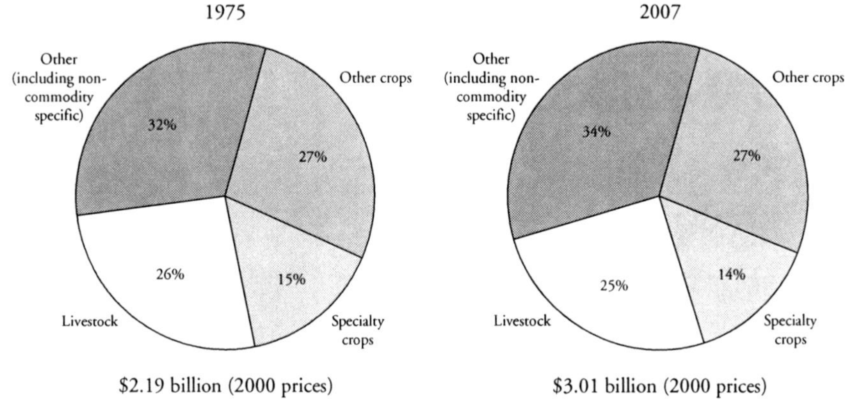

Sources: Extracted by authors from unpublished USDA CRIS data tapes.

Notes: Public agricultural research includes SAES and intramural USDA agricultural R&D spending for 48 states, exclusive of research on forestry, rangeland, recreation and wildlife, game birds and animals, pets, laboratory animals, aquaculture and fisheries, horses, ponies, and mules.

in real spending was much slower after 1970 than in the previous two decades. Setting aside differences resulting from the use of different deflators, comparing Panels a and b in Figure 6-9 reinforces the finding that the more-recent slowdown in agricultural R&D spending is consistent with the trend for U.S. science spending generally. Nevertheless, in all sub-periods total spending on private and public science grew faster than spending on agricultural R&D such that agricultural R&D as a share of total U.S. science spending gradually slipped from 4.0 percent in 1953 to an estimated 2.6 percent in 2006.[18]

Commodity Orientation

Figure 6-10 shows the allocation of total U.S. public agricultural R&D spending (including both USDA intramural and SAES expenditure) over time between commodity-specific and other (i.e., non-commodity specific) research. The shares of spending have been fairly constant over time, with no major discernible trend among the main categories.

Table 6-2 also shows the allocation of the research directed towards specific commodities between crops versus livestock research; among the major catego-

---

18 Real agricultural R&D spending grew by 0.88 percent per year after 1990 (Figure 6-9, Panel c) but this period average masks a recent rebound of sorts. During 2000–2006, total agricultural R&D spending, after adjusting for inflation, grew by 1.74 percent per year, compared with just 0.36 percent per year during the 1990s (and just 0.49 percent per year during the 1980s). This 21st Century rate of growth is still well below the rate of growth during the 1950s (an average of 4.62 percent per year for 1953–1960), the 1960s (3.61 percent per year), and the 1970s (4.05 percent per year).

Table 6-2 Commodity Orientation of U.S. Public Agricultural R&D Spending, 1975–2007

	1975	1980	1990	2000	2007
Expenditures			*millions of dollars (2000 prices)*		
Crops total	934.6	1,178.9	1,220.9	1,229.1	1,227.5
Specialty crops	336.9	412.6	434.2	434.3	420.5
Vegetables	131.5	168.2	195.3	193.9	171.6
Fruits and nuts	148.1	173.0	172.2	170.5	168.7
Ornamentals	57.3	71.5	66.7	69.9	80.1
Other (non specialty crops)	597.7	766.3	786.7	794.9	807.0
Grains and oilseeds	275.6	365.5	412.5	426.9	413.7
Pasture and forage	77.2	110.9	95.2	73.7	67.5
Other crops	244.8	289.9	278.9	294.3	325.8
Livestock total	567.5	735.2	807.1	775.6	766.9
Beef cattle	180.6	248.2	224.3	181.2	195.6
Dairy cattle	142.7	169.8	175.8	162.2	156.1
Poultry	98.7	105.2	116.6	113.4	101.4
Swine	75.2	100.1	116.6	120.3	86.1
Other livestock	70.2	111.8	173.9	198.4	227.8
Other total (includes non-commodity)	689.9	723.5	770.5	834.4	1,023.2
All Research	*2,192.0*	*2,637.6*	*2,798.5*	*2,839.1*	*3,017.7*
Expenditure shares			*percentage*		
Crops total	42.6	44.7	43.6	43.3	40.7
Livestock total	25.9	27.9	28.8	27.3	25.4
Other total (includes non-commodity)	31.5	27.4	27.5	29.4	33.9
Share of crop total					
Specialty crops	36.0	35.0	35.6	35.3	34.3
Vegetables	14.1	14.3	16.0	15.8	14.0
Fruits and nuts	15.8	14.7	14.1	13.9	13.7
Ornamentals	6.1	6.1	5.5	5.7	6.5
Other (non specialty crops)	64.0	65.0	64.4	64.7	65.7
Grains and oilseeds	29.5	31.0	33.8	34.7	33.7
Pasture and forage	8.3	9.4	7.8	6.0	5.5
Other crops	26.2	24.6	22.8	23.9	26.5
Share of livestock total					
Beef cattle	31.8	33.8	27.8	23.4	25.5
Dairy cattle	25.1	23.1	21.8	20.9	20.4
Poultry	17.4	14.3	14.4	14.6	13.2
Swine	13.3	13.6	14.4	15.5	11.2
Other livestock	12.4	15.2	21.5	25.6	29.7

Sources: Extracted by the authors from unpublished USDA CRIS data tapes. Nominal research expenditure data were deflated by a U.S. agricultural research price index reported in Pardey, Andersen and Alston (2009).

Notes: Public agricultural research includes all SAES and intramural USDA spending, exclusive of research on forestry, rangeland, recreation and wildlife, game birds and animals, pets, laboratory animals, aquaculture and fisheries, horses, ponies and mules. "Other total" includes food (not readily associated with specific plant and animal products), economic and other social science research, basic R&D and environmental and resource-related research not directly attributable to a particular commodity.

ries within crops (i.e., grains and oilseeds, pasture and forage, other crops), the main categories of specialty crops (i.e., vegetables, fruits and nuts, and ornamentals) and the most-valuable livestock commodities. The top half of Table 6-2 includes real expenditures (deflated to 2000 values), while the bottom half of the table includes those expenditures expressed as shares of different sub-totals.

While the allocations across major categories have been fairly stable over time, more substantial changes have been made in the allocations within major categories (e.g., consider beef cattle versus other livestock). Specialty crops research has been a fairly constant share of expenditure on crop-specific research (about 35 percent). Crops research has held a fairly constant, but in more recent decades slightly declining, share of total research; inching up from 42.6 percent in 1975 to 44.7 percent in 1980 then drifting down to 40.7 percent by 2007.[19] Combining these two effects, the specialty crops share of total public agricultural research spending was fairly stable, between 14 and 16 percent over the 26 years 1980 through 2007. In turn, the allocation of specialty crops research among major categories was also fairly stable over the 25 year period, with roughly equal shares going to fruit and nuts and to vegetables (14 to 16 percent each out of the 35 percent spent on crops research) and a smaller share going to ornamentals (about 6 percent of the 35 percent). Among the non-specialty crops categories, "grains and oilseeds" increased its share, from 29.5 percent in 1975 to 33.7 percent in 2007. The "pasture and forage crops" category lost ground (from 8.3 percent in 1975 to 5.5 percent in 2007), while a group of "other crops" (including narcotic plants, mint, coffee, cocoa, tea, rubber and miscellaneous crops that were not specifically identified) had about the same share in 2007 as it did in 1975.

Productivity Orientation

Enhanced productivity as a result of agricultural R&D means that consumers have access to a more abundant, cheaper, safer, higher-quality, and more diverse and convenient food supply, perhaps produced with lower stress on the natural resource base and the environment. But the relevant comparison is not against a counterfactual scenario in which productivity would be sustained even without any R&D. In fact, some (privately and socially profitable) agricultural R&D is necessary simply to maintain productivity. If R&D were to cease altogether, the typical scenario would be one of declining agricultural productivity or crop yields, and rising costs, not simply a continuation of current (or baseline) yields and costs. Significant investments in so-called "maintenance" research, particularly in plant breeding, plant pathology, and entomology, are required just to maintain productivity. Various estimates indicate that 35 to 70 percent of U.S.

19 A substantial amount of agricultural R&D not reported as crop-related R&D nonetheless has implications for production of crops generally or a particular crop.

Figure 6-11 Share of SAES Research Oriented to Farm Productivity, 1975–2007

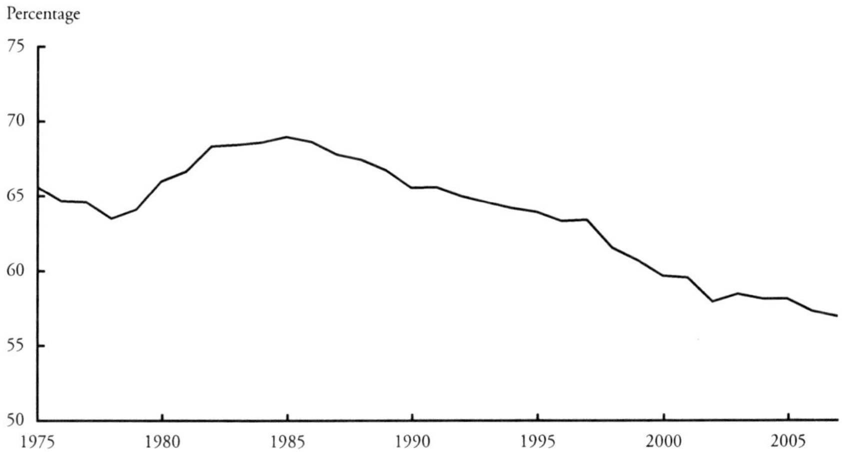

Sources: Extracted by authors from unpublished USDA CRIS data tapes. SAES total (inclusive of forestry research) from Appendix Table 6-1 was used to form productivity shares.

Notes: Details of what constitutes productivity-oriented agricultural R&D given in Appendix III.

agricultural research could be considered as research intended to maintain productivity and prevent it from falling.[20]

Figure 6-9 reveals a gradual ratcheting down in the rate of growth in public agricultural R&D spending during the past several decades. The consequences of that slowdown in spending growth for the future path of productivity may be exacerbated by the fact that the United States has also reduced the share of its total agricultural R&D investment spent on R&D designed to increase, or at least maintain, agricultural productivity.[21] In 1975 around 66 percent ($317.8 million) of all SAES research was so oriented. During the subsequent few years, that share fell a little, before rising to 69 percent in 1985 (Figure 6-11).[22] The subsequent two decades saw a sizable and sustained reduction in the productivity

20 See Heim and Blakeslee (1986), Swallow et al. (1985), and Adusei and Norton (1990) for a range of earlier estimates. Sparger (2009) reported results from a 2008 survey of U.S. agricultural scientists that suggested the share of commodity research directed to maintenance had risen to around 41 percent relative to the 35 percent estimate for the mid-1980s reported by Adusei and Norton (1990).

21 Having classified the reported research-problem-area (RPA) orientation of the individual research programs in each of the SAESs, we could use the CRIS data to estimate the share of total SAES research directed to maintaining or enhancing farm productivity. See Appendix III for more details.

22 This increase might have been in response to concerns about a shortage of world food supplies spurred by a surge in global food prices in the early 1970s (Alston, Beddow and Pardey 2009). As Ruttan (1980, p. 540) noted "Support [for agricultural research] tends to emerge during periods of sharply rising prices and to be rapidly dissipated during periods of relative price stability."

Figure 6-12 Shares of SAES Research Oriented to Farm Productivity, by State

Panel a. State distributions, 1975 and 2007

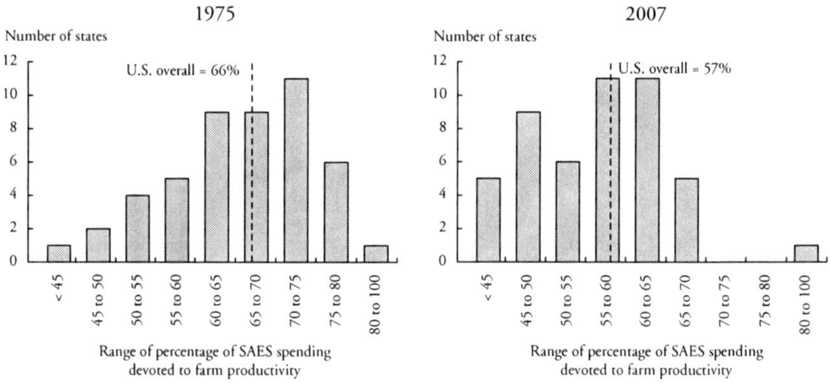

Panel b: Share of SAES research oriented to farm productivity, 2007

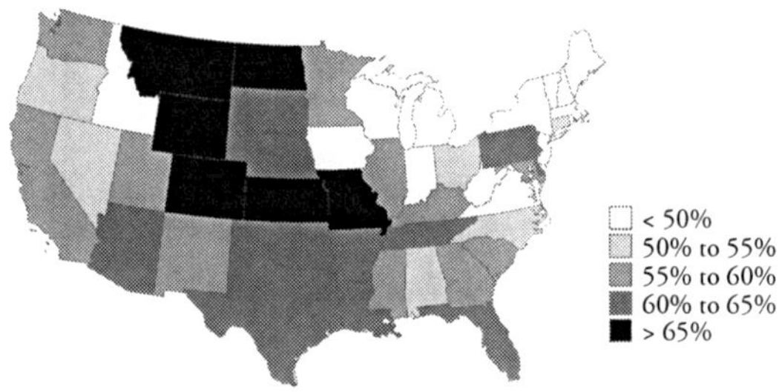

Sources: See Figure 6-11.

orientation of SAES research. By 2007 only 57 percent ($1.9 billion) of SAES research sought to raise or maintain farm productivity.

In Panels b and c of Figure 6-9, period-specific growth rates for productivity-oriented total, public and private R&D spending for various post-1949 periods are included in parentheses, next to the corresponding percentage growth rates for all agricultural R&D spending. The public series is based on the data underlying Figure 6-8, whereas the productivity-oriented private series excludes food (processing) oriented research from the corresponding private total for R&D on food and agriculture. The shift away from productivity-oriented public R&D is most pronounced. During the period 1990–2006, all public (i.e., SAES and intramural USDA) agricultural research grew by 1.05 percent per year, but productivity related agricultural research grew by just 0.21 percent per year. Farm-productivity-oriented agricultural R&D undertaken by the private sector—taken to encompass agricultural input, on-farm oriented research—was estimated to grow faster (1.66 percent per year) than the broader aggregate of all private agricultural

Figure 6-13 Public R&D and Extension Expenditures, 1890–2006

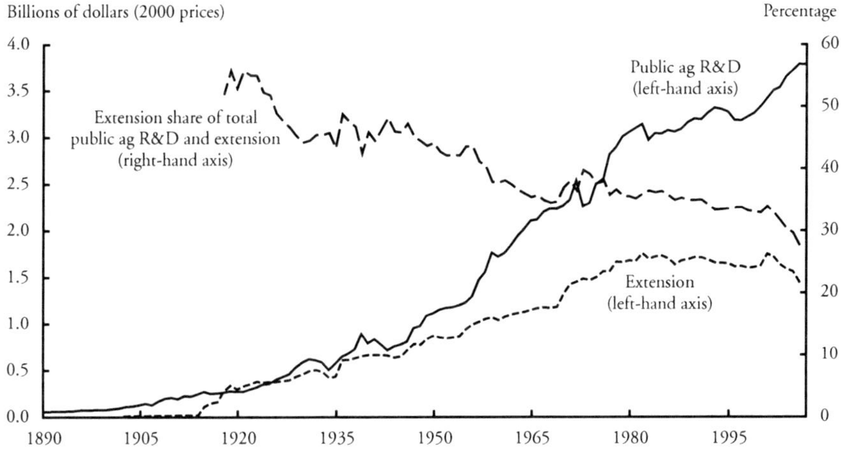

Sources: Public agricultural R&D is the sum of expenditures by the 48 SAESs and intramural USDA agricultural R&D as described in Appendix III. The extension series was obtained from U.S. House of Representatives and USDA CSREES sources as detailed in Appendix III. Nominal extension and research spending were deflated to 2000 prices using an agricultural R&D deflator from Pardey, Andersen and Alston (2009).

Notes: Public agricultural R&D includes SAES and USDA intramural spending, exclusive of forestry research.

and (post-farm) food research (0.70 percent per year), reflecting a shift in the share of private research related to food (Dehmer and Pardey 2010).

The productivity orientation of SAES research varies markedly among U.S. states (Figure 6-12). In 2007, at one extreme barely 37 percent of SAES research in Rhode Island was related to farm productivity, compared with nearly 83 percent in Colorado, at the other extreme. The variation in the share of farm productivity oriented R&D in SAES research among states exhibits some spatial structure. The smaller Northeastern states spent an average of only 50 percent on farm productivity research in 2007, compared with nearly 66 percent in the Mountain and Northern Plains states.

Extension Trends

In 1915, federal funds were made available for the first time to support cooperative extension involving the USDA and various state extension agencies. In that year, almost \$1.5 million of federal funds were combined with \$2.1 million made available from various state and local government sources for a total of \$3.6 million. This total grew by 6.80 percent per year to reach \$1.76 billion by 2006 (Figure 6-13). Extension spending grew hand in hand with public spending on agricultural R&D for much of the first half of the 20th Century. Then, during the period 1950–1980, inflation-adjusted growth in extension spending slowed

Table 6-3 Full-Time Equivalent Personnel in USDA and SAES Research, 1975–2007

	1975	1985	1995	2007
Scientific years		*full-time equivalents*		
SAESs				
Pacific	790	1,109	997	986
Mountain	588	707	692	634
Northern Plains	487	560	546	549
Southern Plains	855	1,007	1,011	910
Central	1,132	1,283	1,393	1,557
Southeast	1,473	1,617	1,600	1,489
Northeast	894	995	1,081	1,347
48 states total	6,219	7,278	7,319	7,472
USDA total	3,650	3,077	2,679	2,581
USDA and SAESs total	9,869	10,355	9,998	10,053
Professional, technical, and clerical years				
SAESs, 48 states total	15,406	23,156	26,278	25,884
USDA total	6,730	6,350	5,611	6,363
USDA and SAESs total	22,136	29,506	31,889	32,247
Full-time equivalent, total				
SAESs, 48 states total	21,624	30,434	33,598	33,357
USDA total	10,381	9,427	8,290	8,944
USDA and SAESs total	32,005	39,861	41,887	42,300

Sources: Extracted by the authors from unpublished USDA CRIS data tapes.

Notes: Researchers working in federal institutions require at least a GS11 ranking to be classified as scientists. Those working at non-federal institutions require at least an assistant professor rank to be so classified.

to 2.19 percent per year, compared with 3.73 percent per year for agricultural R&D. Subsequently, during the period 1980–2006, extension spending shrank by 0.57 percent per year compared with public agricultural R&D which continued to grow, but only by 1.03 percent per year.

Research Personnel

In line with Peterson's (1992) prediction, the demand for experiment station personnel has grown little over the past several decades. The number of scientific years in the SAESs increased by about 1,000 from the mid-1970s to the mid-1980s, but barely budged thereafter (Table 6-3). USDA scientific years declined from the mid-1970s to the mid-1990s until it reached its lowest point in 1998 (with 1,846 scientific years). By 2007, it had increased somewhat to 2,581 scientific years. In 2007, a total of 10,053 scientist-years were employed in the public agricultural R&D system in the United States, nearly 75 percent of whom worked in state experiment stations. Approximately three professional and technical staff-years were employed for every scientist year, for a total of 32,247 scientific, professional and technical full-time equivalent (fte) years in 2007 in the USDA and SAES systems.

Figure 6-14 Total Public Expenditure per Scientific Year, 1970–2007

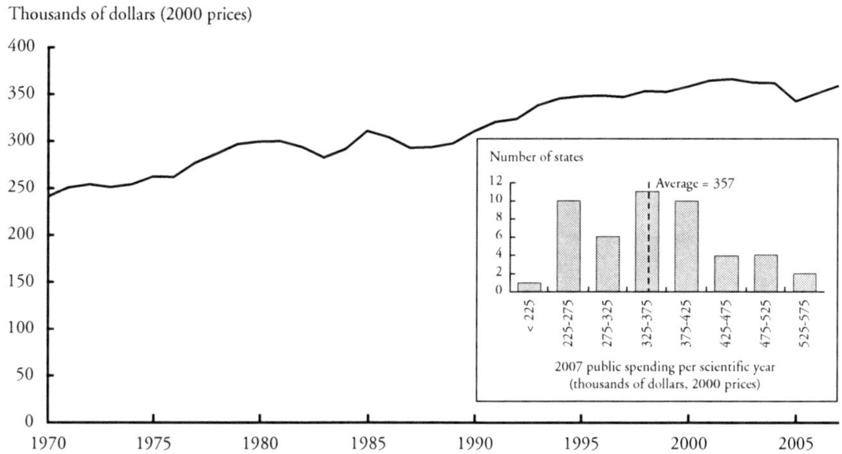

Sources: Extracted by the authors from unpublished USDA CRIS data tapes.

Notes: Data represent total SAES and USDA spending (including forestry) divided by the corresponding full-time-equivalent SAES and USDA research totals.

Since 1970, average spending per public scientist—combining those working in the SAESs and the USDA—trended up in inflation-adjusted terms by 1.09 percent per year, from around $239,046 (2000 prices) per fte scientist in 1970, to $357,337 per fte scientist in 2007 (Figure 6-14). The range around this average is quite large. In 2007, Delaware spent just $214,544 per scientist whereas 21 other states spent more than $375,000 per scientist, all measured in 2000 dollars (Figure 6-14, Inset). This variation reflects differences among the states in the types of research being done (e.g., basic versus applied, livestock versus crop, annual versus perennial plants), the mix, age and skills of scientists and support personnel, and the factor intensities (e.g., capital versus labor versus materials cost shares) of the R&D enterprise, among other things.

6.5 Intensity of Investment

Table 6-4 and Figure 6-15 include various ratios that express research and extension spending relative to alternative measures of agricultural output (farm value-added and agricultural GDP), farm area and numbers, and total and farm population. During the period 2004–2006, on average the United States spent $3.82 on public agricultural R&D for every $100 of farm value-added; almost $1,800 of research spending per farm; and around $2,543 for every square mile of farmed area. The extension spending ratios were typically about half the corresponding research spending ratios. The ratios expressing research spending per farm, farm area and farm population continued to grow throughout the entire

Table 6-4 U.S. Public Agricultural Research and Extension Intensities, 1891–2005

	1891	1910	1930	1950	1970	1990	2005
Relative to farm value-added				*dollars per $100*			
Research	0.04	0.11	0.39	0.45	1.83	3.03	3.82
Extension	0.00	0.01	0.32	0.34	1.05	1.62	1.56
Relative to agricultural GDP				*dollars per $100*			
Research	–	–	–	0.45	1.75	2.49	3.41
Extension	–	–	–	0.34	1.01	1.33	1.40
Relative to farm numbers				*dollars per farm (2000 prices)*			
Research	10.28	29.73	86.71	197.95	768.96	1,480.01	1,766.84
Extension	–	1.97	69.76	151.84	443.02	792.36	727.65
Relative to total population				*dollars per capita (2000 prices)*			
Research	0.75	2.06	4.62	7.31	11.11	12.71	12.51
Extension	–	0.14	3.72	5.61	6.39	6.81	5.16
Relative to farm population				*dollars per capita (2000 prices)*			
Research	1.90	5.93	18.55	48.18	231.52	662.79	1,281.24
Extension	–	0.39	14.92	36.95	133.57	354.84	527.67
Relative to total farm area				*dollars per square mile (2000 prices)*			
Research	47.79	137.89	368.05	597.02	1,316.70	2,060.37	2,542.92
Extension	–	9.13	296.11	458.22	758.18	1,103.07	1,047.43

Sources: For research and extension data, see Figures 6-8 and 6-13 and Appendix III. General population data for 1869–1999 are from Haines and Sutch (2006); values for 2000–2006 are from U.S. Bureau of the Census (2007). Farm population data for 1869–1970 are from U.S. Bureau of the Census (1975, series K-1) and Wells (1937), and 1971–1991 data are from Olmstead and Rhode (2006, series Da 1). Number of farms (1910–1999) and land in farms (1911–1999) are from Olmstead and Rhode (2006, series Da 4 and Da 5, respectively); values for 2000–2006 are from USDA ERS (2007). 1900 and 1890 values for farm numbers are from the U.S. Bureau of the Census (1975, series K-4 and K-5). 1910, 1900 and 1890 values for land in farms are from series K-5 of the same resource. Estimates of farm value-added for 1869–1928 were derived using U.S. Bureau of the Census (1975, series F-127); 1929–2006 are from BEA (2007a, NIPA Table 1.3.5). Agricultural GDP values are from BEA (2007c). Research and extension expenditures are expressed in 2000 prices using the deflator in Pardey, Andersen and Alston (2009).

Notes: Intensities are three-year averages centered on the year noted in the column heading. Research expenditures exclude forestry.

period 1890–2006 (Figure 6-15, Panel a). The stagnation in extension spending over the past several decades meant that extension spending per farm and per square mile of farm area also stalled after 1980 (Figure 6-15, Panel b). Extension spending per farm population continued growing until 1991, as the farm population continued to shrink (Figure 2-4) against a relatively stable trend in extension spending.

Variation in Intensities Among States

The spatial pattern of research (and extension) spending has never been especially congruent with the value of production. Figure 6-16, Panel a plots the state distribution of agricultural research spending intensities (here measuring research

Figure 6-15 U.S. Public Agricultural Research and Extension Intensities, 1890–2006

Panel a. Public agricultural R&D

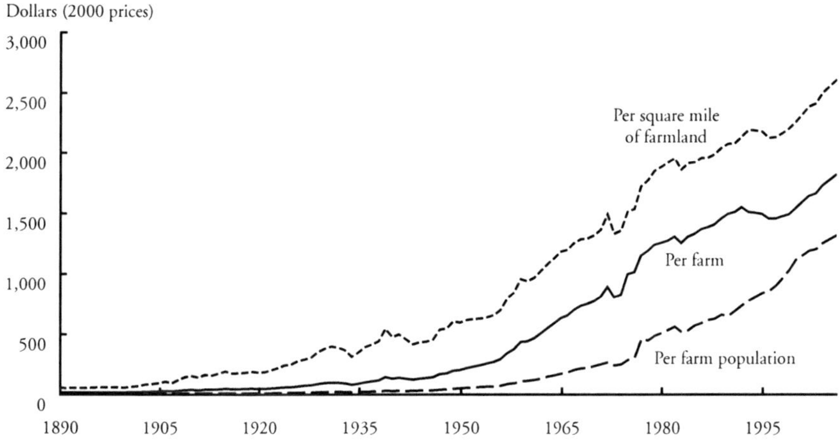

Panel b. Extension

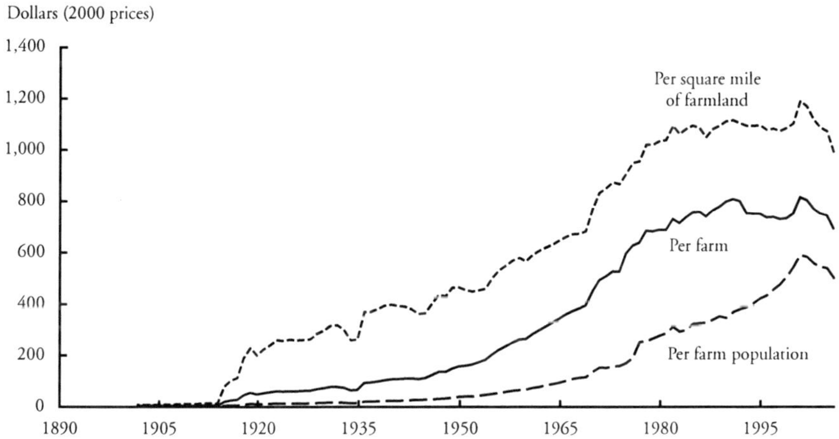

Sources: See Table 6-4.

spending as a percentage of the gross value of agricultural production) for various periods from 1924–1926 to 2003–2005. Panel b plots the same state distributions for the intensity of extension spending. Not only did the (national) median intensity of research and extension spending increase substantially over time, the dispersion of intensities among the states about that median increased markedly as well. During the first half of the 20th Century, the state distribution of research and extension intensities was quite tightly clustered. By the 1970s, and increasingly thereafter, the variation among states became more pronounced, mainly because of rapid growth in intensities in northeastern states like Rhode Island,

Figure 6-16 Distribution of State Agricultural Research and Extension Intensities, 1924–2005

Panel a. Research intensities

Panel b. Extension intensities

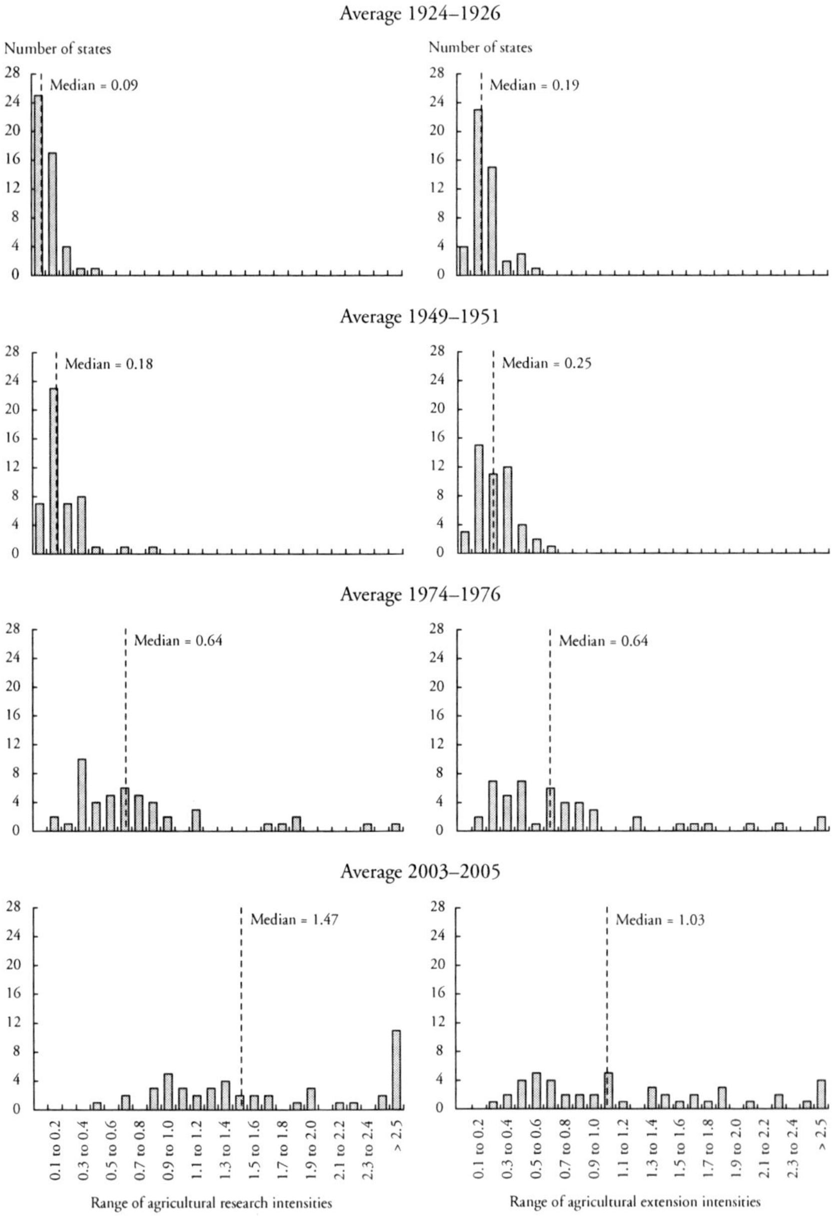

Sources: Agricultural R&D spending excludes forestry, and is from Appendix Table 6-1. See Figure 4-1 for details of value of production series used to form research and extension intensity ratios.

Notes: Plots represent the number of states in each research intensity range for each period. Data are the average intensity ratios for each state over the years in each period.

Figure 6-17 Agricultural Research and Extension Intensities by State, 2003–2005

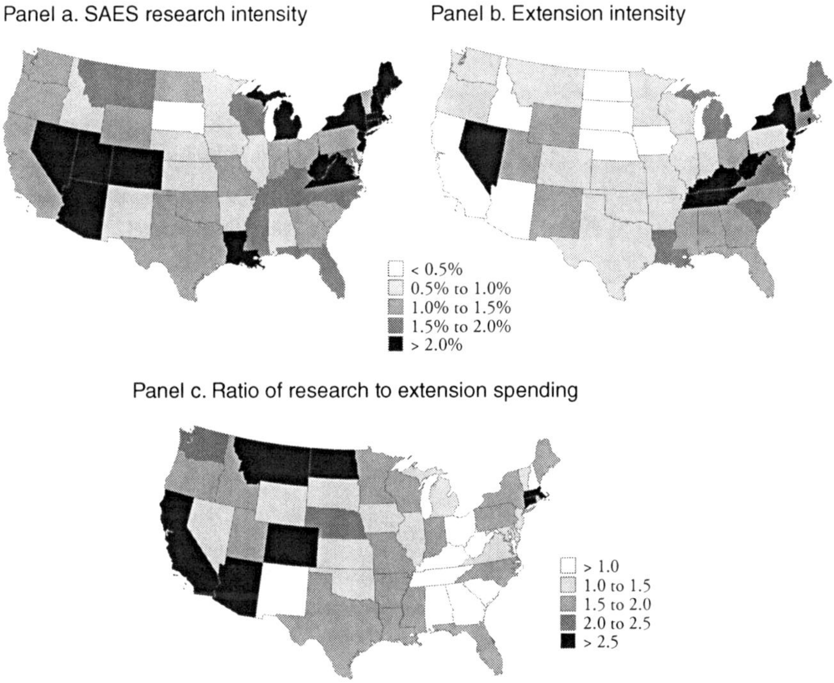

Sources: See Table 6-4 and Figure 6-16.

Massachusetts, New York, Connecticut and New Hampshire. For example, in the mid-1920s, 25 states spent less than 10 cents on research for every $100 of agricultural output. The highest research intensity was 44 cents per $100 (for Rhode Island), which was 24 times the lowest intensity (nearly 2 cents per $100 for Georgia). By the mid-2000s, 37 states spent more than $1 on research for every $100 of output. Rhode Island had a research intensity of $6.83 that topped the 48 states at nearly 15 times greater than that of the bottom-ranked state, South Dakota, whose intensity was $0.47 for every $100 of agricultural output. In 2003–2005, to distribute R&D spending according to the value of production would have required reallocating approximately $538 million of research resources per year from the 28 states with the largest intensities (which tend to be the states with the relatively small shares of national production value) to the 20 states with the smaller intensities.

A geographical perspective on the intensity of investment in research and extension averaged over the 2003–2005 period is given by Figure 6-17. Both research and extension intensities are comparatively high among states in the Northeast. Research intensities also tend to be high in the Mountain and Southeastern states, and those in the Northern Plains (and Central) states are at the lower end of the range. The Pacific and Northern Plains states have among the lowest intensities of investment in extension, typically less than one-third the average extension intensity among the much-higher-ranked Southeastern states (such as Tennessee, South Carolina and Louisiana).

Panel c in Figure 6-17 reveals the spatial distribution of research spending relative to extension spending among states. The range is from a high of $4.92 spent on research for every dollar spent on extension in Arizona to a low of $0.47 spent on research per dollar spent on extension in New Hampshire. Perhaps not surprising given the substantial differences in the sources of funds for research and extension, a high (or low) research intensity ratio is no guarantee of a correspondingly high (or low) research-to-extension spending ratio. For example, averaging over 2003–2005, Rhode Island had the highest research intensity but ranked 22nd in terms of its research-to-extension spending ratio (which is 1.70). Likewise, South Dakota had the lowest research intensity of 0.47 but ranked 32nd in terms of its research-to-extension ratio (of 1.45).

Commodity Congruence

Turning to a consideration of the commodity-by-commodity congruence between research funding and the value of production, Figure 6-18 shows the evolution of agricultural research intensity ratios for broad commodity categories since 1970. The research intensity for livestock has always been below that for crops, but the two have moved together, along with the total intensity for all commodity-specific research (Figure 6-18, Panel a). The overall research intensity ratio (which expresses all public agricultural R&D—i.e., including research targeted to specific commodities plus all non-commodity-specific R&D—relative to the total value of agricultural sales) rose steadily from 0.81 percent in 1970 to 1.60 percent in 2005, compared with the intensity of investment in commodity-specific R&D of 1.1 percent in 2005. This pattern is consistent with the finding that a sizable, and of late growing, share of public agricultural R&D does not target specific commodities. The U.S. public agricultural research agenda has increasingly focused on concerns such as food safety, food security, and the environmental implications of agriculture; programs of research that have little if any impact on enhancing or even maintaining farm-level productivity.

Crop-specific intensity ratios exhibit a variety of patterns (Figure 6-18, Panel b). Including all of the relevant commodities, there has been little change around an almost flat trend line for the intensity of public investment in specialty crops research. In contrast the intensity of investment in grains research (and hence all crop research) increased over time. Notably, however, specialty crops had a higher intensity of public research investment than (mainly grain) crops subject to price

Figure 6-18 Commodity Research Intensity Ratios, 1970–2005

Panel a. Overall intensity ratios

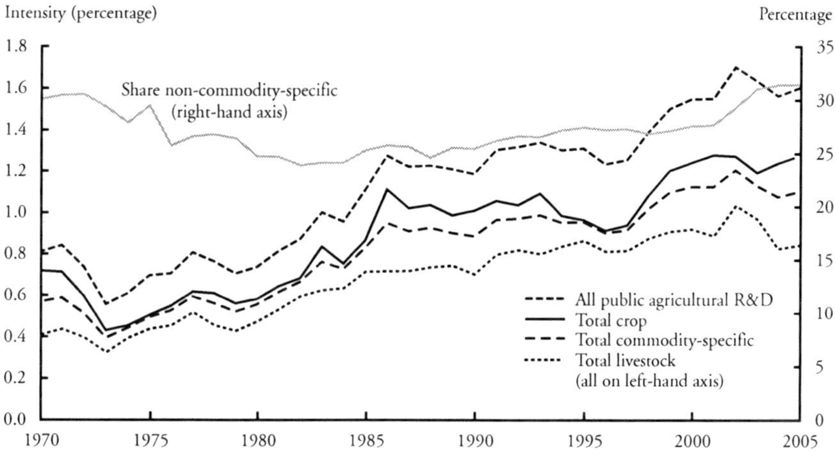

Panel b. Selected crop-specific intensity ratios

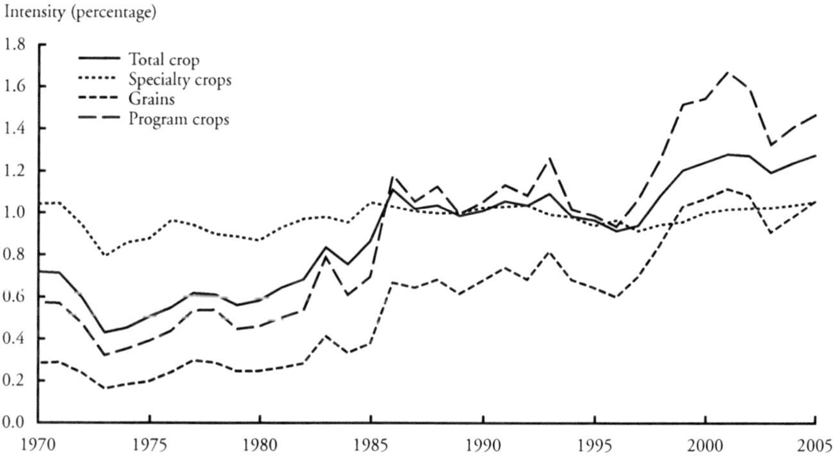

Sources: See Table 6-2 for details of commodity-specific agricultural R&D spending series, and Figure 4-1 for details of the value of production series used to form research intensity ratios.

Notes: Each agricultural research intensity ratio is the ratio of public agricultural research spending to the corresponding value of production. Public agricultural research includes the 48 state total SAES and intramural USDA spending, exclusive of research on forestry, rangeland, recreation and wildlife, game birds and animals, pets, laboratory animals, aquaculture and fisheries, horses, ponies, and mules. In Panel a, the "Total Livestock" series represents all commodity-specific research related to a specific livestock product or to multiple livestock products. The "Total Commodities" research series is the sum of total crops and total livestock research. The share of R&D that is non-commodity specific is also included, along with the ratio of all public agricultural R&D (total commodity plus non-commodity specific R&D) spending to the value of production. The value of production series excludes forestry, aquaculture and fisheries products. Ostensibly, farm gate (or first point of sale) prices and quantities produced (or marketed) by farms are used to form the value of production series. Panel b includes only public research identified as commodity-specific R&D. The "Total Crop" series includes all commodity-specific research related to a specific crop or to multiple crops along with a "Specialty Crops" and a "Grains" research grouping. "Program Crops" represent crops subject to government support programs (see footnote 23 in this chapter).

supports under various U.S. farm programs from 1970 to about the late 1990s.[23] Beginning in the mid 1990s, the intensity of R&D investment in program crops grew substantially to exceed that for specialty crops by a significant margin.

Figure 6-19 provides further commodity-specific detail on the pattern of agricultural output and the amount and intensity of public research spending for 2005. Total research spending on commodity-specific research was divided into SAES and USDA intramural research spending, and the agricultural research intensities were computed by dividing the total commodity-specific research spending by the corresponding gross value of production.

In Figure 6-19, Panel a, there is an apparent but loose concordance between the value of production of a given commodity (shown in the right-hand part of the figure) and the amount of public R&D spending (on the left)—higher-valued commodities garner greater R&D spending. However, the amount of R&D spending does not rise uniformly with the value of production. In Figure 6-19, Panel a, the more valuable commodities tend to have relatively low intensities of R&D spending (middle graph). This is especially apparent when comparing among crops. Figure 6-19, Panel b includes research spending, research intensity ratios, and value of production for a range of more minor (often specialty) crops.[24] The intensity of investment in these crops is often much higher than the intensities of investment in large-value commodities, such as cattle, milk, broilers, corn and soybeans. Large-acreage field crops have comparatively low public research spending per acre (and especially corn, wheat and soybeans, where less than two dollars per acre is spent on publicly performed R&D) while, for the smaller-acreage specialty crops, research spending per acre often exceeds 20 dollars, and in quite a few cases more than 40 dollars (see Alston and Pardey, 2008, Table 1). These spending patterns suggest that there may be economies of scale and size in research—solving a production problem for one acre solves it for all similar acres for any given crop.[25]

Spatial Patterns

Table 6-5 gives some perspective on the geographically dispersed nature of the performance of SAES research. Averaging across all 48 contiguous states, $67.8 million was spent per SAES in 2007, but with a large range around that average. California ranked first with $333.0 million of R&D (performed throughout the

23 "Program crops" represent crops subject to U.S. government price support programs, including corn, soybeans, upland cotton, wheat, rice, feed grains (barley, oats, and grain sorghum) peanuts, oilseeds, lentils, chickpeas, and dry edible beans.

24 The Specialty Crop Competitiveness Act of 2004 (Public Law108-465) defines specialty crops as fruits and vegetables, tree nuts, dried fruits, and nursery crops, including floriculture. Section 7311 (the Specialty Crops Research Initiative) of the 2008 Farm Bill maintained the definition from the 2004 Competitiveness Act.

25 Ruttan (1983) observed that research intensities were comparatively high for a number of smaller crops and questioned whether this allocation of research resources made economic sense.

Figure 6-19 Research Spending versus Value of Production, 2005

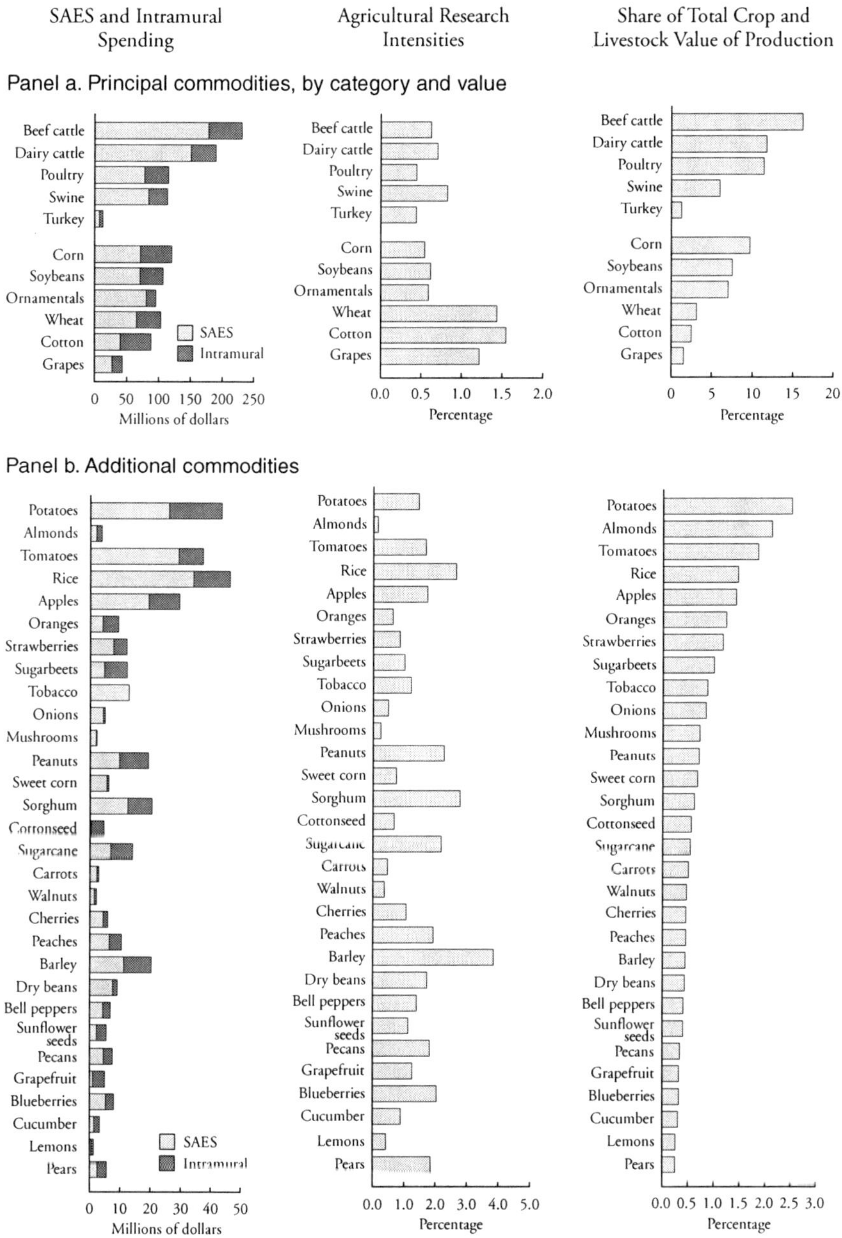

Sources: See Figure 6-18. SAES and intramural agricultural research includes spending as defined in Appendix Table 6-1, excluding forestry spending.

Notes: Value-of-production data described in Appendix II were used to form the research intensity ratio. Beef cattle, dairy cattle (including milk) and swine categories include meat and associated products; poultry includes meat, eggs, and associated products but excludes turkey, which is categorized separately here.

Table 6-5 SAES Research Spending Amounts, Intensities, and Sources of Support, circa 2007

	Performance in 2007		Sources of support (average 2005–2007)				R&D intensity (average 2003–2005)	
Rank	State	Current spending[a]	State	Federal share[b]	State	State share[c]	State	Intensity[d]
Top 10 states		*millions of dollars*		*percentage*		*percentage*		*percentage*
1	California	333.0	Massachusetts	75.3	Georgia	69.4	Rhode Island	6.83
2	New York	185.6	Vermont	70.4	Wyoming	63.0	Massachusetts	6.52
3	Texas	182.2	Rhode Island	67.9	Louisiana	58.5	Nevada	5.48
4	Florida	142.3	Delaware	65.1	New Hampshire	58.1	Connecticut	4.56
5	North Carolina	123.8	Maryland	62.0	New Jersey	56.4	New York	4.30
6	Indiana	111.0	Colorado	58.2	Arkansas	54.9	New Hampshire	3.82
7	Michigan	106.8	South Carolina	57.0	Kentucky	53.7	New Jersey	3.67
8	Wisconsin	106.5	West Virginia	56.1	Oklahoma	53.2	Louisiana	3.31
9	Minnesota	105.9	Montana	55.7	Maine	52.7	Maine	3.24
10	Colorado	104.8	New Mexico	55.5	Florida	48.2	West Virginia	3.23
Bottom 5 states								
44	Wyoming	10.9	Florida	26.4	Vermont	23.6	Illinois	0.82
45	Delaware	9.8	Arkansas	25.1	New York	21.1	Idaho	0.81
46	Vermont	7.5	Nebraska	24.2	Rhode Island	17.6	New Mexico	0.68
47	Rhode Island	6.7	Georgia	19.3	Colorado	13.7	Iowa	0.67
48	New Hampshire	5.8	Louisiana	18.9	Massachusetts	10.3	South Dakota	0.47
Average across all states		*67.8*		*36.9*		*38.9*		*1.35*

Sources: See Figure 6-16.
Notes: Corresponding data for all states are included in Appendix Table 6-2.
[a] SAES spending, exclusive of forestry, in nominal dollars.
[b] Federally sourced share (from all federal agencies) of state's spending total.
[c] State sourced share of state's spending total.
[d] SAES spending (exclusive of forestry research) per $100 of gross value of agricultural output.

state, but with the experiment station located primarily on the campuses of UC Davis, UC Berkeley, and UC Riverside). New Hampshire ranked last, with just $5.8 million spent on research conducted by its State Agricultural Experiment Station.

Where the research is performed is one aspect; who pays for it is another. The changing sources of support for SAES research are discussed in some detail below. For now, Table 6-5 points to very substantial differences among states in terms of who pays for the R&D. States that are smaller in terms of their agricultural R&D investments or their agricultural production or both tend to be more-heavily reliant on federal funding, with states like Massachusetts, Vermont, Rhode Island, and Delaware, all receiving 65 percent or more of their SAES funding from federal sources. However, not all small agricultural R&D states are heavily reliant on federal funding. Wyoming, for example, the forty-fourth ranked state in terms of the total amount of SAES expenditures, ranks second in terms of the share of that spending (63 percent) derived from state sources.[26] At the other end of the spectrum, only 10.3 percent of SAES funding in Massachusetts is paid from state government sources. At the same time, states with larger agricultural sectors tend to spend more on agricultural research than smaller states. The right-hand column in Table 6-5 normalizes SAES spending by the value of agricultural production; a type of agricultural research intensity ratio. On average, $1.35 was spent on SAES research for every $100 of state agricultural output. Three states—Rhode Island, Massachusetts, and Nevada—each spent $5 or more on agricultural research per $100 of agricultural output while eleven states had research intensity ratios less than $1 per $100.

6.6 Sources and Forms of Funding

The economic consequences of agricultural R&D depend on the source of funds and the form it takes as well as the amount, orientation and pattern of spending.

Research

Of the $3.49 billion spent in 2007 on agricultural R&D by the SAESs and related institutions (including schools of veterinary medicine or forestry, and the 1890 institutions), 39.0 percent came from federal sources, 39.2 percent from state government, 7.5 percent from industry grants and contracts, and 14.3 percent from income earned from sales, royalties, and various other sources (Figure 6-20). Research conducted by USDA labs was almost entirely reliant on federal

26 The exceptionally high state share of SAES funding for Wyoming arose because the state annually allocates a portion of it mineral severance taxes to the SAES, and the revenue stream from these taxes was buoyant in the period 2005–2007.

Figure 6-20 Funding Channels for U.S. Public-Sector Agricultural R&D, 2007

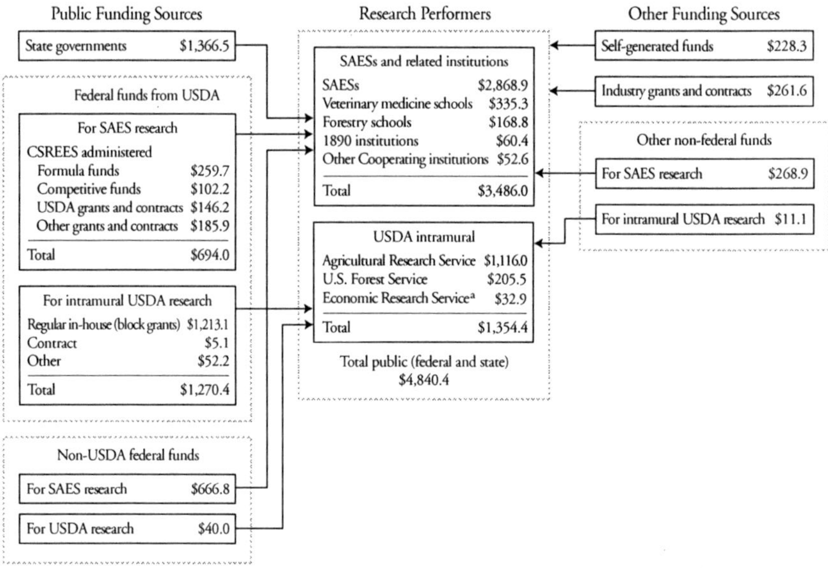

Sources: Compiled by authors from unpublished USDA CRIS data files.
Notes: All data are reported in millions of dollars. SAES series spans 48 states.
[a] ERS intramural expenditures for 2007 were not reported in CRIS; value is for 2006.

government funding; $1.31 billion (or 96.8 percent) of the total of $1.35 billion of that research in 2007 was so funded.

The current structure of funding for SAES research represents a significant departure from past patterns of support. During the founding phases of the SAESs the federal government was a significant source of support, accounting for an average of 68.0 percent of total SAES funding during the decade of the 1890s (Figure 6-21). Putting aside the years of the Great Depression and Second World War, the state-government share of total SAES funding grew fairly steadily from 1890 to a peak of 69.3 percent in 1970. Since then the state government share of SAES funding has declined dramatically, down to 39.3 percent in 2007. Beginning in 1975 funding from industry and self-generated funds was on the rise, accounting for 22.2 percent of total SAES funding in 2007 (with 60.7 percent of SAES funding coming from sources other than state governments; that is industry, self-generated plus federal government funds).

While SAES funding from federal sources has been increasing by an annual average (inflation-adjusted) rate of 3.25 percent per year since 1890 (against the corresponding rate of growth in total SAES funding of 3.68 percent per year), the composition of those funds has changed too. In the United States, the federal government funds agricultural research through a variety of mechanisms. Historically the USDA was the primary federal government agency channeling

Figure 6-21 SAES Research Expenditures by Sources of Funds, 1890–2007

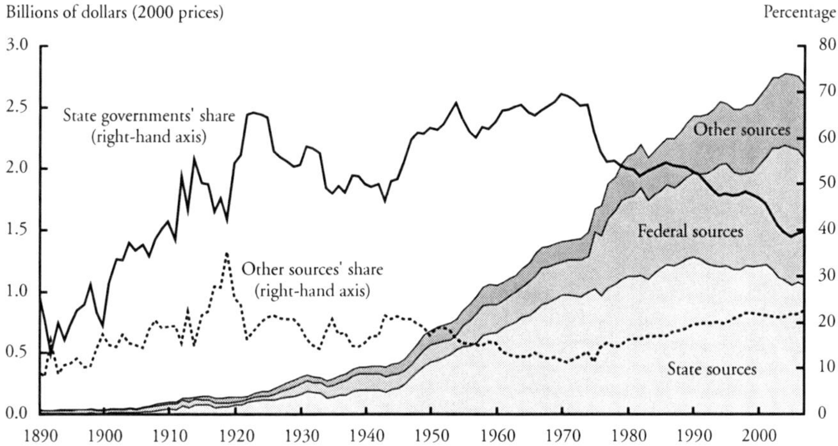

Sources: See Figure 6-8. Nominal research funding data were deflated by a U.S. agricultural research price index reported in Pardey, Andersen and Alston (2009).

Notes: SAES funding refers to 48 contiguous states, excluding Alaska and Hawaii, and includes all R&D performed by the SAESs and other cooperating institutions.

funds to the SAESs, mostly through the Cooperative State Research Education and Extension Service (CSREES), but that has changed.[27] In 1975, the USDA disbursed about 74 percent of the federal funds flowing to the SAESs through a combination of formula funds, grants, and contracts, but by 2007 that had declined to about 50 percent (Figure 6-22). The other half of federal funds is now being disbursed by a wide range of federal agencies, including the National Science Foundation (NSF), the National Institutes of Health (NIH), the Department of Energy (DOE), the Department of Defense (DOD), the U.S. Agency for International Development (USAID) and others. The CSREES share of federal funding for SAES research also declined (from 66 percent in 1975 to 39 percent in 2007), such that CSREES now provides just 16 percent of total SAES funding.

Behind these overall national trends lies a good deal of variation among states in their sources of support and the pattern of change in those funding sources over time. Between 2005 and 2007, federal funding accounted for 36.9

27 While periodic farm bills authorize certain amounts of USDA funds to be used for particular programs, actual expenditures are set annually by agricultural Appropriations Acts. In the Research Title, appropriated amounts have often differed substantially from those authorized. Several grant programs authorized in earlier Research Titles were not appropriated the funds that were expected. In recent years, Congress has also tended to fund more grants specified by members of Congress than the broader grant programs requested by the Administration. Chapter 7 provides more details on the legislation and the role of Congressional earmarks and other elements of Congressional direction of research.

Figure 6-22 USDA Role in Funding SAES Research, 1970–2007

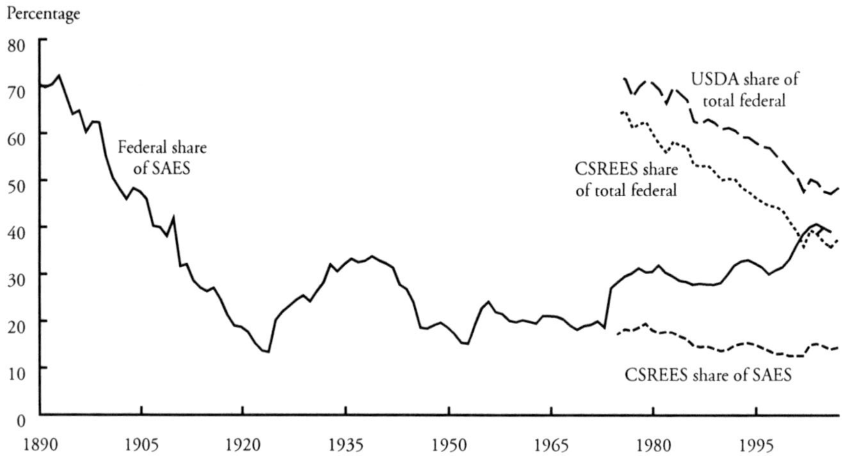

Sources: See Figure 6-8 for data details.

percent of all SAES funding and state governments paid 38.9 percent; such that $1.10 of state funding flowed to the SAESs for every dollar of federal funding support averaged over the period 2000–2007 (Table 6-6). This is well below the $2.81 of state funding for every dollar of federal support in the 1920s. In the 2000s, the Plains and Southeastern regions averaged more than $1.50 from state sources for every dollar of federal support, and the Pacific and Central regions received almost equal shares of federal and state funding, whereas the Mountain and Northeast regions each received less than one dollar of state funding for each dollar coming from the federal government.

Looking state by state since 2000, 20 of the 48 states received more than half their SAES funding from the federal government. Six of the states were heavily reliant on funding from state government, and got no more than a third of their funds from federal government sources—i.e., the ratio of state to federal funding exceeds 2.0 (see also Appendix Table 6-3). In contrast, others were much less dependent on state government sources (in seven states they accounted for less than one-third of the total funding).

Extension

The public provision of extension services in the United States is essentially a state or local activity. Consequently, in 2006, funds from within-state sources accounted for 79 percent of the total funds for extension. Federal funds accounted for the remaining 21 percent, well down from the peak federal share of 62 percent in 1919 (Figure 6-23). In contrast to the funding trend for public R&D, funding for extension from state (mainly state and county government) sources

Table 6-6 Ratio of State-to-Federal Government Support for SAES Research, 1920s–2000s

	1920s	1950s	1980s	2000s
United States	2.81	2.95	1.81	1.10
48 state				
Average	2.81	2.95	1.80	1.11
Minimum	0.04	0.47	0.41	0.18
Maximum	11.04	13.40	4.05	3.28
Selected states				
California	10.15	13.40	2.56	1.09
Minnesota	7.49	4.10	2.97	1.68
Wyoming	0.59	1.66	1.46	2.09
Regions				
Pacific	5.04	8.50	2.04	1.04
Mountain	1.28	1.92	1.20	0.64
Northern Plains	2.32	2.34	2.11	1.53
Southern Plains	2.45	2.38	2.40	1.61
Central	5.95	3.24	1.52	1.03
Southeast	1.74	2.12	2.33	1.50
Northeast	2.25	2.84	1.26	0.75

Sources: For details on research data, see Figure 6-8 and Appendix III.

Notes: The figure for the United States represents the 48 states total. The figure for the 1920s is the simple average of the observations for 1920–1929, and similarly for remaining decades except for the 2000s which is an average of the observations for 2000–2007.

has increased over the past few years from 72 percent in 1990 to 79 percent in 2006. During this period, the share of funding for extension from federal sources dropped from 28 percent in 1990 to 21 percent in 2006 (in contrast to the trends in funding for SAES research where the federal share grew from 28 percent in 1990 to 39 percent in 2007). This reflects a shift of priorities of federal funding away from extension and towards research. A feature of cooperative extension activities that has no parallel with SAES research is that a substantial share of funds is provided by county governments. In 1915, county appropriations accounted for over one-third of within-state funding. Their share rose to a peak of around 47 percent during the late-1930s, then declined to 30 percent in 1970, and has been about 29 percent during the 2000s.

6.7 Conclusion

This chapter began with a review of the changing pattern of privately versus publicly performed agricultural R&D and the place of agricultural research in the overall spectrum of scientific research performed in the United States during the past century or more. This longer-term and broader-based review provided context for a more detailed documentation and discussion of the changes in the performance of public agricultural R&D over the latter half of the 20th Century. The data reveal that the balance between state and federally performed agri-

Figure 6-23 Extension Expenditures by Sources of Funds, 1915–2006

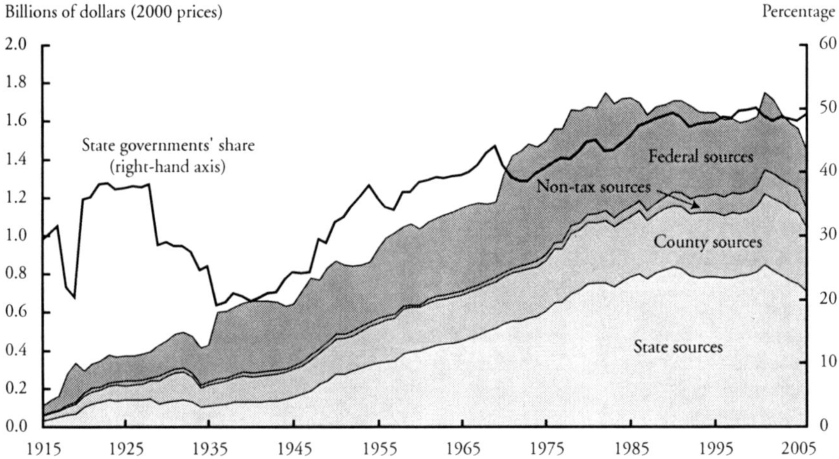

Sources: See Figure 6-13. Nominal extension expenditure data were deflated by a U.S. agricultural research price index reported in Pardey, Andersen and Alston (2009).

cultural research has changed markedly, as has the spatial structure of research performed by the SAESs.

A sustained trend of strong growth in real (inflation-adjusted) R&D spending has given way to a slowdown in the rate of spending growth in recent decades; with the rate of growth in agricultural R&D slowing to a greater extent than overall science spending since the early 1970s. Real spending on extension has effectively been stalled for decades. Combined with these slowdowns has been a shift in the orientation of public agricultural R&D away from preserving or promoting productivity gains in agriculture. This reorientation of agricultural R&D has developed in conjunction with a diversification of support for that research. Notably, while the USDA is still an important conduit for federal government funding for publicly performed agricultural R&D in the United States, its share of federal support has shrunk considerably, with a host of other government agencies now helping to fund the activity. State government funding as a share of total SAES funding has declined too.

Not only have the orientation of the research and sources of support changed, the form of the funding has changed as well. These trends are quantified and discussed in the chapter to follow, along with the evolution of the federal legislative framework that pertains to the funding and conduct of agricultural R&D in the United States.

Appendix Table 6-1 SAESs, USDA Intramural, and Extension Expenditure for the 48 Contiguous States, 1890–2007

	SAES by Source of Funds								
Year	State	Federal	MFS[a]	SAES Total	SAES Total (Excluding Forestry)	USDA Intramural	USDA Plus SAES (Excluding Forestry)	Extension	USDA, SAES and Extension (Excluding Forestry)
					millions of dollars (2000 prices)				
1890	9.6	23.2	3.4	36.1	36.1	12.3	48.4		48.4
1891	6.8	24.1	2.6	33.5	33.5	13.2	46.7		46.7
1892	4.5	24.9	5.6	34.9	34.9	14.4	49.3		49.3
1893	7.0	25.6	3.1	35.7	35.7	15.5	51.1		51.1
1894	5.7	26.5	3.8	35.9	35.9	16.6	52.5		52.5
1895	7.5	26.8	4.2	38.4	38.4	17.5	55.9		55.9
1896	9.2	26.8	4.9	41.0	41.0	22.9	63.8		63.8
1897	9.6	27.0	4.1	40.7	40.7	21.9	62.7		62.7
1898	12.1	26.7	4.5	43.3	43.3	24.1	67.3		67.3
1899	9.0	26.1	5.8	40.9	40.9	26.4	67.3		67.3
1900	7.6	25.6	6.9	40.1	40.1	28.5	68.6		68.6
1901	12.8	25.3	6.7	44.8	44.8	32.0	76.8		76.8
1902	16.3	25.2	7.0	48.5	48.5	36.6	85.1	6.0	91.1
1903	16.3	24.4	8.4	49.1	49.1	51.2	100.3	6.3	106.6
1904	19.2	24.5	7.9	51.7	51.7	54.7	106.3	7.2	113.5
1905	17.3	24.4	7.3	48.9	48.9	69.5	118.5	7.6	126.1
1906	24.0	32.1	9.3	65.3	65.3	69.7	135.0	9.0	144.0
1907	24.7	34.4	13.3	72.4	72.4	46.4	118.8	9.3	128.0
1908	33.9	37.3	18.2	89.4	89.4	68.2	157.6	10.6	168.1
1909	38.0	39.4	17.6	95.0	95.0	92.5	187.5	10.9	198.4
1910	43.5	41.4	19.8	104.7	104.7	94.3	199.0	13.4	212.4
1911	38.8	44.6	19.6	103.0	103.0	80.4	183.4	13.4	196.8
1912	70.5	45.3	20.9	136.7	136.6	80.8	217.4	16.8	234.2
1913	58.2	44.2	29.2	131.6	131.5	79.8	211.2	15.7	227.0

(continued)

Appendix Table 6-1 (continued)

Year	SAES by Source of Funds				SAES Total (Excluding Forestry)	USDA Intramural	USDA Plus SAES (Excluding Forestry)	Extension	USDA, SAES and Extension (Excluding Forestry)
	State	Federal	MFS[a]	SAES Total					
				millions of dollars (2000 prices)					
1914	79.8	43.4	21.1	144.2	144.1	91.7	235.8	13.7	249.5
1915	76.3	43.7	32.7	152.6	152.4	109.0	261.5	109.4	370.8
1916	75.7	42.2	33.8	151.6	151.4	89.1	240.5	143.0	383.5
1917	57.9	37.7	36.6	132.2	132.0	113.3	245.3	159.8	405.1
1918	62.3	34.8	36.6	133.7	133.5	121.1	254.6	275.8	530.3
1919	60.7	32.9	50.6	144.3	144.0	122.6	266.6	335.4	602.0
1920	76.6	28.9	35.4	140.9	140.5	121.8	262.3	294.1	556.3
1921	77.9	28.1	33.0	139.1	138.6	122.4	261.1	327.9	589.0
1922	98.9	29.1	24.5	152.5	152.0	133.4	285.4	347.9	633.3
1923	112.1	28.7	30.7	171.5	170.8	137.2	308.0	374.9	682.9
1924	120.6	28.1	37.2	185.9	185.2	152.7	337.9	368.5	706.5
1925	121.5	27.8	39.3	188.6	187.9	159.1	347.0	372.2	719.2
1926	121.2	46.1	45.6	212.9	212.0	179.6	391.6	373.8	765.4
1927	132.1	55.6	49.3	237.0	236.0	184.0	420.0	381.3	801.3
1928	143.2	64.4	53.6	261.2	260.1	189.0	449.0	390.9	839.9
1929	151.8	73.4	57.9	283.2	281.9	237.6	519.5	428.9	948.5
1930	167.2	82.9	59.0	309.0	307.4	268.7	576.1	455.1	1,031.2
1931	188.2	82.8	53.2	324.2	322.3	288.0	610.3	488.3	1,098.6
1932	177.8	85.2	45.8	308.8	306.7	294.4	601.1	499.2	1,100.3
1933	170.4	88.8	42.3	301.6	299.3	276.9	576.2	478.6	1,054.8
1934	133.3	90.7	48.2	272.2	270.3	224.5	494.8	416.0	910.7
1935	139.9	93.3	59.9	293.1	291.0	270.3	561.3	427.6	988.9
1936	154.9	104.4	53.7	313.0	310.8	325.5	636.3	604.3	1,240.6
1937	157.8	113.5	58.1	329.3	326.9	344.1	671.0	607.5	1,278.5
1938	190.5	124.4	53.7	368.7	365.7	350.3	716.0	626.7	1,342.7

1939	197.2	130.5	55.8	383.5	379.9	504.2	884.1	648.1	1,532.2
1940	193.8	135.8	59.1	388.7	385.3	393.8	779.0	658.1	1,437.2
1941	194.1	134.1	65.7	393.9	390.3	433.8	824.1	657.8	1,481.8
1942	197.8	132.5	66.1	396.4	392.7	375.0	767.6	661.6	1,429.3
1943	178.8	126.2	82.9	387.9	384.1	321.7	705.8	653.7	1,359.5
1944	204.7	117.3	82.9	404.8	401.0	344.4	745.3	631.5	1,376.8
1945	212.0	116.9	88.3	417.3	413.0	353.0	766.1	646.1	1,412.2
1946	243.5	112.9	91.5	447.9	443.1	355.3	798.4	713.0	1,511.4
1947	308.9	103.4	107.1	519.3	513.6	434.1	947.7	777.8	1,725.5
1948	356.4	115.0	113.4	584.8	578.1	388.9	967.0	770.4	1,737.4
1949	393.9	132.5	122.7	649.1	640.8	436.6	1,077.4	832.9	1,910.3
1950	425.8	143.4	116.9	686.1	676.9	424.4	1,101.3	867.3	1,968.6
1951	439.1	141.7	132.5	713.3	703.1	439.9	1,143.0	848.9	1,991.9
1952	460.6	135.6	136.3	732.6	721.8	438.6	1,160.4	840.9	2,001.3
1953	485.1	123.4	135.4	743.9	732.4	435.1	1,167.5	849.3	2,016.8
1954	524.6	127.6	126.5	778.7	766.7	422.6	1,189.3	862.0	2,051.3
1955	546.5	174.7	130.3	851.6	838.3	379.5	1,217.8	937.9	2,155.7
1956	554.4	216.0	135.8	906.2	891.8	393.3	1,285.2	989.2	2,274.4
1957	578.1	243.9	143.7	965.7	949.9	511.1	1,461.0	1,017.3	2,478.3
1958	647.2	239.8	152.2	1,039.2	1,021.8	523.8	1,545.6	1,048.4	2,594.1
1959	655.8	239.6	164.4	1,059.9	1,041.7	710.4	1,752.1	1,064.8	2,816.9
1960	670.7	224.1	161.3	1,056.1	1,037.7	672.6	1,710.4	1,035.1	2,745.4
1961	705.4	224.1	143.0	1,072.6	1,053.2	696.3	1,749.5	1,073.9	2,823.4
1962	728.6	235.0	140.2	1,103.8	1,082.6	752.7	1,835.3	1,094.3	2,929.5
1963	755.8	237.7	140.3	1,133.8	1,111.3	819.3	1,930.7	1,109.9	3,040.6
1964	795.3	243.7	146.4	1,185.4	1,160.4	846.7	2,007.1	1,124.8	3,132.0
1965	808.5	274.4	154.1	1,236.9	1,209.8	886.3	2,096.1	1,145.8	3,241.9
1966	845.7	289.0	173.4	1,308.1	1,279.7	826.1	2,105.8	1,163.8	3,269.7
1967	894.8	298.9	167.3	1,361.0	1,330.1	862.8	2,192.9	1,171.8	3,364.7
1968	91[illegible].9	292.5	163.4	1,367.9	1,334.1	892.1	2,226.3	1,166.8	3,393.0

(continued)

Appendix Table 6-1 (continued)

Year	SAES by Source of Funds				SAES Total (Excluding Forestry)	USDA Intramural	USDA Plus SAES (Excluding Forestry)	Extension	USDA, SAES and Extension (Excluding Forestry)
	State	Federal	MFS[a]	SAES Total					
	millions of dollars (2000 prices)								
1969	942.9	279.7	170.5	1,393.1	1,358.3	866.0	2,224.4	1,176.3	3,400.6
1970	974.0	270.6	160.6	1,405.1	1,374.1	881.1	2,255.2	1,318.7	3,573.9
1971	974.1	283.3	157.8	1,415.2	1,381.2	942.4	2,323.6	1,421.4	3,745.0
1972	966.9	287.4	166.1	1,420.4	1,386.1	1,145.3	2,531.4	1,446.9	3,978.2
1973	956.1	300.4	176.2	1,432.7	1,396.2	853.1	2,249.2	1,480.7	3,730.0
1974	994.3	291.0	198.8	1,484.1	1,443.4	844.4	2,287.8	1,463.5	3,751.3
1975	1,021.5	463.5	187.0	1,671.9	1,621.2	874.6	2,495.8	1,495.8	3,991.6
1976	966.1	488.3	240.5	1,695.0	1,638.0	875.5	2,513.4	1,558.2	4,071.7
1977	1,026.2	562.9	286.7	1,875.8	1,812.2	996.4	2,808.7	1,559.1	4,367.8
1978	1,062.8	591.9	279.8	1,934.5	1,866.9	1,014.1	2,881.1	1,660.3	4,541.4
1979	1,097.0	644.6	299.1	2,040.7	1,965.3	1,036.6	3,001.9	1,654.7	4,656.6
1980	1,119.3	646.5	336.4	2,102.1	2,024.5	1,020.6	3,045.1	1,673.8	4,718.9
1981	1,125.3	654.3	344.8	2,124.4	2,045.8	1,045.2	3,091.0	1,671.2	4,762.2
1982	1,133.7	711.8	356.7	2,202.2	2,129.6	1,002.1	3,131.7	1,751.2	4,882.9
1983	1,097.4	644.0	349.5	2,090.9	2,021.2	943.2	2,964.4	1,692.9	4,657.3
1984	1,143.7	644.8	358.2	2,146.8	2,074.7	959.8	3,034.6	1,714.7	4,749.3
1985	1,182.1	640.6	373.7	2,196.4	2,125.0	905.2	3,030.2	1,724.9	4,755.2
1986	1,219.9	648.3	374.3	2,242.5	2,167.7	898.6	3,066.2	1,698.5	4,764.7
1987	1,209.3	637.0	400.3	2,246.7	2,173.0	877.8	3,050.8	1,631.9	4,682.7
1988	1,231.0	653.0	416.1	2,300.1	2,214.2	866.4	3,080.6	1,673.9	4,754.5
1989	1,265.3	669.7	438.2	2,373.2	2,282.4	869.8	3,152.1	1,688.0	4,840.1
1990	1,278.7	684.7	466.3	2,429.7	2,336.1	856.1	3,192.2	1,707.9	4,900.1
1991	1,263.4	694.3	471.2	2,428.9	2,340.4	842.0	3,182.4	1,704.5	4,886.9
1992	1,222.5	740.1	481.3	2,443.9	2,351.0	900.2	3,251.3	1,682.2	4,933.4
1993	1,205.7	790.6	486.4	2,482.7	2,369.0	939.1	3,308.1	1,650.4	4,958.5

1994	1,205.3	830.2	506.8	2,542.4	2,424.4	866.1	3,290.5	1,646.0	4,936.5
1995	1,207.8	831.8	490.1	2,529.7	2,409.1	856.6	3,265.7	1,642.7	4,908.4
1996	1,176.0	798.2	511.0	2,485.3	2,363.5	810.8	3,174.3	1,608.6	4,782.9
1997	1,178.9	779.0	525.2	2,483.2	2,361.5	812.3	3,173.8	1,612.3	4,786.1
1998	1,209.1	752.6	547.5	2,509.2	2,386.8	825.9	3,212.7	1,593.8	4,806.6
1999	1,198.6	776.2	547.1	2,521.9	2,399.6	852.6	3,252.2	1,601.1	4,853.3
2000	1,212.7	811.1	560.0	2,583.7	2,458.8	861.1	3,319.9	1,621.6	4,941.6
2001	1,214.6	879.1	568.1	2,661.9	2,535.3	871.6	3,406.9	1,746.2	5,153.0
2002	1,180.6	983.9	578.4	2,743.0	2,617.0	877.5	3,494.6	1,712.6	5,207.2
2003	1,119.1	1,046.0	574.9	2,740.1	2,613.8	910.3	3,524.1	1,632.5	5,156.6
2004	1,092.8	1,095.9	580.2	2,768.9	2,638.3	1,004.8	3,643.2	1,584.7	5,227.8
2005	1,056.2	1,107.4	597.9	2,761.5	2,625.5	1,084.9	3,710.4	1,558.4	5,268.8
2006	1,073.2	1,081.1	595.1	2,749.3	2,612.5	1,166.6	3,779.1	1,442.8	5,221.9
2007	1,054.0	1,036.6	593.3	2,684.2	2,549.7	1,230.3	3,779.9	na	na

Sources: Details on the sources of SAES, intramural USDA and extension are provided in Appendix III.

Notes: "SAES Total" includes research performed by the SAESs and other cooperating institutions (here including the 1890 colleges along with veterinary and forestry schools) for the 48 contiguous states (i.e., excluding Alaska and Hawaii). The "SAES total (excluding forestry)" series excludes research conducted by the forestry schools. Spending by forestry schools was directly obtained from USDA CRIS data files for the 1979–2007 period, and estimated by authors for prior years. Nominal research expenditure data were deflated by a U.S. agricultural research price index reported in Pardey, Andersen and Alston (2009).

[a] Miscellaneous fees and sales.

Appendix Table 6-2 Agricultural R&D Performance, Funding Sources, and Intensity, circa 2007

	Performance in 2007[a]		Sources of Support (Average 2005–2007) Federal Share		State Share		R&D Intensity (Average 2003–2005)	
	Rank	Spending	Rank	Share	Rank	Share	Rank	Intensity
		millions of dollars		*percentage*		*percentage*		*percentage*
United States Average		*67.80*		*36.9*		*38.9*		*1.35*
Pacific		*474.21*		*39.9*		*40.4*		*1.12*
California	1	332.96	23	40.1	17	40.9	37	1.05
Oregon	25	61.11	25	39.8	23	39.1	25	1.45
Washington	15	80.15	26	39.5	21	39.5	32	1.21
Mountain		*330.81*		*51.0*		*28.7*		*1.71*
Arizona	18	73.03	17	45.2	31	36.2	13	2.44
Colorado	10	104.78	6	58.2	47	13.7	15	2.19
Idaho	31	35.89	21	41.2	38	31.5	45	0.81
Montana	30	40.40	9	55.7	43	25.2	21	1.66
Nevada	39	20.91	12	54.6	29	37.2	3	5.48
New Mexico	42	14.73	10	55.5	20	40.4	46	0.68
Utah	35	30.16	14	51.3	26	38.5	12	2.46
Wyoming	44	10.92	39	31.5	2	63.0	34	1.13
Northern Plains		*228.21*		*28.9*		*41.7*		*0.84*
Kansas	23	67.85	38	32.6	13	46.8	43	0.87
Nebraska	13	92.44	46	24.2	25	38.6	42	0.91
North Dakota	29	46.77	40	30.1	15	42.1	36	1.06
South Dakota	38	21.15	33	35.8	24	38.9	48	0.47
Southern Plains		*455.33*		*32.9*		*45.1*		*1.31*
Arkansas	24	64.46	45	25.1	6	54.9	39	0.98
Louisiana	19	72.24	48	18.9	3	58.5	8	3.31
Mississippi	16	78.58	22	40.5	35	33.8	19	1.85
Oklahoma	26	57.80	43	27.0	8	53.2	30	1.23
Texas	3	182.24	28	39.1	22	39.5	35	1.06
Central		*758.56*		*40.0*		*36.2*		*1.15*
Illinois	20	71.07	34	35.5	34	34.4	44	0.82

Indiana	6	110.98	29	38.4	30	36.9	27	1.40
Iowa	11	93.88	30	37.7	37	32.9	47	0.67
Michigan	7	106.81	16	45.3	32	35.9	14	2.26
Minnesota	9	105.87	41	29.4	19	40.6	38	0.99
Missouri	12	93.68	19	42.9	40	29.8	28	1.40
Ohio	21	69.75	37	32.8	11	48.0	33	1.14
Wisconsin	8	106.52	13	53.0	36	33.6	20	1.66
Southeast		*588.96*		*34.5*		*47.8*		*1.63*
Alabama	33	32.43	11	55.4	28	37.7	40	0.96
Florida	4	142.26	44	26.4	10	48.2	17	1.95
Georgia	22	68.29	47	19.3	1	69.4	29	1.34
Kentucky	28	51.00	36	33.8	7	53.7	22	1.58
North Carolina	5	123.84	32	36.0	14	45.4	23	1.56
South Carolina	40	20.82	7	57.0	42	25.5	31	1.23
Tennessee	27	52.97	35	35.4	12	47.3	18	1.93
Virginia	14	81.65	24	40.0	18	40.8	11	2.53
West Virginia	41	15.70	8	56.1	33	35.7	10	3.23
Northeast		*418.15*		*47.2*		*29.1*		*2.72*
Connecticut	36	26.73	18	43.6	16	42.1	4	4.56
Delaware	45	9.82	4	65.1	39	30.7	41	0.92
Maine	43	13.85	31	37.0	9	52.7	9	3.24
Maryland	37	21.58	5	62.0	41	27.5	16	1.97
Massachusetts	32	32.74	1	75.3	48	10.3	2	6.52
New Hampshire	48	5.79	20	41.6	4	58.1	6	3.82
New Jersey	34	31.42	42	28.1	5	56.4	7	3.67
New York	2	185.64	15	45.9	45	21.1	5	4.30
Pennsylvania	17	76.38	27	39.3	27	37.7	24	1.49
Rhode Island	47	6.67	3	67.9	46	17.6	1	6.83
Vermont	46	7.53	2	70.4	44	23.6	26	1.42

Sources: R&D data were extracted by the authors from unpublished USDA CRIS data tapes. See Figure 4-1 for details of gross value-of-production data used to form the research intensity ratios. Research intensities express SAES spending exclusive of forestry as a share of the corresponding gross value of agricultural production.

[a] SAES spending, exclusive of forestry, in nominal dollars.

Appendix Table 6-3 Ratio of State-to-Federal Government Support for SAES Research, 1920s–2000s

Region	1920s	1950s	1980s	2000s
United States	*2.81*	*2.95*	*1.80*	*1.11*
Pacific	*5.04*	*8.50*	*2.04*	*1.04*
California	10.15	13.40	2.56	1.09
Oregon	2.39	4.83	1.22	1.01
Washington	2.57	4.89	1.46	0.93
Mountain	*1.28*	*1.92*	*1.20*	*0.64*
Arizona	2.00	2.57	2.44	0.85
Colorado	2.54	2.18	0.41	0.27
Idaho	0.89	2.05	1.57	0.92
Montana	2.57	2.43	1.75	0.51
Nevada	0.04	0.47	1.61	0.75
New Mexico	0.17	1.42	1.89	0.89
Utah	1.44	2.06	1.39	0.93
Wyoming	0.59	1.66	1.46	2.09
Northern Plains	*2.32*	*2.34*	*2.11*	*1.53*
Kansas	2.84	2.84	1.95	1.53
Nebraska	3.01	2.17	1.75	1.60
North Dakota	2.73	2.65	3.46	1.51
South Dakota	0.70	1.56	1.76	1.35
Southern Plains	*2.45*	*2.38*	*2.40*	*1.61*
Arkansas	1.52	1.48	2.21	2.39
Louisiana	1.15	4.83	3.89	3.28
Mississippi	2.97	1.50	1.94	1.03
Oklahoma	0.79	2.57	1.95	1.98
Texas	5.82	2.19	2.34	1.29
Central	*5.95*	*3.24*	*1.52*	*1.03*
Illinois	7.69	3.54	1.23	1.19
Indiana	4.92	2.81	1.31	1.04
Iowa	5.45	3.23	1.45	1.11
Michigan	5.06	3.62	1.45	0.92
Minnesota	7.49	4.10	2.97	1.68
Missouri	0.94	1.12	1.01	0.71
Ohio	10.63	2.79	2.43	1.91
Wisconsin	5.46	4.84	1.05	0.62
Southeast	*1.74*	*2.12*	*2.33*	*1.50*
Alabama	0.98	1.63	1.43	0.92
Florida	3.28	10.07	4.05	2.13
Georgia	0.30	1.75	3.80	2.82
Kentucky	2.16	1.19	1.84	1.73
North Carolina	2.82	2.06	1.95	1.33
South Carolina	1.51	1.30	2.68	0.64
Tennessee	0.92	1.07	1.37	1.51
Virginia	1.47	2.17	1.75	1.15
West Virginia	2.20	0.68	0.75	0.44

(continued)

Appendix Table 6-3 (continued)

Region	1920s	1950s	1980s	2000s
Northeast	*2.25*	*2.84*	*1.26*	*0.75*
Connecticut	3.15	4.10	2.09	1.16
Delaware	0.37	1.28	1.37	0.39
Maine	0.61	1.08	1.01	1.31
Maryland	1.50	1.95	1.87	0.46
Massachusetts	2.74	1.97	0.77	0.18
New Hampshire	0.09	0.64	1.03	1.52
New Jersey	3.73	5.27	2.32	2.15
New York	11.04	6.80	1.20	0.63
Pennsylvania	1.39	1.67	1.04	1.06
Rhode Island	0.07	0.64	0.71	0.41
Vermont	0.04	0.61	0.87	0.44

Sources: For details on research data, see Figure 6-8 and Appendix III.

Notes: The figure for the United States represents the 48 states total. The figure for the 1920s is the simple average of the observations for 1920–1929, and similarly for remaining decades except for the 2000s which is an average of the observations for 2000–2007. The SAES research expenditure data used to construct these estimates are inclusive of forestry research.

CHAPTER 7

The Federal Role

The history of agricultural R&D and related government policy in the United States is one of jointly evolving state and federal, public- and private-sector roles. The private role has always emphasized more-patentable inventions, or at least innovations from which the returns seem more appropriable by a variety of intellectual property rights or other means. In agriculture, in particular, however, it is difficult for individuals to fully appropriate the returns from their research investments, leading to a general consensus that some government action is warranted to ensure an adequate investment in R&D.[1]

In the early years, agricultural innovation was encouraged primarily by state and local governments, and "Societies for the Promotion of Agriculture," through the provision of prizes and demonstrations of best practice, at county fairs and experimental gardens, but with relatively little organized public research.[2] Until 1862, federal government action to encourage investment in agricultural (and other) research was primarily through patent and copyright (and trademark, trade secrecy and eventually other legal means) enabled by Article 1, Section 8 of the U.S. Constitution which became operational on March 4, 1789. The year 1862 was a watershed year with the creation of the U.S. Department of Agriculture and the passage of the Morrill Land Grant College Act, laying the foundation for the modern era of U.S. federal agricultural R&D policy.

This chapter reviews the role of the federal government in enhancing agricultural R&D, first, by developing institutions to provide incentives for private investment; second, by providing resources and incentives to state governments

1 Not all commentators concur that government action is warranted. See, for example, Kealey (1996).

2 Wright (1983) lays out the economic context in which prizes are a more efficient incentive for innovation compared with patents or research contracts. Kerr (1987, pp. 1-2) and Huffman and Evenson (1993, pp. 12-13) describe the role of farmer societies in promoting experimentation in early U.S. agriculture.

J.M. Alston et al., *Persistence Pays: U.S. Agricultural Productivity Growth and the Benefits from Public R&D Spending*, Natural Resource Management and Policy 34,
DOI 10.1007/978-1-4419-0658-8_7,

to conduct agricultural R&D; and third, by funding and conducting agricultural R&D itself.[3]

7.1 Enhanced Incentives to Innovate

Much of the innovation in agriculture over the centuries has been the result of tinkering by farmers and on-farm experimentation—including breeding, screening and selection of plants and animals and the development of improved methods, practices, tools, and mechanical innovations. Before the modern scientific age, great advances in American agricultural productivity resulted from the efforts of plant prospectors who imported new and improved varieties from foreign lands. Walter Bruling of Mississippi imported a new cotton variety from Mexico in 1806 that would become the mainstay of the early American cotton industry; Agoston Haraszthy helped transform the California wine industry by importing several hundred grape varieties from across Europe, North Africa, and the Middle East in the 1860s. In addition to the efforts of private citizens, the USDA sent its scientists to the far corners of the globe in search of better plant varieties.[4] These efforts were particularly fruitful in introducing varieties of wheat and other crops suitable for the arid and harsh conditions on the Great Plains.

Among the more famous inventions in U.S. agriculture attributable to individual inventors, Eli Whitney patented the cotton gin, Cyrus McCormick's mechanical reaper "made bread cheap," John Deere introduced steel-tipped moldboard plows that helped tame the prairies, and Hiram Moore built the first combine harvester (combining a reaper and a thresher in one machine). The list of biological innovators is less well-known but the legendary Luther Burbank who developed scores of new and improved varieties, many of which still bear his name, is representative of thousands of farmer-scientists who by careful selection and, in some cases, hybridization improved the plant varieties available to American farmers.

3 For more details on the institutional history of U.S. agricultural R&D see True (1895, 1900, 1928 and 1937), Baker et al. (1963), Rasmussen and Baker (1972), Rossiter (1975), Waggoner (1976), Bonnen (1986), Kerr (1987), Huffman and Evenson (1993 and 2006a), and Alston and Pardey (1996 and 2006a).

4 As early as the mid-1850s the federal government employed "agricultural explorers" to scout the globe for new plant and seed material for shipping back to the United States (Ryerson 1933, p.117). U.S. Navy expeditions and Consular staff were also regularly used to collect new plant material from countries around the world and ship that material back to the United States. Juma (1989) placed these early seed scouting endeavors in an international context, which is then linked to contemporary interests concerning genetic resources and modern biotechnologies. See also Olmstead and Rhode (2008).

Intellectual Property Rights

In attacking their local problems, farmers throughout history have produced many innovations with no prospects of reaping a significant fraction of their full monetary value. Nonetheless, societies relying exclusively on private market incentives are likely to underinvest in certain kinds of research and support a sub-optimal mix of R&D. The introduction of intellectual property rights, beginning in the United States with patents, trademarks and copyrights in the 18th Century, rates among the more prominent public policy measures intended to stimulate the creation and dissemination of U.S. inventions.[5]

The scope of intellectual property protection in the United States for 150 years after ratification of the U.S. Constitution offered little protection for biological inventions such as new crop varieties (Appendix Table 7-1). Trademarks and trade secrecy laws were applicable, but these did not protect against reverse engineering or self replication, and so the common practice of saving seeds for their own use—or for sharing seed with other farmers or selling to them—did not constitute legal infringement of new seed varieties. Intellectual property protection did apply to product and process inventions related to chemical, mechanical, storage, transport, and food processing inventions, among others. Johnson (1999 and 2006) estimated numbers of patents by sector-of-use and reported a significant number of patents pertaining to agriculture for each year since 1840 (the first year of his data series), with more than 1,000 such patents issued annually for most years after 1881.

Many of the agricultural patents in the middle of the 19th Century dealt with agricultural machinery, implements and devices. Even something as seemingly simple as farm fencing material was heavily patented. Beginning with patent number 63,482 issued on April 2, 1867 to Alphonzo Dabb from Elizabethport, New Jersey for "Improvement in Pickets for Fences and Walls," more than 400 patents were issued for designs and manufacturing methods related just to barbed wire (Clifton 1970; Krell 2003). Like most issued patents, many of those granted for barbed wire designs and manufacturing methods failed to result in commercially successful inventions, but one—granted to Joseph Glidden, a farmer from DeKalb, Illinois, in November 1874—was especially successful. This particular invention spurred the development of the industry that enabled ranchers to fence in the Longhorn cattle of Texas and other livestock throughout the Western United States and many places beyond; a technology that continues to play an important role in managed grazing practices on farms and ranches in the United States and around the world.

5 Other mechanisms such as research prizes, contracts or open-source initiatives may also be effective in generating new innovations in certain circumstances (Wright et al. 2007).

Expanding Scope of Intellectual Property Rights

In the United States, the first steps towards broadening the scope of intellectual property protection to include inventions involving living things began with the Plant Patent Act of 1930. This legislation provided for the protection of asexually reproduced plants, including plants like grape vines, fruit trees, and ornamentals that are propagated through cuttings and graftings (Fowler 1994; Wright et al. 2007). The scope of intellectual property protection for plants was further broadened in 1970 with the introduction of the Plant Variety Protection Act (PVPA), designed to strengthen intellectual property protection for non-hybrid varieties.[6]

In 1980, a sea change in the intellectual property protection of agriculture was heralded in the United States by a key Supreme Court Decision, an Act of Congress, and the award of a fundamental patent. In that year the U.S. Supreme Court held that the class of patentable subject matter included living organisms in the landmark *Diamond v. Chakrabarty* decision.[7] In addition, the 1980 Bayh-Dole Act established the general right of grant recipients (e.g., universities) to apply for patents on most federally-funded research (Mowery et al. 2001).[8] This was complemented by the introduction, also in 1980, of Cooperative Research and Development Agreements (CRADAs) designed specifically to speed the commercialization of federally developed technology (Day-Rubenstein and Fuglie 2000).[9] Finally, Cohen and Boyer, after almost a decade of examination and continuances, were awarded U.S. patent number 4,237,224 in 1980 on their fundamental recombinant DNA technology, which ushered in a new era of genetic modification of plants for agriculture.

---

6 Efforts to analyze the economic effects of plant variety protection legislation in the United States include Perrin, Kunnings and Ihnen (1983), Butler and Marion (1985), Knudson and Pray (1991), Alston and Venner (2002) and Kolady and Lesser (2009). Moschini and Lapan (1997) provided a more general analysis of the economic effects of appropriable agricultural inventions. Janis and Kesan (2002) examined some of the legal principles and practices concerning the U.S. Plant Variety Protection Act.

7 In the early 1970s General Electric brought a powerful test case on the patentability of a living organism (an oil eating bacterium). In 1980, the U.S. Supreme Court (in the case of Diamond v Chakrabarty) ruled in GE's favor, and although the bacterium was never commercialized, a legal basis for patenting life forms had been established.

8 Some of the pressures for strengthening U.S. patent law and expanding its scope originated outside of agriculture. They included the pessimistic perception that the United States had lost its technological edge in the 1970s and that other countries were insufficiently compensating the United States for past innovations. See Landes and Posner (2003) for more perspectives.

9 A CRADA is a contract between a private company and a government agency to work together on a project, in which the private collaborating partner agrees to provide funds, personnel, services, facilities, equipment or other resources needed to conduct a specific research or development effort while the Federal government agrees to provide similar complementary resources. The government and the collaborating partner may share patents and patent licenses, allow one partner to retain exclusive rights to a patent or patent license, or assign licensing rights to facilitate licensing to third-party users.

In the same decade the U.S. federal court structure was reformed. The newly established Court of Appeals of the Federal Circuit was given jurisdiction over all patent appeals (Jaffe 2000), and the result was litigation outcomes more favorable, on average, to patentees. Later in the decade the patentability of both plants and animals was explicitly confirmed. Thus, by coincidence, the patentability of life forms, including plants and animals, was confirmed in the United States just as detection of infringement of life form patents was becoming technologically more feasible, and the prospects for usefully applying biotechnology were rapidly expanding. Until the 1980s, patents on specific genetic characteristics of plants, animals or other life forms would have been problematic if not impossible to enforce because of the difficulty of verifying that the genetic material of the life form in question was within the scope of the patent claims (Wright and Pardey 2006).

Subsequently, biotechnology itself began producing a new stream of potentially valuable innovations, fueled by a surge in health research funding, through the U.S. National Institutes of Health, that had widespread political support. Large investments were also made in the private sector, often founded on technology based on research conducted in universities with public funding. Participants included startups funded by venture capitalists, who typically demanded evidence of patenting as a condition for investment, and existing pharmaceutical and chemical companies. The majority were interested in health applications, though agricultural applications, initially thought to be a component of a "life sciences" approach, also attracted considerable interest.

Thus, the changes in the 1980s in patent law and in biotechnology were complementary in their effects on subsequent agricultural research incentives in the United States. Other developed nations followed, to various degrees, the lead set by the United States in allowing patents on life forms. In the 1990s, the Trade-Related Aspects of Intellectual Property Rights (TRIPS) agreement of the World Trade Organization (WTO) ensured that adoption of intellectual property protection relevant to agricultural research would quickly become a global phenomenon.

Trends in Plant-Related Intellectual Property Rights

Beginning in 1930 with just 18 applications for plant patent protection in the United States, the number of annual applications for intellectual property protection pertaining to plant varieties (including all three forms of intellectual property—plant patents, plant variety protection certificates, and utility patents) grew to 1,352 applications in 2004 (Figure 7-1). As the legal scope of the protection broadened over time, so too did the subject matter of the protection sought. From 1930 to 1970 all of the applications were for plant patents. This was the only form of protection on offer during that period, encompassing vegetatively propagated plants such as vines or fruit trees but not sexually reproduced plants

Figure 7-1 Applications for U.S. Plant Patents, Utility Patents, and Plant Variety Protection Certificates, 1930–2004

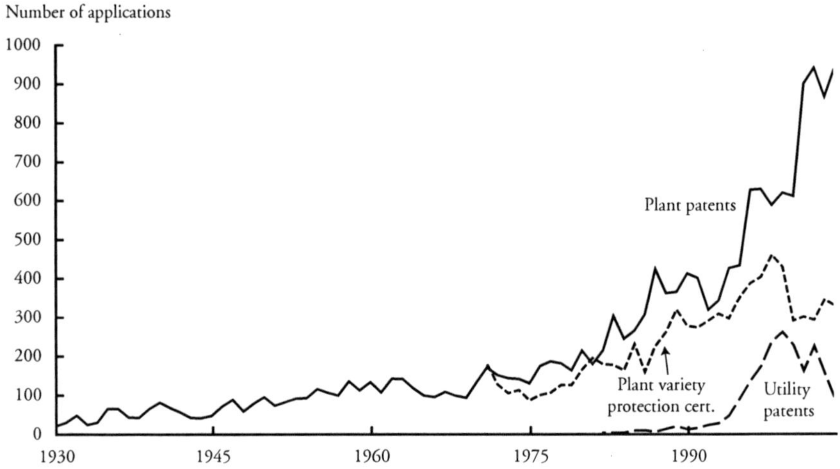

Sources: Koo et al. (2009).

Notes: Consistent with the first issuance of different forms of plant protection in the United States, the data series begins in 1930 for plant patents, in 1971 for plant variety protection certificates, and in 1986 for utility patents.

from seeds. PVPCs first became available in 1970 under the PVPA. A decade later, in 1980, 43 percent of the applications were for Plant Variety Protection Certificates (PVPCs) that offered protection for sexually propagated plants. Applications for utility patents that confer exclusionary rights over specific plant varieties in the United States (be they sexually or asexually propagated) were first lodged in 1982. Applications for this form of protection peaked in 1999, at 259, just 20 percent of the total number of intellectual property applications for plants in that year. Applications for utility patents had fallen to 86 by 2004.

In 1984, 60 percent of all plant-related intellectual property rights were plant patents, and 40 percent were PVPCs. During the decade to follow, annual applications for plant patents grew by an average of 5.61 percent per year, compared with 6.02 percent per year for PVPC applications. Thus PVPCs constituted just 24 percent of the total intellectual property applications lodged for plant varieties in 2004, substantially down from their peak share of 52 percent in 1982.

Changes in the form of varietal protection sought reflect substantial shifts in the types of plants for which applications were lodged. In the 1950s, only asexually propagated plants (including ornamentals, fruits, and vegetables) were subject to intellectual property protection. As Koo et al. (2009) show, during the early 1950s 79 percent of the total protection was for ornamental plants, 19 percent for fruits and 2 percent for tree-related varieties (Figure 7-2). By the five-

Figure 7-2 Crop Orientation of U.S. Intellectual Property Protection, 1950–2004

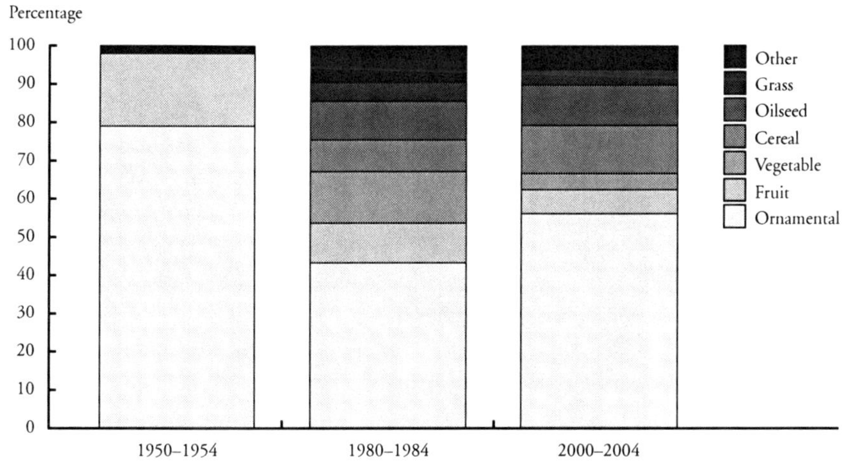

Sources: Koo et al. (2009).

Notes: Consistent with the first issuance of different forms of plant protection in the United States, data for the period 1950–1954 pertain only to plant patents, data for the period 1980–1984 include both plant patents and PVPCs, while data for the period 2000–2004 also include utility patents, though their numbers are quite small.

year period 2000–2004, the rate of applications had grown over fifteen fold—from 423 applications lodged in the period 1950–1954 to 6,638 applications in a comparable five year period spanning 2000–2004—and a more diverse range of types of plants were being protected. High-valued ornamentals accounted for 56 percent of the total applications, fruits and vegetables a further 11 percent. Cereal and oilseed crops of lower unit value constituted just 13 and 11 percent of the total, slightly up on their respective shares of 8 and 10 percent of the corresponding 1980–1984 period totals.

7.2 Organized Agricultural Research and Extension

Policies to develop organized public agricultural research and extension were implemented in parallel with the evolving intellectual property rights that were intended to foster private research investments. Since 1862, which marked both the establishment of the U.S. Department of Agriculture (USDA) and the passage of the Morrill Land Grant College Act, state and federal governments have become progressively more involved through public investments in agricultural R&D. The first Commissioner of Agriculture—the non-cabinet post that originally directed the USDA—was Isaac Newton, who prior to the Department's establishment had been the Superintendent of Agriculture at the Patent Office, with responsibility for the collection and distribution of seeds for new plant varieties.[10] One of the first acts of the new Commissioner was the appointment of a superintendent of the propagating garden, the USDA's first research facility, on what is now part of the Washington D.C. Mall.

The First 100 Years

Active intramural USDA research began immediately after the creation of the Department, with publication of the first research bulletin in 1862, describing the sugar content and suitability for winemaking of several grape varieties (Wetherill 1862). The early years of the USDA were marked by the slow but steady expansion of the Department's internal scientific activities, mostly devoted to "service" work rather than the discovery and development of new knowledge, but leading eventually to the establishment of the Agricultural Research Service (ARS) in 1953.[11] Under the Progressive Era leadership of James "Tama Jim" Wilson, 1897–1913, the USDA budget grew dramatically (by over 700 percent during Wilson's tenure). By 1904, employment of scientists within the USDA—in agencies such as the Bureau of Animal Industry formed in 1884 and the Bureau of Plant Industry established in 1900—surpassed total employment of scientists in the State Agricultural Experiment Stations.

Publicly funded research outside the USDA grew out of the state agricultural stations, developed first in Connecticut by Samuel W. Johnson, based on the prototypes developed in Germany in the 1850s (Ruttan 1982). Following work prior to the Civil War to analyze chemical soil enrichers, Johnson was designated state chemist in 1869, with the formal establishment of the Connecticut Agricultural Experiment Station at Wesleyan University in 1875. At about the same time, experimentation directed to the problems of local farmers was beginning at the state land-grant institutions.[12] USDA funding of external (i.e., extramural)

---

10 Kerr (1987) observed that as a division of the State Department, the Patent Office "... began its agricultural program in the 1820s as the distributor of foreign seeds sent by American consuls to their Washington headquarters. This work continued after the office was transferred to the Department of Interior in 1846 (p. 6)." Henry Ellsworth became Commissioner of Patents in 1836, and "...he secured in 1839 an appropriation of $1,000 for the collection and introduction of seeds and plants and agricultural information. This was the first appropriation ever made for agriculture by an American Congress; here was the beginnings of the United States Department of Agriculture (Ryerson 1933, p. 115)." Fowler (1994, p. 17) reports that the government distribution of seed packages (containing enough seeds to facilitate experimentation) was very popular, with 306,304 packages mailed out in 1862, growing to over 20 million packages in 1897. See also Cooke (2002) for a description of the origins of a seed certification program in the United States.

11 The Department of Agriculture was elevated to an executive department with Cabinet status by a bill signed into law by President Cleveland on February 9, 1889. Less than a week later, then Commissioner Norman Coleman was sworn in as the first Secretary of Agriculture (Baker et al. 1963, pp. 29-30).

12 "The University of California began experiments on its college farm at Berkeley in 1874 in an attempt to win support for the land-grant institution from the state's farmers (Kerr 1987, pp. 12-13)." Eugene Hilgard arrived as Director the following year, and in 1877 the state legislature designated the Berkeley facility as an agricultural experiment station under the control of the University Board of Regents. Agricultural R&D was extended to include activities at Davis in 1906 and

research followed the passage in 1887 of the Hatch Experiment Station Act.[13] In the following years, agricultural experiment stations, supported by a mixture of federal, state, and private funds, and generally located at the various land-grant colleges, opened across the country.

In the early years, extension activities provided local information and technology transfer services to farmers. Eventually, the importance and popularity of extension activities led to legislative support through the Smith-Lever Act of 1914, which created the Cooperative Extension Service and instituted a federal role in extension. During the early 1930s, state support for the experiment stations fell sharply.[14] In response, the Bankhead-Jones Act of 1935 provided additional federal support for research. Several important features of the earlier Smith-Lever Act carried over to the Bankhead-Jones Act; notably, the disbursement of federal funds to the states on a formula basis (20 percent of the funds distributed equally among states, 40 percent based on the state's share of the U.S. rural population, and 40 percent according to its share of U.S. farm population), provided that the federal dollars were matched by state funds. The ensuing years saw further legislative changes (as documented in Appendix Tables 7-2 and 7-3), but the main elements of combined federal and state funding institutions remained unchanged.

More-Recent Legislation

Various legislative initiatives over the years reflected the desire by Congress to direct research funds into particular priority areas, changing the balance between block grant (formula) funds, funds earmarked for specific purposes, and competitive grants, as exemplified by the farm bills during the 1970s and 1980s. In 1977, the USDA's Competitive Research Grants Office (CRGO) was launched and, in 1981, this initiative was continued, along with the reauthorizations of the earmarks and other legislative strictures incorporated in Title XIV of the 1977 Farm Bill. The continuing strong Congressional control over the direction

---

Riverside in 1907 (Scheuring, McCorkle and Lyons 1995). The Minnesota agricultural experiment station was established in St. Paul under its first director, Professor Edward D. Porter, in 1885. Willet Hays, an agronomist, arrived in February 1888 as the experiment station's first researcher. He chaired the organizing committee that founded the American Breeder's Association and was the first editor of the *American Breeders Magazine*, now the *Journal of Heredity* (Hardman and Hansen 2006, p. 2).

13 It took many decades of Congressional deliberations before the USDA was established and sustained funding for agricultural R&D received U.S. government support. Congress failed to act favorably on President Washington's 1796 proposal to create a board of agriculture (Baker et al. 1963). In 1853 "… a bill was introduced in Congress to establish an agricultural department as an independent agency. Not until 1862 [in the midst of a Civil War] did the bill become law [under Abraham Lincoln's signature] and then only in a rather abbreviated form (Kerr 1987, p. 6)."

14 State appropriation for the 48 U.S. contiguous states dropped from $9.8 million in 1931 to $6.3 million in 1934—a contraction of almost 36 percent in just 3 years—before increasing again to $6.5 million in 1935 and $9.3 million by 1938.

of agricultural research was reflected in the priority areas for research funding as described in the legislation; and additional subtitles were added, including specified funding for rangelands and for aquaculture. The 1985 reauthorization continued these patterns of substantial Congressional direction, including a new mandate for quality-enhancing, post-harvest technology (a resurrection of the marketing set-aside). The 1985 Act also included a competitive program for facilities construction at the SAESs.

Stemming from concerns about a U.S. productivity slowdown in the 1970s and a slide in the U.S competitive position in world markets, during the 1980s Congress gave increasing attention to a broad array of legislative instruments designed to stimulate technological change, revive the rate of U.S. productivity growth, and enhance the country's competitive position in world markets.[15] The Bayh-Dole Act of 1980, which generalized the rights of researchers to patent inventions achieved under federal funding in non-defense areas, ushered in a string of legislative initiatives to accelerate the commercialization of new products and processes emerging from federally funded R&D. Some of this legislation was specific to agriculture; some spanned multiple sectors, including agriculture. The Stevenson-Wydler Technology Innovation Act of 1980 encouraged federal laboratories to increase cooperation with the private sector in technology development and transfer; the National Cooperative Research Act of 1984 provided antitrust exemptions for private participation in research consortia; the Federal Technology Transfer Act of 1986 amended the Stevenson-Wydler Act to facilitate the formation of Cooperative Research and Development Agreements (so-called CRADAs)—agreements between collaborating government agencies and private firms designed to speed the development and commercialization of technology; and the Alternative Agricultural Research and Commercialization Act of 1990 directed some of the agricultural research and commercialization efforts of federally funded R&D to new nonfood and nonfeed products derived from agricultural commodities.

The 1990 Farm Bill legislation amended the National Agricultural Research, Extension and Teaching Policy Act of 1977, as previously amended in 1981 and

---

15 As Wright and Pardey (2006) observed, pressures for strengthening U.S. patent law and expanding its scope arose in the 1970s, and originated outside of agriculture. They arose from the concern of business interests with capturing rents on existing technology, as distinct from creation of new incentives for innovation. They also reflected the pessimistic perception that the United States had lost its technological edge in the 1970s to other countries, such as Japan, and that these countries were insufficiently compensating the United States for past innovations (Dutfield 2002). The concerns that a productivity slowdown had afflicted the U.S. economy in the 1970s spawned a large literature to measure and account for this slowdown. In a recent retrospective, Nordhaus (2004, p. 1) noted that "... the [U.S.] productivity slowdown of the 1970s has survived three decades of scrutiny, conceptual refinements, and data revisions. The slowdown was primarily centered in those sectors that were most energy-intensive, were hardest hit by the energy shocks of the 1970s, and therefore had large output declines."

1985, and other related Acts.[16] It extended the pre-existing arrangements, authorized certain new programs, and expanded the purposes of agricultural research and extension.[17] The Act envisaged that federally funded agricultural research and extension would continue to stress mostly conventional objectives for agricultural R&D that address human food and fiber needs, but extended the legislative emphasis on "competitiveness" further into agricultural R&D while also expanding the agricultural research agenda to consider "new uses," "sustainable," and "food-safety" concerns.[18]

The major innovation of the 1990 Farm Bill in the area of research funding was the National Research Initiative (NRI), which authorized a substantial increase in competitive grants, an increase that was not to be specifically earmarked, but rather was to support the development and application of advanced technologies. As in the past, however, the attempt to retain flexibility in the research funding process has been resisted by Congress, which has funded the NRI at well below its authorized levels.[19]

In October 1994 the USDA began implementing a major restructuring—the ninth such attempt since 1945—with the objective of reducing total staff by up to 11,000 and saving $3.6 billion in spending over the subsequent five years, creating a set of Farm Service Centers by closing or moving about one-third (or roughly 1,100) of the Department's offices, and consolidating the Department's agencies from 43 to 29.[20] As part of this restructuring, the functions formerly performed by the Cooperative State Research Service (CSRS) and the Extension Service (ES) were, for the first time in the Department's history, merged into a single agency, the newly created Cooperative State Research, Education, and Extension Service (CSREES). The National Agricultural Library (NAL) was consolidated with the Agricultural Research Service (ARS), which, together with

16 The National Agricultural Research, Extension and Teaching Policy Act of 1977 is set forth as Title XIV of the Food and Agriculture Act of 1977, and the amended provisions are in Title XVI of the Food, Agriculture, Conservation, and Trade (FACT) Act of 1990.

17 For more details of this particular legislation see Kennedy (1990).

18 The 1990 Act extended the authorizations for programs administered by the ARS, CSRS, Extension Service (ES), and other general research programs through 1995 and a few programs were repealed. The Act authorized specific programs such as "Research on Alcohol and Industrial Hydrocarbons," the establishment of a "Food Science and Nutrition Research Center," "International Agricultural Science, Education, and Development," "International Trade Development Centers," "Aquaculture Assistance Program," as well as broadening and extending the "Special Research Grants" and "Competitive Grants" programs. The legislation also emphasized programs in "Sustainable Agricultural Research and Education," "Integrated Pest Management," and "Alternative Agricultural Research and Commercialization." Miscellaneous provisions ranged from research on honeybee diseases to a requirement to reserve one percent of USDA outlays on biotechnology research for biotechnology-environmental risk assessment.

19 See NRC (1989, 1994 and 2000) for more details on the background to and development of this initiative, and a later section in this chapter.

20 For more details on these changes see Davey (1994) and Hall (1994).

CSREES, ERS, and the National Agricultural Statistics Service (NASS) reported to the newly created Under Secretary for Research, Education, and Economics. CSRS, ES and NAL, and the position of Assistant Secretary for Science and Education were abolished. Also abolished was the position of Assistant Secretary for Economics; but a new position of Chief Economist was created to supervise the Economic Outlook Staff, the World Agricultural Outlook Board, and a newly created Office of Risk Assessment and Cost-Benefit Analysis.

The 1998 Farm Bill created the Initiative for Future Agriculture and Food Systems (IFAFS). With an initial authorization of $120 million for each of the fiscal years 1998–2002, IFAFS was reauthorized in the 2002 Farm Bill and slated to increase incrementally to $200 million for FY2007 and every year thereafter. The program was intended to fund research on critical emerging areas under the 1990 Alternative Agricultural Research and Commercialization Act.

The 2008 Farm Bill (named the Food, Conservation and Energy Act) portends further major changes in the way federal funds are directed to and deployed in the U.S. agricultural research system. In October 2009, CSREES was replaced by the newly created National Institute of Food and Agriculture (NIFA). The U.S. President appointed a Director of NIFA to a (once renewable) 6-year term, to administer the research, extension, and education programs supported by federal funding through the USDA. Congress authorized annual appropriations of $700 million for grants in each of the fiscal years 2008 to 2012 to be made on a competitive basis through an Agriculture and Food Research Initiative (AFRI) that combines the authorities of the previous NRI and IFAFS programs. These competitive grants will be awarded on the basis of merit, quality, and relevance for a two-year period up to a maximum of 10 years. The legislation earmarks 60 percent of AFRI funds to fundamental (or basic) research (30 percent of which must involve multidisciplinary teams), and the remaining 40 percent to applied research. There is also a requirement that recipients provide matching funds for applied research that is commodity specific and less than national in scope.

7.3 Forms of Federal Funding

The past changes in policies reflect a mixture of political and economic influences. The economic rationale for government intervention in agricultural R&D is to correct the underinvestment, from the perspective of the broader society, that would otherwise occur. Questions arise about the appropriate form of government intervention, including provision of improved intellectual property rights as discussed in the previous section as well as government funding and production of agricultural R&D. Then within government funding, questions arise about the appropriate "division of labor" between the federal, state, and local governments according to efficient jurisdictions for the provision of particular kinds of public and collective goods, as well as equity considerations. A federal role is justified in many cases both (a) because new technologies are not strictly local in scope, and may often be usefully applied in more than one state (as we quantify in detail in later chapters), and (b) because imperfectly elastic demand for agricultural commodities implies that significant benefits from agricultural research accrue to consumers who are often outside the producing state or region. Joint federal and state funding is a natural outcome where the appropriate jurisdiction is neither individual states acting alone nor the federal government alone, and a significant part of the federal role in agricultural R&D is to partially fund research undertaken by State Agricultural Experiment Stations (SAESs) and in the process to provide inducements for states to do more of particular kinds of research and extension. The forms for federal support to the SAESs have evolved over time, reflecting changing views of research priorities and the appropriate balance between federal and state funding, and how best to achieve it.

Formula and Other Block-Funding Instruments

The core (and many argue, the strength) of the Hatch Act funding of the State Agricultural Experiment Stations, both in its original form and following the 1955 amendments, has been the distribution of block funds with little or no programmatic direction by the federal government. In the original Hatch Act of 1887, the Adams Act of 1906 and the Purnell Act of 1925 which expanded federal support of the SAESs, funding was particularly simple: the appropriated funds were simply divided equally among the various states.[21] The sole control vested by Congress in the USDA was a slowly tightening requirement that the funds be used to support research, rather than some other activity. The 1935 Bankhead-Jones Act imposed a formula that tied SAES support to each state's share of the nation's rural population; a more complicated formula was used in the Research and Marketing Act of 1946, with part of the funds divided equally among states, part distributed on the basis of rural population, and a third part based on farm population. A similar formula was included in the 1955 Hatch Act amendment that replaced the original Hatch, Adams, and Purnell Acts; formula funding also found its way into the 1962 McIntire-Stennis Forestry Research Act, the Research Facilities Act of 1963, and the periodic Farm Bills reauthorizing federal support for the SAESs.

The federal legislation authorizing funding generally includes a requirement for matching funds from the receiving states. In fact this arrangement has been part of the formula funding legislation since the Research and Marketing Act of 1946, which required that federal funds provided through the states to

---

21 Initially $15,000 went to each state. See Appendix Table 7-2 for details.

the SAESs be matched on a one-to-one basis by the state governments.[22] This requirement is consistent with the observation that the benefits from agricultural research are shared between (local) producers and (nationwide) consumers and with an equity-based argument that those who benefit should pay. In many cases the matching requirement is not a binding constraint. When states spend more than is required to receive federal funds, a reduction in federal funding may not necessarily induce a further reduction in state funding of agricultural R&D.

There is, of course, no implication that the formula funds approach is perfect. One could write down (which is certainly easier than implementing) matching rules that take into account both supply and demand elasticities, and the geographical (or jurisdictional) distribution of producers and consumers. Or one might relax the assumption that the best research organization to perform the research is within the same jurisdiction as the population measured in the funding formula. Yet funding decisions are at least in part made within the politically-charged atmosphere of the U.S. Congress, where efforts to improve the technical performance of an allocation procedure can rapidly deteriorate into debates over allocative "fairness" and negotiations that revolve more around where than how money is spent. In this context, the formula funds are understood as a negotiation-proof approximation of one aspect of an efficient allocation scheme; this mechanism may indeed be efficient when one takes into account the substantial transaction costs of the Congressional appropriations process.

Competitive Grants

Another funding mechanism is the investigator-initiated grant, generally awarded following a merit-review competition, typically with substantial input from an extra-governmental peer review procedure. As Alston and Pardey (1996, pp. 297-8) noted, in-principle advantages of competitive grants include: responsiveness and flexibility; potential to attract the best talent through open competition; through professional and peer review, potential to ensure that research resources flow in the directions with the greatest expected payoff; and, capacity to balance and complement other research resources and programs. Possible disadvantages include: competing for grants can be time-consuming and expensive, and adds an element of uncertainty compared with other types of funding arrangements; peer review can easily turn into old-boy networks; competitive grants might be directed in uneconomic directions for political or other reasons (just like other

22 Kerr (1987) reproduces key sections of the Act, Section 204 of which states that "...no payment under any such allotment [of the Act] shall be made for any fiscal year to any State agency in excess of the amount which such State agency makes available out of its own funds for such research. The funds which State agencies are required to make available in order to qualify for such an allotment shall be in addition to any funds now available to such agencies for marketing services and marketing research (Kerr 1987, p. 229)."

types of grants) or in the direction of "good science;" and, it may be inappropriate to have the "tail" of competitive grants "wagging the dog" of SAES research that is substantially supported by core formula and state funding.[23]

The National Science Foundation (NSF) uses competitive approaches almost exclusively in its support of basic research that is not supported by other agencies. The National Institutes of Health (NIH) also has a very large competitive grants program. In fiscal year 2007 NIH made 47,181 such grants, totaling $20.4 billion; an average award of $432,700 per grant (NIH 2008). The USDA has a much smaller competitive grants program, with just 537 grants awarded in 2007, for a total of $165.8 million and an average of $308,752 per grant (Table 7-1). The USDA program is proportionally as well as absolutely smaller: of total USDA spending on agricultural R&D in 2007, just 9.0 percent was allocated as competitive grant funds compared with almost 75 percent of funds spent by the NIH.

Competitive grant processes in the USDA were launched with the formation of the Competitive Research Grants Office (CRGO) under the Congressional authority of the Food and Agricultural Act of 1977. A key motivating factor was the finding of a National Research Council (1972) report—the so-called Pound Report—that "...agricultural research is suffering from an inadequate interaction with the basic disciplines that underlie it (p. 42)" and that "...the Committee...is convinced that there is an inexcusable amount of mediocre and duplicative research and the element of directed research is too great (p. 75)." A peer-reviewed, competitive grants program was proposed as a means of moving the publicly funded agricultural research portfolio towards the more-basic end of the R&D spectrum. The National Research Council (1972, pp. 49-50) stated "... that there is ample justification for increased allocations for the [competitive] grants program to a level that would approximate 20% of the USDA's research budget, at least one half of which would be for basic research related to agriculture." The 1977 Farm Bill authorized $25 million for competitive grants in FY1978 (around 4.9 percent of the USDA's total research budget that year), $30 million in FY1979 growing to $50 million by FY1982. In fact only $14.5 million was obligated in 1979 and an estimated $16.0 million in 1982, well short of the authorized totals prescribed in the enabling legislation.

23 One "wagging the dog" concern is that competitive grants may not cover the full cost of the research they support. In competitive grants, the allowances for overhead costs are often capped (e.g., in the case of the NRI, overhead was not allowed to exceed 14 percent of the budget, whereas many universities charge in excess of 40 percent for overhead costs more generally). Further discussion of the relative merits of competitive grants versus other forms of funding may be found in Bredahl, Bryant and Ruttan (1980), Just and Huffman (1992), Huffman and Just (1994, 1999 and 2000), Huffman and Evenson (2006b), and Huffman et al. (2006).

Table 7-1 Competitive USDA Funding of Agricultural Research, by Institution of Recipient, Fiscal Years 1979, 1991 and 2007

	1979				1991				2007			
	Land Grant[a] Universities	USDA	Other	Total[b]	Land Grant[a] Universities	USDA	Other	Total[b]	Land Grant[a] Universities	USDA	Other	Total[b]
						number						
Proposals received	560	57	244	861	1,777	177	759	2,713	1,401	103	373	1,877
Grants awarded	134	11	48	193	411	29	150	590	377	39	121	537
						percentage						
Share of proposals funded	23.9	19.2	19.7	22.4	23.1	16.4	19.8	21.7	26.9	37.9	6.4	28.6
						millions of dollars						
Funds requested	na	na	na	134.0	415.3	35.3	186.2	636.8	585.4	39.9	145.9	771.2
Funds awarded	9.9	0.6	4.0	14.5	47.2	3.4	18.6	69.2	127.8	5.7	32.3	165.8
						dollars						
Average funds per grant	73,657	56,364	83,542	75,130	114,841	70,560	124,000	117,288	338,993	146,154	266,942	308,752
						percentage						
Share of total grant funds awarded	68.1	4.2	27.7	100.0	68.2	5.5	29.2	100.0	77.0	3.4	19.5	100.0

Sources: Compiled by the authors from USDA SEA (1981) for 1979; from USDA CSRS (1993) for 1991; and from USDA CSREES (2008) for 2007.

Notes: All value data are reported in nominal dollars.

[a] Includes 1862, 1890 and 1984 land grant universities for all 50 states and territories.

[b] Includes other public and private universities and colleges, other federal agencies, and private for- and non-profit organizations.

A subsequent report by the National Research Council (1989, p. 5) recommended expanding the CRGO into a National Research Initiative (NRI) with a proposal to increase the funding to $500 million per year on the premise that:

> (1) The pervasive needs and problems require large amounts of new knowledge and technology for their resolution.... (2) Agricultural research provides a high return on investment. (3) The agricultural research system, as presently funded, is unable to provide the necessary financial support for the quality, amount, and breadth of science and technology necessary to address the problems.

An NRI program was launched as part of the 1990 Farm Bill with the intention of increasing the amount (and possibly the share) of federal research funds committed to agriculture that are disbursed through a competitive grants program. Congress authorized a total of $150 million for competitive agricultural research grants in FY1991. Authorized funding grew incrementally to $500 million by FY1995. Once again, these authorized totals were never reached in practice; a total of $69.2 million was granted in 1991 and $165.8 in 2007, less than 35 percent of the authorized amount (and less than 9 percent of total USDA research funding in 2007).[24]

The 2008 Farm Bill represents yet another Congressional attempt to allocate more of the federal funds for agricultural R&D by peer-reviewed competitive means (versus formula funding, block grant or earmarked means of disbursement). As part of an Agriculture and Food Research Initiative (AFRI), which combines authorities of the previous NRI and IFAFS (Initiative for Future Agriculture and Food Systems) programs, the Bill authorized annual appropriations of $700 million in competitive grants for each of the fiscal years 2008 to 2012.[25]

While the research problem emphasis of the USDA's competitive grants program has changed over the years—usually in the direction of broadening the scope of the problems to be addressed—many of the fundamentals of the program have remained unchanged. To be sure, the program has grown: from 861

24 Here the USDA research funding total was estimated as the total of USDA intramural research spending plus the federal funding through the USDA that is used to conduct research in the SAESs and other cooperating institutions.

25 The IFAFS program was launched as part of the Agricultural Research, Education and Extension Reform (AREER) Act of 1998. Congress authorized funding at $120 million annually for fiscal years 1998 to 2002 to be disbursed on a competitive basis (either as grants, contracts or cooperative agreements) to address emerging areas of interest as prescribed in the Alternative Agricultural Research and Commercialization Act of 1990. Additional targets for funding included research on food safety, agricultural genomes, natural resource management, agricultural biotechnology, high-value agricultural products, product quality, precision agriculture, and bio-based products (Appendix Table 7-2).

Figure 7-3 Competitive Funding of U.S. Agricultural Research, Fiscal Years 1979–2007

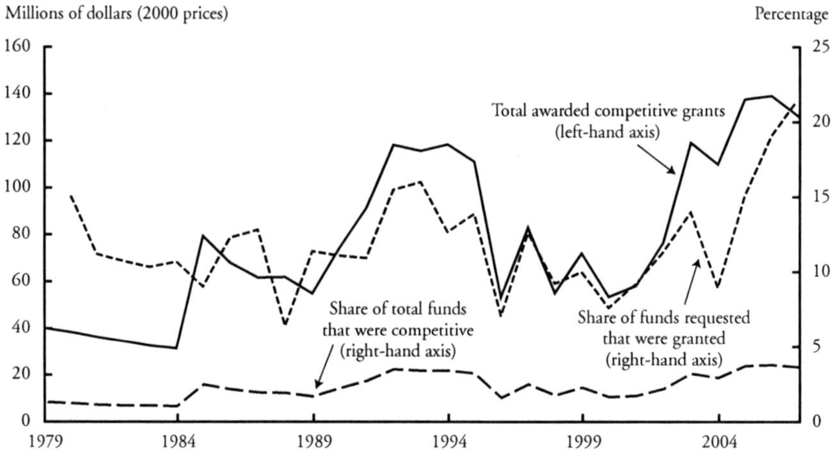

Sources: See Table 7-1. Data for the two fiscal years ending 1982 and 1990 obtained by linear interpolation of respective adjacent years.

proposals received in 1979 (193 grants awarded) to 1,877 proposals lodged (537 granted) in 2007; from a total of $134 million requested by those seeking grants in 1979 ($14.5 million awarded) to $771 million requested (and $166 million awarded) in 2007; and an increase from $75,130 per grant on average in 1979 to $308,752 per grant in 2007 (Table 7-1; Figure 7-3).[26]

In contrast, the share of grant applications funded has grown little (22.4 percent of grant applications funded in 1979 and 28.6 percent in 2007 (with just 10.8 percent of funds sought being granted in 1979 versus 21.5 percent in 2007). The overall institutional orientation of the grants has shown no obvious trend, with between 58 and 77 percent of the competitive funds going to the SAESs, between 16 and 35 percent to other agencies, and typically less than 6 percent to the USDA's own research programs. Starting from a very small base, the nominal amount of funding grew by an average of 8.69 percent per year from 1980 to 2007, and after adjusting for the increased price of agricultural R&D it grew annually by 4.23 percent per year in real terms. Total real federal support for agricultural R&D (including funding provided to the SAESs via the

---

26 Stumpf (1992) pointed out that NRI grants at that time provided funds for an average of around two years, while the NSF and NIH typically fund grantees for three to five years. The NRI data reported in the text and tables in this report represent the totality of NRI funding disbursed by competitive means. NRI (2009) report that "...in FY2007, 318 standard research projects were funded averaging $391,244 for 2.8 years (excluding research career enhancement awards, equipment grants, seed grants, conferences, continuing increments, and supplements). Fifty-one standard integrated research, education, and extension projects were funded in fiscal year 2007 averaging $681,026 for 3.5 years (excluding bridge grants, conferences, continuing increments, and supplements)."

USDA and other federal agencies) grew by 0.50 percent per year over the period 1979–2007. Total USDA funding for agricultural R&D, including USDA funds for intramural research and USDA funds disbursed to the SAESs and other cooperating agencies, grew by only 0.21 percent per year over the same period. Competitive funding as a share of total USDA funding never exceeded 10 percent.

Earmarked Funds

Despite some indications of Congressional intent to shift agricultural R&D funding towards a more competitive allocation model (at least through increases in the amounts authorized for competitive funding over several decades), amounts spent through competitive grants did not increase much. Rather than cede funding allocation decisions to competitive scientific per review processes, Congressional earmarks in the federal funding of public agricultural R&D have been persistent and pervasive. Earmarked funds are allocated by legislative mandate in Congressional appropriations bills to provide funding for specific research projects at specific locations.

Agricultural R&D earmarks were first given legislative expression in 1965 as part of Public Law 89-106. Section 2 of the Act authorized the Secretary of Agriculture "... to make grants, for periods not to exceed five years' duration, to State agricultural experiment stations, colleges, universities, and other research institutions and organizations and to Federal and private organizations and individuals for research...." This became known as the Special Grants Program within USDA CSRS. Law, Tonon and Miller (2008, p. 197) observed that "Even though PL 89–106 was enacted in August 1965, the law was not invoked until the 1969 fiscal year. In what may be considered the earliest "special grants" made under this authority, Congressional appropriators from the Senate earmarked $1,000,000 for cotton research and $400,000 for soybean research (U.S. Congress 1968)."

Offut (1993, pp. 274–275) observed that "Congressional earmarking of research grants is not confined to agriculture. However it has historically found its fullest expression there." Citing a 1992 Office of Management and Budget report she noted:

> FY1992 total science earmarks for both facilities and research amounted to $993 million, of which the single largest portion (almost 20 percent) went for 334 agricultural projects at a cost of $180 million. And, within the appropriation for agriculture, earmarks are not confined to the Cooperative State Research Service (CSRS), the primary source of funds for the land grant universities, but also are found in the Agricultural Research Service (ARS) and the Extension Service (ES). Indeed, the FY1993 ARS appropriations report con-

> tained 61 separate instructions on spending, of which 49 identified specific locations or recipients.... The CSRS appropriations ($484 million in FY1993) accounts for about one-third of Federal spending on agricultural research (CSRS, ARS, ES combined).... Of the $433 million in program funds for CSRS, formula grants under the Hatch Act account for $168 million, a total little changed, in real terms, over the past decade. Of the remaining $265 million, $97.5 million goes to the NRI and about $64 million is earmarked for special grants "with a zip code." These earmarks, some 120 in number, thus account for about 15 percent of the CSRS program spending [U.S. Congress 1993].

Trends in Funding Forms

Table 7-2 summarizes the trends in federal sources and forms of funding to the SAESs over the period 1970–2007. Formula funding as a share of total USDA support to the states shrank from 86.6 percent in 1970 to 37.5 percent in 2007; less than 20 percent of the total federal support to the SAESs in that year, reflecting the substantial decline in the USDA share of federal government funding over this same period. As a share of USDA and total support, most of the increase in competitive funding occurred in the early years of the program, with little upward trend in the NRI share after the mid-1990s. Notably, earmarked or special grants funding also increased. Federal funds allocated by means of Congressional earmarks are now equivalent to those allocated by competitive, peer review processes. Funds allocated by way of formula or as grants and contracts to collaborating institutions still account for 70 percent of USDA research funding to the states, but only 36 percent of all federal funding to the states for agricultural research.

Evidence of the comparative productivity and broader economic payoffs to block versus formula versus competitive forms of funding would be useful in guiding choices about the appropriate mechanism by which to allocate public funds to agricultural R&D. Economists have made a few attempts to estimate econometrically the effects of funding arrangements on the effectiveness of agricultural R&D spending—an ambitious undertaking given the general difficulty of modeling research impacts and resolving particular influences (see, for example, the discussion in Chapter 9), and the tendency for findings to be fragile. Attempts to draw fine econometric distinctions in models of research impacts should be interpreted with care and caution, especially as a basis for suggesting directions for policy. At a minimum, strong caveats should be attached to any inferences about policy, but that is not always done.

Table 7-2 Sources and Forms of Federal Funding to the SAESs, 1970–2007

Year	USDA (Including CSREES Administered)						
	Formula Funds	Competitive Grants	Special Grants	Other Grants and Contracts	Total USDA	Other Federal	Total Federal
Total funds			*thousands of dollars*				
1970	57,451	0	1,581	7,347	66,379	27,731	94,110
1975	81,113	0	10,442	11,432	102,987	35,301	138,288
1980	145,493	34	16,973	28,458	190,959	71,697	262,656
1985	188,233	11,514	21,302	35,941	256,990	112,414	369,404
1990	191,711	31,173	47,605	56,439	326,928	188,606	515,534
1995	213,555	67,876	68,076	90,740	440,247	285,838	726,085
2000	224,056	64,553	50,027	117,270	455,907	380,066	835,972
2005	221,798	91,299	98,778	258,813	670,688	681,350	1,352,038
2007	258,366	101,718	97,567	231,808	689,459	666,002	1,355,461
Funding as share of total USDA			*percentage share*				
1970	86.6	0.0	2.4	11.1	100.0		
1975	78.8	0.0	10.1	11.1	100.0		
1980	76.2	0.0	8.9	14.9	100.0		
1985	73.2	4.5	8.3	14.0	100.0		
1990	58.6	9.5	14.6	17.3	100.0		
1995	48.5	15.4	15.5	20.6	100.0		
2000	49.1	14.2	11.0	25.7	100.0		
2005	33.1	13.6	14.7	38.6	100.0		
2007	37.5	14.8	14.2	33.6	100.0		
Funding as share of total federal			*percentage share*				
1970	61.0	0.0	1.7	7.8	70.5	29.5	100.0
1975	58.7	0.0	7.6	8.3	74.5	25.5	100.0
1980	55.4	0.0	6.5	10.8	72.7	27.3	100.0
1985	51.0	3.1	5.8	9.7	69.6	30.4	100.0
1990	37.2	6.0	9.2	10.9	63.4	36.6	100.0
1995	29.4	9.3	9.1	12.5	60.6	39.1	100.0
2000	26.8	7.7	6.0	14.0	54.5	45.5	100.0
2005	16.4	6.8	7.3	19.1	49.6	50.4	100.0
2007	19.1	7.5	7.2	17.1	50.9	49.1	100.0

Sources: Data extracted by authors from unpublished USDA CRIS data files.

Notes: Series include all U.S. states and territories. USDA formula funds are the sum of Hatch, McIntire-Stennis, Evan Allens, and Animal Health grants administered by CSREES; USDA competitive grants are NRI competitive grants; USDA special grants are CSREES grants; USDA other grants and contracts represent the sum of a range of grants administered by CSREES including cooperative agreements, rural development grants, small business grants, 3D grants funded via Section D of the Smith-Lever Act, other extension grants, RREA grants made under the Renewable Resources Extension Act, SERD grants administered by the Science and Education Resources Development unit of CSREES, and various other grants to the states.

Summarizing results from their statistical assessment of the amount, structure and funding of public agricultural R&D on state productivity, Huffman and Just (1994, p. 754) observed that their:

> … results do not provide any evidence that public or private grant, contract and cooperative agreement funds are more productive than federal formula or state funded research. Rather the results provide evidence that federal formula and state funded research are more productive. … [suggesting that] a reduction in productivity will result from the increasing domination of agricultural research funding by competitive grants.[27]

These strong conclusions rest on a questionable foundation. They hinge on the sign and significance of variables that ostensibly account for the effects of the form of funding on state-specific multi-factor productivity for the period 1973–1982. The form of funding was represented by an estimate of the average share (for 1970, 1975 and 1980) of SAES funds received by way of grants, contracts and cooperative agreements from (a) the federal government, and (b) private business, commodity groups and other nongovernmental agencies. Important additional explanatory variables included the corresponding stocks of public and private R&D spending (formed by aggregating R&D spending from the current and 33 previous years). The maintained hypothesis is that a competitive grants (i.e., form of funding) effect on productivity can be meaningfully disentangled from the myriad other influences on productivity, most notably the size (and structure) of the stock of knowledge formed by accumulating spending on agricultural R&D over the prior 33 years.

This is asking a lot of the data; especially as the dependent productivity variable in the Huffman and Just analysis spans the period 1973–1982, yet competitive funding processes did not begin to influence federal agriculture R&D allocations until FY1978. These timing issues confound an already difficult "needle-in-the-haystack" problem. According to our extractions from USDA CRIS data files, competitive funds accounted for just 0.35 percent (a total of $9.8 million) of the accumulated total of $2.8 billion of the federal funds allocated to SAES research during the period 1949–1982 (the terminal date in the Huffman and Just sample). Competitive funds accounted for just 0.06 percent of all USDA and SAES research spending during this same 33-year period. Even by 2007, just 3.6 percent of all public funding for agricultural R&D performed by the SAESs and USDA was disbursed competitively, including 9.0 percent of all funding for research performed by the USDA (Figure 7-4).

27 Day-Rubenstein et al. (2000) report an earlier econometric attempt to discern the productivity implications of competitive versus formula funding.

Figure 7-4 Total Public, USDA and Competitive Funding for Agricultural R&D, 1979 and 2007

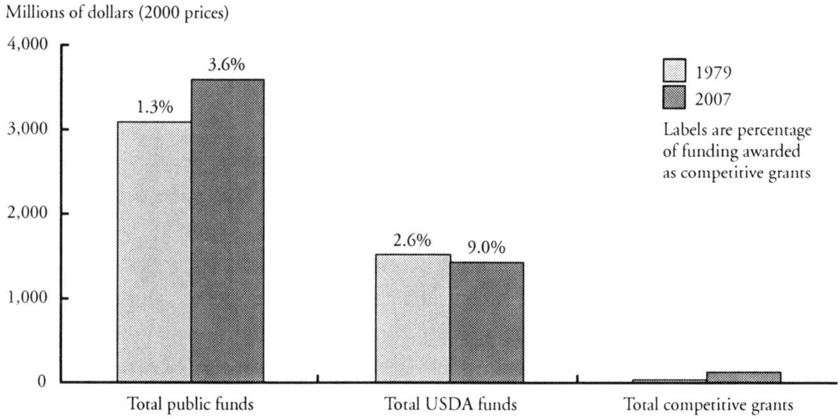

Sources: Data extracted by authors from unpublished USDA CRIS data files.

Notes: Total public funds represent total funding for the 48 SAESs and intramural USDA research.

More recently, Huffman and Evenson (2006b) revisited the same question using more recent data. Their objective was to establish whether federal formula or competitive grant funding of agricultural research has a greater impact on state agricultural productivity. They estimated a model of agricultural productivity using annual data for the 48 contiguous U.S. states over the period 1970–1999, and they found that "...Hatch formula funding has a larger impact on agricultural productivity than federal competitive grant funding, and a reallocation of Hatch formula funds to competitive grant funding would lower agricultural productivity (p. 783)." These findings reinforce the earlier results from Huffman and Just (1994), but are questionable for some of the same reasons, and some additional ones. In particular, the fact that competitive funding was so comparatively unimportant throughout the period of analysis makes it difficult to believe that changes in the observed share of funding in this form had appreciable impacts on productivity patterns. In addition, competitive grants were represented crudely in the model. Knowledge stocks based on a 35-year trapezoidal lag structure applied to total public agricultural research spending were multiplied by a 12-year simple moving average of the state-specific share of SAES funding in the form of competitive grants. The trends in this variable (and corresponding variables for other funding forms) might well have captured various effects of omitted variables or other specification errors. In particular, as documented in Chapter 5, productivity growth slowed in most states since 1990, and during the same period the share of federal formula funding declined while the shares of competitive grants and earmarked funds *both* grew (Table 7-2). This correlation is likely to be little more than a coincidence, but Huffman and Evenson (2006b), like Huffman and Just (1994) twelve years earlier, do not allow for the relevant alternative hypotheses and interpret the observed statistical relationship as a causal one.

7.4 Conclusion

The transition from the 20th to 21st Century saw potentially seismic shifts in the policies, practices, and potentials for the agricultural sciences. In the 1970s, the rate of growth of public investment in agricultural R&D in the United States began to ratchet down, and continued to do so generally, aside from an uptick in several recent years. The most recent legislative changes portend major changes in the way federal funds are disbursed to the states, perhaps implementing a shift towards greater use of competitive processes for allocating federal funding to agricultural R&D. This would bring agricultural research funding through the USDA more into line with mechanisms used to fund research through the NIH or NSF. Whether that will engender efficiencies in the use of these funds is open to conjecture.

As documented in Chapter 6, the place of U.S. public agricultural R&D in the broader spectrum of science is also changing. Public science spending in the United States has shifted its priorities toward health research. The private sector now performs about half of all the food and agricultural R&D in the country, still substantially less than the almost 80 percent private-sector share for all the sciences. In 2000 (the latest year of available global data), the United States still accounted for about 19 percent of the world's agricultural R&D spending. This is substantially less than its corresponding global share of 33 percent in total science spending. Extending recent past trends toward the middle of the 21st Century, the United States is likely to lose (possibly significant) world market share in both total science spending and agricultural R&D spending, although it will remain a leading if not dominant player for decades to come.

What constitutes agricultural R&D changed substantially as the 20th Century drew to a close. U.S. public agricultural research substantially expanded its scope over the past several decades, taking on an ever-broadening portfolio of research interests (to include research on the environment, nutrition, food safety, and bio-energy as well as an increased emphasis on the upstream genetic and genomic sciences), but absent a commensurate expansion in the amount of funds to conduct the research. An important consequence, documented in Chapter 6, was a contraction in the share of agricultural R&D conducted by the SAESs (and the USDA) intended to maintain and enhance agricultural productivity.[28] This shift has been underway since at least the 1970s.

Chapter 5 presented evidence of a sizable slowdown in the rate of growth of U.S. multi-factor productivity, beginning in the early 1990s, several decades after the slowdown in research spending growth took hold. Some of the shifting public science agenda may reflect political pressures on government-mediated funding processes. Some might reflect a perception that the payoffs to more conventional agricultural R&D are waning. Part IV of this book presents new evidence on the relationship between U.S. agricultural R&D spending and productivity growth, and assesses the payoffs to those research-induced productivity gains.

28 The share of overall SAES funding oriented to farm productivity research dropped from 73 percent in 1970 to 57 percent in 2007; for all public (i.e., SAES and USDA intramural) the farm productivity share was 63 percent in 1970 and 56 percent in 2007.

Appendix Table 7-1 Legal and Regulatory Changes Affecting Intellectual Property Rights in U.S. Agriculture, 1790–2001

Year	Legislation, Ruling or Event	Notes
1790	Patent Act of 1790	First U.S. statute pertaining to patents (as referenced in Article 1, Section 8 of the U.S. Constitution). Excluded plant and animal innovations from protection.
1836	Patent Act of 1836	Created the Patent Office and gave it the power to examine (and refuse) patents; the underpinnings of modern patent law.
1930	Plant Patent Act (P.L. 71-245)	The first legislation to protect plant varieties. Provided protection to those who invent or discover new and distinct varieties of asexually propagated plants, other than a tuber propogated plant. Gave the grantee the right to exclude others from asexually reproducing the plant or selling or using the plant so reproduced. The Act did not protect sexually propagated plants, plant parts, or plants found in an uncultivated state. The duration of the plant patent was specified to be 17 years.
1952	Patent Act of 1952 (P.L. 82-593)	Defined "invention" and put forth requirements for patentability; revised procedures for obtaining a patent and operational details pertaining to the Patent Office.
1954	Amendment to the Plant Patent Act (P.L. 83-775)	Made patentable plant seedlings and mutants discovered in an uncultivated state, propagated asexually, and proved to have new characteristics distinct from other known plants.
1961	International Union for the Protection of New Varieties of Plants (UPOV)	Internationally coordinated protection for plant varieties (called plant breeders' rights) adopted in Paris by five UPOV member countries (Belgium, France, Germany, Italy and Netherlands). The convention was subsequently revised in 1972, 1978 and 1991.
1970	Plant Variety Protection Act (PVPA) (P.L. 91-577)	Protected sexually propagated plant varieties for 17 years from date of issuance. Included breeders' and farmers' exemptions. PVP Office responsible for administering the Act was organized within the Agricultural Marketing Service of the U.S. Department of Agriculture.
1970	Patent Cooperation Treaty (PCT)	Unified the procedure for filing patent applications in multiple jurisdictions. The PCT, administered by the World Intellectual Property Organization (WIPO), Geneva, was concluded in 1970, amended in 1979, and modified in 1984 and 2001.
1976	*Yoder Brothers, Inc. v. California-Florida Plant Corp,*. 537 F.2d. 1347, 1382 (5th Cir. 1976)	Ruling invited the argument that even a variety selected as a naturally-occurring mutation or "sport," and asexually reproduced, is "made by the hand of man," and is therefore patentable subject matter.
1980	Amendment to Plant Variety Protection Act (P.L. 96-574)	Expanded the scope of PVPA to encompass "soup vegetables" such as okra, carrots, celery, tomatoes, peppers, and cucumbers. Extended the term of protection to 18 years from date of issue.

1980	*Diamond v. Chakrabarty*, 447 U.S. 303 (1980)	Held that the class of patentable subject matter includes living organisms.
1980	Bayh-Dole Act (P.L. 96-517)	Established the general right of grant recipients (e.g., universities) to apply for patents on most federally-funded research.
1985	*Ex parte Hilbberd*, 227 USPQ 433 (Bd. Pat. App. & Intref. 1990)	Held that seeds, plants, and tissue cultures were subject to utility patents. No longer was an inventor limited to applying for a PVPC or plant patent.
1987–1988	*Ex parte Allen*, 2 USPQ2d 1425, 1426 (Bd. Pat. App. & Interf. 1987), *aff'd mem.*, 846 F.2d 77 (Fed. Cir. 1988)	Held that multicellular organisms (in this case oysters) were patentable.
1994	Amendment to Plant Variety Protection Act (P.L. 103-349)	Harmonized the U.S. PVPA with the 1991 UPOV Convention. Clarified that seed could be on-sold, but could not be sold to another farmer for further production of seeds of the protected variety. Amendment extended protection, to varieties that are "essentially derived" from the protected variety. Tuber propagated plants were also subject to protection and the term of protection increased to 20 years for most crops and 25 years for trees and vines.
1994	*Pioneer Hi-Bred Int'l, Inc.v. Holden Foundation Seed Inc.*, 35 F.3d 1226, 1230 (8th Cir. 1994)	Ruled that identification by private code of fields of inbred parent lines of corn is sufficient to constitute a reasonable effort to maintain secrecy, thus establishing that inbred lines can be protected as trade secrets.
1994	*Advanta USA Inc. v Pioneer Hi-Bred International, Inc*, No. 04-C-238-S, slip op. (W.D. Wisc Oct 27, 2004)	Ruled that submission of sample seeds to the Plant Variety Protection Office as part of an application for a PVPC does not constitute a disclosure that prevents subsequent patentability.
1995	Community Plant Variety Office (CPVO)	Prior to April 27, 1995, when the CPVO was established, a breeder seeking protection for a variety throughout the European Union was required to submit an application to each of the member states. Now with a single application to the CPVO, a breeder can be granted varietal protection rights throughout the European Union. CPVO members currently can exploit both a community plant variety right (CPVR) and a national plant breeders' right in relation to that variety. Individuals or companies from member states of UPOV, but not a member of the European Union, can also apply, provided that an agent domiciled in the Community has been nominated. The duration of CPVR protection is twenty-five years for most crops, and thirty years for potato, vine, and tree varieties.
1995	*Imazio Nursery, Inc. v. Dania Greenhouse*, 69 F.3d1560, 1569 (Fed. Cir. 1995), *cert. denied*, 518 U.S. 1018 (1996)	Court held that to show infringement of a plant patent, the patent owner must prove that the alleged infringing plant is an asexually reproduced progeny of the patented plant. A mere demonstration of morphological identity between the patented and alleged infringing varieties was found insufficient to meet this standard, and actual evidence of "copying" was required. Independent creation was held to be a defense against the claim of infringement of plant patents.

(continued)

Appendix Table 7-1 (continued)

Year	Legislation, Ruling or Event	Notes
1995	*Asgrow Seed Co. v. Winterboer*, 513 U.S. 179 (1995)	The PVPA protects owners of novel seed varieties against unauthorized sales of their seed for replanting purposes. An exemption, however, allows farmers to make some sales of protected variety seed to other farmers. This case raised the question of whether there is a limit to the quantity of protected seed that a farmer can sell under this exemption. The court held that under the PVPA, a farmer may only sell the amount of saved seed that would be required for the purpose of replanting the farmer's own acreage.
1998	Plant Patent Amendment Act (P.L. 105-289)	Extended the life of a plant patent to 20 years. Rights prior to 1998 enabled the grantee to exclude others from asexually reproducing the plant or selling or using the plant so reproduced. To these rights were added exclusion rights for offering for sale the protected plant or any of its parts, and for importing the plant.
2001	*J.E.M. Ag Supply, Inc v. Pioneer Hi-Bred, Inc.*, 534 U.S. 124 (2001)	Permitted dual protection for plants, both a utility patent and a PVPC, or a utility patent and a plant patent.

Sources: Pardey, Koo and Nottenburg (2004), Hanson and Highlander (2004), Wright et al. (2007), USDA (2005) and Koo et al. (2009).

Appendix Table 7-2 History of Major Legislation Affecting the Conduct and Federal Funding of Research in the USDA, SAESs and Other Cooperating Institutions, 1862–2008

Year	Legislation		
1862	Act of Congress (Chapter 72, 37 Congress, Session 2)	*Provisions*	Introduced a Commissioner of Agriculture and the Department of Agriculture (USDA) to take over agricultural science functions of the Patent Office.
1862	First Morrill Act (Chapter 130, 37 Congress, Session 2)	*Provisions*	Each state could establish and maintain at least one college to (without excluding other scientific and classical studies, and including military tactics) teach courses related to agriculture and mechanical arts in order to promote the liberal and practical education of the industrial classes.
		Comments	Established the land-grant system.
		Funding Details and Mechanisms	Each state was to receive 30,000 acres of land for each Senator and Representative in Congress. States where not enough public land was available were given script to public land in other states; the income from the land was to be used for operating expenses (construction, purchase and repair of buildings were excluded).
1887	Hatch Act (Chapter 314, 49 Congress, Session 2)	*Provisions*	Each state could establish an experiment station to conduct original research or verify experiments on subjects bearing directly to the agricultural industry of the United States. Stations were to be established under direction of land-grant colleges, but exceptions were permitted.
		Comments	Established the SAES.
		Funding Details and Mechanisms	Each qualifying state was to receive $15,000 per year.
1890	Second Morrill Act (Chapter 841, 51 Congress, Session 1)	*Provisions*	First proposed in 1872. Gave direct annual appropriations to each state to further support land-grant colleges.
		Comments	Forbade racial discrimination in admission to colleges receiving the funds and gave rise to the so-called "1890 colleges."
		Funding Details and Mechanisms	Congress gave each qualifying state $15,000 in the first year, increasing by $1,000 per year for subsequent years until the annual amount reached $25,000.

(continued)

Appendix Table 7-2 (continued)

Year	Legislation		
1906	Adams Act (P.L. 59-47)	*Provisions*	Each state could receive additional federal funding to pay the necessary expenses of conducting original research and experiments.
		Comments	Put more emphasis on science and accountability; coincided with the formation of ESCOP.
		Funding Details and Mechanisms	Each qualifying state could receive a maximum of an additional $15,000 per year. Each state was entitled to an increase of $5,000 for the first year and $2,000 over the previous year's sum for five subsequent years.
1925	Purnell Act (P.L. 68-458)	*Provisions*	Each state could receive additional federal funding for research to (a) establish and maintain a permanent and efficient agricultural industry and (b) develop and improve the rural home and rural life.
		Comments	First emphasis on economics, home economics, and sociology.
		Funding Details and Mechanisms	Each qualifying state could receive a maximum of $30,000 per year. Each state was entitled to an increase of $10,000 for the first year and $5,000 over the previous year's sum for four subsequent years.
1930	Ransdell Act (P.L. 71-251)	*Provisions*	Reorganized, expanded and redesignated the Laboratory of Hygiene (established in 1887) as the National Institute of Health (later to become the National Institutes of Health, P.L. 80-655).
		Funding Details and Mechanisms	Appropriated $750,000 for the construction of facilities and research fellowships.
1935	Bankhead-Jones Act (P.L. 74-182)	*Provisions*	SAES and USDA could receive additional funding for research into basic problems of agriculture; research relating to quality improvement, new and improved methods of production and distribution, and new and extended uses and markets for agricultural commodities; and research relating to conservation, development, and recreational use of land and water.
		Comments	Established formula funding and federal-state matching grants.
		Funding Details and Mechanisms	Appropriated a maximum of $5 million per year, with $3 million to the SAES, to be increased by $1 million per year for each of five years. Funds to be distributed to the states on the basis of their proportions of the U.S. rural population and each state must match federal contribution with nonfederal funding of the SAES.
1946	Research and Marketing Act (P.L. 79-733)	*Provisions*	SAES and USDA could receive additional funding for marketing and utilization research, and for regional research involving two or more states on a problem of regional significance.
		Comments	Introduced open-ended appropriations. Linked agricultural R&D to national welfare. Stated that the goal of Congress was to maintain a balanced farming and industrial economy. Established the National Advisory Committee. Committee of Nine was formed. Included the first use of congruence principle in funding formulas.

Year	Legislation		
		Funding Details and Mechanisms	Increased total SAES funding by $2.5 million in FY1947 and FY1948; increased by $5 million for each of FY1949, 1950 and 1951; with additional funds as Congress deemed necessary for additional years. Allocated among states: 20% equally among states; 26% according to state shares of U.S. rural population; 26% according to shares of U.S. farm population; 25% for regional research; 3% for administrative costs incurred by the USDA. Authorized grants for "new uses" research to increase by $3 million per year from FY1947 to FY1951, with additional funds thereafter as Congress deemed necessary. Funds for cooperative research into farm product utilization were authorized to rise from $1.5 million in FY1947 to $6 million after FY1950; reauthorized $2 million Special Research Fund provided for in the Bankhead-Jones Act of 1935. Title II authorized an additional $2.5 million in FY1947, increasing to $20 million per year after FY1950, for marketing research, carried out cooperatively with SAES and other public and private institutions, on a matching grant basis.
1950	National Science Foundation Act (P.L. 81-507)	*Provisions*	Established the National Science Foundation as an independent agency in the executive branch of the government.
		Funding Details and Mechanisms	Appropriated to the Foundation a sum not to exceed $0.5 million for the fiscal year ending June 30, 1951, and not to exceed $15 million for each fiscal year thereafter.
1953		*Comments*	By executive order, most USDA research was consolidated into a new agency, the Agricultural Research Service (ARS).
1955	Amended Hatch Act (P.L. 84-352)	*Provisions*	Authorized the conduct of research contributing to the maintenance of a permanent and effective agricultural industry in the United States, including research basic to the problems of agriculture in its broadest aspects, and research related to the development and improvement of the rural home and rural life and the maximum contribution of agriculture to the welfare of the consumer. Removed restrictions on using funds for buildings, but Hatch funds still had to be spent within the year awarded.
		Comments	Retained allocation formulas, matching grant requirements, and "open-ended" appropriations. Congress rejected a proposal to reduce marketing research by 20% and insisted that earmarking apply to all increases in appropriations.
		Funding Details and Mechanisms	Consolidated federal funding for SAES into two accounts (formula funds and regional research funds). No set annual amounts were established. Funds were allocated according to the formula from the Research and Marketing Act: 20% equally among states; 26% according to a state's share of the U.S. rural population; 26% according to a state's share of the U.S. farm population; 25% for cooperative regional research; 3% for administrative costs incurred by the USDA.

(continued)

Appendix Table 7-2 (continued)

Year	Legislation		
1961		*Comments*	Economic Research Service was established as a separate agency within the USDA.
1962	McIntire-Stennis Forestry Research Act (P.L. 87-788)	*Provisions*	Made funding available to SAES, land grant colleges and forestry schools for forestry research—including reforestation, woodlands and related watershed management, outdoor recreation, wildlife habitats, wood utilization, and such other studies as may be necessary to obtain the fullest and most effective use of forest resources.
		Comments	Coincided with the formation of the Cooperative State Research Service (CSRS) in 1961–1963. CSRS was given authority to administer appropriations under McIntire-Stennis.
		Funding Details and Mechanisms	A formula allocated $10,000 to each state, 40% of the remainder was allocated according to a state's share of the nation's total commercial forest land, 40% according to the value of its annual timber cut, and 20% according to its contribution of non-federal forestry research dollars. In both FY1964 and FY1965, $1 million was appropriated, 2% of CSRS-managed funds (by FY1974 this figure had increased to over $6 million annually, 7% of CSRS-managed funds, and by FY1984 it was up to almost $13 million or 6% of combined federal funding to the states for agricultural R&D).
1965	Research Facilities Act (P.L. 88-74)	*Provisions*	Earmarked funds to be matched by the states for the construction, acquisition, and remodeling of buildings, laboratories, and other capital facilities. Supported new construction only of facilities for research on hazardous chemicals used in farming. Allowed each station to obligate its annual share over three years for the first time.
		Comments	IR-4 "National Program of Clearances of Chemicals for Minor and Specialty Uses" was launched in 1963. Current Research Information System (CRIS) was established in the 1960s.
		Funding Details and Mechanisms	The formula resembled that in the amended Hatch Act: one-third of funds were allocated equally among states; one-third according to their share of rural residents; one-third according to the share of farm population. Total allocations were $3.2 million in 1965; $2 million per year in 1966, 1967, and 1968; none in 1969; $1 million in 1970; and none thereafter.
1965	Public Law 89-106	*Provisions*	Established the "Specific Research Grants" program to finance selected projects to address specific problems of constituent concern or multistate problems, to run for a maximum of five years. Later became the "Special Grants" program.
		Comments	National Agricultural Research Advisory Committee (NARAC) was established in 1961. Producer-dominated commodity-oriented research councils declined, and were abandoned in 1970.
		Funding Details and Mechanisms	CSRS would call annually for proposals in areas singled out by Congress for special attention. In FY1966, $1.6 million was offered; in FY1967–1970, $1.7 million per year. $283,000 per year was allocated to the sixteen "1890 Institutions."
1972	Rural Development Act (P.L. 92-419)	*Provisions*	Title V authorized funding for the SAES and Extension Service to carry out research and extension related to rural development and small-farms.

Year	Act		
		Comments	In 1971, Congress granted $75,000 to each of four rural development centers. Congress recommended that SAES devote $3 million of Hatch appropriations to community improvement research.
		Funding Details and Mechanisms	The Act authorized up to $10 million for FY1974, $15 million for 1975, and $20 million for FY1976. Actual expenditures were much less. $3 million was provided in each of the first three years, split between extension and research, allocated among the SAES on a basis similar to the Hatch formula except that 10% was reserved for interstate projects. Funding continued at $3 million per year for another four years after the initial authorization expired in 1977.
1972	Technology Assessment Act (P.L. 92-484)	*Provisions*	Created the Office of Technology Assessment with responsibility to the legislative branch of government.
		Comments	The basic function of the Office of Technology Assessment was to provide early indications of the probable beneficial and adverse impacts of the applications of technology and to develop other coordinate information which may assist the Congress.
1977	National Agricultural Research, Extension and Teaching Policy Act (Title XIV) of the Food and Agriculture Act (P.L. 95-113)	*Provisions*	Continued and strengthened amended Hatch programs. Subtitle C initiated a new USDA Competitive Grants program for plant science and nutrition research, open to all scientists, to be awarded on a competitive basis to private- and public-sector organizations, including SAESs, all colleges and universities, other research organizations, federal agencies and individuals. Continued the Special Grants program. Dropped the requirement that 20% of amended Hatch funds be earmarked for marketing research.
		Comments	Other new earmarked grants were also introduced (e.g., energy research, animal health). Established the Joint Council and Users Advisory Board as a priority-setting and accountability mechanism. Amended the 1965 Special Research Grants Act to authorize a competitive research grant program at USDA.
		Funding Details and Mechanisms	Hatch formula funds were strengthened with $120 million called for in FY1978 and increases of $25 million per year up to $220 million in FY1982. Allocation was basically as specified in previous arrangements and formulas. A competitive grants program authorized additional spending of $25 million in FY1978, $30 million in FY1979, $35 million in 1980, $40 million in FY1981 and $50 million in FY1982.
1980	Bayh-Dole Act (P.L. 96-517)	*Provisions*	Authorized federal agencies to (1) apply for, obtain, and maintain patents or other forms of protection in the United States and in foreign countries on inventions in which the federal government owns a right, title, or interest; (2) grant nonexclusive, exclusive, or partially exclusive licenses under federally owned patent applications, patents, or other forms of protection obtained, royalty-free or for royalties or other consideration, and on such terms and conditions as determined appropriate in the public interest; (3) undertake all other suitable and necessary steps to protect and administer rights to federally owned inventions on behalf of the federal government either directly or through contract; and (4) transfer custody and administration, in whole or in part, to another federal agency, of the right, title, or interest in any federally owned invention.

(continued)

Appendix Table 7-2 (continued)

Year	Legislation		
1980	Stevenson-Wydler Technology Innovation Act (P.L. 96-480)	*Provisions*	Included several provisions to stimulate the development of technologies: (1) established organizations in the executive branch to study and stimulate technology; (2) promoted technology development through the establishment of centers for industrial technology; (3) stimulated improved utilization of federally funded technology developments by state and local governments and the private sector; (4) provided recognition of individuals and companies which have made outstanding contributions in technology; and (5) encouraged the exchange of scientific and technical personnel among academia, industry, and federal laboratories.
1981	Agriculture and Food Act (P.L. 97-98)	*Provisions*	Extended the 1977 Act for four years. Introduced a $10 million annual rangeland research program and a $7.5 million annual acquaculture research program.
		Comments	Congress effectively promised not to replace, but to supplement, formula funds with competitive grants. The scope of the competitive grants program was expanded with a biotechnology initiative that included animal science.
		Funding Details and Mechanisms	Funding formula was the same as the 1977 Act. Hatch funds were authorized to rise from $220 million in FY1982 to $250 million in FY1985. Hatch funds were guaranteed at a minimum of 25% of USDA expenditures in cooperative programs.
1982	Small Business Innovation Development Act (P.L. 97-219) Amended 1992 (P.L. 102-564)	*Provisions*	Earmarked 1.5% of federal extramural research funds to small businesses (increased to 2.5% in 1993).
1984	National Cooperative Research Act (P.L. 98-462)	*Comments*	Provided antitrust exemptions for private participation in research consortia.
1985	Food Security Act of 1985 (P.L. 98-198)	*Provisions*	Extended the 1981 Act for four years. Added a new subtitle to promote agricultural productivity. Earmarked funds for marketing research were reintroduced ($10 million per year) along with trade development centers at land-grant universities (on a matching basis). Established a research and education program on sustainable agriculture.
		Comments	USDA was permitted to fund competitive grants for facilities at SAESs.
		Funding Details and Mechanisms	Funding formula was the same as in the 1981 Act. Hatch funds were to grow only 4% per year, while competitive grants were authorized to increase substantially, especially for biotechnology research. Hatch funding of $270 million in FY1986 was to increase to $310 million for FY1990. Competitive grants funding was to increase from $50 million in FY1985 to $70 million in FY1986 and subsequent years.

1986	Federal Technology Transfer Act of 1986 (P.L. 99-502)	*Provisions*	Amended the Stevenson-Wydler Technology Innovation Act of 1980 to facilitate the formation of Cooperative Research and Development Agreements (CRADAs).
		Comments	CRADAs are agreements between collaborating government agencies and private firms designed to speed the development and commercialization of technology. Private corporations participating in a CRADA may file patents and retain patent rights on inventions developed by the CRADA, while the government retains the right to license the patents.
1990	Food, Agriculture, Conservation and Trade Act (P.L. 101-624)	*Provisions*	Extended the 1985 Act for four years. Title 16, Section 1615 provided for the inception of the National Competitive Initiative, commonly called the National Research Initiative (NRI).
		Comments	The legislation directed the USDA to emphasize "high-priority research" on national and regional research and commercialization needs regarding plant systems; animal systems; nutrition, food quality, and health; natural resources and the environment; engineering, products, and processes (including new uses and products from traditional and non-traditional crops); and, markets, trade, and policy research.
		Funding Details and Mechanisms	Congress authorized competitive grant funding at $150 million for FY1991, $275 million for FY1992, $350 million for FY1993, $400 million for FY1994, and $500 for FY1995, of which (a) not less than 10% for FY 1991, 20% for FY1992, and 30% for FY1993 and thereafter was for multidisciplinary research; (b) not less than 20% was for mission-linked systems research; and (c) not less than 10% was for grants to strengthen research and education opportunities.
1990	Alternative Agricultural Research and Commercialization Act (P.L. 101-624)	*Provisions*	Through the encouragement of and the provision of assistance to agricultural research, development, and commercialization, one Subtitle directed, to the maximum extent possible, research and commercialization efforts toward the production of new nonfood, nonfeed products made from agricultural commodities that can be raised by family-sized agricultural producers. Established an independent entity within USDA, the Alternative Agriculture Research and Commercialization Center, to promote industrial uses for agricultural commodities.
		Funding Details and Mechanisms	Grants made, and contracts and cooperative agreements entered into, by the Alternative Agriculture Research and Commercialization Center were to be selected on a competitive basis on the recommendation of a peer review system established by the Center. Peer reviewers were required to have expertise in commercial production, product development, processing, and marketing of agricultural commodities as well as in scientific research. Selection criteria were based on the likelihood that the project will result in creating or improving economically viable commercial nonfood, nonfeed products, applications, processes, or technologies that involve the use of raw or processed agricultural commodities. Established in the U.S. Treasury a fund called the Alternative Agricultural Research and Commercialization Revolving Fund. Authorized appropriations to the Fund were $10 million in FY1991 increasing in steps annually to $75 million in FY1995 to 2000.

(continued)

Appendix Table 7-2 (continued)

Year	Legislation		
1994	Department of Agriculture Reorganization Act (P.L. 103-354)	*Provisions*	Merged the Cooperative State Research Service (CSRS) and the Extension Service (ES) into a single agency, the newly created Cooperative State Research, Education and Extension Service (CSREES). The National Agricultural Library (NAL) was consolidated with the Agricultural Research Service (ARS) which together with CSREES, ERS, and the National Agricultural Statistics Service (NASS) report to the newly created Under Secretary for Research, Education and Economics.
		Comments	Created CSREES.
1995	National Technology Transfer and Advancement Act (P.L. 104-113)	*Comments*	Granted CRADA cooperators the first right of negotiation for an exclusive license for a pre-negotiated field of use of any innovation developed under the agreement.
1996	Federal Agricultural Improvement and Reform (FAIR) Act (P.L. 104-127).	*Provisions*	Established the National Agricultural Research, Extension, Education, and Economics Advisory Board to advise USDA on national research priorities and policies. The Board replaced three separate advisory committees.
		Funding Details and Mechanisms	Established a Fund for Rural America through a direct transfer of U.S. Treasury funds to the USDA. Part of the fund was to support competitive research grants for projects that addressed international competitiveness, environmental stewardship, and rural community enhancement.
1998	Agricultural Research, Education and Extension Reform (AREER) Act (P.L. 105-185)	*Provisions*	Created the Initiative for Future Agriculture and Food Systems (IFAFS), funded at $120 million annually from FY 1998–2002.
		Funding Details and Mechanisms	The Act authorized IFAFS funds for critical emerging research related to future food production, environmental quality and natural resource management, farm income, and activities carried out under the Alternative Agricultural Research and Commercialization Act. It also funded new initiatives through IFAFS on the following priority areas: food safety, agricultural genome, natural resource management, agricultural biotechnology, alternative commodity production, and farm profitability. Other high priorities included: partnerships for high-value agriculture, product quality, precision agriculture, biobased products, crop diversification, integrated research, education and extension competitive grants program, improving the viability of small and medium size dairy, livestock, and poultry operations; and research regarding diseases of wheat and barley. The Act also authorized the Secretary of Agriculture to make competitive grants for research, education, or information dissemination related to precision agriculture.

2000	Technology Transfer Commercialization Act (P.L. 106-404)	*Provisions*	Established that a federal agency may grant an exclusive or partially exclusive license on a federally owned invention only if: (1) granting the license is a reasonable and necessary incentive to (a) call forth the investment capital and expenditures needed to bring the invention to practical application; or (b) otherwise promote the invention's utilization by the public; (2) the federal agency finds that the public will be served by the granting of the license, as indicated by the applicant's intentions, plans, and ability to bring the invention to practical application or otherwise promote the invention's utilization by the public, and that the proposed scope of exclusivity is not greater than reasonably necessary to provide the incentive for bringing the invention to practical application, as proposed by the applicant, or otherwise to promote the invention's utilization by the public; (3) the applicant makes a commitment to achieve practical application of the invention within a reasonable time, which time may be extended by the agency upon the applicant's request and the applicant's demonstration that the refusal of such extension would be unreasonable; (4) granting the license will not tend to substantially lessen competition or create or maintain a violation of the federal antitrust laws; and (5) in the case of an invention covered by a foreign patent application or patent, the interests of the federal government or United States industry in foreign commerce will be enhanced.
2002	Farm Security and Rural Investment Act (P.L. 107-171)	*Provisions*	Established a biosecurity planning and response program. Established grant programs for biotechnology risk assessment research and biotechnology research on crops important for developing countries. The Agricultural Research Service (ARS) was required to undergo a comprehensive review of its purpose, efficiency, effectiveness, and impact on agricultural research. The Secretary of Agriculture was required to appoint a task force, to complete the review and report its findings before June 2003.
		Comments	Reauthorized and established new agricultural research and extension programs. Extended previous funding provisions to FY 2007, replacing dollar amounts with "such sums as are necessary to carry out" the research. Expressed the "sense of Congress" that agricultural research funding double over the next 5 years.
		Funding Details and Mechanisms	IFAFS funding levels were set at $120 million in FY2004, increasing to $140 million in FY2005, $160 million in FY2006, and $200 million in FY2007 and each year thereafter. The Secretary was authorized to make competitively awarded "Research Equipment Grants" of $500,000 or less per institution, for special research equipment to colleges, universities, and SAESs engaged in food and agricultural science. Authorized and encouraged the USDA to jointly issue requests for proposals (RFPs), peer review proposals, and award grants with other federal agencies to reduce duplication of research and administrative functions. Added 20 new high-priority research and extension initiative areas to the 24 existing areas, including 5 new areas in natural resources and the environment. A Bovine Johne's disease control program and a program on Karnal Bunt research were added.

(continued)

Appendix Table 7-2 (continued)

Year	Legislation		
2004	Specialty Crop Competitiveness Act (P.L. 108-465)	*Provisions*	Authorized research and extension grants for the purpose of improving the efficiency, productivity and profitability of specialty crop production in the United States. Special emphasis was to be given to research and extension related to the phase-out of methyl bromide usage.
		Funding Details and Mechanisms	Title III of the Act authorized $5 million for each of the years 2005–2009 for research on specialty crops. The Specialty Crops Research Initiative (Section 7311) of the 2008 Farm Bill (P.L. 110-246) continued to earmark funding for specialty crops. Funds of the Commodity Credit Corporation were to be made available to carry out this Section, specifically $30 million FY2008 and $50 million for each fiscal year 2009–2012. In addition, Congress authorized an additional $100 million for each of fiscal years 2008–2012 to carry out specialty crops research.
2008	Food, Conservation, and Energy Act (P.L. 110-246)	*Provisions*	Title VII established the National Institute of Food and Agriculture (NIFA) to replace CSREES as of October 1, 2009. All programs previously under the authority of CSREES, including capacity and infrastructure programs, competitive programs, cooperative state research programs, cooperative extension programs, and education programs were placed under NIFA's authority. NIFA Director is appointed by the President to 6-year term and can be reappointed to an additional 6-year term. The Director is responsible for: organizing offices within NIFA to administer research, extension, and education programs; carrying out research, education, and extension activities of USDA; ensuring that NIFA carries out research priorities of Under Secretary for Research, Education, and Economics (REE); determining appropriate balance between fundamental and applied research; promoting use of competitive grants. Title VII, Section 7406 authorized competitive grant funding under an Agriculture and Food Research Initiative (AFRI) for fundamental and applied research, extension, and education to address food and agricultural sciences. AFRI combined the authorities of previous NRI and IFAFS programs.
		Comments	Created the National Institute of Food and Agriculture (NIFA) to replace CSREES; also created the Agriculture and Food Research Initiative (AFRI) to replace and restructure NRI and IFAFS.
		Funding Details and Mechanisms	Authorized annual appropriations of $700 million for grants in each of fiscal years 2008–2012. AFRI funds were available for obligation for a 2-year period beginning in the fiscal year for which funds are first made available, up to a maximum term of 10 years. The Secretary can retain no more than 4% for administrative costs. Grants awarded by AFRI must be evaluated on basis of merit, quality, and relevance. Priority areas include: plant health and production and plant products; animal health and production and animal products; food safety, nutrition, and health; renewable energy, natural resources, and environment; agriculture systems and technology; agriculture economics and rural communities.

	Specified that 60% of AFRI funds should be allocated to fundamental (or basic) research, and 40% of funds should be allocated to applied research. In addition, directed that 30% of AFRI fundamental research grants fund research by multidisciplinary teams. Authorized the Secretary to direct AFRI funds for development of capabilities in agricultural, food, and environmental sciences through grants to: institutions to allow for improvement of research, development, technology transfer, and education capacity, with not less than 25% of funds set aside for fellowships for pre- and post-doctoral researchers in agricultural science; beginning researchers fewer than 5 years from their initial career track positions; small, mid-sized, and minority-serving institutions previously unsuccessful in obtaining competitive grants; institutions in states that have been unsuccessful in obtaining grants based on 3-year rolling average of funding levels.
	Required AFRI recipients to provide matching funds for applied research that is commodity specific and less than national in scope. Equipment purchases also require matching funds, but the Secretary can waive this requirement for purchases under $25,000 by institutions in lower 1/3 of federal funds received if equipment has multiple uses. Limited research equipment purchases to not more than 2% of AFRI funds for fundamental research and prohibited the use of AFRI funds for construction.
	Required the President to submit a single budget line item reflecting the total amount requested for research, education, and extension activities as part of annual budget submission.

Sources: Huffman and Evenson (1993, Table 1.6), Kerr (1987), NRC (1989 and 1994), Pollack and Lynch (1991), NAS (1992), USDA (1996), Rawson (1997), Young (2008), NSF (2009a), and NIH (2009).

Appendix Table 7-3 History of Major Legislation Affecting Conduct and Federal Funding of Cooperative Extension

Year	Legislation		
1914	Smith-Lever Act (P.L. 63-95)	*Provisions*	Created Cooperative Extension Service to aid in diffusing among the people useful and practical information on subjects relating to agriculture and home economics, and to encourage its application.
		Funding Mechanism	Provided lump-sum grants of $10,000 per state ($480,000 total) and additional formula funding. Formula funds were allocated on the basis of a state's share of the U.S. rural population. Formula funding was phased in over 7 years, with a maximum total funding of $4.1 million. The formula funds were to be matched by state, county, college, local authority, or individual contributions.
1928	Capper-Ketcham Act (P.L. 70-475)	*Provisions*	Provided for the expansion of Cooperative Extension Service.
		Funding Mechanism	Provided an additional lump sum grant of $20,000 per state ($980,000 total per year) and an additional $500,000 starting in 1929 to be allocated by formula.
1935	Bankhead-Jones Act (P.L 74-182)	*Provisions*	Provided for the expansion of Cooperative Extension Service.
		Funding Mechanism	Provided an additional lump sum grant of $20,000 per state ($980,000 total per year) and an additional $8 million to be allocated to states by formula in 1936 and an additional $1 million for each of the next 4 years. Formula funds were to be allocated according to each state's share of the U.S. farm population, with no matching required.
1945	Bankhead-Flannagan Act (P.L.79-76)	*Provisions*	Provided for further development of Cooperative Extension Service.
		Funding Mechanism	Required that two percent of the federal appropriation was for federal administration, 4% was set aside for the Secretary for special need allocation, and 94% was distributed by a formula based on state's share of the U.S. farm population.
1953	Amended Smith-Lever Act (P.L. 83-83)	*Provisions*	Consolidated 9 existing Acts, provided for appropriations for federal extension staff in the USDA.
		Funding Mechanism	Provided that subsequent increases be allocated as follows: 4% for special needs, 48% based on a state's share of the U.S. rural population, and 48% based on a state's share of the U.S. farm population.
1955	Smith-Lever Amendment (P.L. 84-360)	*Funding Mechanism*	Included provisions that allowed for special nonformula funds.
1962	Smith-Lever Amendment (P.L. 87-749)	*Funding Mechanism*	Froze distribution of current federal funds to each state. Designated that subsequent increases be allocated as follows: 4% to the federal service, and of the remainder, 20% in equal proportions to all states, 40% according to a state's share of the U.S. rural population, and 40% according to its share of the U.S. farm population.

1972	Rural Development Act (P.L. 92-419)	*Provisions*	Title V authorized research and extension activities related to rural communities, including activities outside of agriculture.
		Funding Mechanism	Funds were to be distributed as: 4% for federal administration, 10% for multi-state work, 20% equally distributed among states, and 33% each according to a state's share of the U.S. rural and U.S. farm populations.
1977	National Agricultural Research, Extension and Teaching Policy Act (Title XIV) of the Food and Agriculture Act (P.L. 95-113)	*Funding Mechanism*	Ammended Title V of the 1972 Rural Development Act so that 4% of the funds were allocated for federal administration, 19% were allocated among the states to conduct small-farm research programs, and 77% were allocated among the states to conduct small-farm extension programs.
1978	Renewable Resources Extension Act (P.L. 95-306)	*Provisions*	Authorized funding for extension programs pertaining to forests, rangeland, fish, wildlife and other renewable resources.
		Funding Mechanism	Authorized $15 million for the fiscal year ending September 30, 1979, and $15 million for each of the subsequent nine fiscal years. Generally, states were eligible for funds appropriated under this Act according to the respective capabilities of their private forests and range-lands for yielding renewable resources and the relative needs for such resources identified in the periodic Renewable Resource Assessment provided for in Section 3 of the Forest and Rangeland Renewable Resources Planning Act of 1974 and the periodic appraisal of land and water resources provided for in Section 5 of the Soil and Water Resources Conservation Act of 1977.
1981	Agriculture and Food Act (P.L. 97-98)	*Funding Mechanism*	Rural development extension funds became part of Smith-Lever formula appropriation.
1985	Food Security Act (P.L. 98-198)	*Provisions*	Established a research and education program on sustainable agriculture.
1994	Department of Agriculture Reorganization Act (P.L. 103-354)	*Provisions*	Merged the Cooperative State Research Service (CSRS) and the Extension Service (ES) into a single agency, the newly created Cooperative State Research, Education and Extension Service (CSREES). The National Agricultural Library (NAL) was consolidated with the Agricultural Research Service (ARS) which together with CSREES, ERS, and the National Agricultural Statistics Service (NASS) report to the newly created Under Secretary for Research, Education and Economics.
1994	Elementary and Secondary Education Reauthorization Act (P.L.103-382)	*Provisions*	Conferred land grant status on 29 Native American colleges, with authorization for an endowment fund and annual agricultural appropriations for teaching and extension.

(continued)

Appendix Table 7-3 (continued)

Year	Legislation		
1998	Agricultural Research, Education and Extension Reform (AREER) Act (P.L. 105-185)	*Provisions*	The Secretary of Agriculture was required to develop protocols for evaluating the success of multi-state, multi-institutional, and multi-disciplinary extension activities and joint research and extension activities in addressing critical agricultural issues.
		Funding Mechanism	Matching funds requirements under the Hatch Act of 1887 and Smith-Lever Act were made consistent. Specified that no payments are to be made from the allotted funds to a state in excess of the amount that the state makes available out of non-federal funds for cooperative extension work. If a state fails to comply with the requirement to provide matching funds for a fiscal year, the Secretary of Agriculture shall withhold payment to the state for that fiscal year an amount equal to the difference between (a) the amount that would be allotted and paid to the state if the full amount of matching funds were provided by the state, and (b) the amount of matching funds actually provided by the state. The Secretary of Agriculture shall reapportion amounts withheld for lack of matching funds among the states satisfying the matching requirement for that fiscal year. Any reapportioned funds are also subject to the matching requirement.
2002	Farm Security and Rural Investment Act (P.L. 107-171)	*Funding Mechanism*	Twenty new high-priority research and extension initiative areas were added to the twenty-four existing areas, including five new areas in natural resources and the environment. A Bovine Johne's disease control program was added.
2008	Food, Conservation, and Energy Act (P.L. 110-246)	*Provisions*	Established the National Institute of Food and Agriculture (NIFA) to replace USDA's Cooperative State Research, Education, and Extension Service (CSREES). NIFA was given authority to administer research funds and programs which include capacity and infrastructure programs, competitive programs, cooperative state research programs, cooperative extension programs, education programs, and all other CSREES authorities.
		Funding Mechanism	Provided competitive grant funding under an Agriculture and Food Research Initiative (AFRI) for fundamental and applied research, extension, and education programs to address food and agricultural sciences. AFRI combined the authorities of previous NRI and IFAFS programs. (See Appendix Table 7-2 for more details)
			Required the President to submit a single budget line item reflecting the total amount requested for research, education, and extension activities as part of annual budget submission.

Sources: Huffman and Evenson (1993, Table 1.7) and sources for Appendix Table 7-2.

APPENDIX III

U.S. Public Agricultural Research and Extension Series

The U.S. public research and extension data used throughout this volume consist of several interrelated data sets developed by Philip Pardey with major assistance from Connie Chan-Kang (and, especially at the formative stages of the series in the late 1980s, Michelle Hallaway), now at the University of Minnesota's International Science and Technology Practice and Policy (InSTePP) center.

State Agricultural Experiment Stations (SAESs)

Total Expenditures

Research expenditures consist of annual observations of the funds appropriated or made available to each state agricultural experiment station and other cooperating institutions in the same state for the period 1889–2007.[1] Expenditures are designated according to three broad sources of support (federal government sources, state government sources, and miscellaneous fees and sales) and aggregated by research performer (i.e., specified on a "by performer" basis).

The state-specific SAES research expenditure data sets compiled for this study drew from a number of sources, including the annual *Report on the Agricultural Experiment Stations* (or variants thereof), published over the years by USDA (1890), Atwater (1891), Harris (1892 and 1893), True (1894 and 1898–1901), USDA Office of Experiment Stations (1895, 1897, 1902–1915, 1916, 1918–1926, 1926–1954) and USDA Agricultural Research Service (1955–1960 and 1961). After 1960, the report was published annually by the USDA Cooperative State Experiment

1 See OECD (2002) for the commonly accepted standards used to compile and report science indicators that we also sought to follow here. We adopted the premise that funds made available or appropriated for research and extension were obligated or spent in the fiscal year in which they were committed. Through fiscal year 1976, the fiscal year was July 1–June 30; beginning October 1976 the fiscal year was October 1–September 30. The 3-month period from July 1, 1976 through September 30, 1976 was reported as a separate fiscal period known as the "transition quarter" (see USDA CSRS 1977). To avoid an accounting-induced discontinuity in the R&D series, we set aside expenditures incurred during this transition quarter. All data are reported on a fiscal year (FY) ending basis, and so, for example, FY 2000–2001 is designated year 2001 data.

Station Service (later known as the Cooperative State Research Service, CSRS, and then the Cooperative State Research, Education and Extension Service, CSREES) from 1961 to 1975 as the *Funds for Research at State Agricultural Experiment Stations* (or variants thereof). The *Inventory of Agricultural Research* was published by USDA RPDES (1967–1969), USDA SES (1970–1972), USDA CSRS (1972–1977), USDA SEA (1979–1981), USDA CSRS (1982–1994), and USDA CSREES (1995–1998).[2] Beginning in 1970, data were also made available in electronic file format from the USDA's Current Research Information Service (or USDA CRIS), a USDA agency formed in 1967 with the express purpose of documenting the pattern of agricultural R&D spending by the SAESs and their cooperating agencies, as well as agencies of the USDA. Summary digests of the CRIS data are available on-line at http://cris.csrees.usda.gov/fsummaries.html.

We compiled SAES expenditures as hand-tallied data for the period 1889–1979 and electronic extractions from detailed versions of the annual USDA CRIS data files for the period 1980–2007.[3] With overlapping hand-tallied and electronically supplied data available for the period 1970–1986, 1980 was selected as the year in which to splice the two sources of data together. A careful comparison of data from both sources indicated discrepancies between the published *Inventory* series and the corresponding figures extracted from the CRIS data files in the early-1970s. By the mid-1970s, SAES research expenditure estimates from both sources tracked each other closely, and they continued to do so until FY1995–1996, which is the last year of data published in the *Inventory of Agricultural Research*.

The state-specific components of the hand-tallied SAES expenditure series for the years 1889–1979 include:

- SAES expenditures using funds from all federal government sources
- SAES expenditures using funds from all non-federal government sources (including state government funds and miscellaneous fees and sales, MFS)
- SAES expenditures using MFS, a subset of non-federal funds
- total SAES expenditures (defined as the sum of all expenditures of funds from the federal government and all non-federally sourced funds)
- SAES expenditures funded from state government sources (estimated by subtracting MFS funds from all non-federally sourced funds).

The counterpart series for the 1980–2007 data extracted from the USDA CRIS files include:

- SAES federally sourced expenditures (the sum of three sub-totals reported in the CRIS files, namely "CSREES Admin Funds," "Other USDA" and "Other Federal" funds)

---

2 From 1969 to 1981, the *Inventory* was published as a three-volume set. Publication of Volume I was discontinued in 1982, and Volumes II and III were combined into a single format in 1983.

3 Personnel at USDA CRIS have been especially generous in periodically providing these data tapes over the past several decades and assisting Pardey and Chan-Kang in extracting and interpreting compilations made from these files. Special thanks are recorded here to Dennis Unglesbee, Allen Moore, Ed Kane and other colleagues from USDA CRIS for their outstanding help over the years.

- SAES non-federally sourced expenditures (the sum of "State Appropriations" and MFS-sourced funds, described next)
- SAES MFS-sourced funds available (the sum of "Self-Generated Funds," "Industry Grants/Agreements," and "Miscellaneous non Federal Funds," a subset of SAES non-federally-sourced expenditures)
- SAES total expenditures (the sum of all federal and non-federally sourced funds)
- SAES expenditures of funds from state government sources, taken in this instance to be the CRIS series of "State Appropriations."

Minnesota and Vermont Corrections

As part of the diagnostic and cleaning processes in compiling the SAES expenditure series, a detailed analysis of the Minnesota data extracted from the CRIS data files revealed some abnormally large and implausible jumps in the agricultural research spending time series. Notably, the reported "Other Federal Funds" series for Minnesota went from $70 million in 2004 down to $12 million in 2005 then jumped to an implausible $288 million in 2006. After much investigation using unpublished University of Minnesota budget files, the problem was identified as a gross misreporting of the relevant expenditures by a "state cooperating agency" (in the parlance of CRIS), specifically the University of Minnesota Veterinary School.[4] In some years, data from this agency were not reported and therefore were not included in the CRIS totals for Minnesota. In other years the agency, administratively part of the University's large Health Science unit, erroneously reported to CRIS *all* federal funding (including most likely *all* funding from the National Institutes of Health) coming to the Health Sciences units at the University, rather than reporting only the amount of federally-sourced funding spent specifically on veterinary medicine research. We determined that this reporting error caused the Minnesota total (and thereby SAES totals reported by CRIS for the United States) for FY2007 to be overstated by $298 million. Thus, the Minnesota total for FY2007 reported in USDA CRIS (2008, Table B) is $437.9 million compared with our corrected estimate of $139.9 million. These under- and over-reporting problems for the veterinary school at the University of Minnesota persisted, on and off, back to 1980 and were corrected in all the national and state SAES spending totals reported in this volume.

Total spending in 2007 by the Vermont "SAES and other cooperating institutions" was substantially underreported; in USDA CRIS (2008, Table B) the reported value for Vermont "Total Funds" was $3.5 million in 2007 compared with $10.3 million in 2006. An analysis of the CRIS data files revealed that the $3.5 million included funding for the forestry school and other cooperating institutions (OCI funds in CRIS parlance), and vastly underreported SAES funding for that year. We took the 2006 estimate of SAES funds available ($7.5 million, the $10.3 million net of OCI funds) as the best indication of the corresponding 2007 figure,

4 We gratefully acknowledge and thank Lynn Moore for her efforts to help us identify and resolve this substantial data problem.

added that to the reported 2007 OCI and forestry school figures to get a corrected 2007 Vermont "SAES and other cooperating institutions" total of $10.4 million for 2007.

The reported 50-state total for the SAESs and other cooperating institutions (including forestry schools, Washington, D.C., and all U.S. territories) for fiscal year 2007 is $3,776,628,000 (USDA CRIS 2008, Table A) versus our corrected estimate of $3,486,022,833, with the difference reflecting our corrections for both Minnesota and Vermont.

Scope of Included Research

Our analysis is intended to evaluate the economic effects of public R&D from a performer (i.e., SAES and USDA) perspective. The SAES total expenditures described throughout this volume, and used for the empirical work presented mainly in Part IV include all expenditures on agricultural research conducted by the agricultural experiment stations and selected cooperating institutions.[5] Likewise, all of the research conducted by the USDA in Beltsville, Maryland and at USDA facilities located throughout the country is counted as intramural USDA research. These SAES and USDA research aggregates include a host of different types of R&D that have been subjectively classified and referred to by users as short- versus long-duration research, basic versus more applied research, crops- versus livestock-related research, on-farm versus off-farm, and productivity- versus non-productivity-oriented R&D. Changes in the emphasis or orientation of any one of these components (or for that matter any other dimension) of the portfolio of research conducted by the SAES (and the USDA) could affect the aggregate research-cum-productivity relationship and the estimated payoffs to that research.

Alston and Pardey (2001) discussed attribution problems in evaluating the economic returns to investments in agricultural R&D. The essence of the issue is to assure a proper concordance between the costs of R&D and the benefits attributable to those costs. Based on their arguments about potential attribution bias, from a research performer perspective it would make sense to measure all of the on- and off-farm economic effects of the disparate (and changing) portfolio that constitutes SAES and USDA research. However, the estimates in this study will reflect only the measured effects of public research (and extension) on farm productivity.[6] Thus, it makes sense to seek to include all of the types of agricultural and non-agricultural research that affect farm productivity—be it relevant research performed domestically or overseas, by public or private agencies, or by research institutions deemed within the realm of agriculture or not—and, by the same token, to exclude all of the types of research that are not meant to influence agricultural productivity.

In studies in which the streams of research costs do not appropriately match the corresponding stream of benefits, the measures of research benefits are difficult to interpret and vulnerable to attribution biases.[7] To address some of these attribution problems, the

5 The SAES (and USDA) series are net of forestry research, unless otherwise stated.

6 Thus, for instance they do not reflect benefits from any non-market or environmental impacts that could not be expected to be reflected in conventional productivity measures and conventional measures of research benefits (e.g., public benefits and costs from changes in natural resource stocks or changes in environmental pollution resulting from agricultural R&D).

7 From an alternative perspective, these could be construed as "aggregation" biases, stemming from the varied and changing composition of the measurable research totals that are reported as "agricultural research."

series of studies undertaken jointly by Huffman and Evenson (see Huffman 2009, pp. 15-16) and some done jointly by those authors with various collaborators (see, for example, Yee and Huffman 2001, p. 8) sought to identify a subset of "non-productivity" related research and to exclude that from their agricultural research spending totals. After careful consideration, we opted for practical reasons not to pursue this approach. Specifically, we took the view that the available data are insufficient to provide a reasonable and plausible basis for parsing out components of the aggregate for the hundred years of state-specific SAES and USDA intramural R&D spending used to construct the knowledge stocks in Part IV of this book. Cross-referencing the discussion in Huffman (2009) with the information provided in Huffman and Evenson (1993, pp. 113-116), it seems they parsed data for all of the years in their various R&D series using disaggregated data that were available or estimated for just six years (1920, 1925, 1951, 1964, 1969 and 1984) on the commodity-orientation or research-problem-cum-discipline-focus. It is not clear if these disaggregated data were available only at a national level or for all 48 contiguous states, especially for the earlier years. The classification schemes have not been consistent over time and the basis for compiling these data has varied (e.g., the 1920 and 1925 estimates are shares of projects allocated to broad research disciplines, while the more-recent data are compilations of research expenditures by research problem area). In addition, it is not clear from Huffman (2009) whether the substantial (and potentially inconsistent) reconfiguration of the research problem areas (RPAs) used by CRIS to reclassify the SAES and USDA data in 1998 was factored into the more-recent R&D compilations used by Huffman and Evenson to calculate their research capital stocks.

The knowledge stocks we develop are used to account for agricultural productivity growth. The numerator of our productivity measure is an output aggregate that excludes forestry. Likewise the farm-oriented scope of the input aggregate that forms the denominator in our productivity measure also effectively excludes inputs into forestry because most U.S. farms produce little if any outputs that could be construed as forestry related. We determined that it was feasible to exclude forestry research from the research knowledge stocks estimated in this study.[8] By construction, our intramural USDA series excludes research performed by the USDA Department of Forestry. To exclude forestry from the SAES spending totals required some effort, tailored to the specifics of our SAES data sources. For the more-recent years (after 1979) we could simply exclude spending by forestry schools when extracting SAES totals from the CRIS data files. To remove research spending by forestry schools from the pre-aggregated expenditure totals for years prior to 1980, we contacted all the forestry schools to request these data. We obtained founding dates for those schools that did not provide information on research expenditures. For these schools, we extracted total SAES expenditures for the period 1970–1979. We backcasted spending by forestry schools as a share of total SAES spending, and deducted the implied forestry school spending from the reported totals for the SAESs and other cooperating institutes for the years prior to 1980.

---

8 Huffman (2009, p. 14, footnote 8) notes "My most recent measures of public agricultural research expenditures also exclude all types of forestry research. The primary reason is that forest products are a relatively unimportant output of farms in all but a few states."

RPA (Research Problem Area) and Commodity Focus

To gain insight into the changing composition of research we parsed our research spending totals for the more recent decades into various categories using the CRIS crop commodity, field-of-science, and RPA codes as classified in USDA CRIS (1993, 1998 and 2005). Unfortunately the CRIS coding structure does not allow for all of the groupings that may be of policy interest, and the coding structure has changed over time making it difficult to achieve consistency in the groupings over time. The switch to a new coding scheme in 1998 was particularly problematic.[9] Some of the changes implemented by the committee that revised the classification scheme in 1998 resulted in many of the old RPAs each being dispersed among several of the new RPAs. Using unpublished documentation and technical assistance from CRIS personnel, we devised a scheme to crossmatch the old (i.e., pre-1998) RPA classification scheme with the new (post-1997) scheme to facilitate a reasonably consistent grouping of research expenditures into the following six broad (and for the compilations reported here, distinct and exhaustive) classes: (a) farm productivity, (b) environment, forestry and fish, (c) basic genomics, (d) economics, (e) post-farm, and (f) other research, including off-farm productivity.

Similarly, and again with considerable help from CRIS personnel, an extraction routine using crop commodity codes was devised to group research according to its principal commodity focus. Our public agricultural research expenditure totals exclude forestry research (unless otherwise indicated). And, for the post-1979 period at least, the series used to assess the commodity and productivity orientation of R&D also excluded research on rangeland, recreation and wildlife, game birds and animals, pets, laboratory animals, aquaculture and fisheries, horses, ponies, and mules. Our Total Crop series (for example, Figure 6-18) includes all commodity-specific research related to a specific crop or to multiple crops along with a Specialty Crops and a Grains research grouping. Program Crops represent crops subject to government support programs (see footnote 23, Chapter 6). Total Livestock research represents all commodity-specific research related to a specific livestock product or to multiple livestock products. Total Commodities research is defined as the sum of total crops and total livestock research. We also identify a Non-commodity Specific R&D total that includes all of the remaining agricultural research that was not otherwise allocated to a specific crop or livestock category.

Intramural USDA Research

The intramural USDA research expenditure series (net of forestry research) draws from two primary sources. For the period 1889–1999, the series was developed by hand tallies of various U.S. Department of Treasury reports to the U.S. House of Representatives; for the period after 1999 we performed electronic extractions from the CRIS data files.[10] Using the

9 Another set of classification changes occurred in October 2005. RPAs were renamed Knowledge Areas (KA), and these KA categories were expanded to include additional research, education, and extension designations not identified in the RPA classification (USDA CRIS 2005).

10 These sources were U.S. Department of Treasury (1889 and 1890, 1894–1907, 1908–1911, 1912–1926, 1927–1939, 1940–1975, 1976–1983, and 1984–2000). Patricia Zambrano's considerable help in compiling these data is gratefully acknowledged.

Treasury reports we compiled the most disaggregated figures available, often parsing out individual account categories within the totals for specific agencies. These account categories facilitated compilation of a time series of R&D expenditures that drew on information regarding the creation, closure and merger status of agencies and bureaus within the USDA, as well as information concerning the changing research versus non-research (e.g., regulatory) activities of these agencies.[11] Since many USDA bureaus, and even some of the reported projects identified within a relevant bureau, carried out regulatory as well as R&D functions, we augmented the disaggregated appropriations and expenditure data with information (in the form of allocative rules of thumb) obtained from knowledgeable sources within USDA to develop estimates of a series of R&D appropriations and expenditures separate from a series related to regulatory (and other) functions.[12]

For the period 1970–2007, estimates of USDA intramural spending were available in the CRIS electronic data files. However, for several years where we had both hand-tallied estimates and the CRIS estimates, there were substantial differences between the two series. CRIS personnel advised us that the electronic estimates may not consistently include spending by all USDA agencies. Based on their advice, we used a five-year moving average of growth rates to extrapolate USDA intramural spending for 2001–2007. Growth rates from the hand-tallied series were used up to 2000, and were supplemented with the growth rates from the electronically extracted CRIS series for 2001–2007 as necessary. For example, intramural expenditures for 2002 were estimated using the average of year-to-year growth rates from the hand-tallied series for 1997–2000 and the growth rate from the CRIS series for 2000–2001.

Extension Expenditures

State-specific data on sources of funds allocated for cooperative extension work were compiled by hand from a variety of published and unpublished sources to develop an estimate of total

11 For example, the Agricultural Research Service (ARS) did not exist as such until November 1953. To construct an R&D series for the antecedent agencies of ARS for the period 1889–1953 we tracked data for each of the bureaus that were consolidated into ARS in fiscal year 1953–1954 (and, where required, compiled data for specific programs within each bureau). The relevant bureaus, as of 1954, included the Bureau of Animal Industry (BAI), the Bureau of Plant Industry Soil and Agricultural Engineering (BPI), the Bureau of Entomology and Plant Quarantine (BEPQ), the Bureau of Agricultural and Industrial Chemistry (BAIC), the Bureau of Human Nutrition and Home Economics (BHE), and the Bureau of Dairy Industry (BDI). These bureaus—with the exception of BAI—were not established until at least 1907, and thereafter went through several name changes that sometimes involved changing regulatory and R&D-related responsibilities. Thus, rather than simply track bureau totals, we collected information for the activities and projects listed under each bureau that we identified as pertaining to R&D.

12 We were very careful to separate research spending from other functions, recognizing that not doing so may cause large errors in the data. For example, the USDA intramural spending series presented in Huffman and Evenson (1993, Appendix Table 4A, p.128) contain some questionable spikes. They present two series from 1888 to 1990 that represent "Chemical, Biological, and Physical Science Research" and "Economics and Statistics Research" conducted by the USDA, the sum of which represents total USDA intramural research spending. Their "Chemical, Biological, and Physical Science Research" time series reports $31.9 million in 1946, $54.7 million in 1947, $69.8 million in 1948, $46.1 million in 1949, and $27.4 million in 1950. For their total USDA time series, spikes involving year-on-year changes of greater than 40 percent occurred in years 1890, 1901, 1909, 1922, 1947 and 1976. Some of these spikes may indicate aggregation errors associated with unrecorded agency merger, creation and closure activity, coupled with changes in the research, regulatory and other functions performed by these agencies. The large jump in the series from 1975 to 1976 apparently stems from the inclusion of the transition quarter (i.e., the three-month period occasioned by a shift from a fiscal year ending June 30 to a fiscal year ending September 30) in the figure for 1976, such that the data reported by Huffman and Evenson for this year

funding for state cooperative extension work. Data for the period 1915–1983 were obtained from a variety of published sources, including U.S. House of Representatives (1925–1929, 1930–1941, 1952 and 1954–1984), USDA (1915, 1917, 1918–1922 and 1925, 1941–1949 and 1953). Data for the period 1984–2005 were obtained from USDA CSREES (1980–2006), except for 1989, which was obtained by linear interpolation.[13] Total funding for extension was parsed according to the source of funding, which for the period 1980–2006 entailed funds from federal sources (including the Amended Smith-Lever and Agricultural Marketing Acts), state and college, county, and non-tax funds. Entries for some components were incomplete for certain states for certain years (especially the period 2000–2006). We identified and examined these missing source-of-fund observations, and, where deemed appropriate, they were estimated by linear interpolation (often between adjacent observations) of the share of respective source-of-funds component.

Research Deflator

A substantial share of the total costs of agricultural research (around 68 percent in recent years) consists of the salaries and fringe benefits paid to scientists and their professional support staff. The per-unit cost of a scientist has typically increased at a faster pace than the overall rate of inflation, such that increases in general price indexes like the implicit GDP deflator or the consumer price index (CPI) tend to understate the rate of change in the price of scientists. To generate estimates of the real costs of agricultural R&D spending used throughout this volume, the corresponding nominal expenditure series was deflated by an agricultural R&D price index developed by Pardey, Andersen and Alston (2009). This price index differentiates among four cost categories: labor (scientists and support staff), operating expenses (electricity, heat, chemicals, books, and so on) land and buildings, and equipment. The relative cost shares of these expenditure classes varied over the years. For example, during the establishment phases of many SAESs (i.e., during the early part of the 20th Century), capital expenditures accounted for 20–28 percent of total SAES expenditures, compared with an estimated 8 percent in recent years.

---

include expenditures and appropriations incurred for a 15-month rather than a 12-month period (see Huffman and Evenson 1993, Table 4.3, note c).

13 The authors obtained unpublished reports and data compilations from a variety of CSREES personnel over the years to develop this part of the time series. Special thanks go to Don Prindle, Tina Buch, Janet Downey, and Barry Sims for their generous assistance.

PART IV

Models of R&D and Productivity

Parts II and III document the changes in U.S. agricultural inputs, outputs, and productivity during the 20th Century, and the development of agricultural R&D policies that contributed to that evolution in U.S. agriculture. The remainder of the book is devoted to formally modeling the linkages between agricultural productivity in the United States over the period 1949–2002 and public investments in agricultural R&D by federal and state governments during the longer period 1890–2002. In this Part, we review evidence and approaches from previous studies of agricultural R&D and productivity (Chapter 8) as a basis for the development and estimation of our own models (Chapters 9 and 10), to be used to derive estimates of returns to research and other implications in Chapter 11.

CHAPTER 8

Research Lags and Spillovers

Modeling and measuring the productivity consequences of R&D is a tricky business. The challenge in attributing productivity to R&D is to establish which research, conducted by whom, and when, was responsible for a particular productivity increase. In other words, in modeling the effects of research on agricultural productivity the two principal areas of difficulty are in the treatment of knowledge spillovers (i.e., the "by whom" part of the attribution problem) and in identifying the lag structure linking research spending, knowledge stocks, and productivity (i.e., the "when" part).

The "by whom" part can have various elements, relating to knowledge spillovers among different fields of science, different firms within an industry, different industries within a country or other geopolitical entity, or among countries. The emphasis here is on the spatial component: spillovers of technology among geopolitical entities, within the United States. The problem is to attribute credit for a state's agricultural productivity growth among state-specific SAES research and extension investments, and intramural USDA research. Past studies have imposed unduly restrictive constraints on spillover relationships that have influenced their findings. Similar concerns arise with the treatment of the "when" aspect in modeling R&D lags. Research takes a long time to affect production, and then it affects production for a long time. Since the typical study has available only a single, short, time series of annual data, the usual practice has been to impose arbitrary restrictions on the structure and length of the research lag, probably resulting in biased estimates.

This chapter reviews previous work on modeling the spatial and temporal aspects of the linkages between research investments and productivity. Evidence is presented about particular technologies that supports relatively long R&D lags and substantial spatial spillovers.

J.M. Alston et al., *Persistence Pays: U.S. Agricultural Productivity Growth and the Benefits from Public R&D Spending*, Natural Resource Management and Policy 34,
DOI 10.1007/978-1-4419-0658-8_8,

Table 8-1 Research Lag Length in Rate of Return Studies, by Year of Publication

Characteristic	Number of Estimates	Year of Publication 1958–1969	1970–1979	1980–1989	1990–1998	1958–1998
Research lag length	*count*			*percentage of estimates*		
0 to 10 years	253	9.7	6.2	17.9	12.7	13.4
11 to 20 years	537	41.9	22.0	38.8	22.8	28.5
21 to 30 years	376	0.0	20.7	12.0	25.9	19.9
31 to 40 years	178	0.0	4.3	5.6	14.3	9.4
40 up to ∞ years	141	0.0	9.5	6.6	7.6	7.5
∞ years	102	35.5	7.5	2.9	5.4	5.4
Unspecified[a]	109	12.9	13.1	3.2	4.9	5.8
Unclear[b]	190	0.0	16.7	12.7	6.3	10.1
Total	*1,886*	*100.0*	*100.0*	*100.0*	*100.0*	*100.0*

Sources: Adapted from Alston et al. (2000a).

Notes: This table is based on the full sample of 292 publications reporting 1,886 observations.

[a] Unspecified estimates are those for which the research lag length is not made explicit.

[b] Lag length is unclear.

8.1 R&D Lags in Econometric Models

Over the past 50 years, agricultural economists have conducted hundreds of studies of the contributions of public agricultural research and extension to productivity growth and the broader economic performance of the U.S. agricultural sector.[1] In many of those studies, a measure of multi-factor (or total factor) productivity is regressed against a research stock variable, defined as a weighted sum of real research expenditures over some number of past years, often with a view to estimating the rate of return to research.[2] Other variables, such as weather indexes, are often included as well. Sometimes the variables are expressed in logarithms. The specification of the research stock variable is critical, especially the lag length. Table 8-1 summarizes the variation in maximum research lag lengths used in rate-of-return studies published over the years, 1958–1998. The 1,886 estimates of rates of return to agricultural R&D reflect maximum research lags mainly in the range of 10–30 years. Models with quite short lags have been popular. Over 40 percent of all of the estimates were from studies allowing for a maximum lag of 20 years or less, and 13 percent of the estimates published in 1990–1998 allowed for maximum lags of less than 11 years.

1 Much of this effort can be attributed to Theodore Schultz and his students and other colleagues at the University of Chicago, and those who studied under them. Significant contributors to this literature associated directly with the University of Chicago include D. Gale Johnson, Vernon Ruttan, Zvi Griliches, Robert Evenson, G. Edward Schuh, Willis Peterson, Bruce Gardner and Wallace Huffman.

2 A comprehensive reporting and evaluation of this literature is provided by Alston et al. (2000a).

Only a few studies have presented much in the way of formal theoretical justification for the particular lag models they employed in modeling returns to agricultural research. A common conception is that the lag relationship between research investments and productivity will entail an initial "gestation" lag (before research has any effects), an "adoption" lag during which the lag weights rise to a maximum, and eventually, declining weights as the impact of past research investments on current productivity fades. Alston, Norton and Pardey (1995) sketched out a conceptual framework, in which agricultural production uses service flows from a stock of knowledge, that captures these features.[3] In this formulation, agricultural R&D contributes to the development of a stock of useful knowledge; some elements of which may depreciate through obsolescence or other changes, but some knowledge may last forever so the overall lag is infinite. As a practical matter, these effects can be modeled using a finite distributed lag that approximates the underlying infinite distributed lag, and represents the confounded effects of the lags in the knowledge creation and adoption process and the dynamics of depreciation of the knowledge stock.[4] The resulting overall lag length will be longer than that between research and the creation of knowledge alone, and the research lag coefficients will represent a hybrid of the effects of research on innovations, the uptake and depreciation of knowledge and technological innovations, and the consequences of the omission of the longer lags.[5] Alston and Pardey (2001) argued that the truncation of the R&D lag length in econometric models is likely to lead to larger rate-of-return estimates.[6]

Table 8-2 summarizes the results from past econometric studies of returns to agricultural research across countries, classified according to the length and form of the research lag. Most studies have used short lags and shorter lags tend to coincide with larger estimated rates of return. Until quite recently, it was common to restrict the lag length to be less than 20 years. In the earliest studies,

3 Studies of the returns to industrial R&D typically refer to a research stock, or a knowledge stock to which current R&D contributes, but may not provide much detail on how the knowledge stock is constructed.

4 Noting Boulding's (1966) point that knowledge does not physically deteriorate, Griliches (1979) and Pakes and Shankerman (1987) argue that its value to the firm who owns a patent does depreciate, owing to displacement by new innovations and rising appropriability problems. For further discussion on the creative destruction of knowledge stocks through private R&D, see Caballero and Jaffe (1993).

5 In such a model, as longer research lags are progressively introduced, we might expect to see both an improvement in the model in general, and an increasing resolution of the parameters as meaningful representations of the impact of past research on current net increments to knowledge.

6 If the omission of longer lags of R&D investments represents the omission of relevant explanatory variables, and R&D investments are strongly positively correlated over time, the weights on the shorter lags will be biased upward. Calculations of the rate of return will also be biased up, so long as the effect of the higher values for short lag weights more than compensates for restricting weights on the longer lags to be zero. This is quite likely when calculations of rates of return heavily discount benefits in the distant future, as happens with a large internal rate of return, which is typical.

Table 8-2 Lag Structures and Rates of Return to Agricultural R&D

	Estimates		Rate of Return				
Characteristic	Number	Share of Total	Mean	Mode	Median	Minimum	Maximum
Research lag length	*count*	*percentage*		*percent per year*			
0 to 10	370	20.9	90.7	58	56.0	-56.6	1,219.0
11 to 20	490	27.7	58.5	49	43.7	-100.0	677.0
21 to 30	358	20.2	152.4	57	53.9	0.0	5,645.0
31 to 40	152	8.6	64.0	40	41.1	0.0	384.4
40 to ∞ years	113	6.4	29.3	20	19.0	0.3	301.0
∞ years	57	3.2	49.9	20	35.0	-14.9	260.0
Unspecified	205	11.6	48.7	25	34.5	1.1	337.0
Unclear	27	1.5	43.1	27 and 60	38.0	9.0	125.0
Gestation lag							
Included	468	59.2	65.5	46	47.1	-14.9	526.0
Omitted	314	39.7	96.7	95	58.8	0.0	1,219.0
Unspecified or unclear	8	1.0	25.1	na	24.1	6.9	55.0
Total	790	100.0	77.5	46 and 58	50.2	-14.9	1,219.0
Spillovers							
Spillins	291	16.7	94.5	95	68.0	0.0	729.7
Spillouts	70	4.0	73.7	95	46.4	8.9	384.4
No spillovers	1,428	81.7	78.8	49 and 57	40.0	-100.0	5,645.0

Sources: Based on data reported in Alston et al. (2000a).

Notes: This table is based on a full sample of 292 publications reporting 1,886 observations. For all characteristics, the sample excludes two extreme outliers and includes rates of returns to research only for research and extension combined so that the maximum sample size is 1,772. For the research gestation lag, the sample includes only observations from studies that explicitly documented the structure of their lag, resulting in a sample size of 790 observations. For spillovers, 25 observations were lost owing to incomplete information, resulting in a sample size of 1,747 observations. Some estimates have spillover effects in both directions.

available time series were short and lag lengths were very short, but the more recent studies have tended to use longer lags. Along with lag-length restrictions, most studies have restricted the lag distribution to be represented by a small number of parameters, both because the time span of the data set is usually not much longer than the assumed maximum lag length, and because the individual lag parameter estimates are unstable and imprecise given the high degree of collinearity between multiple series of lagged research expenditures.[7] Both types of restrictions can have significant effects on the empirical assessment of research benefits. The direction and magnitude of the bias in estimated rates of return to R&D from restricting the length and shape of the lag profile are empirical issues, but we suspect the bias has been upwards. This suspicion is supported to some

7 Common types of lag structures used to construct a research stock include the de Leeuw or inverted-V (e.g., Evenson 1967), polynomial (e.g., Davis 1980; Leiby and Adams 1991; Thirtle and Bottomley 1988), and trapezoidal (e.g., Huffman and Evenson 1989, 1992, 1993 and 2006a; Evenson 1996). A small number of studies have used free-form lags (e.g., Ravenscraft and Scherer 1982; Pardey and Craig 1989; Chavas and Cox 1992).

extent by a formal analysis of the evidence in the literature (Alston et al. 2000a) and by inspection of Table 8-2.

In many cases, especially the earlier studies, the available data did not permit using or testing for longer R&D lags. Pardey and Craig (1989) used a free-form lag structure to model the relationship between agricultural productivity and public-sector agricultural research, and found "... strong evidence that the impact of research expenditures on agricultural output may persist for as long as thirty years (p. 9)" and that "... long lags—at least thirty years—may be necessary to capture all of the impact of research on agricultural output (p. 18)." While several studies have followed this advice, until recently none tested how much longer than 30 years the lag should be, nor did they consider the problem in the context of an infinite lag structure. Building on Pardey and Craig (1989), work by Alston, Craig and Pardey (1998) supported a research lag of at least 35 years and up to 50 years for U.S. agricultural research. In the work reported in this volume, we take that finding as a datum and try alternative functional forms (and shapes) for the lag distribution subject to a desire for parsimony in terms of the number of parameters to be estimated.

A problem in the kind of work undertaken by Alston, Craig and Pardey (1998), among many others, is that it is difficult to estimate a very long lag structure using a single time series. Alston, Craig and Pardey (1998) had access to a longer time series than in many other studies, and this meant they could test for longer lags. At the same time, however, extending the lag meant they imposed a stronger assumption about the length of time over which the structure of the model was assumed to be stable. If the structure cannot be expected to be stable over reasonably long time periods, in some senses the problem is intractable. Intuitively, going to the level of individual states would seem to be a way of increasing the total number of degrees of freedom for estimating the research lag structure. In fact, however, as we discuss in Chapter 9, once we have to measure the effects of technology spillovers among the states, we have fewer rather than more degrees of freedom. It is necessary to impose an even greater number of restrictive assumptions if we are to estimate the state-level relationships. Nevertheless, if these other restrictions are reasonable and right, the state-level data will enable us to estimate the other elements with greater precision. In our own application using long-run, state-specific data on U.S. agriculture (in Chapter 10 of this book), we test for longer lags, and find in favor of a gamma lag distribution model with a much longer research lag than most previous studies used—a research lag of at least 35 years and up to 50 years for U.S. agricultural research, with a maximum lag weight around year 24.[8] These lags are substantially longer

---

8 Some other studies, beginning from an examination of the time-series structure of the data, rather than reflection about the structural relationships, have implicitly extended the lag length and found lower rates of return (e.g., Myers and Jayne 1997).

than those found in most previous studies, but are justified by other evidence that is available on the time consumed by the research-innovation-adoption process in agriculture, as discussed and documented in the following sections.

8.2 Stylized Facts about R&D Lags in Agriculture

In aggregative models, the lags between R&D investments and productivity reflect the dynamics of knowledge creation and depreciation, averaged in some sense across the different types of knowledge and technology. Some stylized facts about individual technological innovations offer insights into our arguments about the R&D lag structure for agriculture and, by analogy, industry more generally. Consider crop improvement research using conventional breeding techniques. Figure 8-1 represents the costs and benefits over time from an investment in R&D that leads to the successful development of a new variety that is adopted by some growers for a time. Costs are incurred in the early years, in the processes of research, development, and facilitating early adoption. And in some cases, "maintenance" research might be required over the life of a technology, to sustain its usefulness and use.[9]

The first phase, the "research lag," takes at least several years. This phase includes experimental work in crossing parental lines, planting and growing the resulting seed in experimental trials, evaluating the results and making selections for further development. The next phase, the "development lag" takes several more years, as selected varieties are evaluated and modified prior to commercial development, and then seed is multiplied into commercial quantities for sale. For some types of technologies, such as biotech crop varieties, the development lag phase is extended by the several years spent developing and providing information required for regulatory approval, before the technology can be released for adoption (e.g., see Kalaitzandonakes, Alston and Bradford 2006). Even for relatively applied work, such as the development of new crop varieties, the R&D lag can be 5–10 years or longer.

During the "adoption lag" the new variety is progressively adopted and planted in larger quantities, and the net benefits progressively increase until eventually a maximum is reached. The adoption lag reflects the time it takes for individual farmers to learn about the new variety and evaluate its usefulness in their specific environments, and in many instances it reflects further time spent adapting the

9 Olmstead and Rhode (2002) referred to this as the "Curse of the Red Queen" (see also Dalrymple 2004). In Lewis Carroll's *Through the Looking Glass* the Red Queen said, "It takes all the running you can do, to keep in the same place." This colorful metaphor has a parallel in naturally evolving biological systems to which the Red Queen principle was introduced by Leigh Van Halen who broached the notion in his 1973 paper titled "A New Evolutionary Law," arguing that for a species within an evolutionary system, continuing development is needed to maintain its fitness relative to the systems within which it co-evolves.

Figure 8-1 A Stylized Representation of Research Benefits and Costs for Varietal Development

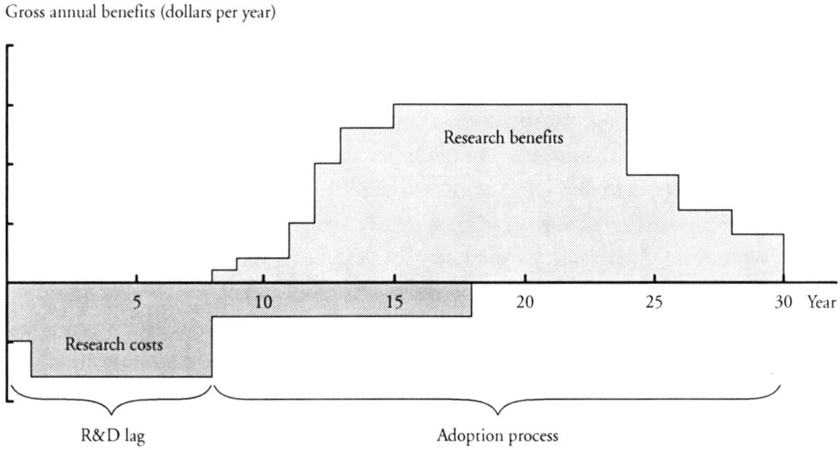

Sources: Developed by the authors.

variety to better suit different agroecological conditions.[10] It may also reflect lags as the market beyond the farm adapts to make use of the products of the new technology. For instance, it takes time for the food processing industry and consumers to adapt to the introduction of a new product innovation such as canola, which was derived from rape seed that was not edible for humans (Phillips and Khachatourians 2001). Consumer or other market resistance has dramatically slowed the industrial adoption of many significant innovations in agriculture and the food industry—e.g., pasteurization of milk, irradiation of food, chemical pesticides, and transgenic crop varieties—with implications for the shape of the lag profile for those innovations. In some cases government regulation reinforces market resistance (e.g., see Just, Alston and Zilberman 2006).

The diffusion of agricultural innovations has a uniquely spatial dimension, since the applicability of the innovation varies systematically with location, and this aspect adds to the time spent evaluating and adapting technologies for local adoption. This process of diffusion of a given innovation often can take a further 5–10 years, depending on the nature of the technology and information systems. In years past, a significant role of agricultural extension services was to facilitate the transmission of information about new farming technologies, to accelerate adoption and shorten the adoption lags. Other innovations, in terms of modern communications technologies and improvements in education of farmers, have

10 Evenson and Kislev (1975) made fundamental contributions to the study of the economics of innovation and adoption of agricultural technology. Subsequently, the lag to adoption was the focus of a suite of decision-theoretic models developed by economists including Pakes (1978), Lindner, Fisher and Pardey (1979) and Feder and O'Mara (1982).

made that traditional role of extension less important and contributed directly to shortening adoption lags. Benefits might flow indefinitely, but for stereotypical technologies, the rate of benefits will decline over time, as shown in Figure 8-1. Eventually, the particular variety will be disadopted by some farmers as it becomes less effective against evolving pests and diseases or is made obsolete by the development of superior varieties. But in many cases a variety may serve as breeding stock, contributing to the varieties that replace it, with vintage carry-over effects. Hence, the benefit stream will continue to flow so long as the variety *or its offspring* continue to be grown by some farmers.

Combining these various elements of lags, it is easy to imagine a typical varietal technology with a research and development lag of 5–10 years, in which no benefits are earned, followed by an extended adoption phase, with peak benefits in the range of 15–25 years after the initial investment, and sustained use after the peak, with benefits extending for a further 10 years and longer. Some other types of research (for instance, genomics and proteomics) may have significantly longer lags, especially the more fundamental types of research that lead to the most important and valuable types of innovations, some of which ultimately may be built into the new varieties. When innovations are embodied in livestock breeds or perennial crops that last for many years or decades, the biological dynamics add to both the research and adoption lags; similarly when innovations are embodied in durable physical capital such as tractors or combine harvesters. Some other types of public investments, including applied research and extension, might have significantly shorter R&D lags and less-enduring impacts. When we model the effects of aggregate R&D spending on multi-factor productivity, the R&D lag profile represents an average of the complete range of different types of agricultural R&D and their impacts across the entire range of agriculture.

The flows of benefits represented by the R&D lag profile in Figure 8-1 are analogous to the flows of benefits associated with investments in a perennial crop, such as a vineyard or an orchard. Depending on the crop and variety, it may take 3–5 years after planting before a tree or vine crop begins to achieve commercial yields and a further 5–10 years before it achieves its maximum yield. Then some varieties may stay in production indefinitely (such as chestnuts or premium wine varieties), whereas others (such as almonds or oranges) have declining yields as they age and are grubbed out and replaced after 20 years or so.[11]

---

11 In this sense, extension may be like alfalfa, which is a perennial crop that has a payoff within the first year of production but continues to yield benefits for a number of years until eventually the field is replanted with alfalfa or some other crop. Another example is strawberries, which have been drifting in the direction of being grown as an annual crop; and extension may have drifted analogously.

Figure 8-2 Trapezoidal, Gamma, and Geometric R&D Lag Models

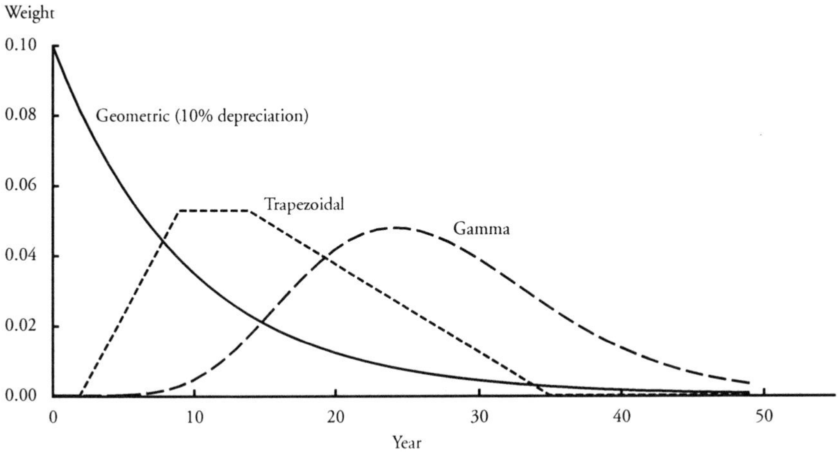

Sources: Developed by the authors.

In contrast, the R&D lag profile, used in the stereotypical study of industrial R&D (see Appendix 8-1 for detailed discussion), is a geometric lag as drawn in Figure 8-2, which is more analogous to the flow of benefits from an investment in a machine with a fairly short commercial life expectancy, such as an automobile. In this representation, benefits begin immediately with the investment and are at their maximum at that time, reflecting maximum adoption, maximum effectiveness, or both.[12] There is no allowance for the research, development, and adoption lags. From the outset, the assumed pattern of benefits is consistent with the tail end of the process in Figure 8-1, in which benefits are declining because of disadoption or obsolescence. Figure 8-2 also includes a trapezoidal lag model from Huffman and Evenson (1993) and the gamma lag distribution model that we prefer based on results presented in later chapters. It can be seen that these lag distributions are very different from the geometric model used in applications to industrial R&D, and much more like the perennial crop yield pattern. It is not just biological factors that make the biological analogy relevant for agricultural R&D. The same analogy is relevant for general industrial R&D: it typically takes many years to grow and develop a technology before it can begin to bear fruit, and then it may continue to bear fruit for many more years. But the standard industrial R&D model does not reflect these conceptions.

12 The geometric lag distribution on Figure 8-2 is drawn based on a 10 percent depreciation rate. It is common in the industrial R&D literature to apply an even less plausible depreciation rate of 15 percent, implying, in effect, an even shorter lag.

8.3 Evidence on Research-Innovation-Adoption Lags

A consideration of the research and adoption processes for major crop varietal innovations, and selected mechanical innovations, provides some sense of the time lags between investment in research, development, and extension and the uptake and use of the resulting innovations in farmers' fields. Drawing on Chan-Kang and Pardey (2009) we begin with a discussion of wheat varietal development. Next we present research and development timelines and adoption curves for hybrid corn (in the mid-twentieth century) and biotech corn (more recently), and then adoption curves for several mechanical technologies.

Wheat

Wheat breeding became a case study of the successful application of science to the agricultural economy following a series of important advances, with notable developments beginning in the 1940s. Two well-known events were the identification and application of the dwarfing characteristic to increase grain yield potential and the development of a "shuttle breeding" technique.[13] However, systematic breeding for resistance to various rust fungi, the development of broad-habitat varieties (e.g., improved drought or salinity tolerance), breeding for specific quality characteristics (such as protein content, cooking quality, grain size, shape, and color, and milling characteristics), and the development of new breeding techniques, like "shuttle breeding," have also been important.[14]

Over the period 1900–2003, a total of 1,051 new wheat varieties gained commercial significance in the United States (Chan-Kang and Pardey 2009). The pace of release and uptake of new varieties varied over time. Prior to 1960 the average was 3.46 new commercial varietal introductions per year; consisting of an average of 1.55 varieties per year for 1900–1919, increasing to 4.43 varieties per year for 1920–1959. Thereafter the pace of varietal release picked up even more to average 19.4 varieties per year for 1960–2003.

---

13 Dwarfing refers to a characteristic of the wheat (and other grain) plant, where the growth of the plant's stalk is limited, increasing the harvest index so that more of the plant's energy is directed to the production of the edible wheat grain, rather than inedible straw (Syme 1970). "Shuttle breeding" was deployed by a team led by Norman Borlaug to speed up the breeding process. They used two breeding cycles per year, shuttling successive breeding cycles between an irrigated, sea-level environment in Sonora in the northwest corner of Mexico, and the cool, rainfed highland plateau around Toluca. The materials planted in November in Sonora and harvested in early May were transferred to Toluca for immediate planting. Selections at this site were in turn harvested in November and sent back to Sonora for immediate planting (Borlaug 1982, p.69).

14 Rust fungi attack the leaves and stems of the wheat plants, threatening wheat yields. Since the various fungi are able to mutate, a particular control method can only work temporarily: the disease evolves in response to biological or chemical controls, and eventually reappears in a new form. Breeding has traditionally been one of the main responses to rust infestations—new varieties are developed that resist the locally-dominant rust strains, and are replaced when new rusts appear to which those varieties are not resistant. Regional variation in the characteristics of rust strains has been one of the reasons for localizing breeding work.

Figure 8-3 U.S. Wheat Varietal Vintages, 1920–2003

Panel a. Average age of wheat and rice varieties

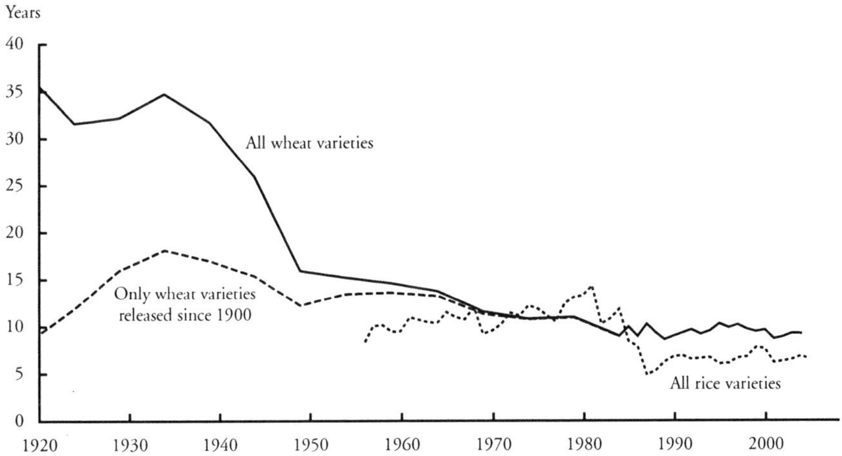

Panel b. Average age of 5 and 10 oldest and youngest wheat varieties

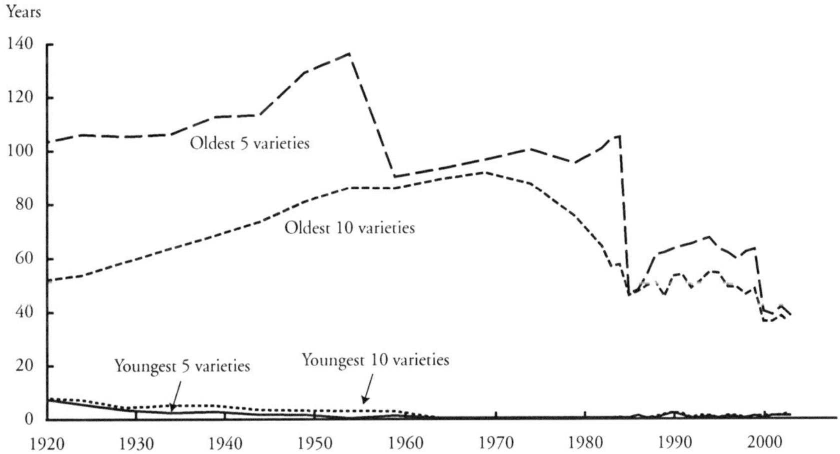

Sources: Chan-Kang and Pardey (2009).

Notes: The age of any given wheat variety was calculated by subtracting the year when the variety was planted from the year when it was released. To estimate the average age in Panel a, we weighted each varietal age by its respective area share for each year. In Panel b, the estimates represent the average age of the oldest 5 or 10 varieties and youngest 5 or 10 varieties in each year, so the pool of varieties in each group changes over time.

A corollary of the increased rate of varietal release was a reduction in the average age of wheat varieties, taking account of the acreage planted and the age since initial release of each variety, as shown in Figure 8-3, Panel a. Considering all planted wheat varieties, their (area-weighted) average age was 32.7 years during the 1920s, dropping to 13.2 years by the 1960s. Counting only those varieties developed or discovered after 1900, the average age was still 12.3 years by 2003. Figure 8-3, Panel a also shows a similar vintage profile for rice. The area-weighted average age of all rice varieties planted in the United States since 1999 was 6.6 years (since 1956 the average age has been 9.1 years). Figure 8-3, Panel b decomposes the vintage profiles for wheat, and shows that the (area-weighted) average age of the oldest ten varieties in use still averaged 38.7 years for the post-1999 period (when these ten varieties were planted on only 1.04 percent of the wheat acres in the United States). The ten youngest varieties in use, accounting for just 0.71 percent of the U.S. wheat acreage after 1999, had an average age of 1.09 years.

Allowing for the 5–10 years it takes to breed a new variety, these vintage profiles (measuring the average age of varieties in use in years from their date of release) underscore the notion that decades elapse before the productivity gains from investments in crop varietal research are fully realized. Notably, even these vintage profiles understate the length of the lags involved because they abstract from the cumulative and intrinsically time-intensive nature of the varietal improvement research that gives rise to new varieties. The history of older varieties, which are found in the family trees of most wheats bred in the United States, is reasonably well documented. For example, *Turkey Red*, a hard red winter wheat directly introduced from Turkey, and *Marquis*, a Canadian-bred (1911) hard red spring wheat crossed from *Calcutta* (an Indian landrace) and *Red Fife* (an 1842 landrace introduction from Germany) accounted for more than a quarter of all U.S. wheat acreage around the beginning of the 20th Century.

By the mid-1990s the most popular variety was *Karl*, a classic cross of well-established, short-statured plains varieties, and the second-most popular variety was *Pioneer 2375*, a hard red spring wheat released in 1989. *Pioneer 2375* represented the contemporary culmination of the spring-wheat breeding revolution and its pedigree reflects many years of intensive breeding activity. One grandparent, *Lark*, is a direct derivative of a CIMMYT line (bred by a private U.S. breeder from several CIMMYT lines). Other recent ancestors, including *Olaf*, *Chris*, and *Era*, are the products of continuing work by breeders in North Dakota and elsewhere to incorporate rust resistance into varieties suitable for spring wheat production on the Northern Plains. The pedigree is complex, and demonstrates the ability of modern wheat breeders to isolate desirable traits from a wide variety of wheat strains, and incorporate those traits into lines suitable for production in diverse environments.

Table 8-3 reveals that nearly one-quarter, or 31 of the 133 documented varietal nodes, in the *Pioneer 2375* pedigree were developed or discovered prior to 1920; more than 60 years prior to the release of the variety. Almost one-half of the documented nodes pre-date 1960. Notably, the variety is an agglomera-

Table 8-3 Attributes of the Wheat Variety, Pioneer 2375

Period and Origin	Pedigree Nodes	
	Number	Share
Period	*count*	*percentage*
Pre-1900	19	14.3
1900–1920	12	9.0
1921–1940	17	12.8
1941–1960	16	12.0
1961–1980	13	9.8
No date	56	42.1
Total	*133*	*100.0*
Origin		
Minnesota	7	5.3
Rest of United States	36	27.1
Rest of world	74	55.6
Unknown	16	12.0
Total	*133*	*100.0*

Sources: Chan-Kang and Pardey (2009).

Notes: To construct this table the dates of release and origin of 133 unique varieties representing nodes in this pedigree were identified.

tion of genetic material obtained from disparate locales. Only 5.3 percent of the documented nodes involve Minnesota material; more than half of the genetic material had its origin outside the United States.

Given that the average age of wheat varieties in use has stabilized at about 10 years, if it takes 5–10 years to develop a variety, the average lag between applied varietal research investment and resulting impacts in farmers fields may be in the range of 15–25 years, but with impacts clearly extending beyond the average lag, and perhaps more so in the past when varieties turned over more slowly. But the research effects must persist even longer (and, conversely, the implied research lag must be even longer) given the role of today's varieties as parents of the varieties that will replace them, and the persistence of the impacts through the offspring (and across subsequent generations) of the research that created the parents. As the example of *Pioneer 2375* shows, the persistent effects of a varietal innovation can last for decades after the variety itself ceases to be grown in farmers' fields.

Hybrid Corn

Griliches' (1957a) analysis of the generation and dissemination of hybrid corn technology throughout the United States was a seminal study in the economics of diffusion and the spatial spillover of an agricultural technology. Here we revisit and update some aspects of that analysis, focusing on the implications for R&D lags. Appendix Table 8-1 represents a timeline of key events in the development of hybrid corn. The relevant history goes back thousands of years to the beginning of agriculture. Even if we focus on the modern, scientific era and the relatively applied work focused on hybrid corn, the story began at least 20 years before commercial planting of hybrid corn became significant, and 40 years before the adoption process had been completed, in the sense that the percentage of corn planted to hybrids had reached a stable maximum.

In 1918, Donald F. Jones working at the Connecticut Agricultural Experiment Station suggested the use of the double cross (involving a cross between two single inbred lines of a particular crop variety) as a practical and effective means of realizing hybrid vigor in corn that George H. Shull and others had begun pursuing using single-cross methods a decade earlier. Through an expanding number of inbreeding projects at various state experiment stations, and research conducted by the USDA's Bureau of Plant Industry, seeds developed with this technology were gradually bred for various local agroecologies and began spreading among the various states, beginning in the early 1930s in Iowa. Thus the R&D or innovation lag was at least 10 years and may have been 20–30 years.

The time path of the adoption process is interesting, too. Figure 8-4, Panel a includes an updated and extended version of the adoption curve for hybrid corn, as initially presented by Griliches (1957a) and revised by Dixon (1980).[15] The first hybrid corn seed sales were in Connecticut in 1920 and in Iowa four years later, but it took until the early 1930s before commercially successful seed in sufficient quantities became more-widely available and the technology took off, initially in the Corn Belt states and then spreading farther afield. Iowa had 10 percent of its corn acreage planted to hybrids in 1936 (with 90 percent of its corn acreage so planted just four years later), while it took until 1948 before Alabama—a state with distinctive agroecological attributes compared with the principal Corn Belt states—had 10 percent of its corn acreage under hybrids. This delay reflected lags in the "availability" of hybrid seed suitable for a particular state (or for the agroecologies dominant in that state) and lags in the uptake or "acceptance" of the technology once suitable seed became available. By 1950, 80 percent and by 1960, almost all of the corn grown in the United States was hybrid corn. Looking across all the states, the technology diffusion process was spread over more like 30 years, reflecting the envelope of adoption processes that were much more rapid in any individual state.

---

15 Dixon (1980) used additional data on the uptake of hybrid corn, beyond that reported by Griliches in 1957, to re-estimate the rate of acceptance and the ceiling rate of adoption of hybrid corn. Dixon's results were "… supportive of Griliches' finding of a close association between the variability in the rates of diffusion across states on the one hand, and yield per acre and acres per farm on the other (1980, p. 1,460)." In a rejoinder to Dixon's paper Griliches observed "…my model (as of 1955–1957) is clearly wrong in retrospect both because of its assumption of a constant ceiling [level of adoption] and because the underlying process did not follow a fixed logistic curve exactly.… I would now rectify the model so that the ceiling is itself a function of economic variables that change over time (1980a, p. 1,463)." In a recent working paper, Sutch (2008) discusses the roles of synthetic fertilizer and Henry Agard Wallace as contributors to the yield and adoption of hybrid corn, respectively.

Figure 8-4 Uptake of Biological Technologies for Corn, 1930–2008

Panel a. Share of corn acreage planted with hybrids

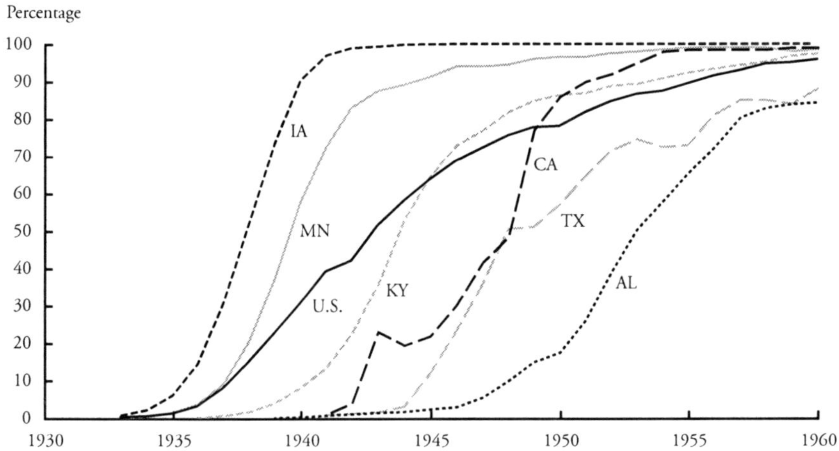

Panel b. Share of corn acreage planted with genetically engineered varieties

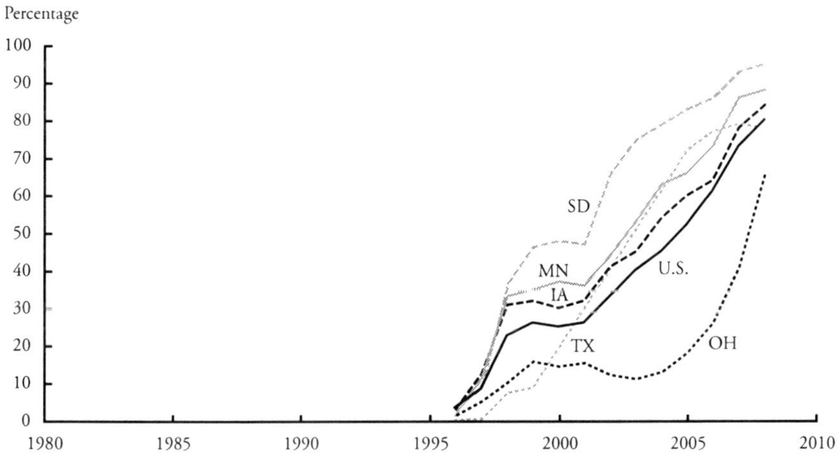

Sources: Pardey, Alston and Ruttan (2010). Panel a. Area shares of hybrid corn were obtained from USDA Agricultural Statistics (various years). Panel b. Data on genetically engineered varieties were calculated using confidential data from Doane for the pre-2000 period and USDA ERS data on biotech crops (http://www.ers.usda.gov/Data/BiotechCrops/) for the post-1999 period combined with data on crop area harvested from USDA (various years) *Agricultural Statistics*.

Notes: The data in Panel b came from two sources with substantial differences. USDA ERS data beginning in 2000 were backcasted using the state-specific rates of change from Doane.

If we think of the entire research, development, and adoption process for hybrid corn as having begun as late as 1918 (if not in the early 1900s with Shull and others), then the total process that had been accomplished by 1960 took place over a period of at least 40 years and possibly decades longer. Moreover, hybrid corn continues to be grown today, in the range of 100 years since the focused research that led to those initial innovations began to take hold. It seems reasonable to imagine that a relatively long overall R&D lag, with a significant gestation lag, would be required to represent the links between investment in hybrid corn research and the resulting impacts on aggregate agricultural productivity, though it is not clear just how long those lags should be nor what shape the lag distribution should assume.

Biotech Corn

The most recent revolution in corn seed technology began to take effect in farmers' fields half a century after the hybrid corn revolution. Modern biotechnology encompasses a range of innovations, including genetically engineered crop varieties. Among these, corn, soybeans, cotton, and canola are the most important biotech crops.[16] Corn was one of the first biotech crops to achieve commercial success. The two main types of innovations in corn and the other main biotech crops confer either (a) herbicide tolerance (in particular tolerance to the broad-spectrum herbicide glyphosate marketed by Monsanto originally under the brand name Roundup®), allowing enhanced weed control at lower cost, or (b) insect pest resistance, achieved by inserting genes from *Bacillus thuringiensis*, or *Bt*, a bacterium that produces insecticides naturally, such that the corn plants themselves express the insecticide.[17]

Notably, different types of *Bt* corn have been introduced with resistance to different insect pests, including the European corn borer (first released for commercial use in 1997) and the Western corn root worm (first released for commercial use in 2006), among others. These have been "stacked" with one another as well as herbicide tolerance ("roundup-ready" corn was first released for commercial use in 1996), to achieve multiple pest resistance jointly with herbicide tolerance.[18] Hence, biotech corn is not a single, simple innovation. Rather, the research to achieve these new outcomes separately, to combine them with one another, and to incorporate them into new corn varieties suited to different agro-

---

16 The perception of market resistance (from consumers or political organizations) has prevented the development and use of biotech varieties for major food crops such as rice and wheat while also slowing the development and use of biotech varieties for feedgrains, oilseeds, and fiber crops. Pardey et al. (2007) and the references therein give details on the uptake of biotech crops in an international context.

17 Alston, Pardey and Ruttan (2008) report technology timelines for two commercially successful efforts to develop biotech crop varieties, specifically the Roundup Ready® soybean event 40-3-2 and the YieldGard® corn borer technology.

18 The first herbicide tolerant and insect resistant corn varieties were approved for use in mid-1995. Since then a further 14 different regulatory approvals have been granted for genetically engineered corn varietal innovations with tolerance of different herbicides, resistance to different insect pests, or some combination. Significant adoption of each of these varieties began in the year when its regulatory approval was granted. These details were provided by Nicholas Kalaitzandonakes (personal communication, September 2008).

ecologies or with enhanced other characteristics, has continued in parallel with the adoption process that started in the 1990s.

In Figure 8-4, Panel b we can see the pattern of uptake of biotech corn among the main U.S. corn-growing states and in the nation as a whole. Genetically engineered (GE) corn was first planted on U.S. farmers' fields in the mid-1990s. The adoption-cum-diffusion process for GE crops is not yet complete; the technology itself is continuing to evolve, and the maximum adoption rate has not yet been achieved, but by 2008, 80 percent of U.S. corn acreage was planted to GE varieties. Like hybrid corn, biotech corn has been adopted at different rates in different states, but perhaps for different reasons.[19] This as-yet incomplete process over less than 15 years represents only part of the relevant time lag. To that we must add the time spent conducting relatively basic and applied research to develop and evaluate the technology, and the time (and money) spent after the technology had been developed to meet the requirements for regulatory approval by a range of government agencies (e.g., Kalaitzandonakes, Alston and Bradford 2006).

Compared with the adoption-cum-diffusion process for hybrid corn within the United States (Figure 8-4, Panel a), the process for biotech corn appears to have been a little faster (Figure 8-4, Panel b). All states began to adopt biotech corn together, without the slower spatial diffusion among states that characterized hybrid corn, possibly because of improved communications and farmer education, perhaps assisted by public extension services. Thus biotech corn achieved 80 percent adoption within 13 years compared with 19 years for hybrid corn. However, other elements of the process may be getting longer. For instance, the process of regulatory approval may have added a further 5–10 years to the R&D lag (and this regulatory approval lag for biotech crops appears to be growing over time). Given a range of 10 20 years spent on R&D to develop the technologies that enabled the creation of biotech crops, and then the time spent to develop the initial varieties and improve them, the overall process of innovation in the case of biotech corn may have taken 20–30 years so far.[20] The implied R&D lag may be in the same range as that for the hybrid corn varietal revolution, upon which this latest corn varietal revolution is building.[21]

---

19 The demand for biotech crop varieties varies among locations, depending on the prevalence of weed and pest problems that they address, on the price charged by the technology providers, and on the perceived market discount or other penalty from the use of the biotech crop variety. Thus some farmers in some locations will never adopt biotech crop varieties, whereas hybrid corn varieties are more generally superior to non-hybrids, given local adaptation, and they do not entail risk of market discounts or other side effects.

20 A more complete analysis would also account for the international adoption of these technologies and the implications for the United States through the resulting price impacts.

21 The cumulative nature of the crop improvement process is clearly evident in the case of corn; the GE innovations of the late 20th Century such as herbicide tolerance or insect resistance are

Uptake of Other Innovations by U.S. Agriculture

In addition to biological innovations, of which genetic improvement of crop varieties has been an important component, agriculture has adopted many other types of innovations. *Mechanical technologies* (especially labor-saving machines for cultivation and harvest and the like), transformed agriculture especially in the early part of the 20th Century; *chemical technologies* such as those embodied in fuels, synthetic fertilizers, pesticides, and growth promotants, had greater impacts in the second half of the 20th Century; *information technologies*, involving computers, electronics, robotics, remote sensing, and geographic information systems (GIS) technologies, are mainly a relatively recent and contemporary phenomenon, though the telephone and telegraph can be seen as earlier examples.[22] Each of these broad categories, like biological innovations, includes a broad range of different types of specific innovations, and we have only partial information on the research and adoption processes. Relatively good information is available on the uptake by farmers of some specific, important innovations that can serve as illustrative examples. Figure 8-5, Panel a shows the pattern of adoption of three types of innovations on U.S. farms: tractors, electrification, and telephones.[23] Panel b, for comparison, includes the national adoption curves for hybrid corn and GE corn (as represented in more detail in Figure 8-4), along with GE soybeans.

In 1920, 7 percent of U.S. farms had electricity. This percentage grew in a classic sigmoid shape to over 90 percent within the following 30 years. The adoption process for telephones was much different. The percentage of farms with telephones fell from 40 percent in 1920 to 25 percent in 1940, reflecting, perhaps, the effects of the Depression and World War II.[24] Then from 1940 forward the number of farms with telephones grew roughly in line with the number of farms with tractors, from around one-quarter to about two-thirds by 1960. All of these changes reflect changes in both the numerator and the denominator of the

---

themselves being bundled into hybrid corn varieties that are the progeny of an early 20th Century innovation.

22 Olmstead and Rhode (2000 and 2008) provide a broader coverage of the transformation of American agriculture during the years 1910–1990. They give some emphasis to the very significant role played by technological innovation, and their coverage of mechanization, transportation and communication, and the related work by economists, is more complete than ours, which is deliberately selective.

23 These are national aggregate percentages. We also have data at the state level and data on other innovations (such as the adoption of combines) that are the subject of continuing research.

24 Both the telephone and electricity required investment in infrastructure. Public policies, notably New Deal programs including the Rural Electrification Administration (REA) and the Tennessee Valley Authority (TVA) affected the development of the supply of electricity and its availability in rural areas (see, for example, Emmons 1993). The availability of these technologies and their uptake by individual farmers depended on other economic circumstances as well. Goldin (1947) describes the moribund state of the U.S. telephone industry during the 1930s. See also studies cited by Olmstead and Rhode (2000).

measures of technology use per farm, because the number of farms was changing rapidly, especially during the latter half of the 20th Century. The number of farms fell from 6.4 million in 1920 to 6.0 million in 1940, then dropped to 3.6 million by 1960. Moreover, it was the smaller and economically less-successful farms that were going out of business and the remaining farms were becoming larger and changing in other ways, factors that would have been strongly related to their use of newer technologies.

The case of tractors warrants particular attention because we have more and better data on the use of tractors on farms, and because the displacement of horses and mules transformed agriculture so dramatically.[25] Figure 8-5, Panel a shows that the adoption process extended over 50 years, from before 1920, when less than 5 percent of farms had tractors, through to the early 1970s, when the fraction of farms with tractors stabilized at almost 90 percent. This simple picture conceals many complications, such as those associated with the changing numbers of farms and the changing definition of what constitutes a farm for statistical purposes. It is an aggregate across different states and different agro-ecologies and production systems that may have adopted tractors sooner or later, faster or slower. And it is an aggregation across types of tractors. Over the 50 years to 1970, and the 40 years since then, tractors have continued to evolve and improve in many ways (see discussion in Chapter 3).[26] Thus, it could be quite misleading simply to count tractors at a point in time as well as over time, when the characteristics of tractors are so variable. And, like biotech corn, it would be a mistake to conceive of the tractor as an episodic innovation that was introduced at a point in time and gradually adopted in unchanged form from that point on. Rather, the tractor represented a continuum of innovations, the adoption of which both enabled and was enabled by the progressive consolidation of farms into larger units that could exploit the economies of size, scale and specialization afforded by mechanization.

In Figure 8-5, comparing the adoption curves for corn and soybean varieties in Panel b with those for tractors, electricity, and telephones in Panel a, one common point emerges. The adoption process for agricultural innovation takes time—in the range of 15–30 years for broad classes of varietal innovations (such as hybrid corn or biotech crops at the level of the nation, as compared with individual crop varieties in a particular locale), and in the range of 30–50 years for major mechanical innovations (such as tractors and combines) and for

25 Olmstead and Rhode (2001) provide an insightful analysis of the adoption of tractors in U.S. agriculture, drawing out the role of induced changes in prices of horses and mules over space and time, and the feed grains they both produced and consumed, as determinants of the adoption decisions that were exogenous to individual farmers but endogenous to the sector as a whole.

26 Improved features include such things as pneumatic tires, suspension, hydraulic systems, power take-offs, fuel efficiency, horsepower, driver safety and comfort (including cushioned seats, air conditioned cabs, stereo systems), four-wheel drive, and computerized driving systems.

Figure 8-5 Uptake of Agricultural Technologies in the United States, 1920–2008

Panel a. Share of farms using tractors, electricity, and telephones

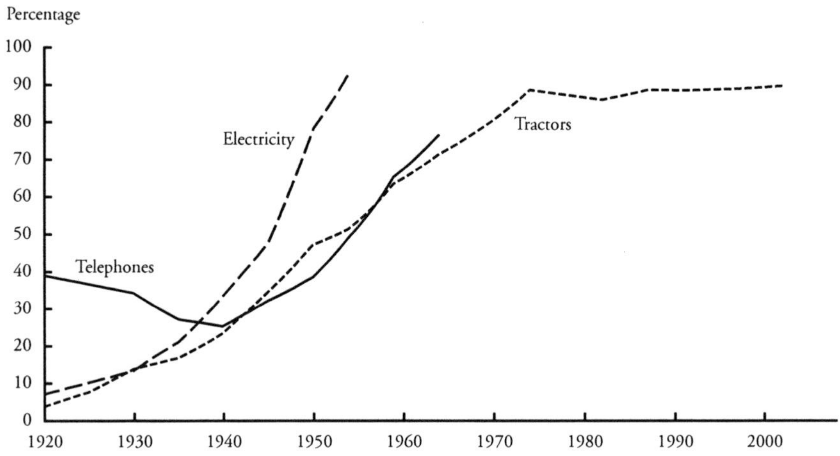

Panel b. Share of acreage planted to different types of corn and soybean varieties

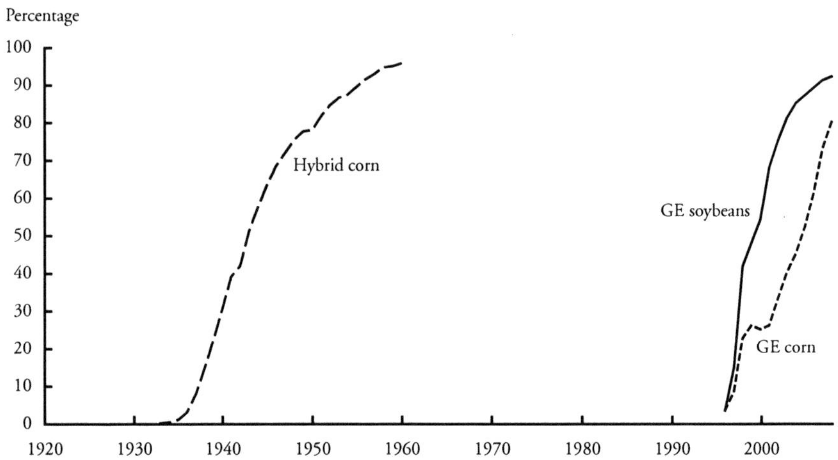

Sources: Panel a. Developed by the authors from U.S. Bureau of the Census (various years). Panel b. see Figure 8-4 sources.

Notes: The plots in Panel a represent linear interpolations between adjacent agricultural census years. The shares were constructed from data on the number of farms reporting tractors, electricity, telephone, and the total numbers of farms. See notes to Figure 8-4 for details on Panel b data.

other significant technologies (such as the telephone and electricity). These facts alone suggest that the time lags between investing in research that contributed to the development of this technology, and reaping the resulting benefits, could be quite long. To the lags from adoption must be added the R&D lags which themselves are hard to pinpoint but potentially also very long.

8.4 Spatial Aspects of the R&D Attribution Problem

Compared with the research lag structure, the issue of spatial attribution has received less attention in the literature on agricultural R&D, and has been approached differently in the literature on industrial R&D (see Appendix 8.1 for detailed discussion). In the more-recent literature, however, increasing attention has been paid to accounting for the fact that knowledge created within a particular geopolitical entity can have impacts on technology elsewhere, with implications that may matter to both the creators of the spillouts and the recipients of the spillins.

Previous Work on Agricultural Technology Spillovers

Some of the earliest work on these matters was done in applications to agriculture.[27] As discussed above, Griliches' (1957a) analysis of the generation and dissemination of hybrid-corn technology throughout the United States was a seminal study in the economics of diffusion and the spatial spillover of an agricultural technology. The 40-year diffusion process reflected lags in the "availability" of hybrid seed suitable for a particular state (or for the agroecologies dominant in that state) and lags in the uptake or "acceptance" of the technology once suitable seed became available. Hybrid-corn technology, and Griliches' study of it, demonstrated the spatial spillovers of an important biological innovation, and the roles of federal and state public laboratories as well as private firms in the spread of the technology.

While much can be learned from studies of spillovers of particular technologies, they provide only a partial picture of the spillover consequences of R&D.[28] Other studies have sought to assess the overall effects of agricultural research on productivity with regression-based methods using more aggregate (region- or state-specific as well as national) measures of R&D. Among these, for example Huffman and Evenson (1993) found that a sizable share (upwards of 45 percent) of the benefits from research conducted in U.S. State Agricultural Experiment Stations was earned as interstate spillovers. Whether they were concerned with spillovers or not, the past studies have imposed implicit or explicit assumptions about the spatial spillover effects of agricultural research based on geopolitical boundaries. For example, most past studies of the effects of U.S. agricultural research on productivity have implicitly assumed that agricultural research is totally fungible, such that U.S. national agricultural output depends on the national

27 Alston (2002) reviewed the literature on agricultural technology spillovers, with particular attention to the U.S. applications. The discussion here draws on that review and extends it.

28 For example, Evenson and Kislev (1973) analyzed spillovers related to wheat and maize research, Araji, White and Guenthner (1995) looked at spillovers regarding potato research, Maredia, Ward, and Byerlee (1996), and Traxler and Byerlee (2001) investigated wheat spillovers, and Pardey et al. (2006) looked at spillovers related to soybean, edible bean and upland rice research. Alston et al. (2000a) list further studies.

aggregate of U.S. spending on public agricultural R&D, regardless of where it was spent or by whom (e.g., Griliches 1964; Evenson 1967; White and Havlicek 1982; Chavas and Cox 1992; Alston, Craig and Pardey 1998).

In contrast, some studies at the level of individual states proposed that research efforts by individual states have spillover effects only among states within the same (subnational) geopolitical region, while research outside a region does not affect its agricultural productivity. The grouping of states into regions and the specifics of the spillin variables vary among these studies. For instance, several studies, beginning with Huffman and Evenson (1989, pp. 11–21), incorporated geoclimatic information while retaining the restriction that technology spillovers occur only among neighboring states within contiguous geopolitical regions.[29]

Drawing on earlier work by Evenson (1988 and 1989), Huffman and Evenson (1989) defined a composite own-state and spillin research variable, R^*, as:

$$(8.1) \qquad R_i^* = R_i + (1 - \alpha)\, RSS_i + (1 - 2\alpha)\, RSR_i\,,$$

where R_i^* is the constructed stock for state i, R_i is the own-state research stock, RSS_i is the research stock for other states in the same geoclimatic subregion as state i (excluding state i's stock), and RSR_i is the research stock for other states in the same geoclimatic region as state i but in different subregions (i.e., excluding RSS_i). If state i had more than one geoclimatic region, the above expression was computed for each relevant region and a weighted sum was formed where the weights represented the region's "relative importance." Separate stocks were formed for crop-related research (for which α was estimated to be 0.5) and livestock-related research (for which α was estimated to be zero). The assignment of states to regions and sub-regions was based on the geographical concordance of state boundaries and the 16 geoclimatic regions and 34 geoclimatic subregions described in USDA (1957). By construction, research conducted in a significant dairy state such as New York does not affect productivity in Wisconsin; nor, for example, does Florida research spill over to California (and vice versa), two states with significant beef and citrus production.

Other studies have used other spatial groupings. Khanna, Huffman and Sandler (1994) grouped states into six regions using a classification scheme devised by the Economic Research Service of the USDA (in conjunction with the geoclimatic classification from Evenson 1989) where for each state in each region a spillover variable consisted of the pool of research done by other states in the same region. McCunn and Huffman (2000) grouped the 48 states into seven regions, each containing contiguous states. In their study of the spillover effects of U.S. agricultural R&D, Yee and Huffman (2001) experimented with alternative state groupings, but settled on the McCunn and Huffman configuration

29 The same or a similar set of constructed spillover weights were used by Huffman and Evenson (1992, 1993, 2001 and 2006a), Huffman and Just (1999), and McCunn and Huffman (2000).

when constructing a spillin stock of publicly generated knowledge as the sum of public research stocks of all states in the relevant region less the state's own research stock.[30]

Many studies, however, simply ignored the effects of research in other states or by the federal government (e.g., Norton and Ortiz 1992; Leiby and Adams 1991; Alston, Pardey and Carter 1994), and almost all of the regression-based studies of agricultural R&D have ignored the possibility of international spillovers, unless they were specifically emphasizing that possibility (two exceptions are the studies by Bouchet, Orden and Norton 1989 and Schimmelpfennig and Thirtle 1999). On the other hand, studies of the effects of the CGIAR centers on agricultural productivity in adopting countries using other than regression methods have emphasized the spillins of technology (e.g., Brennan and Fox 1995; Pardey et al. 1996; Brennan, Singh and Lewin 1997; Brennan and Bantilan 1999; Brennan 2007). Looking more broadly at the literature, few studies of national systems, irrespective of the method used, have allowed for either spillins or spillouts—in their meta-analysis, Alston et al. (2000a) identified less than 20 percent of studies allowing for *any* spillovers. The modeling decisions—either to ignore spillovers or represent them using measures based on proximity—have been at least to some extent driven by the limitations of available data and the requirements for parsimonious models. Even when we are conscious of the possibility of interstate or international spillover effects (and not totally hamstrung by data limitations), it is not clear what we ought to do about them. Clearly, however, restrictive assumptions are inevitable.

In Chapter 9 we develop and apply an adaption of the approach that was suggested by Jaffe (1986 and 1989) for modeling firm-to-firm technology spillovers, to represent state-to-state spillovers of knowledge resulting from agricultural research in the United States. This approach uses an index of agroecological similarity (based on a comparison of state-specific output mix vectors) to represent state-to-state spillover potential. Like precedent approaches in the literature, this approach involves the application of arbitrary, restrictive assumptions, but we suggest that the approach is more reasonable than prior approaches that either base spillover potential on spatial proximity alone, or ignore spillovers altogether.

---

30 One of the alternatives investigated by Yee and Huffman involved grouping states into nine "commodity clusters" based on a cluster analysis of SAESs conducted by the Committee on the Future of the Colleges of Agriculture in the Land Grant System (NRC 1995, Table 7-4 on p. 94 and Figure 7-4 on p. 95). The clusters were identified by the three commodities or commodity groups that were allocated the greatest percentage of research funding. The clusters often included mainly adjoining states, but not always. For instance, cluster 2 for vegetables, citrus, and other fruits included California, Florida, and Hawaii. This approach based on research emphasis may not be ideal for representing potential research spillovers. For instance, California is not included in any of the clusters that incorporate dairy cattle (clusters 3, 7, and 9) even though it is by far the largest dairy state in the nation.

In our empirical work we present some limited comparisons of the alternatives and their implications.

8.5 Conclusion

Over the past 20 years, the literature on modeling the relationship between research and productivity has increasingly paid attention to addressing spatial and temporal dimensions of the links between research spending and productivity. Compared with the literature on non-agricultural industrial R&D, the literature on agricultural R&D has addressed these aspects in different, often more satisfactory, ways. With respect to the lag structure, in particular, agricultural economists have used models that are more intuitively plausible—perhaps especially for agriculture given the nature of the biological lags both in the research process and in adoption—and that stand up better to statistical tests. With respect to technology spillovers, agricultural economists have emphasized spillovers between geopolitical regions rather than between firms, which makes sense in view of the comparatively atomistic structure of agriculture and the site-specific nature of much agricultural technology. Much of the work in the following chapters is devoted to dealing with these aspects of modeling U.S. agricultural productivity, and the implications of particular modeling choices for our findings.

Appendix Table 8-1 Technology Timeline for Hybrid Corn

Date	Notes
Circa 5000 B.C.	Date of wild corn cobs excavated by Dr. Richard MacNeish from caves in Tehuacán Valley located in southern Puebla and northern Oaxaca, Mexico. Intact corn cobs ranged in length from 19–25 mm.
1500–900 B.C.	Early Tripsacoid corn appeared in Tehuacán Valley, suggesting a corn type resulting from introgression of Tripsacum or teosinte (*Zea Mexicana*). Generally larger in size than wild corn.
1716	Cotton Mather from Massachusetts observed and was the first to document the effects of cross-pollination in corn.
1735 and 1739	James Logan of Philadelphia conducted the first published accounts of controlled pollination of corn and described the actions of wind borne pollen.
Circa 1871	Charles Darwin conducted greenhouse experiments and observed hybrid vigor in corn. In his 1877 book *Effects of Cross- and Self-Fertilization in the Vegetable Kingdom* Darwin documented how inbreeding reduced vigor, and crossbreeding restored it.
1877	Professor William Beal at Michigan Agricultural College (now Michigan State University), a correspondent with Charles Darwin, conducted the first controlled crosses between varieties of corn for the sole purpose of increasing yields through hybrid vigor.
1847–1893	Robert Reid, followed by his son James Reid (originally from Cincinnati but after 1946 operating from a farm near Peoria, Illinois) developed *Reid Yellow Dent*, based on progeny from a cross between a (late maturing) southern dent variety, *Gordon Hopkins* (from the Shenandoah Valley, Virginia), and an (early maturing) New England variety, *Little Yellow* (otherwise known as *Early Yellow Flint*, an 8–10 row flint style corn grown by Indians in northeastern United States for centuries). Reid corn, as it was known, had 10-inch ears with 18–24 straight rows of kernels per ear, and, importantly had a maturity period appropriate for central Illinois. It served as the breeding base of Eugene Funk's *Funk Yellow Dent*. These two dent corns were the basis for some of the most widely used inbreds in U.S. commercial corn production.
1900	The Dutch botanist Hugo de Vries, the German botanist Correns, and the Austrian agronomist Tschermark independently and at about the same time published studies on the laws of heredity that had been anticipated in the 1866 paper by the Austrian monk Gregor Mendel. When Mendel's paper was published in the Proceedings of the Natural History Society of Brünn, it had little impact and was cited about three times over the next thirty-five years.
1902–1910	Perry G. Holden (previously of Funk Seeds, and earlier a student of William Beal), came to Iowa State College, Ames in 1902 and was instrumental in mass education of farmers that popularized *Reid Yellow Dent* corns throughout Iowa.
1905–1912	George H. Shull (a personal friend of de Vries, Correns and Tschermark), who in 1904 arrived at the Carnegie Institution's Cold Springs Harbor Laboratory in Long Island, Connecticut, conducted a series of controlled crosses with corn from which he was able to gain a correct understanding of the effects of inbreeding and cross breeding. His results were published in two papers; one in 1908, the other in 1909. The 1908 paper titled "The Composition of a Field of Maize" was a report read to the American Breeders Association in Washington, D.C. wherein Shull drew a number of conclusions: 1) an ordinary field of corn consists of a series of very complex hybrids; 2) the decline in vigor that occurs as a result of self-fertilization is due to a gradual increase in homozygosity; 3) the goal of the corn breeder should be not to find the best pure lines but rather to identify and maintain the best hybrid combinations. His 1909 paper titled "A Pure Line Method of Corn Breeding" described a single-cross method of hybrid corn production in which the progeny of a single cross between two inbred lines constitute the seed corn to be used for planting on farms.

(continued)

Appendix Table 8-1 (continued)

Date	Notes
1905–1909	Edward M. East, formerly at the University of Illinois where he had begun conducting inbreeding experiments to understand the causes of poor yields in repeated selections of varieties chosen for high protein, arrived at the Connecticut Agricultural Experiment Station, with one generation of corn in-breds in hand. Working at the same time and independently of Shull, East contributed extensively to the development of the modern corn hybrid, and, arguably, deserves as much credit as Shull (see Wallace and Brown 1988, p. 108).
1910–1915	East left for Harvard in 1910 and the corn inbreeding and crossing work at Connecticut was taken over by Herbert K. Hayes in 1911. Hayes left for the University of Minnesota in 1915 (where he had a major impact on mid-western agriculture through his teaching, research and seminal publications over the subsequent three decades). He was replaced by Donald F. Jones.
1917	Jones developed the "double-cross" hybrid, wherein four inbred lines (A, B, C and D) are crossed pairwise (i.e., B x A and C x D), making two single crosses, then the two single crosses are crossed (i.e., [B x A] x [C x D]) giving a double cross, instead of simply crossing two inbred lines to create a single-cross hybrid corn variety. Given that the inbreds being used at the time had poor vigor, a single-cross method was an impractical basis for commercial hybrid development. The double-cross method realized a more assured and cost-effective supply of hybrid seed, thus paving the way for commercial hybrid seed production.
1918	F.D. Richey of the USDA discovered *Lancaster Sure Crop*, developed by Isaac Hershey, Lancaster County, Pennsylvania, an early maturing flinty corn.
1921	M.L. Mosher, a county agent, discovered George Krug (a farmer in Wouford County, Central Illinois) and high yielding *Krug Corn*, the progeny of a Nebraska strain of *Reid Yellow Dent* corn and *Iowa Gold Mine*.
1922	Iowa State Experiment station began a program of corn inbreeding and Richey was largely instrumental for including *Lancaster Sure Crop* and various strains of *Reid Yellow Dent* into this breeding program.
1933	First commercial plantings of *Hybrid Iowa 939* developed by Merle Jenkins. This is the first widely adapted hybrid, performing well in Iowa, Illinois, Indiana and Ohio.
1936	Ben Duddleston of Purdue University released *Indian WF9* (*Wilson Farm Row 9*) developed from *Reid Yellow Dent*. In 1935 it became one part of hybrid *U.S. 13*, the first widely popular double-cross hybrid.
1960	Vastly improved inbred lines resulted in an almost complete shift from double- to single-cross (or modified-single-cross) hybrid corn within a decade. Single-cross hybrids typically lead to higher-yielding hybrids than seed developed by double-cross methods.

Sources: Developed by Alson, Pardey and Ruttan (2008) based on information in Wallace and Brown (1988), Duvick (2001) and Smith, Betrán and Runge (2004).

Appendix 8-1 Models of Industrial R&D

The literature on models of agricultural R&D and its effects on productivity can be seen as a subset of the broader literature on industrial R&D, but it has developed in some different directions, partly reflecting the different industrial structure and the important role of public research in agriculture (see Chapter 6 for some details), and partly because of differences in the nature of production and technology in agriculture. For these kinds of reasons, the modeling of technology spillovers has taken a very different path in the industrial R&D literature, emphasizing inter-industry spillovers more than inter-regional spillovers as such. This appendix reviews some key points, highlighting some concerns with the typical R&D lag structure employed in models of industrial R&D.

R&D Lags in Models of Industrial R&D

In the more general industrial R&D literature, views about the research lag structure are often reflected in terms of assumptions about the rate of geometric depreciation of the knowledge stock (the converse of the overall lag length that has more often been the key parameter of the research lag in agricultural R&D studies, as discussed by Alston et al. 2000a). The industrial R&D literature reports a range of estimates of geometric depreciation rates used in the creation of R&D capital stocks, but the rates are generally large, implying much shorter effective research lag lengths than found by studies of agricultural R&D that explicitly tested for lag lengths.[31]

Using sectoral-level data, Adams (1990) estimated an annual depreciation rate for basic research of 0.09 to 0.13, while Nadiri and Prucha (1996) estimated a rate of 0.12 for industrial R&D. Based on this and other evidence, the U.S. Bureau of Economic Analysis (BEA) used a straight-line life span that corresponds to a geometric depreciation rate of 0.11 in constructing estimates of R&D net capital stocks in 1994 (Carson, Grimm and Moylan 1994). This rate implies that only 10 percent of today's knowledge stock will remain in use in 20 years' time. The U.S. Bureau of Labor Statistics, BLS (1989) used a slightly smaller rate of 10 percent as its central estimate to develop economy-wide estimates of the stocks of useful knowledge, which also implies a rapid rundown in these stocks. BLS (1989) also considered annual depreciation rates of 0 and 20 percent, and noted that the choice of a specific rate of depreciation had important implications for the effect of R&D on productivity growth. In one earlier study using firm-level data, Griliches (1980b) considered depreciation rates of 0, 10 and 20 percent; in another (Griliches 1986), 15 percent. Coe and Helpman (1995) suggested a depreciation rate of 5 percent for research applied to business-sector R&D capital, implying a much longer-lived effective stock. Coe and Helpman are in the distinct minority with their comparatively low depreciation rate (and implied long-lived effects of

---

31 Somewhat shorter lags may be appropriate for linking privately performed R&D to productivity using firm-specific data (particularly for the purpose of estimating the private returns to R&D). An argument for shorter lags has even more force in this context when the preponderance of the within-firm R&D involves developmental work based on the prior (and freely available) innovative effort of others. However, there are reasons for thinking the lags are likely to be longer for models that use sectoral or economy-wide data, even if the focus is solely on assessing the productivity effects of private research. In any event, as argued by Alston, Pardey and Ruttan (2008), the relevant lag distribution is still likely to be of a different form than the typical geometric model imposes, and the overall lag is likely to be substantially longer than assumed in the typical model of industrial R&D (since they encompass often sequential invention, development, regulatory and adoption processes).

research on productivity). For instance, Hall and Mairesse (1995) explored the relationship between R&D and productivity using 16 years of R&D data for French manufacturing firms, for which they formed an R&D capital stock using depreciation rates of 15, 25, and (implicitly) 100 percent.

The same general thinking prevails in contemporary work. Sliker (2007) summarized the methodology used to create the knowledge capital stocks reported in the 2007 version of the U.S. BLS satellite accounts for R&D.[32] The measure in the satellite accounts incorporates R&D spending by business, government and non-profit institutions, and so ostensibly represents a measure of the stock of knowledge that is appropriate for economy-wide considerations. In a companion paper Mead (2007) canvassed the economics literature related only to business and industry-specific studies as a basis for informing decisions regarding the choice of R&D depreciation rates used to construct the economy-wide U.S. BLS measures, and concluded that "… the 15 percent depreciation rate for R&D capital that is commonly assumed in studies of the net return to [business] R&D capital is consistent with the empirical evidence, which seems to indicate that the range of 15–20 percent is correct for the depreciation rate of business R&D (2007, p. 5)." The five studies of industry-specific R&D reviewed by Mead (2007) reported R&D depreciation rates ranging from -11 to 52 percent.[33]

The Australian government's Productivity Commission (2007) recently published a report on *Public Support for Science and Innovation* supported by a working paper by Shanks and Zheng (2006) that reported an extensive review of literature and new econometric results on the relationship between business R&D and economy-wide productivity for the Australian economy. This work was subject to considerable professional and public scrutiny. The main model used in that study entailed an R&D capital stock with a depreciation rate of 15 percent applied to business enterprise research and development, consistent with the central tendency of the range of adjusted industry-specific R&D depreciation rates used by BLS in constructing the 2007 total R&D capital stocks for the United States.

It is reasonable to presume that the work by the BLS and the Australian Productivity Commission is consistent with the mainstream of views in the economics profession, and can be treated as a contemporary benchmark. Yet these widely adopted models in the industrial research literature are fundamentally implausible, even when applied to industrial research of the most applied and immediate nature, but especially when applied to the more substantial research that typically takes time. Moreover, a geometric lag model implies that research has its maximum effect on productivity immediately in the year when the

32 The 2007 version of these R&D satellite accounts can be obtained online at http://www.bea.gov/industry/index.htm#satellite. See, also, Robbins and Moylan (2007).

33 The industry-level studies included Lev and Sougiannis (1996), Ballester, Garcia-Ayuso and Livnat (2003), Bernstein and Mamuneas (2006), Hall (2006) and Huang and Diewert (2007). In constructing their measures of stocks, the BLS put aside the Hall (2006) estimates, averaged the industry-specific depreciation rates reported in the remaining four studies, and then scaled down these mid-points "... so the recommended rates are more closely centered on a value of 15 and that the overall ranking of industry-level rates suggested by the literature is preserved (Mead 2007, p. 6)." The rationale for excluding the R&D depreciation rates reported by Hall (2006) was "...because the rates that are presented in the first portion of the [Hall] study, which are based on a production function seem unreasonably low, and the rates that are presented in the second portion of the paper, which are based on a market valuation model, seem unreasonably high (Mead 2007, p. 5)." The basis for determining that these estimates were "unreasonable" was not discussed.

investment is made, allowing no time for the processes of research, knowledge creation, development of technology, and adoption. Such assumptions may be plausible when applied to an aggregate of physical capital that is at its best and most productive at the time of purchase (e.g., see Andersen, Alston and Pardey 2007). However, knowledge capital takes time to create and become effective, after which it may depreciate very slowly (and even then perhaps only because of obsolescence rather than any physical deterioration) if at all. The implied relationship between research investments and the knowledge stock in use, and thus the effect of research on productivity, must have a very different shape than that implied by the analytically convenient but otherwise undesirable geometric depreciation model.

In addition, and possibly more important, the relevant lag between research investments and productivity impacts is likely to be much longer than those implied by the typically assumed rates of geometric depreciation. For instance, in a model with a geometric depreciation rate of 15 percent, the marginal impact of research would have declined to less than half of its initial value after five years, and less than 20 percent after ten years. Many research investments take at least five and possibly as many as ten years before they begin to have any effect on productivity. Thus, a model with a 15 percent geometric depreciation rate imposes much different timing of the research impact, with a generally much shorter research lag structure than can be justified in view of the typical research lags likely to be found in reality. The resulting estimates of model parameters and the implied elasticities of productivity with respect to research, benefit-cost ratios, and internal rates of return are likely to have been significantly distorted.

The benchmark model of industrial R&D with no research, development, and adoption lags, and relatively rapid geometric depreciation, has stood the test of time at least in the sense that it continues to be widely used. Some questions have been raised about its implications and whether they can be reconciled with the data. In a paper he presented at a conference in Melbourne in 1996 (subsequently published as Griliches 1996 and 2001), Zvi Griliches identified a conundrum, which was recently revisited by Bronwyn Hall (2006 and 2007). Paraphrasing Griliches (1996 and 2001), Hall observed that "... the measurement of the depreciation of R&D assets is the central unsolved problem in the measurement of the returns to research (2007, p. 2)." The lag relationship between research and productivity is clearly at issue. Our work suggests that the issue goes beyond the specification of the depreciation process to the specification of the processes of knowledge creation and adoption, which have been omitted altogether from the models that treat current research as an increment to the knowledge stock, that begins to depreciate immediately.

Spillovers in Models of Industrial R&D

The industrial R&D literature has also analyzed spatial spillovers, typically the transfer of technologies among countries, although the preponderance of these studies analyzed firm-to-firm or industry-to-industry spillovers. A feature of many of these studies is that research by others has not been treated as fully fungible or perfectly substitutable. Rather, research investments undertaken by different firms or different industries are weighted in some way such that the weights become smaller as the "distance" between firms or industries, however conceived, increases.

Griliches (1992) pointed out that the earlier weighting schemes were based on notions of "vertical borrowing," in which innovations at one stage of a multistage production process gave rise to innovations upstream or downstream. Quoting Griliches (1992; S35-S36), for example, "Brown and Conrad (1967) used the input-output table to measure the 'closeness' of industries proportional to their purchases from each other, while Terleckyj (1974) used the capital and intermediate inputs purchases matrix weights, assuming that 'borrowed' R&D is embodied in purchased inputs."

Griliches (1992) also suggested that various studies have used notions of "horizontal borrowing" in which they devised weights of various sorts to represent the "intellectual-scientific-technological" proximity among firms and industries. Griliches (1992; S37-38) characterized these alternatives as including the use of: (a) the U.S. National Science Foundation's applied R&D product-field-by-industry table as the basis for a distance metric, on the assumption that if an industry is doing R&D on some other industry's products it is somehow technologically closer than if it is not (Raines 1968; Schankerman 1979); (b) company industrial diversification data from the U.S. Census of Enterprise or Compustat data to compute a measure of closeness based on sales-demand space (Jaffe 1986); (c) information on rates of cross-referencing of patents across product fields to infer the technological distance between them, or a cross classification of patents (e.g., Scherer 1982 and 1984; Englander, Evenson and Hanazaki 1988) or innovations (Robson, Townsend and Pavitt 1988; Sterlacchini 1989) by industry of production and industry of use as a means of mapping the "flow-thru" of R&D expenditures from performing to using industries; and (d) the diversification of a firm's patenting activity among technologically determined patent classes to infer overlap and closeness measures for inventive activity (e.g., Jaffe 1986 and 1988).

Jaffe (1986 and 1988) constructed a measure of an available pool of outside R&D for each firm, with the R&D of other firms being weighted inversely to their estimated technological distance from the particular firm, and validated his measure by including own and outside R&D variables in estimating production functions and number of patents for these firms. Bernstein (1989), Bernstein and Nadiri (1988 and 1989) and Mohnen and Lepine (1991) estimated cost functions using industry-level data for multiple countries wherein R&D variables for each industry from each country are treated as separate explanatory variables. Aside from the difficulties of obtaining good price data for the variable inputs as well as physical and R&D capital, multicollinearity among the respective R&D series must have bedeviled their efforts to identify statistically significant sources of R&D spillovers.

More recently, beginning with the work of Coe and Helpman (1995), a series of studies have viewed trade as the primary mechanism by which international R&D spillovers occur.[34] Using national aggregate data, Coe and Helpman related R&D to productivity in a production function framework that includes national R&D capital stocks and various aggregate measures of foreign capital stocks; one is a simple sum of the foreign R&D capital stocks of each country's set of major trading partners, the second is a bilateral import-share weighted average of the R&D capital stocks of each countries' major trading partners. Based on the notion that the extent of international technology diffusion is related to geographic distance,

34 See also Coe, Helpman and Hoffmaister (1997), Lichtenberg and Pottelsberghe de la Potterie (1998) and Bayoumi, Coe and Helpman (1999).

Keller (2001) estimated a variant of the Coe and Helpman model in which domestic and foreign R&D capital stocks are made conditional on the bilateral distance between R&D-using and -producing countries, and found in favor of the notion that geography plays a statistically significant role in accounting for the spillover consequences of R&D.[35]

---

35 Keller (2001) denominates the geographic distance between countries as the shortest distance between the capital cities of the countries.

CHAPTER 9

Models of Research and Productivity

In this chapter we develop the structure of our models for estimating the effects of U.S. public agricultural research on U.S. agricultural productivity. We begin by laying out a general model relating research spending to agricultural productivity. Because this general specification includes too many parameters to be estimated individually with any degree of precision, some restrictions must be imposed. A conventional approach is to model productivity as a function of knowledge stocks that are created as a result of past research and can be represented using a distributed lag model defined by a small number of parameters. In this chapter we describe our approach for creating research knowledge stocks, including the specification of the research lag structure and state-to-state (and federal-to-state) spillovers used to construct the knowledge stocks. In later chapters we evaluate the effects of specification choices on our estimates and the implied benefit-cost ratios.

9.1 Modeling Productivity and Knowledge Stocks

The basis of the model presented here is that agricultural production (or productivity) in every U.S. state (excluding Alaska and Hawaii) depends on past public agricultural research and extension conducted by itself and other states, and on intramural research conducted by the USDA in federal laboratories. A state's productivity might also depend on private agricultural research conducted in the United States, on overseas agricultural R&D, and on nonagricultural R&D. However, for the time being we set these aspects aside and concentrate on how to model the productivity-enhancing effects of elements of U.S. public-sector agricultural R&D.

J.M. Alston et al., *Persistence Pays: U.S. Agricultural Productivity Growth and the Benefits from Public R&D Spending*, Natural Resource Management and Policy 34,
DOI 10.1007/978-1-4419-0658-8_9,

We can express this model in general terms, mathematically, as:

$$(9.1) \qquad MFP_{i,t} = f_i\left(\mathbf{R}_t, \mathbf{E}_t\right)$$

where $MFP_{i,t}$ is multi-factor productivity in state i in year t, and $\mathbf{R}_t$ is a 49 × (L_R+1) matrix in which each element, $R_{j,t-k}$, is the investment in public agricultural R&D made by state j (for j = 1, . . ., 48) or the USDA (for j = 49) in year t–k (for k = 0 to L_R), and L_R represents the maximum research lag length between public research done by any state and its effect on productivity in any state. Similarly, $\mathbf{E}_t$ is a 48 × (L_E+1) matrix of state-specific extension investments with each element $E_{j,t-k}$ in state j and year t–k (for k = 0 to L_E), where L_E represents the maximum lag length between public extension spending and its effect on productivity.

As it is written, equation (9.1) allows for the effects of research and extension spending on productivity to vary by type (research versus extension), funding source (j), and timing (k). Even if we were to restrict the maximum research lag lengths, L_R and L_E, to 30 years (shorter than recent work supports for L_R), we would have to estimate 3,007 (= 49 × 31 + 48 × 31) separate research and extension effects for each state; and thus we would have to estimate 144,336 (= 3,007 × 48) research and extension effects across the 48 states. Clearly, the flexibility of a general specification is extremely costly in terms of the number of effects to be estimated. Hence, we must look for ways to reduce the number of parameters to be estimated by imposing reasonable restrictions and, where possible, assessing the influence of those restrictions on results.

We can reduce the number of parameters to be estimated by relating productivity to knowledge stocks resulting from past investments in agricultural R&D rather than to the year-specific investments, and imposing structure on how investments accumulate into knowledge stocks (i.e., reducing flexibility in how research effects vary depending on their timing).[1] In this approach, each state employs its own state-specific knowledge stock that results from past investments in agricultural R&D made by itself, by other states, and by the USDA.[2] This conception does not change the econometric problem; however, in a subsequent step the number of parameters can be reduced by imposing restrictions on how those state-specific knowledge stocks are created.

1 The concept of a research knowledge stock in the context of models of productivity is far from new, beginning, for example, with the work of Minasian (1962 and 1969) and Evenson (1967) (see also Griliches 1979). It has now become reasonably conventional in studies of effects of research on productivity, in general as well as in agriculture, to involve this concept at least implicitly (e.g., see Shanks and Zheng 2006). Alston, Norton and Pardey (1995) argued for the explicit use of the concept of research knowledge stocks in developing models of productivity for broader conceptual reasons, not just for empirical convenience (as elaborated in Chapter 8).

2 The stock of knowledge is not directly observable. Here, as in most studies, we use as a proxy an accumulated measure of past investments in production of knowledge (real research expenditure or research quantity)—i.e., a research input measure as a proxy for research output, accumulated over time. This procedure involves a number of nontrivial assumptions.

One such restriction is to assume that state-to-state knowledge spillovers are from pre-aggregated state-specific knowledge stocks, rather than disaggregated R&D streams. If each state transforms its own R&D into a stock of research-based knowledge and a stock of extension-based knowledge, from which there are spillovers into other states, then productivity in each of the 48 states depends on 97 knowledge stocks—one own-state research stock, one own-state extension stock, 47 other-state research stocks, 47 other-state extension stocks, and one federal research stock:[3]

$$(9.2) \qquad MFP_{i,t} = g_i\left(SR_{1,t}, SR_{2,t}, \ldots, SR_{49,t}, SE_{1,t}, SE_{2,t}, \ldots, SE_{48,t}\right),$$

where the research knowledge stock, $SR_{j,t}$ from each state or from USDA intramural labs (j = 49) is defined by its past research investments as:

$$(9.3) \qquad SR_{j,t} = r_j\left(R_{j,t}, R_{j,t-1}, \ldots, R_{j,t-L_R}\right),$$

where r_j denotes the function that transforms past research expenditures in state j (j = 1, . . . , 49) into the current (year t) knowledge stock in the same state, with a maximum lag of L_R years. Similarly, the extension-based knowledge stock from state j is defined as a function of its past extension expenditure as:

$$(9.4) \qquad SE_{j,t} = e_j\left(E_{j,t}, E_{j,t-1}, \ldots, E_{j,t-L_E}\right).$$

The specification in equation (9.2) has 97 effects per state (i.e., a total of 97×48 = 4,656 effects). To measure these effects we have to define the 49 research knowledge stocks, each of which includes L_R+1 effects, as in equation (9.3), and 48 extension knowledge stocks, each of which includes L_E+1 effects, as in equation (9.4). Assuming, as before, a maximum lag of 30 years for each of the 97 knowledge stocks, we have to measure 3,007 research effects, but if we assume that equations (9.3) and (9.4) are the same across states, we only have to do this once, rather than once per state.[4] Hence, the total number of separate effects to be measured has been reduced from 97×31×48 = 144,336 to (97×31 = 3,007)+(97×48 = 4,656) = 7,663. The number of effects to be measured is greatly reduced by making this type of separability assumption, in which we first create state-spe-

3 A somewhat less restrictive specification would allow for past research spending to spill across state borders before being transformed into useful knowledge stocks. By assuming that research is accumulated into knowledge stocks before spilling across borders, we are imposing a restriction that the rate at which spending accumulates into knowledge stocks is the same regardless of which state adopts the results.

4 This might appear to be a restrictive assumption, imposing that the effect of research in any state on agricultural productivity occurs with the same timing in the own state and in all other states—in other words, the research lag profile is the same for spillover effects as for own effects, and is the same for all states. But it is mild compared with what has been typically done, and mild compared with what is necessary to implement a model.

cific knowledge stocks (as a distributed lag of own-state research and extension for each state) and then define spillover effects in terms of these stocks.

Even with the restrictive assumptions already made, 7,663 effects are too many to try to measure without imposing additional restrictions on them. Here, we are interested especially in distinguishing between the effects within any state of (a) research conducted by that state, and (b) spillin effects of research conducted by other states or by the USDA.[5] Hence, as a further simplification, instead of 47 individual other-state research-knowledge stocks and a federal knowledge stock, we include a single research spillover stock, for each state, to represent the aggregation of those 48 effects in that state.[6]

Adopting this approach, the model in equation (9.2) becomes:

$$(9.5) \qquad MFP_{i,t} = g_i\left(SR_{i,t}, SE_{i,t}, SSR_{i,t}, SSE_{i,t}\right),$$

where, in state i and year t, $SR_{i,t}$ is the own stock of knowledge from past research investments in state i, $SE_{i,t}$ is the stock of knowledge from past extension investments in state i, $SSR_{i,t}$ is the spillover stock of knowledge from past research investments in other states and by the USDA, and $SSE_{i,t}$ is the spillover stock of knowledge from past extension investments in other states.[7] To implement this approach, we assume a linear, additive state-to-state spillover relationship, such that:

$$(9.6) \qquad SSR_{i,t} = \sum_{j \neq i} \omega_{ij} SR_{j,t}, \; SSE_{i,t} = \sum_{j \neq i} \omega_{ij} SE_{j,t},$$

where ω_{ij} is a spillover coefficient, a weight that measures the contribution of a unit of the knowledge stock created in state j to the spillover knowledge stock used in state i.[8]

In the remainder of this chapter, we discuss issues relating to the construction of knowledge stocks and the spillover measures, and describe the particular specification choices used in our base model. Specific assumptions about how research spending accumulates into knowledge stocks and how knowledge stocks

5 We have classified research expenditures according to the performer rather than the funding source. The USDA helps fund some SAES research but in our model this is treated as state research, separate from the intramural research that is both funded and conducted by USDA.

6 In preliminary work we attempted to estimate separate spillover effects of research conducted by the federal government and research conducted by all other states. The consequent multicollinearity problems led us to aggregate the federal and state spillover knowledge stocks into a single variable.

7 In our baseline model we allow for interstate spillovers of extension as well as research effects, but we also try models in which the extension knowledge stock does not involve any interstate spillover effects.

8 In a more-general specification, we might allow these spillover coefficients to vary over time, by defining ω_{ijt} rather than the special case with $\omega_{ijt} = \omega_{ij}$ for all years, t.

spill into other states are discussed in Sections 9.2 and 9.3, respectively. Issues related to functional form and model selection are discussed in Chapter 10.

9.2 Specification of R&D Lag Distributions

The distributed lag relationship between a state's past research investments and its current knowledge stock is specified in general terms in equation (9.3). As described in Chapter 8, previous econometric studies of the effects of agricultural research on productivity have almost invariably imposed some structure to reduce the number of lag weights to be estimated and to impose other prior beliefs on the shape or length of the lag (see Alston et al. 2000a and 2000b for details). In the present context, restrictions must be imposed as a practical matter to reduce the number of parameters to be estimated. In addition, however, we might wish to restrict all lag weights to be non-negative and to change smoothly from one lag to the next. These restrictions can be imposed by the judicious choice of a functional form to represent the relationship between past research and the current state-specific knowledge stock.

Theory does not give us much guidance on how far to go in terms of imposing (untested) restrictions on econometric models in general, and on this type of econometric model in particular. All untested restrictions are to some extent arbitrary and will condition the results from estimation, possibly in undesirable ways. On the other hand, our experience with models of research and productivity has led us to think that there is a tendency among some authors to be overly optimistic about the number of research lag parameters that can be meaningfully estimated. In other words, more flexible models might avoid some consequences of specification bias but might at the same time introduce other problems—a greater likelihood of results that are nonsensical, fragile and unstable, or imprecise.[9]

Based on considerations of this nature, Griliches (1979, p. 106) suggested that "it is probably best to *assume* a functional form for the lag distribution on the basis of prior knowledge and general considerations and not to expect the data to answer such fine questions." In this study we assumed that the relationship between research and the knowledge stock within each state could be characterized using a single lag distribution for all states. The lag distribution was defined in terms of (a) an overall lag length, (b) a gestation lag, (c) a functional form (we used a gamma distribution, but for purposes of comparison, we also

---

9 Other authors working in this area have reached similar conclusions for similar reasons and perhaps with greater force because most studies have had much more limited data (typically only a single time series for a much shorter number of years)—for some contemporary examples, see Hall and Scobie (2006), Huffman and Evenson (2006a and 2006b), and Mullen (2007).

tried a trapezoidal distribution), and (d) within the functional form, parameters that determined the shape of the distribution.

Gamma Lag Distribution

The lag distribution determines the weights to be applied to past research expenditures, and the knowledge stock is the sum of the weighted expenditures:

$$(9.7) \qquad SR_{i,t} = \sum_{k=0}^{L_R} b_k^R R_{i,t-k}; \; SE_{i,t} = \sum_{j=0}^{L_E} b_j^E E_{i,t-j},$$

where L_R and L_E are the total lag lengths for research and extension, respectively, the b_k^Rs and b_j^Es are the lag weights defined by the alternative lag distributions, and the lag weights sum to one:

$$(9.8) \qquad \sum_{k=0}^{L_R} b_k^R = 1; \; \sum_{j=0}^{L_E} b_j^E = 1.$$

The gamma distribution was chosen as a functional form because it embodies several characteristics that are desirable for the present purpose. First, all lag weights determined by the function are non-negative. Second, the shape implied is relatively smooth. Third, the gamma distribution is unimodal, and typically implies increasing weight over some range of lags (while, for instance, new technologies are increasingly adopted), then decreasing weights that taper to zero (as older technologies become less relevant). Fourth, the distribution can be skewed to give more weight to more recent or more distant lags. Finally, it can be characterized by only two parameters.

The research lag weights (b_k^R) implied by the gamma distribution are:

$$(9.9) \qquad b_k^R = \frac{(k-g+1)^{(\delta/1-\delta)} \lambda^{(k-g)}}{\sum_{k=0}^{L_R} \left[(k-g+1)^{(\delta/1-\delta)} \lambda^{(k-g)} \right]} \text{ for } L_R \geq k > g; \text{ otherwise } b_k^R = 0; \; \sum_{k=0}^{L_R} b_k^R = 1,$$

where g is the gestation lag before research begins to affect productivity, and δ and λ are parameters that define the shape of the distribution ($0 \leq \delta < 1$ and $0 \leq \lambda < 1$). Hence, the research knowledge stocks were defined as:

$$(9.10) \qquad SR_{i,t} = \sum_{k=0}^{L_R} b_k^R R_{i,t-k} = \sum_{k=0}^{L_R} \left(\frac{(k-g+1)^{(\delta/1-\delta)} \lambda^{(k-g)}}{\sum_{k=0}^{L_R} \left[(k-g+1)^{(\delta/1-\delta)} \lambda^{(k-g)} \right]} \right) R_{i,t-k}.$$

We assumed a gestation lag of $g = 0$ years, given that several distributions implied by combinations of δ and λ have weights very close to zero for small values of k. We focused our estimation efforts on specifications with a maximum lag length, L_R, of 50 years. This approach was based on our own previous experience with similar data and models (e.g., Alston, Craig and Pardey 1998; Alston, Pardey and

Carter 1994) and some limited pretesting as a part of the present study, as well as a predisposition to allow for "generously" long lags. The sensitivity of the results to the maximum lag lengths allowed is explored in later chapters.

Figure 9-1 shows several lag distributions for different values of the parameters δ and λ. In each graph, the number of years since the R&D investment (i.e., k) varies along the horizontal axis. The value on the vertical axis is the weight that spending receives k years after it has been made—i.e., the contribution of a \$1 investment k years ago to the current knowledge stock. The location of the peak of each distribution indicates how many years it takes for research to have its largest impact on the knowledge stock. This graph demonstrates the variety of shapes that the gamma distribution can take. Based on our prior beliefs about the nature of the effects of research, we expect the lag weights to be very small for a few years, increase for several years, and then eventually to decline. The graphs in Figure 9-1 indicate that δ and λ values must exceed 0.5 to generate a plausible lag distribution. Accordingly, we constructed an 8×8 grid of feasible gamma distributions, shown in Figure 9-2. Knowledge stocks were constructed using each set of lag weights, and one model was estimated for each cell in the grid.[10]

Trapezoidal Lag Distribution

The trapezoidal form for the lag distribution also satisfies our criterion of strictly positive lag weights and parametric parsimony. In addition, it has been applied in several studies of state- or national-level U.S. agricultural R&D impacts (e.g., Huffman and Evenson 1992, 1993, 2001, 2006a and 2006b; Huffman and Just 1994; McCunn and Huffman 2000; and Alston, Pardey and Carter 1994). We opted to try this alternative as a check on the results from the gamma lag distribution model, and as a link with the prior literature, but without seeking to optimize the details of the specification for our dataset.

The trapezoidal model used here is taken from Huffman and Evenson (1993), and shown in Figure 9-3 along with selected gamma distributions. The trapezoidal specification of the research lag structure includes a gestation lag of two years before research has any impact. Over the next seven years, the lag weights increase linearly, then for a further six years the weights are constant, and finally they decline linearly for 20 years. Hence, a total of 35 lagged research expenditures are included. We applied the identical lag structure to all of the various federal and state-specific research knowledge stocks; and, in our base model, also to extension knowledge stocks.

10 Ideally, we would estimate values for δ and λ directly that best fit the data. However, when we attempted to do so the models failed to converge, so we were forced to conduct a grid search instead. Thirtle, Piesse and Schimmelpfennig (2008) attempted to estimate parameters of a gamma distribution, applied to agricultural R&D lags in UK agriculture, but their estimation also failed to converge and they rejected this model in favor of others they tried. They used a different functional form than we do for the gamma distribution weights.

Figure 9-1 Potential Gamma Distribution Shapes

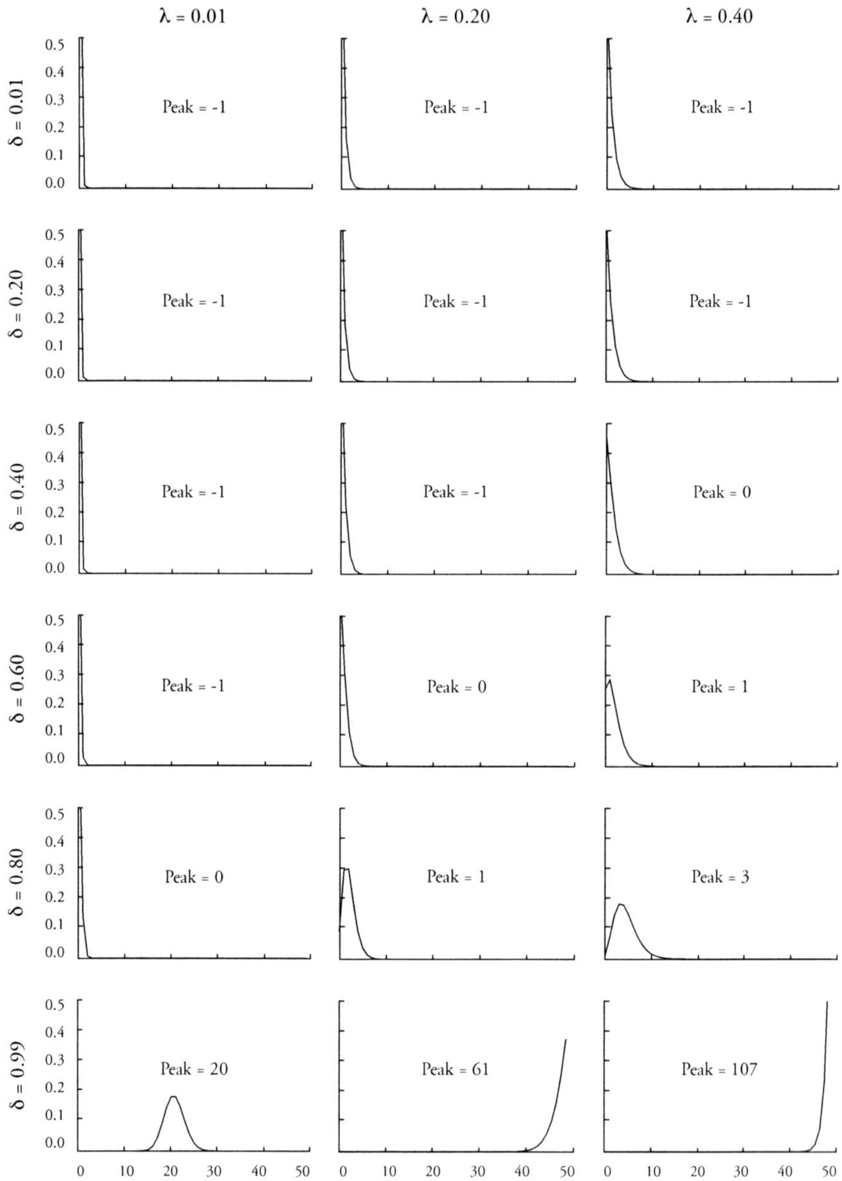

Sources: Developed by the authors.

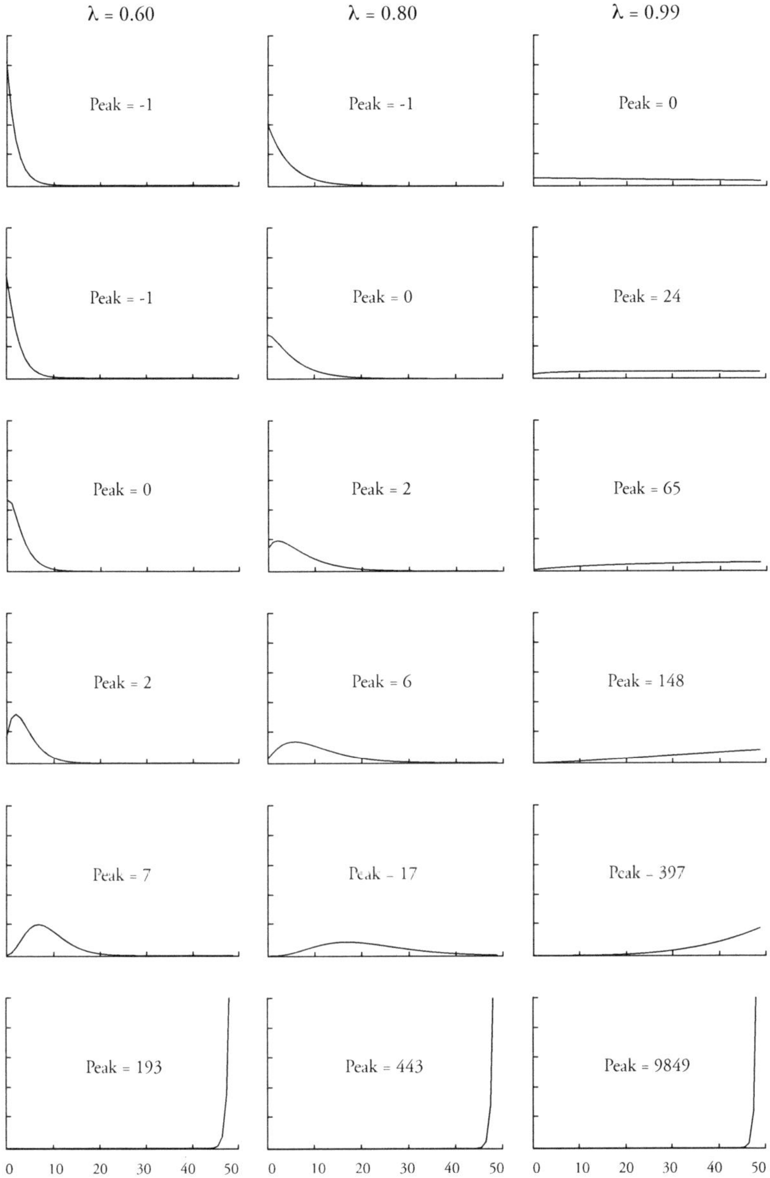

Notes: The number of years since R&D investment is on the horizontal axis, and the weight that year's spending receives is on the vertical axis. The peak year indicates the lag year in which the distribution peaks (how long it takes spending to have its largest impact on the knowledge stock).

Figure 9-2 Gamma Distribution Parameters and Shapes Used in Estimation

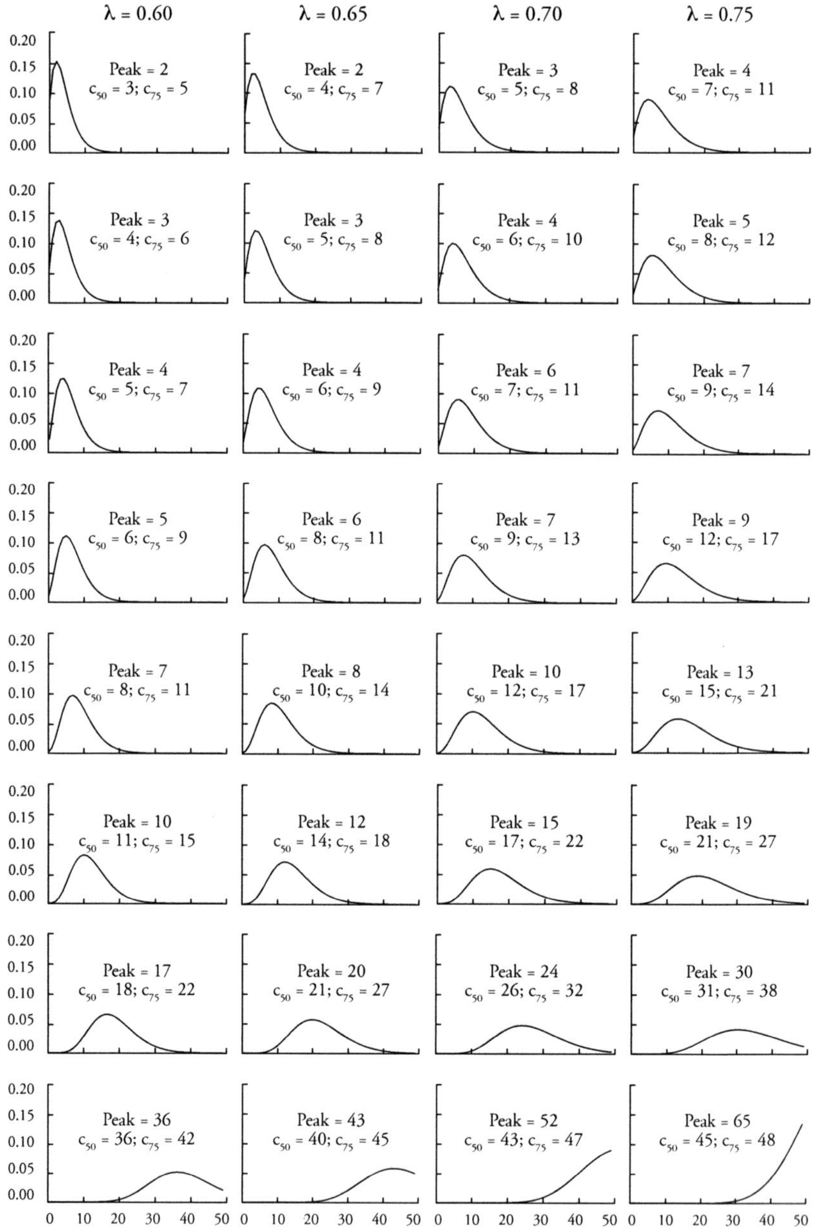

Sources: Developed by the authors.

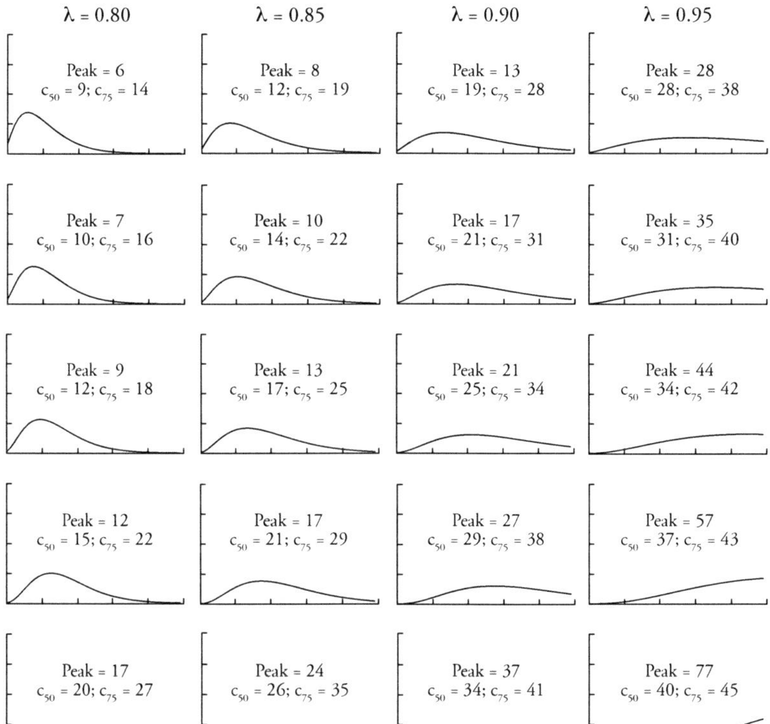

Notes: See notes to Figure 9-1. In each gamma distribution, c_{50} indicates the number of years it takes for a dollar of spending to add 50 cents to the knowledge stock (i.e., half of the effects of the spending have accumulated). Similarly, c_{75} indicates the number of years it takes for 75 percent of the impact of spending to accumulate.

Figure 9-3 Trapezoidal Distribution Shape Compared with Gamma Distributions

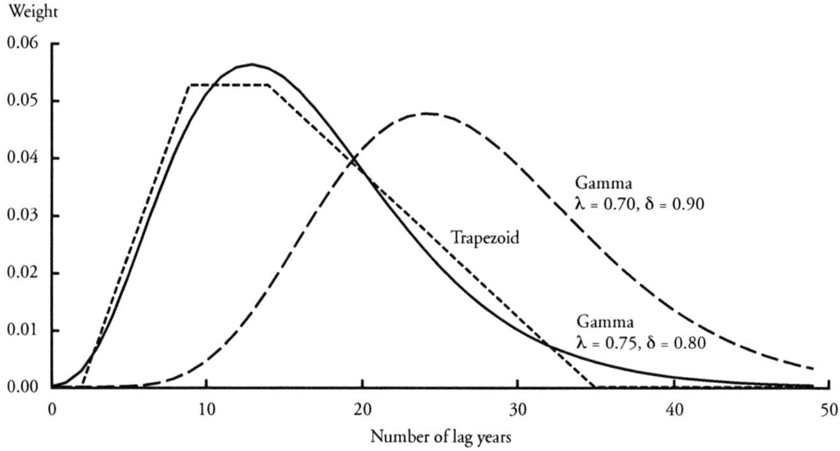

Sources: Developed by the authors.

Influence of Lag Specification on Knowledge Stocks

Table 9-1 summarizes SAES spending and the corresponding own-state stock of knowledge from past research investments for the three lag distributions shown in Figure 9-3. Column 1 of Table 9-1 shows average annual SAES spending for 1949–2002 and, in parentheses, the average annual percentage change in SAES spending. Figures are included for all 48 states combined, for particular selected states, and for regional aggregates. Columns 2 through 4 show the corresponding values for the average annual knowledge stock and average annual percentage change in the knowledge stock over time using each of the three alternative lag distributions.

As described above, the knowledge stock is a weighted sum of spending. Accordingly, if spending were fairly constant over time, then the average knowledge stock would be roughly equal to the average spending (since the lag weights are normalized to sum to one). However, observed spending has changed over time, so the average knowledge stock differs from average spending. Comparing the average SAES spending with the average knowledge stock highlights the importance of the lag distribution in determining the knowledge stocks. For each specification used to determine the lag weights, the stock of knowledge is smaller than the average spending amount. This reflects the upward trend in spending, and the fact that in any year, the most recent years of spending receive relatively small weight. The effect is particularly pronounced in column 2, where the gamma distribution is characterized by $\lambda = 0.70$ and $\delta = 0.90$, and peaks later than the other two distributions represented in columns 3 and 4, as shown in Figure 9-3.

Table 9-1 Summary of Average Annual SAES Spending and Average Annual Own-State Research Knowledge Stocks (Excluding Extension) Using Three Alternative Lag Specifications, 1949–2002

State or Region	SAES Spending (1)	Knowledge Stocks: Gamma (λ=0.70, δ=0.90) (2)	Knowledge Stocks: Gamma (λ=0.75, δ=0.80) (3)	Knowledge Stocks: Trapezoid (4)
	millions of dollars (2000 prices)[a]			
United States Total	1,656	751	1,070	1,083
	(2.65)	(4.79)	(4.23)	(4.22)
48 state				
Average	34.5	15.6	22.3	22.6
	(2.62)	(3.95)	(3.50)	(3.50)
Minimum	4.5	3.0	3.8	3.8
	(0.51)	(1.95)	(1.38)	(1.37)
Maximum	160.1	67.7	100.0	101.3
	(4.34)	(6.77)	(5.81)	(5.78)
Selected states				
California	160.1	67.7	100.0	101.3
	(3.17)	(4.93)	(4.31)	(4.31)
Minnesota	54.6	24.5	34.4	34.8
	(2.66)	(3.37)	(3.54)	(3.55)
Wyoming	8.3	5.4	6.7	6.8
	(0.78)	(3.08)	(2.22)	(2.23)
Regions				
Pacific	235.5	101.9	148.6	150.5
	(2.99)	(4.79)	(4.23)	(4.22)
Mountain	140.2	59.7	87.2	88.3
	(3.22)	(3.97)	(3.83)	(3.84)
Northern Plains	118.9	52.3	76.1	77.1
	(3.16)	(4.09)	(4.00)	(4.00)
Southern Plains	216.8	94.0	137.0	138.8
	(2.77)	(4.66)	(4.07)	(4.06)
Central	376.1	177.3	244.4	247.2
	(2.69)	(3.50)	(3.37)	(3.36)
Southeast	349.7	148.2	221.8	224.7
	(2.92)	(4.90)	(4.33)	(4.32)
Northeast	218.8	117.2	154.6	156.3
	(2.24)	(3.23)	(2.70)	(2.70)

Sources: Developed by the authors using SAES spending data (exclusive of forestry) described in Appendix III.

Notes: The gamma distribution model in column 2 was the best-fitting distribution for the logarithmic model and the model in column 3 was the best for the linear model in the base specification. U.S. total excludes Alaska and Hawaii.

[a] Figures in parentheses are average annual percentage growth rates of knowledge stocks.

The average rates of growth in SAES spending relative to the average growth rates in the knowledge stocks also reveal an interesting relationship. For each lag specification, the average rate of growth in the knowledge stock is larger than the average rate of growth in SAES spending. While SAES spending has increased for most states, the rate of growth decreased in the last 10 to 20 years of the period. Total SAES spending increased, on average, by 2.65 percent per year between 1949 and 2002. However, it increased by 4.38, 2.81, and 3.88 percent per year during the 1950s, 1960s and 1970s, respectively, but only by 1.43 and 0.95 percent during the 1980s and 1990s, respectively. Average annual growth for the period 1949–2002 in all SAES knowledge stocks combined was 4.79, 4.23, and 4.22 percent per year for the three lag distributions. The higher rates of growth in the knowledge stocks relative to growth in spending (particularly at the state and regional levels) reveal the time that it takes for changes in spending to show up in the knowledge stock. The relatively large growth in knowledge stocks reflects the earlier growth in SAES spending, while the slower growth in SAES spending in the last 20 years will have more pronounced effects on knowledge stocks in years beyond our data set.

The lag distribution determines the time it takes for a change in spending to have its biggest effect on the stock of knowledge, and how big that effect will be. The later the lag distribution peaks, the longer it takes for a change in spending to affect the knowledge stock. Because SAES spending has tended to increase over time, lag distributions that peak later will result in smaller knowledge stocks since it takes longer for the spending increase to be fully incorporated in the knowledge stocks. Similarly, because rates of growth in SAES spending have decreased over time, lag distributions that peak later will result in higher rates of growth in knowledge stocks. While these relationships are true by construction (i.e., because of the specifications we impose), they reflect a fairly realistic representation of the temporal aspects of knowledge accumulation.

The knowledge stocks resulting from the second gamma lag distribution (column 3) and the trapezoidal specification (column 4) are quite similar, which is not surprising given the similar shapes of the two lag distributions (shown in Figure 9-3). Knowledge stocks implied by the first gamma distribution (column 2) are quite different because it peaks so much later than the other distributions.

9.3 Spillover Coefficients and Knowledge Stocks

In some senses it is unnatural to be modeling the effects of agricultural science in terms of spillovers among geopolitical entities such as U.S. states. From the standpoint of many agricultural technologies, whose potential is circumscribed by nature, geopolitical boundaries are irrelevant; it is agroecological factors that matter, and notions of the applicability and spillovers of technologies across agroecological zones seem much more natural.[11] Nevertheless, we model tech-

11 Much agricultural technology is characterized by site-specificity, related to agroecological conditions, which defines the size of the relevant market in a way that is much less common in nonagricultural industrial R&D. One way to think of this is in terms of the unit costs of making local

nology spillovers among geopolitical regions for two practical reasons. First, most of the data that are available on commodity prices and quantities and R&D are collected by and on the basis of geopolitical entities. Second, many of the policy questions that give rise to an interest in agricultural technology spillovers relate to geopolitical entities—spillovers among countries or states.[12]

A Measure of Spillover Potential Based on Output Mix

In what follows we define measures of spillover potential, to be used to aggregate state-specific agricultural research stocks, based on agroecological similarity of states rather than geographic proximity or geopolitical congruence (as in some previous approaches based on USDA regions). Our measures of agroecological similarity (or proximity) are adapted from an approach developed by Jaffe (1986)—see, also, Griliches (1979)—and used subsequently by Jaffe (1989), Adams (1990), and Park (1995) to measure inter-firm or inter-industry spillover effects.

The variant used by Jaffe (1989) is closest to what we use here. Jaffe (1989) used characteristics of their patent portfolios to define a measure of technological closeness among firms. Noting that technological proximity is defined by the direction in which the vectors of characteristics are pointing, but not necessarily their length, Jaffe (1989) proposed a measure called the angular separation of the vectors, which is equal to the cosine of the angle between them. We use agroecological characteristics of agriculture in the different states to define their technological "closeness" to one another in the same way as Jaffe (1989) used characteristics of their patent portfolios to define technological closeness among firms.

Various agroecological characteristics of agriculture might be used for this purpose, such as GIS measures of climate and characteristics of the land, measures of the mix of agricultural products produced, or measures of the mix of inputs used. Alternatively, information on the nature of each state's agricultural research portfolio might be used to define spillover potential; or a combination of two or more of these indexes might be used. Here we have opted to use information about the mix of outputs produced by the individual states to define an index of

---

research results applicable to other locations (say, by adaptive research), which must be added to the local research costs. Alston and Pardey (1999, p. 18) noted that as the size of the research enterprise increases, unit costs are likely to decline at first (because economies of size are relatively important) but will eventually rise (as the costs of agroecological, technological, or other elements of economic distance become ever-more important).

12 Ideally, we would combine information on both agroecologies (as a determinant of technology potential) within geopolitical units and geopolitical barriers to adoption to obtain a picture of potential geopolitical spillovers of agricultural technologies. Alston et al. (2009) combined information on applicability of technology, defined by agroecological zones, with other information on the geopolitical location of agroecological zones, to define the adoption of technologies within states in Latin America.

agroecological proximity between any pair of them, which we use as an index of technological spillover potential. Intuitively, the more similar is the output mix between a pair of states, the more likely it is that one of those states, conducting research directed towards its own agriculture, will produce knowledge that is applicable in the other. This intuition is more clearly relevant for commodity-oriented research than more-basic research or research related to, say, natural resources. But, even still, differences in the types of basic or resources-related research done among states are likely to be driven to some extent by elements of the natural environment that might be well proxied by the output mix.

Using output mix as a proxy, summary measure of agroecological similarity, the vector of output (value) shares $f_i = (f_{i1}, \ldots, f_{iM})$ locates state i in M-dimensional agroecological space. The corresponding measure of technological spillover potential is defined as:

$$(9.11) \quad \omega_{ij} = \frac{\sum_{m=1}^{M} f_{im} f_{jm}}{\left(\sum_{m=1}^{M} f_{im}^2\right)^{1/2} \left(\sum_{m=1}^{M} f_{jm}^2\right)^{1/2}},$$

where f_{im} is the value of production of output m as a share of the total value of agricultural output in state i, such that these shares fall between zero and one and sum to one (i.e., there are a total of M different outputs across the 48 states, and $0 \leq f_{im} \leq 1$ and $\Sigma_m f_{im} = 1$). To define corresponding "spillover coefficients" for measuring the state-specific impacts of USDA research stocks (i.e., $\omega_{iF} = \omega_{i49}$, for $i = 1, \ldots, 48$), we applied equation (9.11) to index the similarity of each state's vector of output shares and the national vector of output shares. Paraphrasing Jaffe (1989, p. 88), in a sense, ω_{ij} measures the degree of overlap of f_i and f_j. The numerator will be large when states i and j have very similar output mixes. The denominator normalizes the measure to be one when f_i and f_j are identical. Hence, ω_{ij} will be zero for pairs of states with no overlap in their output mix and one for pairs of states with an identical output mix; and for the in-between cases, $0 < \omega_{ij} < 1$. It is conceptually similar to a correlation coefficient. Like a correlation coefficient, it is symmetric: $\omega_{ij} = \omega_{ji}$; and, $\omega_{ii} = 1$.[13]

Estimates of Spillover Coefficients

The spillover measure defined in equation (9.11) was applied to the U.S. state-level data on U.S. agricultural output for the period 1949–2002, as described

13 This symmetry characteristic may not be desirable in some settings where we think technology spillovers might be more likely to be one-directional because of differences in the nature of research being undertaken (for whatever reason), or differences in institutional aspects that may affect the adoption of research results in otherwise similar settings.

in Chapter 4.[14] The spillover coefficients were computed for each state-state combination for every year; in addition, year-specific spillover coefficients were calculated for each state relative to the United States as a whole (which we term the federal-state spillover coefficient). Appendix Table 9-1 includes the average values of the annual state-state spillover coefficients for 1949–2002 (these are the values used in our econometric models, described in Chapter 10). The dimensions of this matrix are such that it is difficult to talk usefully even about the annual average, or about the matrix for a particular year (since the diagonal elements are all equal to one, and the matrix is symmetric, we only need to report the off-diagonal elements, but this still leaves 1,128 elements for each year).[15]

Table 9-2 includes summary information for the federal-state and state-state spillover coefficients. Column 1 shows the average spillover coefficient for each state with all other states and across all years during the period 1949–2002, column 2 shows the spillover coefficient between the state in that row and the state, identified by postal abbreviation in column 3, with which it has the highest spillover coefficient. The federal-state spillover coefficient (shown in the first row) averaged across all states is 0.65. Missouri has the largest coefficient ($\omega_{MO,F}$ = 0.91) and is therefore the most similar to the country as a whole. Other rows in Table 9-2 show the same measures for state-state spillover coefficients. For example, the average of $\omega_{CA,j}$ over all states j is 0.50, and Pennsylvania is most similar to California ($\omega_{CA,PA}$ = 0.71). Compared with the federal-state spillovers, the state-state spillover coefficients are generally smaller (reflecting the fact that any state is likely to be less like any other individual state than an average of all states including itself), and they vary more across states.

The next four columns in Table 9-2 (columns 4 through 8) show the number of states with federal-state or state-state spillover coefficients in the range of values specified. For instance, in the first row, 13 states have ω_{iF} between 0.75 and 1.00 (reflecting a high degree of "overlap" with the national output mix) whereas, in the second row, none of the states has such a high degree of overlap with the output mix in California. The frequency counts indicate the shape of the distribution of states according to their similarity with the specified base state. Notably, some states clearly have a skewed distribution (e.g., North Caro-

14 The estimates are based on the set of M = 74 output categories in the InSTePP series defined in Appendix II, including 9 livestock commodities, 16 field crops, 40 fruits and vegetables, 4 tree nuts, implicit quantities of nursery and greenhouse products, plus 4 miscellaneous items including implicit quantities of machines rented out by farmers, Conservation Reserve Program acreage, mushrooms and hops. The latest version of the InSTePP series represents a revised and updated version of data published by Acquaye, Alston and Pardey (2003) and originally developed and used by Craig and Pardey (1996a). More complete descriptions can be found in Pardey et al. (2009a).

15 The complete matrix is appended so the interested reader may look up state pairs of interest. Appendix Table 9-1 includes states arranged by region to facilitate a casual analysis of inter- and intra-regional similarity. Formatting of the entries indicates whether they have increased or decreased over time.

Table 9-2 Summary of Federal-State and State-State Spillover Coefficients Among States, 1949–2002

	Average	Maximum		Number of States with Average ω_{ij} Value in Range					Share of Production Value from States with Average ω_{ij} in Range				
	All States (1)	Value (2)	State (3)	0.00–0.35 (4)	0.35–0.50 (5)	0.50–0.60 (6)	0.60–0.75 (7)	0.75–1.00 (8)	0.00–0.35 (9)	0.35–0.50 (10)	0.50–0.60 (11)	0.60–0.75 (12)	0.75–1.00 (13)
United States	0.65	0.91	MO	1	7	7	20	13	0.00	0.07	0.09	0.48	0.35
Pacific													
California	0.50	0.71	PA	7	16	9	15	0	0.29	0.36	0.17	0.18	0.00
Oregon	0.55	0.82	UT	8	8	13	11	7	0.27	0.10	0.25	0.26	0.12
Washington	0.46	0.79	OR	13	14	12	6	2	0.36	0.27	0.24	0.11	0.03
Mountain													
Arizona	0.41	0.82	TX	19	15	5	6	2	0.37	0.35	0.06	0.16	0.07
Colorado	0.51	0.94	WY	16	9	6	4	12	0.19	0.38	0.13	0.07	0.23
Idaho	0.47	0.81	OR	17	8	10	8	4	0.36	0.16	0.31	0.12	0.05
Montana	0.41	0.92	KS	24	8	1	7	7	0.47	0.22	0.03	0.15	0.12
Nevada	0.48	0.95	WY	16	12	3	9	7	0.25	0.32	0.12	0.17	0.13
New Mexico	0.51	0.91	NV	12	13	5	10	7	0.20	0.31	0.10	0.27	0.12
Utah	0.57	0.87	NV	7	10	5	17	8	0.19	0.16	0.08	0.49	0.07
Wyoming	0.43	0.95	NV	21	8	4	5	9	0.37	0.30	0.06	0.10	0.17
Northern Plains													
Kansas	0.47	0.93	OK	18	9	5	7	8	0.25	0.35	0.11	0.14	0.15
Nebraska	0.49	0.93	SD	14	9	6	10	8	0.24	0.16	0.08	0.18	0.33
North Dakota	0.35	0.87	MT	26	10	3	6	2	0.57	0.23	0.05	0.10	0.05
South Dakota	0.53	0.93	NE	12	9	3	14	9	0.13	0.24	0.05	0.37	0.21
Southern Plains													
Arkansas	0.36	0.90	MS	29	8	4	4	2	0.59	0.24	0.09	0.05	0.03
Louisiana	0.41	0.71	MS	15	22	5	5	0	0.17	0.55	0.16	0.13	0.00
Mississippi	0.40	0.90	AR	27	7	5	6	2	0.52	0.25	0.06	0.13	0.04
Oklahoma	0.51	0.93	CO	14	13	2	8	10	0.21	0.44	0.03	0.15	0.17
Texas	0.50	0.88	NM	14	11	4	12	6	0.22	0.34	0.15	0.23	0.06
Central													

Illinois	0.37	0.98	IN	28	9	2	2	6	0.46	0.19	0.03	0.04	0.28
Indiana	0.41	0.98	IL	25	11	2	3	6	0.39	0.22	0.03	0.06	0.29
Iowa	0.41	0.96	IN	19	17	2	3	6	0.31	0.33	0.03	0.06	0.26
Michigan	0.57	0.88	WI	4	15	4	18	6	0.08	0.26	0.05	0.45	0.16
Minnesota	0.55	0.95	OH	5	20	7	6	9	0.06	0.39	0.11	0.10	0.34
Missouri	0.55	0.88	MN	9	10	8	12	8	0.05	0.27	0.14	0.21	0.33
Ohio	0.53	0.95	MN	6	20	7	8	6	0.06	0.39	0.09	0.18	0.28
Wisconsin	0.50	0.96	NY	11	15	6	10	5	0.22	0.40	0.09	0.23	0.07
Southeast													
Alabama	0.46	0.91	GA	15	18	4	7	3	0.23	0.52	0.07	0.11	0.07
Florida	0.30	0.52	CA	33	13	1	0	0	0.79	0.11	0.09	0.00	0.00
Georgia	0.42	0.91	AL	20	17	0	8	2	0.25	0.61	0.00	0.12	0.02
Kentucky	0.46	0.82	TN	12	18	10	3	4	0.13	0.40	0.29	0.11	0.07
North Carolina	0.32	0.84	SC	30	11	1	3	2	0.62	0.29	0.01	0.05	0.03
South Carolina	0.45	0.84	TN	15	17	7	4	4	0.18	0.53	0.13	0.08	0.08
Tennessee	0.61	0.85	VA	2	8	8	24	5	0.01	0.09	0.16	0.62	0.12
Virginia	0.59	0.87	WV	0	11	17	14	5	0.00	0.18	0.45	0.32	0.05
West Virginia	0.58	0.87	VA	1	12	12	19	3	0.06	0.23	0.21	0.47	0.03
Northeast													
Connecticut	0.41	0.88	MA	22	7	6	7	5	0.53	0.20	0.05	0.19	0.03
Delaware	0.23	0.80	MD	39	3	1	3	1	0.86	0.05	0.02	0.06	0.01
Maine	0.32	0.70	NH	28	13	5	1	0	0.70	0.24	0.06	0.00	0.00
Maryland	0.49	0.80	DE	11	12	12	8	4	0.20	0.34	0.25	0.17	0.04
Massachusetts	0.40	0.89	NJ	25	8	4	6	4	0.60	0.16	0.03	0.20	0.01
New Hampshire	0.45	0.88	NY	24	5	5	5	8	0.59	0.12	0.07	0.12	0.09
New Jersey	0.39	0.89	RI	25	9	6	3	4	0.61	0.14	0.11	0.14	0.01
New York	0.45	0.98	VT	22	5	7	8	5	0.58	0.07	0.13	0.13	0.09
Pennsylvania	0.53	0.95	NY	8	17	5	11	6	0.15	0.46	0.08	0.22	0.09
Rhode Island	0.35	0.89	NJ	27	8	6	2	4	0.66	0.15	0.14	0.04	0.01
Vermont	0.41	0.98	NY	23	8	7	4	5	0.60	0.10	0.10	0.10	0.10

Sources: Developed by the authors using InSTePP data.

lina and Tennessee), whereas other states have a more bi-modal distribution (e.g., California and Michigan).

The final five columns in Table 9-2 (columns 9 through 13) show the same distribution as in columns 4 through 8 but, rather than each state in the appropriate range receiving equal weight, state-specific shares of U.S. value of agricultural production (averaged over 1949–2002) were used to weight each state in the distribution (for example, the thirteen states with federal-state spillover coefficients, ω_{iF} between 0.75 and 1.00 accounted for 35 percent of the U.S. value of agricultural production). These measures of the distribution of similarity, given by spillover coefficients weighted by the value of production, may provide a better indication of a state's spillout potential than the distribution of unweighted spillover coefficients. For instance (looking at column 8), Kansas has state-state spillover coefficients greater than 0.75 with eight other states, and so does Nebraska. However (looking at column 13), the eight states that are similar to Kansas account for 14 percent of the U.S. value of production, while the eight states that are similar to Nebraska are more important (in terms of their agricultural industries), as they account for 32 percent of the total U.S. value of agricultural production. Thus, Nebraska has a potential to generate technological spillovers to other states that will influence a larger value of production and thus will generate larger spillover benefits.

To the extent that the value of agricultural production is a good indicator of research spending, the same coefficients also provide an indication of the potential for a state to benefit from spillins from R&D conducted in other states. Hence, the summary in Table 9-2 provides some indication of the potential for each state to realize spillins from R&D conducted in other states and to boost agricultural productivity in other states through its own R&D investments (i.e., to provide spillouts to other states).

Federal-State Spillover Coefficients—Spatial Patterns and Trends

Although the average values of the spillover coefficients over 1949–2002 are used in the econometric analysis, it is useful to examine how the coefficients have changed over time, particularly in light of the changes in production patterns since 1949 (see Chapter 4). The federal-state spillover coefficients (ω_{iF}) represent an "average" spillover relationship between each state, *i*, and all the other states combined. An examination of these coefficients gives a general sense of the movements in the spillover coefficients over time. Table 9-3 shows several descriptive statistics summarizing the federal-state spillover coefficients for the period 1949–2002. The average federal-state spillover coefficients vary substantially across states, as seen in column 1. Column 2 of Table 9-3 shows the rank of the state to indicate how it compares with all other states in terms of its similarity to the United States as a whole. Columns 3 and 4 indicate state-by-state how the

Table 9-3 Federal-State Spillover Coefficients Among States, 1949–2002

	Descriptive Statistics, 1949–2002				Trend Coefficient
	Mean (1)	Rank (2)	Minimum (3)	Maximum (4)	(5)
Pacific					
California	0.66	26	0.55	0.76	-0.52*
Oregon	0.73	15	0.60	0.83	-0.37*
Washington	0.61	31	0.50	0.72	-0.19*
Mountain					
Arizona	0.59	35	0.41	0.77	0.45*
Colorado	0.76	13	0.67	0.81	0.12*
Idaho	0.64	28	0.53	0.75	-0.12*
Montana	0.60	33	0.45	0.75	-0.02
Nevada	0.68	23	0.53	0.78	0.33*
New Mexico	0.72	20	0.58	0.82	0.22*
Utah	0.78	11	0.69	0.84	0.03
Wyoming	0.63	29	0.49	0.75	-0.07
Northern Plains					
Kansas	0.73	16	0.60	0.82	0.14*
Nebraska	0.84	7	0.74	0.91	-0.15*
North Dakota	0.53	38	0.37	0.72	-0.22*
South Dakota	0.86	5	0.75	0.90	-0.01
Southern Plains					
Arkansas	0.52	40	0.43	0.61	-0.27*
Louisiana	0.62	30	0.46	0.76	-0.45*
Mississippi	0.58	36	0.47	0.75	-0.43*
Oklahoma	0.74	14	0.65	0.86	-0.10*
Texas	0.72	19	0.61	0.81	0.29*
Central					
Illinois	0.72	18	0.59	0.83	-0.49*
Indiana	0.76	12	0.63	0.86	-0.49*
Iowa	0.78	10	0.65	0.83	-0.32*
Michigan	0.85	6	0.69	0.90	-0.11*
Minnesota	0.90	3	0.80	0.95	-0.21*
Missouri	0.91	1	0.83	0.95	-0.17*
Ohio	0.87	4	0.77	0.93	-0.25*
Wisconsin	0.71	21	0.62	0.82	-0.35*

(continued)

federal-state spillover coefficients varied over 1949–2002. For many states, the range of ω_{iF} values is quite wide.

We might expect coefficients to have become smaller over time, as individual states have tended to become more specialized in their mix of agricultural production, but for many states the coefficients trended up, not down. To explore this aspect, the time series of federal-state spillover coefficients for each state was regressed on a time trend to estimate whether the state became more or less similar (or neither) to the United States as a whole. The resulting trend coefficient for each state, expressed as a percentage of the average federal-state spillover coeffi-

Table 9-3 (continued)

	Descriptive Statistics, 1949-2002				Trend Coefficient
	Mean (1)	Rank (2)	Minimum (3)	Maximum (4)	(5)
Southeast					
Alabama	0.65	27	0.43	0.87	-1.25*
Florida	0.40	46	0.33	0.52	0.02
Georgia	0.61	32	0.44	0.83	-1.06*
Kentucky	0.71	22	0.60	0.86	0.12
North Carolina	0.48	43	0.38	0.57	0.63*
South Carolina	0.67	25	0.56	0.79	0.19*
Tennessee	0.90	2	0.84	0.95	-0.03
Virginia	0.84	8	0.76	0.90	-0.05
West Virginia	0.79	9	0.52	0.87	-0.53*
Northeast					
Connecticut	0.49	42	0.34	0.62	-0.66*
Delaware	0.32	48	0.23	0.40	0.42*
Maine	0.38	47	0.19	0.54	0.09
Maryland	0.68	24	0.58	0.81	-0.35*
Massachusetts	0.47	44	0.33	0.64	-1.01*
New Hampshire	0.54	37	0.41	0.63	-0.03
New Jersey	0.50	41	0.36	0.67	-0.80*
New York	0.59	34	0.47	0.69	-0.30*
Pennsylvania	0.72	17	0.65	0.81	-0.19*
Rhode Island	0.41	45	0.23	0.62	-1.64*
Vermont	0.53	39	0.38	0.63	-0.31*

Sources: Developed by the authors using InSTePP data.

Notes: The entries in column 5 are coefficients on linear trends fitted to ω_{iF} for 1949–2004, expressed as a percentage of the average ω_{iF} over the relevant time period. An asterisk, "*", indicates a coefficient is statistically significantly different from zero at the 5 percent level of significance.

cient for that state, is included in column 5 of Table 9-3. The estimated trend coefficients confirm that state-specific production patterns have evolved differently among the states relative to the United States as a whole. The time trend was not statistically significantly different from zero for ten states. However, over the period 1949–2004, 29 states became less similar to the United States, with negative and statistically significant trend coefficients, while nine states became more similar to the United States over time, with positive and statistically significant trend coefficients. The interpretation of the reason for an increase or decrease in similarity to the United States is somewhat ambiguous because the output mix of the United States as a whole changed over the same period of time.

A further geographical perspective on the spillover coefficients is given by Figure 9-4. In Panel a, states with larger average federal-state spillover coefficients are shaded darker on a map of the United States. A few spatial patterns are clear; for instance, eastern states tended to be less similar to the nation as a whole, and mid-western states tended to be more similar to the nation as a whole. Shading

Figure 9-4 Federal-State Spillover Coefficients

Panel a. Average, 1949–2002 Panel b. Trend coefficient (percent per year)

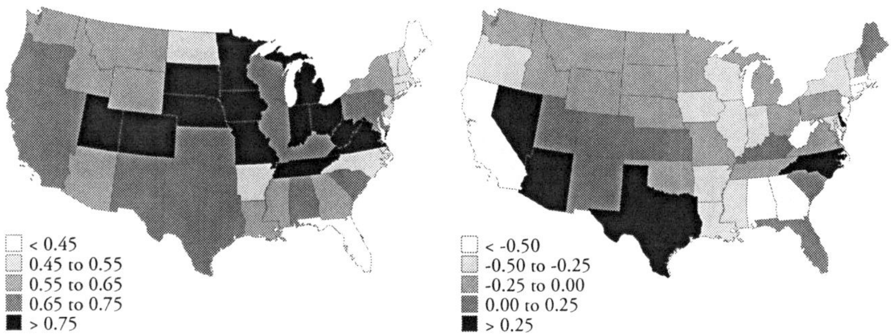

Sources: Developed by the authors using InSTePP data.

in Panel b indicates the sign and magnitude of the estimated trend coefficient described above (again, expressed as a percentage of the average federal-state spillover coefficient). Most states had a small (but possibly statistically significant) trend in the spillover coefficient. Eleven states had negative trend coefficients between -0.50 and -0.25. For those states, the downward trend was equivalent to between 0.25 and 0.50 percent of the average spillover coefficient. Only four states (specifically Alabama, Georgia, Massachusetts, and Rhode Island) had downward trends greater than 1 percent, and none of the states had an upward trend greater than 1 percent.

State-to-State Spillover Coefficients—Spatial Patterns and Trends

Additional insights can be obtained by similarly analyzing state-state spillover coefficients. In Figure 9-5, we show the average annual spillover coefficients over 1949–2002 between each other state and California (Panel a), Wyoming (Panel b), Iowa (Panel c), and Minnesota (Panel d). As in Panel a of Figure 9-4, darker shades reflect greater similarity between the shaded state and the state of comparison. These maps show that agroecological similarity can be quite independent of geographic proximity. For instance, comparatively few states are very similar to California in terms of their mix of outputs, but those that are similar are not necessarily close to California geographically. In contrast, a number of states have an output mix that is quite similar to that of Wyoming, but they all tend to be close to Wyoming and to one other. The different spatial distributions of spillover coefficients for Iowa and Minnesota are particularly striking. The two states are quite similar ($\omega_{IA,MN} = \omega_{MN,IA} = 0.89$), and several other states have high spillover coefficients with both Iowa and Minnesota. However, Iowa has many more states with $\omega_{IA,i} < 0.35$ whereas, on average, Minnesota is more similar to a larger number of (and more geographically dispersed) states.

Figure 9-5 State-State Spillover Coefficients, Selected States, Average 1949–2002

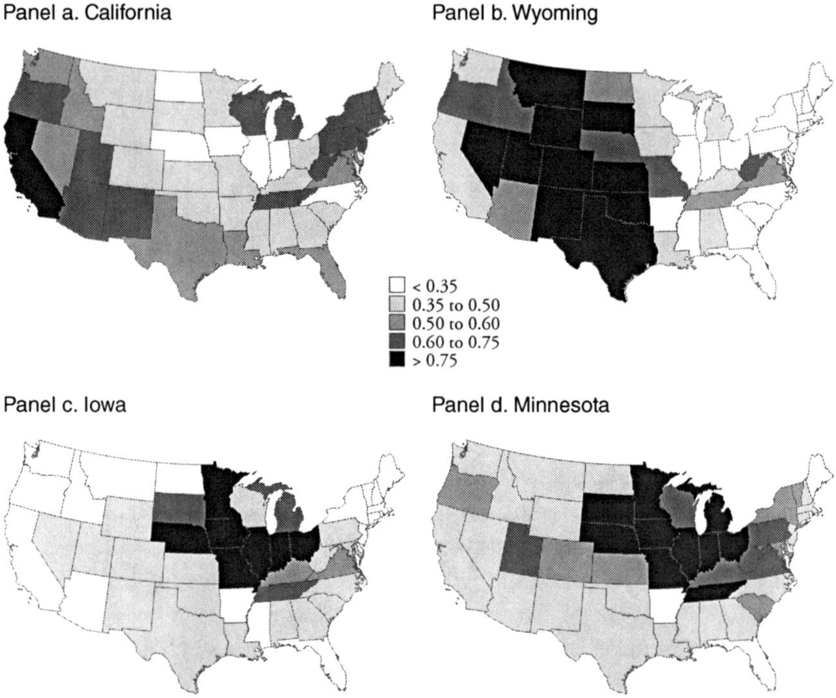

Sources: Developed by the authors using InSTePP data.

These observations support the view that our measures of agroecological similarity are different from previous measures that emphasize geographical proximity, and we would suspect that they are different in desirable ways relative to the present purpose.

To assess the extent by which state-state spillover coefficients changed over the past 50 years, we estimated time trends for the time series of each ω_{ij} (i.e., for every i and j). Appendix Table 9-2 includes a summary of the time trends in the state-state spillover coefficients (found by expressing the trend coefficient as a percentage of the average ω_{ij} across years, then averaging across all states j). The distributions of the trend coefficients differ quite substantially across states. For instance, 33 of the estimated trend coefficients for Mississippi were negative and statistically significant, whereas North Carolina had 31 trend coefficients that were positive and statistically significant. Figure 9-6 maps the trends in the state-state spillover coefficients for California, Wyoming, Iowa, and Minnesota. The maps reveal some interesting differences among states. In particular, while Iowa on average was less similar to many states than Minnesota was (shading in the map for Iowa in Figure 9-5 is generally lighter than shading in the correspond-

Figure 9-6 Trends in State-State Spillover Coefficients, Percent per Year

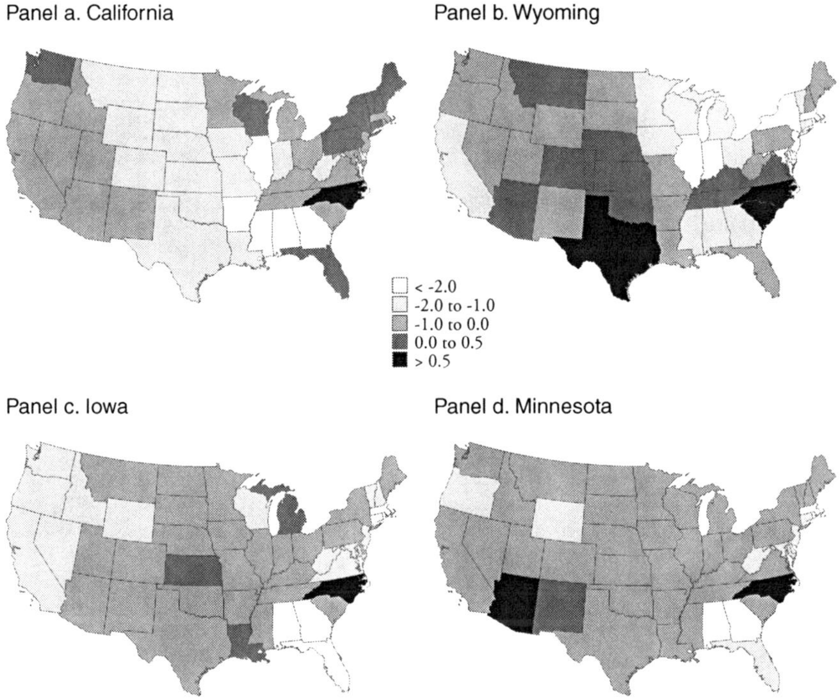

Sources: Developed by the authors using InSTePP data.

ing map for Minnesota), Iowa appears to have become even less similar to more states than Minnesota has over the period 1949–2004 (generally lighter shading in Panel c than in Panel d in Figure 9-6).

Huffman and Evenson (and others) have used alternative measures of spillover potential in a number of studies of the payoff to agricultural R&D. In most cases, these measures are based primarily on geographic proximity. A simplistic specification for spillover coefficients is μ_{ij}, where $\mu_{ij} = 1$ if states i and j are in the same geographic region and $\mu_{ij} = 0$ otherwise. This measure may be a reasonable approximation for spillover potential in some applications.

Spillin Knowledge Stocks

To investigate the implications of this aspect of model specification choice for the time path of spillin knowledge stocks, measures of knowledge stocks were created using a number of specifications, as summarized in Table 9-4. This table includes six sets of spillover knowledge stocks using two alternative specifications of spillover coefficients and the three lag distributions used in Table 9-1 and shown in Figure 9-3. In each case, the knowledge stocks include only SAES and

Table 9-4 **Summary of Average SAES Spillin Knowledge Stocks using Three Alternative Lag Distributions and Two Alternative Specifications of Spillover Coefficients, 1949–2002**

	Lag Specification					
	Gamma (λ=0.70, δ=0.90)		Gamma (λ=0.75, δ=0.80)		Trapezoidal	
	Spillover Coefficients		Spillover Coefficients		Spillover Coefficients	
	ω_{ij} (output mix)	μ_{ij} (USDA regions)	ω_{ij} (output mix)	μ_{ij} (USDA regions)	ω_{ij} (output mix)	μ_{ij} (USDA regions)
State or Region	(1)	(2)	(3)	(4)	(5)	(6)
48 state	*millions of dollars (2000 prices)*[a]					
Average	669.1	599.8	902.8	776.6	912.8	784.4
	(3.66)	(3.34)	(2.99)	(2.44)	(2.98)	(2.43)
Minimum	330.7	535.0	449.2	685.4	454.2	692.0
	(3.55)	(3.19)	(2.87)	(2.25)	(2.86)	(2.24)
Maximum	911.4	663.2	1,230.2	858.9	1,243.7	867.6
	(3.75)	(3.59)	(3.07)	(2.71)	(3.06)	(2.70)
Selected states						
California	670.4	535.0	902.0	685.4	911.9	692.0
	(3.62)	(3.30)	(2.94)	(2.32)	(2.94)	(2.31)
Minnesota	867.4	653.6	1,163.7	846.7	1,176.3	855.2
	(3.60)	(3.30)	(2.92)	(2.49)	(2.91)	(2.48)
Wyoming	624.6	555.1	846.3	717.2	855.6	724.3
	(3.69)	(3.31)	(3.03)	(2.41)	(3.03)	(2.39)
Regions						
Pacific	2,058.6	1,706.2	2,776.7	2,207.4	2,807.2	2,229.4
	(3.64)	(3.39)	(2.98)	(2.45)	(2.97)	(2.43)
Mountain	5,464.3	4,424.4	7,393.4	5,704.2	7,474.9	5,760.4
	(3.69)	(3.30)	(3.02)	(2.38)	(3.01)	(2.37)
Northern Plains	2,826.2	2,159.9	3,802.9	2,775.2	3,844.3	2,802.4
	(3.62)	(3.29)	(2.96)	(2.34)	(2.95)	(2.33)
Southern Plains	3,177.6	2,879.8	4,302.3	3,731.9	4,349.8	3,769.1
	(3.70)	(3.40)	(3.03)	(2.46)	(3.02)	(2.45)
Central	6,245.8	5,247.7	8,380.4	6,804.4	8,471.4	6,873.1
	(3.59)	(3.30)	(2.92)	(2.50)	(2.91)	(2.49)
Southeast	6,144.4	5,692.9	8,300.2	7,505.3	8,391.6	7,583.2
	(3.67)	(3.55)	(3.00)	(2.66)	(2.99)	(2.64)
Northeast	6,200.8	6,680.7	8,380.5	8,550.4	8,472.9	8,633.7
	(3.67)	(3.23)	(3.01)	(2.30)	(3.00)	(2.29)

Sources: Developed by the authors using InSTePP value-of-production data described in Appendix II and SAES spending data described in Appendix III.

Notes: The gamma distribution model in columns 1 and 2 was the best-fitting distribution for the logarithmic model and the model in columns 3 and 4 was the best for the linear model in the base specification.

[a] Figures in parentheses are average annual percentage growth rates of knowledge stocks.

USDA intramural spending (i.e., extension spending is excluded for the current purposes, although it is included in spillin stocks in the base model). In addition, the numbers included reflect averages over 1949–2002 for each state or region.

Columns 1 and 2 of Table 9-4 describe the spillover knowledge stocks when the gamma lag distribution characterized by $\lambda = 0.70$ and $\delta = 0.90$ is used to create the knowledge stocks (this is the preferred lag distribution from the base model estimated in logarithmic form). Column 1 summarizes the spillin knowledge stocks using our measure of output-mix similarity, ω_{ij}. Column 2 refers to knowledge stocks using regional dummies, μ_{ij}. For most states and regions, the knowledge stocks are smaller in column 2 than column 1.

Columns 3 and 4 of Table 9-4 show the corresponding spillin knowledge stocks when an alternative gamma lag distribution is used ($\lambda = 0.75$, $\delta = 0.80$), and columns 5 and 6, similarly, when the 35-year trapezoidal distribution is used. Across all three lag structures (i.e., columns 1–2 versus columns 3–4 versus columns 5–6), variations in the structure of spillover coefficients have similar implications. Specifically, moving from left to right across the columns within a pair, spillin knowledge stocks tend to decrease, the range of spillin knowledge stocks across states gets wider, and the average annual percentage growth in knowledge stocks gets smaller. The implications of the influence of spillover coefficients are more thoroughly analyzed in Chapters 10, 11, and 12.

9.4 More About Extension Knowledge Stocks

We conducted some preliminary analysis with various models using a data set that ended in 1991, which we subsequently revised and extended to 2002. In that preliminary analysis we found that it was not possible to estimate satisfactory models with separate knowledge stocks for own-state research, own-state extension, state-state spillovers, and federal-state spillovers, without imposing strong additional parametric restrictions. Even after combining state-state and federal-state spillins into a single spillin knowledge stock, the multicollinearity among own-state research, own-state extension, and spillin knowledge stocks appeared to have caused fragile estimates and, in some cases, nonsensical results (such as negative elasticities of productivity with respect to research). Because our focus is on the returns to research spending, our goal was primarily to control for the effects of extension funding. In doing so, we needed to consider how to create extension knowledge stocks and how they should be combined with other knowledge stocks to minimize the effects of multicollinearity. In particular, we needed to make decisions about what lag weights should be used to construct extension knowledge stocks, and whether their effects should be allowed to spill over to other states.

The appropriate lag distribution for creating extension knowledge stocks depends on how quickly findings from extension work are put into practice, and how lasting their effects are. The extent to which the nature of extension-funded work differs from other types of publicly funded agricultural research is likely to vary across time and space. Certainly, the focus of extension work has been on conducting more-applied research, disseminating research findings, and facilitating the adoption of new technologies. Hence, one might speculate that the lag structure should be quite different from that used for other types of research, reflecting more immediate but perhaps shorter-lived impacts of extension funding—for instance, Huffman and Evenson (1993) applied a type of geometric lag distribution to extension, including a total of four extension expenditures with lag weights of 0.50, 0.25, 0.125, and 0.125 for lags of 0-3 years. Complicating the issue further is the changing nature of extension and SAES-funded work, the division between which has become increasingly blurred in recent years. A related factor is the rise of "private extension services" that are often "bundled" with the purchase of off-farm (materials) inputs, the use of which increased substantially during the latter half of the 20th Century, as documented in Chapter 3.

The extent to which the benefits from extension spending may spill over state borders is another empirical question with no easy answers. Because extension work tends to be more applied, one may argue that it is more focused on local growing conditions and on facilitating adoption within state boundaries, implying that spillovers from this type of work are minimal. However, there are no barriers to the communication of extension findings. Hence, we might expect states to enjoy some spillovers from extension funding, but the relative extent and duration of extension spillovers compared with research spillovers is unclear.

Strong priors about the nature of extension research and the degree to which the benefits spill across state lines would clarify specification choices, but there is little theoretical or empirical basis for one approach over another. We opted to treat extension spending exactly as we treated research spending in our base model. Extension spending was accumulated into an extension knowledge stock using the same gamma lag weights as were used to aggregate research spending. The two stocks were then combined into an own-state knowledge stock. In keeping with the equivalent treatment of research and extension, extension knowledge stocks were allowed to spill over to other states.

Our primary justification for these decisions is the recognition that any state's SAES funding supports a heterogeneous research portfolio including activities across the spectrum from basic to applied, with varying degrees of geographic specificity, and with a variety of years until fruition and obsolescence. In treating extension funding the same as research funding, we have simply increased the number (and perhaps the range or heterogeneity) of projects with each state's research and extension portfolio.

In the absence of a theoretical justification for any particular treatment of extension vis-à-vis research, we were also careful to examine the implications of the priors we imposed for the results. In doing so, we constructed alternative sets of knowledge stocks and estimated models using those alternatives as well. Table

Table 9-5 Summary of Annual Average Extension Spending and Average Own-State Extension Knowledge Stocks Using Four Alternative Lag Specifications, 1949–2002

		Extension Knowledge Stocks			
State or Region	Extension Spending (1)	Gamma (λ=0.70, δ=0.90) (2)	Gamma (λ=0.75, δ=0.80) (3)	Trapezoid (4)	Short Geometric (5)
		millions of dollars (2000 prices)[a]			
United States total	1,388	839	1,068	1,078	1,372
	(1.36)	(3.61)	(2.89)	(2.85)	(1.64)
48 state					
Average	28.9	17.5	22.2	22.4	28.6
	(1.42)	(2.87)	(2.16)	(2.13)	(1.38)
Minimum	2.9	1.9	2.4	2.4	2.9
	(-0.35)	(1.62)	(0.80)	(0.75)	(-0.49)
Maximum	75.5	45.3	59.0	59.5	74.7
	(3.03)	(4.15)	(3.78)	(3.75)	(3.01)
Selected states					
California	69.0	37.1	50.1	50.7	68.1
	(1.68)	(3.92)	(3.11)	(3.08)	(1.78)
Minnesota	37.6	19.6	26.1	26.4	36.9
	(2.25)	(3.00)	(2.69)	(2.65)	(2.18)
Wyoming	7.5	5.1	6.2	6.2	7.5
	(0.44)	(2.35)	(1.79)	(1.75)	(0.41)
Regions					
Pacific	116.8	65.7	86.6	87.5	115.4
	(1.58)	(3.61)	(2.89)	(2.85)	(1.64)
Mountain	90.0	53.7	68.2	68.8	88.9
	(1.64)	(2.81)	(2.26)	(2.22)	(1.62)
Northern Plains	90.5	56.6	70.8	71.4	89.6
	(1.40)	(2.74)	(2.10)	(2.07)	(1.34)
Southern Plains	207.2	130.6	165.4	166.8	205.4
	(1.21)	(3.07)	(2.14)	(2.10)	(1.14)
Central	326.5	196.7	248.9	251.2	322.4
	(1.65)	(2.87)	(2.21)	(2.18)	(1.56)
Southeast	367.9	208.4	273.5	276.2	363.6
	(1.59)	(3.35)	(2.61)	(2.57)	(1.56)
Northeast	188.6	127.4	154.3	155.6	187.1
	(1.16)	(2.43)	(1.70)	(1.67)	(1.08)

Sources: Developed by the authors using extension spending data described in Appendix III.

Notes: The gamma distribution model in column 2 was the best-fitting distribution for the logarithmic model and the model in column 3 was the best for the linear model in the base specification. U.S. total excludes Alaska and Hawaii.

[a] Figures in parentheses are average annual percentage growth rates of knowledge stocks.

9-5 summarizes extension spending and the corresponding own-state stock of extension knowledge from past extension investments for the three lag distributions shown in Figure 9-3 and for the shortened geometric lag distribution used by Huffman and Evenson (1993).

The first column of Table 9-5 shows average annual extension spending over the period 1949–2002 and the average annual percentage change in extension spending for all states combined, for regional aggregates, and for particular states. The average spending on extension for all states combined was approximately \$1.4 billion, compared with \$1.7 billion for SAES spending (both in real 2000 dollars). Extension spending as a whole grew more slowly between 1949 and 2002, with average annual percentage growth of 1.36 percent, compared with 2.65 percent for SAES spending. In addition, the rate of growth in extension spending has decreased over time, particularly since the 1960s. Extension spending grew by 2.42 percent per year in the 1960s, 2.38 percent per year during the 1970s, but only 0.20 percent per year in the 1980s, and 0.02 percent per year for 1990–2002.

Columns 2 through 5 of Table 9-5 show the average knowledge stock and average annual percentage change in the knowledge stock over time using the four alternative lag distributions. The first three extension knowledge stocks reflect the same patterns that were described above for the state research knowledge stocks. The last lag distribution is quite different because it peaks immediately and because each year of spending affects the knowledge stock for only four years. In this case, the size and average percentage growth of the knowledge stock is very similar to the size and average percentage growth of the corresponding spending series.

The extension knowledge stocks summarized in Table 9-5 and several others were used in alternative models. In several alternative specifications, we used the geometric lag weights from Huffman and Evenson (1993) to create extension knowledge stocks before combining them with research stocks; in some other specifications, extension knowledge was excluded from spillin stocks; and finally, in some specifications the extension knowledge stock entered the model separately, as specified in equation (9.4). Highlights of the differences in results among the alternative models are presented in the following chapters.

9.5 Weather

Natural inputs have a measurable and important effect on agricultural production and productivity, yet their inclusion in economic production or supply models is problematic, even for models that relate inputs to a single output like corn or wheat. The empirical problems are doubly difficult in models that link inputs to aggregate measures of output like "all crops" or "all agricultural output." The geographical unit of analysis matters too. The effect of weather on crop yields, and agricultural production more generally, is location specific such that observations at ever-larger spatial aggregates (e.g., U.S. counties versus states versus the nation) make it increasingly difficult to conceive of appropriate weather metrics.

In regression models designed to account for observed variation in production or crop yields, one approach is to introduce meteorological variables as components of weather such as average or extreme measures of temperature, sunlight, precipitation, or wind velocity—or transformations thereof (such as cumulative degree days, evapo-transpiration rates, frost events, or soil moisture)—as explanatory variables.[16] To account for yield or production that is the outcome of lengthy cropping seasons, in which the timing of each component of weather can matter, along with the amount, some analysts use time-dated weather attributes rather than seasonal averages or totals. For instance, studies have used daily, weekly, or monthly measures of moisture, temperature and related weather attributes at a specific point in the growing cycle of a plant (e.g., at planting, or emergence, or flowering)—see, for example, Kaylen, Wade and Frank (1992, pp. 515-516).

Another approach is to recognize that the relationship between production (or yield) and weather involves complex, typically non-linear, and often time-sensitive interactions among each of the weather variables and, in many cases, between weather and other input variables that affect production (such as the types, quantities, and timing of the use of seed varieties, fertilizer, pesticides, herbicides, and labor).[17] Many of these subtle, but empirically sensitive interaction effects are difficult to address by the inclusion of particular weather variables. For instance, average rainfall masks aspects of the timing of rainfall such that "abnormal" (either high or low) rainfall at planting or flowering from year to year may have measurable production consequences absent any measurable variation in the total amount of annual or seasonal precipitation. Moreover, more or less rain at certain times in the growing season may induce a larger or smaller yield effect for a given amount and timing of, say, nitrogen fertilizer. And there may be interactions between the timing of rainfall and the application of other inputs such as fungicides.

Doll (1967, p.81) observed that "Oury [1965], Stallings [1960 and 1961], and Shaw [1964] reject the use of meteorological variables—primarily on the grounds that the functional relationship between these variables and yield is not known." Stallings (1960 and 1961) recognized that weather has both a direct and an indirect effect on crop yields. Direct effects relate to the biological growth processes of a plant that are affected by light, temperature, moisture and other natural factors. Regarding the indirect effects, Stallings (1961, p. 1156) noted

16 According to Shaw (1964), Wallace (1920) was the first to use regression techniques to study the relationship between crop yield and weather.

17 Omitting important attributes of weather from an agricultural production function can lead to the specification bias problem identified by Griliches (1957b). For example, omitting rainfall from a set of explanatory variables that also include land, labor, capital and fertilizer can cause the estimated coefficient on fertilizer to be upwardly biased to the extent that fertilizer and rainfall are complements in production.

that "The intensity of certain insect infestations and plant diseases…is affected by weather. These effects may not be wholly the direct results of weather in a particular year. They may be affected by weather factors in previous years."

To address this complexity, Stallings opted to instrument weather by first fitting a linear trend line to crop yield data for corn, oats, barley, wheat, soybeans, cotton and tobacco (to control for factors that varied linearly over time) and then creating a "weather index" consisting of each years' observed experimental yield expressed as a percentage of the computed trend yield; essentially the same method used by Wallace in 1920 to investigate the influence of weather in corn yields.[18] In our assessment of the relationship between agricultural R&D and state-specific productivity growth in Chapter 10, we follow the Stallings tradition by using a proxy variable for weather; in our case a state-specific index of range and pasture conditions on September 1 of each year, as reported by USDA (see Appendix II). Not all states grow all crops (making a yield deviations index based on any particular crop problematic), whereas all states support grazing activities and consequently report a range and pasture condition index.[19]

9.6 Conclusion

This chapter has developed the general form of the productivity models to be estimated in Chapter 10. To do so, it has drawn on the review of literature in Chapter 8, and applied the ideas from previous work in the light of the discussion of R&D spending and institutions in Chapters 6 and 7, and data available on inputs, outputs and productivity as reviewed in Chapters 3 through 5.

A key issue in the previous literature has been the "attribution problem" as discussed by Alston and Pardey (2001). This problem has two parts. First, what was the role of research compared with other factors affecting productivity? Second, within research, which research conducted when, and by whom, was responsible for a particular productivity change? Here we have focused on the attribution of impacts of U.S. public agricultural research and extension. The temporal aspect of the attribution problem is treated by the choice of R&D lag distribution models. The availability of data in unusually long-time series allows us to explore the role of different lag specifications in influencing findings, and we have adopted a flexible gamma lag distribution with a maximum length of 50 years as our baseline model against which to explore these issues. The use of state-level panel data increases our degrees of freedom for estimating the lag

---

18 The Stallings weather index or variants thereof were used by Griliches (1960a), Hathaway (1959), Johnson (1952), Shumway and Chang (1980) and Lopez and Ramos (1998).

19 Other regression studies that use proxies for weather in this manner include Houck and Gallagher (1976) and Ryan (1977).

distribution structure, but only if we are willing to impose restrictions on the spatial dimension.

The spatial aspect of the attribution problem is treated by allowing for state-state spillovers of R&D impacts. The yield-increasing, cost-reducing or other productivity-enhancing effects of agricultural R&D tend to be location specific because agricultural production is biologically based and dependent on agroecological conditions. Agricultural research done in one state is likely to be targeted to the constraints and production opportunities most pertinent to that state. Even so, it is also likely to have consequences for other states. In conducting state-specific assessments of the economic consequences of agricultural R&D, it is therefore important to account for state-to-state spillovers of knowledge and technology resulting from research. Intuitively, research spillovers are likely to be greater when agriculture is more similar between states—i.e., where the technological distance between the states is shorter. We have developed an index of spillover potential based on the similarity of the output mix between pairs of states, which seems to have desirable features compared with indexes based entirely on spatial proximity. Analysis of the properties of these indexes over space and time in this chapter has revealed that they are different from indexes based on proximity, and they are reasonably stable over time, justifying our use of the average annual values over the sample period.

Other modeling choices concern the distinction between research and extension, and the likely lag distributions and spillover potential for extension spending. In our baseline model we treat research and extension as fungible (as we do with elements of research within that category and elements of extension within that category), but in the econometric estimation we explore alternatives and evaluate their implications. The econometric results are reported and discussed in Chapter 10, which is next, and the implications for returns to research are explored in Chapter 11.

Appendix Table 9-1 Spillover Coefficients, Sample Means, 1949–2002

			Pacific			Mountain								Northern Plains			
		Fed	**CA**	**OR**	**WA**	**AZ**	**CO**	**ID**	**MT**	**NV**	**NM**	**UT**	**WY**	**KS**	**NE**	**ND**	**SD**
Pacific	California	*0.66*	1.00	*0.67*	0.55	*0.69*	*0.49*	*0.54*	*0.36*	*0.53*	*0.64*	*0.69*	*0.42*	*0.37*	*0.35*	*0.29*	*0.42*
	Oregon	*0.73*	*0.67*	1.00	*0.79*	**0.52**	*0.80*	*0.81*	*0.78*	*0.74*	0.70	*0.82*	*0.69*	*0.75*	*0.58*	*0.69*	*0.69*
	Washington	*0.61*	0.55	*0.79*	1.00	**0.39**	*0.60*	*0.77*	*0.68*	**0.51**	**0.51**	*0.67*	*0.44*	*0.67*	*0.42*	*0.73*	*0.51*
Mountain	Arizona	**0.59**	*0.69*	**0.52**	**0.39**	1.00	**0.58**	**0.48**	**0.48**	**0.62**	*0.79*	**0.59**	0.56	**0.48**	0.43	0.32	**0.51**
	Colorado	**0.76**	*0.49*	*0.80*	*0.60*	**0.58**	1.00	*0.76*	0.87	0.92	0.84	0.84	0.94	**0.88**	0.82	*0.64*	0.89
	Idaho	*0.64*	*0.54*	*0.81*	*0.77*	**0.48**	*0.76*	1.00	*0.74*	**0.71**	**0.66**	*0.76*	*0.66*	*0.69*	*0.52*	*0.70*	*0.62*
	Montana	0.60	*0.36*	*0.78*	*0.68*	**0.48**	0.87	*0.74*	1.00	0.75	0.68	0.71	**0.81**	*0.92*	*0.65*	*0.87*	0.77
	Nevada	**0.68**	*0.53*	*0.74*	**0.51**	**0.62**	0.92	**0.71**	0.75	1.00	0.91	**0.87**	*0.95*	**0.73**	*0.69*	0.46	0.81
	New Mexico	**0.72**	*0.64*	0.70	**0.51**	*0.79*	0.84	**0.66**	0.68	0.91	1.00	**0.82**	*0.83*	0.69	*0.65*	0.44	0.75
	Utah	0.78	*0.69*	*0.82*	*0.67*	**0.59**	0.84	*0.76*	0.71	**0.87**	**0.82**	1.00	*0.80*	0.70	*0.63*	*0.53*	0.74
	Wyoming	0.63	*0.42*	*0.69*	*0.44*	0.56	0.94	*0.66*	**0.81**	*0.95*	*0.83*	*0.80*	1.00	**0.78**	0.73	*0.51*	0.83
Northern Plains	Kansas	**0.73**	*0.37*	*0.75*	*0.67*	**0.48**	**0.88**	*0.69*	*0.92*	**0.73**	0.69	0.70	**0.78**	1.00	**0.80**	*0.81*	**0.85**
	Nebraska	*0.84*	*0.35*	*0.58*	*0.42*	0.43	0.82	*0.52*	*0.65*	*0.69*	*0.65*	*0.63*	0.73	**0.80**	1.00	*0.50*	0.93
	North Dakota	*0.53*	*0.29*	*0.69*	*0.73*	0.32	*0.64*	*0.70*	*0.87*	0.46	0.44	*0.53*	*0.51*	*0.81*	*0.50*	1.00	0.62
	South Dakota	0.86	*0.42*	*0.69*	*0.51*	**0.51**	0.89	*0.62*	0.77	0.81	0.75	0.74	0.83	**0.85**	0.93	0.62	1.00
Southern Plains	Arkansas	*0.52*	*0.40*	*0.27*	*0.20*	*0.46*	*0.26*	*0.20*	0.23	*0.26*	*0.39*	*0.27*	*0.25*	0.27	*0.27*	0.19	0.30
	Louisiana	*0.62*	*0.53*	*0.41*	*0.30*	*0.60*	*0.42*	*0.34*	0.33	*0.44*	*0.55*	*0.46*	*0.40*	0.39	0.42	0.25	0.47
	Mississippi	*0.58*	*0.48*	*0.31*	*0.23*	*0.64*	*0.32*	*0.25*	0.26	*0.32*	*0.49*	*0.33*	*0.30*	0.30	*0.33*	0.20	*0.37*
	Oklahoma	*0.74*	*0.49*	*0.81*	*0.65*	0.62	0.93	*0.72*	0.92	**0.85**	*0.82*	0.80	**0.88**	0.93	*0.73*	*0.73*	0.84
	Texas	**0.72**	*0.60*	**0.65**	**0.44**	*0.82*	**0.80**	**0.56**	**0.67**	**0.79**	*0.88*	**0.72**	**0.79**	**0.72**	**0.67**	**0.44**	**0.73**
Central	Illinois	*0.72*	*0.19*	*0.25*	*0.20*	*0.15*	*0.36*	*0.21*	*0.21*	*0.22*	*0.23*	*0.26*	*0.23*	*0.41*	*0.76*	0.26	0.63

	Indiana	*0.76*	*0.25*	*0.29*	*0.25*	0.17	*0.37*	*0.25*	*0.22*	*0.23*	*0.25*	*0.31*	*0.23*	*0.43*	*0.76*	*0.28*	*0.65*
	Iowa	*0.78*	*0.24*	*0.32*	*0.22*	0.24	*0.47*	*0.27*	*0.29*	*0.36*	*0.36*	*0.37*	*0.37*	0.48	*0.83*	0.27	*0.75*
	Michigan	*0.85*	0.66	*0.65*	*0.63*	**0.38**	*0.52*	*0.57*	*0.35*	0.46	**0.50**	*0.69*	*0.35*	*0.48*	*0.63*	*0.39*	*0.61*
	Minnesota	*0.90*	*0.49*	*0.52*	*0.47*	**0.36**	*0.55*	*0.49*	*0.39*	*0.47*	**0.49**	*0.62*	*0.42*	0.55	*0.79*	0.41	*0.77*
	Missouri	*0.91*	*0.44*	*0.57*	*0.43*	0.47	0.69	*0.50*	0.55	0.62	*0.62*	*0.64*	0.61	**0.70**	*0.85*	0.46	0.87
	Ohio	*0.87*	*0.47*	*0.51*	*0.45*	**0.29**	*0.47*	*0.41*	*0.33*	*0.37*	**0.39**	*0.52*	*0.31*	*0.51*	*0.74*	*0.38*	*0.68*
	Wisconsin	*0.71*	0.66	*0.53*	**0.54**	**0.39**	*0.40*	**0.52**	*0.24*	**0.46**	**0.51**	0.71	*0.29*	*0.33*	*0.42*	*0.24*	*0.46*
Southeast	Alabama	*0.65*	*0.48*	*0.43*	*0.29*	*0.49*	*0.42*	*0.32*	*0.32*	*0.40*	*0.50*	*0.42*	*0.39*	*0.37*	*0.44*	*0.23*	*0.46*
	Florida	0.40	**0.52**	**0.43**	**0.27**	**0.27**	0.29	*0.27*	*0.19*	0.29	**0.30**	0.36	*0.24*	*0.21*	*0.22*	*0.14*	*0.25*
	Georgia	*0.61*	*0.40*	*0.33*	*0.26*	*0.33*	*0.29*	*0.23*	*0.20*	*0.25*	*0.35*	*0.33*	*0.23*	*0.27*	*0.37*	*0.18*	*0.37*
	Kentucky	0.71	*0.37*	*0.44*	0.34	**0.34**	**0.51**	0.38	**0.38**	**0.48**	**0.47**	**0.52**	**0.45**	**0.47**	**0.59**	**0.30**	**0.60**
	North Carolina	**0.48**	**0.25**	**0.24**	**0.18**	**0.16**	**0.18**	0.14	**0.11**	**0.13**	0.16	**0.22**	**0.11**	**0.18**	0.27	0.12	**0.25**
	South Carolina	**0.67**	*0.45*	**0.38**	**0.23**	*0.44*	**0.33**	0.26	**0.25**	**0.29**	*0.40*	**0.37**	**0.26**	**0.33**	0.41	**0.22**	0.41
	Tennessee	0.90	*0.63*	0.62	0.47	0.63	**0.62**	0.50	**0.47**	**0.61**	0.69	**0.68**	**0.55**	**0.58**	0.67	**0.37**	**0.71**
	Virginia	0.84	*0.59*	*0.62*	*0.53*	**0.43**	**0.59**	0.53	**0.44**	**0.58**	**0.57**	0.71	**0.50**	0.52	*0.58*	0.35	0.62
	West Virginia	*0.79*	*0.62*	*0.66*	*0.57*	0.47	0.67	*0.56*	0.50	0.68	0.65	*0.79*	0.62	0.55	*0.59*	*0.35*	*0.65*
Northeast	Connecticut	*0.49*	**0.64**	**0.54**	*0.44*	**0.24**	*0.22*	*0.31*	*0.11*	**0.24**	**0.28**	*0.50*	*0.12*	*0.14*	*0.13*	*0.12*	*0.18*
	Delaware	**0.32**	*0.16*	*0.15*	*0.13*	*0.04*	*0.08*	*0.09*	*0.04*	*0.05*	*0.06*	*0.10*	*0.04*	*0.09*	*0.15*	*0.06*	*0.12*
	Maine	0.38	0.46	0.43	**0.46**	**0.21**	0.22	**0.60**	**0.11**	**0.25**	**0.26**	**0.40**	*0.12*	0.12	*0.11*	0.15	0.15
	Maryland	*0.68*	*0.52*	*0.48*	*0.42*	**0.24**	*0.31*	*0.34*	*0.20*	*0.28*	**0.30**	*0.47*	*0.21*	*0.29*	*0.39*	*0.22*	*0.37*
	Massachusetts	*0.47*	*0.64*	**0.55**	*0.46*	**0.23**	*0.21*	*0.31*	*0.10*	**0.23**	**0.26**	*0.49*	*0.12*	*0.14*	*0.13*	*0.12*	*0.18*
	New Hampshire	0.54	**0.70**	**0.60**	**0.58**	**0.32**	0.28	**0.49**	0.15	**0.34**	**0.38**	0.62	*0.17*	*0.19*	*0.17*	*0.17*	*0.24*
	New Jersey	*0.50*	*0.62*	**0.56**	*0.41*	**0.21**	*0.23*	*0.26*	*0.12*	0.20	0.23	*0.44*	*0.12*	*0.18*	*0.21*	*0.14*	*0.23*
	New York	*0.59*	**0.70**	*0.53*	**0.58**	**0.35**	*0.30*	**0.49**	*0.17*	**0.38**	**0.44**	0.67	*0.19*	*0.22*	*0.23*	*0.20*	*0.29*
	Pennsylvania	*0.72*	**0.71**	*0.59*	0.59	**0.38**	*0.40*	**0.52**	*0.25*	**0.44**	**0.49**	0.73	*0.28*	*0.33*	*0.39*	*0.26*	*0.43*
	Rhode Island	*0.41*	*0.60*	**0.57**	*0.40*	0.18	*0.20*	*0.33*	*0.08*	*0.18*	*0.19*	*0.40*	*0.10*	*0.12*	*0.11*	*0.11*	*0.14*
	Vermont	*0.53*	**0.64**	*0.46*	**0.52**	**0.34**	*0.26*	**0.45**	*0.14*	**0.36**	**0.42**	**0.65**	*0.17*	*0.19*	*0.16*	*0.16*	*0.24*

(continued)

Appendix Table 9-1 (continued)

		Southern Plains					Central							
		AR	**LA**	**MS**	**OK**	**TX**	**IL**	**IN**	**IA**	**MI**	**MN**	**MO**	**OH**	**WI**
Pacific	California	*0.40*	*0.53*	*0.48*	*0.49*	*0.60*	*0.19*	*0.25*	*0.24*	0.66	*0.49*	*0.44*	*0.47*	0.66
	Oregon	*0.27*	*0.41*	*0.31*	*0.81*	*0.65*	*0.25*	*0.29*	*0.32*	*0.65*	*0.52*	*0.57*	*0.51*	**0.53**
	Washington	*0.20*	*0.30*	*0.23*	*0.65*	*0.44*	*0.20*	*0.25*	*0.22*	*0.63*	*0.47*	*0.43*	*0.45*	**0.54**
Mountain	Arizona	*0.46*	*0.60*	*0.64*	0.62	*0.82*	*0.15*	0.17	0.24	**0.38**	**0.36**	0.47	**0.29**	**0.39**
	Colorado	*0.26*	*0.42*	*0.32*	0.93	**0.80**	*0.36*	*0.37*	*0.47*	*0.52*	*0.55*	0.69	*0.47*	*0.40*
	Idaho	*0.20*	*0.34*	*0.25*	*0.72*	**0.56**	*0.21*	*0.25*	*0.27*	*0.57*	*0.49*	*0.50*	*0.41*	**0.52**
	Montana	0.23	0.33	0.26	0.92	**0.67**	*0.21*	*0.22*	*0.29*	*0.35*	*0.39*	0.55	*0.33*	*0.24*
	Nevada	*0.26*	*0.44*	*0.32*	**0.85**	**0.79**	*0.22*	*0.23*	*0.36*	0.46	*0.47*	0.62	*0.37*	**0.46**
	New Mexico	*0.39*	*0.55*	*0.49*	*0.82*	*0.88*	*0.23*	*0.25*	*0.36*	**0.50**	**0.49**	*0.62*	**0.39**	**0.51**
	Utah	*0.27*	*0.46*	*0.33*	0.80	**0.72**	*0.26*	*0.31*	*0.37*	*0.69*	*0.62*	*0.64*	*0.52*	0.71
	Wyoming	*0.25*	*0.40*	*0.30*	**0.88**	**0.79**	*0.23*	*0.23*	*0.37*	*0.35*	*0.42*	0.61	*0.31*	*0.29*
Northern Plains	Kansas	0.27	0.39	0.30	0.93	**0.72**	*0.41*	*0.43*	0.48	*0.48*	0.55	**0.70**	*0.51*	*0.33*
	Nebraska	*0.27*	0.42	*0.33*	*0.73*	**0.67**	*0.76*	*0.76*	*0.83*	*0.63*	*0.79*	*0.85*	*0.74*	*0.42*
	North Dakota	0.19	0.25	0.20	*0.73*	**0.44**	0.26	*0.28*	0.27	*0.39*	0.41	0.46	*0.38*	*0.24*
	South Dakota	0.30	0.47	*0.37*	0.84	**0.73**	0.63	*0.65*	*0.75*	*0.61*	*0.77*	0.87	*0.68*	*0.46*
Southern Plains	Arkansas	1.00	*0.66*	0.90	*0.38*	*0.54*	*0.30*	*0.31*	*0.29*	*0.25*	*0.34*	0.49	0.36	*0.19*
	Louisiana	*0.66*	1.00	*0.71*	*0.46*	*0.63*	**0.39**	0.39	0.39	*0.44*	0.49	0.60	0.50	*0.39*
	Mississippi	0.90	*0.71*	1.00	*0.44*	*0.64*	*0.33*	*0.33*	*0.33*	*0.32*	*0.39*	*0.54*	*0.41*	*0.26*
	Oklahoma	*0.38*	*0.46*	*0.44*	1.00	**0.84**	*0.27*	*0.29*	*0.38*	*0.46*	*0.48*	*0.67*	*0.42*	*0.36*
	Texas	*0.54*	*0.63*	*0.64*	**0.84**	1.00	*0.26*	*0.27*	0.36	0.42	0.44	**0.63**	0.38	0.37
Central	Illinois	*0.30*	**0.39**	*0.33*	*0.27*	*0.26*	1.00	0.98	*0.94*	0.66	0.86	*0.81*	*0.90*	*0.41*

	Indiana	*0.31*	0.39	*0.33*	*0.29*	*0.27*	0.98	1.00	*0.96*	0.70	0.89	*0.83*	*0.93*	*0.47*
	Iowa	*0.29*	0.39	*0.33*	*0.38*	0.36	*0.94*	*0.96*	1.00	0.65	0.89	*0.87*	*0.87*	*0.44*
	Michigan	*0.25*	*0.44*	*0.32*	*0.46*	0.42	0.66	0.70	0.65	1.00	0.88	*0.69*	0.88	*0.88*
	Minnesota	*0.34*	0.49	*0.39*	*0.48*	0.44	0.86	0.89	0.89	0.88	1.00	*0.88*	*0.95*	*0.75*
	Missouri	0.49	0.60	*0.54*	*0.67*	**0.63**	*0.81*	*0.83*	*0.87*	*0.69*	*0.88*	1.00	*0.86*	*0.53*
	Ohio	**0.36**	*0.50*	*0.41*	*0.42*	*0.38*	*0.90*	*0.93*	*0.87*	0.88	*0.95*	*0.86*	1.00	*0.68*
	Wisconsin	**0.19**	*0.39*	*0.26*	*0.36*	*0.37*	*0.41*	*0.47*	*0.44*	*0.88*	*0.75*	*0.53*	*0.68*	1.00
Southeast	Alabama	**0.84**	*0.51*	0.85	*0.51*	*0.62*	*0.35*	*0.38*	*0.40*	*0.39*	*0.44*	*0.56*	*0.44*	*0.33*
	Florida	0.17	0.29	0.20	0.28	**0.29**	*0.15*	*0.17*	*0.17*	**0.38**	*0.27*	*0.26*	0.30	*0.32*
	Georgia	**0.72**	*0.40*	**0.70**	*0.37*	*0.45*	*0.37*	*0.41*	*0.40*	*0.40*	*0.44*	*0.49*	*0.46*	*0.34*
	Kentucky	**0.28**	0.38	**0.34**	**0.47**	**0.45**	*0.51*	*0.54*	0.55	*0.56*	0.62	0.63	*0.61*	*0.49*
	North Carolina	**0.39**	0.22	**0.37**	**0.21**	**0.22**	0.32	0.36	**0.36**	**0.35**	**0.38**	**0.38**	**0.40**	*0.25*
	South Carolina	0.63	*0.52*	0.67	**0.39**	*0.50*	*0.45*	0.48	0.45	**0.47**	0.52	0.59	0.56	*0.36*
	Tennessee	*0.60*	*0.68*	*0.70*	**0.64**	0.72	*0.58*	*0.61*	*0.64*	*0.71*	*0.75*	*0.83*	*0.75*	*0.63*
	Virginia	**0.50**	*0.44*	**0.51**	**0.59**	**0.56**	*0.45*	*0.51*	*0.51*	*0.71*	*0.69*	*0.69*	*0.67*	*0.68*
	West Virginia	**0.51**	*0.43*	**0.53**	0.67	**0.64**	*0.34*	*0.39*	*0.43*	*0.66*	*0.62*	*0.64*	*0.56*	*0.67*
Northeast	Connecticut	*0.19*	*0.27*	*0.21*	*0.23*	0.25	*0.13*	*0.22*	*0.14*	*0.63*	*0.39*	*0.26*	*0.45*	*0.62*
	Delaware	**0.62**	*0.16*	**0.50**	**0.13**	**0.15**	*0.21*	*0.23*	*0.19*	*0.20*	*0.22*	0.23	*0.25*	*0.16*
	Maine	*0.22*	*0.21*	*0.21*	0.17	**0.20**	*0.09*	*0.16*	*0.11*	**0.46**	0.31	*0.20*	0.31	**0.49**
	Maryland	**0.58**	*0.35*	**0.54**	*0.34*	0.34	*0.44*	*0.48*	*0.41*	*0.68*	*0.59*	*0.50*	*0.63*	*0.63*
	Massachusetts	*0.15*	*0.27*	*0.19*	*0.22*	*0.24*	*0.15*	*0.21*	*0.15*	*0.64*	*0.40*	*0.27*	*0.45*	*0.64*
	New Hampshire	*0.18*	*0.31*	*0.22*	*0.27*	**0.29**	*0.15*	*0.23*	*0.17*	**0.74**	*0.49*	*0.31*	*0.49*	0.79
	New Jersey	*0.19*	*0.30*	*0.22*	*0.23*	0.25	*0.27*	*0.31*	*0.25*	*0.64*	*0.43*	*0.32*	*0.53*	*0.52*
	New York	*0.15*	*0.34*	*0.21*	*0.29*	*0.29*	*0.22*	*0.29*	*0.23*	*0.82*	*0.59*	*0.37*	*0.56*	**0.96**
	Pennsylvania	*0.25*	*0.38*	*0.31*	*0.39*	**0.38**	*0.37*	*0.44*	*0.39*	*0.88*	*0.71*	*0.51*	*0.68*	0.95
	Rhode Island	*0.14*	*0.23*	*0.16*	*0.19*	*0.21*	*0.13*	*0.18*	*0.12*	*0.57*	*0.32*	*0.22*	*0.41*	*0.50*
	Vermont	*0.14*	*0.32*	*0.20*	*0.26*	*0.26*	*0.15*	*0.22*	*0.17*	*0.75*	*0.53*	*0.32*	*0.48*	**0.95**

(continued)

Appendix Table 9-1 (continued)

		Southeast									Northeast										
		AL	FL	GA	KY	NC	SC	TN	VA	WV	CT	DE	ME	MD	MA	NH	NJ	NY	PA	RI	VT
Pacific	California	*0.48*	**0.52**	*0.40*	*0.37*	**0.25**	*0.45*	*0.63*	*0.59*	*0.62*	**0.64**	*0.16*	0.46	*0.52*	*0.64*	**0.70**	*0.62*	**0.70**	**0.71**	*0.60*	**0.64**
	Oregon	*0.43*	**0.43**	*0.33*	*0.44*	**0.24**	**0.38**	0.62	*0.62*	*0.66*	**0.54**	*0.15*	0.43	*0.48*	**0.55**	**0.60**	**0.56**	*0.53*	*0.59*	**0.57**	*0.46*
	Washington	*0.29*	**0.27**	*0.26*	0.34	**0.18**	**0.28**	0.47	*0.53*	*0.57*	*0.44*	*0.13*	**0.46**	*0.42*	*0.46*	**0.58**	*0.41*	**0.58**	0.59	*0.40*	**0.52**
Mountain	Arizona	*0.49*	**0.27**	*0.33*	**0.34**	**0.16**	*0.44*	0.63	**0.43**	0.47	**0.24**	*0.04*	**0.21**	**0.24**	**0.23**	**0.32**	**0.21**	**0.35**	**0.38**	0.18	**0.34**
	Colorado	*0.42*	0.29	*0.29*	**0.51**	**0.18**	**0.33**	**0.62**	**0.59**	0.67	*0.22*	*0.08*	0.22	*0.31*	*0.21*	0.28	*0.23*	*0.30*	*0.40*	*0.20*	*0.26*
	Idaho	*0.32*	*0.27*	*0.23*	0.38	0.14	0.26	0.50	0.53	*0.56*	*0.31*	*0.09*	**0.60**	*0.34*	*0.31*	**0.49**	*0.26*	**0.49**	**0.52**	*0.33*	**0.45**
	Montana	*0.32*	*0.19*	*0.20*	**0.38**	**0.11**	**0.25**	**0.47**	**0.44**	0.50	*0.11*	*0.04*	**0.11**	*0.20*	*0.10*	0.15	*0.12*	*0.17*	*0.25*	*0.08*	*0.14*
	Nevada	*0.40*	0.29	*0.25*	**0.48**	**0.13**	**0.29**	**0.61**	**0.58**	0.68	**0.24**	*0.05*	**0.25**	*0.28*	**0.23**	**0.34**	0.20	**0.38**	**0.44**	*0.18*	**0.36**
	New Mexico	*0.50*	**0.30**	*0.35*	**0.47**	0.16	*0.40*	0.69	**0.57**	0.65	**0.28**	*0.06*	**0.26**	**0.30**	**0.26**	**0.38**	0.23	**0.44**	**0.49**	*0.19*	**0.42**
	Utah	*0.42*	0.36	*0.33*	**0.52**	**0.22**	**0.37**	**0.68**	0.71	*0.79*	*0.50*	*0.10*	**0.40**	*0.47*	*0.49*	0.62	*0.44*	0.67	0.73	*0.40*	**0.65**
	Wyoming	*0.39*	*0.24*	*0.23*	**0.45**	**0.11**	**0.26**	**0.55**	**0.50**	0.62	*0.12*	*0.04*	*0.12*	*0.21*	*0.12*	*0.17*	*0.12*	*0.19*	*0.28*	*0.10*	*0.17*
Northern Plains	Kansas	*0.37*	*0.21*	*0.27*	**0.47**	**0.18**	**0.33**	**0.58**	0.52	0.55	*0.14*	*0.09*	0.12	*0.29*	*0.14*	*0.19*	*0.18*	*0.22*	*0.33*	*0.12*	*0.19*
	Nebraska	*0.44*	*0.22*	*0.37*	**0.59**	0.27	0.41	0.67	*0.58*	*0.59*	*0.13*	*0.15*	*0.11*	*0.39*	*0.13*	*0.17*	*0.21*	*0.23*	*0.39*	*0.11*	*0.16*
	North Dakota	*0.23*	*0.14*	*0.18*	**0.30**	0.12	**0.22**	**0.37**	0.35	*0.35*	*0.12*	*0.06*	0.15	*0.22*	*0.12*	*0.17*	*0.14*	*0.20*	*0.26*	*0.11*	*0.16*
	South Dakota	*0.46*	*0.25*	*0.37*	**0.60**	**0.25**	0.41	**0.71**	0.62	*0.65*	*0.18*	*0.12*	0.15	*0.37*	*0.18*	*0.24*	*0.23*	*0.29*	*0.43*	*0.14*	*0.24*
Southern Plains	Arkansas	**0.84**	0.17	**0.72**	**0.28**	**0.39**	0.63	*0.60*	**0.50**	**0.51**	*0.19*	**0.62**	*0.22*	**0.58**	*0.15*	*0.18*	*0.19*	*0.15*	*0.25*	*0.14*	*0.14*
	Louisiana	*0.51*	0.29	*0.40*	0.38	0.22	*0.52*	*0.68*	*0.44*	*0.43*	*0.27*	*0.16*	*0.21*	*0.35*	*0.27*	*0.31*	*0.30*	*0.34*	*0.38*	*0.23*	*0.32*
	Mississippi	0.85	0.20	**0.70**	**0.34**	**0.37**	0.67	*0.70*	**0.51**	**0.53**	*0.21*	**0.50**	*0.21*	**0.54**	*0.19*	*0.22*	*0.22*	*0.21*	*0.31*	*0.16*	*0.20*
	Oklahoma	*0.51*	0.28	*0.37*	**0.47**	**0.21**	**0.39**	**0.64**	**0.59**	0.67	*0.23*	**0.13**	0.17	*0.34*	*0.22*	*0.27*	*0.23*	*0.29*	*0.39*	*0.19*	*0.26*
	Texas	*0.62*	**0.29**	*0.45*	**0.45**	**0.22**	*0.50*	0.72	**0.56**	**0.64**	0.25	**0.15**	**0.20**	0.34	*0.24*	**0.29**	0.25	*0.29*	**0.38**	*0.21*	*0.26*
Central	Illinois	*0.35*	*0.15*	*0.37*	*0.51*	0.32	*0.45*	*0.58*	*0.45*	*0.34*	*0.13*	*0.21*	*0.09*	*0.44*	*0.15*	*0.15*	*0.27*	*0.22*	*0.37*	*0.13*	*0.15*
	Indiana	*0.38*	*0.17*	*0.41*	*0.54*	0.36	0.48	*0.61*	*0.51*	*0.39*	*0.22*	*0.23*	*0.16*	*0.48*	*0.21*	*0.23*	*0.31*	*0.29*	*0.44*	*0.18*	*0.22*
	Iowa	*0.40*	*0.17*	*0.40*	0.55	**0.36**	0.45	*0.64*	*0.51*	*0.43*	*0.14*	*0.19*	*0.11*	*0.41*	*0.15*	*0.17*	*0.25*	*0.23*	*0.39*	*0.12*	*0.17*

	Michigan	*0.39*	**0.38**	*0.40*	*0.56*	**0.35**	**0.47**	*0.71*	*0.71*	*0.66*	*0.63*	*0.20*	**0.46**	*0.68*	*0.64*	**0.74**	*0.64*	*0.82*	*0.88*	*0.57*	*0.75*
	Minnesota	*0.44*	*0.27*	*0.44*	0.62	**0.33**	0.52	*0.75*	*0.69*	*0.62*	*0.39*	*0.22*	0.31	*0.59*	*0.40*	*0.49*	*0.43*	*0.59*	*0.71*	*0.32*	*0.53*
	Missouri	*0.56*	*0.26*	*0.49*	0.63	**0.38**	0.59	*0.83*	*0.69*	*0.64*	*0.26*	*0.23*	*0.20*	*0.50*	*0.27*	*0.31*	*0.32*	*0.37*	*0.51*	*0.22*	*0.32*
	Ohio	*0.44*	0.30	*0.46*	*0.61*	**0.40**	0.56	*0.75*	*0.67*	*0.56*	*0.45*	*0.25*	0.31	*0.63*	*0.45*	*0.49*	*0.53*	*0.56*	*0.68*	*0.41*	*0.48*
	Wisconsin	*0.33*	*0.32*	*0.34*	*0.49*	*0.25*	*0.36*	*0.63*	*0.68*	*0.67*	*0.62*	*0.16*	**0.49**	*0.63*	*0.64*	0.79	*0.52*	**0.96**	0.95	*0.50*	**0.95**
Southeast	Alabama	1.00	0.28	**0.91**	0.40	**0.46**	0.64	*0.68*	**0.67**	**0.71**	*0.33*	**0.71**	*0.33*	**0.75**	*0.29*	*0.31*	*0.32*	*0.27*	*0.41*	*0.29*	*0.23*
	Florida	0.28	1.00	*0.27*	*0.26*	**0.24**	**0.30**	**0.37**	0.39	*0.36*	**0.46**	**0.13**	**0.26**	**0.36**	**0.46**	**0.42**	**0.49**	*0.34*	0.38	**0.48**	*0.30*
	Georgia	**0.91**	*0.27*	1.00	*0.49*	**0.63**	0.70	*0.65*	0.74	**0.65**	*0.43*	**0.74**	*0.36*	**0.78**	*0.33*	*0.33*	*0.34*	*0.28*	*0.43*	*0.29*	*0.24*
	Kentucky	0.40	*0.26*	*0.49*	1.00	*0.79*	0.79	**0.82**	*0.82*	0.57	*0.45*	**0.18**	0.20	*0.50*	*0.34*	*0.33*	*0.29*	*0.38*	*0.49*	*0.22*	*0.35*
	North Carolina	**0.46**	**0.24**	**0.63**	*0.79*	1.00	**0.84**	0.63	0.74	**0.42**	*0.48*	**0.38**	0.20	**0.57**	0.33	**0.26**	**0.29**	*0.21*	**0.33**	**0.25**	*0.18*
	South Carolina	0.64	**0.30**	0.70	0.79	**0.84**	1.00	*0.84*	**0.78**	**0.54**	0.51	**0.34**	0.24	**0.58**	0.38	**0.35**	**0.40**	*0.30*	0.42	**0.30**	*0.26*
	Tennessee	*0.68*	**0.37**	*0.65*	**0.82**	0.63	*0.84*	1.00	0.85	*0.73*	*0.53*	**0.29**	0.31	0.64	*0.48*	0.51	*0.47*	*0.53*	*0.64*	*0.40*	*0.50*
	Virginia	**0.67**	0.39	0.74	*0.82*	*0.74*	**0.78**	0.85	*1.00*	*0.87*	*0.63*	**0.45**	*0.42*	*0.79*	*0.55*	*0.60*	*0.50*	*0.62*	*0.73*	*0.44*	*0.58*
	West Virginia	**0.71**	*0.36*	**0.65**	0.57	*0.42*	**0.54**	*0.73*	*0.87*	*1.00*	*0.54*	**0.48**	*0.44*	*0.75*	*0.53*	*0.61*	*0.48*	*0.62*	*0.73*	*0.44*	*0.59*
Northeast	Connecticut	*0.33*	**0.46**	*0.43*	*0.45*	*0.48*	0.51	*0.53*	*0.63*	*0.54*	1.00	*0.21*	*0.58*	*0.60*	*0.88*	0.86	0.84	*0.71*	*0.75*	0.84	*0.65*
	Delaware	**0.71**	**0.13**	**0.74**	**0.18**	**0.38**	**0.34**	**0.29**	**0.45**	**0.48**	*0.21*	1.00	*0.32*	**0.80**	*0.17*	*0.17*	*0.17*	*0.13*	*0.24*	*0.16*	*0.11*
	Maine	*0.33*	**0.26**	*0.36*	0.20	0.20	0.24	0.31	*0.42*	*0.44*	*0.58*	*0.32*	1.00	*0.46*	*0.48*	*0.70*	*0.42*	0.55	0.57	*0.52*	**0.49**
	Maryland	**0.75**	**0.36**	**0.78**	*0.50*	**0.57**	**0.58**	0.64	0.79	*0.75*	*0.60*	**0.80**	*0.46*	1.00	*0.57*	*0.59*	*0.54*	*0.60*	*0.71*	*0.52*	*0.56*
	Massachusetts	*0.29*	**0.46**	*0.33*	*0.34*	0.33	0.38	*0.48*	*0.55*	*0.53*	*0.88*	*0.17*	*0.48*	*0.57*	1.00	*0.85*	*0.89*	*0.72*	*0.74*	*0.88*	*0.66*
	New Hampshire	*0.31*	**0.42**	*0.33*	*0.33*	**0.26**	**0.35**	0.51	*0.60*	*0.61*	0.86	*0.17*	*0.70*	*0.59*	*0.85*	1.00	*0.79*	0.88	*0.87*	*0.79*	0.82
	New Jersey	*0.32*	**0.49**	*0.34*	*0.29*	**0.29**	**0.40**	*0.47*	*0.50*	*0.48*	0.84	*0.17*	*0.42*	*0.54*	*0.89*	*0.79*	1.00	*0.60*	*0.66*	**0.89**	*0.50*
	New York	*0.27*	*0.34*	*0.28*	*0.38*	*0.21*	*0.30*	*0.53*	*0.62*	*0.62*	*0.71*	*0.13*	0.55	*0.60*	*0.72*	0.88	*0.60*	1.00	*0.95*	*0.60*	0.98
	Pennsylvania	*0.41*	0.38	*0.43*	*0.49*	**0.33**	0.42	*0.64*	*0.73*	*0.73*	*0.75*	*0.24*	0.57	*0.71*	*0.74*	*0.87*	*0.66*	*0.95*	1.00	*0.62*	**0.92**
	Rhode Island	*0.29*	**0.48**	*0.29*	*0.22*	**0.25**	**0.30**	*0.40*	*0.44*	*0.44*	0.84	*0.16*	*0.52*	*0.52*	*0.88*	*0.79*	**0.89**	*0.60*	*0.62*	1.00	*0.52*
	Vermont	*0.23*	*0.30*	*0.24*	*0.35*	*0.18*	*0.26*	*0.50*	*0.58*	*0.59*	*0.65*	*0.11*	**0.49**	*0.56*	*0.66*	0.82	*0.50*	0.98	**0.92**	*0.52*	1.00

Sources: Developed by the authors using InSTePP value-of-production data described in Appendix II.

Notes: Entries are ω_{ij} averaged over 1949-2002. Entries in bold have positive and statistically significant (at the 5 percent level of significance) time trends over 1949-2004. Italicized entries have negative and statistically significant time trends over the same period of time (also at the 5 percent level of significance).

Appendix Table 9-2 Trends in Spillover Coefficients Among States, 1949–2004

	Trend in Fed-State (ω_{iF})	Trends in State-State Spillover Coefficients			Number of State-State Spillover Coefficients with Trends that are			
		Average	Minimum	Maximum	Negative Significant	Negative	Positive	Positive Significant
United States	na	-0.22	-1.64	0.63	29	35	13	9
Pacific								
California	-0.52	-0.89	-2.98	0.52	36	37	10	7
Oregon	-0.37	-0.48	-2.42	1.75	34	35	12	10
Washington	-0.19	-0.45	-1.96	1.45	31	32	15	12
Mountain								
Arizona	0.45	0.41	-3.43	2.64	11	14	33	26
Colorado	0.12	-0.31	-1.99	1.21	26	31	16	8
Idaho	-0.12	-0.54	-2.62	1.26	32	34	13	10
Montana	-0.02	-0.54	-2.65	1.19	26	34	13	9
Nevada	0.33	0.04	-2.19	2.31	17	23	24	20
New Mexico	0.22	0.13	-3.23	3.29	18	24	23	18
Utah	0.03	-0.44	-3.11	1.25	26	33	14	10
Wyoming	-0.07	-0.82	-3.49	1.06	32	35	12	9
Northern Plains								
Kansas	0.14	-0.49	-3.68	1.13	24	30	17	12
Nebraska	-0.15	-0.80	-3.99	0.80	36	39	8	3
North Dakota	-0.22	-0.74	-3.38	0.64	29	38	9	4
South Dakota	-0.01	-0.47	-3.23	0.79	25	35	12	6
Southern Plains								
Arkansas	-0.27	-0.80	-3.91	2.34	30	37	10	8
Louisiana	-0.45	-0.83	-2.92	0.39	33	39	8	1
Mississippi	-0.43	-0.83	-3.53	2.98	33	39	8	7
Oklahoma	-0.10	-0.47	-2.12	1.98	29	33	14	9
Texas	0.29	0.05	-2.12	1.21	15	21	26	23
Central								
Illinois	-0.49	-1.37	-3.41	0.39	40	45	2	1
Indiana	-0.49	-1.26	-3.56	0.25	40	44	3	0
Iowa	-0.32	-0.98	-3.78	0.99	37	43	4	1
Michigan	-0.11	-0.48	-2.73	1.41	32	38	9	7
Minnesota	-0.21	-0.65	-3.34	0.78	33	44	3	3
Missouri	-0.17	-0.56	-3.38	0.91	32	36	11	3
Ohio	-0.25	-0.56	-2.42	0.96	37	42	5	3
Wisconsin	-0.35	-0.73	-3.35	2.25	34	37	10	8
Southeast								
Alabama	-1.25	-1.51	-3.61	1.82	36	39	8	7
Florida	0.02	-0.12	-2.42	1.80	18	28	19	18
Georgia	-1.06	-1.37	-2.83	1.06	38	39	8	7
Kentucky	0.12	-0.12	-3.11	1.98	20	26	21	17
North Carolina	0.63	0.57	-1.07	2.48	5	11	36	31
South Carolina	0.19	0.28	-1.52	3.15	10	16	31	20
Tennessee	-0.03	-0.13	-1.13	1.52	23	28	19	12
Virginia	-0.05	-0.20	-2.18	1.79	23	30	17	14
West Virginia	-0.53	-0.84	-4.07	1.86	29	34	13	9

(continued)

Appendix Table 9-2 (continued)

	Trend in Fed-State (ω_{iF})	Trends in State-State Spillover Coefficients			Number of State-State Spillover Coefficients with Trends that are			
		Average	Minimum	Maximum	Negative Significant	Negative	Positive	Positive Significant
Northeast								
Connecticut	-0.66	-0.99	-4.22	1.73	36	39	8	6
Delaware	0.42	-0.91	-4.22	3.15	32	33	14	14
Maine	0.09	-0.35	-3.68	3.29	20	29	18	12
Maryland	-0.35	-0.64	-2.12	1.78	34	36	11	10
Massachusetts	-1.01	-1.36	-4.00	1.43	40	41	6	5
New Hampshire	-0.03	-0.46	-3.68	2.60	27	33	14	12
New Jersey	-0.80	-1.06	-3.17	1.80	37	39	8	6
New York	-0.30	-0.84	-3.35	2.73	36	38	9	7
Pennsylvania	-0.19	-0.45	-2.47	2.33	33	36	11	8
Rhode Island	-1.64	-2.00	-4.07	1.47	40	41	6	5
Vermont	-0.31	-0.88	-3.61	3.06	35	36	11	10

Sources: Developed by the authors using InSTePP value-of-production data described in Appendix II.

Notes: Entries on the first row of the table describe state-federal spillover coefficients.

CHAPTER 10

Econometric Estimation and Results

The implementation of the general model developed in Chapter 9 requires some specific choices about the detail of the model, beginning with the functional form. In the present chapter we discuss those choices, and present and interpret the resulting econometric estimates, along with the results of some analysis of the sensitivity of the estimates to model specification choices. In Chapter 11 we report the results from using the econometric estimates to compute a range of benefit-cost ratios for alternative types of research spending, and in Chapter 12 we interpret and assess the results from both the econometric estimation and the benefit-cost analysis.

10.1 Estimation Procedure

Based on the discussion in Chapter 9, the model to be estimated has the following general form:

$$(10.1)\quad MFP_{i,t} = f\left(SK_{i,t}, SS_{i,t}, Z_{i,t}\right).$$

In this model, state-specific multi-factor productivity in agriculture depends on (a) a state-specific knowledge stock from own-state public agricultural R&D (including extension), $SK_{i,t}$, (b) a state-specific spillover knowledge stock from both agricultural R&D (including extension) conducted by other states and intramural research conducted in USDA labs, $SS_{i,t}$, and (c) a variable (or variables) representing the effects of weather and other uncontrolled factors, $Z_{i,t}$.[1]

Importantly, this specification does not include any variables to represent the stocks of knowledge from private agricultural research conducted in the United

1 The R&D knowledge stock, $SK_{i,t}$, is the sum of the research knowledge stock, $SR_{i,t}$, and the extension knowledge stock, $SE_{i,t}$, discussed in Chapter 9. We used only one variable to represent effects of weather on productivity, a state-specific pasture and rangeland condition index, measured in September for each year, $PRC_{i,t}$.

J.M. Alston et al., *Persistence Pays: U.S. Agricultural Productivity Growth and the Benefits from Public R&D Spending*, Natural Resource Management and Policy 34,
DOI 10.1007/978-1-4419-0658-8_10,

States or internationally, agricultural research conducted in other countries, or nonagricultural research. The reason for excluding these variables is that appropriate data in suitably long time series simply are not available. The omission of these variables could lead to biases in the estimated effects of the included knowledge stocks if the omitted stocks are correlated with the included stocks. However, private research effects are largely embodied in inputs and, to the extent that the benefits are captured through royalties or the equivalent, may not have much impact on measured productivity compared with an equivalent public research achievement provided to farmers for free. In addition, our adjustments for changes in input and output quality will have dealt with some of these impacts. This view is supported to some extent by some recent work by Huffman and Evenson (2006b).[2] Even so, we are conscious of the potentially biasing effects of omitting private agricultural R&D (as well as omitting U.S. nonagricultural research and international research), and we explore this issue in Chapter 12.

Underpinning the general representation in equation (10.1), a number of specification choices were made, allowing us to aggregate the different past research and extension investments into knowledge stocks, as described in Chapter 9. These choices were based on a combination of review of findings from previous work, our own past experience with similar models, and some limited pretesting with our own data in an earlier version of the current work (the data have since been substantially revised and extended from 1991 to 2002). Specifically, we assumed that all 48 states have the same research lag distribution for aggregating past own-state research and extension expenditures into a knowledge stock. The lag distribution is represented by a gamma distribution with a maximum lag of 50 years, the shape of which is defined in turn by the two parameters of the gamma distribution, λ and δ ($0 \leq \lambda < 1$, $0 \leq \delta < 1$). The same lag distribution applies to federal intramural USDA research. This lag distribution allows for positive contributions to the current stock from up to 50 years of past expenditures on research and extension, but particular values of λ and δ can imply a much shorter effective maximum lag because the tail of the distribution can represent a very small portion of the overall density.

Further, it is assumed that the spillover knowledge stock can be constructed for each state as a weighted sum of all of the other 47 own-state knowledge

---

2 Most studies of the effects of public agricultural research on productivity have not incorporated an explicit measure of private research. In a significant and rare exception, Huffman and Evenson (2006b) attempted to account for private research effects in an analysis using U.S. state-level data (see, also, Huffman and Evenson 1993 and 2006a). In the absence of suitably long time series of private research expenditures, they used state-specific production weights applied to four classes of commodity-specific patent data, to define state-specific annual flows of private research outputs, which they aggregated into state-specific stocks by applying trapezoidal lag weights over a 19-year period and summing. The resulting measure of "private agricultural research capital" did not make a statistically significant contribution to either of the productivity models that Huffman and Evenson (2006b) reported.

stocks and the USDA intramural knowledge stock, where the weights are based on indexes of agroecological similarity, ω_{ij} for states i and j, computed using data on the agricultural output mix. The state-specific estimates of own-state and spillover knowledge stocks are thus quantified by combining (a) the matrix of spillover coefficients, ω_{ij}, with (b) a pair of gamma distribution parameters, λ and δ, defining the research lag structure, and (c) data on past research and extension expenditures.

A first step towards econometric estimation is to choose a functional form for the model. A natural candidate is a linear model. Assuming a linear form for equation (10.1), replacing Z with PRC (a state-specific pasture and range condition index, representing relevant weather variation, as described in Chapter 9), and appending a residual, yields:

$$(10.2a)\quad MFP_{i,t} = \beta_i + \beta_K SK_{i,t} + \beta_S SS_{i,t} + \beta_Z PRC_{i,t} + e_{i,t}.$$

Alternatively, assuming a model that is linear in logarithms implies:

$$(10.2b)\quad \ln MFP_{i,t} = \eta_i + \eta_K \ln SK_{i,t} + \eta_S \ln SS_{i,t} + \eta_Z \ln PRC_{i,t} + e_{i,t}.$$

In this specification, the coefficients are elasticities rather than multipliers of MFP with respect to the knowledge stocks. In either case this model corresponds to a fixed-effects structure in which state-specific intercepts (β_i or η_i) are included, and the changes in productivity with respect to the various knowledge stocks, and the marginal impact of the weather index, are equal across the states.[3]

We could substitute into equation (10.2a) or equation (10.2b) the expressions from Chapter 9 defining the knowledge stock variables as functions of the lagged research and extension variables, spillover coefficients, and the lag weights as a function of the gamma distribution parameters λ and δ—equations (9.6), (9.10), and (9.11).[4] In principle it would be possible to estimate this model using nonlinear regression methods but, after some limited experimentation we concluded it would be difficult to do so in practice because the models generally failed to converge.

We opted instead to use a type of grid-search procedure, in which we assigned a range of alternative values for the lag distribution parameters (λ and

3 It is a restricted case of a more-general model in which the slopes as well as the intercepts are allowed to vary across states. We established early in this project that we would not attempt to estimate the model with the full set of state-specific slope and intercept dummies. Doing so would be likely to result in implausible estimates for at least some states and a more parsimonious specification is generally preferable.

4 The result would be an equation expressing productivity in each state as a linear function of a large number of spending variables (representing up to 50 lagged research and extension expenditures in 48 states and by the USDA). The coefficients on the spending variables would be complicated nonlinear functions of the underlying parameters: λ and δ, β_K and β_S, and 1,152 ω_{ij} parameters.

δ), then constructed the knowledge stock variables using these parameters along with the expenditures on research and extension and the spillover coefficients (ω_{ij}), and then estimated the model using these constructed stocks.[5] By repeating this procedure using different values for λ and δ, we were able to search for the values of these parameters that, jointly with the estimated values for the other parameters (β_i, β_K, β_S, and β_Z or η_i, η_K, η_S, and η_Z), would best fit the data. Combining the following eight possible values for both λ and δ (0.60, 0.65, 0.70, 0.75, 0.80, 0.85, 0.90, 0.95), a fixed maximum lag (50 years in most cases), and no gestation lag, yields a total of 64 possible combinations, for which the implied distribution shapes are plotted in Figure 9-2. A very wide range of shapes and effective lag lengths are encompassed by the range of parameter values tried. We initially thought we might conduct a further search over a finer grid, but upon review of our econometric results with the 64 lag distributions, we concluded that it would not be informative to do so because the top-ranked models were not meaningfully different.

More formally, the estimation procedure included the following steps:

1. Choose a pair of values for λ and δ corresponding to one of the 64 possible combinations given the set of eight possible values for each.

2. Compute the gamma distribution weights given the selected values for λ and δ, a given fixed maximum lag (50 years in most cases), and no gestation lag (see equation 9.9).

3. Construct own-state knowledge stocks (see equation 9.10) for the years 1949–2002, for each of the 48 states, using the lag weights from step 2 combined with the own-state research and extension expenditures for the previous 50 years; similarly for the USDA intramural research stocks applying the same lag weights to USDA intramural research expenditure.

4. Construct state-specific spillover knowledge stocks (see equation 9.6) for each of the 48 states, as a weighted sum of the own-state knowledge stocks for the other 47 states and USDA intramural research, with each stock weighted by the appropriate spillover coefficient, ω_{ij}, as defined by equation (9.11) and presented in Section 9.3.

5. Estimate the regression model in equation (10.2) using these constructed stocks. Compute and store the implied values for model statistics (sum of squared errors, parameter values and their standard errors and approximate t-values) and transformations such as elasticities.

5 This approach of estimating productivity models with pre-constructed research knowledge stocks is standard in much of the relevant previous work. Our important departure in this context from most of the previous work is to search across the range of possibilities for the lag distribution involved in constructing that stock, and test amongst them, rather than simply impose one.

6. Repeat steps 1-5 until all 64 models, corresponding to the 64 different lag distribution shapes, have been estimated.

7. Compare and evaluate the models in terms of goodness of fit, and the implied values for parameters and so on.

8. Repeat steps 1-7 for alternative model specifications, such as alternative functional forms.[6]

10.2 Base Model Estimates

We estimated the model in equation (10.2), and variations on it, using the procedures described above with annual data on agricultural productivity for the United States, for each of the 48 contiguous U.S. states over the period 1949–2002, and annual data on agricultural research and extension expenditure by the federal and state governments, for the period 1890–2002; all constructed as described in the previous chapters. In these models:

- $MFP_{i,t}$ is a Fisher ideal index (i.e., a discrete approximation to a divisia index) of multi-factor agricultural productivity in state i in year t, constructed as described and documented in Chapter 5 and Appendix II.[7]

- $SK_{i,t}$ is the own-state stock of knowledge in state i in year t from own-state government spending on agricultural research and extension over the previous 50 years, in real terms, constructed as described in Chapter 9 using one of the 64 lag distributions corresponding to a particular pair of parameters for the gamma distribution.

- $SS_{i,t}$ is the state-specific spillover stock of knowledge in state i in year t from federal and other-state government spending on agricultural research and extension over the previous 50 years, in real terms, constructed as described in Chapter 9 using the same lag distribution parameters as for $SK_{i,t}$.

- $PRC_{i,t}$ is a state-specific pasture and rangeland condition index, measured in September for each year. The index is published by the Economics, Statistics, and Market Information System (ESMIS) branch of the USDA.

- $e_{i,t}$ is a residual, assumed to be independent and identically distributed over states and years.

---

6 Using this procedure we estimated more than 2,700 different regressions for comparison.

7 The InSTePP dataset represents a revised and updated version of data published by Acquaye, Alston and Pardey (2003) and originally developed and used by Craig and Pardey (1996a). Pardey et al. (2009a) provide further details on the construction of the data, which are presented and discussed in Chapters 3 through 5.

Simple summary statistics for these variables are presented in Table 10-1. The models were all estimated using various estimation procedures, as described in the next sections, in STATA 9.0.

Lag Structure for Knowledge Stocks

The base model treats state-specific research and extension symmetrically, such that the same lag weights and spillover coefficients apply, as though for each state we have a single fungible R&D variable that includes both research and extension. This model was estimated first using ordinary least squares with state-specific intercepts, which is a "fixed effects" panel data estimator.[8] We tried specifications that were either linear in logarithms or linear in levels of the variables. Appendix Table 10-1 summarizes the results for the linear model (in Panel a) and the logarithmic model (in Panel b). Each of the 64 cells in Panels a and b of Appendix Table 10-1 corresponds to a particular shape for the research lag distribution used to create the knowledge stocks, defined by the values for λ and δ as shown in the table. The shaded cells represent cases where we thought the lag distribution shape was questionable on prior grounds. Each cell includes information on the elasticities of *MFP* with respect to each of the knowledge stocks (computed at every data point and averaged across states and years), the sum of the squared errors (SSE) and the rank of the model in terms of SSE (where 1 refers to the model with smallest SSE and 64 the largest).

In the case of the linear model (Panel a), the highest-ranked model is obtained with values for $\lambda = 0.75$ and $\delta = 0.80$ implying a peak lag weight at year 13; the second-ranked model has $\lambda = 0.80$ and $\delta = 0.75$ implying a peak lag weight at year 12; and so on.[9] In the case of the logarithmic model (Panel b), the highest-ranked model is obtained with values for $\lambda = 0.70$ and $\delta = 0.90$ implying a peak lag weight at year 24; the second-ranked model has $\lambda = 0.65$ and $\delta = 0.90$ implying a peak lag weight at year 20; and so on. Thus the linear and logarithmic models imply different shapes of the lag distributions, and the choice between these models is likely to matter for the findings.

To provide a different perspective on the pattern of results than given by Appendix Table 10-1, Table 10-2 summarizes the main results for the highest-ranked eight linear models (Panel a) and the highest-ranked eight logarithmic models (Panel b), arranged in rank order, highest to lowest from left to right. Among the (linear in levels) models in Panel a, the shape of the lag distribution was fairly similar across the top-ranked models compared with other models that

8 We established that a fixed-effects estimator was preferred to a random-effects estimator using Hausman's (1978) specification test for fixed or random effects. The results of the test are presented along with additional diagnostic tests in Table 10-3.

9 In the linear model, the SSE is shown as 2.39 million for the top five-ranked models, but differences in the SSEs are apparent when we allow for more than two decimal digits, allowing us to rank the models as shown.

Table 10-1 Simple Summary Statistics, Data for the Productivity Model

Symbol	Variable Name	Definition	Value Description	Value
$MFP_{i,t}$	Multi-factor agricultural productivity	Ratio of Fisher index of aggregate output to Fisher index of aggregate input in state *i* and year *t* (see Chapter 5 for details)	Minimum across all years and states	74.7
			Maximum across all years and states	481.8
			Average across all years	
			All states	181.3
			California	176.1
			Minnesota	173.4
			Wyoming	142.2
$SK_{i,t}$	Own-state stock of knowledge	Constructed using 50 years of own-state government spending on agricultural research and extension (in real 2000 dollars) and specification of gamma lag distribution	Preferred lag distribution for linear model ($\lambda = 0.75$, $\delta = 0.80$)	
			Minimum across all years and states	$6.3 million
			Maximum across all years and states	$150.1 million
			Average across all years and states	$44.5 million
			Preferred lag distribution for logarithmic model ($\lambda = 0.70$, $\delta = 0.90$)	
			Minimum across all years and states	$5.0 million
			Maximum across all years and states	$104.8 million
			Average across all years and states	$33.1 million
			(see Tables 9-1 and 9-5 for state- and region-specific average research and extension knowledge stocks)	
$SS_{i,t}$	State-specific spillin stock of knowledge	Constructed using federal and other-state government spending on agricultural research and extension (in real 2000 dollars), specification of lag distribution, and ω_{ij}'s used as weights	Preferred lag distribution for linear model ($\lambda = 0.75$, $\delta = 0.80$)	
			Minimum across all years and states	$279.5 million
			Maximum across all years and states	$3,142.7 million
			Average across all years and states	$1,387.8 million
			Preferred lag distribution for logarithmic model ($\lambda = 0.70$, $\delta = 0.90$)	
			Minimum across all years and states	$548.2 million
			Maximum across all years and states	$1,436.0 million
			Average across all years and states	$1,050.9 million
			(see Table 9-4 for state- and region-specific average spillin knowledge stocks)	
$PRC_{i,t}$	Pasture and rangeland condition index	Measured in September for each year (published by the Economics, Statistics, and Market Information System (ESMIS) branch of the USDA)	Minimum across all years and states	8.0
			Maximum across all years and states	107.0
			Average across all years	
			All states	74.3
			California	73.3
			Minnesota	73.4
			Wyoming	78.0

Sources: Developed by the authors based on information described in Appendix II and Appendix III.

Table 10-2 Summary of Results for the Base Model, Top-Ranked Models

Panel a. Linear model

Model Details	**Model Results**							
Model rank by SSE	1	2	3	4	5	6	7	8
Lag distribution characteristics								
λ	0.75	0.80	0.85	0.65	0.85	0.70	0.80	0.85
δ	0.80	0.75	0.65	0.85	0.70	0.85	0.70	0.60
Peak lag year	13	12	10	12	13	15	9	8
RMSE	30.36	30.36	30.36	30.37	30.39	30.40	30.40	30.41
Elasticities with respect to								
Own-state research (R)	0.06	0.06	0.06	0.06	0.06	0.06	0.06	0.07
Own-state extension (E)	0.06	0.07	0.07	0.06	0.07	0.06	0.07	0.07
Own-state R&E	*0.13*	*0.13*	*0.13*	*0.13*	*0.13*	*0.12*	*0.13*	*0.13*
SAES spillins	0.18	0.18	0.19	0.19	0.17	0.17	0.20	0.20
Intramural spillins	0.17	0.17	0.17	0.17	0.16	0.16	0.17	0.18
Extension spillins	0.19	0.19	0.20	0.20	0.19	0.19	0.20	0.20
All spillins combined	*0.54*	*0.54*	*0.55*	*0.55*	*0.52*	*0.52*	*0.57*	*0.58*

Panel b. Logarithmic model

Model Details	**Model Results**							
Model rank by SSE	1	2	3	4	5	6	7	8
Lag distribution characteristics								
λ	0.70	0.65	0.80	0.75	0.85	0.90	0.60	0.80
δ	0.90	0.90	0.85	0.85	0.80	0.75	0.90	0.80
Peak lag year	24	20	24	19	24	27	17	17
RMSE	22.46	22.52	22.49	22.59	22.52	22.56	22.71	22.68
Elasticities with respect to								
Own-state research (R)	0.15	0.13	0.15	0.13	0.15	0.16	0.12	0.14
Own-state extension (E)	0.18	0.15	0.18	0.16	0.18	0.19	0.13	0.15
Own-state R&E	*0.32*	*0.28*	*0.33*	*0.29*	*0.33*	*0.35*	*0.25*	*0.29*
SAES spillins	0.07	0.09	0.07	0.10	0.07	0.06	0.12	0.10
Intramural spillins	0.07	0.10	0.07	0.10	0.07	0.06	0.11	0.10
Extension spillins	0.09	0.11	0.08	0.11	0.08	0.07	0.13	0.12
All spillins combined	*0.24*	*0.31*	*0.22*	*0.30*	*0.22*	*0.19*	*0.36*	*0.31*

Sources: Developed by the authors.

Notes: SSE refers to the goodness of fit of the model. RMSE refers to the root mean square prediction error for *MFP* in levels from the model, whether it was estimated in logarithms, first differenced, or not. This statistic was computed for every model using the predicted values of the dependent variable transformed as necessary to make un-differenced predictions of *MFP* in levels. The elasticities refer to elasticities of *MFP* with respect to the own- and spillover-research knowledge stocks.

did not fit as well (see Figure 9-2). The peak lag varied somewhat but the implied values for the elasticities of *MFP* with respect to the various knowledge stocks were very similar across the eight models. A similar story holds for the (linear in logarithms) models in Panel b. Specifically, while the peak lag varied somewhat, the implied values for the elasticities of *MFP* with respect to the various knowledge stocks and other model statistics were very similar across the eight models.

From this perspective, the results appear to be robust. That is, given the choice of either the linear or logarithmic functional form, and other specification choices, the results appear to be insensitive to variations in the gamma distribution parameters. However, the choice of functional form does appear to significantly influence the results. We will return to this question later.

Alternative Estimators

The standard specification issues related to functional form, simultaneous equations, omitted variables, and measurement errors may be present in any econometric model, but in panel-data models additional issues also arise related to the disturbance terms between different panels (i.e., states). The classical assumption is that the error terms are independent and identically distributed across states and time; however, the variance of the errors terms may not be constant within panels (differ over time for a given state), between panels (differ in cross-section for a given year), or both. The disturbances may be independent or contemporaneously correlated between panels, and may be serially correlated, with either a common autocorrelation coefficient for all panels, or panel-specific autocorrelation coefficients. The standard specification errors as well as the panel data issues can have important implications for the consistency and the efficiency of the parameter estimates.

All of the results reported in Appendix Table 10-1 and Table 10-2 were obtained using a fixed effects (FE) model applied to the panel data under the assumption that the residuals were i.i.d. random variables—independent and identically distributed across states and years. Some diagnostic testing indicated that this assumption is violated, as is likely given the size of our panel data set. For each functional form, we calculated a modified Wald statistic for group-wise heteroskedasticity in the residuals of a fixed-effects regression model, indicating rejection of the hypothesis of homoskedastic residuals, as well as a Breusch-Pagan (1980) statistic for independence of the disturbances, which indicated rejection of the hypothesis of independence.[10] We also tested for the presence of first-order serial correlation in the residuals of a linear panel data model using a test devised by Wooldridge (2002), which indicated rejection of the hypothesis of no first-order serial correlation. The results of these tests, as well as Hausman's specification test for random or fixed-effects, are summarized in Table 10-3. The results for the preferred linear model are in Panel a, and the results for the preferred logarithmic model are in Panel b.

These findings led to the estimation of two varieties of panel data estimators, a feasible generalized least squares (FGLS) estimator and a panel corrected

10 Greene (2000, pp. 598 and 601) provides details of these testing procedures.

Table 10-3 Diagnostic Tests for Panel Data Estimators

Panel a. Linear model (λ = 0.75, δ = 0.80)

Test	Distribution	Null Hypothesis	Test Statistic	P-Value
Modified Wald	$\chi^2(48)$	$\sigma_i^2 = \sigma_j^2 \ \forall \ i, j$	5,692	0.0000
Breusch-Pagan Lagrange-Multiplier	$\chi^2(1,128)$	$\text{cov}[e_{it}, e_{jt}] = 0 \ \forall \ i, j, t$ and $i \neq j$	18,922	0.0000
Wooldridge	F(1,47)	No first-order autocorrelation ($\rho = 0$)	13.42	0.0006
Hausman	$\chi^2(3)$	Difference in coefficients is not systematic	7,137	0.0000

Panel b. Logarithmic model (λ = 0.70, δ = 0.90)

Test	Distribution	Null Hypothesis	Test Statistic	P-Value
Modified Wald	$\chi^2(48)$	$\sigma_i^2 = \sigma_j^2 \ \forall \ i, j$	965.27	0.0000
Breusch-Pagan Lagrange-Multiplier	$\chi^2(1,128)$	$\text{cov}[e_{it}, e_{jt}] = 0 \ \forall \ i, j, t$ and $i \neq j$	9,838	0.0000
Wooldridge	F(1,47)	No first-order autocorrelation ($\rho = 0$)	47.79	0.0000
Hausman	$\chi^2(3)$	Difference in coefficients is not systematic	94.23	0.0000

Sources: Developed by the authors.

Notes: i and j denote different states, t denotes year. σ^2 = residual variance, e = residual, and ρ = autocorrelation coefficient.

standard errors (PCSE) estimator.[11] Additionally, we tried three alternative structures for the error terms: the first assumes the error terms are heteroskedastic (unequal error variances among different states) but are uncorrelated; the second assumes the error terms are heteroskedastic and correlated across states but serially uncorrelated; the third assumes the error terms are heteroskedastic and correlated across states, with a common first-order autoregressive (AR1) disturbance term. That is, letting i and j denote different states and t denote the year, the three alternative sets of assumptions are:

(a) $\sigma_i^2 \neq \sigma_j^2$ but $\text{cov}\left[e_{it}, e_{jt}\right] = 0$ and $\text{cov}\left[e_{it}, e_{i,t-1}\right] = 0$;

11 The PCSE estimator is OLS with a correction for standard errors, $\hat{\beta}_{PCSE} = \left(X'X\right)^{-1} X'Y$, $\text{Var}\left(\hat{\beta}_{PCSE}\right) = \left(X'X\right)^{-1} X'\hat{\Omega}^{-1}X\left(X'X\right)^{-1}$, $\hat{\Omega} = \hat{\Sigma} \otimes I_{T\times T}$, and $\hat{\Sigma} = \hat{\varepsilon}_i'\hat{\varepsilon}_j / T$, where $\hat{\varepsilon}_i$ and $\hat{\varepsilon}_j$ are vectors of the OLS residuals for state i and state j. If an autocorrelation model is estimated, a Prais-Winston procedure is used, and therefore the coefficient estimates (as well as the standard errors) differ slightly from those obtained from OLS. The FGLS estimator is: $\hat{\beta}_{FGLS} = \left(X'\hat{\Omega}^{-1}X\right)^{-1} X'\hat{\Omega}^{-1}Y$, $\text{Var}\left(\hat{\beta}_{FGLS}\right) = \left(X'\hat{\Omega}^{-1}X\right)^{-1}$, $\hat{\Omega} = \hat{\Sigma} \otimes I_{T\times T}$, and $\hat{\Sigma} = \hat{\varepsilon}_i'\hat{\varepsilon}_j / T$, where $\hat{\varepsilon}_i$ and $\hat{\varepsilon}_j$ are the OLS residuals for state i and state j.

(b) $\sigma_i^2 \neq \sigma_j^2$ and $\text{cov}\left[e_{it}, e_{jt}\right] \neq 0$ but $\text{cov}\left[e_{it}, e_{i,t-1}\right] = 0$; and

(c) $\sigma_i^2 \neq \sigma_j^2$ and $\text{cov}\left[e_{it}, e_{jt}\right] \neq 0$ and $\text{cov}\left[e_{it}, e_{i,t-1}\right] \neq 0$.

The regression results from the different estimation procedures are presented in Table 10-4 where, once again, Panel a refers to variations of the top-ranked linear model and Panel b refers to variations of the top-ranked logarithmic model. The first column of Table 10-4 provides the results from the preferred model as presented in the first column of Table 10-2 (i.e., based on Ordinary Least Squares (OLS) estimation of equation 10.2 assuming fixed effects), but with additional details. The other columns in Table 10-4 represent the results from the application of alternative estimation procedures to the same model for comparison, holding the structure of the lag distribution constant.[12] We compare the results from fixed effects (FE) estimators with those from applying random effects (RE), feasible generalized least squares (FGLS), and panel corrected standard errors (PCSE) estimators. We include state-specific intercept terms in each of the FGLS and PCSE models to facilitate comparisons with the FE model. Table 10-4 includes, for each estimation procedure, the estimated coefficients of *MFP* with respect to the various knowledge stocks, and the associated *t*-statistics, elasticities, and R^2 when applicable.

The primary reason for presenting results from these different estimation procedures was to demonstrate that we obtained very similar estimates, providing evidence that our choice of our model specification and estimation procedure are not driving the results. The features of the structure of the error terms revealed by our diagnostic testing, such as group-wise heteroskedasticity, contemporaneous correlation among the states, and first-order autocorrelation in the error terms had little impact on the resulting estimates. In other words, the various constraints that are implied by our preferred FE model compared to a FGLS or PCSE model come at a small statistical 'price.' Group-wise heteroskedasticity, contemporaneous correlation, and first-order autocorrelation primarily affect the efficiency of estimates, which is not a concern given the large sample size and the asymptotic properties of the different estimators. Next, we examine the possibly more serious issue of unit roots and the potential for spurious regression results.

12 We would be interested to know whether applying our grid search procedure with the alternative specifications would yield the same lag specification; however, in the FGLS models the total sum of squares cannot be neatly decomposed into an explained sum of squares and a residual sum of squares, so we were unable to use our criterion of minimum SSE for model selection. We did apply the RE estimator to each of the 64 lag specifications, and the one yielding the smallest root mean square error with RE estimation was the one that minimized the SSE in the FE specification. A similar model selection criterion was not available for the FGLS estimation procedures.

Table 10-4 Comparison of Alternative Estimators for the Base Model

Panel a. Linear model ($\lambda = 0.75$, $\delta = 0.80$, Peak lag year = 13)

	Estimation Procedure							
Model Details	**FE**	**RE**	**PCSE Het**	**PCSE Het/CC**	**PCSE Het/CC/ AR1**	**FGLS Het**	**FGLS Het/CC**	**FGLS Het/CC/ AR1**
Parameter Estimates								
Growing Conditions								
Coefficient ($\hat{\beta}_Z$)	0.2709	0.2660	0.2709	0.2709	0.2918	0.2651	0.2557	0.2760
Standard Error	0.0432	0.0437	0.0444	0.0637	0.0334	0.0293	0.0044	0.0041
Elasticity	*0.1111*	*0.1090*	*0.1111*	*0.1111*	*0.1201*	*0.1087*	*0.1048*	*0.1136*
Own-State R&D								
Coefficient ($\hat{\beta}_K$)	0.5110	0.4926	0.5110	0.5110	0.4990	0.3951	0.5098	0.4933
Standard Error	0.0397	0.0390	0.0428	0.0215	0.0753	0.0309	0.0028	0.0103
Elasticity	*0.1254*	*0.1209*	*0.1254*	*0.1254*	*0.1229*	*0.0970*	*0.1251*	*0.1215*
Spillover R&D								
Coefficient ($\hat{\beta}_S$)	0.0692	0.0693	0.0692	0.0692	0.0695	0.0642	0.0692	0.0691
Standard Error	0.0017	0.0017	0.0015	0.0014	0.0048	0.0011	0.0003	0.0013
Elasticity	*0.5301*	*0.5308*	*0.5301*	*0.5301*	*0.5340*	*0.4920*	*0.5298*	*0.5309*
R^2	0.7343	0.7343	0.7972	0.7972	0.4657			

Panel b. Logarithmic model ($\lambda = 0.70$, $\delta = 0.90$, peak lag year = 24)

	Estimation Procedure							
Model Details	**FE**	**RE**	**PCSE Het**	**PCSE Het/CC**	**PCSE Het/CC/ AR1**	**FGLS Het**	**FGLS Het/CC**	**FGLS Het/CC/ AR1**
Parameter estimates								
Growing conditions								
Coefficient ($\hat{\eta}_Z$)	0.1106	0.1091	0.1106	0.1106	0.1035	0.1057	0.1033	0.0967
Standard error	0.0098	0.0100	0.0101	0.0158	0.0098	0.0085	0.0021	0.0020
Elasticity	*0.1106*	*0.1091*	*0.1106*	*0.1106*	*0.1035*	*0.1057*	*0.1033*	*0.0967*
Own-state R&D								
Coefficient ($\hat{\eta}_K$)	0.3223	0.2484	0.3223	0.3223	0.3136	0.3075	0.3211	0.3110
Standard error	0.0173	0.0156	0.0170	0.0206	0.0406	0.0153	0.0018	0.0053
Elasticity	*0.3223*	*0.2484*	*0.3223*	*0.3223*	*0.3136*	*0.3075*	*0.3211*	*0.3110*
Spillover R&D								
Coefficient ($\hat{\eta}_S$)	0.2350	0.3054	0.2350	0.2350	0.2361	0.2455	0.2363	0.2410
Standard error	0.0173	0.0157	0.0170	0.0209	0.0397	0.0153	0.0037	0.0101
Elasticity	*0.2350*	*0.3054*	*0.2350*	*0.2350*	*0.2361*	*0.2455*	*0.2363*	*0.2410*
R^2	0.8761	0.8752	0.8999	0.8999	0.9256			

Sources: Developed by the authors.

Notes: FE denotes fixed-effects, RE denotes random effects, PCSE denotes ordinary least squares with panel corrected standard errors, and FGLS denotes feasible generalized least squares estimates. Each estimation procedure includes state-level indicator variables except for the RE model.

"Het" corrects for group-wise heteroskedasticity; "Het/CC" corrects for group-wise heteroskedasticity and contemporaneous correlation of residuals; "Het/CC/AR1" corrects for group-wise heteroskedasticity, contemporaneous correlation, and first-order autocorrelation of residuals.

All coefficient estimates are statistically significantly different from zero at the 1 percent level of significance.

The elasticities refer to elasticities of *MFP* with respect to the own-state and spillover R&D knowledge stocks, where the own-state R&D stock variable combines own-state research and extension, and the state-specific spillover variable is based on the R&D stock combining research and extension. Subsequent tables refer to the research stock, excluding extension, and thus the elasticities are different.

Unit Roots—First-Difference Models

Measures of productivity in U.S. agriculture are typically non-stationary. We performed augmented Dickey-Fuller tests for the presence of a unit root in each of the state-specific measures of *MFP* both in natural units and in logarithms, and in each state we could not reject the null hypothesis of a unit root. When we applied the same tests to the first differences of the state-specific *MFP* series, the tests indicated that the hypothesis of a unit root could be rejected, meaning the series are integrated of order one.[13] This finding suggests the potential for spurious regression results if standard estimation procedures are applied to the base model. To explore this possibility, we estimated the base model in first-difference form (i.e., the same model but without an intercept and with all the variables entering as first-differences) for all 64 lag distribution shapes and for both the linear model and the logarithmic model.[14]

In the case of the linear model, the resulting estimates of the elasticities of productivity with respect to own-state research and spillover research were generally very similar between the base model in levels of variables and its first-difference counterpart for any given definition of the research lag distribution. However, the ranking of models according to lag distribution shapes was different when the model was estimated in first-difference form. The effects of first-differencing the data were somewhat more pronounced for the model estimated in logarithms.

Panel a of Table 10-5 compares the elasticities and standard errors from the linear model estimated in levels (the "linear model") and first-differences (the "first-difference model"). The upper half of Panel a includes the results for the six top-ranked lag distribution models (by SSE) estimated using the un-differenced data, as reported in Table 10-2 (Panel a) and the corresponding results from estimating each of the same models in first-difference form. It can be seen that the corresponding elasticity estimates are virtually identical between the two versions (whether differenced or not) for a given research lag distribution. The lower half of Panel a mirrors the upper half, except that the top-ranked lag distribution models were found by estimating the model in first-difference form, and then we included the corresponding results from estimating each of the same models in levels. Importantly, the use of differenced data resulted in a different ranking of the lag distribution models, but the implied lag distribution shapes were generally similar for the top few ranked models. The peak lags tended to be earlier for the first-difference model (8–10 years for the top three models) than for the base model estimated with un-differenced data (10–13 years) but the estimated elasticities fell within a narrow range across all of the sets reported in Panel a of

13 The tests were performed for each state.

14 Appendix Table 10-2 includes results for the full set of 64 models estimated using the first-differenced data, for comparison with Appendix Table 10-1.

Table 10-5 Effects of First Differencing on Base Model Results

Panel a. Linear model

Model Details	**Model Results**					
Models ordered by linear model rankings						
Model rankings						
Linear model rank	1	2	3	4	5	6
Difference model rank	8	5	2	16	7	12
Lag distribution parameters						
λ	0.75	0.80	0.85	0.65	0.85	0.70
δ	0.80	0.75	0.65	0.85	0.70	0.85
Peak lag year	13	12	10	12	13	15
Root mean squared error (RMSE)						
Linear model	30.36	30.36	30.36	30.37	30.39	30.40
Difference model	33.98	33.98	33.99	34.00	34.04	34.07
Implied elasticities						
Linear model						
Own research	0.13	0.13	0.13	0.13	0.13	0.12
Spillover research	0.54	0.54	0.55	0.55	0.52	0.52
Difference model						
Own research	0.11	0.12	0.12	0.11	0.11	0.10
Spillover research	0.54	0.54	0.56	0.56	0.52	0.52
Models ordered by first-difference model rankings						
Model rankings						
Difference model rank	1	2	3	4	5	6
Linear model rank	8	3	7	16	2	24
Lag distribution parameters						
λ	0.85	0.85	0.80	0.80	0.80	0.80
δ	0.60	0.65	0.70	0.65	0.75	0.60
Peak lag year	8	10	9	7	12	6
Root mean squared error (RMSE)						
Difference model	34.08	33.99	34.07	34.32	33.98	34.61
Linear model	30.41	30.36	30.40	30.54	30.36	30.72
Implied elasticities						
Difference model						
Own research	0.13	0.12	0.13	0.14	0.12	0.15
Spillover research	0.59	0.56	0.58	0.62	0.54	0.64
Linear model						
Own research	0.13	0.13	0.13	0.14	0.13	0.14
Spillover research	0.58	0.55	0.57	0.60	0.54	0.62

(continued)

Table 10-5: 0.10 to 0.15 for the elasticity of *MFP* with respect to the own-state knowledge stock, 0.52 to 0.64 for the elasticity of *MFP* with respect to the state-specific spillover knowledge stock.

Panel b of Table 10-5 compares the elasticities and standard errors from the model estimated in logarithms of the variables (the "logarithmic model") and first-differences of logarithms (the "growth model"). The upper half of Panel

Table 10-5 (continued)

Panel b. Logarithmic model

Model Details	**Model Results**					
Models ordered by logarithmic model rankings						
Model rankings						
Logarithmic model rank	1	2	3	4	5	6
Growth model rank	4	1	11	3	14	19
Lag distribution parameters						
λ	0.70	0.65	0.80	0.75	0.85	0.90
δ	0.90	0.90	0.85	0.85	0.80	0.75
Peak lag year	24	20	24	19	24	27
Root mean squared error (RMSE)						
Logarithmic model	22.46	22.52	22.49	22.59	22.52	22.56
Growth model	27.68	27.70	27.65	27.70	27.69	27.82
Implied elasticities						
Logarithmic model						
Own research	0.32	0.28	0.33	0.29	0.33	0.35
Spillover research	0.24	0.31	0.22	0.30	0.22	0.19
Growth model						
Own research	0.24	0.15	0.24	0.15	0.22	0.24
Spillover research	0.28	0.43	0.29	0.44	0.31	0.27
Models ordered by growth model rankings						
Model rankings						
Growth model rank	1	2	3	4	5	6
Logarithmic model rank	2	7	4	1	8	10
Lag distribution parameters						
λ	0.65	0.60	0.75	0.70	0.80	0.85
δ	0.90	0.90	0.85	0.90	0.80	0.75
Peak lag year	20	17	19	24	17	17
Root mean squared error (RMSE)						
Growth model	27.70	27.75	27.70	27.68	27.76	27.77
Logarithmic model	22.52	22.71	22.59	22.46	22.68	22.67
Implied elasticities						
Growth model						
Own research	0.15	0.09	0.15	0.24	0.14	0.16
Spillover research	0.43	0.53	0.44	0.28	0.46	0.42
Logarithmic model						
Own research	0.28	0.25	0.29	0.32	0.29	0.31
Spillover research	0.31	0.36	0.30	0.24	0.31	0.29

Sources: Developed by the authors.

Notes: See notes to Table 10-2. "Growth model" refers to the model using first-differenced logarithms of the variables.

b includes the results for the six top-ranked lag distribution models (by SSE) estimated using the un-differenced data, as reported in Table 10-2 (Panel b), and the corresponding results from estimating each of the same models in first-difference form. The lower half of Panel b mirrors the upper half, except that the top-ranked lag distribution models were found by estimating the logarithmic model in first-difference or growth-rate form, and then we included the corresponding results from estimating each of the same models in logarithms. Again, the use of differenced data resulted in a different ranking of the lag distribution models, but the implied lag distributions for the few top-ranked models were generally of similar shapes. The peak lags tended to be earlier for the growth rate model (17–20 years for the top three models) than for the logarithmic model (20–24 years). Compared with the counterparts for the linear model in Panel a, in the logarithmic model the elasticities were more sensitive to first-differencing the data, and the range of estimated elasticities across all of the sets reported in Panel b of Table 10-5 was larger: 0.09 to 0.35 for the elasticity of *MFP* with respect to the own-state knowledge stock, 0.19 to 0.53 for the elasticity of *MFP* with respect to the state-specific spillover knowledge stock. This reflects mainly variation in the elasticities with changes in the lag distribution for the growth model; the elasticities for the logarithmic model were essentially constant across all the lag distribution shapes shown in Panel b of Table 10-5.

The implications of these differences for benefit-cost ratios are explored in Chapter 11 and Chapter 12. However, the fact that in most instances first-differencing resulted in very similar estimates of elasticities for a given lag distribution shape, and quite similar findings with respect to the shape of the lag distribution (albeit different specific rankings of particular distributions) gives us some confidence in using the results from the un-differenced model, which has some advantages for other purposes, including computation of benefit-cost ratios. In other words, these results support the view that the unit root problem is not causing spurious results in the base model estimated with the data in levels.

10.3 Sensitivity of Results to Model Variations

As mentioned at the beginning of this chapter, the base model entails a host of assumptions, many of which we are treating as maintained hypotheses for much if not all of what we do here. But some of these assumptions can be varied at reasonable cost, and it is of interest to examine the sensitivity of results to some key choices. In this section we report results from alternative assumptions about (a) functional form for the model, (b) the shape of the knowledge stock for extension (whether it is identical to that for research) and whether the same spillover weights should be applied to extension as for research, and (c) the maximum lag length (whether it could be shorter than 50 years).

Functional Form—Logarithmic Model

In models of effects of research on productivity, the most common specification has been a "double-log" model in which the variables enter in logarithms rather than natural units. To check the role, if any, of functional form in influencing the results, we estimated the base model with the variables in both levels and logarithms. The resulting estimates of the elasticities of productivity with respect to own-state research and spillover research were generally quite different between the base model in levels of variables and its logarithmic counterpart for any given definition of the research lag distribution, as was the ranking of models according to lag distribution shapes.

Table 10-6 compares the elasticities and other aspects between the linear model and the logarithmic model. Panel a of Table 10-6 includes the results for the six top-ranked lag distribution models (by SSE) estimated using the data in natural units, as reported in Table 10-2. It also includes the corresponding results from estimating each of the same models in logarithms. Panel b of Table 10-6 mirrors Panel a, except that the top-ranked lag distribution models were found by estimating the model in logarithms, and then we included the corresponding results from estimating each of the same models in levels.

The use of logarithms resulted in a very different ranking of the lag distribution models. The peak lags were much later for the logarithmic model (20-24 years for the top three models) than for the linear model (10-13 years). The estimated elasticities were generally fairly constant across lag distribution shapes for either the linear model or logarithmic model, but quite different between the linear model and the logarithmic model for any given lag distribution shape. For the linear model, across all of the results reported in Table 10-6 the range of elasticities was 0.12 to 0.13 for the elasticity of *MFP* with respect to the own-state knowledge stock; 0.43 to 0.55 for the elasticity of *MFP* with respect to the spillover knowledge stock. For the logarithmic model the elasticity with respect to the own-state knowledge stock was much larger, generally, and the elasticity with respect to the spillover knowledge stock was somewhat smaller, generally: 0.24 to 0.35 for the elasticity of *MFP* with respect to the own-state knowledge stock; 0.19 to 0.41 for the elasticity of *MFP* with respect to the spillover knowledge stock. These comparisons indicate that the choice of functional form may have significant implications for the findings with respect to the benefits from research, and those aspects are explored in detail in later chapters.

Like some previous tables, Table 10-6 includes an estimate of the root mean squared (prediction) error (RMSE) for *MFP* from each model. The RMSE was calculated by using the estimated model to predict the values of *MFP* in levels (which required transformations of predictions from models estimated in logarithms or differences) and calculating the square root of the average squared prediction errors across all the states and years of the sample data. As shown in Table 10-6, in every instance the RMSE for the logarithmic model was smaller than the RMSE for the corresponding linear model.[15] These statistics would support

15 Recall, referring back to Table 10-5, in every instance the RMSE for the model using un-differenced data was smaller than the RMSE for the corresponding first-difference model.

Table 10-6 Effects of Functional Form on Base Model Results

Panel a. Estimates ordered by linear model rankings

Model Details	Model Results					
Model rankings						
Linear model rank	1	2	3	4	5	6
Logarithmic model rank	21	22	23	24	18	15
Lag distribution parameters						
λ	0.75	0.80	0.85	0.65	0.85	0.70
δ	0.80	0.75	0.65	0.85	0.70	0.85
Peak lag year	13	12	10	12	13	15
Root mean squared error (RMSE)						
Linear model	30.36	30.36	30.36	30.37	30.39	30.40
Logarithmic model	23.05	23.05	23.21	23.27	22.92	22.85
Implied elasticities						
Linear model						
Own research	0.13	0.13	0.13	0.13	0.13	0.12
Spillover research	0.54	0.54	0.55	0.55	0.52	0.52
Logarithmic model						
Own research	0.26	0.27	0.28	0.24	0.29	0.26
Spillover research	0.38	0.37	0.37	0.41	0.34	0.37

Panel b. Estimates ordered by logarithmic model rankings

Model Details	Model Results					
Model rankings						
Logarithmic model rank	1	2	3	4	5	6
Linear model rank	32	21	30	18	26	29
Lag distribution parameters						
λ	0.70	0.65	0.80	0.75	0.85	0.90
δ	0.90	0.90	0.85	0.85	0.80	0.75
Peak lag year	24	20	24	19	24	27
Root mean squared error (RMSE)						
Logarithmic model	22.46	22.52	22.49	22.59	22.52	22.56
Linear model	31.00	30.68	30.95	30.60	30.86	30.95
Implied elasticities						
Logarithmic model						
Own research	0.32	0.28	0.33	0.29	0.33	0.35
Spillover research	0.24	0.31	0.22	0.30	0.22	0.19
Linear model						
Own research	0.12	0.12	0.12	0.12	0.12	0.12
Spillover research	0.43	0.47	0.43	0.48	0.44	0.43

Sources: Developed by the authors.

Notes: See notes to Table 10-2.

the use of the estimates from the logarithmic model rather than linear model, but such findings to this point are conditional on the other aspects of the specification of the base model.

Extension Lag Distribution and Extension Spillovers

The base model treats extension and research symmetrically, in terms of the overall lag length and shape, and the interstate spillover effects. This treatment is equivalent to adding annual state-specific research and extension expenditures together into a single R&D expenditure series before computing own-state and spillover knowledge stocks. To examine the implications of this structure, we estimated the equivalent model but with variations in the assumptions about the extension lag structure and extension spillovers. First, we tried a model holding the extension lag structure the same as the research lag structure, but assuming only the research knowledge stock (and not the extension knowledge stock) had spillover effects on other states (so extension was left out of the spillover knowledge stocks). Second, we tried a model with an extension lag structure taken from Huffman and Evenson (1993 and 2006a)—a type of geometric lag distribution for extension, including a total of four extension expenditures with lag weights of 0.50, 0.25, 0.125, and 0.125 for lags of 0 to 3 years—but applying the gamma lag distribution to research and allowing spillovers from both research and extension knowledge stocks.

Table 10-7 compares the elasticities and RMSEs from the base model with extension spillovers and the alternative model without extension spillovers. Panel a refers to the linear model and Panel b refers to the logarithmic model. In each panel of Table 10-7, the upper half includes the results for the six top-ranked lag distribution models (by SSE) estimated using the base model specification, and the corresponding results from estimating each of the same models without extension spillovers. The lower half mirrors the upper half, except that the top-ranked lag distribution models were found by estimating the model without extension spillovers, and then we included the corresponding results from estimating each of the same models with extension spillovers. For a given logarithmic or linear functional form, the lag distribution models were ranked almost identically between the models with and without extension spillovers, and the implied elasticities were very similar both across specifications and across lag distributions for a given specification—especially in the case of the linear model.

Across all of the sets reported in Table 10-7 for the linear model (Panel a) the elasticity of *MFP* with respect to the own-state knowledge stock ranged from 0.12 to 0.13; the elasticity of *MFP* with respect to the spillover knowledge stock ranged from 0.46 to 0.50 for the model without extension spillovers compared with a slightly higher range of 0.52 to 0.55 for the base model, with extension spillovers. For the logarithmic model (Panel b) the elasticity of *MFP* with respect to the own-state knowledge stock ranged from 0.25 to 0.30 for the model without extension spillovers compared with a slightly higher range of 0.28 to 0.35 for the base model with extension spillovers; the elasticity of *MFP* with respect to the spillover knowledge stock ranged from 0.18 to 0.41 for the model without

Table 10-7 Effects of Alternative Treatment of Interstate Extension Spillovers

Panel a. Linear model

Model Details	**Model Results**					
Estimates ranked by model with extension spillovers						
Model rankings						
With spillovers model rank	1	2	3	4	5	6
No spillovers model rank	1	2	3	5	6	4
Lag distribution parameters						
λ	0.75	0.80	0.85	0.65	0.85	0.70
δ	0.80	0.75	0.65	0.85	0.70	0.85
Peak lag year	13	12	10	12	13	15
Root mean squared error (RMSE)						
With spillovers model	30.36	30.36	30.36	30.37	30.39	30.40
No spillovers model	30.55	30.55	30.56	30.58	30.59	30.57
Implied elasticities						
With spillovers model						
Own research	0.13	0.13	0.13	0.13	0.13	0.12
Spillover research	0.54	0.54	0.55	0.55	0.52	0.52
No spillovers model						
Own research	0.13	0.13	0.13	0.13	0.13	0.13
Spillover research	0.48	0.48	0.50	0.49	0.47	0.46
Estimates ranked by model without extension spillovers						
Model rankings						
No spillovers model rank	1	2	3	4	5	6
With spillovers model rank	1	2	3	6	4	5
Lag distribution parameters						
λ	0.75	0.80	0.85	0.70	0.65	0.85
δ	0.80	0.75	0.65	0.85	0.85	0.70
Peak lag year	13	12	10	15	12	13
Root mean squared error (RMSE)						
No spillovers model	30.55	30.55	30.56	30.57	30.58	30.59
With spillovers model	30.36	30.36	30.36	30.40	30.37	30.39
Implied elasticities						
No spillovers model						
Own research	0.13	0.13	0.13	0.13	0.13	0.13
Spillover research	0.48	0.48	0.50	0.46	0.49	0.47
With spillovers model						
Own research	0.13	0.13	0.13	0.12	0.13	0.13
Spillover research	0.54	0.54	0.55	0.52	0.55	0.52

(continued)

extension spillovers compared with a slightly narrower range of 0.19 to 0.31 for the base model, with extension spillovers.

In short, the estimation results were quite insensitive to the treatment of extension spillovers, given the maintained hypothesis that the extension and research lag distribution shapes were identical. Looking at the RMSEs, for the linear model in every instance the model with extension spillovers slightly outper-

Table 10-7 (continued)

Panel b. Logarithmic model

Model Details	**Model Results**					
Estimates ranked by model with extension spillovers						
Model rankings						
With spillovers model rank	1	2	3	4	5	6
No spillovers model rank	1	2	3	5	4	6
Lag distribution parameters						
λ	0.70	0.65	0.80	0.75	0.85	0.90
δ	0.90	0.90	0.85	0.85	0.80	0.75
Peak lag year	24	20	24	19	24	27
Root mean squared error (RMSE)						
With spillovers model	22.46	22.52	22.49	22.59	22.52	22.56
No spillovers model	22.41	22.46	22.40	22.51	22.44	22.47
Implied elasticities						
With spillovers model						
Own research	0.32	0.28	0.33	0.29	0.33	0.35
Spillover research	0.24	0.31	0.22	0.30	0.22	0.19
No spillovers model						
Own research	0.27	0.25	0.30	0.29	0.29	0.28
Spillover research	0.19	0.20	0.18	0.41	0.40	0.39
Estimates ranked by model without extension spillovers						
Model rankings						
No spillovers model rank	1	2	3	4	5	6
With spillovers model rank	1	2	3	5	4	6
Lag distribution parameters						
λ	0.70	0.65	0.80	0.85	0.75	0.90
δ	0.90	0.90	0.85	0.80	0.85	0.75
Peak lag year	24	20	24	24	19	27
Root mean squared error (RMSE)						
No spillovers model	22.41	22.46	22.40	22.44	22.51	22.47
With spillovers model	22.46	22.52	22.49	22.52	22.59	22.56
Implied elasticities						
No spillovers model						
Own research	0.27	0.25	0.30	0.29	0.29	0.28
Spillover research	0.19	0.20	0.18	0.40	0.41	0.39
With spillovers model						
Own research	0.32	0.28	0.33	0.33	0.29	0.35
Spillover research	0.24	0.31	0.22	0.22	0.30	0.19

Sources: Developed by the authors.

Notes: See notes to Table 10-2.

formed the model without extension spillovers. In contrast, for the logarithmic model in every instance the model without extension spillovers slightly outperformed the model with extension spillovers.

Table 10-8 compares the elasticities and standard errors from the base model with the 50-year gamma distribution weights for extension and an alternative

Table 10-8 Effects of Alternative Extension Lag Distribution Models

Panel a. Linear model

Model Details	**Model Results**					
Estimates ranked by model with 50-year gamma extension lag weights						
Model rankings						
Gamma model rank	1	2	3	4	5	6
Geometric model rank	21	22	27	25	19	11
Lag distribution parameters						
λ	0.75	0.80	0.85	0.65	0.85	0.70
δ	0.80	0.75	0.65	0.85	0.70	0.85
Peak lag year	13	12	10	12	13	15
Root mean squared error (RMSE)						
Gamma model	30.36	30.36	30.36	30.37	30.39	30.40
Geometric model	30.70	30.71	30.82	30.81	30.65	30.57
Implied elasticities						
Gamma model						
Own research	0.13	0.13	0.13	0.13	0.13	0.12
Spillover research	0.54	0.54	0.55	0.55	0.52	0.52
Geometric model						
Own research	0.15	0.15	0.15	0.17	0.16	0.17
Spillover research	0.63	0.62	0.62	0.70	0.67	0.70
Estimates ranked by model with 4-year geometric extension lag weights						
Model rankings						
Geometric model rank	1	2	3	4	5	6
Gamma model rank	21	32	18	12	30	26
Lag distribution parameters						
λ	0.65	0.70	0.75	0.60	0.80	0.85
δ	0.90	0.90	0.85	0.90	0.85	0.80
Peak lag year	20	24	19	17	24	24
Root mean squared error (RMSE)						
Geometric model	30.39	30.43	30.44	30.47	30.48	30.50
Gamma model	30.68	31.00	30.60	30.46	30.95	30.86
Implied elasticities						
Geometric model						
Own research	0.14	0.15	0.15	0.14	0.17	0.17
Spillover research	0.70	0.65	0.64	0.69	0.71	0.70
Gamma model						
Own research	0.12	0.12	0.12	0.12	0.12	0.12
Spillover research	0.47	0.43	0.48	0.50	0.43	0.44

(continued)

model with 4-year geometric extension weights for extension from Huffman and Evenson (1993 and 2006a). Panel a includes the results for the linear model and Panel b includes the results for the logarithmic model. In each panel, the upper half includes the results for the six top-ranked lag distribution models (by SSE) estimated using the base model specification (with a 50-year gamma distribution applied to extension), and the corresponding results from each of the same mod-

Table 10-8 (continued)

Panel b. Logarithmic model

Model Details	**Model Results**					
Estimates ranked by model with 50-year gamma extension lag weights						
Model rankings						
Gamma model rank	1	2	3	4	5	6
Geometric model rank	2	1	5	3	6	10
Lag distribution parameters						
λ	0.70	0.65	0.80	0.75	0.85	0.90
δ	0.90	0.90	0.85	0.85	0.80	0.75
Peak lag year	24	20	24	19	24	27
Root mean squared error (RMSE)						
Gamma model	22.46	22.52	22.49	22.59	22.52	22.56
Geometric model	23.73	23.71	23.85	23.86	23.94	24.05
Implied elasticities						
Gamma model						
Own research	0.32	0.28	0.33	0.29	0.33	0.35
Spillover research	0.24	0.31	0.22	0.30	0.22	0.19
Geometric model						
Own research	0.08	0.02	0.24	0.11	0.23	0.15
Spillover research	0.67	0.74	0.56	0.64	0.56	0.59
Estimates ranked by model with 4-year geometric extension lag weights						
Model rankings						
Geometric model rank	1	2	3	4	5	6
Gamma model rank	2	1	4	7	3	5
Lag distribution parameters						
λ	0.65	0.70	0.75	0.60	0.80	0.85
δ	0.90	0.90	0.85	0.90	0.85	0.80
Peak lag year	20	24	19	17	24	24
Root mean squared error (RMSE)						
Geometric model	23.71	23.73	23.86	23.92	23.85	23.94
Gamma model	22.52	22.46	22.59	22.71	22.49	22.52
Implied elasticities						
Geometric model						
Own research	0.02	0.08	0.11	0.02	0.24	0.23
Spillover research	0.74	0.67	0.64	0.74	0.56	0.56
Gamma model						
Own research	0.28	0.32	0.29	0.25	0.33	0.33
Spillover research	0.31	0.24	0.30	0.36	0.22	0.22

Sources: Developed by the authors.

Notes: See notes to Table 10-2.

els estimated alternatively with geometric extension lags. The lower half of each panel mirrors the upper half except that the top-ranked lag distribution models were found by estimating the model with geometric extension lags, and then we included the corresponding results from estimating each of the same models using the base specification with gamma extension lags.

Consider first the linear model in Panel a. The use of the Huffman and Evenson geometric lag structure for extension resulted in a very different ranking of the lag distribution models compared with the base model with gamma distribution lags. The peak research lags were much later for the alternative model (18–32 years for the top three models) than for the base model (10–13 years). This result seems intuitively reasonable. In the base model, both extension and research have the same lag distribution with a peak lag of 10–13 years, representing an "average" of some research and extension expenditures that take effect with very long lags and other research and extension expenditures that take effect with very short lags. In the alternative model, a much shorter extension lag is imposed (the peak weight is in the current year, with a lag of zero) and the research lag becomes commensurately longer, leaving the overall average lag across the combined research and extension spending similar to that from the base model. Even though the research lag distribution is significantly different, the estimated elasticities did not appear to be very sensitive to either the specification or the implied lag distribution shapes. Across all of the results reported in Panel a of Table 10-8 the elasticity of *MFP* with respect to the own-state knowledge stock ranged from 0.12 to 0.17; the elasticity of *MFP* with respect to the spillover knowledge stock ranged from 0.43 to 0.55 for the base model with gamma extension weights, compared with a slightly higher range of 0.62 to 0.71 for the alternative model, with Huffman and Evenson geometric extension lag weights.

Now, consider the logarithmic model in Panel b. Unlike the linear model, the use of the Huffman and Evenson geometric lag structure for extension resulted in a quite similar ranking of the gamma lag distribution models for research compared with the base model that has identical gamma distribution lags for both research and extension. The peak lags were in a narrow range (19–24) years for the top three gamma distribution models across both specifications of the extension lag. In the case of the logarithmic model, the elasticities were sensitive to the specification of the form of the extension lag. Across the sets of estimates reported in Panel b of Table 10-8 the elasticity of *MFP* with respect to the own-state knowledge stock ranged from 0.25 to 0.35 for the base model that has gamma extension lag weights compared with 0.02 to 0.24 for the alternative model that has Huffman and Evenson geometric extension lag weights; the elasticity of *MFP* with respect to the spillover knowledge stock ranged from 0.19 to 0.36 for the base model using gamma extension weights, compared with 0.56 to 0.74 for the alternative model, using Huffman and Evenson geometric extension lag weights.

Considering RMSEs, the base model with the 50-year gamma distribution lag weights for extension outperforms its counterpart with the 4-year geometric Huffman and Evenson lag weights in every instance for the logarithmic functional form—though in some instances the differences are fairly small. Because

Table 10-9 Effects of Alternative Specifications of Extension Knowledge Stocks

	Gamma Extension Lags				Geometric Extension Lags			
	Linear		Logarithmic		Linear		Logarithmic	
Extension Spillovers	Yes (1)	No (2)	Yes (3)	No (4)	Yes (5)	No (6)	Yes (7)	No (8)
RMSE	30.36	30.55	22.46	22.41	30.39	30.56	23.71	23.21
Lag distribution parameters								
λ	0.75	0.75	0.70	0.70	0.65	0.60	0.65	0.65
δ	0.80	0.80	0.90	0.90	0.90	0.90	0.90	0.90
Peak lag year	13	13	24	24	20	17	20	20
Model rankings								
Model 1 rank	1	1	21	22	21	3	22	15
Model 2 rank	1	1	21	22	21	3	22	15
Model 3 rank	32	33	1	1	2	27	2	5
Model 4 rank	32	33	1	1	2	27	2	5
Model 5 rank	21	19	2	2	1	14	1	1
Model 6 rank	12	8	7	8	4	1	4	2
Model 7 rank	21	19	2	2	1	14	1	1
Model 8 rank	21	19	2	2	1	14	1	1
Implied elasticities with respect to								
Own-state SAES	0.06	0.06	0.15	0.12	0.02	0.03	0.00	0.01
Own-state extension	0.06	0.07	0.18	0.15	0.12	0.16	0.01	0.03
All own-state combined	*0.13*	*0.13*	*0.32*	*0.27*	*0.14*	*0.20*	*0.02*	*0.04*
SAES spillins	0.18	0.25	0.07	0.09	0.09	0.15	0.10	0.17
IM spillins	0.17	0.23	0.07	0.10	0.11	0.17	0.11	0.20
Extension spillins	0.19	0.00	0.09	0.00	0.49	0.00	0.53	0.00
All spillins combined	*0.54*	*0.48*	*0.24*	*0.19*	*0.70*	*0.32*	*0.74*	*0.38*

Sources: Developed by the authors.

Notes: See notes to Table 10-2.

it changes the research lag shape and the mean lag for the linear model, and the elasticities for the logarithmic model, the treatment of the extension lag is likely to have significant implications for the findings with respect to the benefits from research, which we explore in later chapters.

Synthesis of Results on Functional Form and Extension Lags

Table 10-9 summarizes the main points from our examination of the implications of key specification choices. For each of eight alternative specifications, the table includes the results for the top-ranked gamma lag distribution model. Since the results for a given specification have been shown to be stable across at least the eight highest-ranked lag distribution models (by SSE), the top-ranked model in each case can be taken as representative. The eight alternatives in the table combine three binary specification choices: (a) the use of the 50-year gamma distribution lag weights for extension versus the 4-year geometric Huffman-Evenson lag weights, (b) the linear versus logarithmic functional form, and (c) extension effects that are confined to the state making the investment, versus extension effects with interstate spillovers, the same as for research investments.

Across all the models shown in Table 10-9, the lowest RMSE is for the model in column 4, which represents the logarithmic model with the same gamma distribution lag weights applied to extension as to research, but no extension spillovers. This model is slightly superior, statistically, to the equivalent model with extension spillovers in column 3, which is our base model in logarithms. These two models are essentially equivalent statistical models with the identical lag structure, although they do imply some slight differences in elasticities and will have different economic implications. Comparing these two models to their counterparts in columns 7 and 8, it can be seen that the use of Huffman and Evenson's 4-year geometric lag weights for extension, rather than the statistically preferred 50-year gamma distribution lag weights for extension, has quite significant implications for the elasticities and other parameters. Compared with the base model, the use of the geometric lag distribution for extension resulted in much smaller elasticities of *MFP* with respect to own-state investments in SAES research and extension; but much larger elasticities of *MFP* with respect to spillovers from investments in intramural research by the USDA, and in SAES research and extension by other states. Finally, comparing the statistically superior logarithmic model in columns 3 and 4, with its linear counterparts in columns 1 and 2, the linear model tends to result in significantly smaller elasticities of *MFP* with respect to own-state investments in SAES research and extension, and larger elasticities of *MFP* with respect to spillovers from investments in intramural research by the USDA and in SAES research and extension by other states.

Alternative Research Spillover Models

Our base model includes state-state spillovers from both research and extension, with state-specific spillover knowledge stocks computed using a measure of agroecological proximity based on an index of similarities in the output mix between states. For comparison, we also report results from otherwise identical models using two alternative state-to-state spillover structures: one that assumes no research spillovers between states, such that $\beta_S = 0$ in equation (10.2a) and $\eta_S = 0$ in equation (10.2b); another that assumes state-to-state spillover coefficients are equal to 1 between pairs of states within the seven regions defined in Appendix II and zero otherwise (this is similar to an approach used by Evenson (1988 and 1999) as discussed in Chapter 8). Table 10-10 compares the results between the baseline model, this alternative specification of spillover weights based on geopolitical rather than agroecological proximity, and a model without any spillover effects.

In Table 10-10, comparing columns 1 and 2 for the linear model (or columns 4 and 5 for the logarithmic model), it can be seen that the results are very simiar between models that use our estimated state-state and federal-state spill-

Table 10-10 Effects of Alternative Specifications of Interstate Spillovers

	Linear			Logarithmic		
Model Details	**Spillovers by Output Mix (1)**	**Spillovers by USDA Regions (2)**	**No Spillovers (3)**	**Spillovers by Output Mix (4)**	**Spillovers by USDA Regions (5)**	**No Spillovers (6)**
RMSE	30.36	27.75	38.52	22.46	22.23	22.77
Lag distribution parameters						
λ	0.75	0.70	0.95	0.70	0.65	0.95
δ	0.80	0.85	0.70	0.90	0.90	0.65
Peak lag year	13	15	44	24	20	35
Model rankings						
Model 1 rank	1	6	36	32	21	31
Model 2 rank	9	1	24	25	13	17
Model 3 rank	39	36	1	14	23	4
Model 4 rank	21	15	19	1	2	14
Model 5 rank	21	13	15	5	1	14
Model 6 rank	28	25	4	10	17	1
Implied elasticities with respect to						
Own-state SAES	0.06	0.04	0.20	0.15	0.12	0.24
Own-state extension	0.06	0.04	0.22	0.18	0.14	0.29
All own-state combined	*0.13*	*0.08*	*0.42*	*0.32*	*0.25*	*0.53*
SAES spillins	0.18	0.09	0.00	0.07	0.05	0.00
IM spillins	0.17	0.43	0.00	0.07	0.25	0.00
Extension spillins	0.19	0.10	0.00	0.09	0.06	0.00
All spillins combined	*0.54*	*0.62*	*0.00*	*0.24*	*0.35*	*0.00*

Sources: Developed by the authors.

Notes: See notes to Table 10-2.

over coefficients, and otherwise identical models in which the state-state spillover coefficients are 1 for states within the same USDA region, and 0 otherwise, and all federal-state spillover coefficients are 1. While the elasticities and other model statistics were minimally affected, this difference in the definition of the spillover knowledge stock has very different implications for the interpretation of sources of productivity growth, especially in those states such as California or Florida for which geopolitical proximity is not a good indicator of agroecological similarity.

A more extreme restriction is to assume the state-to-state spillover coefficients are zero, as has been done implicitly in most of the state-level studies (e.g., Norton and Ortiz 1992; Leiby and Adams 1991; Alston, Pardey and Carter 1994). In Table 10-10 the results for models that do not include any federal-state or state-state spillovers are shown in columns 3 and 6 for the linear and logarithmic forms, respectively. By conventional standards, such a model might appear to be quite satisfactory. However, it is statistically dominated by models that include the spillover effects. And as would be anticipated (and consistent with the suggestions of Alston and Pardey 2001), the omission of the spillover effects resulted in much larger elasticities of *MFP* with respect to the own-research knowledge stocks than in the model that included spillovers. Hence, the omission (or other misspecification) of the spillover impacts might have led to substantial upward biases in estimates of own-state rates of return to research in some previous studies. These implications of this aspect of the specification are explored in Chapters 11 and 12.

Alternative Lag Distribution Models

Our base model assumes a gamma distribution for the lag weights used in constructing the research and extension knowledge stocks. We also estimated the same model using a trapezoidal form for the lag distribution. The trapezoidal model is taken from Huffman and Evenson (1992, 1993 and 2006a), and includes a total of 35 lagged research expenditures, with weights defined as described in Chapter 9. In the first variant of this model, as we did with the gamma distribution in the base model, we applied the same weights to both research and extension in creating the own-state research and extension knowledge stocks that were then used to create the state-specific spillover knowledge stocks. In an alternative variant, we combined the trapezoidal research lag model with the geometric extension lag model. We estimated both of these models using the linear and logarithmic functional forms.

The results from these 35-year trapezoidal lag-distribution models are compared with their counterpart best-fitting 50-year gamma distribution models in Table 10-11—i.e., comparing columns 1 and 2, columns 3 and 4, columns 5 and 6, and columns 7 and 8, respectively. Comparing columns 1 and 2 for the linear model, the RMSE (for predictions of *MFP* in levels) from the trapezoidal lag distribution model is almost identical to that from using the otherwise identical base model with the gamma lag distribution applied to research and extension combined. In the case of the logarithmic model (comparing columns 5 and 6), the RMSE is slightly larger for the trapezoidal lag specification than for the gamma lag specification. The estimated elasticities are also relatively insensitive to this aspect of specification choice, especially for the linear models. Comparing columns 3 and 4 for the linear case and even more so comparing columns 7 and 8 for the logarithmic case, somewhat larger differences in results are found between the gamma and trapezoidal models of the research lag when they are combined with the Huffman-Evenson 4-year geometric extension lag. Even so, the patterns of elasticities are similar comparing estimates made using the trapezoidal lag rather than the gamma lag for research. That is, the differences in results between the trapezoidal lag model and the gamma lag model are moderate; even though the lag distributions have somewhat different shapes and different lengths (Figure 9-3). This is especially true for the preferred model in which the same lag distribution is applied to both research and extension.

Table 10-11 Effects of Alternative Research Lag Distribution Shapes

	Linear				Logarithmic			
	Equal Research and Extension Lags		Short Geometric Extension Lags		Equal Research and Extension Lags		Short Geometric Extension Lags	
Model Details	**(1)**	**(2)**	**(3)**	**(4)**	**(5)**	**(6)**	**(7)**	**(8)**
Research lag								
Maximum years	50	35	50	35	50	35	50	35
Lag form	gamma	trapezoid	gamma	trapezoid	gamma	trapezoid	gamma	trapezoid
Extension lag								
Maximum years	50	35	4	4	50	35	4	4
Lag form	gamma	trapezoid	geometric	geometric	gamma	trapezoid	geometric	geometric
RMSE	30.36	30.35	30.39	30.70	22.46	23.06	23.71	24.43
Implied elasticities with respect to								
Own-state SAES	0.06	0.06	0.02	0.06	0.15	0.12	0.00	0.08
Own-state extension	0.06	0.07	0.12	0.09	0.18	0.13	0.01	0.11
All own-state	*0.13*	*0.13*	*0.14*	*0.16*	*0.32*	*0.26*	*0.02*	*0.19*
SAES spillins	0.18	0.18	0.09	0.19	0.07	0.13	0.10	0.16
IM spillins	0.17	0.17	0.11	0.18	0.07	0.12	0.11	0.15
Extension spillins	0.19	0.19	0.49	0.27	0.09	0.14	0.53	0.24
All spillins	*0.54*	*0.54*	*0.70*	*0.64*	*0.24*	*0.38*	*0.74*	*0.55*

Sources: Developed by the authors.

Notes: See notes to Table 10-2. All of these models assume that the same spillover coefficients apply to both research and extension knowledge stocks.

Maximum Lag Length

To this point, our analysis has been based on a maintained assumption of an overall lag length of 50 years in the gamma distribution model used to define the lag weights. In many of the estimations, however, very little effective weight was placed on the longer lags, and it may have been feasible to have applied a much shorter overall lag. This is a potentially important point. Previous studies have often used much shorter lags, especially the earliest studies, and in previous work we have suggested that this choice may have resulted in upwards biased estimates of returns to research (e.g., Alston, Norton and Pardey 1995; Alston, Craig and Pardey 1998; Alston et al. 2000a). However, many studies do not have sufficient data to estimate (or test for) lag lengths as long as 50 years, so it is useful to explore the effects of restrictions on the overall lag length on the estimation results and the implied benefit-cost ratios to provide general advice on this question and to examine our own findings.

Table 10-12 shows the effects of variations in the maximum research lag, from 50 years down to 35 years or 20 years, on results from both the base model (i.e., the model with the same gamma lag distribution research and extension) and an alternative model (i.e., with a gamma lag distribution for research and the

Table 10-12 Effects of Alternative Specifications of Maximum Lag Length

Panel a. Linear model

	Gamma Extension Lag Weights with Gamma Research Lags Over			4-Year Geometric Extension Lag with Gamma Research Lags Over		
Model Details	**50 years (1)**	**35 years (2)**	**20 years (3)**	**50 years (4)**	**35 years (5)**	**20 years (6)**
RMSE	30.36	30.35	30.39	30.39	30.36	30.54
Lag distribution parameters						
λ	0.75	0.80	0.95	0.65	0.70	0.90
δ	0.80	0.75	0.70	0.90	0.90	0.90
Peak lag year	13	12	44	20	24	84
Model rankings						
Model 1 rank	1	2	36	21	32	6
Model 2 rank	2	1	30	21	31	52
Model 3 rank	17	21	1	16	23	36
Model 4 rank	21	2	18	1	2	37
Model 5 rank	30	31	8	2	1	28
Model 6 rank	34	38	26	19	16	1
Implied elasticities with respect to						
Own-state research (R)	0.06	0.06	0.06	0.02	0.09	0.06
Own-state extension (E)	0.06	0.07	0.06	0.12	0.09	0.09
Own-state R&E	*0.13*	*0.13*	*0.12*	*0.14*	*0.18*	*0.16*
SAES spillins	0.18	0.18	0.18	0.09	0.27	0.17
IM spillins	0.17	0.17	0.17	0.11	0.21	0.17
Extension spillins	0.19	0.19	0.19	0.49	0.26	0.26
All spillins combined	*0.54*	*0.54*	*0.55*	*0.70*	*0.74*	*0.60*

(continued)

Huffman and Evenson geometric lag for extension).[16] All of the models reported in this table allow for state-state spillover effects of both research and extension, but as demonstrated previously in this chapter, the results are likely to be insensitive to the treatment of extension spillovers. Again, Panel a refers to the linear model and Panel b refers to the logarithmic model.

Looking across the models in Table 10-12, a number of interesting results emerge. First, the model with a 35-year maximum lag is generally preferred (in terms of the RMSE) over its counterparts with 20 or 50 year lags. Second, the statistically preferred gamma lag distribution shape when the model is estimated with a 20-year maximum lag is generally implausible, rising throughout the relevant range with an implied peak lag weight outside the range. Third, in the model with the gamma distribution weights for extension, for both the linear and logarithmic functional forms, the elasticities are essentially identical between the 35-year lag and corresponding 50-year lag models (and even for the 20-year

16 In practice, for a given pair of gamma distribution parameters, the lag distribution for 35 years has the identical shape to that for the 50 years lag distribution over its first 35 years, at which point it is truncated. In either case we normalized the weights such that they sum to one.

Table 10-12 (continued)

Panel b. Logarithmic model

Model Details	Gamma Extension Lag Weights with Gamma Research Lags Over			4-Year Geometric Extension Lag with Gamma Research Lags Over		
	50 years (1)	35 years (2)	20 years (3)	50 years (4)	35 years (5)	20 years (6)
RMSE	22.46	22.47	23.06	23.71	23.60	24.01
Lag distribution parameters						
λ	0.70	0.70	0.70	0.65	0.70	0.85
δ	0.90	0.90	0.90	0.90	0.90	0.90
Peak lag year	24	24	24	20	24	54
Model rankings						
Model 1 rank	1	1	1	2	1	42
Model 2 rank	1	1	1	5	1	26
Model 3 rank	1	1	1	3	1	13
Model 4 rank	2	2	2	1	2	30
Model 5 rank	1	1	1	2	1	22
Model 6 rank	9	9	9	16	9	1
Implied elasticities with respect to						
Own-state research (R)	0.15	0.14	0.10	0.00	0.06	0.08
Own-state extension (E)	0.18	0.16	0.11	0.01	0.12	0.11
Own-state R&E	*0.32*	*0.30*	*0.21*	*0.02*	*0.18*	*0.19*
SAES spillins	0.07	0.09	0.13	0.10	0.14	0.15
IM spillins	0.07	0.09	0.13	0.11	0.14	0.15
Extension spillins	0.09	0.11	0.15	0.53	0.27	0.24
All spillins combined	*0.24*	*0.28*	*0.41*	*0.74*	*0.55*	*0.54*

Sources: Developed by the authors.

Notes: The base model (columns 1, 2, and 3) applies the same gamma distribution lag to research and extension and the "alternative" model (columns 4, 5, and 6) applies Huffman and Evenson's geometric lag distribution to extension. See notes to Table 10-3.

lag model); even so, the benefit-cost ratios are likely to be greater for the 35-year model because it will have larger weights on the shorter lags. In the model with the Huffman-Evenson geometric extension lag weights, however, the elasticities are somewhat more sensitive to the maximum research lag length, especially for the logarithmic model.

The same points are illustrated graphically in Figure 10-1. In the upper left quadrant (which refers to results for the linear model reported in columns 1-3 of Table 10-12, Panel a, with the same gamma lag distribution applied to both research and extension), the three plots refer to the lag distributions from the models with maximum lags of 20, 35, and 50 years. The models with lags of 35 and 50 years are virtually indistinguishable from one another, whereas the model with a maximum lag of 20 years has lag weights rising throughout the range. A similar story holds in Panel c (corresponding to results reported in columns 1-3 of Table 10-12, Panel b, for the logarithmic model with the same lag distribution applied to research and extension).

Figure 10-1 Top-Ranked Research Lag Distributions with Maximum Lag Length of 20, 35, and 50 Years

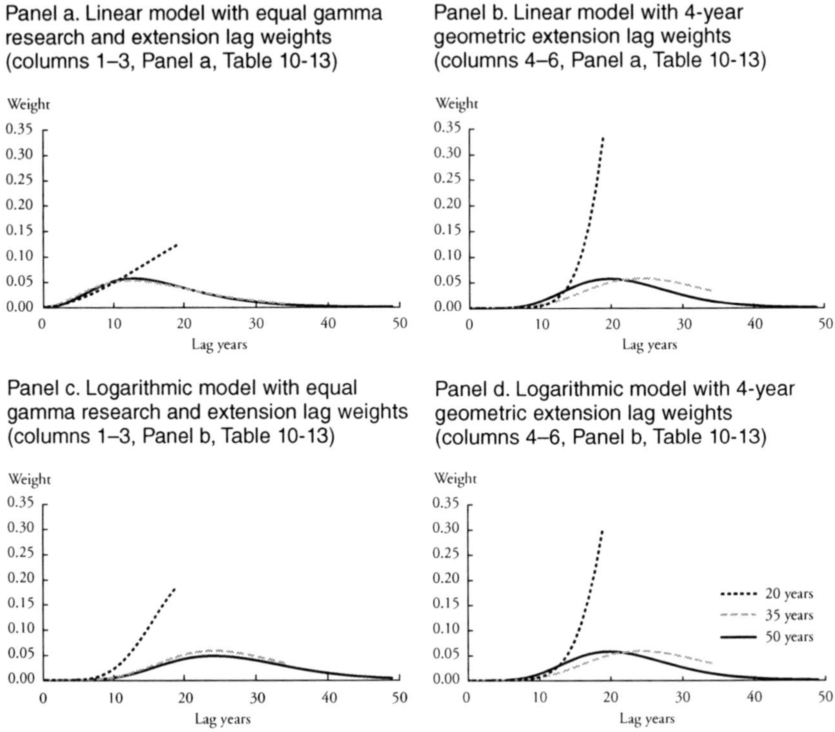

Sources: Developed by the authors.

Some interesting contrasts are apparent between the models that use 4-year geometric extension weights relative to the models that use the same gamma distribution weights for extension as for research—that is, in Figure 10-1, comparing the models in Panel a with their counterparts in Panel b, and comparing the models in Panel c with their counterparts in Panel d. In the case of the linear model the imposition of a very short geometric lag on the impacts of extension resulted in generally longer research lags; in the case of the logarithmic model the effects of imposing the short extension lag were less clear. Finally, when using the same gamma lag distribution model for extension as research, all three lag distributions in Panel a of Figure 10-1 (for the linear model) are substantially to the left of their counterparts in Panel c (for the logarithmic model), implying shorter overall lags with the linear model. In contrast, when using the 4-year geometric lag for extension, the estimated lag distributions in Panel b (for the linear model) are very similar to their counterparts in Panel d (for the logarithmic model).

In sum, restricting the maximum lag from 50 years to 35 years had little impact on any of the results when the same gamma lag distribution was applied to both research and extension, but had some impact on the findings for the research lag distribution when the 4-year geometric distribution was imposed for extension lags. However, restricting the maximum lag to 20 years had profound impacts. The resulting (generally implausible) lag distribution shapes—in which the lag weight rose to a maximum at the 20-year constraint for both linear and logarithmic functional forms, regardless of the treatment of the lag distribution for extension—reflect the strong relationships in the data that support findings of lagged research impacts that last much longer than 20 years after the research investment was made.

10.4 Interpretation and Assessment

The base model was defined as a model that is linear in levels or logarithms of the variables, in which own-state extension and research were treated symmetrically in terms of (a) the 50-year gamma lag distribution used to create knowledge stocks, (b) their spillover effects on other states, and (c) their marginal impacts on *MFP* (i.e., effectively own-state research and extension were treated as though they could be combined within the state before accumulating into a stock and allowing for spillover effects from that stock). The model effectively includes two knowledge stock variables (an own-state R&E stock and a state-specific spillover R&E stock variable), a state-specific weather index, and a state-specific intercept, corresponding to a fixed effects (FE) error structure when estimated by OLS. The results from this model are satisfactory in the sense that, for a broad range of lag distribution characteristics (defined by the range of gamma distribution characteristics) the estimated elasticities are generally reasonable and insensitive to this aspect of the specification.

The estimates of the base model are summarized in Table 10-2 for the top ranked eight from the total of 64 gamma lag distribution models estimated for that specification. Across these top-ranked models, the elasticities of *MFP* with respect to knowledge stocks from own-state extension and research and state-specific spillover knowledge stocks differ between the two functional forms but fall within narrow ranges for a given form—for the linear model, the elasticities are 0.12 to 0.13 for the own-state research and extension knowledge stock, and 0.52 to 0.58 for the state-specific stock of state-to-state and federal-state research and extension knowledge spillovers; for the statistically preferred logarithmic model the elasticities are 0.25 to 0.35 for the own-state research and extension knowledge stock, and 0.19 to 0.36 for the state specific stock of state-to-state and federal-state research and extension knowledge spillovers. In either case the elasticities seem plausible.

We applied a number of diagnostic tests to this model, and the tests indicated a rejection of the classical assumptions of serially and contemporaneously independent, homoskedastic residuals. However, when we applied alternative estimators, the feasible generalized least squares (FGLS) estimates were essentially indistinguishable from the OLS estimates of the base model. These findings indicate that the failure of the classical assumptions to hold has not resulted in serious consequences for the estimates, and we can use the OLS estimates of the models with reasonable confidence. Augmented Dickey-Fuller tests indicated the presence of unit roots in the *MFP* series in each state, but not in the first differences of these data. We estimated the linear and logarithmic forms of the base model in first-differences of the data, and the resulting estimates were similar to those from the same model estimated with the un-differenced data. Although the ranking of models according to lag distribution parameters was different, the implied lag distribution shapes were similar, and the implied elasticities were also very similar. Again, the implication is that we can use the OLS estimates obtained using the un-differenced data with reasonable confidence. Nevertheless, in later chapters we explore the implications of using first-differenced data for the benefit-cost ratios.

The base model entails a number of strong, maintained hypotheses. We evaluated the implications of several key specification choices, including (a) the functional form of the model (linear in logarithms versus linear in levels in the base model), (b) the extension lag distribution (Huffman and Evenson's four-year geometric lag distribution versus the same 50-year gamma lag distribution as applied to research in the base model), (c) differential treatment of research and extension spillovers, (d) specification of research and extension spillovers (none at all or spillovers based on USDA regions versus spillovers based on product mix similarities, as in the base model), (e) the functional form of the research lag distribution (Huffman and Evenson's trapezoidal model versus the 50-year gamma lag distribution as applied to research in the base model), and (f) the maximum research lag length (20 or 35 years versus 50 years in the base model). The results from this analysis of sensitivity of results to specification choices were mainly predictable and generally plausible.

Among these aspects of the specification, the choice of functional form for the model appears potentially to have relatively important implications. Certainly the best-fitting lag distribution model had a different shape and peak lag, and implied quite different albeit still plausible elasticities of *MFP* with respect to knowledge stocks, when the model was estimated in logarithms rather than levels of the variables. It seems likely that this aspect could have important implications in particular for estimated benefit-cost ratios.

Important differences were found when we tried the much shorter Huffman-Evenson geometric lag distribution for extension, rather than treat extension symmetrically with SAES research and apply the same 50-year gamma lag weights. The results made more intuitive sense and the prediction errors were smaller from the base model, which is preferred for these reasons over the Huffman-Evenson model. The results were not sensitive to whether we allowed for interstate extension spillovers, however. Nor were they sensitive to whether we used the 35-year trapezoid versus the 50-year gamma lag distribution, or a 35-year versus a 50-year gamma distribution. This reflects the fact that the preferred gamma distribution had very small weights on the lags beyond 35 years, and had a similar shape to the trapezoid otherwise, especially in the case of the linear model. However, the statistical results were sensitive to further shortening the maximum lag to 20 years, and the resulting models were unsatisfactory compared with the models that included longer lags. These results suggest that unduly restricting the length of the research lag would lead to biased estimates.

Other sensitivity analysis indicated that inappropriate specification of spillover effects would result in biased estimates of various parameters of interest (e.g., if spillover effects are omitted) and distorted inferences (e.g., when we impose a restriction that spillover effects are based on proximity if in fact they are based on agroecological similarity). Chapter 11 presents benefit-cost ratios and other performance measures implied by the base model and the main alternatives, drawing out the nature of these types of implications of specification choices for findings. Chapter 12 presents a more formal assessment.

Appendix Table 10-1 Summary of Results for the Base Model, 64 Lag Distributions

Panel a. Linear model

δ		λ 0.60	0.65	0.70	0.75	0.80	0.85	0.90	0.95
0.60	Rank	64	62	45	35	24	8	9	25
	SSE	2.70	2.65	2.58	2.51	2.45	2.40	2.40	2.46
	η_{Own}	0.17	0.16	0.15	0.15	0.14	0.13	0.13	0.12
	η_{Spill}	0.72	0.70	0.68	0.66	0.62	0.58	0.52	0.45
0.65	Rank	63	53	38	27	16	3	15	31
	SSE	2.66	2.60	2.54	2.47	2.42	2.39	2.41	2.48
	η_{Own}	0.16	0.16	0.15	0.14	0.14	0.13	0.12	0.11
	η_{Spill}	0.70	0.69	0.66	0.64	0.60	0.55	0.49	0.43
0.70	Rank	58	43	33	20	7	5	23	36
	SSE	2.61	2.55	2.49	2.44	2.40	2.39	2.44	2.51
	η_{Own}	0.16	0.15	0.14	0.14	0.13	0.13	0.12	0.11
	η_{Spill}	0.69	0.67	0.64	0.61	0.57	0.52	0.46	0.41
0.75	Rank	42	34	22	11	2	17	29	40
	SSE	2.55	2.50	2.44	2.40	2.39	2.42	2.48	2.55
	η_{Own}	0.15	0.14	0.14	0.13	0.13	0.12	0.12	0.11
	η_{Spill}	0.66	0.64	0.61	0.58	0.54	0.49	0.43	0.39
0.80	Rank	28	19	10	1	14	26	37	44
	SSE	2.48	2.43	2.40	2.39	2.41	2.47	2.53	2.58
	η_{Own}	0.14	0.13	0.13	0.13	0.12	0.12	0.11	0.10
	η_{Spill}	0.63	0.60	0.57	0.54	0.49	0.44	0.40	0.37
0.85	Rank	13	4	6	18	30	39	46	51
	SSE	2.41	2.39	2.40	2.43	2.48	2.54	2.58	2.60
	η_{Own}	0.13	0.13	0.12	0.12	0.12	0.11	0.10	0.09
	η_{Spill}	0.58	0.55	0.52	0.48	0.43	0.39	0.37	0.35
0.90	Rank	12	21	32	41	47	55	56	54
	SSE	2.40	2.65	2.58	2.51	2.45	2.40	2.40	2.46
	η_{Own}	0.12	0.12	0.12	0.11	0.10	0.09	0.08	0.08
	η_{Spill}	0.50	0.47	0.43	0.40	0.37	0.35	0.34	0.33
0.95	Rank	59	61	60	57	52	48	49	50
	SSE	2.62	2.62	2.62	2.61	2.60	2.60	2.60	2.60
	η_{Own}	0.10	0.09	0.08	0.08	0.07	0.07	0.07	0.07
	η_{Spill}	0.37	0.35	0.34	0.33	0.33	0.32	0.32	0.32

(continued)

Appendix Table 10-1 (continued)

Panel b. Logarithmic model

δ		λ 0.60	0.65	0.70	0.75	0.80	0.85	0.90	0.95
0.60	Rank	61	57	52	46	39	27	20	12
	SSE	42.63	41.21	39.54	37.61	35.53	33.57	32.18	31.77
	η_{Own}	0.26	0.26	0.26	0.26	0.26	0.27	0.31	0.36
	η_{Spill}	0.53	0.51	0.50	0.48	0.45	0.40	0.31	0.20
0.65	Rank	58	53	48	40	32	23	13	14
	SSE	41.60	40.10	38.37	36.45	34.50	32.83	31.81	31.84
	η_{Own}	0.26	0.26	0.26	0.25	0.26	0.28	0.32	0.36
	η_{Spill}	0.52	0.50	0.48	0.46	0.43	0.37	0.28	0.17
0.70	Rank	55	50	43	37	26	18	9	19
	SSE	40.33	38.75	37.00	35.16	33.44	32.14	31.55	32.15
	η_{Own}	0.26	0.25	0.25	0.25	0.26	0.29	0.33	0.36
	η_{Spill}	0.50	0.49	0.47	0.45	0.41	0.34	0.24	0.15
0.75	Rank	49	44	38	29	22	10	6	25
	SSE	38.73	37.11	35.41	33.77	32.41	31.58	31.52	32.95
	η_{Own}	0.25	0.24	0.24	0.25	0.27	0.31	0.35	0.34
	η_{Spill}	0.49	0.47	0.45	0.42	0.37	0.29	0.19	0.13
0.80	Rank	41	36	28	21	8	5	17	35
	SSE	36.70	35.14	33.64	32.38	31.55	31.29	32.14	34.65
	η_{Own}	0.24	0.24	0.24	0.26	0.29	0.33	0.35	0.30
	η_{Spill}	0.47	0.45	0.42	0.38	0.31	0.22	0.15	0.14
0.85	Rank	31	24	15	4	3	16	33	45
	SSE	34.18	32.90	31.90	31.27	31.16	32.06	34.52	37.57
	η_{Own}	0.23	0.24	0.26	0.29	0.33	0.35	0.31	0.22
	η_{Spill}	0.44	0.41	0.37	0.30	0.22	0.15	0.14	0.18
0.90	Rank	7	2	1	11	30	42	51	56
	SSE	31.53	31.06	31.00	31.72	33.82	36.85	39.46	41.12
	η_{Own}	0.25	0.28	0.32	0.35	0.32	0.24	0.17	0.12
	η_{Spill}	0.36	0.31	0.24	0.17	0.14	0.17	0.21	0.24
0.95	Rank	34	47	54	59	60	62	63	64
	SSE	34.62	37.71	40.21	41.70	42.47	42.87	43.08	43.20
	η_{Own}	0.30	0.23	0.15	0.10	0.08	0.06	0.05	0.05
	η_{Spill}	0.16	0.18	0.22	0.25	0.26	0.26	0.27	0.27

Sources: Developed by the authors.

Notes: SSE is the sum of squared errors from the estimated model, and is in millions for the linear model in Panel a. Rank reflects the model's rank by SSE, where the top-ranked model has the smallest SSE. η_{Own} is the elasticity of MFP with respect to state's own research and extension knowledge stock, η_{Spill} is the elasticity of MFP with respect to knowledge spillins.

Appendix Table 10-2 Summary of Results for First-Differenced Versions of the Base Model, 64 Lag Distributions

Panel a. First differences of levels

		λ							
δ		**0.60**	**0.65**	**0.70**	**0.75**	**0.80**	**0.85**	**0.90**	**0.95**
0.60	Rank	44	40	32	20	6	1	11	37
	SSE	585	584	583	582	582	581	582	584
	η_{Own}	0.12	0.13	0.14	0.15	0.14	0.13	0.11	0.10
	η_{Spill}	0.65	0.66	0.66	0.65	0.62	0.58	0.49	0.38
0.65	Rank	41	35	26	14	4	2	21	43
	SSE	584	583	583	582	581	581	582	584
	η_{Own}	0.13	0.14	0.15	0.15	0.14	0.12	0.10	0.10
	η_{Spill}	0.66	0.66	0.65	0.63	0.60	0.54	0.45	0.35
0.70	Rank	34	28	19	13	3	7	33	45
	SSE	583	583	582	582	581	582	583	585
	η_{Own}	0.14	0.15	0.15	0.14	0.13	0.11	0.10	0.09
	η_{Spill}	0.66	0.65	0.63	0.60	0.57	0.50	0.41	0.32
0.75	Rank	29	25	17	10	5	22	42	49
	SSE	583	583	582	582	582	582	584	586
	η_{Own}	0.15	0.15	0.14	0.13	0.11	0.10	0.09	0.09
	η_{Spill}	0.63	0.62	0.60	0.57	0.53	0.45	0.36	0.28
0.80	Rank	31	27	15	8	18	36	47	53
	SSE	583	583	582	582	582	584	586	587
	η_{Own}	0.15	0.14	0.12	0.11	0.10	0.09	0.09	0.09
	η_{Spill}	0.59	0.58	0.56	0.53	0.46	0.38	0.30	0.25
0.85	Rank	30	16	12	23	38	48	51	56
	SSE	583	582	582	582	584	586	587	588
	η_{Own}	0.12	0.11	0.10	0.09	0.09	0.09	0.09	0.08
	η_{Spill}	0.56	0.55	0.51	0.44	0.37	0.30	0.25	0.23
0.90	Rank	9	24	39	46	50	54	58	60
	SSE	582	583	584	585	587	588	589	590
	η_{Own}	0.09	0.09	0.09	0.09	0.09	0.08	0.07	0.07
	η_{Spill}	0.49	0.43	0.36	0.30	0.26	0.23	0.22	0.21
0.95	Rank	52	55	57	59	61	62	63	64
	SSE	587	588	589	590	591	592	593	593
	η_{Own}	0.09	0.08	0.07	0.07	0.06	0.06	0.06	0.05
	η_{Spill}	0.25	0.23	0.21	0.21	0.19	0.18	0.17	0.16

(continued)

Appendix Table 10-2 (continued)

Panel b. First differences of logarithms

δ		λ 0.60	0.65	0.70	0.75	0.80	0.85	0.90	0.95
0.60	Rank	56	52	46	38	25	16	9	21
	SSE	14.52	14.48	14.46	14.44	14.42	14.40	14.39	14.41
	η_{Own}	0.05	0.06	0.08	0.10	0.11	0.12	0.15	0.22
	η_{Spill}	0.60	0.60	0.60	0.58	0.56	0.53	0.46	0.30
0.65	Rank	51	45	39	29	20	12	10	23
	SSE	14.48	14.45	14.44	14.43	14.41	14.40	14.40	14.42
	η_{Own}	0.06	0.08	0.10	0.11	0.12	0.13	0.17	0.23
	η_{Spill}	0.60	0.59	0.58	0.57	0.55	0.51	0.41	0.26
0.70	Rank	41	37	31	26	18	8	15	33
	SSE	14.45	14.44	14.43	14.42	14.41	14.39	14.40	14.43
	η_{Own}	0.08	0.10	0.12	0.12	0.12	0.14	0.20	0.23
	η_{Spill}	0.59	0.58	0.56	0.55	0.53	0.48	0.35	0.23
0.75	Rank	35	36	32	22	13	6	19	42
	SSE	14.43	14.44	14.43	14.42	14.40	14.39	14.41	14.45
	η_{Own}	0.11	0.13	0.13	0.12	0.12	0.16	0.24	0.20
	η_{Spill}	0.56	0.55	0.54	0.54	0.51	0.42	0.27	0.22
0.80	Rank	43	40	28	17	5	14	34	50
	SSE	14.45	14.44	14.43	14.40	14.39	14.40	14.43	14.48
	η_{Own}	0.14	0.13	0.11	0.10	0.14	0.22	0.25	0.12
	η_{Spill}	0.53	0.53	0.54	0.53	0.46	0.31	0.20	0.25
0.85	Rank	44	27	7	3	11	30	48	55
	SSE	14.45	14.42	14.39	14.38	14.40	14.43	14.47	14.51
	η_{Own}	0.10	0.08	0.09	0.15	0.24	0.27	0.14	0.03
	η_{Spill}	0.55	0.56	0.53	0.44	0.29	0.18	0.24	0.30
0.90	Rank	2	1	4	24	47	53	57	59
	SSE	14.38	14.38	14.39	14.42	14.46	14.50	14.53	14.56
	η_{Own}	0.09	0.15	0.24	0.29	0.18	0.05	0.00	0.00
	η_{Spill}	0.53	0.43	0.28	0.17	0.21	0.29	0.30	0.28
0.95	Rank	49	54	58	60	61	62	63	64
	SSE	14.47	14.51	14.54	14.56	14.59	14.61	14.64	14.66
	η_{Own}	0.13	0.02	-0.02	-0.01	0.00	0.01	0.02	0.02
	η_{Spill}	0.25	0.32	0.32	0.29	0.26	0.23	0.22	0.20

Sources: Developed by the authors.

Notes: SSE is the sum of squared errors from the estimated model, and is in thousands for the first-differences model in Panel a. Rank reflects the model's rank by SSE, where the top-ranked model has the smallest SSE. η_{Own} is the elasticity of MFP with respect to state's own research and extension knowledge stock, η_{Spill} is the elasticity of MFP with respect to knowledge spillins.

CHAPTER 11

Productivity Patterns and Research Benefits

In Chapter 10 we reported the results from estimating models of productivity as a function of variables representing agricultural research and extension knowledge stocks. Various transformations of these models can be used to derive implications that are of interest to economists and policymakers. For instance, we can use the estimated model to evaluate the roles of policies in influencing the past time path and spatial pattern of agricultural productivity. Alternatively, we can use the model to evaluate the future time path and spatial pattern of agricultural productivity given actual past and likely future research spending patterns or alternative counterfactual spending patterns. Or, we can compare productivity patterns under alternative scenarios of research spending patterns and infer measures such as benefit-cost ratios or internal rates of return.

In this chapter we report the results from such uses of the estimates of our preferred, base gamma distribution model, and we discuss the sensitivity of our findings to model specification choices. First, the estimated model was used to conduct a growth-accounting exercise, in which the productivity growth predicted by the model was attributed among the various forms of public research and extension knowledge stocks. Second, the same model was used to simulate the impacts of marginal counterfactual changes in past federal research spending, and state-by-state spending on research or extension, and the results were used to compute estimates of national and state benefits and benefit-cost ratios. Third, the same model was used to project future productivity growth to 2050 under alternative assumptions about the likely time path of state and federal research and extension spending over the coming decades.

J.M. Alston et al., *Persistence Pays: U.S. Agricultural Productivity Growth and the Benefits from Public R&D Spending*, Natural Resource Management and Policy 34,
DOI 10.1007/978-1-4419-0658-8_11,

11.1 Growth Accounting

As described in Chapter 10, in the base model research and extension are treated symmetrically, with the same gamma lag distribution weights and the same spill-over coefficients, and with the variables entering either in natural values (equation 11.1a) or in logarithms (equation 11.1b) as follows:

$$\text{(11.1a)}\quad MFP_{i,t} = \beta_i + \beta_K SK_{i,t} + \beta_S SS_{i,t} + \beta_Z PRC_{i,t} + e_{i,t}$$

$$\text{(11.1b)}\quad \ln MFP_{i,t} = \eta_i + \eta_K \ln SK_{i,t} + \eta_S \ln SS_{i,t} + \eta_Z \ln PRC_{i,t} + e_{i,t}\,.$$

In this model, state-specific multi-factor productivity in agriculture depends on (a) a state-specific knowledge stock from own-state public agricultural R&D (including extension), $SK_{i,t}$, (b) a state-specific spillover knowledge stock from both agricultural R&D (including extension) conducted by other states and intramural research conducted in USDA labs, $SS_{i,t}$, and (c) a pasture and range condition index, used to represent the effects of weather, $PRC_{i,t}$.

In this section we report the results from using the estimates of this model to apportion state-specific growth attributable to public agricultural R&D among the various sources, including (a) own-state research and extension expenditures, (b) research and extension expenditures by other states, and (c) intramural USDA research expenditures. We develop ideas first with the linear model, which is simpler for linear partitioning of this sort, and then present counterparts for the logarithmic model, which is preferred statistically and for other reasons. Then we present and discuss estimates from both.

Growth Accounting Procedures

Given the linear aggregation of the elements of the knowledge stocks, the linear model in equation (11.1a) can be represented as:

$$\text{(11.2)}\quad MFP_{i,t} = \beta_i + \beta_K\left(SE_{i,t} + SR_{i,t}\right) + \beta_S\left(SSE_{i,t} + SSR_{i,t} + SSF_{i,t}\right) + \beta_Z PRC_{i,t} + e_{i,t}\,.$$

Thus, we can partition the own-state R&D knowledge stock ($SK_{i,t}$) into its components of an own-state extension knowledge stock ($SE_{i,t}$) and an own-state research knowledge stock ($SR_{i,t}$), and we can partition the state-specific spillover knowledge stock ($SS_{i,t}$) into its components of spillins from (a) extension spending by other states ($SSE_{i,t}$), (b) research spending by other states ($SSR_{i,t}$), and (c) USDA intramural research ($SSF_{i,t} = \omega_{iF} SF_t$), where $SS_{i,t} = SSE_{i,t} + SSR_{i,t} + SSF_{i,t}$. Consequently, we can use the estimated parameters to compute elements of the year-to-year changes in *MFP* attributable to changes in own-state and spillover R&D knowledge stocks, and their underlying components.

Year-to-year predicted growth in state-specific *MFP* attributable to growth in each of the knowledge stocks of interest can be computed as follows, where, for any variable x, $\Delta x_t = x_t - x_{t-1}$:

(11.3) $\Delta MFP^E_{i,t} = \hat{\beta}_K \Delta SE_{i,t}$ (own-state extension)

(11.4) $\Delta MFP^R_{i,t} = \hat{\beta}_K \Delta SR_{i,t}$ (own-state SAES research)

(11.5) $\Delta MFP^K_{i,t} = \hat{\beta}_K \Delta SK_{i,t}$ (total own-state extension and SAES research)

and $\Delta MFP^K_{i,t} = \Delta MFP^E_{i,t} + \Delta MFP^R_{i,t}$

(11.6) $\Delta MFP^{SE}_{i,t} = \hat{\beta}_S \Delta SSE_{i,t}$ (state-state extension spillins)

(11.7) $\Delta MFP^{SR}_{i,t} = \hat{\beta}_S \Delta SSR_{i,t}$ (state-state SAES research spillins)

(11.8) $\Delta MFP^{SF}_{i,t} = \hat{\beta}_S \Delta SSF_{i,t} = \hat{\beta}_S \omega_{iF} \Delta SF_t$ (federal-state research spillins)

(11.9) $\Delta MFP^S_{i,t} = \hat{\beta}_S \Delta SS_{i,t}$ (total spillins)

and $\Delta MFP^S_{i,t} = \Delta MFP^{SE}_{i,t} + \Delta MFP^{SR}_{i,t} + \Delta MFP^{SF}_{i,t}$.

The sum of these terms is the total state-specific annual productivity growth attributable to public-sector agricultural research and extension investments:

(11.10) $\Delta MFP^T_{i,t} = \Delta MFP^K_{i,t} + \Delta MFP^S_{i,t}$

$= \left(\Delta MFP^E_{i,t} + \Delta MFP^R_{i,t}\right) + \left(\Delta MFP^{SE}_{i,t} + \Delta MFP^{SR}_{i,t} + \Delta MFP^{SF}_{i,t}\right) \cdot$

Since these are predicted changes from a model that is linear in the levels of the variables, the growth is measured linearly as changes in the level of the *MFP* index (from a base of 100 in 1949) rather than exponentially as proportional or percentage changes. Dividing each of the elements of equation (11.10) by the total and multiplying by 100 yields estimates of the percentage shares of annual growth in productivity attributable to each element (i.e., percentages that sum to 100 percent across the various elements of public-sector agricultural research and extension) as follows:

(11.11) $SG^X_{i,t} = 100 \times \left(\Delta MFP^X_{i,t} / \Delta MFP^T_{i,t}\right)$,

for $X = K, E, R, S, SE, SR, SF$, and T.

The components of growth in the index of *MFP* in equations (11.3) through (11.9) can also be expressed in proportional change terms, relative to the value of the index, as follows (for $X = K, E, R, S, SE, SR, SF$, and T):

$$(11.12)\quad \%\Delta\, MFP^{X}_{i,t} = 100 \times \frac{\Delta\, MFP^{X}_{i,t}}{\frac{1}{2}\left(\hat{MFP}_{i,t} + \hat{MFP}_{i,t-1}\right)},$$

where $\hat{MFP}_{i,t}$ is the predicted value of $MFP_{i,t}$ from the model. In our application we use the annual values of the knowledge stock variables but, to eliminate extreme fluctuations in the measure, we use the state-specific sample mean rather than the annual value of the weather index, $PRC_{i,t}$.

The measures presented so far are from the linear form of the base model. Precisely the same formulas (equations 11.3 through 11.12) are applicable when the model is estimated in first differences rather than levels of the variables, so it is straightforward to estimate all of the same measures of components of growth attributable to the different knowledge stocks from the first-difference model if it were preferred to the model estimated in levels.

Comparable measures are also straightforward to obtain when the model is estimated in logarithms rather than in levels. Specifically, suppose we start with the model in equation (11.1b), which is equivalent to equation (11.1a) except that the variables enter in logarithms rather than natural units:

$$(11.13)\quad \ln MFP_{i,t} = \eta_i + \eta_K \ln SK_{i,t} + \eta_S \ln SS_{i,t} + \eta_Z \ln PRC_{i,t} + e_{i,t}.$$

Then, we can use the estimated parameters to compute elements of the year-to-year proportional changes in *MFP* attributable to changes in own-state and spillover R&D knowledge stocks, and their underlying components, as follows (where, for any variable x, $\Delta \ln x_t = \ln x_t - \ln x_{t-1}$):

$$(11.14)\quad \Delta \ln MFP^{E}_{i,t} = \hat{\eta}_K \left(\frac{SE_{i,t}}{SK_{i,t}}\right) \Delta \ln SE_{i,t} \quad \text{(own-state extension)}$$

$$(11.15)\quad \Delta \ln MFP^{R}_{i,t} = \hat{\eta}_K \left(\frac{SR_{i,t}}{SK_{i,t}}\right) \Delta \ln SR_{i,t} \quad \text{(own-state SAES research)}$$

$$(11.16)\quad \Delta \ln MFP^{K}_{i,t} = \hat{\eta}_K \Delta \ln SK_{i,t} \quad \text{(own-state extension and SAES research)}$$

$$\text{and } \Delta \ln MFP^{K}_{i,t} = \Delta \ln MFP^{E}_{i,t} + \Delta \ln MFP^{R}_{i,t}$$

$$(11.17)\quad \Delta \ln MFP^{SE}_{i,t} = \hat{\eta}_S \left(\frac{SSE_{i,t}}{SS_{i,t}}\right) \Delta \ln SSE_{i,t} \quad \text{(state-state extension spillins)}$$

$$(11.18)\quad \Delta \ln MFP^{SR}_{i,t} = \hat{\eta}_S \left(\frac{SSR_{i,t}}{SS_{i,t}}\right) \Delta \ln SSR_{i,t} \quad \text{(state-state SAES research spillins)}$$

$$(11.19)\quad \Delta \ln MFP_{i,t}^{SF} = \hat{\eta}_S \left(\frac{SSF_{i,t}}{SS_{i,t}} \right) \Delta \ln SSF_{i,t} \text{ (federal-state research spillins)}$$

$$(11.20)\quad \Delta \ln MFP_{i,t}^{S} = \hat{\eta}_S \Delta \ln SS_{i,t} \text{ (total spillins)}$$

$$\text{and } \Delta \ln MFP_{i,t}^{S} = \Delta \ln MFP_{i,t}^{SE} + \Delta \ln MFP_{i,t}^{SR} + \Delta \ln MFP_{i,t}^{SF}.$$

$$(11.21)\quad \Delta \ln MFP_{i,t}^{T} = \Delta \ln MFP_{i,t}^{K} + \Delta \ln MFP_{i,t}^{S}$$

$$= \left(\Delta \ln MFP_{i,t}^{E} + \Delta \ln MFP_{i,t}^{R}\right) + \left(\Delta \ln MFP_{i,t}^{SE} + \Delta \ln MFP_{i,t}^{SR} + \Delta \ln MFP_{i,t}^{SF}\right).$$

As with the linear model, dividing each of the elements of equation (11.21) by the total and multiplying by 100 yields estimates of the percentage shares of annual proportional growth in productivity attributable to each element as follows:

$$(11.22)\quad SG_{i,t}^{X} = 100 \times \left(\Delta \ln MFP_{i,t}^{X} / \Delta \ln MFP_{i,t}^{T}\right),$$

for $X = K, E, R, S, SE, SR, SF$, and T. If we wish, alternatively, to compute the growth as changes in the level of the *MFP* index (from a base of 100 in 1949) rather than exponentially, we can multiply the proportional changes by the value of the index (or the average of the current and lagged values of the index). That is, for $X = K, E, R, S, SE, SR, SF$, and T:

$$(11.23)\quad \Delta MFP_{i,t}^{X} = \Delta \ln MFP_{i,t}^{X} \times \tfrac{1}{2}\left(M\hat{F}P_{i,t} + M\hat{F}P_{i,t-1}\right).$$

Again, the state-specific average of the pasture and range condition index is used to calculate the predicted *MFP* index.

Growth Accounting Results—Contributors to Growth in MFP

We applied the growth accounting procedures, described in equations (11.1) through (11.23) to the estimated models documented in Chapter 10. In Appendix Table 11-1, we report the state-specific averages of the annual figures over 1950 to 2002 for the predicted growth rates in *MFP* attributable to research and extension knowledge stocks, and the shares of that total growth attributable to the different components of each knowledge stock. Panel a summarizes these results for the best-fitting linear model, and Panel b includes results from the preferred logarithmic model. Appendix Table 11-2 replicates Appendix Table 11-1 but instead of percentage shares of the total it includes the amounts of productivity growth attributable to the different knowledge stocks. In both of these tables, the states are listed within regions and, as well as state-specific figures for each of the 48 states, for each region we report the simple average of the estimates for the states in that region; we also report the simple average across all 48 states. Table

11-1 replicates the information in Appendix Table 11-1, just for the regional and national averages, and for a selection of states of interest (California, Minnesota, and Wyoming), as well as the minimum, maximum, and average across the 48 states for each element.

A primary partitioning is between growth attributable to own-state investments in research and extension, and growth attributable to spillins from investments by other states in research and extension or by the USDA in intramural research. This partitioning is sensitive to the functional form of the model. Both the linear and logarithmic models indicate that knowledge and technology spillovers have accounted for a very significant share of the total productivity growth experienced in U.S. agriculture.[1] However, the shares of growth attributable to spillovers are significantly larger for the linear model (in Panel a of Table 11-1) than the logarithmic model (in Panel b of Table 11-1).

Column 8 of Table 11-1 shows estimates of the state-by-state average annual year-to-year growth in *MFP* attributed to public-sector agricultural research and extension. Using the linear model, across the 48 states, the average annual year-to-year growth in *MFP* attributed to public-sector agricultural research and extension ranges from 0.59 to 3.43 percent per year, with a 48-state average of 1.77 percent per year. Less than one-fifth (19.0 percent) of this *MFP* growth is attributable to own-state research and extension—11.6 percent to own-state SAES research and 7.3 percent to own-state extension (Panel a, columns 1, 2 and 3). The share attributable to spillins from all sources ranges from 48.6 to 97.0 percent, averaging 81.0 percent across the states (Panel a, column 7). This 81.0 percent is comprised of 18.9 percent attributable to intramural USDA research, 38.0 percent attributable to research conducted by other states, and 24.1 percent attributable to extension conducted by other states (Panel a, columns 4, 5, and 6). These rates differ among the states, with relatively large variances in the own-state research and extension impacts, compared with the spillover impacts, but in every state the spillover elements account for a substantial share of the average annual productivity growth. The very small share of productivity growth attributable to own-state research and extension is a striking feature of this model, and a point of significant difference between it and the logarithmic model, discussed next.

Using the logarithmic model, across the 48 states, the average annual year-to-year growth in *MFP* attributed to public-sector agricultural research and extension ranges from 1.38 percent per year to 2.42 percent per year, with a 48-state average of 1.87 percent per year (Table 11-1, Panel b, column 8). Own-state research and extension accounts for more than half (56.7 percent) on average

1 These models did not include variables to represent many alternative potential influences on productivity, and the estimates therefore may reflect some omitted variables bias and may have consequently overstated the extent to which public agricultural research caused own-state or interstate productivity growth. The potential implications are explored in Chapter 12.

Table 11-1 Productivity Growth Attributable to Knowledge Stocks, 1949–2002

Panel a. Linear model

	Own			Spillins				Average Annual
State	SAES (1)	Extension (2)	Total (3)	SAES (4)	USDA (5)	Extension (6)	Total (7)	%Δ MFP (8)
48 state	*percentage share of change in MFP attributable to knowledge stock*							*percent*
Average	11.6	7.3	19.0	38.0	18.9	24.1	81.0	1.77
Minimum	1.5	1.2	3.0	22.4	11.5	14.6	48.6	0.59
Maximum	37.6	19.7	51.4	48.3	23.4	29.9	97.0	3.43
Selected states								
California	37.6	13.8	51.4	22.4	11.5	14.6	48.6	3.09
Minnesota	15.1	9.3	24.3	34.1	19.4	22.1	75.7	2.37
Wyoming	2.7	2.2	4.9	44.8	22.7	27.6	95.1	1.68
Regions								
Pacific	21.5	9.0	30.5	32.9	16.1	20.5	69.5	2.25
Mountain	7.1	3.3	10.5	42.4	21.0	26.1	89.5	1.77
Northern Plains	11.3	5.8	17.1	37.8	21.1	23.9	82.9	1.59
Southern Plains	15.2	10.1	25.3	34.9	17.5	22.3	74.7	1.83
Central	14.0	9.4	23.4	34.4	19.8	22.3	76.6	2.33
Southeast	14.3	11.4	25.7	34.5	17.2	22.6	74.3	1.78
Northeast	6.7	4.2	11.0	43.1	18.7	27.2	89.0	1.26

Panel b. Logarithmic model

	Own			Spillins				Average Annual
State	SAES (1)	Extension (2)	Total (3)	SAES (4)	USDA (5)	Extension (6)	Total (7)	%Δ MFP (8)
48 state	*percentage share of change in MFP attributable to knowledge stock*							*percent*
Average	30.6	26.0	56.7	16.5	12.7	14.1	43.3	1.87
Minimum	17.3	14.2	40.8	13.0	9.3	10.6	32.9	1.38
Maximum	46.1	35.6	67.1	23.9	16.8	20.1	59.2	2.42
Selected states								
California	44.2	20.7	64.9	13.3	10.4	11.4	35.1	2.26
Minnesota	34.0	24.3	58.4	15.1	13.3	13.3	41.6	1.82
Wyoming	28.3	22.2	50.6	18.6	15.0	15.8	49.4	1.68
Regions								
Pacific	39.3	22.7	62.0	14.7	11.1	12.2	38.0	2.12
Mountain	34.3	23.2	57.6	16.2	12.6	13.6	42.4	1.88
Northern Plains	34.1	23.9	57.9	15.4	13.4	13.2	42.1	1.86
Southern Plains	29.6	29.2	58.8	15.6	12.2	13.4	41.2	2.00
Central	29.5	27.3	56.8	15.6	14.0	13.6	43.2	1.83
Southeast	28.3	31.2	59.5	15.3	11.8	13.4	40.5	2.03
Northeast	27.5	23.2	50.7	19.6	13.1	16.6	49.3	1.66

Sources: Developed by the authors.

of the total *MFP* growth (compared with only one-fifth for the linear model), a share that ranges from 40.8 percent to 67.1 percent across the states. Of this total, own-state research accounts for 30.6 percent (ranging from 17.3 to 46.1 percent) and own-state extension accounts for a slightly smaller share of 26.0

percent (from 14.2 to 35.6 percent). The share attributable to spillins ranges from 32.9 to 59.2 percent, averaging 43.3 percent across the states (Panel b, column 7), half as much as indicated by the linear model but nonetheless an important element of productivity growth in every state. This 43.3 percent is comprised of 12.7 percent attributable to intramural USDA research, 16.5 percent attributable to research conducted by other states, and 14.1 percent attributable to extension conducted by other states (columns 4, 5, and 6). While the *MFP* growth contributed by spillins in the logarithmic model is very similar for every state, ranging from 0.79 to 0.82 percent per year across all the states (Appendix Table 11-2, Panel b, column 7), this relatively fixed amount represents a much more variable share of the total state-specific growth, which varies from 1.38 to 2.42 percent per year (Table 11-1, Panel b, column 8). In addition, the value of this contribution will be different for different states, according to the sizes of their agricultural sectors.

In both the linear and logarithmic models the variation in results among the states is systematic, with spillovers being relatively important for the smaller agricultural states (like Wyoming, or various New England states) and less so for the larger states (like California or Texas), especially in the linear model. States with smaller agricultural sectors and correspondingly smaller SAESs—especially if they are also states in which the agricultural sector is not too different from that in the nation as a whole—are likely to have comparatively large shares attributable to spillover effects and comparatively small shares attributable to own-state research and extension.

The patterns of results summarized in Table 11-1 (and presented more completely in Appendix Tables 11-1 and 11-2) are illustrated graphically in Figure 11-1, in which Panel a represents the linear model and Panel b represents the logarithmic model. The states are ordered according to their total estimated *MFP* growth over the period, which is presented in parentheses after each state name. The contributions of own-state research and extension are measured to the left of the vertical axis and the contributions of spillins from extension and research conducted by other states or the USDA are measured to the right. The total length of the bar for each state thus represents the total growth in *MFP* attributable to the various knowledge stocks.

Comparing the two panels, the logarithmic model resulted in much less variation among states in the total predicted productivity growth and its attribution among the different knowledge stocks. In particular, the amounts of growth attributed to the different elements of spillovers are almost identical among states in the logarithmic model, but quite variable among states using the linear model. This result is largely an artifact of the functional form. The logarithmic form implies elasticities of productivity with respect to knowledge stocks that are the same for all states, regardless of their size. Spillover knowledge stocks are fairly similar among states and hence the growth attributable to spillovers is fairly similar among states. In contrast, the linear form implies equal multipliers of productivity with respect to knowledge stocks. Hence the elasticities of productivity with respect to knowledge stocks are positively related to the size of the knowledge stock, which is itself positively correlated with the size of the state's agriculture (for own-state research impacts). Consequently, larger states tend to have larger rates of productivity growth attributable to their own (themselves generally larger) knowledge stocks because the elasticities are larger even though the same coefficient, $\hat{\beta}_K$, applies to all states.

In principle, either set of results could be plausible—i.e., the increment to productivity could be proportional to the size of the increment in the relevant knowledge stock, a constant multiplier effect of knowledge stocks on productivity as implied by the linear model, or it could be a constant elasticity relationship as implied by the logarithmic model. However, the actual productivity growth has been similar across all 48 states even though they have had very different absolute growth in their knowledge stocks, which is more difficult to reconcile with a linear model and a constant multiplier. This aspect is reflected in the patterns of predicted *MFP* growth. The constant multiplier feature of the linear model, whereby the multiplier is equal across all sizes of states, necessarily implies comparatively fast predicted (and generally overstated) productivity growth in larger states that have experienced greater absolute growth in their knowledge stocks (like California and Texas); the converse is true in the smaller states for which predicted productivity growth is comparatively low and generally understated by the linear model. The logarithmic model imposes different restrictions on the patterns across states, but the results seem generally more consistent with prior expectations.

Effects of Specification Choices on Growth Accounting Results

In Chapter 10 we reported the results from a range of alternative models, allowing for different forms of research and extension lag distributions—including different maximum lag length, different lag shapes, and asymmetric treatment of research and extension in terms of lag distribution shape or spillover effects. In terms of statistical performance and other characteristics we prefer the base model over these alternatives; and, between the linear and logarithmic (and first-differenced versions of the linear and logarithmic) versions of the base model, we prefer the logarithmic model on the whole. Even so, it is of interest to consider the implications of the alternatives for findings with respect to the attribution of responsibility for productivity growth and, later, for benefit-cost ratios and so on. In this section we present and compare growth accounting results from a range of alternative models, summarized in terms of (a) the predicted growth rate of *MFP* and (b) the share of that growth attributable to own-state research and extension. We present ranges and averages of state-specific figures, along with

Figure 11-1 Productivity Growth Partitioned Among Knowledge Stocks, 1949–2009

a. Linear model

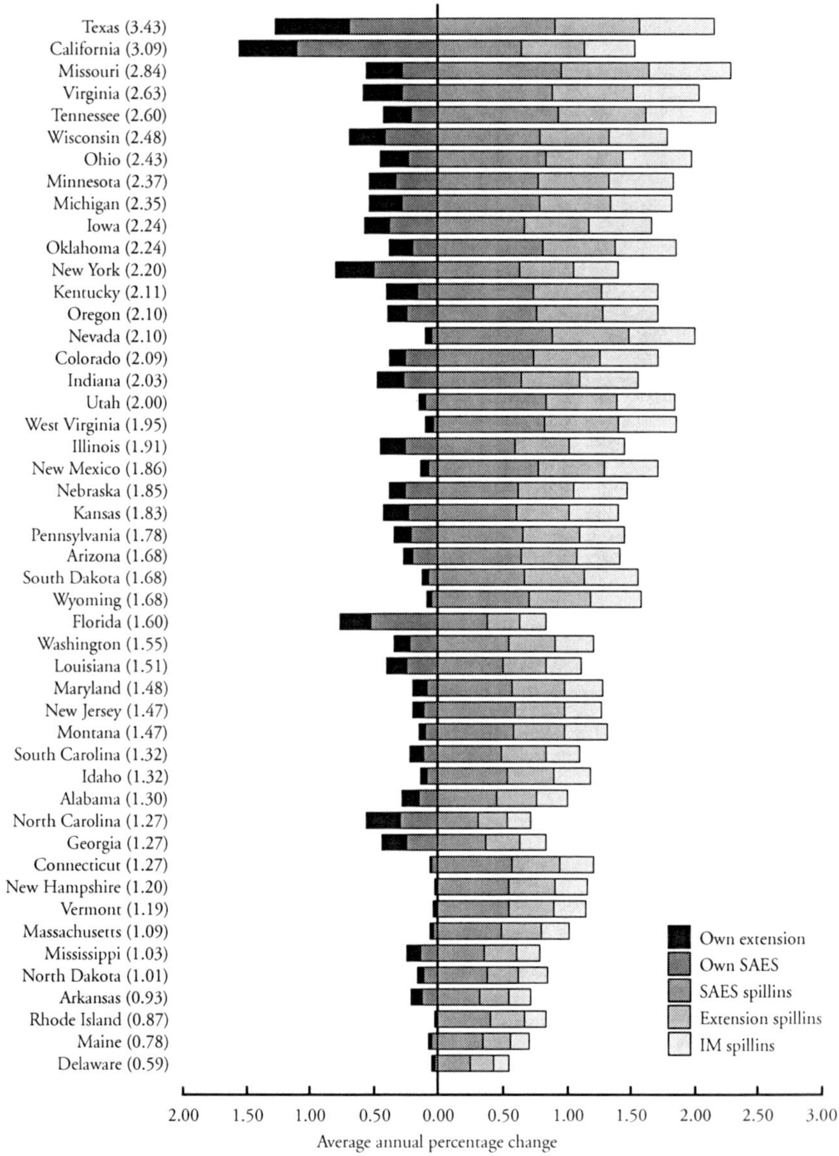

(continued)

Figure 11-1 (continued)

b. Logarithmic model

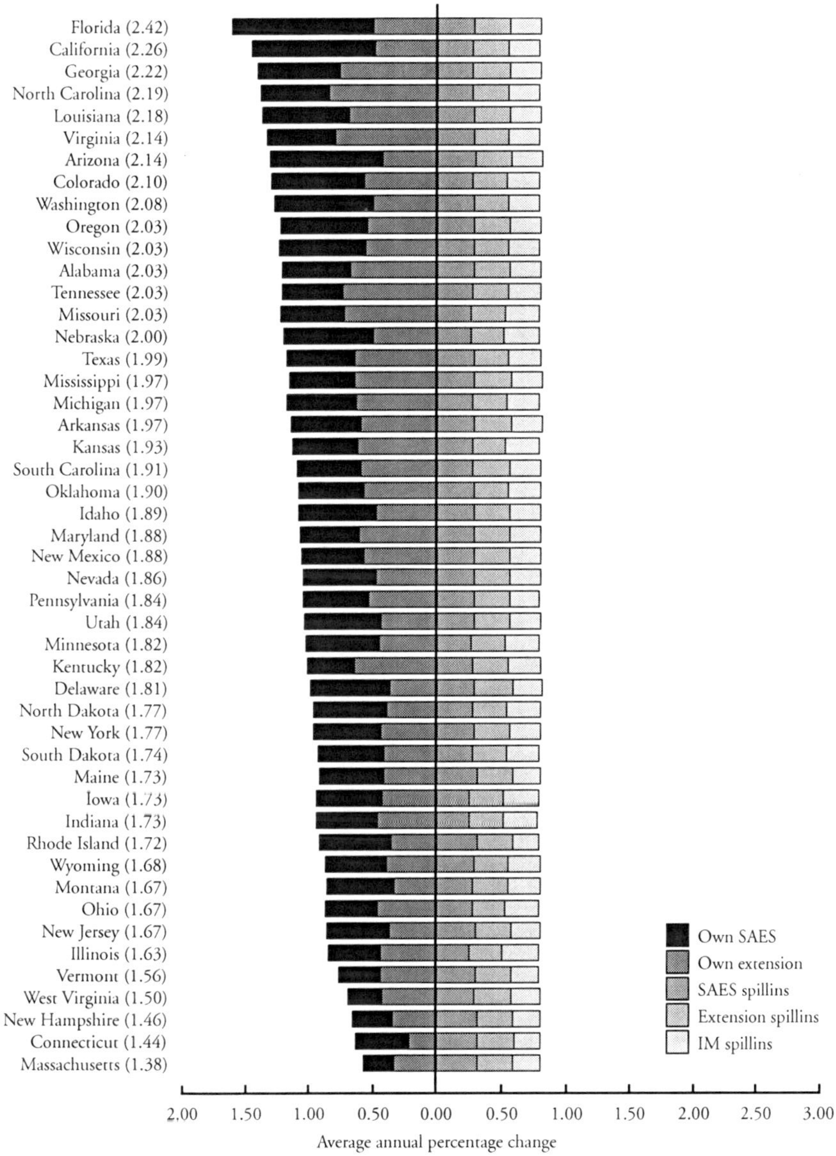

Sources: Developed by the authors.

Table 11-2 MFP Growth Accounting—Effects of Functional Form, 1949–2002

State	Linear (1)	First-Difference (2)	Logarithmic (3)	Growth (4)
RMSE	30.36	34.08	22.46	27.70
Lag distribution parameters				
λ	0.75	0.85	0.70	0.65
δ	0.80	0.60	0.90	0.90
Peak lag year	13	8	24	20
48 states	*average annual percentage predicted change in MFP (percentage share of growth attributed to own-state R&E in parentheses)*			
Average	1.77	1.85	1.87	1.80
	(19.0)	(18.5)	(56.7)	(26.1)
Minimum	0.59	0.52	1.38	1.56
	(3.0)	(2.5)	(40.8)	(13.6)
Maximum	3.43	3.22	2.42	2.05
	(51.4)	(50.9)	(67.1)	(35.8)
Selected states				
California	3.09	3.22	2.26	1.96
	(51.4)	(50.9)	(64.9)	(33.2)
Minnesota	2.37	2.84	1.82	1.80
	(24.3)	(25.0)	(58.4)	(28.7)
Wyoming	1.68	1.60	1.68	1.71
	(4.9)	(4.5)	(50.6)	(20.4)

Sources: Developed by the authors.

state-specific figures for California, Minnesota, and Wyoming. In each case we present the results using the best-fitting gamma distribution for the particular model specification (and we report the parameters of that gamma distribution and peak lag year), along with the root mean square prediction error (RMSE) for *MFP* in levels based on the predictions from that model.

Table 11-2 includes results for the best-fitting linear, first-differenced linear, logarithmic, and first-differenced logarithmic (or growth) model, in columns 1 through 4, respectively. This table replicates in slightly different format the findings, already reviewed, showing that the linear and logarithmic model yield different values for the total predicted growth in *MFP* attributable to research and extension, and that the linear model attributes a much greater share to spillovers (and a much smaller share to own-state research and extension) compared with the logarithmic model. The results from the first-difference model are almost identical to those from the linear model; the results from the first-differenced logarithmic model (the "growth" model) are generally in between, but closer to those from the linear model than the logarithmic model.

Table 11-3 includes corresponding results for models that entail different specifications of the lag distribution applied to extension. A primary distinction is between models that applied the same 50-year gamma lag distribution to both research and extension (columns 1 through 4) versus otherwise equivalent

Table 11-3 MFP Growth Accounting—Effects of Extension Lag Model, 1949–2002

	Gamma Extension Lags				Geometric Extension Lags			
	Linear Model		Logarithmic Model		Linear Model		Logarithmic Model	
Extension Spillovers	Yes (1)	No (2)	Yes (3)	No (4)	Yes (5)	No (6)	Yes (7)	No (8)
RMSE	30.36	30.55	22.46	22.41	30.39	30.56	23.71	23.21
Lag distribution parameters								
λ	0.75	0.75	0.70	0.70	0.65	0.60	0.65	0.65
δ	0.80	0.80	0.90	0.90	0.90	0.90	0.90	0.90
Peak lag year	13	13	24	24	20	17	20	20
	average annual percentage predicted change in MFP (percentage share of growth attributed to own-state R&E in parentheses)							
48 states								
Average	1.77	2.34	1.87	2.29	1.82	2.27	1.76	2.44
	(19.0)	(15.0)	(56.7)	(45.3)	(18.1)	(15.8)	(22.8)	(17.4)
Minimum	0.59	0.81	1.38	1.83	0.61	0.77	1.46	2.19
	(3.0)	(2.2)	(40.8)	(29.8)	(2.5)	(2.1)	(3.9)	(2.7)
Maximum	3.43	4.34	2.42	2.82	3.35	4.15	2.08	2.77
	(51.4)	(43.7)	(67.1)	(56.3)	(50.6)	(46.5)	(35.2)	(27.9)
Selected states								
California	3.09	3.75	2.26	2.66	3.18	3.82	1.92	2.61
	(51.4)	(43.7)	(64.9)	(53.7)	(50.6)	(46.5)	(30.6)	(23.7)
Minnesota	2.37	3.11	1.82	2.21	2.50	3.12	1.82	2.46
	(24.3)	(19.1)	(58.4)	(47.1)	(24.0)	(21.1)	(27.5)	(21.5)
Wyoming	1.68	2.31	1.68	2.10	1.70	2.18	1.62	2.28
	(4.9)	(3.7)	(50.6)	(39.3)	(4.0)	(3.1)	(14.4)	(10.6)

Sources: Developed by the authors.

models that applied the Huffman-Evenson 4-year geometric lag distribution to extension (columns 5 through 8). Another distinction is between models that applied the same spillover weights to extension and research versus otherwise equivalent models that did not allow for extension spillovers. Combining these options yielded four specifications, each of which was estimated in linear and logarithmic form. We can see the main implications of these alternatives by comparing columns in the highlighted row, representing the average values across the 48 states.

First, disallowing extension spillovers (comparing columns 1 versus 2, 3 versus 4, 5 versus 6, and 7 versus 8) results in a substantially greater estimate of total *MFP* growth attributable to research and extension knowledge stocks (greater by 0.4 to 0.6 percent per year) of which in every instance, perhaps surprisingly, a *smaller* share is attributed to own-state research and extension and hence a *larger* share is attributed to spillovers, even though they now must come entirely from SAES research or USDA research since extension spillovers are not allowed. Second, the use of the Huffman-Evenson 4-year geometric lag distribution for extension, rather than the 50-year gamma distribution had only modest impacts on the results from the linear model (i.e., comparing columns 1 and 2 with columns 5 and 6, respectively). However, the use of the 4-year geometric lag distribution for extension significantly changed the share of growth attributable to own-state R&E for the logarithmic model (i.e., comparing columns 3 and 4 with columns 7 and 8, respectively). Third, the use of the 4-year geometric lag distribution for extension resulted in smaller differences between the linear and logarithmic model in the share of growth attributable to own-state R&E (i.e., comparing columns 7 and 8 with columns 5 and 6, respectively) than when the same 50-year gamma distribution was applied to both extension and research (i.e., comparing columns 3 and 4 with columns 1 and 2, respectively).

These results reveal some complex interactions between the effects of the functional form for the model (linear versus logarithmic), the structure of the lag distribution for extension (4-year geometric versus 50-year gamma), and the treatment of extension spillovers, in jointly influencing the findings regarding the total growth in *MFP* attributed to research and extension knowledge stocks and the share of that total attributable to own-state research and extension.[2] It remains to be seen whether the benefit-cost analysis results are as sensitive to these same factors.

11.2 Analysis of State and National Benefits and Costs

The growth accounting exercise provides a useful depiction of the shares of total productivity growth attributable to different components of the public-sector agricultural research and extension effort. The same partitioning could be applied to a measure of the total benefits from productivity growth. These total benefits are approximately equal to the state-specific proportional growth in productivity multiplied by the corresponding state-specific value of production, either year-by-year or on average over the period. The resulting figures would correspond to a total, *ex post* benefit measure that could be compared with a corresponding total cost measure to derive an *average* benefit-cost ratio or internal rate of return. Alternatively we could use the same productivity model to compute the *marginal* benefit associated with a hypothetical change in the research investment, *ex ante* or *ex post*. Here we compute the state-specific (private, in some sense) and national (social, in some sense) benefits from a small (one thousand dollar) change in a particular year (1950) in expenditures (a) on research by a particular state,

2 Appendix Tables 11-3, 11-4 and 11-5 report similar types of comparisons for the models presented in Tables 10-10, 10-11, and 10-12. These models incorporate different treatments of the research lag in terms of (a) the basis for research and extension spillovers (based on output mix, versus USDA regions, or not allowed at all), (b) the lag distribution form (i.e., gamma versus trapezoid research lags, combined with alternative specifications of the extension lag), and (c) the overall lag length for the gamma model (a maximum lag of 20 or 35 years versus 50 years). These variations in specification had mostly modest effects on the predicted *MFP* growth attributed to research and extension, and the relative importance of own-state versus spillin effects. One clear exception is the models that entirely precluded spillins.

(b) on extension by a particular state, or (c) on USDA intramural research by the federal government. In computing the social benefits, we take into account that both federal and state-specific research will have effects on all the states.

The gross annual research benefits (*GARB*) to state *i* in year *t* were computed using the following approximation:

$$(11.24)\quad GARB_{i,t} = \Delta \ln MFP_{i,t} V_{i,t}$$

where $V_{i,t}$ is the real (in year 2000 dollars) value of agricultural production in state *i* in year *t*, and $\Delta \ln MFP_{i,t}$ is the proportional change in agricultural productivity in state *i* in year *t*, associated with the simulated one thousand dollar change in research or extension spending in a particular state or federally in 1950.[3] For the linear model, the simulated proportional change in *MFP* is equal to the simulated value of the index with the counterfactual amount of research spending (MFP^1) minus the simulated value of the index with the actual amount of research spending (MFP^0), all divided by the average of the two values of *MFP*:

$$(11.25)\quad \Delta \ln MFP_{i,t} = \frac{MFP^1_{i,t} - MFP^0_{i,t}}{\frac{1}{2}\left(MFP^1_{i,t} + MFP^0_{i,t}\right)}.$$

For the logarithmic model, the simulated proportional change in *MFP* is simply equal to $\Delta \ln MFP = \ln MFP^1 - \ln MFP^0$. Then, in either case, the present value in the year 2002 of benefits accruing to state *i* (PVB_i) was computed using a (correspondingly real) discount rate of $r = 3$ percent per year.

$$(11.26)\quad PVB_i = \sum_{t=1950}^{2002} GARB_{i,t}\left(1+r\right)^{2002-t} = \sum_{t=1950}^{2002} \Delta \ln MFP_{i,t} V_{i,t}\left(1+r\right)^{2002-t}.$$

The benefit-cost ratio for that one thousand dollar investment is given by dividing the present value of benefits by the present value of the costs—$PVC = \$1,000\ (1+r)^{53}$ (= \$4,650 for $r = 3$ percent). Hence, marginal benefit-cost ratios (or benefits per dollar of additional expenditure) were computed as $B^k_i / C^k_i = PVB^k_i / \$4,650$, where the superscript *k* denotes which of (a) federal re-

3 This approximation is likely to be reasonably valid as a measure of the total benefits for a small research-induced change in production, as a result of a comparatively small change in the research investment. However, to the extent that research induces price changes, the benefits will be distributed between producers and consumers, depending on the elasticities of supply and demand, and this might imply differences in spatial distribution of benefits, compared with our analysis that implicitly presumes that all of the benefits from increased productivity in a state are enjoyed within that state (i.e., accruing to producers or assuming an absence of interstate and international trade). This "distortion" will itself be unevenly distributed. Some states produce commodities for which the United States as a whole, let alone an individual state, does not appreciably influence the world price; but California, for instance, significantly influences world prices for a substantial share of its production, and a big share of its production is consumed in other states. This means there are greater spillouts of California's research benefits than for most other states, associated with research-induced price changes, which we have not accounted for here.

Table 11-4 Marginal Benefit-Cost Ratios—Regional and National Averages

State or Region	Linear Model			Logarithmic Model		
	State R&E "Private" (1)	State R&E "Social" (2)	USDA Intramural (3)	State R&E "Private" (4)	State R&E "Social" (5)	USDA Intramural (6)
Total			47.0			17.5
48 states						
Average	10.0	39.7	1.0	21.0	32.1	0.4
Minimum	0.2	14.2	0.0	2.4	9.9	0.0
Maximum	43.9	74.4	4.6	57.8	69.2	1.6
Selected states						
California	42.3	68.9	3.8	33.3	43.4	1.4
Minnesota	22.6	62.3	2.8	40.6	55.4	0.8
Wyoming	2.2	31.9	0.2	12.7	23.6	0.1
Regions						
Pacific	17.9	47.2	1.6	21.8	32.9	0.6
Mountain	3.7	35.2	0.3	20.0	31.6	0.1
Northern Plains	11.2	44.4	1.2	42.4	54.5	0.5
Southern Plains	13.7	41.7	1.3	20.2	31.0	0.5
Central	23.4	58.8	2.5	33.7	46.8	0.8
Southeast	6.7	36.9	0.6	15.1	26.7	0.3
Northeast	3.0	26.8	0.2	9.4	18.4	0.1

Sources: Developed by the authors.

search expenditures, (b) one of the 48 state-specific research expenditures, or (c) one of the 48 state-specific extension expenditures was increased by $1,000 in 1950 to generate the stream of benefits being evaluated.

Base Model Results

Recall that in the base model, own-state research and extension are treated symmetrically (the same spillover coefficients and the same lag distribution weights from a 50-year gamma distribution apply to research and extension). Because we have treated state-specific research and extension symmetrically, as fungible elements of the own-state knowledge stock, the "private" benefit-cost ratio for SAES research in any state is the same as the "private" benefit-cost ratio for extension; the same is true for the "social" benefit-cost ratios for state government expenditures on research and extension.

Complete results from the various experiments conducted using the base model estimated in either linear form or logarithmic form are included in Appendix Table 11-6 (which includes the estimated benefit-cost ratios) and Appendix Table 11-7 (which corresponds to Appendix Table 11-6 except that the entries are internal rates of return instead of benefit-cost ratios).[4] Table 11-4 sum-

4 The internal rates of return are presented mainly for purposes of comparison with other studies, we do not put great stock in the specific values. Among other potential problems, the computation presumes that the funds can be reinvested at the computed rate of return, which becomes implau-

Table 11-5 Marginal Internal Rates of Return—Regional and National Averages

	Linear Model		Logarithmic Model	
State or Region	**"Private"**	**"Social"**	**"Private"**	**"Social"**
	rate of return to USDA intramural research spending, percent per year			
		65.9		18.7
48 states	*rate of return to state spending on research and extension, percent per year*			
Average	23.4	59.4	18.9	22.7
Minimum	-8.0	34.8	7.4	15.3
Maximum	68.3	85.8	27.6	29.1
Selected states				
California	61.9	79.6	24.1	26.1
Minnesota	45.0	76.0	24.7	27.3
Wyoming	9.5	53.6	16.8	20.9
Regions				
Pacific	33.8	64.8	20.2	23.5
Mountain	13.2	56.3	19.0	22.7
Northern Plains	28.2	62.4	24.9	27.0
Southern Plains	29.6	61.1	19.5	22.7
Central	45.5	74.2	23.1	25.9
Southeast	21.2	57.6	17.6	22.0
Northeast	9.2	49.0	14.0	19.0

Sources: Developed by the authors.

marizes the benefit-cost ratios in Appendix Table 11-6 in terms of the regional averages (the simple average of the entries for the states within each region), the minimum, maximum, and simple average across the 48 states, and state-specific entries for some selected states (California, Minnesota, and Wyoming). In Table 11-4 (and Appendix Table 11-6), for each state and for each model, the entries are measures of the marginal benefits per dollar of expenditure (a type of benefit-cost ratio), including the benefits from the state's expenditures on research and extension combined as they accrue to itself (the state's "private" benefits) and the nation as a whole (the "social" benefits, including both the "private" benefits and the "spillover" benefits to the other 47 states), and the state's benefits from USDA intramural research expenditures. All of these figures are in common terms, expressing real, marginal benefits per dollar invested (associated with a small change in expenditure in 1950). Table 11-5 provides the corresponding regional and national summary information on the internal rates of return from Appendix Table 11-7.

The interesting patterns to consider in these tables are (a) between "private" and "social" returns to R&D that in this case includes both research and extension, (b) between "private" and "social" returns across states, and (c) between

sible when the streams of benefits are very large relative to the streams of costs such that the implied rate of return is very large.

Figure 11-2 Own-State and National Benefit-Cost Ratios for SAES Research

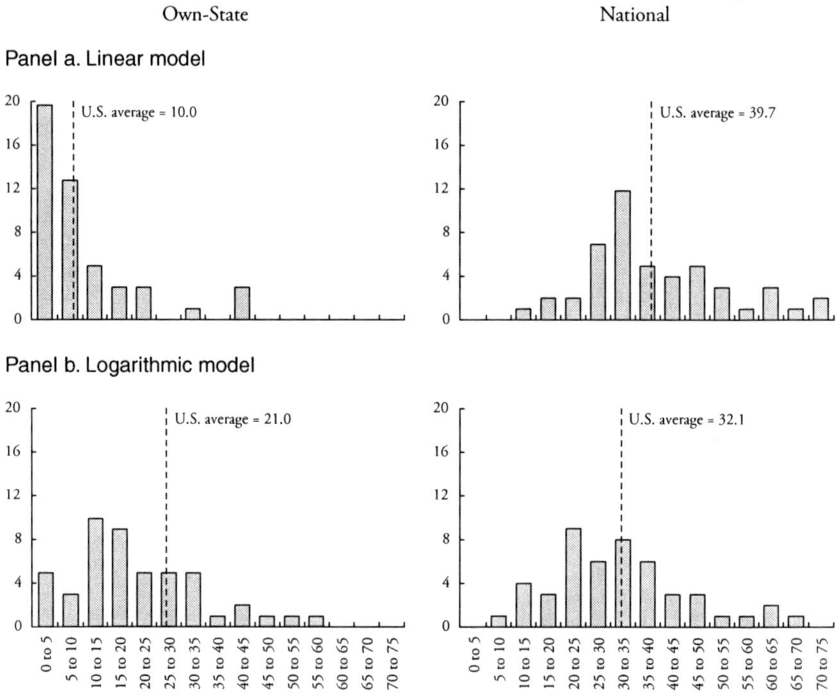

Sources: Developed by the authors.

social returns to federal intramural research versus state R&D spending.[5] By comparing the findings between the linear model and the logarithmic model we can examine the sensitivity of the findings to this dimension of modeling choice. These comparisons are most easily made in the context of the summary measures in Tables 11-4 and 11-5, while we can refer to the more complete versions in Appendix Table 11-6 and Appendix Table 11-7 for information on particular states. In addition, Figures 11-2 and 11-3 include graphical and geographical representations of the benefit-cost ratios from Appendix Table 11-6.

Within a row in Table 11-4, comparing columns 1 and 2 for the linear model and columns 4 and 5 for the logarithmic model, we can compare the "private" payoff to that state from investing in R&E (i.e., research-cum-extension) versus

5 These tables also allow us to compare the estimates of internal rates of return and benefit-cost ratios, and to compare our results with those from other studies. The computed rates of return to research are not unlike the typical results for studies of agricultural R&D (as summarized by Alston et al. 2000a, for instance). The ranking of states according to their rates of return to research is the same as the ranking according to benefit-cost ratios, in this instance, because the research lag structure is common.

Figure 11-3 Spatial Distribution of Own-State and National Marginal Benefits per Dollar of SAES Research

Own-State National

Panel a. Linear model

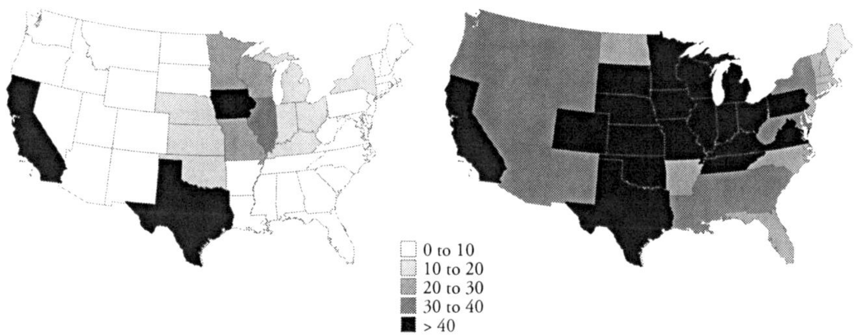

Panel b. Logarithmic model

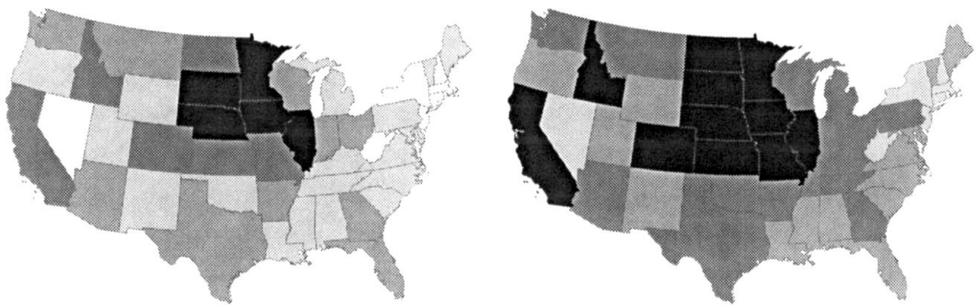

Sources: Developed by the authors.

the “social” payoff to the nation as a whole; the difference between these two is the spillover benefit per dollar of spending. Similarly, the left-hand side panels in Figures 11-2 and 11-3 represent the “private” benefit-cost ratios while the right-hand side panels show the “social” benefit-cost ratios. This comparison indicates the magnitude of the distortion in incentives for a state to conduct the quantity and mixture of agricultural research that will generate the greatest national payoff, if it attaches no value to interstate spillouts of its research results.

Consider first the results from using the linear model. Across all the states, the “private” benefit-cost ratio for state R&D exhibits a wide range, from 0.2:1 to 44:1 (and the corresponding internal rates of return range from -8 to 68). Panel a of Figure 11-2 shows that although a few states have quite large own-state benefit-cost ratios, they are less than 10:1 for more than half of the states, with an average 10:1 across all states (and a corresponding average internal rate of return of 23 percent per year). Panel a of Figure 11-3 shows that the largest “private” benefit-cost ratios are in states with very large agricultural sectors (California, Texas, and Iowa), while most states in the Central region have benefit-cost ratios exceeding the national average. The "social" benefit cost-ratio ranges from 14:1 to 74:1, around an average of 40:1 (and the corresponding internal rates of return range from 35 to 86 with an average of 59 percent per year). Panel a of Figure 11-2 highlights the variability of "social" benefit-cost ratios across states, and the corresponding panel of Figure 11-3 highlights that most states in or near the Central region tend to have relatively high "social" benefit-cost ratios. USDA intramural research yielded a national benefit-cost ratio of 47:1 (an internal rate of return of 66 percent per year), in the same general range as the social benefit-cost ratio for research and extension conducted by states.

The results from the logarithmic model are systematically different in ways that make sense given what we have seen already about these two alternatives. In particular, the logarithmic model attributes a greater share of productivity growth to own-state research and extension, allowing a smaller role for spillovers. With this model, across all the states, the marginal own-state payoff to state R&E ranges from 2:1 to 58:1 (and the corresponding internal rates of return range from 7 to 28 with an average of 19 percent per year). Panel b of Figure 11-2 shows the wider range of "private" benefit-cost ratios, compared with the linear model (in Panel a). Further, the average own-state payoff is about double that of the linear model. Similarly, the national "social" benefit cost-ratio ranges from 10:1 to 69:1, around an average of 32:1 (and the internal rates of return range from 15 to 29 with an average of 23 percent per year). Compared with the linear model, the logarithmic model yielded generally smaller national ("social") benefit-cost ratios even though the own-state ("private") benefit-cost ratios are generally larger, because the spillover benefits are much smaller, though still significant. USDA intramural research yielded a social benefit-cost ratio of 18:1 (an internal rate of return of 18.7 percent per year), generally lower than the social benefit-cost ratio for research and extension conducted by states.

Accounting for Patterns in Base Model Results

The pattern of the private and social payoffs across states can be understood better by examining the equations for the determinants of the present value of benefits, which differ between the linear and logarithmic models. The total "social" benefits from research spending by a particular state include the own-state "private" benefits accruing within the state and the cross-state "spillover" benefits accruing in other states. Summing the total benefits from equation (11.26) across states, after substituting for $\Delta\ln MFP_{i,t}$ from equation (11.25) the total national benefits are, in present value terms:

$$(11.27)\quad PVB_{US} = \sum_{i=1}^{48} PVB_i = \sum_{i=1}^{48} \sum_{t=1950}^{2002} \left(MFP_{i,t}^{1} - MFP_{i,t}^{0}\right)\left(\frac{V_{i,t}}{\bar{MFP}_{i,t}}\right)(1+r)^{2002-t},$$

$$\text{where } \bar{MFP}_{i,t} = \tfrac{1}{2}\left(MFP_{i,t}^{1} + MFP_{i,t}^{0}\right).$$

Drawing on the details in Chapter 9 (equations 9.6 and 9.7) and Chapter 10 (equation 10.2a), in the linear model, the own-and cross-state changes in *MFP* in year t caused by a \$1,000 increase in research spending in 1950 in state i are given, respectively, by:

$$(11.28)\quad MFP_{j,t}^{1} - MFP_{j,t}^{0} = \begin{cases} \hat{\beta}_K\, b_{t-1950} \text{ if } j = i \\ \hat{\beta}_S\, b_{t-1950}\, \omega_{ij} \text{ if } j \neq i \end{cases}$$

where $\hat{\beta}_K$ is the estimated coefficient representing the marginal effect of a change in the own-state knowledge stock on *MFP*; $\hat{\beta}_S$ is the estimated coefficient representing the marginal effect of a change in the spillover knowledge stock on *MFP*; b_{t-1950} is the lag coefficient representing the impact on the year t knowledge stock of a unit change in research spending in 1950, and ω_{ij} is the spillover coefficient representing the effect of a change in the own-state knowledge stock in state i on the state-specific spillover knowledge stock in state j.

Equation (11.28) shows that the change in productivity in any year attributable to a change in own-state agricultural research spending is the same in every state (because the same lag distribution weights and the same regression parameter, β_K, apply to every state). Further, the measure of benefits from a given productivity increase, $GARB_{i,t}$ in equation (11.26), is directly proportional to the value of agricultural production, $V_{i,t}$. Substituting equation (11.28) into equation (11.27) and organizing the terms yields an equation that combines these points. This equation represents a particular case of equation (11.27) (for the linear functional form) and provides a measure of the present value of benefits to the nation (i.e., the national social benefits) from a marginal change in research spending by state i:

$$(11.29)\quad PVB_{US}^{i} = \hat{\beta}_K \sum_{t=1950}^{2002} b_{t-1950}\left(\frac{V_{i,t}}{\bar{MFP}_{i,t}}\right)(1+r)^{2002-t} + \hat{\beta}_S \sum_{j\neq i}^{48} \omega_{ij} \sum_{t=1950}^{2002} b_{t-1950}\left(\frac{V_{j,t}}{\bar{MFP}_{j,t}}\right)(1+r)^{2002-t}.$$

The first term in this equation represents the own-state research benefits and the second term represents the spillover benefits to other states.

In equation (11.29) the state-by-state differences in benefits from own-state research mainly reflect differences among states in the sizes of their agricultural sectors over the period being studied. Hence, those states with a comparatively large "private" benefit-cost ratio were states with comparatively large agricultural sectors.[6] The differences in the "social" payoffs among states reflect this aspect (the size of the agricultural sector in the state conducting the research, which determines the "private" benefit) as well as the variation in the extent of benefits from spillovers to other states. The spillover benefits depend on the degree of agricultural output similarity between the state conducting the research and each other state, the state-state spillover coefficients, weighted by the size of the agricultural sector in the recipient state. For instance, the difference in social benefits between California and Ohio ($56 versus $69) reflects a substantially larger private payoff in California ($42 versus $17 in Ohio) that is partly offset by larger spillover benefits from Ohio ($39 versus $27 in California).

In the third column of benefit-cost ratios in either Table 11-4 or Appendix Table 11-6, the state-specific payoff per dollar of federal intramural research ranges from less than 5 cents (in Delaware, Maine, Massachusetts, Nevada, New Hampshire, Rhode Island, and Vermont) up to over $4 (in Iowa and Texas). In the case of intramural USDA research, the "own-state" payoff is zero, and the total payoff is represented by the spillover term from equation (11.29) as:

$$(11.30)\quad PVB_{US}^{F} = \hat{\beta}_S \sum_{j=1}^{48} \omega_{Fj} \sum_{t=1950}^{2002} b_{t-1950} \left(\frac{V_{j,t}}{\bar{MFP}_{j,t}} \right) (1+r)^{2002-t}.$$

As for own-state research, the productivity growth attributable to federal agricultural research is very similar across states, with differences reflecting the differences in federal-state spillover coefficients (ω_{Fj}). This means that the state-by-state differences in benefits from federal research largely reflect differences among states in the sizes of their agricultural sectors over the period being studied: states with a comparatively large benefit-cost ratio for federal research had comparatively large agricultural sectors.

The logarithmic model is different. Summing the total benefits from equation (11.26) across states, after substituting for $\Delta \ln MFP$ in this case yields:

$$(11.31)\quad PVB_{US} = \sum_{i=1}^{48} PVB_i = \sum_{i=1}^{48} \sum_{t=1950}^{2002} \left(\ln MFP_{i,t}^{1} - \ln MFP_{i,t}^{0} \right) V_{i,t} (1+r)^{2002-t}.$$

Analogously to equation (11.28) for the linear model, the own-and cross-state changes in MFP in year t caused by a $1,000 increase in research spending in 1950 in state i are given by:

$$(11.32)\quad \ln MFP_{j,t}^{1} - \ln MFP_{j,t}^{0} = \begin{cases} \dfrac{\hat{\eta}_K}{SK_{i,t}} b_{t-1950} & \text{if } j = i \\ \dfrac{\hat{\eta}_S}{SS_{j,t}} b_{t-1950}\, \omega_{ij} & \text{if } j \neq i \end{cases}$$

6 This is an artifact of the model but is not an unreasonable result to have imposed by construction. Everything else equal, we might expect those states with larger agricultural sectors also to have comparatively large benefits from productivity growth induced by changes in their own research or extension investments.

where $\hat{\eta}_K$ is the estimated elasticity of *MFP* with respect to a change in the own-state knowledge stock; $\hat{\eta}_S$ is the estimated elasticity of *MFP* with respect to a change in the spillover knowledge stock; and the other parameters are as previously defined.

Equation (11.32) shows that the percentage change in productivity in any state attributable to a change in own-state agricultural research spending is inversely proportional to the state-specific knowledge stock, an important difference from the counterpart for the linear model. Offsetting this, as in the linear model, the measure of benefits from a given productivity increase, $GARB_i$ in equation (11.26), is directly proportional to the value of agricultural production.

Substituting equation (11.32) into equation (11.31) and organizing the terms yields an equation that combines these points and measures the marginal present value of benefits to the nation from a change in research expenditure in state *i*:

$$(11.33)\quad PVB^{i}_{US} = \hat{\eta}_K \sum_{t=1950}^{2002} b_{t-1950} \left(\frac{V_{i,t}}{SK_{i,t}} \right) (1+r)^{2002-t} + \hat{\eta}_S \sum_{j\neq 1}^{48} \omega_{ij} \sum_{t=1950}^{2002} b_{t-1950} \left(\frac{V_{j,t}}{SS_{j,t}} \right) (1+r)^{2002-t}.$$

The first term in this equation represents the own-state research benefits and the second term represents the spillover benefits to other states. In the case of intramural USDA research the total payoff is represented correspondingly by:

$$(11.34)\quad PVB^{F}_{US} = \hat{\eta}_S \sum_{j=1}^{48} \omega_{Fj} \sum_{t=1950}^{2002} b_{t-1950} \left(\frac{V_{j,t}}{SS_{j,t}} \right) (1+r)^{2002-t}.$$

In both of these equations, the measures of private and social benefits depend on the relative sizes of the state-specific value of production and the corresponding state-specific own-state or spillin research and extension knowledge stocks.[7] In the linear model, the state-by-state differences in benefits from own-state research mainly reflected differences among states in the sizes of their agricultural sectors over the period being studied. In the logarithmic model, this effect is offset somewhat by differences in the size of state-specific knowledge stocks, which tend to be larger for states having larger agricultural sectors, but perhaps not proportionately so (agricultural research intensities tend to be lower for states with larger agricultural sectors). Hence, as with the linear model, larger agricultural states tend to have comparatively large private and social benefit-cost ratios for research and extension, but the relationship is not as clear and pronounced as in the case of the linear model.

State-State Comparisons of "Private" and "Social" Benefits

The interstate differences in marginal own-state and national benefits per dollar of SAES research or extension are illustrated graphically in Figure 11-4 for

7 The inverse of this ratio ($SS_{j,t} / V_{j,t}$) can be seen as a type of "knowledge intensity" ratio.

Figure 11-4 Spillover and Own-State Elements of Marginal Benefits per Dollar of SAES Research

Panel a. Linear model

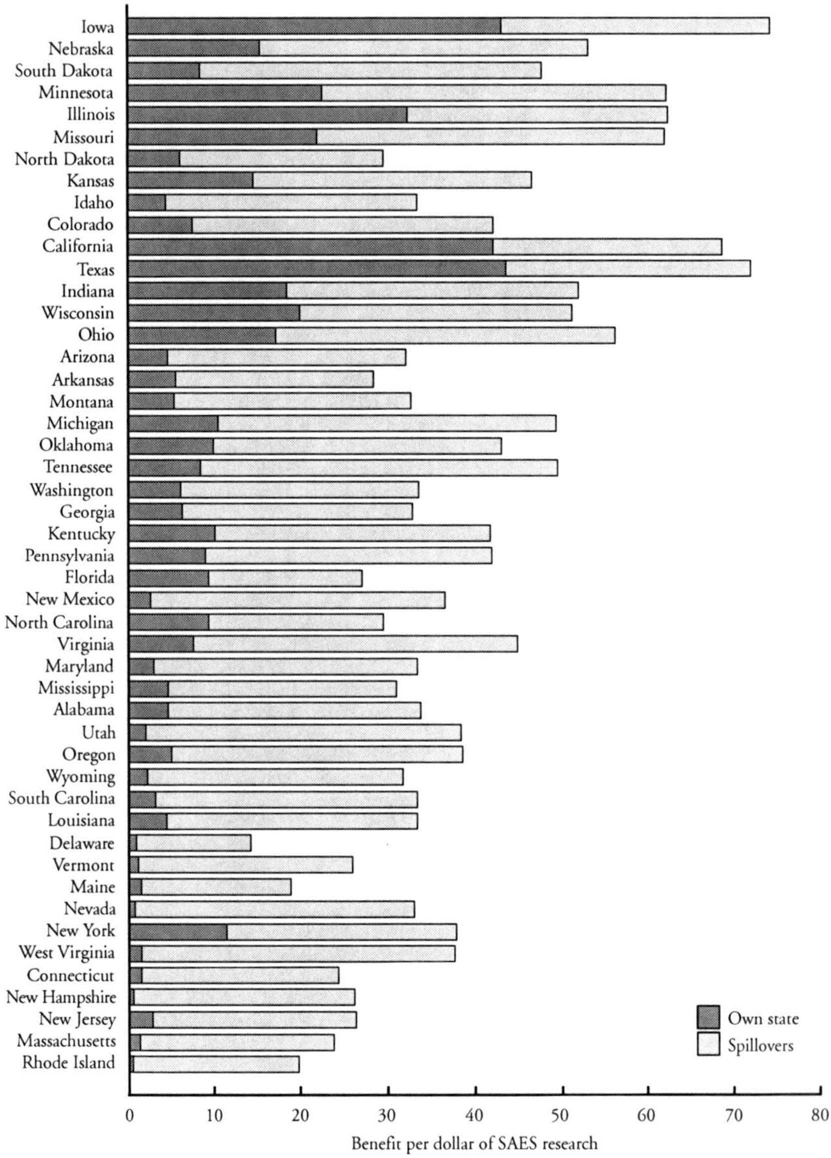

(continued)

Figure 11-4 (continued)

Panel b. Logarithmic model

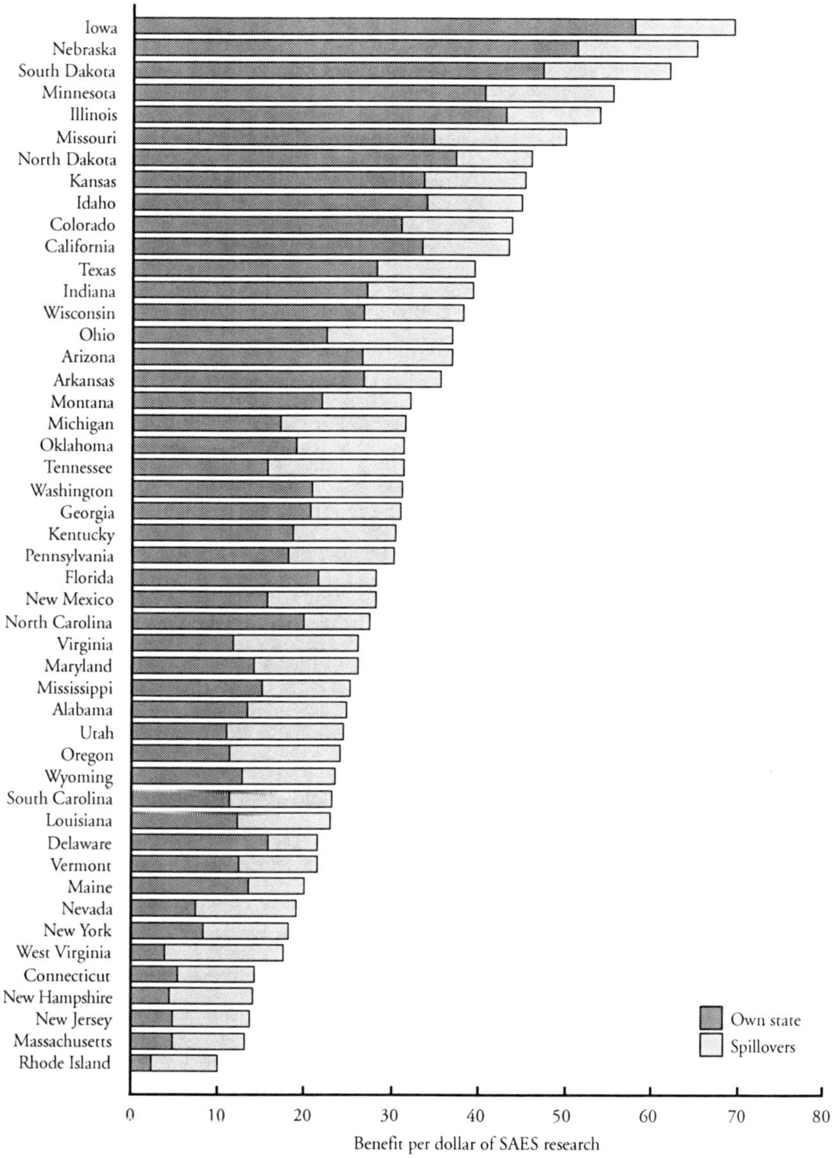

Sources: Developed by the authors.

both the linear model (Panel a) and the logarithmic model (Panel b). For each state and for each model, the figures show the total marginal benefit-cost ratio for state-specific agricultural R&D, partitioned into the own-state (or private) benefit (darker shaded) and the spillover benefits to other states (lighter shaded). The states are ranked according to the total social marginal benefit-cost ratio from the logarithmic model.

Spillover benefits represent a larger share of total benefits for the linear model than for the logarithmic model in every state. This finding follows directly from the econometric results in which the linear model had a comparatively large elasticity of *MFP* with respect to the spillover knowledge stock and a comparatively small elasticity of *MFP* with respect to the own-state knowledge stock. For both models, but especially for the logarithmic model, the spillover benefits are relatively constant across the states and thus variation in the own-state benefits drives most of the inter-state differences in national benefits from SAES research and extension. Hence, for both models, spillovers typically represent a smaller share of the total benefits in those states where own-state benefits are comparatively large.

The own-state benefits vary more across states for the linear model than the logarithmic model because they are proportional to the size of the agricultural sector in the linear model, and thus the total benefits and the own-state and spillover shares vary more across states for the linear model than for the logarithmic model. Spillover benefits to other states are worth between \$13 and \$41 per dollar in the linear model and between \$6 and \$16 per dollar in the logarithmic model; and in some states—especially states having smaller agricultural sectors—the spillover benefits account for the lion's share of the national benefits, especially in the case of the linear model.

Comparing columns 1 and 3 of Table 11-4 for the linear model, and columns 4 and 6 for the logarithmic model, we can see the difference between the benefits to the state from a marginal investment in its own research versus a marginal investment in federal research (the difference indicates the payoff to the state from diverting a dollar from USDA intramural research to the individual SAES or vice versa). In California, the linear model indicates that a marginal dollar of USDA research is worth \$4 (\$1 in the logarithmic model), compared with \$42 for California SAES research (\$33 for the logarithmic model). Adding up the state-by-state benefits from federal research (Appendix Table 11-6, columns 3 and 6, respectively, for the linear and logarithmic models) across all the states provides a measure of the national or "social" benefits from a marginal increase in federal research expenditure from the two models. The resulting value of \$47 per dollar (\$18 per dollar from the logarithmic model) can be compared with the national (social) benefits from a marginal increase in spending by each of the SAESs, shown in column 2, which ranges from \$14 to \$74 across the states in the linear model (\$10 to \$69 in the logarithmic model).

Table 11-6 Marginal Benefit-Cost Ratios—Effects of Functional Form

State	Linear (1)	First-Difference (2)	Logarithmic (3)	Growth (4)
RMSE	30.36	34.08	22.46	27.70
Lag distribution parameters				
λ	0.75	0.85	0.70	0.65
δ	0.80	0.60	0.90	0.90
Peak lag year	13	8	24	20
48 states		*own-state benefit-cost ratio (national benefit-cost ratio in parentheses)*		
Average	10.0	11.2	21.0	10.7
	(39.7)	(46.3)	(32.1)	(32.2)
Minimum	0.2	0.2	2.4	1.4
	(14.2)	(16.7)	(9.9)	(15.9)
Maximum	43.9	51.3	57.8	29.4
	(74.4)	(84.5)	(69.2)	(52.1)
Selected states				
California	42.3	47.6	33.3	16.4
	(68.9)	(79.1)	(43.4)	(35.9)
Minnesota	22.6	24.2	40.6	20.4
	(62.3)	(71.2)	(55.4)	(48.8)
Wyoming	2.2	2.4	12.7	6.6
	(31.9)	(37.4)	(23.6)	(27.5)

Sources: Developed by the authors.

Effects of Alternative Specification Choices

In this section—paralleling the analysis of the effects of specification choices on the growth accounting—we present and compare the benefit-cost results from a range of alternative models. The results are summarized in terms of (a) the "private" benefit from own-state research and extension, (b) the "social" benefit from own-state research and extension, and (c) the social benefit from USDA intramural research. We present national averages of state-specific figures, along with state-specific figures for California, Minnesota, and Wyoming. In each case, as appropriate, we present the results using the best-fitting gamma distribution for the particular model specification (and we report the parameters of that gamma distribution and peak lag year) along with the root mean square prediction error (RMSE) for *MFP* in levels based on the predictions from that model.

Table 11-6 includes results for the linear, first-differenced linear, logarithmic, and first-differenced logarithmic (or growth) model, in columns 1 through 4, respectively. This table replicates in slightly different format the findings, already reviewed, showing that the linear and logarithmic model yield different private and social benefit-cost ratios for research and extension. Specifically, the linear model indicates generally greater social benefits, with a much greater share attributed to spillovers (and a much smaller share to own-state research and extension), compared with the logarithmic model. Comparing columns 1 and 2, the results from the first-difference model are generally quite similar to those from the linear model, but the private and social benefit-cost ratios are always larger for the first-difference model, reflecting differences in elasticity estimates and R&D lag distributions between the preferred models for the two specifications. Comparing columns 3 and 4, first differencing had a much larger impact on the results from the logarithmic model. The first-differenced logarithmic (or growth) model implied generally (but not always) smaller benefit-cost ratios than the linear, first-difference, or logarithmic models. Compared with the logarithmic model, the growth model had similar spillover benefits combined with smaller own-state benefits (similar to the own-state benefits from the linear model for middle-sized states).

Looking at the 48-state average estimates, the alternative models implied an own-state (or "private") marginal benefit-cost ratio in the range of 10:1 to 21:1, and an overall national (or "social") marginal benefit-cost ratio in the range of 32:1 to 46:1. The effect of the choice of functional form has significant implications for both the total benefit and its distribution, but across the functional forms the message is clear and consistent, that the own-state, spillover, and national benefits are very large relative to the costs.

Table 11-7 includes corresponding results for models that entail different specifications of the lag distribution applied to extension. First, as noted in section 11.1, disallowing extension spillovers (comparing columns 1 versus 2, 3 versus 4, 5 versus 6, and 7 versus 8) results in a substantially greater estimate of total *MFP* growth attributable to research and extension knowledge stocks of which a smaller share is attributed to own-state research and extension and hence a larger share is attributed to spillovers. Consequently, while the own-state benefits from research were only marginally affected, ruling out extension spillovers resulted in substantially larger estimates of the spillover benefits and thus the national benefits from SAES research in every state. Second, the use of the Huffman-Evenson 4-year geometric lag distribution for extension, rather than the 50-year gamma distribution had only modest impacts on the results from the linear model (i.e., comparing columns 1 and 2 with columns 5 and 6, respectively). However, comparing columns 3 and 4 with columns 7 and 8, the use of the 4-year geometric lag distribution for extension significantly changed the results for the logarithmic model. The linear and logarithmic models yielded very different results when the same 50-year gamma distribution was applied to both extension and research, but these differences all but vanished when the Huffman-Evenson 4-year geometric lag distribution was applied to extension. These results reveal some complex interactions between the effects of the functional form for the model (linear versus logarithmic) and the structure of the lag distribution for extension (4-year geometric versus 50-year gamma) and the treatment of extension spillovers, in jointly influencing the findings regarding the national (social) benefit-cost ratios

Table 11-7 Marginal Benefit-Cost Ratios—Effects of Extension Lag Model

	Gamma Extension Lags				4-Year Geometric Extension Lags			
	Linear Model		Logarithmic Model		Linear Model		Logarithmic Model	
Extension Spillovers	Yes (1)	No (2)	Yes (3)	No (4)	Yes (5)	No (6)	Yes (7)	No (8)
RMSE	30.36	30.55	22.46	22.41	30.39	30.56	23.71	23.21
Lag distribution parameters								
λ	0.75	0.75	0.70	0.70	0.65	0.60	0.65	0.65
δ	0.80	0.80	0.90	0.90	0.90	0.90	0.90	0.90
Peak lag year	13	13	24	24	20	17	20	20
48 states	*own-state benefit-cost ratio (national benefit-cost ratio in parentheses)*							
Average	10.0	10.3	21.0	20.3	8.8	10.3	9.3	9.5
	(39.7)	(52.1)	(32.1)	(37.7)	(34.5)	(47.5)	(31.4)	(42.7)
Minimum	0.2	0.2	2.4	2.3	0.1	0.2	1.3	1.3
	(14.2)	(19.6)	(9.9)	(14.1)	(12.5)	(17.6)	(16.2)	(23.9)
Maximum	43.9	45.7	57.8	55.9	39.7	46.0	27.8	28.5
	(74.4)	(88.4)	(69.2)	(73.6)	(66.6)	(84.9)	(50.5)	(64.5)
Selected states								
California	42.3	43.7	33.3	32.2	36.1	42.9	13.5	13.9
	(68.9)	(81.1)	(43.4)	(48.0)	(58.9)	(76.1)	(33.5)	(44.0)
Minnesota	22.6	23.4	40.6	39.3	20.3	23.9	18.0	18.4
	(62.3)	(79.2)	(55.4)	(62.1)	(54.6)	(73.5)	(47.2)	(62.1)
Wyoming	2.2	2.3	12.7	12.3	2.0	2.4	6.6	6.8
	(31.9)	(44.1)	(23.6)	(29.2)	(27.8)	(39.6)	(28.1)	(38.9)

Sources: Developed by the authors.

for SAES research, and the distribution of the benefits between own-state and spillover benefits to other states.

The lower panels of Appendix Tables 11-3, 11-4, and 11-5 include marginal private and social benefit-cost ratios for the alternative model specifications discussed in Chapter 10.

Our base model allowed for state-to-state and federal-state spillovers of impacts from research and extension knowledge stocks, where the spillover coefficients were based on indexes of output-mix similarity. To evaluate the effects of this dimension of the specification, we also tried two other specifications of spillovers, and the results are reported in Appendix Table 11-3. First, we tried a model with spillovers based on spatial proximity alone, in which spillover coefficients were 1 if the two states came from the same region, and 0 if they were from different regions, as used in some previous published work (discussed in Chapter 8). Second, we tried a model from which spillover effects were excluded altogether. Columns 1, 2, and 3 of Appendix Table 11-3 show the results from the linear model with (a) the baseline specification of spillovers, (b) spillovers based on USDA regions, and (c) no spillovers. Columns 4, 5, and 6 of Appendix Table 11-3 show the corresponding results from the logarithmic model.

Compared with the base model, the use of the specification in which spillovers are based on USDA regions resulted in smaller benefit-cost ratios generally, but the size of these impacts was much more pronounced for the linear model than the logarithmic specification. In the linear model both the own-state (or "private") and the national (or "social") benefit-cost ratios were roughly halved, on average, across the 48 states, but with considerable variation in the impacts among states, as a result of this change in the specification of spillover effects. In addition, the policy implications may differ because the states to which the implied spillover benefits flow may be far away from the own state in the base specification but are necessarily near neighbors in the alternative. In either case the spillover impacts are large and represent a substantial share of the total national benefits from SAES research, especially in the linear model.

If these effects are ignored and all of the growth in *MFP* is attributed to own-state research and extension, then the estimates of social and private benefit-cost ratios can be seriously biased. When spillovers are ignored, the estimated own-state benefit-cost ratios from the linear model are approximately doubled compared with the base model; more so compared with the model based on USDA regions. In the case of the logarithmic model, the bias in the own-state benefit-cost ratios from eliminating the possibility of spillovers is generally larger in magnitude, but represents a smaller percentage of the already larger estimated benefit-cost ratios.

Appendix Table 11-4 includes results for the linear and logarithmic models, in each case comparing (a) the base model (in which the same 50-year gamma lag distribution is applied to both research and extension) with (b) a model applying an alternative 35-year trapezoidal lag distribution (as developed by Huffman and Evenson and applied by themselves and various others) to both research and extension, (c) a model applying the 50-year gamma distribution to research and an alternative 4-year geometric lag distribution to extension (as applied by Huffman and Evenson and various others), and (d) a model combining the 35-year trapezoidal distribution for research and the 4-year geometric lag distribution for extension.

In the case of the linear model (the first four columns of results in Appendix Table 11-4) these variations in the specifications of the research and extension lag distributions had relatively small effects on the benefit-cost ratios (shown in the lower portion of Appendix Table 11-4). The combination of the 50-year gamma lag distribution for research with the 4-year geometric lag for extension resulted in somewhat lower benefit-cost ratios generally, whereas the results for the other two models were much the same as for the base model (in column 1). Perhaps it was because of its use of shorter lag lengths for both research and extension that the model combining Huffman and Evenson's trapezoidal lag distribution for research with their geometric lag for extension resulted in larger estimates of benefit-cost ratios, generally, but the size of the difference was fairly small in every case.

The same variations in specification of the lag distribution had more pronounced effects on the results from the logarithmic model (the last four columns of results in Appendix Table 11-4). As previously noted, in the base specification, the logarithmic model (column 5) resulted in generally larger private benefit-cost ratios but often smaller social benefit-cost ratios, compared with the linear model (column 1). When the 50-year gamma lag distribution was replaced with the 35-year trapezoidal distribution, applied to both research and extension, the difference in "private" benefit-cost ratios between the linear and logarithmic models became more pronounced while the difference in "social" benefit-cost ratios became smaller. However, the use of the 4-year geometric lag distribution for extension, combined with either the 50-year gamma lag distribution or the 35-year trapezoidal distribution for research, yielded benefit-cost ratios that were generally quite similar between the logarithmic and linear models.

Again, the results reveal that our findings concerning benefit-cost ratios and the distribution of benefits from SAES research are governed by complex interactions between elements of model specification choice: lag distribution forms, lag length, and functional form for the model. Nevertheless, the main findings are fairly robust and the range of results across models is reasonable. Looking at the 48-state average estimates, the alternative models in Appendix Table 11-4 imply an own-state (or "private") marginal benefit-cost ratio in the range of 9:1 to 21:1 and an overall national (or "social") marginal benefit-cost ratio in the range of 31:1 to 43:1.

Finally, we considered the effects of imposing restrictions on the overall lag length, since most previous studies used much shorter lags than we have used here. First, we tried reducing the maximum number of lags in the gamma distribution applied to both research and extension from 50 years to either 35 years or 20 years. Second, we tried a model with a 4-year geometric lag distribution applied to extension and a gamma distribution applied to research with maximum lags of 50 years, 35 years or 20 years. The results from these six alternative specifications are reported in Appendix Table 11-5, with the linear model reported in Panel a, and the logarithmic model reported in Panel b.

In the linear model (Panel a) the benefit-cost ratios were very similar across all of the alternative specifications, and appeared not to be very sensitive to this aspect. In the case of the logarithmic model (Panel b) the benefit-cost ratios were sensitive to the specification of the extension lag (as previously discussed) but were not very sensitive to the specification of the research lag length given the specification of the extension lag. This finding was somewhat surprising, initially, since the alternative specifications implied quite different research lag distribution parameters, and we expected this aspect to influence the regression

Table 11-8 Growth Rates of Agricultural R&E Spending, by Decade, 1949–2002

	1949–2002	1949–1960	1960–1970	1970–1980	1980–1990	1990–2002
United States						
SAES	2.65	4.38	2.81	3.88	1.43	0.95
Extension (Ext)	1.36	1.98	2.42	2.38	0.20	0.02
Intramural (IM)	1.32	3.93	2.70	1.47	-1.76	0.21
SAES + Ext + IM	1.89	3.30	2.64	2.78	0.38	0.51
48 states		*average annual percentage growth in SAES spending*				
Average	2.48	4.59	2.70	3.37	1.19	0.69
Minimum	0.55	0.45	-0.86	-3.85	-4.39	-5.55
Maximum	4.49	12.84	6.24	9.93	5.79	12.62
Selected states						
California	3.17	6.12	2.10	4.12	2.06	1.50
Minnesota	2.63	4.04	3.01	4.10	1.62	0.64
Wyoming	0.55	3.08	1.25	-3.10	3.93	-2.11
Regions						
Pacific	2.88	4.98	2.51	4.05	1.25	1.64
Mountain	3.03	4.95	2.13	4.95	1.88	1.39
Northern Plains	3.12	7.24	3.62	4.28	-0.56	1.01
Southern Plains	2.53	3.98	1.10	5.03	1.07	1.52
Central	2.60	4.04	2.96	2.99	1.91	1.24
Southeast	2.81	4.73	3.77	4.72	1.03	0.13
Northeast	2.02	2.90	2.94	1.83	2.73	0.04
48 states		*average annual percentage growth in extension spending*				
Average	1.33	2.03	2.36	2.29	0.01	0.12
Minimum	-0.53	-0.01	-0.70	-0.30	-2.62	-5.11
Maximum	2.99	4.23	5.75	4.78	3.44	4.00
Selected states						
California	1.58	3.30	2.25	2.86	0.12	-0.40
Minnesota	2.13	1.46	3.63	3.79	1.30	0.81
Wyoming	0.25	0.29	0.32	2.24	0.10	-1.36
Regions						
Pacific	1.52	3.18	1.87	2.50	-0.12	0.23
Mountain	1.60	2.45	1.61	3.26	-0.56	1.22
Northern Plains	1.27	1.86	2.41	2.40	-0.22	0.08
Southern Plains	1.08	1.90	1.41	3.06	-0.99	0.12
Central	1.47	1.72	2.73	2.38	-0.16	0.80
Southeast	1.50	1.73	3.08	2.54	1.03	-0.49
Northeast	1.02	2.02	2.52	0.87	1.18	-1.17

(continued)

coefficients and the benefit-cost ratios. However, for a given set of gamma distribution coefficients, in our approach the specification of a shorter maximum lag meant literally truncation of the lag distribution, with rescaling so the weights would sum to one. In some cases, then, if the weights on the long lags were small, the truncation of the distribution may be immaterial. In some other cases, the truncation of the lag may result in a different set of gamma distribution coefficients that implies a fairly similar set of lag weights, even though the parameters

Table 11-8 (continued)

	1949–2002	1949–1960	1960–1970	1970–1980	1980–1990	1990–2002
48 states	*average annual percentage growth in SAES and extension spending combined*					
Average	1.91	3.14	2.48	2.87	0.67	0.54
Minimum	0.40	0.92	0.23	-2.48	-2.51	-2.82
Maximum	3.51	6.79	5.25	7.62	3.96	8.43
Selected states						
California	2.67	5.07	2.15	3.71	1.49	1.02
Minnesota	2.42	2.93	3.26	3.97	1.49	0.71
Wyoming	0.40	1.71	0.84	-0.45	1.95	-1.76
Regions						
Pacific	2.41	4.25	2.27	3.51	0.82	1.24
Mountain	2.42	3.74	1.90	4.25	0.98	1.33
Northern Plains	2.19	4.29	3.07	3.49	-0.42	0.64
Southern Plains	1.81	2.81	1.27	4.01	0.10	0.92
Central	2.06	2.82	2.85	2.70	0.98	1.06
Southeast	2.08	2.93	3.39	3.59	1.03	-0.17
Northeast	1.56	2.44	2.73	1.37	2.03	-0.46

Sources: Based on public agricultural R&D spending data described in Appendix III.

seem quite different. In yet other cases, the combination of a different lag distribution (with larger weights on earlier years) with a smaller estimated elasticity of *MFP* with respect to the knowledge stock could result in similar benefit-cost ratios, and we suspect that some offsetting changes of this nature may be reflected in some results. In any event, across the linear and logarithmic models and the six alternative lag specifications, the results were quite robust: the 48-state average "private" benefit-cost ratio ranged from 9:1 to 21:1 and the 48-state average "social" benefit-cost ratio ranged from 30:1 to 41:1.

11.3 Prospective Productivity Patterns

The estimated model is also useful for projecting the consequences of alternative research investment profiles for the future time path of productivity patterns, state-by-state and nationally. A first step is to choose a reasonable baseline scenario for future research spending, but it is not obvious how to define this baseline. As discussed in Chapter 6, the long-term trend over the past 50 years has been one of real growth in total spending nationally on public research and extension, but with slower growth in some states, and a decline in the relative importance of extension and for most years USDA intramural research. What should we assume about the next 50 years given these past trends? An examination of the trends may be helpful for this decision.

As shown in Table 11-8, over the years 1949–2002, aggregate (inflation adjusted) spending on public agricultural R&D (including USDA intramural research and state-specific spending on research and extension) grew at an average rate of 1.89 percent per annum (state-specific data are included in Appendix Table 11-8). This average annual growth rate reflects a general downward trend in the growth rate from 3.30 percent in the 1950s to 2.64 percent in the 1960s, a slight recovery to 2.78 percent in the 1970s, and serious decline to 0.38 percent in the 1980s, with a slight recovery to 0.51 percent over 1990–2002. Spending growth has recovered somewhat in more recent years, but seems unlikely to return to the past long-term average rate.

Within that aggregate, the annual growth rate of USDA intramural research (which averaged 1.32 percent over 1949–2002) declined faster than the growth rate of total public agricultural R&D spending, from 3.93 percent in the 1950s to 2.70 percent in the 1960s, 1.47 percent in the 1970s, -1.76 percent per year in the 1990s, and 0.21 percent over 1990–2002. Spending on extension also has generally grown more slowly than total public spending (the annual growth rate averaged 1.36 percent over 1949–2002), and the average annual growth has declined relatively rapidly, especially in recent decades, from 1.98 percent in the 1950s to 2.42 percent in the 1960s, 2.38 percent in the 1970s, 0.20 percent in the 1980s, and 0.02 percent per year over 1990–2002. This reflects a range of spending growth across the individual states, with some rapidly reducing their spending on extension and others increasing (the average annual state-specific growth rates for extension spending over 1949–2002 ranged from -0.53 percent to 2.99 percent across the 48 states).

Spending by the SAESs, partly supported by the federal government, has grown rapidly compared with the other components of national spending on public agricultural R&D, but with considerable differences among the states (the annual growth rate over 1949–2002 averaged 2.48 percent across the states, ranging from a minimum of 0.55 percent to a maximum of 4.49 percent). Like the other components, spending by the SAESs has been generally growing but at a declining rate over time. The annual growth in total spending by the SAESs averaged 4.38 percent in the 1950s, 2.81 percent in the 1960s, 3.88 percent in the 1970s, 1.43 percent in the 1980s, and 0.95 percent over 1990–2002. Each of these averages reflects a range across the states. In every sub-period at least some SAESs experienced negative spending growth, and even in the most-recent decade some SAESs had quite rapid expenditure growth.

Against this background, we opted to define a baseline scenario in which we projected average annual growth of expenditure for the years 2003–2050 (for each state-specific element of research and extension, and federal intramural research) at its respective average annual growth rate over the historical period 1949–2002. These longer-term past growth rates of spending are generally high compared with the recent past. To examine the implications of alternative spending patterns, we defined an alternative scenario in which we projected expenditure growth for each state-specific element of research and extension, and

Table 11-9 Predicted Past and Projected Future MFP Growth, 1949–2050

	Linear Model				Logarithmic Model			
	Predicted MFP Growth		Projected MFP Growth (2003–2050)		Predicted MFP Growth		Projected MFP Growth (2003–2050)	
	1949–2002	1990–2002	Optimistic	Pessimistic	1949–2002	1990–2002	Optimistic	Pessimistic
48 states				*average annual percentage change*				
Average	1.72	0.82	1.45	0.71	1.82	1.09	0.88	0.52
Minimum	0.57	0.07	0.77	0.31	1.42	0.26	0.24	-0.39
Maximum	3.23	1.81	2.08	1.71	2.42	1.90	1.41	1.23
Selected states								
California	3.07	1.60	2.08	1.05	2.15	1.49	1.16	0.75
Minnesota	2.41	1.30	1.98	1.71	1.84	1.54	1.29	1.23
Wyoming	1.60	0.42	1.46	0.73	1.57	0.31	0.45	0.00
Regions								
Pacific	2.24	1.09	1.69	0.92	2.06	1.14	1.02	0.75
Mountain	1.69	0.82	1.57	0.83	1.78	1.15	1.05	0.76
Northern Plains	1.53	0.72	1.42	0.70	1.78	1.11	0.91	0.52
Southern Plains	1.75	1.07	1.31	0.61	1.96	1.56	0.78	0.49
Central	2.26	0.95	1.73	1.05	1.76	1.00	1.00	0.74
Southeast	1.68	0.96	1.41	0.52	1.94	1.36	0.81	0.32
Northeast	1.31	0.45	1.21	0.53	1.67	0.65	0.71	0.29

Sources: Developed by the authors.

Notes: For the optimistic scenario, spending was extrapolated using 1949–2002 growth rates; for the pessimistic alternative scenario, spending was extrapolated using 1990–2002 growth rates.

federal intramural research at its respective average annual growth rate over the more-recent period 1990–2002. This approach means we will have some states with negative expenditure growth and some with very rapid positive growth in some elements of the total, and we consequently might want to exercise caution in interpreting the specific results for certain states.

We projected spending on each element of research and extension, computed the corresponding knowledge stocks, and then computed the corresponding values for *MFP* for each state, for both the optimistic baseline scenario (extrapolating spending using 1949–2002 growth rates) and the pessimistic alternative scenario (extrapolating spending using 1990–2002 growth rates) using the linear and logarithmic specifications of the base model. Table 11-9 shows a summary of the projected productivity growth (state-specific details are shown in Appendix Table 11-9), under the two scenarios. The main results can be seen in the plot of the projected time path of the national average of the state-specific indexes of *MFP* (with each individual state-specific index of *MFP* weighted by its average share of national value of agricultural production over the period 1949–2002), shown in Figure 11-5 (Panel a is for the linear model, Panel b is for the logarithmic model). Under the optimistic spending projection, *MFP* grows steadily throughout the entire period of the projection, continuing the long-term trend

Figure 11-5 Projected MFP under Optimistic and Pessimistic Research and Extension Spending Projections, 2003–2050

Panel a. Linear model

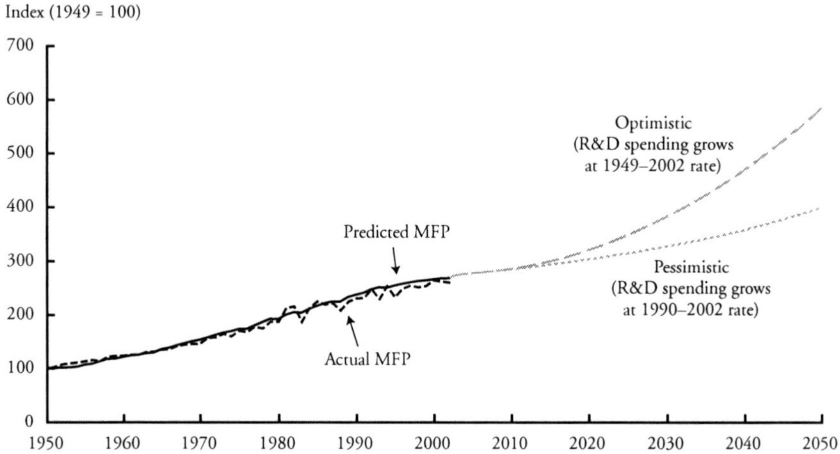

Panel b. Logarithmic model

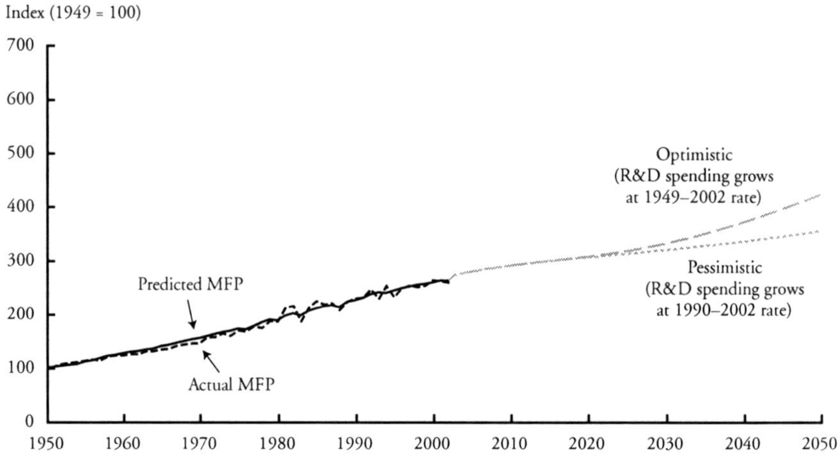

Sources: Developed by the authors.

established in the latter half of the 20th Century. In contrast, under the pessimistic projection, *MFP* grows much more slowly, and at a diminishing rate, perpetuating the productivity slowdown that we identified as beginning in the 1990s (discussed in more detail in Chapter 5).

To understand these graphs it is useful to reflect on the stock-flow relationship between research spending, knowledge, and productivity. In all of our models (and, indeed, in all of the models in the literature), agricultural productivity depends on a finite distributed lag of research spending. Consequently, if research spending is static over the long term (i.e., with constant spending over a period at least as long as the maximum research lag) such that the knowledge stock is in a steady state, then *MFP* will also be in a steady state. In other words, growth in spending is necessary for growth in the knowledge stock and thus growth in productivity (see Box 11-1). The long research lags mean that constant research spending could be associated with a growing knowledge stock (if the current constant spending is high relative to the past) or shrinking knowledge stock (if the current constant spending is low relative to the past), and thus with constant research spending *MFP* could approach its steady-state constant value from above or below.

In both of our scenarios we projected continuing positive growth in spending such that productivity would be projected to continue to increase, and not to approach a steady state with zero growth. Total research spending had been growing through 2002, but at a generally decreasing rate, such that the knowledge stock was growing, but at a decreasing rate. A continuation of the recent relatively slow growth in spending, as in the pessimistic scenario, implies that productivity would continue to grow but at a decreasing rate—a continuation of the productivity slowdown identified in Chapter 5. In contrast, a return to more rapid spending growth as in the optimistic scenario implies an increase in the growth rate of the knowledge stock and an accelerating growth rate of productivity until it settles onto the faster long-run path implied by faster growth in spending. The pessimistic scenario may be more realistic than the optimistic alternative in view of recent policy trends. In this scenario agricultural productivity is projected to continue to grow but only slowly (0.52 percent per year) compared with the past 50 years or so (1.82 percent per year), and compared with recent growth rates in other countries.

Box 11-1 Growth in Research and Growth in Productivity

Conventional and widely used models of agricultural (or industrial) R&D and productivity assume that productivity in year t (Q_t) depends on the current stock of useful knowledge (SK_t), which is based on a distributed lag (weighted sum) of L_R past annual flows of agricultural research investment (R_t):

$$Q_t = f(SK_t) \text{ and } SK_t = \sum_{k=0}^{L_R} b_k R_{t-k} \quad \text{(B11.1)}$$

Most such models impose a finite lag relationship, such that $L_R < 30$ years (Alston et al. 2000; Chapter 8 this volume). Some models assume an infinite lag but use a functional form such that the weights become negligible for lags beyond 30 years (or less).

For simplicity, suppose we are in a long-run steady state, in which research spending is constant over the relevant number of years. In this scenario, the knowledge stock also will be constant as will be the level of productivity. In other words, if research spending is constant (over at least the L_R years over which today's research has an impact on increasing the future stock of useful knowledge), this model implies productivity will also be constant.

The implication is that the steady-state spending on R&D is all effectively maintenance research, required to maintain the effective stock of knowledge and thus maintain productivity. Growth in productivity requires growth in R&D spending, and a slowdown in the rate of growth of the amount spent per year implies a slowdown (eventually) in the rate of growth of productivity. This may be seen as an extreme case or intuitively unreasonable. Surely some research leads to enduring increments to knowledge (at least, much more enduring than is allowed by the typically short, finite lags included in many empirical productivity models) such that productivity will continue to grow even if research is static? The logic of the equations is inescapable: if R&D spending is constant over the relevant number of years, then so will productivity be constant.

The intuitive objection is really an objection about the length of the lag, L_R. An alternative extreme view is that research-induced increments to knowledge last forever, such that the appropriate value is $L_R = \infty$. With this model, any positive spending on R&D implies a net increase in the stock of knowledge and causes productivity to increase in perpetuity. But our empirical work using aggregative data suggests that the appropriate value for L_R (as a relevant average value for the aggregate of all R&D) is less than 50 years and most studies have used well less than 35 years. Further, plenty of other evidence suggests that knowledge and technology depreciate or become obsolete, pests and diseases co-evolve, and therefore much of the current research spending is maintenance research (see, for example, Chapter 6).

As a practical matter, in the context of the present study, we are not talking about the implications of going to zero growth in spending (though it may be an interesting case to consider). We are suggesting that a reduction in the (positive) growth rate of spending on agricultural R&D that leaves spending nevertheless positive and still growing implies a reduction in the growth rate of productivity. The dynamics of this relationship are complex but the fundamental forces at play are revealed by the simple mathematics of the pair of equations in (B11.1).

Appendix Table 11-1 Growth Attributable to Knowledge Stocks, by State, 1949–2002

Panel a. Linear model

State	Own			Spillins				Average Annual	
	SAES	Extension	Total	SAES	USDA	Extension	Total	%Δ MFP	Rank
	percentage share of change in MFP attributable to knowledge stock							*percent*	
Pacific	*21.5*	*9.0*	*30.5*	*32.9*	*16.1*	*20.5*	*69.5*	*2.25*	
California	37.6	13.8	51.4	22.4	11.5	14.6	48.6	3.09	2
Oregon	12.4	5.6	18.0	39.0	18.8	24.1	82.0	2.10	14
Washington	14.5	7.5	22.0	37.2	18.0	22.8	78.0	1.55	29
Mountain	*7.1*	*3.3*	*10.5*	*42.4*	*21.0*	*26.1*	*89.5*	*1.77*	
Arizona	13.3	3.9	17.2	39.7	18.6	24.6	82.8	1.68	25
Colorado	14.8	5.8	20.5	36.7	19.6	23.2	79.5	2.09	16
Idaho	7.0	3.5	10.5	42.8	20.7	26.0	89.5	1.32	35
Montana	6.9	2.7	9.6	42.3	22.0	26.1	90.4	1.47	33
Nevada	3.1	2.4	5.5	44.9	22.0	27.5	94.5	2.10	15
New Mexico	4.4	3.2	7.6	44.1	21.2	27.1	92.4	1.86	21
Utah	5.0	2.9	8.0	44.0	20.9	27.1	92.0	2.00	18
Wyoming	2.7	2.2	4.9	44.8	22.7	27.6	95.1	1.68	27
Northern Plains	*11.3*	*5.8*	*17.1*	*37.8*	*21.1*	*23.9*	*82.9*	*1.59*	
Kansas	13.9	9.6	23.5	35.1	19.6	21.8	76.5	1.83	23
Nebraska	14.7	6.7	21.3	35.0	20.8	22.8	78.7	1.85	22
North Dakota	12.2	4.6	16.9	38.5	20.7	23.9	83.1	1.01	44
South Dakota	4.3	2.5	6.8	42.7	23.4	27.1	93.2	1.68	26
Southern Plains	*15.2*	*10.1*	*25.3*	*34.9*	*17.5*	*22.3*	*74.7*	*1.83*	
Arkansas	14.1	8.6	22.7	35.9	17.5	24.0	77.3	0.93	45
Louisiana	15.9	9.6	25.5	34.9	17.4	22.1	74.5	1.51	30
Mississippi	13.6	9.2	22.8	36.1	17.5	23.6	77.2	1.03	43
Oklahoma	8.7	7.3	16.0	39.5	20.1	24.3	84.0	2.24	11
Texas	23.5	16.0	39.6	28.1	15.0	17.3	60.4	3.43	1
Central	*14.0*	*9.4*	*23.4*	*34.4*	*19.8*	*22.3*	*76.6*	*2.33*	
Illinois	13.0	10.0	23.0	33.5	21.4	22.2	77.0	1.91	20
Indiana	14.5	9.0	23.5	33.4	20.8	22.3	76.5	2.03	17
Iowa	17.8	8.7	26.5	31.8	20.3	21.5	73.5	2.24	10
Michigan	13.3	9.6	22.9	35.9	18.7	22.5	77.1	2.35	9
Minnesota	15.1	9.3	24.3	34.1	19.4	22.1	75.7	2.37	8
Missouri	11.2	8.5	19.7	36.3	20.5	23.4	80.3	2.84	3
Ohio	9.8	9.2	19.0	36.9	20.5	23.6	81.0	2.43	7
Wisconsin	17.3	11.3	28.5	33.6	16.9	21.0	71.5	2.48	6
Southeast	*14.3*	*11.4*	*25.7*	*34.5*	*17.2*	*22.6*	*74.3*	*1.78*	
Alabama	11.9	9.8	21.7	36.6	17.8	23.9	78.3	1.30	36
Florida	33.5	16.0	49.4	24.0	11.5	15.0	50.6	1.60	28
Georgia	19.8	15.7	35.5	29.6	15.1	19.8	64.5	1.27	38
Kentucky	7.9	11.4	19.3	37.1	19.3	24.3	80.7	2.11	13
North Carolina	24.6	19.7	44.3	25.0	13.3	17.5	55.7	1.27	37
South Carolina	8.6	8.8	17.3	38.3	18.8	25.6	82.7	1.32	34
Tennessee	8.3	8.0	16.3	39.0	19.7	25.1	83.7	2.60	5
Virginia	12.1	11.3	23.5	35.7	17.8	23.1	76.5	2.63	4
West Virginia	2.0	2.1	4.1	45.4	21.4	29.0	95.9	1.95	19

(continued)

Appendix Table 11-1 (continued)

State	Own SAES	Own Extension	Own Total	Spillins SAES	Spillins USDA	Spillins Extension	Spillins Total	Average Annual %Δ MFP	Rank
	percentage share of change in MFP attributable to knowledge stock							*percent*	
Northeast	*6.7*	*4.2*	*11.0*	*43.1*	*18.7*	*27.2*	*89.0*	*1.26*	
Connecticut	3.4	1.3	4.7	46.7	18.9	29.7	95.3	1.27	39
Delaware	5.5	2.6	8.1	42.3	19.7	29.9	91.9	0.59	48
Maine	6.3	3.0	9.2	44.5	18.6	27.6	90.8	0.78	47
Maryland	6.4	7.1	13.5	40.7	19.3	26.5	86.5	1.48	31
Massachusetts	3.8	2.5	6.4	46.1	18.8	28.7	93.6	1.09	42
New Hampshire	1.5	1.5	3.0	47.8	19.8	29.3	97.0	1.20	40
New Jersey	7.1	5.7	12.8	42.5	18.5	26.2	87.2	1.47	32
New York	24.3	13.0	37.3	29.8	14.3	18.6	62.7	2.20	12
Pennsylvania	12.2	6.8	19.0	38.5	18.3	24.3	81.0	1.78	24
Rhode Island	1.8	1.2	3.0	48.3	19.1	29.6	97.0	0.87	46
Vermont	1.9	1.7	3.6	47.2	20.1	29.0	96.4	1.19	41
Average	*11.6*	*7.3*	*19.0*	*38.0*	*18.9*	*24.1*	*81.0*	*1.77*	

Panel b. Logarithmic model

State	Own SAES	Own Extension	Own Total	Spillins SAES	Spillins USDA	Spillins Extension	Spillins Total	Average Annual %Δ MFP	Rank
	percentage share of change in MFP attributable to knowledge stock							*percent*	
Pacific	*39.3*	*22.7*	*62.0*	*14.7*	*11.1*	*12.2*	*38.0*	*2.12*	
California	44.2	20.7	64.9	13.3	10.4	11.4	35.1	2.26	2
Oregon	35.4	24.4	59.7	15.7	11.7	12.9	40.3	2.03	10
Washington	38.2	23.1	61.3	15.1	11.2	12.3	38.7	2.08	9
Mountain	*34.3*	*23.2*	*57.6*	*16.2*	*12.6*	*13.6*	*42.4*	*1.88*	
Arizona	44.8	19.0	63.8	14.2	10.2	11.8	36.2	2.14	7
Colorado	38.5	25.7	64.2	13.4	11.0	11.4	35.8	2.10	8
Idaho	35.0	23.4	58.5	16.1	12.1	13.3	41.5	1.89	23
Montana	33.5	18.1	51.7	18.0	14.9	15.4	48.3	1.67	40
Nevada	32.7	25.6	58.3	16.0	12.3	13.5	41.7	1.86	26
New Mexico	27.9	28.5	56.4	16.9	12.7	14.1	43.6	1.88	25
Utah	33.9	23.3	57.3	16.6	12.3	13.9	42.7	1.84	28
Wyoming	28.3	22.2	50.6	18.6	15.0	15.8	49.4	1.68	39
Northern Plains	*34.1*	*23.9*	*57.9*	*15.4*	*13.4*	*13.2*	*42.1*	*1.86*	
Kansas	29.2	29.7	59.0	15.1	13.2	12.7	41.0	1.93	20
Nebraska	39.2	22.8	62.0	13.5	12.5	11.9	38.0	2.00	15
North Dakota	36.2	20.3	56.5	16.2	13.6	13.7	43.5	1.77	32
South Dakota	31.6	22.6	54.3	16.7	14.5	14.5	45.7	1.74	34
Southern Plains	*29.6*	*29.2*	*58.8*	*15.6*	*12.2*	*13.4*	*41.2*	*2.00*	
Arkansas	30.8	27.7	58.4	15.6	11.8	14.1	41.6	1.97	19
Louisiana	33.6	28.9	62.5	14.4	11.0	12.1	37.5	2.18	5
Mississippi	28.2	29.7	57.9	16.0	12.1	14.1	42.1	1.97	17
Oklahoma	27.2	28.6	55.8	16.7	13.4	14.0	44.2	1.90	22
Texas	28.5	31.0	59.5	15.3	12.5	12.7	40.5	1.99	16

(continued)

Appendix Table 11-1 (continued)

State	Own			Spillins				Average Annual	
	SAES	Extension	Total	SAES	USDA	Extension	Total	%Δ MFP	Rank
	percentage share of change in MFP attributable to knowledge stock							*percent*	
Central	*29.5*	*27.3*	*56.8*	*15.6*	*14.0*	*13.6*	*43.2*	*1.83*	
Illinois	25.4	26.0	51.4	16.7	16.8	15.1	48.6	1.63	43
Indiana	29.1	25.6	54.7	15.7	15.3	14.2	45.3	1.73	37
Iowa	31.0	23.4	54.4	15.7	15.6	14.3	45.6	1.73	36
Michigan	29.5	30.6	60.1	15.2	12.1	12.6	39.9	1.97	18
Minnesota	34.0	24.3	58.4	15.1	13.3	13.3	41.6	1.82	29
Missouri	27.8	33.4	61.2	14.2	12.4	12.2	38.8	2.03	14
Ohio	25.5	27.7	53.3	17.0	14.9	14.9	46.7	1.67	41
Wisconsin	33.8	27.0	60.8	15.1	11.5	12.6	39.2	2.03	11
Southeast	*28.3*	*31.2*	*59.5*	*15.3*	*11.8*	*13.4*	*40.5*	*2.03*	
Alabama	28.0	30.7	58.7	15.7	11.9	13.8	41.3	2.03	12
Florida	46.1	21.0	67.1	13.0	9.3	10.6	32.9	2.42	1
Georgia	32.0	32.6	64.6	13.3	10.3	11.8	35.4	2.22	3
Kentucky	22.0	34.0	56.0	16.3	13.3	14.5	44.0	1.82	30
North Carolina	28.3	35.3	63.6	13.4	10.8	12.1	36.4	2.19	4
South Carolina	27.2	30.5	57.7	15.8	12.1	14.4	42.3	1.91	21
Tennessee	26.3	33.8	60.1	15.1	11.8	13.0	39.9	2.03	13
Virginia	27.6	35.6	63.2	14.1	10.7	12.0	36.8	2.14	6
West Virginia	17.3	27.5	44.8	21.0	15.7	18.4	55.2	1.50	45
Northeast	*27.5*	*23.2*	*50.7*	*19.6*	*13.1*	*16.6*	*49.3*	*1.66*	
Connecticut	27.9	14.2	42.1	23.2	14.7	20.0	57.9	1.44	47
Delaware	34.7	20.2	54.8	16.9	12.2	16.1	45.2	1.81	31
Maine	30.8	22.9	53.7	18.7	12.0	15.6	46.3	1.73	35
Maryland	25.4	32.3	57.7	16.3	11.9	14.2	42.3	1.88	24
Massachusetts	17.4	23.4	40.8	23.9	15.2	20.1	59.2	1.38	48
New Hampshire	22.4	22.0	44.5	22.4	14.5	18.7	55.5	1.46	46
New Jersey	29.1	22.3	51.4	19.4	13.1	16.2	48.6	1.67	42
New York	31.2	23.3	54.5	17.6	13.1	14.8	45.5	1.77	33
Pennsylvania	29.0	26.9	55.9	17.2	12.5	14.4	44.1	1.84	27
Rhode Island	32.9	20.6	53.5	19.2	11.6	15.7	46.5	1.72	38
Vermont	21.9	27.1	49.0	20.4	13.6	17.0	51.0	1.56	44
Average	*30.6*	*26.0*	*56.7*	*16.5*	*12.7*	*14.1*	*43.3*	*1.87*	

Sources: Developed by the authors.

Appendix Table 11-2 Productivity Growth Partitioned Among Knowledge Stocks, by State, 1949–2002

Panel a. Linear model

State	Own			Spillins				Total	Rank
	SAES	Extension	Total	SAES	IM	Extension	Total		
	average annual percentage change in MFP								
Pacific	*0.52*	*0.24*	*0.76*	*0.65*	*0.37*	*0.46*	*1.48*	*2.25*	
California	1.10	0.45	1.55	0.65	0.40	0.49	1.54	3.09	2
Oregon	0.25	0.14	0.39	0.77	0.43	0.52	1.71	2.10	14
Washington	0.23	0.12	0.35	0.55	0.30	0.36	1.20	1.55	29
Mountain	*0.12*	*0.06*	*0.18*	*0.72*	*0.40*	*0.48*	*1.60*	*1.77*	
Arizona	0.20	0.06	0.27	0.65	0.34	0.43	1.42	1.68	25
Colorado	0.25	0.12	0.37	0.74	0.46	0.51	1.72	2.09	16
Idaho	0.09	0.05	0.14	0.54	0.29	0.35	1.18	1.32	35
Montana	0.11	0.04	0.15	0.59	0.34	0.39	1.32	1.47	33
Nevada	0.06	0.04	0.10	0.89	0.51	0.60	2.00	2.10	15
New Mexico	0.08	0.06	0.14	0.77	0.42	0.52	1.72	1.86	21
Utah	0.09	0.06	0.15	0.83	0.45	0.56	1.84	2.00	18
Wyoming	0.05	0.04	0.09	0.71	0.41	0.47	1.59	1.68	27
Northern Plains	*0.17*	*0.10*	*0.27*	*0.57*	*0.36*	*0.39*	*1.32*	*1.59*	
Kansas	0.24	0.19	0.43	0.61	0.38	0.41	1.40	1.83	23
Nebraska	0.25	0.12	0.37	0.62	0.42	0.44	1.47	1.85	22
North Dakota	0.12	0.05	0.17	0.38	0.22	0.25	0.84	1.01	44
South Dakota	0.08	0.05	0.12	0.67	0.42	0.46	1.55	1.68	26
Southern Plains	*0.28*	*0.22*	*0.50*	*0.58*	*0.34*	*0.40*	*1.33*	*1.83*	
Arkansas	0.13	0.08	0.21	0.33	0.17	0.23	0.72	0.93	45
Louisiana	0.24	0.16	0.40	0.50	0.28	0.34	1.11	1.51	30
Mississippi	0.14	0.10	0.24	0.36	0.19	0.25	0.79	1.03	43
Oklahoma	0.20	0.18	0.38	0.82	0.48	0.56	1.86	2.24	11
Texas	0.70	0.57	1.27	0.91	0.59	0.66	2.16	3.43	1
Central	*0.31*	*0.23*	*0.53*	*0.76*	*0.50*	*0.54*	*1.80*	*2.33*	
Illinois	0.26	0.20	0.45	0.59	0.43	0.43	1.46	1.91	20
Indiana	0.27	0.19	0.47	0.64	0.46	0.46	1.56	2.03	17
Iowa	0.37	0.20	0.57	0.67	0.50	0.50	1.67	2.24	10
Michigan	0.28	0.25	0.53	0.79	0.48	0.55	1.82	2.35	9
Minnesota	0.33	0.20	0.53	0.77	0.51	0.55	1.84	2.37	8
Missouri	0.28	0.27	0.55	0.95	0.64	0.69	2.29	2.84	3
Ohio	0.23	0.22	0.45	0.84	0.55	0.60	1.98	2.43	7
Wisconsin	0.41	0.28	0.69	0.78	0.46	0.55	1.79	2.48	6
Southeast	*0.22*	*0.20*	*0.42*	*0.60*	*0.34*	*0.43*	*1.36*	*1.78*	
Alabama	0.15	0.13	0.29	0.45	0.24	0.31	1.01	1.30	36
Florida	0.52	0.24	0.76	0.38	0.20	0.25	0.84	1.60	28
Georgia	0.24	0.20	0.44	0.37	0.21	0.26	0.84	1.27	38
Kentucky	0.16	0.24	0.40	0.74	0.44	0.53	1.71	2.11	13
North Carolina	0.29	0.27	0.56	0.31	0.18	0.23	0.71	1.27	37
South Carolina	0.11	0.11	0.22	0.49	0.27	0.35	1.10	1.32	34
Tennessee	0.20	0.22	0.42	0.94	0.56	0.68	2.17	2.60	5
Virginia	0.29	0.30	0.59	0.88	0.52	0.64	2.04	2.63	4
West Virginia	0.05	0.05	0.10	0.83	0.45	0.58	1.85	1.95	19

(continued)

Appendix Table 11-2 (continued)

State	Own			Spillins				Total	Rank
	SAES	Extension	Total	SAES	IM	Extension	Total		
	average annual percentage change in MFP								
Northeast	*0.10*	*0.07*	*0.17*	*0.51*	*0.25*	*0.34*	*1.09*	*1.26*	
Connecticut	0.05	0.02	0.07	0.57	0.25	0.38	1.20	1.27	39
Delaware	0.03	0.02	0.05	0.25	0.12	0.18	0.55	0.59	48
Maine	0.05	0.02	0.07	0.34	0.15	0.22	0.71	0.78	47
Maryland	0.09	0.10	0.19	0.58	0.30	0.40	1.28	1.48	31
Massachusetts	0.04	0.03	0.07	0.49	0.22	0.32	1.02	1.09	42
New Hampshire	0.02	0.02	0.03	0.55	0.25	0.36	1.16	1.20	40
New Jersey	0.11	0.09	0.20	0.59	0.29	0.39	1.27	1.47	32
New York	0.49	0.30	0.80	0.63	0.35	0.43	1.40	2.20	12
Pennsylvania	0.21	0.13	0.34	0.65	0.35	0.44	1.45	1.78	24
Rhode Island	0.02	0.01	0.03	0.41	0.17	0.26	0.84	0.87	46
Vermont	0.02	0.02	0.04	0.54	0.25	0.35	1.15	1.19	41
Average	*0.21*	*0.15*	*0.36*	*0.62*	*0.36*	*0.43*	*1.41*	*1.77*	

Panel b. Logarithmic model

State	Own			Spillins				Total	Rank
	SAES	Extension	Total	SAES	IM	Extension	Total		
	average annual percentage change in MFP								
Pacific	*0.81*	*0.51*	*1.33*	*0.29*	*0.24*	*0.27*	*0.80*	*2.12*	
California	0.97	0.49	1.47	0.28	0.24	0.27	0.79	2.26	2
Oregon	0.69	0.54	1.23	0.29	0.24	0.27	0.80	2.03	10
Washington	0.78	0.50	1.28	0.29	0.24	0.27	0.80	2.08	9
Mountain	*0.61*	*0.46*	*1.08*	*0.29*	*0.25*	*0.27*	*0.81*	*1.88*	
Arizona	0.89	0.43	1.32	0.30	0.24	0.28	0.82	2.14	7
Colorado	0.73	0.57	1.30	0.28	0.25	0.27	0.80	2.10	8
Idaho	0.62	0.47	1.09	0.29	0.24	0.27	0.80	1.89	23
Montana	0.53	0.33	0.86	0.28	0.26	0.27	0.81	1.67	40
Nevada	0.57	0.48	1.05	0.29	0.24	0.27	0.81	1.86	26
New Mexico	0.50	0.57	1.07	0.29	0.24	0.27	0.81	1.88	25
Utah	0.60	0.44	1.04	0.29	0.24	0.27	0.80	1.84	28
Wyoming	0.48	0.39	0.87	0.29	0.25	0.27	0.81	1.68	39
Northern Plains	*0.58*	*0.48*	*1.06*	*0.27*	*0.26*	*0.26*	*0.80*	*1.86*	
Kansas	0.51	0.63	1.13	0.28	0.26	0.26	0.80	1.93	20
Nebraska	0.71	0.50	1.21	0.26	0.27	0.26	0.79	2.00	15
North Dakota	0.58	0.39	0.97	0.28	0.26	0.26	0.80	1.77	32
South Dakota	0.52	0.41	0.94	0.27	0.26	0.26	0.80	1.74	34
Southern Plains	*0.56*	*0.63*	*1.19*	*0.29*	*0.25*	*0.28*	*0.81*	*2.00*	
Arkansas	0.55	0.60	1.15	0.29	0.24	0.29	0.82	1.97	19
Louisiana	0.68	0.70	1.38	0.29	0.24	0.27	0.80	2.18	5
Mississippi	0.51	0.64	1.16	0.29	0.24	0.29	0.82	1.97	17
Oklahoma	0.52	0.57	1.09	0.29	0.25	0.27	0.81	1.90	22
Texas	0.53	0.65	1.18	0.29	0.26	0.27	0.81	1.99	16

(continued)

Appendix Table 11-2 (continued)

	Own			Spillins					
State	SAES	Extension	Total	SAES	IM	Extension	Total	Total	Rank
			average annual percentage change in MFP						
Central	*0.52*	*0.52*	*1.04*	*0.27*	*0.26*	*0.26*	*0.79*	*1.83*	
Illinois	0.41	0.44	0.84	0.25	0.28	0.25	0.79	1.63	43
Indiana	0.48	0.46	0.94	0.26	0.27	0.26	0.79	1.73	37
Iowa	0.51	0.43	0.94	0.26	0.28	0.26	0.79	1.73	36
Michigan	0.54	0.63	1.18	0.28	0.24	0.26	0.79	1.97	18
Minnesota	0.59	0.45	1.03	0.27	0.26	0.26	0.79	1.82	29
Missouri	0.51	0.72	1.23	0.27	0.26	0.26	0.79	2.03	14
Ohio	0.41	0.47	0.87	0.27	0.26	0.26	0.79	1.67	41
Wisconsin	0.68	0.56	1.24	0.28	0.24	0.27	0.79	2.03	11
Southeast	*0.56*	*0.67*	*1.22*	*0.28*	*0.24*	*0.28*	*0.80*	*2.03*	
Alabama	0.54	0.68	1.22	0.29	0.24	0.28	0.81	2.03	12
Florida	1.12	0.50	1.62	0.29	0.23	0.27	0.80	2.42	1
Georgia	0.65	0.77	1.42	0.28	0.24	0.28	0.80	2.22	3
Kentucky	0.38	0.64	1.01	0.28	0.25	0.28	0.80	1.82	30
North Carolina	0.54	0.85	1.39	0.27	0.24	0.28	0.80	2.19	4
South Carolina	0.50	0.60	1.10	0.28	0.24	0.29	0.81	1.91	21
Tennessee	0.49	0.74	1.23	0.28	0.24	0.27	0.80	2.03	13
Virginia	0.54	0.80	1.34	0.29	0.24	0.27	0.80	2.14	6
West Virginia	0.26	0.43	0.69	0.29	0.24	0.28	0.81	1.50	45
Northeast	*0.45*	*0.40*	*0.86*	*0.30*	*0.22*	*0.28*	*0.80*	*1.66*	
Connecticut	0.42	0.22	0.63	0.31	0.21	0.29	0.81	1.44	47
Delaware	0.63	0.36	1.00	0.29	0.23	0.30	0.81	1.81	31
Maine	0.51	0.42	0.93	0.31	0.21	0.28	0.80	1.73	35
Maryland	0.46	0.61	1.08	0.29	0.23	0.28	0.80	1.88	24
Massachusetts	0.24	0.33	0.57	0.31	0.21	0.28	0.81	1.38	48
New Hampshire	0.32	0.34	0.66	0.31	0.21	0.28	0.80	1.46	46
New Jersey	0.49	0.37	0.87	0.30	0.22	0.28	0.80	1.67	42
New York	0.53	0.44	0.97	0.30	0.24	0.27	0.80	1.77	33
Pennsylvania	0.51	0.54	1.05	0.29	0.23	0.27	0.80	1.84	27
Rhode Island	0.56	0.36	0.92	0.32	0.20	0.28	0.80	1.72	38
Vermont	0.33	0.44	0.77	0.31	0.22	0.28	0.80	1.56	44
Average	*0.55*	*0.52*	*1.07*	*0.29*	*0.24*	*0.27*	*0.80*	*1.87*	

Sources: Developed by the authors.

Appendix Table 11-3 MFP Growth Accounting and Marginal Benefit-Cost Ratio—Effects of Interstate Spillovers Specification

	Linear Model With Spillovers Defined Based on			Logarithmic Model With Spillovers Defined Based on		
	Output Mix (1)	USDA Regions (2)	No Spillovers (3)	Output Mix (4)	USDA Regions (5)	No Spillovers (6)
RMSE	30.36	27.75	38.52	22.46	22.23	22.77
Lag distribution parameters						
λ	0.75	0.70	0.95	0.70	0.65	0.95
δ	0.80	0.85	0.70	0.90	0.90	0.65
Peak lag year	13	15	44	24	20	35
	average annual percentage predicted change in MFP (percentage share of growth attributed to own-state R&E in parentheses)					
48 states						
Average	1.77	1.75	1.51	1.87	1.81	1.86
	(19.0)	(13.5)	(100.0)	(56.7)	(43.1)	(100.0)
Minimum	0.59	1.08	0.14	1.38	1.34	1.13
	(3.0)	(1.6)	(100.0)	(40.8)	(27.1)	(100.0)
Maximum	3.43	2.71	11.23	2.42	2.29	2.69
	(51.4)	(47.8)	(100.0)	(67.1)	(53.7)	(100.0)
Selected states						
California	3.09	2.16	11.23	2.26	2.11	2.49
	(51.4)	(47.8)	(100.0)	(64.9)	(51.9)	(100.0)
Minnesota	2.37	2.17	1.71	1.82	1.82	1.78
	(24.3)	(18.0)	(100.0)	(58.4)	(46.5)	(100.0)
Wyoming	1.68	1.60	0.43	1.68	1.64	1.57
	(4.9)	(3.7)	(100.0)	(50.6)	(35.9)	(100.0)
	own-state benefit-cost ratio (national benefit-cost ratio in parentheses)					
48 states						
Average	10.0	6.4	26.0	21.0	17.6	33.7
	(39.7)	(20.2)	(26.0)	(32.1)	(24.8)	(33.7)
Minimum	0.2	0.1	0.4	2.4	2.3	4.5
	(14.2)	(7.1)	(0.4)	(9.9)	(6.6)	(4.5)
Maximum	43.9	29.9	145.8	57.8	48.5	90.0
	(74.4)	(63.2)	(145.8)	(69.2)	(62.4)	(90.0)
Selected states						
California	42.3	24.4	145.8	33.3	27.0	56.0
	(68.9)	(26.9)	(145.8)	(43.4)	(28.8)	(56.0)
Minnesota	22.6	14.3	56.3	40.6	33.6	62.8
	(62.3)	(53.2)	(56.3)	(55.4)	(49.4)	(62.8)
Wyoming	2.2	1.5	5.5	12.7	10.9	20.7
	(31.9)	(7.7)	(5.5)	(23.6)	(15.3)	(20.7)

Sources: Developed by the authors.

Appendix Table 11-4 MFP Growth Accounting and Marginal Benefit-Cost Ratios—Effects of Research Lag Distribution Shapes

	Linear Model				Logarithmic Model			
Research lag								
Maximum lag, years	50	35	50	35	50	35	50	35
Lag distribution form	gamma	trapezoid	gamma	trapezoid	gamma	trapezoid	gamma	trapezoid
Extension lag								
Maximum lag, years	50	35	4	4	50	35	4	4
Lag distribution form	gamma	trapezoid	geometric	geometric	gamma	trapezoid	geometric	geometric
RMSE	30.36	30.35	30.39	30.70	22.46	23.06	23.71	24.43
	average annual percentage predicted change in MFP (percentage share of growth attributed to own-state R&E in parentheses)							
48 states								
Average	1.77	1.77	1.82	1.80	1.87	1.75	1.76	1.70
	(19.0)	(18.9)	(18.1)	(18.5)	(56.7)	(40.0)	(22.8)	(24.6)
Minimum	0.59	0.59	0.61	0.59	1.38	1.35	1.46	1.41
	(3.0)	(3.0)	(2.5)	(2.3)	(40.8)	(20.2)	(3.9)	(6.4)
Maximum	3.43	3.43	3.35	3.43	2.42	2.15	2.08	2.02
	(51.4)	(51.4)	(50.6)	(51.4)	(67.1)	(52.4)	(35.2)	(37.2)
Selected states								
California	3.09	3.10	3.18	3.26	2.26	2.02	1.92	1.87
	(51.4)	(51.4)	(50.6)	(51.4)	(64.9)	(48.8)	(30.6)	(32.4)
Minnesota	2.37	2.37	2.50	2.50	1.82	1.83	1.82	1.79
	(24.3)	(24.4)	(24.0)	(25.2)	(58.4)	(45.9)	(27.5)	(30.7)
Wyoming	1.68	1.68	1.70	1.67	1.68	1.57	1.62	1.53
	(4.9)	(4.9)	(4.0)	(3.5)	(50.6)	(31.1)	(14.4)	(13.9)
	own-state benefit-cost ratio (national benefit-cost ratio in parentheses)							
48 states								
Average	10.0	10.1	8.8	10.7	21.0	19.8	9.3	11.8
	(39.7)	(40.3)	(34.5)	(42.9)	(32.1)	(41.2)	(31.4)	(38.2)
Minimum	0.2	0.2	0.1	0.2	2.4	3.4	1.3	2.2
	(14.2)	(14.4)	(12.5)	(15.3)	(9.9)	(18.0)	(16.2)	(20.2)
Maximum	43.9	44.6	39.7	48.0	57.8	53.5	27.8	34.0
	(74.4)	(75.6)	(66.6)	(80.5)	(69.2)	(75.4)	(50.5)	(61.0)
Selected states								
California	42.3	42.9	36.1	44.6	33.3	29.2	13.5	16.4
	(68.9)	(69.9)	(58.9)	(73.5)	(43.4)	(48.8)	(33.5)	(40.4)
Minnesota	22.6	23.0	20.3	24.7	40.6	37.9	18.0	23.4
	(62.3)	(63.4)	(54.6)	(67.7)	(55.4)	(66.2)	(47.2)	(58.3)
Wyoming	2.2	2.2	2.0	2.4	12.7	12.4	6.6	8.0
	(31.9)	(32.4)	(27.8)	(34.6)	(23.6)	(32.9)	(28.1)	(33.2)

Sources: Developed by the authors.

Appendix Table 11-5 MFP Growth Accounting and Marginal Benefit-Cost Ratios—Effects of Maximum Lag Length

Panel a. Linear Model

	Gamma Extension Lag Weights with Gamma Research Lags Over			4-Year Geometric Extension Lag with Gamma Research Lags Over		
	50 years (1)	35 years (2)	20 years (3)	50 years (4)	35 years (5)	20 years (6)
RMSE	30.36	30.35	30.39	30.39	30.36	30.54
Lag distribution parameters						
λ	0.75	0.80	0.95	0.65	0.70	0.90
δ	0.80	0.75	0.70	0.90	0.90	0.90
Peak lag year	13	12	44	20	24	84
	average annual percentage predicted change in MFP (percentage share of growth attributed to own-state R&E in parentheses)					
48 states						
Average	1.77	1.78	1.72	1.82	1.83	1.71
	(19.0)	(18.9)	(18.8)	(18.1)	(18.0)	(19.4)
Minimum	0.59	0.59	0.57	0.61	0.62	0.57
	(3.0)	(2.9)	(2.5)	(2.5)	(2.3)	(2.4)
Maximum	3.43	3.45	3.36	3.35	3.33	3.22
	(51.4)	(51.4)	(51.5)	(50.6)	(50.0)	(53.6)
Selected states						
California	3.09	3.12	3.00	3.18	3.17	3.11
	(51.4)	(51.4)	(51.5)	(50.6)	(49.9)	(53.4)
Minnesota	2.37	2.38	2.31	2.50	2.51	2.36
	(24.3)	(24.5)	(24.6)	(24.0)	(23.5)	(25.8)
Wyoming	1.68	1.68	1.64	1.70	1.72	1.58
	(4.9)	(4.9)	(4.9)	(4.0)	(4.2)	(3.8)
48 states	*own-state benefit-cost ratio (national benefit-cost ratio in parentheses)*					
Average	10.0	10.3	9.7	8.8	8.5	9.5
	(39.7)	(41.0)	(39.6)	(34.5)	(33.1)	(36.1)
Minimum	0.2	0.2	0.2	0.1	0.1	0.1
	(14.2)	(14.7)	(14.3)	(12.5)	(12.0)	(12.8)
Maximum	43.9	45.7	42.4	39.7	38.7	42.9
	(74.4)	(76.8)	(73.5)	(66.6)	(64.5)	(70.7)
Selected states						
California	42.3	43.5	41.8	36.1	34.5	40.2
	(68.9)	(71.0)	(68.5)	(58.9)	(56.3)	(63.8)
Minnesota	22.6	23.4	21.9	20.3	19.7	21.8
	(62.3)	(64.4)	(61.9)	(54.6)	(52.6)	(57.3)
Wyoming	2.2	2.3	2.2	2.0	1.9	2.3
	(31.9)	(33.0)	(32.0)	(27.8)	(26.6)	(28.8)

(continued)

Appendix Table 11-5 (continued)

Panel b. Logarithmic Model

	Gamma Extension Lag Weights with Gamma Research Lags Over			4-Year Geometric Extension Lag with Gamma Research Lags Over		
	50 years (1)	35 years (2)	20 years (3)	50 years (4)	35 years (5)	20 years (6)
RMSE	22.46	22.47	23.06	23.71	23.60	24.01
Lag distribution parameters						
λ	0.70	0.70	0.70	0.65	0.70	0.85
δ	0.90	0.90	0.90	0.90	0.90	0.90
Peak lag year	24	24	24	20	24	54
	average annual percentage predicted change in MFP (percentage share of growth attributed to own-state R&E in parentheses)					
48 states						
Average	1.87	1.85	1.70	1.76	1.78	1.66
	(56.7)	(50.4)	(33.5)	(22.8)	(22.4)	(24.4)
Minimum	1.38	1.36	1.33	1.46	1.48	1.37
	(40.8)	(33)	(14.4)	(3.9)	(2.9)	(7.2)
Maximum	2.42	2.36	2.02	2.08	2.11	1.98
	(67.1)	(61.9)	(46.3)	(35.2)	(34.8)	(37.5)
Selected states						
California	2.26	2.21	1.90	1.92	1.94	1.82
	(64.9)	(59.1)	(42)	(30.6)	(30)	(32.6)
Minnesota	1.82	1.83	1.78	1.82	1.84	1.74
	(58.4)	(53.1)	(39.4)	(27.5)	(26.7)	(30.1)
Wyoming	1.68	1.66	1.56	1.62	1.65	1.49
	(50.6)	(43.3)	(26.5)	(14.4)	(14.7)	(14.4)
	own-state benefit-cost ratio (national benefit-cost ratio in parentheses)					
48 states						
Average	21.0	20.4	14.8	9.3	8.8	10.4
	(32.1)	(34.3)	(36.3)	(31.4)	(30.1)	(33.7)
Minimum	2.4	2.4	2.5	1.3	1.1	1.7
	(9.9)	(11.7)	(17.2)	(16.2)	(15.3)	(17.6)
Maximum	57.8	56.7	39.5	27.8	27.0	29.4
	(69.2)	(71.0)	(63.0)	(50.5)	(48.9)	(55.0)
Selected states						
California	33.3	31.5	22.2	13.5	13.1	14.7
	(43.4)	(44.1)	(41.8)	(33.5)	(32.3)	(35.8)
Minnesota	40.6	39.7	27.2	18.0	17.0	19.8
	(55.4)	(58.1)	(55.6)	(47.2)	(45.2)	(50.7)
Wyoming	12.7	12.4	9.2	6.6	6.3	7.3
	(23.6)	(26.0)	(29.8)	(28.1)	(27.1)	(29.7)

Sources: Developed by the authors.

Appendix Table 11-6 Marginal Benefit-Cost Ratios from the Base Models, by State

	Linear Model			Logarithmic Model		
State or Region	State R&E "Private" (1)	State R&E "Social" (2)	USDA Intramural (3)	State R&E "Private" (4)	State R&E "Social" (5)	USDA Intramural (6)
Pacific	*17.9*	*47.2*	*1.6*	*21.8*	*32.9*	*0.6*
California	42.3	68.9	3.8	33.3	43.4	1.4
Oregon	5.1	38.8	0.5	11.3	24.1	0.2
Washington	6.2	33.7	0.5	20.9	31.2	0.3
Mountain	*3.7*	*35.2*	*0.3*	*20.0*	*31.6*	*0.1*
Arizona	4.6	32.4	0.4	26.6	36.9	0.2
Colorado	7.6	42.3	0.8	31.1	43.8	0.3
Idaho	4.4	33.7	0.4	34.0	44.8	0.2
Montana	5.5	32.8	0.4	22.0	32.2	0.2
Nevada	0.8	33.1	0.1	7.3	19.2	0.0
New Mexico	2.6	36.7	0.3	15.6	28.2	0.1
Utah	2.0	38.6	0.2	11.0	24.5	0.1
Wyoming	2.2	31.9	0.2	12.7	23.6	0.1
Northern Plains	*11.2*	*44.4*	*1.2*	*42.4*	*54.5*	*0.5*
Kansas	14.7	46.7	1.5	33.6	45.3	0.7
Nebraska	15.4	53.2	1.8	51.3	64.9	0.8
North Dakota	6.1	29.8	0.4	37.3	46.0	0.3
South Dakota	8.6	47.9	1.0	47.4	61.7	0.4
Southern Plains	*13.7*	*41.7*	*1.3*	*20.2*	*31.0*	*0.5*
Arkansas	5.5	28.5	0.4	26.8	35.7	0.4
Louisiana	4.5	33.6	0.4	12.2	23.0	0.2
Mississippi	4.6	31.1	0.4	15.1	25.3	0.3
Oklahoma	10.1	43.3	1.0	19.0	31.4	0.3
Texas	43.9	72.2	4.3	28.2	39.4	1.1
Central	*23.4*	*58.8*	*2.5*	*33.7*	*46.8*	*0.8*
Illinois	32.5	62.5	3.2	43.0	53.8	1.3
Indiana	18.6	52.2	1.9	27.1	39.4	0.7
Iowa	43.2	74.4	4.6	57.8	69.2	1.6
Michigan	10.5	49.5	1.2	17.1	31.5	0.3
Minnesota	22.6	62.3	2.8	40.6	55.4	0.8
Missouri	22.1	62.1	2.7	34.7	49.9	0.6
Ohio	17.3	56.4	2.0	22.4	37.0	0.5
Wisconsin	20.1	51.4	1.9	26.7	38.3	0.6
Southeast	*6.7*	*36.9*	*0.6*	*15.1*	*26.7*	*0.3*
Alabama	4.7	33.9	0.4	13.4	24.8	0.3
Florida	9.4	27.4	0.5	21.6	28.2	0.4
Georgia	6.3	33.0	0.5	20.5	31.0	0.4
Kentucky	10.2	42.0	1.0	18.5	30.5	0.3
North Carolina	9.4	29.7	0.6	19.9	27.5	0.5
South Carolina	3.2	33.7	0.3	11.2	23.1	0.1
Tennessee	8.5	49.7	1.0	15.7	31.3	0.2
Virginia	7.5	45.1	0.9	11.8	26.3	0.2
West Virginia	1.5	37.8	0.2	3.8	17.6	0.0

(continued)

Appendix Table 11-6 (continued)

State or Region	Linear Model: State R&E "Private" (1)	Linear Model: State R&E "Social" (2)	Linear Model: USDA Intramural (3)	Logarithmic Model: State R&E "Private" (4)	Logarithmic Model: State R&E "Social" (5)	Logarithmic Model: USDA Intramural (6)
Northeast	*3.0*	*26.8*	*0.2*	*9.4*	*18.4*	*0.1*
Connecticut	1.5	24.5	0.1	5.4	14.2	0.0
Delaware	0.9	14.2	0.0	15.8	21.5	0.0
Maine	1.6	18.9	0.1	13.5	20.1	0.1
Maryland	2.9	33.7	0.3	14.1	26.1	0.1
Massachusetts	1.3	23.9	0.1	4.7	13.3	0.0
New Hampshire	0.5	26.3	0.0	4.4	14.0	0.0
New Jersey	2.9	26.5	0.2	4.7	13.7	0.1
New York	11.4	38.1	0.9	8.3	18.1	0.3
Pennsylvania	9.1	42.2	0.9	18.0	30.3	0.3
Rhode Island	0.2	19.8	0.0	2.4	9.9	0.0
Vermont	1.2	26.2	0.1	12.4	21.5	0.0
Average	*10.0*	*39.7*	*1.0*	*21.0*	*32.1*	*0.4*

Sources: Developed by the authors.

Appendix Table 11-7 Marginal Internal Rates of Return from the Base Models, by State

State or Region	Linear Model "Private"	Linear Model "Social"	Logarithmic Model "Private"	Logarithmic Model "Social"
	rate of return to state spending, percent per year			
Pacific	*33.8*	*64.8*	*20.2*	*23.5*
California	61.9	79.6	24.1	26.1
Oregon	19.1	59.7	16.3	21.3
Washington	20.5	55.0	20.3	23.1
Mountain	*13.2*	*56.3*	*19.0*	*22.7*
Arizona	16.9	54.0	22.1	24.5
Colorado	22.8	61.3	22.5	25.2
Idaho	15.8	54.6	23.3	25.5
Montana	19.4	54.2	20.4	23.1
Nevada	1.3	54.9	13.0	19.1
New Mexico	11.1	57.8	18.1	22.2
Utah	9.1	59.7	16.0	21.3
Wyoming	9.5	53.6	16.8	20.9
Northern Plains	*28.2*	*62.4*	*24.9*	*27.0*
Kansas	33.5	64.2	23.3	25.6
Nebraska	34.3	68.8	26.3	28.4
North Dakota	20.1	51.0	23.8	25.5
South Dakota	25.1	65.7	26.3	28.4
Southern Plains	*29.6*	*61.1*	*19.5*	*22.7*
Arkansas	17.8	49.6	21.4	23.6
Louisiana	16.5	55.0	16.8	21.0
Mississippi	16.9	52.7	18.3	21.7
Oklahoma	28.3	62.6	19.1	22.8
Texas	68.3	85.8	21.9	24.5
Central	*45.5*	*74.2*	*23.1*	*25.9*
Illinois	53.5	75.6	25.1	27.0
Indiana	40.7	69.7	21.7	24.6
Iowa	62.6	83.1	27.6	29.1
Michigan	30.6	68.2	19.1	23.4
Minnesota	45.0	76.0	24.7	27.3
Missouri	47.0	77.6	24.3	27.1
Ohio	41.3	73.9	20.2	24.0
Wisconsin	43.4	69.7	22.1	24.8
Southeast	*21.2*	*57.6*	*17.6*	*22.0*
Alabama	17.1	55.1	17.1	21.3
Florida	24.8	47.6	20.5	22.4
Georgia	20.2	53.9	20.3	23.2
Kentucky	28.9	62.1	19.2	22.8
North Carolina	26.7	51.1	20.6	22.8
South Carolina	13.3	55.5	16.1	20.9
Tennessee	27.4	68.5	18.4	23.3
Virginia	26.1	65.4	16.7	22.0
West Virginia	6.3	59.3	9.7	18.9

(continued)

Appendix Table 11-7 (continued)

State or Region	Linear Model "Private"	Linear Model "Social"	Logarithmic Model "Private"	Logarithmic Model "Social"
	rate of return to state spending, percent per year			
Northeast	*9.2*	*49.0*	*14.0*	*19.0*
Connecticut	6.6	47.5	11.8	17.6
Delaware	2.1	34.8	17.9	20.0
Maine	6.5	40.9	17.5	20.1
Maryland	12.1	55.3	17.5	21.7
Massachusetts	5.3	46.8	10.8	17.0
New Hampshire	-1.4	49.2	10.6	17.5
New Jersey	13.5	49.8	11.3	17.5
New York	32.5	60.1	14.2	19.1
Pennsylvania	27.9	62.8	19.1	22.8
Rhode Island	-8.0	42.4	7.4	15.3
Vermont	4.3	49.1	16.2	20.0
Average	*23.4*	*59.4*	*18.9*	*22.7*

Sources: Developed by the authors.

Appendix Table 11-8 Growth Rates of State-Specific Agricultural R&E Spending, by Decade, 1949–2002

	1949–2002	1949–1960	1960–1970	1970–1980	1980–1990	1990–2002
	average annual percentage change					
United States						
SAES	2.65	4.38	2.81	3.88	1.43	0.95
Extension (Ext)	1.36	1.98	2.42	2.38	0.20	0.02
Intramural (IM)	1.32	3.93	2.70	1.47	-1.76	0.21
SAES + Ext + IM	1.89	3.30	2.64	2.78	0.38	0.51
Pacific	*2.41*	*4.25*	*2.27*	*3.51*	*0.82*	*1.24*
California	2.67	5.07	2.15	3.71	1.49	1.02
Oregon	2.12	3.72	1.84	3.74	-0.60	1.81
Washington	1.81	2.22	3.12	2.56	-0.46	1.61
Mountain	*2.42*	*3.74*	*1.90*	*4.25*	*0.98*	*1.33*
Arizona	3.51	6.79	2.93	4.91	1.90	1.13
Colorado	3.31	4.48	2.64	7.62	1.27	0.91
Idaho	2.43	4.79	1.38	3.98	-0.62	2.38
Montana	1.41	2.43	0.65	2.51	-0.99	2.18
Nevada	3.28	3.91	4.90	3.54	0.60	3.36
New Mexico	1.74	3.17	1.88	0.58	2.94	0.29
Utah	2.18	2.42	0.78	5.52	0.69	1.59
Wyoming	0.40	1.71	0.84	-0.45	1.95	-1.76
Northern Plains	*2.19*	*4.29*	*3.07*	*3.49*	*-0.42*	*0.64*
Kansas	1.99	3.96	2.88	3.48	0.34	-0.40
Nebraska	2.76	4.03	5.25	3.68	-0.64	1.57
North Dakota	2.05	4.91	0.23	5.23	-1.23	1.01
South Dakota	1.56	4.75	2.61	0.81	-0.97	0.48
Southern Plains	*1.81*	*2.81*	*1.27*	*4.01*	*0.10*	*0.92*
Arkansas	2.10	4.62	1.13	4.20	-0.80	1.26
Louisiana	1.56	3.59	1.55	3.87	-1.83	0.61
Mississippi	1.34	0.92	1.39	4.50	-0.80	0.84
Oklahoma	1.63	2.43	0.55	2.26	0.97	1.83
Texas	2.11	2.83	1.43	4.42	1.46	0.65
Central	*2.06*	*2.82*	*2.05*	*2.70*	*0.98*	*1.06*
Illinois	1.54	1.06	3.62	0.53	1.25	1.33
Indiana	1.48	1.84	1.42	4.50	0.15	-0.22
Iowa	2.25	3.22	0.98	3.31	3.08	0.87
Michigan	2.64	5.20	2.06	3.72	0.85	1.36
Minnesota	2.42	2.93	3.26	3.97	1.49	0.71
Missouri	1.96	3.03	4.53	1.16	0.34	0.83
Ohio	1.88	2.52	4.91	1.02	-0.09	1.12
Wisconsin	2.21	3.07	1.97	3.43	0.39	2.12
Southeast	*2.08*	*2.93*	*3.39*	*3.59*	*1.03*	*-0.17*
Alabama	1.07	1.65	2.57	2.95	0.44	-1.76
Florida	2.59	2.88	4.24	4.02	2.47	-0.16
Georgia	2.80	5.74	3.47	3.84	1.38	-0.14
Kentucky	1.94	2.96	3.40	2.31	0.26	0.88
North Carolina	2.12	3.30	3.50	3.31	0.82	-0.04
South Carolina	1.36	1.05	3.10	5.14	1.18	-2.82
Tennessee	1.79	1.85	3.35	4.35	-0.80	0.47
Virginia	1.98	3.41	3.77	3.78	1.63	-2.04
West Virginia	2.50	1.83	1.36	1.24	-1.47	8.43

(continued)

Appendix Table 11-8 (continued)

	1949–2002	1949–1960	1960–1970	1970–1980	1980–1990	1990–2002
			average annual percentage change			
Northeast	*1.56*	*2.44*	*2.73*	*1.37*	*2.03*	*-0.46*
Connecticut	1.12	1.66	2.75	-2.48	1.08	2.29
Delaware	1.92	5.17	0.56	3.70	1.72	-1.23
Maine	1.45	2.07	3.11	2.59	1.13	-1.20
Maryland	2.13	4.94	2.11	1.96	3.96	-1.82
Massachusetts	0.60	1.59	1.86	-0.52	2.59	-2.09
New Hampshire	1.79	1.89	2.06	1.34	2.03	1.63
New Jersey	1.04	2.68	4.08	1.49	-2.47	-0.43
New York	1.74	1.76	3.17	1.64	2.67	-0.18
Pennsylvania	1.75	2.67	1.95	1.50	3.19	-0.26
Rhode Island	0.66	3.59	2.71	2.60	-2.51	-2.70
Vermont	1.00	2.60	2.93	0.89	0.60	-1.64

Sources: Developed by the authors using InSTePP data.

Appendix Table 11-9 Predicted Past and Projected Future MFP Growth by State, 1949–2050

	Linear Model				Logarithmic Model			
	Predicted MFP Growth		Projected MFP Growth (2003–2050)		Predicted MFP Growth		Projected MFP Growth (2003–2050)	
	1949–2002	1990–2002	Optimistic	Pessimistic	1949–2002	1990–2002	Optimistic	Pessimistic
	average annual percentage change							
Pacific	*2.24*	*1.09*	*1.69*	*0.92*	*2.06*	*1.14*	*1.02*	*0.75*
California	3.07	1.60	2.08	1.05	2.15	1.49	1.16	0.75
Oregon	2.13	0.96	1.64	0.93	1.98	0.96	1.01	0.78
Washington	1.53	0.73	1.35	0.77	2.04	0.98	0.89	0.72
Mountain	*1.69*	*0.82*	*1.57*	*0.83*	*1.78*	*1.15*	*1.05*	*0.76*
Arizona	1.57	0.84	1.72	0.80	2.00	1.34	1.41	0.88
Colorado	1.95	0.95	1.82	0.86	1.94	1.54	1.36	0.82
Idaho	1.28	0.77	1.35	0.76	1.84	1.34	1.07	0.87
Montana	1.53	0.59	1.36	0.81	1.68	0.87	0.81	0.79
Nevada	1.98	1.08	1.70	0.98	1.77	1.54	1.35	1.18
New Mexico	1.70	0.82	1.52	0.81	1.75	0.87	0.88	0.72
Utah	1.89	1.09	1.60	0.86	1.72	1.41	1.07	0.82
Wyoming	1.60	0.42	1.46	0.73	1.57	0.31	0.45	0.00
Northern Plains	*1.53*	*0.72*	*1.42*	*0.70*	*1.78*	*1.11*	*0.91*	*0.52*
Kansas	1.71	0.68	1.51	0.63	1.81	0.90	0.92	0.37
Nebraska	1.72	0.74	1.64	0.89	1.84	1.11	1.14	0.80
North Dakota	1.00	0.75	1.10	0.55	1.74	1.67	0.90	0.57
South Dakota	1.71	0.70	1.43	0.72	1.72	0.76	0.67	0.33
Southern Plains	*1.75*	*1.07*	*1.31*	*0.61*	*1.96*	*1.56*	*0.78*	*0.49*
Arkansas	0.89	0.73	1.05	0.44	1.92	1.66	0.88	0.54
Louisiana	1.44	0.91	1.25	0.56	2.12	1.55	0.68	0.37
Mississippi	0.99	0.78	1.01	0.44	1.93	1.67	0.70	0.45
Oklahoma	2.18	1.12	1.57	0.92	1.87	1.16	0.84	0.72
Texas	3.23	1.81	1.69	0.66	1.94	1.77	0.79	0.37
Central	*2.26*	*0.95*	*1.73*	*1.05*	*1.76*	*1.00*	*1.00*	*0.74*
Illinois	1.80	0.70	1.54	0.98	1.55	0.72	0.87	0.71
Indiana	1.91	0.69	1.48	0.72	1.61	0.82	0.78	0.40
Iowa	2.20	1.04	1.78	0.93	1.69	0.95	1.11	0.73
Michigan	2.31	0.98	1.84	0.98	1.93	1.05	1.12	0.74
Minnesota	2.41	1.30	1.98	1.71	1.84	1.54	1.29	1.23
Missouri	2.59	0.99	1.80	0.95	1.92	1.04	0.95	0.59
Ohio	2.35	0.70	1.69	0.96	1.57	0.70	0.90	0.66
Wisconsin	2.49	1.20	1.72	1.13	2.02	1.20	1.00	0.83
Southeast	*1.68*	*0.96*	*1.41*	*0.52*	*1.94*	*1.36*	*0.81*	*0.32*
Alabama	1.23	0.95	1.08	0.38	1.96	1.65	0.51	0.13
Florida	1.61	1.31	1.42	0.38	2.42	1.90	1.00	0.44
Georgia	1.21	0.96	1.41	0.37	2.12	1.81	1.09	0.41
Kentucky	1.99	0.88	1.55	0.75	1.72	0.96	0.86	0.55
North Carolina	1.18	0.68	1.26	0.36	2.06	1.21	0.95	0.42
South Carolina	1.24	0.85	1.14	0.36	1.82	1.57	0.63	-0.05
Tennessee	2.40	1.22	1.65	0.77	1.91	1.40	0.83	0.46
Virginia	2.42	0.99	1.65	0.55	1.99	1.16	0.86	0.10
West Virginia	1.84	0.77	1.51	0.74	1.42	0.60	0.56	0.44

(continued)

Appendix Table 11-9 (continued)

	Linear Model				Logarithmic Model			
	Predicted MFP Growth		Projected MFP Growth (2003–2050)		Predicted MFP Growth		Projected MFP Growth (2003–2050)	
	1949–2002	1990–2002	Optimistic	Pessimistic	1949–2002	1990–2002	Optimistic	Pessimistic
	average annual percentage change							
Northeast	*1.31*	*0.45*	*1.21*	*0.53*	*1.67*	*0.65*	*0.71*	*0.29*
Connecticut	1.35	0.40	1.27	0.67	1.47	0.26	0.76	0.79
Delaware	0.57	0.07	0.77	0.31	1.76	0.75	0.86	0.64
Maine	0.80	0.22	0.95	0.40	1.72	0.81	0.74	0.20
Maryland	1.39	0.60	1.34	0.50	1.77	0.75	0.93	0.22
Massachusetts	1.18	0.39	1.12	0.46	1.45	0.49	0.44	-0.13
New Hampshire	1.29	0.51	1.24	0.60	1.52	0.68	0.90	0.69
New Jersey	1.56	0.29	1.28	0.56	1.69	0.47	0.49	0.17
New York	2.36	1.13	1.58	0.65	1.83	0.96	0.89	0.46
Pennsylvania	1.75	0.68	1.50	0.68	1.75	0.51	0.96	0.50
Rhode Island	0.96	0.20	1.00	0.43	1.82	0.67	0.24	-0.39
Vermont	1.22	0.48	1.23	0.59	1.56	0.79	0.56	0.09

Sources: Developed by the authors.

Notes: For the optimistic scenario, spending was extrapolated using 1949–2002 growth rates; for the pessimistic alternative scenario, spending was extrapolated using 1990–2002 growth rates.

PART V

Interpretation and Synthesis

This Part of the book is devoted to interpreting the results from the econometric modeling and benefit-cost analysis in Part IV and providing a summary and synthesis of the main findings. Chapter 12 provides the interpretation. It begins with a summary of the results in Chapter 11. Then we systematically explore how the findings are influenced both by factors that are determined by the analyst, and by other factors that are aspects of the reality being modeled. Some of these relationships can be identified by consideration of the equations for the present value of benefits, as discussed in Chapter 11. However, to explore the quantitative importance of those factors and the role of specification choices, we conducted some statistical analysis of the patterns of results across states and specifications—a type of meta-analysis in which the explanatory variables are the characteristics of the model specification and agriculture in the states being modeled. Chapter 13 concludes the book with a summary and synthesis.

CHAPTER 12

Interpretation and Assessment of Benefit-Cost Findings

Agricultural production, input use, and productivity have been evolving over time, with substantially different patterns among U.S. states; so, too, has the pattern of spending on agricultural research and extension by the federal and state governments. In our econometric models linking these patterns of R&D spending and agricultural productivity, we have imposed a great deal of structure on the research lag and state-to-state spillover relationships. So long as they are appropriate and do not lead to estimation bias, these restrictions are helpful in reducing the number of free parameters to be estimated and improving the precision with which they are estimated. The resulting estimates indicate strong linkages between research and extension spending and productivity, and high payoffs to past investments. They also signal slower future productivity growth, especially if the past slowdown in the rate of growth in spending on farm-productivity-oriented research and extension spending will be sustained into the future.

In any study such as this, reasonable questions can (and should) be asked about the findings before we can decide how to use them. Are the findings plausible? Will they stand up to a common-sense scrutiny? Are the findings generally consistent with previous published work, and thus reinforced by and reinforcing the prior literature, or are they systematically different—and if so what is implied by the differences? What role has been played by our own decisions, versus the evolving patterns of R&D spending and agricultural production in the data, in determining the pattern of findings across states and over time? In this chapter we answer these questions. We summarize and interpret our findings, explain the patterns in our results, and assess the contribution.

J.M. Alston et al., *Persistence Pays: U.S. Agricultural Productivity Growth and the Benefits from Public R&D Spending*, Natural Resource Management and Policy 34, DOI 10.1007/978-1-4419-0658-8_12,

12.1 Summary of Main Findings

In Chapter 11, we used the econometric estimation results from Chapter 10 to identify the sources of past productivity growth, to compute implied benefit-cost ratios, and to examine the implications of recent actual past and projected future research investments for productivity growth, paying particular attention to evaluating the role of our specification choices in determining our results. Here, we present a brief summary of the main findings to set the stage for the present chapter, which is devoted to interpretation and assessment. In this interpretation and assessment we distill the main messages from a consideration of the entire body of evidence we have assembled and generated in this volume, rather than focus on the results for any particular state or on any specific detail of our study. We are conscious of the fact that choices made by the analyst in generating and analyzing data can distort findings, and so we pay particular attention to that possibility in this summary.

Sources of Growth

In Chapter 10 we identified a preferred model specification that used a gamma lag distribution model, with a maximum lag of 50 years, to represent the lagged impacts of research and extension on productivity, and with research and extension entering symmetrically in terms of both the lag distribution and the state-to-state spillovers. We estimated the model in both linear and logarithmic form. Although the statistical results and the economic implications supported a preference for the logarithmic model, throughout the analysis in Chapter 11 we reported full results from the linear model for comparison with the logarithmic model, since this aspect of the specification had relatively large effects on the results. Here, to simplify the discussion and focus on the main points we concentrate on the results from the preferred logarithmic model.

In the preferred, logarithmic model the average annual year-to-year growth in predicted *MFP* over the period 1949–2002 attributed to public-sector agricultural research and extension ranges, across the 48 states, from 1.38 percent per year to 2.42 percent per year, with a 48-state average of 1.87 percent per year. On average, own-state research accounts for 30.6 percent of this total growth (varying between 17.3 and 46.1 percent among states) and own-state extension accounts for 26.0 percent (varying between 14.2 and 35.6 percent). Spillins account for the remaining 43.3 percent of the growth (32.9 to 59.2 percent)—with 12.7 percent attributable to intramural USDA research, 16.5 percent attributable to research conducted by other states, and 14.1 percent attributable to extension conducted by other states. The predicted *MFP* growth contributed by spillins is very similar for every state, ranging from 0.79 to 0.82 percent per year across all the states, but this relatively fixed amount represents a much more variable share of the total state-specific growth. The variation in results among the states is systematic. States with smaller agricultural sectors and correspondingly smaller SAESs—especially if they are also states in which the agricultural sector is not too different from that of the nation as a whole—are likely to have comparatively large shares of their productivity growth attributable to spillins and comparatively small shares attributable to own-state research and extension.

We explored the implications of alternative specifications of the model for the growth accounting results and found that the functional form for the model (linear versus logarithmic), the structure of the lag distribution for extension (4-year geometric versus 50-year gamma), and the treatment of extension spillovers, jointly influenced the findings regarding the total predicted growth in *MFP* attributed to research and extension knowledge stocks, and the share of that total attributable to own-state research and extension.

Benefit-Cost Analysis

The implications of these and other aspects of the model for benefit-cost results are of particular interest. Table 12-1 summarizes some key features of the estimates of marginal benefit-cost ratios presented in Chapter 11, to illustrate the main findings and the potential role of modeling choices. In this table the results from alternative models are presented relative to our preferred, base model (shaded), in which SAES research and extension enter symmetrically, with a 50-year gamma lag distribution, and the variables are in logarithms unless otherwise specified. For each model we present the minimum, maximum, and average of the marginal benefit-cost ratios across the 48 states, as would result from a small increase in SAES research in 1950.[1]

The first block of results in Table 12-1 shows the effects of using an alternative (linear) functional form and the effects of first-differencing the variables in either the linear or logarithmic model. The second block of results shows the effects of alternative treatments for extension, to allow for a different lag model (a 4-year geometric lag for extension rather than a 50-year gamma lag) and a different spillover structure (no extension spillovers rather than the same spillovers as for SAES research). The third block of results shows the effect of alternative specifications of the research and extension lag distributions. The base model uses a 50-year gamma lag for both research and extension. The alternatives include a 35-year trapezoidal lag for research and extension, or a 4-year geometric lag for extension combined with either (a) a 50-year gamma lag for research or (b) a 35-year trapezoidal lag for research. The fourth block of results shows the effects of alternative spillover models for research and extension when the same 50-year gamma lag distribution is applied to both. The base model has spillovers

1 In many cases the same benefit-cost ratio would apply for extension because it enters symmetrically with SAES research, as in the base model, but this is not true in those cases where extension has a different lag distribution or different spillover specification from that used for SAES research.

Table 12-1 Marginal Benefit-Cost Ratios for SAES and USDA Intramural Research

Model	Own-State ("Private") Benefit-Cost Ratio for SAES Research			National ("Social") Benefit-Cost Ratio for SAES Research			National ("Social") Benefit-Cost Ratio for USDA IM Research
	Minimum	Maximum	Average	Minimum	Maximum	Average	Total
Functional form							
Logarithmic	2.4	57.8	21.0	9.9	69.2	32.1	17.5
Growth (first-difference logarithmic)	1.4	29.4	10.7	15.9	52.1	10.7	33.7
Linear	0.2	43.9	10.0	14.2	74.4	39.7	47.0
First-difference linear	0.2	51.3	11.2	16.7	84.5	46.3	55.4
Extension treatment (logarithmic model)							
50 gamma lags with spillovers	2.4	57.8	21.0	9.9	69.2	32.1	17.5
50 gamma lags without spillovers	2.3	55.9	20.3	14.1	73.6	37.7	27.3
4 geometric lags with spillovers	1.3	27.8	9.3	16.2	50.5	31.4	34.7
4 geometric lags without spillovers	1.3	28.5	9.5	23.9	64.5	42.7	52.0
Lag distribution for research (R) and extension (E) (logarithmic model)							
50-year gamma, R&E	2.4	57.8	21.0	9.9	69.2	32.1	17.5
35-year trapezoid, R&E	3.4	53.5	19.8	18.0	75.4	41.2	33.6
50-year gamma, R; 4-year geometric, E	1.3	27.8	9.3	16.2	50.5	31.4	34.7
35-year trapezoid, R; 4-year geometric, E	2.2	34.0	11.8	20.2	61.0	38.2	41.3
Spillovers (logarithmic model)							
Based on output mix	2.4	57.8	21.0	9.9	69.2	32.1	17.5
Based on USDA regions	2.3	48.5	17.6	6.6	62.4	24.8	60.5
No spillovers	4.5	90.0	33.7	4.5	90.0	33.7	n/a
Research lag length (logarithmic model)							
50-year gamma, R&E	2.4	57.8	21.0	9.9	69.2	32.1	17.5
35-year gamma, R&E	2.4	56.7	20.4	11.7	71.0	20.4	21.9
20-year gamma, R&E	2.5	39.5	14.8	17.2	63.0	36.3	33.7
50-year gamma, R; 4-year geometric, E	1.3	27.8	9.3	16.2	50.5	31.4	34.7
35-year gamma, R; 4-year geometric, E	1.1	27.0	8.8	15.3	48.9	30.1	33.4
20-year gamma, R; 4-year geometric, E	1.7	29.4	10.4	17.6	55.0	33.7	36.6

Sources: Developed by the authors.

based on the output mix and the alternatives have either (a) no spillovers or (b) spillovers based on geographic proximity, occurring only within USDA regions. Finally, the fifth block of results shows the effects of alternative settings of the total length of the gamma lag distribution for research (50, 35, or 20 years) when either the same lag distribution applies to extension, or a 4-year geometric lag applies to extension.

Across all the models summarized in Table 12-1, some consistent patterns emerge in the estimates. First, in every case the national (social) benefit-cost ratios for SAES research are well greater than 1.0 in every state, and the average values across the 48 states are quite large. Across the models, the 48-state average marginal social benefit-cost ratio was between 10:1 and 50:1. If we leave out the first-differenced linear model and the growth model, which yielded the extreme values and were reported mainly for illustrative purposes, the range is smaller: from 20:1 to 43:1. Thus the maximum estimate across models is a little more than twice the minimum and the estimate from the preferred model is in the middle of that range at 32:1.

Second, these social benefit-cost ratios for SAES research are large relative to the own-state (private) benefit-cost ratios. In all but two of the models (the linear model in levels or in first-difference form), the marginal own-state benefit cost ratio was greater than 1.0 in every state, and the average value across the 48 states was much greater than 1.0 in every model. Across the models, the 48-state average of the marginal own-state benefit-cost ratios ranged from 9:1 to 34:1. If we leave out the (clearly misspecified) model that precludes spillovers, which was reported mainly for illustrative purposes, the range is smaller: from 9:1 to 21:1. Again, the maximum estimate across models is a little more than twice the minimum estimate, but in this case the estimate from the preferred model is also the maximum across models, 21:1.

Third, the different models imply a range of estimates for the marginal social benefit-cost ratio for USDA intramural research, from 18:1 to 61:1. The lowest estimate is from our preferred logarithmic model. Most of the other models yielded substantially larger estimates of the marginal social benefit-cost ratio for USDA intramural research.

The implication of these results is that specification choices do influence the results, but not in ways that change the primary messages: (a) the social benefits from agricultural research and extension are generally very large relative to the costs, though the benefit-cost ratios vary among states systematically depending on the characteristics of the states, and (b) the spillover benefits are an important component of the total benefits, such that the national benefits are much greater than the own-state benefits from SAES research and extension.

If accurate, the high own-state and even higher national marginal benefit-cost ratios represent evidence of past underinvestment in public agricultural research by both the state and federal governments. In the rest of this chapter we further examine these findings, their credibility, and the appropriate interpretation. We conduct a statistical meta-analysis to explore the roles of characteristics of both the models applied, and the state-specific patterns of production and research spending being modeled, as they influence the estimates of national and state benefits and costs from spending by the state and national governments on agricultural R&D. After presenting the results from that formal statistical analysis we consider some supplementary evidence as a type of check on the credibility of the benefit-cost results derived from the econometric analysis.

12.2 Determinants of Benefits

In Chapter 11, we presented some analytical results showing the roles of particular factors in influencing benefit-cost ratios, and we conducted some sensitivity analysis by estimating alternative model specifications and examining their implications. In this section we explore the roles of factors that are determined by the analyst and factors that are aspects of the data being modeled as determinants of the findings.

Analytical Results

We presented equations in Chapter 11 representing the present value of benefits from a $1,000 increase in research spending in 1950. Given that the cost is given and fixed, these equations also represent benefit-cost ratios (scaled by a constant). The relevant equations are restated in Table 12-2. The first three entries (rows 1–3) are equations for the linear model that represent marginal private (own-state) benefit-cost ratios for SAES research, marginal social (national) benefit-cost ratios for SAES research, and marginal social (national) benefit-cost ratios for USDA intramural research. The next three entries (rows 4–6) are counterpart equations for the logarithmic model. The variables and parameters in these equations are all defined in Chapter 11. These equations are useful for considering the effects of differences among states, in influencing the pattern of benefit-cost ratios among them, for a given set of model parameters. The meta-analysis quantifies the effects of these same characteristics of states jointly with the characteristics of model specification that can have direct effects as well as indirect effects through their influence on the parameter estimates.

Data for the Meta-Analysis

The data for the meta-analysis include state-specific estimates of the benefit-cost ratio (the left-hand side variable), and measures of the factors (characteristics of the model or the state) that may have influenced the estimates. The meta-analysis is based on a total of 15 different specifications of the model of *MFP* for a given functional form. The extensive nature of our data set allowed us to estimate numerous models with a variety of specifications. We have a clear preference for the logarithmic model discussed at length in Chapters 10 and 11, based on an

Table 12-2 Analytic Results for Determinants of Benefit-Cost Ratios

Equations for the Present Value of Benefits for a Marginal Increase in Research Spending in 1950

Panel a. Linear model

(1) "Private" benefits from SAES research and extension

$$\hat{\beta}_K \sum_{t=1950}^{2002} b_{t-1950} \left(\frac{V_{i,t}}{M\bar{F}P_{i,t}} \right) (1+r)^{2002-t}$$

(2) "Social" benefits from SAES research and extension

$$\hat{\beta}_K \sum_{t=1950}^{2002} b_{t-1950} \left(\frac{V_{i,t}}{M\bar{F}P_{i,t}} \right) (1+r)^{2002-t} + \hat{\beta}_S \sum_{j\neq 1}^{48} \omega_{ij} \sum_{t=1950}^{2002} b_{t-1950} \left(\frac{V_{j,t}}{M\bar{F}P_{j,t}} \right) (1+r)^{2002-t}$$

(3) "Social" benefits from USDA intramural research

$$\hat{\beta}_S \sum_{j=1}^{48} \omega_{Fj} \sum_{t=1950}^{2002} b_{t-1950} \left(\frac{V_{j,t}}{M\bar{F}P_{j,t}} \right) (1+r)^{2002-t}$$

Panel b. Logarithmic model

(4) "Private" benefits from SAES research and extension

$$\hat{\eta}_K \sum_{t=1950}^{2002} b_{t-1950} \left(\frac{V_{i,t}}{SK_{i,t}} \right) (1+r)^{2002-t}$$

(5) "Social" benefits from SAES research and extension

$$\hat{\eta}_K \sum_{t=1950}^{2002} b_{t-1950} \left(\frac{V_{i,t}}{SK_{i,t}} \right) (1+r)^{2002-t} + \hat{\eta}_S \sum_{j\neq 1}^{48} \omega_{ij} \sum_{t=1950}^{2002} b_{t-1950} \left(\frac{V_{j,t}}{SS_{j,t}} \right) (1+r)^{2002-t}$$

(6) "Social" benefits from USDA intramural research

$$\hat{\eta}_S \sum_{j=1}^{48} \omega_{Fj} \sum_{t=1950}^{2002} b_{t-1950} \left(\frac{V_{j,t}}{SS_{j,t}} \right) (1+r)^{2002-t}$$

Sources: Developed by the authors.

examination of the results from all of the models estimated. Here, we present an analysis of results from various specifications of the logarithmic model.

Alternative specifications allowed for differences in the overall lag length, the basis for calculating knowledge spillovers, and the treatment of extension spending. Each alternative specification of the productivity model involved 64 estimations (one for each gamma lag distribution), making for a total of 960 combinations. For each of these estimated models we conducted the full benefit-cost analysis. So, for each regression model we have estimates of 48 state-specific marginal own-state ("private") benefit-cost ratios for SAES research, 48 state-specific marginal national ("social") benefit-cost ratios for SAES research, and 48 state-specific marginal benefit-cost ratios for USDA intramural research.[2] Hence, we were able to estimate three separate corresponding meta-analysis models: one for each type of benefit-cost ratio. In defining the data for the meta-analysis, we ruled out benefit-cost ratios from 23 of the lag distribution models, because they peaked very early (before 5 years) or very late (after 45 years), leaving a total of 41 feasible lag distribution models. Combining 41 lag distributions with 15 model specifications implies a maximum total of 615 feasible combinations.

The variables included as regressors are defined in Table 12-3. They include variables to represent both characteristics of the models from which the estimates of benefit-cost ratios were derived, and characteristics of the states to which they apply. Given that we are focusing on the logarithmic model, we have set aside the role of functional form. The remaining relevant characteristics of the models are represented by dummy variables to measure the effects relative to the default specification in terms of the specification of the extension variable, and the representation of spillover effects. Based on the analytical results summarized in Table 12-2, we identified several relevant characteristics of the states, including the inverse of the agricultural research and extension intensity, the numerator of that ratio (the value of production) and the denominator (the expenditure on research and extension), the growth rate of spending on research and extension, and the average *MFP* (an indication of average productivity growth since the indexes begin at 100 in 1949). These state characteristics could all have non-linear effects on the benefit-cost ratios, so we included quadratic terms as well. In addition, for the social benefit-cost ratios, spillovers are important and we included a measure of the state's spillover propensity, the average of its spillover coefficients with other states.

Regression Results

Three sets of regression results were generated, each using a different subset of the data. The first set of regression results were obtained after restricting the sample to the benefit-cost ratios from only the best-fitting lag distribution model (out of the 41 possible lag distribution models) for each specification of the logarithmic model. This approach is designed to account for variation in results among states and across models, given that the lag-distribution model was selected according to goodness of fit, in keeping with the approach that we used in Chapter 10. In this case we had a total of 672 observations of the marginal own-state "private" benefit-cost ratio for SAES research, one for each of 48 states from each

2 For some of these models research and extension enter symmetrically and the state-specific private or social marginal benefit-cost ratio for extension is the same as that for research; but this is not the case for other models where extension and research enter the model separately. To allow comparisons across as many models as possible we modeled only the determinants of the benefit-cost ratios for SAES research.

Table 12-3 Variables Included as Regressors in the Meta-Analysis

	Variable Name	Variable Type	Default Case	Alternative Case
Model characteristics				
Extension lag	EX-LAG-GEOM	0–1 dummy	50-year gamma	4-year geometric
Extension spillovers	NO-EXT-SPILL	0–1 dummy	Same as research	None
Extension entering	SEP-EXT-VAR	0–1 dummy	With research	Separately
Research spillovers	R-SPILL-USDA	0–1 dummy	Output omegas	USDA region omegas
	R-SPILL-ZERO	0–1 dummy		No spillovers ($\omega_{ij} = 0$)
	R-SPILL-ALL	0–1 dummy		All spillovers ($\omega_{ij} = 1$)
Maximum lag length	R-LAG-35	0–1 dummy	50 years	35 years
	R-LAG-20	0–1 dummy		20 years
Peak lag year	PEAKLAG	Integer 0–50 years		
State characteristics[a]				
Inverse ARI (*V/R*)	INV-ARI	Continuous		
Inverse ARI squared[b]	INV-ARI-SQ	Continuous		
Output value (*V*)	VALUE	Continuous		
Output value squared	VALUE-SQ	Continuous		
Spending (*R*)	R-SPEND	Continuous		
Spending squared	R-SPEND-SQ	Continuous		
Spending growth (*G*)	RS-GROWTH	Continuous		
Spending growth squared	RS-GROWTH -SQ	Continuous		
MFP	MFP	Continuous		
MFP squared	MFP-SQ	Continuous		
Spillover potential	AV-OMEGA	Continuous		

Sources: Developed by the authors.

[a] The average value of the state characteristics from 1949–2002 was included as a regressor.

[b] ARI includes research and extension spending.

of 14 alternative model specifications, to be used as data for a regression.[3] The 672 corresponding observations of the marginal state-specific national benefit-cost ratio for SAES research were used for a second regression. And the further 672 corresponding observations of the marginal state-specific benefit-cost ratio for USDA intramural research (i.e., the state-specific benefits from additional USDA research spending which has to be summed across states to compute the national "social" benefits) were used for a third regression. Appendix Table 12-1 summarizes the results from these three regressions.

Alternative results were obtained by applying different restrictions to the total sample of benefit-cost ratios. A second set of regressions, reported in Table 12-4, used the benefit-cost ratios from the top 10 (out of the 41 possible) lag distribution models. In this case we had a total of 6,528 observations to be used as data in the regression for each of the three types of benefit-cost ratio. A third set of regressions, reported in Appendix Table 12-2, used the results from all

3 For one of the 15 model specifications (the model with only 20 research lags and 4 extension lags included), the top-ranked lag distribution model was one of the 23 that were judged infeasible, hence the sample size is 14 × 48 = 672 instead of 15 × 48 = 720.

Table 12-4 Meta-Analysis Results—Top Ten Lag Distributions, Logarithmic Model

Explanatory Variable		Dependent Variable, State-Specific Benefit-Cost Ratio for		
		SAES "Private"	SAES "Social"	USDA IM
		coefficient estimate (p-value in italics)		
Extension lag	EXT-LAG-GEOM	**-9.35**	**-3.26**	**0.20**
		0.00	*0.00*	*0.00*
Extension spillovers	NO-EXT-SPILL	-0.31	**-10.24**	**-0.32**
		0.30	*0.00*	*0.00*
Extension entering separately	SEP-EXT-VAR	**31.53**	**23.19**	**-0.26**
		0.00	*0.00*	*0.00*
Research spillovers	R-SPILL-USDA	-0.62	**7.95**	**0.56**
		0.20	*0.00*	*0.00*
	R-SPILL-ZERO	**13.62**	**18.41**	**-0.84**
		0.00	*0.00*	*0.00*
	R-SPILL-ALL	**2.66**	**27.94**	**-0.34**
		0.00	*0.00*	*0.00*
Peak lag year	PEAKLAG	-0.02	**-0.38**	**-0.01**
		0.35	*0.00*	*0.00*
Maximum lag length	R-LAG-35	-1.17	**8.39**	**0.32**
		0.00	*0.00*	*0.00*
	R-LAG-20	0.26	**3.76**	**0.12**
		0.44	*0.00*	*0.00*
Inverse ARI	INV-ARI	**30.03**	**32.69**	-0.14
		0.00	*0.00*	*0.08*
Inverse ARI squared	INV-ARI-SQ	1.01	0.58	**0.13**
		0.26	*0.52*	*0.00*
Output value	VALUE	0.22	0.31	**0.16**
		0.50	*0.36*	*0.00*
Output value squared	VALUE-SQ	-0.02	-0.02	0.00
		0.28	*0.29*	*0.13*
R&E spending	R-SPEND	35.34	**70.30**	**2.23**
		0.07	*0.00*	*0.01*
R&E spending squared	R-SPEND-SQ	-69.11	**-309.78**	**-15.68**
		0.39	*0.00*	*0.00*
R&E spending growth	RS-GROWTH	-0.09	-0.99	0.02
		0.91	*0.22*	*0.54*
R&E spending growth squared	RS-GROWTH-SQ	**0.59**	**0.79**	-0.01
		0.00	*0.00*	*0.17*
MFP	MFP	0.00	-0.06	**0.00**
		0.98	*0.13*	*0.00*
MFP squared	MFP-SQ	0.00	**0.00**	**0.00**
		0.51	*0.02*	*0.01*
Spillover potential	AV-OMEGA		**53.92**	**-0.38**
			0.00	*0.00*
Intercept		-6.53	3.27	**1.07**
		0.07	0.38	0.00
N		**6,528**	**6,528**	**6,528**
R^2		**0.80**	**0.80**	**0.80**

Sources: Developed by the authors.

of the feasible lag distribution models. In this case we had a total of 29,520 observations to be used as data for a regression for each of the three types of benefit-cost ratio.[4]

Table 12-4 and Appendix Tables 12-1 and 12-2 are structured identically. The first column represents the results from the regression model of own-state ("private") benefit-cost ratios for SAES research; the second is for the model of national ("social") benefit-cost ratios for SAES research; and the third is for the state-specific benefit-cost ratios for USDA intramural research. For each right-hand side variable, the regression coefficient is listed, and the number below it in italics is the corresponding p-value for the test of the null hypothesis that the coefficient is zero. Entries are in bold if the p-value is less than 0.05.

Comparing results among the three tables, we can see the effects of expanding the sample size from 672 to 6,528 or 29,520 by including alternative lag distributions, not just the best-fitting one. The explanatory power of the models remains high, with R^2 values still close to 80 percent for each model. Comparing the estimates for a given model across Table 12-4 and Appendix Tables 12-1 and 12-2, most of the parameter estimates are similar but the precision of the estimates is improved with the increases in sample size such that many more of them are statistically significant when all of the estimates are used in the analysis. Most of the explanatory variables representing characteristics of the states did not contribute significantly to any of the regression models in Appendix Table 12-1, but several of these explanatory variables contributed significantly to at least one of the regression models in Table 12-4.[5] In contrast, all of the variables representing model specification choices contributed significantly to at least one of the models for all of the sub-samples.

We use the results from Table 12-4 as representative of the results presented in the other two tables. Taking this approach, the results in Table 12-4 show a range of effects relative to the baseline model specification. Some aspect of how extension spending was incorporated in the model affected each of the benefit-cost ratios. For example, the use of the 4-year geometric lag for extension resulted in a statistically significant and substantial decrease in the estimates of both the own-state and national benefits from SAES research (by \$9.35 and \$3.26 per dollar) but a corresponding significant and substantial increase in the estimated benefits from USDA intramural research (by \$0.20 per dollar, equivalent to

---

4 If all of the top 10 lag distributions were feasible in all 15 models, we would have a total of $15 \times 48 \times 10 = 7{,}200$ observations of benefit-cost ratios for the regression models in Table 12-4, rather than the 6,528 that remain after dropping infeasible models. Appendix Table 12-2 uses results from the 41 feasible lag distributions for all 15 models and for 48 states: $15 \times 48 \times 41 = 29{,}520$.

5 Several of these variables were not expected to contribute to the regression for benefit-cost ratios from the logarithmic model of *MFP* but were expected to contribute to the regression for benefit-cost ratios from the linear model of *MFP*, and were included in these regressions to preserve an option of comparing results for the linear and logarithmic specifications.

$9.60 across the 48 states). Restricting benefits from extension spending to the state in which the investment was made (i.e., disallowing extension spillovers) had a significant and substantial negative effect on the national benefit-cost ratio for SAES spending ($10.24 per dollar) and on the benefits from USDA intramural funding ($0.32 per dollar per state, or $15.36 over all 48 states). In a few models in which a stock for extension knowledge was created separately and entered the model separately, the estimated own-state and national benefits from SAES spending increased dramatically (by $31.53 and $23.19, respectively) and the benefits from USDA intramural spending decreased.

Our baseline for incorporating research spillovers in the models of productivity was to use the measures of similarity in output mixes to create spillover knowledge stocks. Using geographic proximity instead increased estimated social benefits from SAES research and from USDA intramural research significantly (by $7.95 per dollar and $0.56 per dollar per state). Two extreme treatments were also tried: disallowing spillovers and imposing no restrictions on spillovers. Both of the extreme specifications affected the benefit-cost ratio in the same direction in each of the regressions (and all of the effects were statistically significant). While there is no generally accepted method for dealing with technological spillovers in this type of analysis, these meta-results show how the specification of spillovers can substantially influence findings.

The lag structure used to convert past research expenditures into a knowledge stock was investigated fairly extensively in the analysis described in Chapters 9 and 10. The meta-regression results summarize the influence of lag shape on the estimated benefit-cost ratios. While the year in which the lag distribution peaked had an insignificant effect on the own-state benefits from SAES research, it had a negative and statistically significant effect on the social benefits from SAES research and from USDA intramural research. These effects are smaller than one might expect, but could be driven by our exclusion of lag structures we deemed infeasible. Shortening the lag to include only 35 or 20 years of past research spending had similar effects: an insignificant effect on own-state benefits from SAES research and positive, statistically significant, and substantial effects on the other two benefit-cost ratios.

The estimated effects of several characteristics of states were in line with the analytical results discussed in Chapter 11 and shown in Table 12-2. Specifically, states with relatively small agricultural research intensities (i.e., relatively large inverse-ARIs) tended to have greater estimated benefits from SAES research. While the inverse-ARI was statistically insignificant as a determinant of benefits from USDA intramural research, its square had a positive and statistically significant effect. The components of ARI (output value and research and extension spending), and their squares, had mixed effects on estimated benefits that are difficult to disentangle because of the squared terms. Notably, the squares of the average rates of growth in research and extension spending and in *MFP* had positive and statistically significant effects on some of the benefit-cost ratios. Finally, and in line with analytical solutions in Table 12-2, states that were more similar, on average, to other states tended to generate higher social payoffs from their SAES research.

12.3 Plausibility of Estimates—Various Perspectives

Our measures of benefit-cost ratios are large, and it is natural to be skeptical. One way to address skepticism about high estimated benefit-cost ratios is to set aside the complex models and simply compute the value of the growth in agricultural productivity (which is simple to calculate and not controversial) and compare it with the cost of agricultural research. In this section we present simple measures of this nature. These simple measures abstract from the issues of spatial spillovers and R&D lags that were central to our econometric analysis in Chapters 10 and 11. We also present some information about those relationships that, like our simple benefit-cost comparisons, avoids the joint hypothesis of model specification. Before turning to these simple measures and spillover relationships, we compare our results with others reported in the professional literature, a different kind of check on plausibility.

Comparison with Results in the Literature

We prefer to use benefit-cost ratios to measure returns to research but for purposes of comparison we also computed internal rates of return. Alston et al. (2000a) conducted a meta-analysis of 292 studies that reported estimates of returns to agricultural R&D. The authors (Table 12, p. 55) reported an overall mean internal rate of return for their sample of 1,852 estimates of 81.3 percent per annum, with a mode of 40 percent, and a median of 44.3 percent. After dropping some outliers and incomplete observations, they conducted regression analysis using a sample of 1,128 estimates with a mean of 64.6 percent per annum, a mode of 28 percent, and a median of 42.0 percent. The main mass of the distribution of internal rates of return reported in the literature is between 20 and 80 percent per annum.[6] Other reviews of the literature may not have covered the same studies or in the same ways, but nevertheless reached similar general conclusions—for instance, Evenson (2002), and Fuglie and Heisey (2007). Relative to the mainstream of the literature, our preferred logarithmic model yielded estimates at the lower end of the range for both national and own-state annual rates of return to state and federal agricultural R&D—around 20 percent. Specifically, our es-

6 When characterizing the evidence from the literature, economists often use a range like this or perhaps even narrower, such as 20–60 percent per annum (e.g., Fuglie and Heisey 2007), but as discussed by Alston et al. (2000a and 2000b) such selective reporting of the literature may be misleading, giving a false impression of both the average and the size of the range around it.

timates of own-state "private" rates of return ranged from 7.4 to 27.6 percent, with an average of 18.9 percent per annum across the states and our estimates of national "social" rates of return ranged from 15.3 to 29.1 percent, with an average of 22.7 percent per annum across the states.[7] The estimated national internal rate of return to USDA intramural research was 18.7 percent per annum.

The Value of Productivity Growth

The value of U.S. agricultural output increased from $29.9 billion in 1949 to $173.3 billion in 2002 in nominal terms.[8] After dividing by the GDP deflator to account for inflation, the value of agricultural output actually decreased from $183.0 billion in 1949 to $166.3 billion in 2002, although it increased to $191.5 billion in 2006 (all in real 2000 dollar values). While the real value of output stagnated, the output quantity more than doubled as a result of growth in agricultural productivity. Long-term and sustained growth in productivity is attributed primarily to various forms of technological change. Technological change results from innovations adopted by farmers, but the potential sources of these innovations are many. Some innovations are the result of tinkering by individual farmers and trial and error on farms. More often and especially more recently, a greater share of agricultural innovation can be traced to more-organized and collectivized scientific and industrial research and development efforts conducted and funded by both government and the private sector. Here we estimate the value of this productivity growth, make alternative assumptions about the share attributable to public U.S. agricultural research, and compare that estimate of the benefits with various measures of the cost of the relevant research investments.

As documented in Chapter 5, in annual rate-of-change terms, aggregate U.S. agricultural output increased by 1.68 percent per annum over the period 1949–2002; aggregate inputs used in agriculture declined by 0.11 percent per annum, and so measured MFP grew by 1.78 percent per annum. Compounding the growth rate of 1.78 percent per year over 53 years, the index of productivity grew from 100 in 1949 to about 257 in 2002. That is, if inputs had been held constant at the 1949 quantities, output would have increased by a factor of 2.57. In other words, of the actual output in 2002, only 39 percent (i.e., 100/257 = 0.39) could be accounted for by conventional inputs using 1949 technology, holding productivity constant. The remaining 61 percent (i.e., 157/257 = 0.61)

7 The linear model yielded generally larger estimates, with a bigger range across the states: across the 48 states the average own-state "private" rate of return to SAES research and extension was 23.4 percent per annum and the average "social" rate of return was 59.4 percent per annum, while the social rate of return to USDA intramural research was 65.9 percent per annum, closer to the mainstream. As noted, however, we prefer the logarithmic model results; partly because the linear model implies some implausible patterns in rates of return or benefit-cost ratios among states.

8 Here we are using the 74 item output measure from the InSTePP production accounts that was used for the econometric estimations (see Appendix II).

Figure 12-1 U.S. Agricultural Output Value Attributable to Productivity Growth, 1949–2002

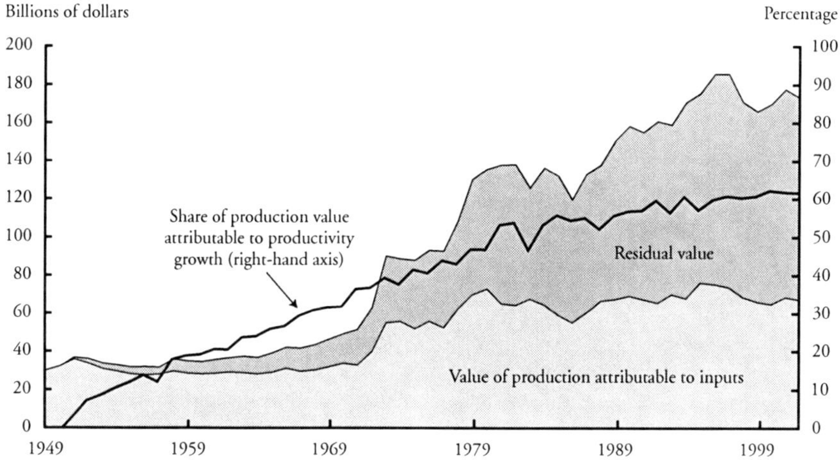

Sources: Developed by the authors.

Notes: Residual value is the value of production attributable to productivity growth.

is accounted for by the 157 percent increase in productivity. Hence, of the total production, worth \$173.3 billion in 2002, only 39 percent or \$67.3 billion could be accounted for by conventional inputs using 1949 technology, and the remaining \$106.0 billion is attributable to the factors that gave rise to improved productivity. Among these factors is new technology, developed and adopted as a result of agricultural research and extension.

Figure 12-1 represents these ideas and measures graphically over the period 1949–2002. If U.S. agricultural productivity had stayed constant at the 1949 value of 100, the actual pattern of total output would have followed the pattern of total input (i.e., in every year, the index of output would be equal to the index of input). Figure 12-1 shows the actual value of output (AV_t) divided into two parts: (a) the lower part, representing what the value of output would have been, given the actual input quantities, if productivity had not grown since 1949—i.e., hypothetical value, $HV_t = AV_t * (100 / MFP_t)$; and (b) the upper part, the value of additional output attributable to productivity growth—i.e., residual value, $RV_t = AV_t - HV_t = AV_t * (MFP_t - 100) / MFP_t$. As productivity increases over time, the share of the value of production that is attributable to productivity growth increases.

Figure 12-2 shows graphs corresponding to Figure 12-1 for a selection of individual U.S. states, with different patterns of growth of production, productivity, and input use, including our three reference states (California, Minnesota, and Wyoming) as well as three others (Mississippi, New York, and North Da-

Figure 12-2 Output Value Attributable to Productivity Growth, Selected States, 1949–2002

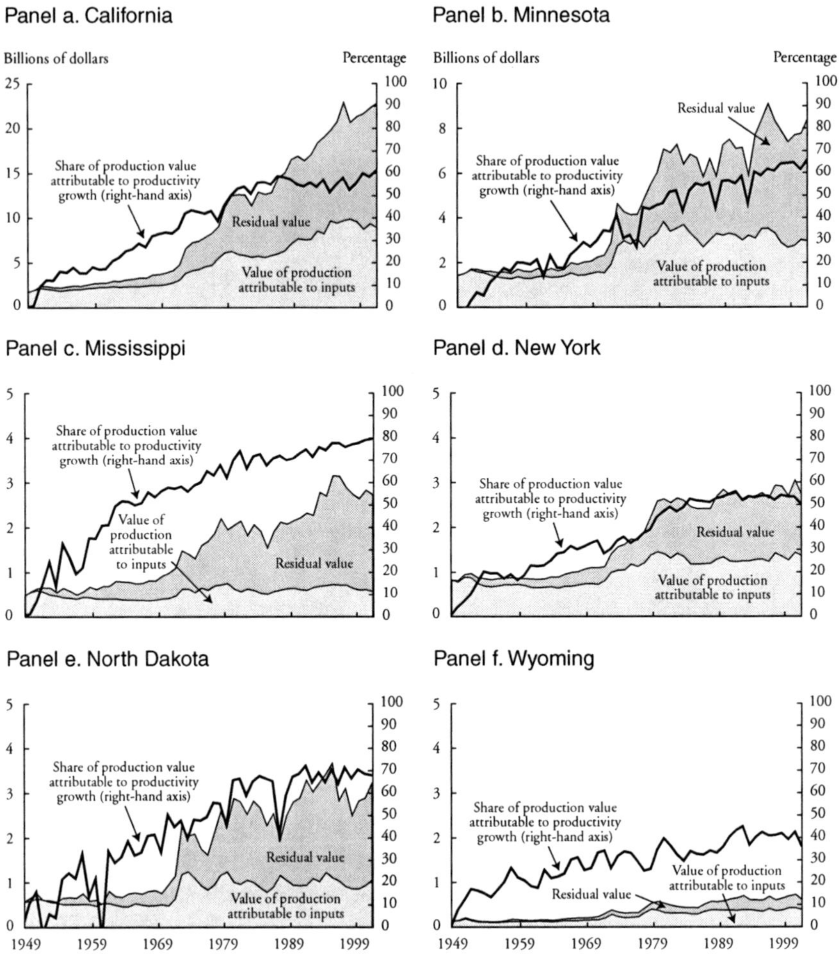

Sources: Developed by the authors.

Notes: Residual value is the value of production attributable to productivity growth.

kota). These graphs illustrate the roles of the size of the agricultural sector and the rate of productivity growth in determining the benefits from productivity growth, and how they differ among states. Such differences will account for a significant share of the measures of benefits from productivity growth, and thus the benefits from productivity growth attributable to research and extension, regardless of what procedure is used to measure those benefits.

Appendix Table 12-3 presents state-by-state estimates of the output value in 2002 attributable to productivity growth since 1949, both in dollars and as a

Table 12-5 Agricultural Output Value Attributable to Productivity Growth

State	Total Value of Agricultural Output in 2002	2002 Output Value Attributable to Productivity Growth Since 1949		Agricultural Research and Extension Intensity	
		Value	Share of Total	1975	2002
	billions of dollars		*percentage*	*percentage*	
United States	173.3	106.0	61.2	1.3	3.2
48 state					
Average	3.6	2.2	57.7	1.9	4.6
Minimum	0.1	0.0	35.9	0.3	1.0
Maximum	22.8	13.9	79.1	11.7	23.8
Selected states					
California	22.8	13.9	60.8	0.9	1.7
Minnesota	8.4	5.5	65.1	0.6	1.8
Wyoming	0.6	0.2	35.9	1.5	2.6
Regions					
Pacific	29.8	18.5	61.9	1.01	1.94
Mountain	13.6	7.8	56.9	1.08	2.83
Northern Plains	19.1	12.1	63.2	0.60	1.59
Southern Plains	22.7	14.4	63.2	1.14	2.78
Central	50.0	28.7	57.4	0.64	2.24
Southeast	27.2	18.2	67.0	1.71	3.88
Northeast	10.8	6.3	58.0	2.17	5.15

Sources: Developed by the authors.

Notes: Agricultural research and extension intensities are the dollars of spending per $100 of agricultural output value, and thus are percentages.

percentage share of the total output value. Table 12-5 summarizes the information across states and regions. Among the 48 states, these shares (of the total value of agricultural output in 2002 attributable to growth in productivity since 1949) averaged 58 percent but ranged from as low as 36 percent (Wyoming) to as high as 79 percent (Mississippi). Table 12-5 also includes summaries of our estimates of the state-by-state agricultural research intensity ratio (state-specific spending on research and extension per $100 of the value of output) in 1975 and 2002 (complete details of state-specific measures are included in Appendix Table 12-3).[9] In 2002, the ARI averaged $4.60 per $100 of agricultural production across the states. The 2002 ARIs ranged from $0.96 (South Dakota) to $23.83 (West Virginia), but in states with substantial agricultural sectors, spending was less than $10 per $100 of agricultural value in 2002.

9 These ARIs differ from those included in Chapter 6 because they include both state research and extension spending in the numerator and because the value of production in the denominator is from the InSTePP series of value of agricultural output rather than the constructed value-of-production series used in Chapter 6. See Appendix II for details about the two output series.

Simple Approximate Benefit-Cost Ratios

To summarize the stream of values attributable to output growth, the yearly residual values, RV_t (defined above) were expressed in constant dollar terms by dividing the nominal values by the GDP deflator based at 1.00 in the year 2000. The deflated values were compounded forward at a real interest rate of 3 percent per annum and evaluated in the year 2002. The stream of values of agricultural output attributable to productivity improvements is equivalent to a one-time payment of more than $7.4 trillion in 2002, an enormous benefit from improved agricultural productivity in the United States during the post-WWII period.

These benefits from productivity growth are attributable to various things, such as public and private investments in agricultural research and extension in the United States and elsewhere, improvements in infrastructure, investments in education and improvements in human capital (and other changes in input and output quality that may have not been fully taken into account in the indexing procedures used to measure productivity), and spillovers of knowledge and technology from other (nonagricultural) industries. Here, we propose a crude partitioning, based on various pieces of information. First, in constructing the data used to measure productivity, we made adjustments for measurable changes in input quality, so it may be reasonable to presume that public and private research are responsible for most if not all of the measured productivity growth. Second, since private and public agricultural research expenditures nowadays are of broadly comparable magnitudes perhaps a reasonable approximation is to assign equal shares, such that half the measured growth is attributable to public investments in agricultural research and extension and the other half is attributable to private investments.[10]

Table 12-6 includes various alternative approximations of benefit-cost ratios using the method described above. In each case, the benefits refer to the value of productivity gains since 1949 compounded forward over 54 years to 2002. The costs refer to expenditures on agricultural research and extension over various time periods, all compounded forward to 2002. Both costs and benefits were converted into real terms using the GDP deflator. The different sets of estimates reflect different assumptions about (a) the time period over which research expenditures are to be counted, (b) the share of the total benefits attributed to the defined stream of public agricultural research and extension spending (50 percent versus 100 percent), and (c) the real discount rate to be used to accumulate

---

10 Griliches (1964, p. 968) and Evenson (1967, p. 1424) attributed agricultural research benefits similarly for the same reasons. However, this is perhaps too conservative since private-sector agricultural research spending in the United States has only recently caught up with public-sector spending, and would be much less than equal over the entire 20th Century, which may be the relevant time period. In addition, some of the consequences of private research have been accounted for already through the input-quality adjustments that were made, especially in relation to capital inputs in which many private research-induced technological changes are embodied.

Table 12-6 Simple Approximate Average Benefit-Cost Ratios, Benefits over 54 Years, 1949–2002

	Research Costs Accumulated over the Years						
	1949–2002	1910–2002	1939–1992	1929–1982	1939–1992	1929–1982	1929–1982
	Benefits 100% Attributable to Public R&D				Benefits 50% Attributable to Public R&D		
	$r = 0.03$				$r = 0.03$		$r = 0.05$
State or Region	(1)	(2)	(3)	(4)	(5)	(6)	(7)
United States	22.8	16.5	23.8	25.6	11.9	12.8	8.7
48 state							
Average	26.5	19.1	28.1	30.4	14.0	15.2	10.5
Minimum	4.4	3.2	5.1	5.4	2.5	2.7	1.9
Maximum	74.7	51.7	76.0	77.7	38.0	38.8	27.6
Selected states							
California	36.9	30.2	41.3	48.5	20.7	24.2	17.0
Minnesota	44.2	31.8	49.1	55.6	24.6	27.8	19.0
Wyoming	17.5	11.6	17.1	17.0	8.5	8.5	6.1
Regions							
Pacific	32.1	25.8	35.6	41.1	17.8	20.5	14.3
Mountain	25.1	18.5	27.5	30.5	13.8	15.3	10.5
Northern Plains	54.1	39.5	58.1	63.6	29.0	31.8	22.2
Southern Plains	23.7	17.6	24.9	27.3	12.4	13.6	8.4
Central	35.3	25.2	37.7	40.6	18.8	20.3	13.7
Southeast	23.6	18.1	25.3	28.6	12.6	14.3	10.1
Northeast	17.6	11.8	17.9	18.1	8.9	9.0	6.3

Sources: Developed by the authors.

costs and benefits forward to 2002 (3 percent versus 5 percent). State-specific details are provided in Appendix Table 12-4.

The first column (column 1) refers to the estimates given by the ratio of benefits over the period 1949–2002 relative to the total expenditure over the same period 1949–2002, presuming 100 percent of the benefits are attributable to the public R&D investments, and using a discount rate of 3 percent. The resulting estimates are average benefit-cost ratios, since they compare total benefits with total costs, rather than marginal benefit-cost ratios, as were reported in Chapter 11 and in previous sections of the present chapter. These average benefit-cost ratios are generally quite large, averaging 26.5 across the 48 states, but with a wide range—from 4.4 (Nevada) to 74.7 (South Dakota). This range reflects the fact that across the states, the research intensity ratios tend to be inversely correlated with the size of the agricultural sector. As well as the average of the state-specific estimates, we report estimates at the regional and national levels. The national aggregate ratio compares total benefits from productivity growth with total national expenditures on agricultural research and extension, including USDA intramural research. This estimate of the approximate average benefit-cost ratio from public agricultural research and extension is 22.8.

The estimates in column 1 are biased estimates of the true benefit-cost ratios, for several reasons. First, R&D lags mean that we have left out some of the relevant costs (research expenditures prior to 1949 will have contributed to productivity growth between 1949 and 2002) and some of the relevant benefits (research expenditures between 1949 and 2002 will generate benefits for many years after 2002). Depending on the pattern of benefits and costs over time and the effects of discounting, these two sources of bias could be offsetting. However, given the generally rising pattern of research expenditures and the annual flows of benefits from productivity gains, we would expect the effect of the understatement of benefits to outweigh the effect of the understatement of costs, biasing the benefit-cost ratios down on balance.

Second, as mentioned, up to half of the total benefits may be attributable to private research. Third, spillover effects mean that some (perhaps half, on average, if our econometric estimates are to be believed) of a state's productivity growth will be attributable to expenditures by other states and the federal government; conversely, some of the national benefits from a state's research expenditures will accrue as productivity gains in other states (again, perhaps half, on average, if our econometric estimates are to be believed).[11] In the estimates at the regional level reported in Table 12-6, the distortions associated with state-to-state spillovers will be much smaller, and in the estimates at the national level they will be absent (since they are based on regional or national *MFP* indexes, and, in the case of regional benefit-cost ratios, incorporate intra-regional spillover effects).

The estimates in other columns of Table 12-6 represent attempts to correct for some of these potential sources of bias. In addition, we illustrate the effects of the choice of discount rate. The estimates in columns 2, 3, and 4 of Table 12-6 compare the benefits over 1949–2002 with the costs over different intervals, as a crude way of allowing for the role of research lags, maintaining the assumption of 100 percent attribution and a real discount rate of 3 percent per year.

First, in column 2 we compare the benefits over 1949–2002 with the costs over 1910–2002, which should incorporate any research expenditures that may have affected productivity growth over 1949–2002. These estimates of benefit-cost ratios ignore the benefits from productivity gains generated between 1910 and 1949 and after 2002. Incorporating the research costs incurred between 1910 and 1949 reduced the benefit-cost ratios somewhat (by about one fourth on average). The effects were modest because research expenditures were com-

11 If these two sources of errors were exactly offsetting, we could interpret the state-specific estimates as representing national (social) benefit-cost ratios from state-specific investments in agricultural research and extension. This approximation is likely to be misleading in particular cases since the relative importance of spillin versus spillout effects varies considerably across states, as discussed later in this section.

paratively low in the early years even after accounting for inflation and the time-value of money. The national estimate of the benefit-cost ratio from public agricultural research and extension was reduced from 22.8 to 16.5.

The estimates in column 3 of Table 12-6 compare the benefits over 1949–2002 with the costs over 1939–1992. This approach includes research expenditures for 10 years before benefits begin, and includes benefits for 10 years after expenditures end, and thus makes some adjustment for both of the (potentially offsetting) sources of bias in column 1. The resulting benefit-cost ratios in column 3 are generally larger than their counterparts in column 1, but not by much. The state-specific benefit-cost ratios range from 5.1 to 76.0, averaging 28.1 across the 48 states. The national average benefit-cost ratio is 23.8.

The estimates in column 4 compare the benefits over 1949–2002 with the costs over 1929–1982, including research expenditures for 20 years before benefits begin, and benefits for 20 years after expenditures end. The resulting benefit-cost ratios in column 4 are slightly larger again than their counterparts in column 1. The state-specific benefit-cost ratios range from 5.4 to 77.7, averaging 30.4 across the 48 states, and the national average benefit-cost ratio is 25.6.

The estimates in columns 5 and 6 show the effects of an alternative attribution assumption—that only 50 percent (rather than 100 percent) of the benefits would be attributable to the corresponding stream of research costs. The resulting benefit-cost ratios are all exactly half of their counterparts in columns 3 and 4. Any alternative assumption about the percentage attribution could be applied by scaling the benefit-cost ratios in the same fashion.

Finally, the estimates in column 7 show the effects of using a 5 percent discount rate rather than a 3 percent discount rate on the estimates with 50 percent attribution of benefits over 1949–2002 and costs over 1929–1982 (as shown in column 6). This treatment reduced the benefit-cost ratios by a factor of about one-third. We have included these estimates to illustrate the role of the choice of discount rate, but a discount rate of 3 percent is more appropriate for public investments of this type.

The estimates in Table 12-6 were not very sensitive to variations in the period over which costs were computed to compare with benefits. They were more sensitive to reducing the share of benefits attributable to public agricultural R&D, since the ratio is directly proportional to this share. Using an appropriate discount rate of 3 percent and some reasonable allowance for R&D lags (comparing benefits over 1949–2002 with costs over 1929–1982), the approximate measure of the national benefit-cost ratio could be as high as 25.6 (the upper bound with 100 percent attribution, in column 4) or as low as 12.8 (the lower bound with 50 percent attribution, in column 6). In column 4, the corresponding upper-bound estimates of regional benefit-cost ratios range from 18.1 to 63.6; the state-specific benefit-cost ratios range from 5.4 to 77.7, and

Table 12-7 Benefit-Cost Ratios—Econometric Estimates versus Approximations

	Logarithmic Model, Marginal BCR		Approximate Average BCR: Costs 1929–1982, Benefits 1949–2002	
State or Region	State R&E "Private" (1)	State R&E "Social" (2)	100% Attribution (3)	50% Attribution (4)
United States (includes USDA intramural)			25.6	12.8
USDA intramural		17.5		
48 states				
Average	21.0	32.1	30.4	15.2
Minimum	2.4	9.9	5.4	2.7
Maximum	57.8	69.2	77.7	38.8
Selected states				
California	33.3	43.4	48.5	24.2
Minnesota	40.6	55.4	55.6	27.8
Wyoming	12.7	23.6	17.0	8.5
Regions				
Pacific	21.8	32.9	41.1	20.5
Mountain	20.0	31.6	30.5	15.3
Northern Plains	42.4	54.5	63.6	31.8
Southern Plains	20.2	31.0	27.3	13.6
Central	33.7	46.8	40.6	20.3
Southeast	15.1	26.7	28.6	14.3
Northeast	9.4	18.4	18.1	9.0

Sources: Developed by the authors.

the simple average of these 48 estimates is 30.4. In column 6, the corresponding lower-bound estimates of regional benefit cost ratios range from 9.0 to 31.8; the state-specific benefit-cost ratios range from 2.7 to 38.8 and the simple average of these 48 estimates is 15.2.

Comparison of Approximations with Econometric Estimates

In Table 12-7 and Appendix Table 12-5 we compare estimates of approximate *average* benefit-cost ratios with the preferred estimates of *marginal* social benefit-cost ratios derived from the econometric estimation, using the model in logarithms, taken from Appendix Table 11-6. Columns 1 and 2 show the estimates of marginal private and social benefit-cost ratios from the econometric model and columns 3 and 4 show the approximate measures, comparing benefits over 1949–2002 with costs over 1929–1982, and allowing for either 100 percent or 50 percent attribution. The estimates of marginal social benefit cost ratios in column 2 are remarkably similar to the estimates of approximate average benefit-cost ratios with 100 percent attribution in column 3, while the estimates of state-specific (private) marginal benefit-cost ratios in column 1 are more comparable to the approximate average benefit-cost ratios with 50 percent attribution in column 4.

Figure 12-3 Spatial Distribution of Benefit-Cost Ratios—Econometric Estimates versus Approximations

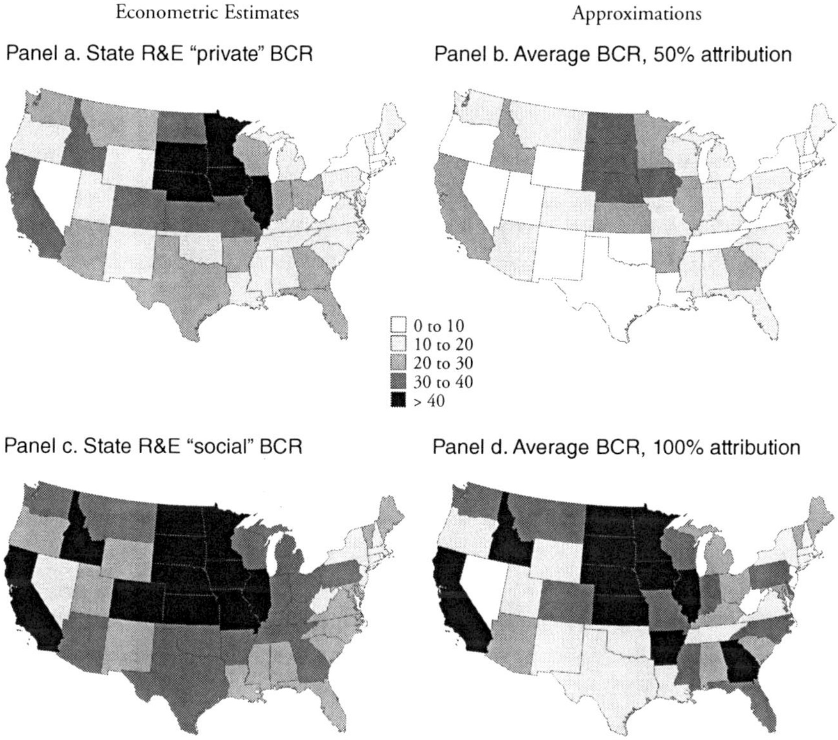

Sources: Developed by the authors.

Figure 12-3 shows graphically how the patterns of estimates across the states compare between the marginal benefit-cost ratios from the econometric model and the average approximate benefit-cost ratios. This comparison shows that the simple approximation procedure generates estimates that are on a similar general scale to those from the econometric estimation and simulation approach, and with some similar patterns across states. This similarity between the two sets of estimates reflects the central role of the fundamental characteristics of the data—the relatively large value of productivity growth compared with the value of research expenditures, especially in the largest agricultural states—in determining the findings. Thus the potential for modeling assumptions to have determined the benefit-cost findings from the econometric analysis is limited.

Analytical Representation of the Simple Approximation

The approximate measures have an advantage in that they avoid the complications of econometric estimation but they entail ad hoc assumptions about the share of benefits attributable to agricultural research and extension, and about the matching of research expenditures against a corresponding period of flows of benefits. Importantly, however, they provide estimates on a similar scale to those that are derived using the more-difficult and less-transparent econometric approaches, and they illustrate how estimates of benefit-cost ratios are driven by fundamental relationships between rates of productivity growth and their cumulative value, compared with the corresponding figures for annual spending on agricultural R&D.

A relatively simple mathematical model can be used to demonstrate those linkages, and to show how we can extend the general findings to other settings. Consider a scenario in which a policy is implemented to spend a fixed real amount, R per year on agricultural R&D in perpetuity. Given a constant real discount rate of r, the present value of the costs of this research investment is equal to:

$$(12.1)\quad PVC_t = \sum_{n=0}^{\infty} R\left(1+r\right)^{-n} = \frac{R}{r}.$$

After a gestation lag of L years, this stream of research investments contributes to a compound annual rate of agricultural productivity growth of g in perpetuity. In any future year, the benefits are equal to the difference between the actual value of production, given the productivity growth, and the value in the absence of productivity growth. Assume, for simplicity, that in the absence of this research spending, the real value of agricultural production would be constant at V per year (i.e., $V_{t+n} = V$ for all values of n). Then, if $n \geq L$:

$$(12.2)\quad B_{t+n} = \left(\left(1+g\right)^{n-L} - 1\right)V.$$

The present value of this stream of benefits is equal to:

$$(12.3)\quad PVB_t = \sum_{n=0}^{\infty} B_{t+n}\left(1+r\right)^{-n} = \sum_{n=L}^{\infty}\left(\left(1+g\right)^{n-L} - 1\right)V\left(1+r\right)^{-n} = \left(1+r\right)^{-L}\frac{V}{r}\left(\frac{g}{r-g}\right).$$

Defining the benefit-cost ratio, BCR, as equal to the present value of benefits divided by the present value of costs,

$$(12.4)\quad BCR = \frac{PVB_t}{PVC_t} = \left(1+r\right)^{-L}\frac{V}{r}\left(\frac{g}{r-g}\right)\left(\frac{R}{r}\right)^{-1} = \left(1+r\right)^{-L}\frac{g}{(r-g)}\left(\frac{V}{R}\right).$$

Suppose we use values of $r = 0.03$ (i.e., a real interest rate of 3 percent per annum), $L = 10$ years, $g = 0.02$ (i.e., a compound productivity growth rate of 2 percent per year attributable to R&D), and $V/R = 25$ (corresponding to an agricultural research intensity ratio of $i = 0.04$). Using these values, the discount factor is $(1+r)^{-L} = 0.61$, and $BCR = 37.2$.

Table 12-8 presents the corresponding benefit-cost ratios for a range of values of the parameters in equation (12.4). It can be seen that the benefit-cost ratio is directly proportional to the inverse research intensity ratio (i.e., inversely

Table 12-8 Approximate Benefit-Cost Ratios Implied by a Range of Parameter Values

	Discount Rate, r = 3 percent per annum		Discount Rate, r = 5 percent per annum	
Inverse Research Intensity, R/V	Research Lag, L = 10 years	Research Lag, L = 20 years	Research Lag, L = 10 years	Research Lag, L = 20 years
	productivity growth, g = 2 percent per year			
50 (i = 2 percent)	74.4	55.4	20.5	12.6
25 (i = 4 percent)	37.2	27.7	10.2	6.3
	productivity growth, g = 1 percent per year			
50 (i = 2 percent)	18.6	13.8	7.7	4.7
25 (i = 4 percent)	9.3	6.9	3.8	2.3

Sources: Developed by the authors based on formulas in the text.

proportional to research spending as a share of the value of output), such that doubling the research intensity halves the benefit-cost ratio. The benefit-cost ratios are similarly sensitive to the other parameters. In particular, if the annual productivity growth rate associated with the given research intensity is reduced from 2 percent (in the top half of the table) to 1 percent (in the bottom half of the table), the benefit-cost ratios are reduced by well more than half; if the discount rate is increased from 3 percent to 5 percent per annum, again the benefit-cost ratios are reduced by more than half; and if the research gestation lag is doubled from 10 to 20 years, the benefit-cost ratios are reduced by about one-third. Combining these changes, the most favorable combination of parameters results in a benefit-cost ratio that is about 30 times the benefit-cost ratio implied by the least favorable combination, but the least-favorable combination is highly unlikely to reflect actual parameter values, and even so implies a benefit-cost ratio of well more than one.

Spatial Spillovers

As noted above, the approximate benefit-cost ratios at the level of individual states do not account for spillin effects on productivity coming from either USDA intramural research, or research and extension from other states; nor do they account for the effects of a state's research spilling out to yield benefits from productivity improvements in other states. This means that, to the extent that spillovers matter, the approximate benefit-cost ratios will be biased up as measures of own-state (private) benefits from state-specific investments in agricultural research and extension. The same measures may be more accurate as measures of national (social) benefit-cost ratios, if the value of the benefits a state receives through spillins from other states and the USDA is approximately equal to the value of the benefits it confers through spillouts to other states. However, spillover impacts are not likely to be symmetric, depending on whether a state is large in research (which influences whether it is likely to generate large spillover benefits for other states) or large in agriculture (and thus likely to receive large benefits from a given productivity gain), and on its pattern of agroecological similarity with other states that are large in agriculture or research or both. These determinants of spillover potential are discussed in Chapter 9 and reflected in our econometric results in Chapters 10 and 11.

Here we present some measures of spillover potential based on our spillover coefficients (reflecting similarity of output mix between states), and the state-specific scale of investment in agricultural research and extension. These measures are free from other modeling assumptions and provide some insight into the results from the econometric models and the comparison between the benefit-cost ratios based on the econometric results (which reflect allowance for spillovers) and the approximate benefit-cost ratios (which do not). Table 12-9 includes two sets of measures of spillovers from state-specific expenditures on research and extension. The first set, in the first three columns of numbers, were computed using spillover coefficients based on state-to-state similarities in the mixture of agricultural outputs, as defined in Chapter 9. The second set use spillover coefficients equal to one between pairs of states that are within the same USDA region, and zero between pairs of states from different regions. Panel a includes estimates computed based on expenditures in 2002 alone (more complete state-specific details are reported in Appendix Table 12-6), and Panel b includes estimates based on expenditures over the period 1949–2002 (more complete state-specific details are reported in Appendix Table 12-7). We discuss the estimates in the upper half of Table 12-9 first, referring to just one year's expenditure.

Consider the first set of measures, in the first three columns. The first column shows a measure of the potential for a state to receive spillins of technology from other states. For a given state, we weighted expenditures in each other state and in intramural USDA labs by the corresponding spillover coefficients, thus transforming those interstate measures into equivalent amounts of own-state expenditures on research and extension. Thus, the numbers in the first column represent the value of research and extension spillins to each state from all other states and the USDA labs, measured in equivalents of own-state research spending (i.e., not in terms of the benefits that would flow from that spending). The first entry is the sum across the 48 states and the second entry is the average of the state-specific entries across the 48 states.

The next column shows the corresponding measure of spillouts of technology to other states, measured in equivalents of own-state research spending by the recipient states. For a given state we weighted its research expenditures by the sum of spillover coefficients between that state and all other states. Thus the numbers in the second column represent the value of research spillouts from each state to all other states. Again, the first entry is the sum across the 48 states and the second entry is the average of the state-specific entries across the 48 states.

Table 12-9 Spillover Potentials, Expenditures by States on Research and Extension

State or Region	Based on Output Mix: Spillins	Spillouts	Ratio	Based on USDA Regions: Spillins	Spillouts	Ratio
	millions of dollars (2000 prices)			*millions of dollars (2000 prices)*		
Panel a. 2002 expenditures						
United States total	125,767	97,186	1.29	71,217	27,973	2.55
48 state						
Average	2,620	2,025	2.69	1,484	583	4.46
Minimum	1,351	102	0.30	1,083	62	0.60
Maximum	3,573	8,808	18.93	1,871	2,064	23.09
Selected states						
California	2,611	8,808	0.30	1,083	747	1.45
Minnesota	3,299	3,798	0.87	1,827	1,032	1.77
Wyoming	2,475	303	8.17	1,256	104	12.04
Panel b. 1949–2002 expenditures						
United States total	7,783,624	5,558,130	1.40	4,996,437	1,629,201	3.07
48 state						
Average	162,159	115,794	2.48	104,092	33,942	4.90
Minimum	84,856	10,625	0.36	80,580	6,613	0.76
Maximum	221,717	448,576	10.87	127,843	122,857	15.79
Selected states						
California	162,851	448,576	0.36	80,580	38,066	2.12
Minnesota	206,218	194,546	1.06	121,599	52,852	2.30
Wyoming	151,203	28,562	5.29	87,788	9,833	8.93

The third column is the ratio of spillins to spillouts, as measured in the first two columns. Hence, in California, for example, the total value of spillins from all other states and the USDA in 2002 was $2.6 billion, the total value of spillouts was $8.8 billion, and the ratio of spillins to spillouts was 0.30. This reflects the fact that California is a large state in terms of its total research spending (spending $374 million on research and extension in 2002), and generates relatively large spillovers to other states (the average of the spillover coefficients between California and other states was 0.50, and the spillover coefficient between California and the nation as a whole was 0.66).

Across all the states, the average value of spillins per state was $2.6 billion, the average value of spillouts per state was $2.0 billion, and the average of the state-specific ratios of spillins to spillouts was 2.69. The value exceeding one reflects the fact that spillins include intramural research, but not just that. The total value of spillins across the 48 states was $125.8 billion and the total value of spillouts was $97.2 billion, with a national ratio of spillins to spillouts of 1.29. The difference between this national ratio and the average of the state-specific ratios reflects the inequality of states, with many (especially smaller) states receiving relatively large spillins compared with spillouts they generate for other states. The states with comparatively small spillin-to-spillout ratios tend to be those with comparatively large agricultural experiment stations—California (0.30), New York (0.55), Texas (0.49), Florida (0.62), Minnesota (0.87), North Carolina (0.72), Wisconsin (0.74), Georgia (0.76), Iowa (0.85), and Michigan (0.81). Many of the states with comparatively large spillin-to-spillout ratios are found in the Mountain and Northeast regions, typically states with relatively small agricultural sectors and small experiment stations.

The corresponding numbers in the last three columns of Table 12-9, based on USDA regions rather than output mixes, tell a very different story in terms of the size of measured spillovers, the patterns across states, and the relative importance of spillins relative to spillouts. Both measures of spillover potential are reduced when we impose the restriction that spillovers occur only among states in the same region. However, spillouts are relatively more restricted, such that the spillin-to-spillout ratios are, on average, much greater than when estimates of spillovers are based on similarity of the output mix. In several states where we estimated substantial spillouts using the measure based on the output mix (like California, Florida, and Texas) much smaller spillover benefits are implied when we assume those benefits accrue only to states in the same region.

As noted, the entries in Panel a of Table 12-9 are based on just one year's research spending data. We computed corresponding measures of spillins and spillouts using data on research spending over the 54 years 1949–2002, compounded forward to 2002 using a real interest rate of 3 percent per annum. The entries reported in Panel b of Table 12-9 represent the present value of research spillins to each state from all other states and the USDA labs over 1949–2002 and the present value of research spillouts to all other states 1949–2002. Again these are measured in equivalents of own-state research spending, not in terms of the benefits that would flow from that spending. The patterns in the results are very similar to those for 2002 spending alone, as can be seen by comparing the ratios of spillins to spillouts between Panels a and b of Table 12-9. In California, for example, the present value in 2002 of spillins over 1949–2002 was $162.9 billion, the present value in 2002 of spillouts over 1949–2002 was $448.6 billion, and the ratio of spillins to spillouts was 0.36 (compared with 0.30 for 2002 spending). Across all of the states, the average value of spillins per state was $162 billion, the average value of spillouts per state was $116 billion, and the average of the state-specific ratios of spillins to spillouts was 2.48 (compared with 2.69 for 2002 spending). The total value of spillins across the 48 states was $7.8 trillion and the total value of spillouts was $5.6 trillion, with a national ratio of spillins to spillouts of 1.40 (compared with 1.29 for 2002 spending). The same states that had comparatively small spillin-spillout ratios using data just for 2002 also had comparatively small spillin-spillout ratios using data for 1949–2002—

Figure 12-4 Spatial Distribution of Ratio of Potential Spillins to Potential Spillouts

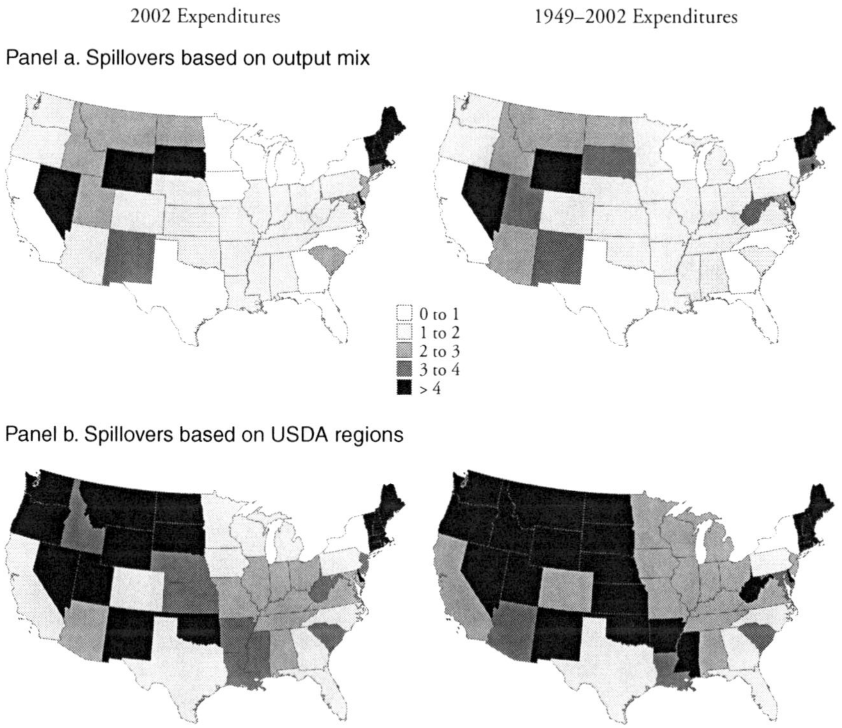

Sources: Developed by the authors.

California (0.36), New York (0.57), Texas (0.57), North Carolina (0.74), Florida (0.75), Georgia (0.87), Wisconsin (0.89), Michigan (1.01), Minnesota (1.06), and Iowa (1.09).

Figure 12-4 shows the spatial distribution of spillin-to-spillout potential using 2002 expenditures (maps on the left) and 1949–2002 expenditures (maps on the right) using the alternative spillover coefficients (based on output mix in Panel a and on regions in Panel b). States with no shading provide more spillover benefits (as spillouts) than they receive (as spillins) from other states (i.e., the spillin-spillout ratio is less than one). For shaded states, darker shading indicates that the state receives a greater benefit of spillins from other states per dollar of spillouts it provides to other states. The spatial patterns are fairly similar regardless of which measure of expenditures (i.e., 2002 or 1949–2002) is used, and which measure is used to indicate spillovers. In all four maps, California, Texas, and Florida are the most lightly shaded (receiving the least spillins per dollar of spillouts provided). Several states in the Central and Southeast regions also receive comparatively small spillins relative to the spillouts they provide to other states.

Appendix Table 12-1 Meta-Analysis Results—Best-Fitting Lag Distribution, Logarithmic Model

Explanatory Variable		Dependent Variable, State-Specific Benefit-Cost Ratio for		
		SAES "Private"	SAES "Social"	USDA IM
		coefficient estimate (p-value in italics)		
Extension lag	EXT-LAG-GEOM	**-8.01**	-1.16	**0.22**
		0.00	*0.14*	*0.00*
Extension spillovers	NO-EXT-SPILL	-0.46	**-10.13**	**-0.31**
		0.58	*0.00*	*0.00*
Extension entering separately	SEP-EXT-VAR	**25.67**	**18.74**	**-0.23**
		0.00	*0.00*	*0.00*
Research spillovers	R-SPILL-USDA	0.00	**8.31**	**0.64**
		1.00	*0.00*	*0.00*
	R-SPILL-ZERO	**7.26**	**21.17**	**-0.56**
		0.00	*0.00*	*0.00*
	R-SPILL-ALL	1.48	**27.70**	**-0.30**
		0.29	*0.00*	*0.01*
Peak lag year	PEAKLAG	**0.55**	**-0.34**	**-0.03**
		0.00	*0.04*	*0.00*
Maximum lag length	R-LAG-35	**-5.22**	**7.05**	**0.40**
		0.00	*0.00*	*0.00*
	R-LAG-20	-0.98	**2.17**	**0.10**
		0.28	*0.02*	*0.01*
Inverse ARI	INV-ARI	**29.50**	**32.30**	-0.14
		0.00	*0.00*	*0.59*
Inverse ARI squared	INV-ARI-SQ	0.98	0.51	0.14
		0.69	*0.84*	*0.22*
Output value	VALUE	0.37	0.44	**0.16**
		0.69	*0.64*	*0.00*
Output value squared	VALUE-SQ	-0.03	-0.02	0.00
		0.57	*0.59*	*0.60*
R&E spending	R-SPEND	19.96	57.03	2.26
		0.72	*0.30*	*0.37*
R&E spending squared	R-SPEND-SQ	-15.09	-265.03	-16.17
		0.95	*0.24*	*0.11*
R&E spending growth	RS-GROWTH	-0.55	-1.41	0.02
		0.80	*0.53*	*0.82*
R&E spending growth squared	RS-GROWTH-SQ	0.74	0.93	-0.01
		0.16	*0.08*	*0.67*
MFP	MFP	0.02	-0.04	0.00
		0.84	*0.69*	*0.30*
MFP squared	MFP-SQ	0.00	0.00	0.00
		0.97	*0.51*	*0.38*
Spillover potential	AV-OMEGA		**52.42**	**-0.46**
			0.00	*0.03*
Intercept		-20.00	1.07	**1.42**
		0.06	*0.92*	*0.00*
N		**672**	**672**	**672**
R^2		**0.81**	**0.82**	**0.81**

Sources: Developed by the authors.

Appendix Table 12-2 Meta-Analysis Results—All Lag Distributions, Logarithmic Model

		Dependent Variable, State-Specific Benefit-Cost Ratio for		
Explanatory Variable		**SAES "Private"**	**SAES "Social"**	**USDA IM**
		coefficient estimate (p-value in italics)		
Extension lag	EXT-LAG-GEOM	**-7.02**	**-1.49**	**0.18**
		0.00	*0.00*	*0.00*
Extension spillovers	NO-EXT-SPILL	**0.31**	**-11.95**	**-0.40**
		0.03	*0.00*	*0.00*
Extension entering separately	SEP-EXT-VAR	**30.33**	**23.02**	**-0.24**
		0.00	*0.00*	*0.00*
Research spillovers	R-SPILL-USDA	**2.47**	**12.16**	**0.61**
		0.00	*0.00*	*0.00*
	R-SPILL-ZERO	**24.99**	**26.18**	**-1.14**
		0.00	*0.00*	*0.00*
	R-SPILL-ALL	**1.36**	**35.45**	**-0.31**
		0.00	*0.00*	*0.00*
Peak lag year	PEAKLAG	**-0.28**	**-0.82**	**-0.02**
		0.00	*0.00*	*0.00*
Maximum lag length	R-LAG-35	0.15	**6.88**	**0.22**
		0.36	*0.00*	*0.00*
	R-LAG-20	0.20	**2.99**	**0.09**
		0.24	*0.00*	*0.00*
Inverse ARI	INV-ARI	**29.82**	**32.52**	**-0.23**
		0.00	*0.00*	*0.00*
Inverse ARI squared	INV-ARI-SQ	**1.28**	**0.96**	**0.19**
		0.00	*0.05*	*0.00*
Output value	VALUE	0.24	**0.38**	**0.19**
		0.15	*0.03*	*0.00*
Output value squared	VALUE-SQ	**-0.02**	-0.02	**0.00**
		0.05	*0.06*	*0.00*
R&E spending	R-SPEND	**36.44**	**80.25**	**3.96**
		0.00	*0.00*	*0.00*
R&E spending squared	R-SPEND-SQ	**-101.54**	**-409.04**	**-25.32**
		0.01	*0.00*	*0.00*
R&E spending growth	RS-GROWTH	-0.46	**-1.50**	0.03
		0.25	*0.00*	*0.13*
R&E spending growth squared	RS-GROWTH-SQ	**0.63**	**0.86**	**-0.02**
		0.00	*0.00*	*0.00*
MFP	MFP	**0.04**	-0.01	-0.01
		0.03	*0.50*	*0.00*
MFP squared	MFP-SQ	0.00	0.00	**0.00**
		0.20	*0.08*	*0.00*
Spillover potential	AV-OMEGA		**66.94**	**-0.34**
			0.00	*0.00*
Intercept		**-4.58**	**6.56**	**1.39**
		0.01	*0.00*	*0.00*
N		**29,520**	**29,520**	**29,520**
R^2		**0.77**	**0.80**	**0.81**

Sources: Developed by the authors.

Appendix Table 12-3 Agricultural Output Value Attributable to Productivity Growth, by State, 2002

State	Total Value of Agricultural Output in 2002	2002 Output Value Attributable to Productivity Growth since 1949		Agricultural Research and Extension Intensity	
		Value	Share of Total	1975	2002
	billions of dollars		*percent*	*percent*	
Pacific	*29.8*	*18.5*	*61.9*	*1.01*	*1.94*
California	22.8	13.9	60.8	0.93	1.71
Oregon	2.3	1.4	58.4	1.95	4.17
Washington	4.7	3.0	64.0	0.87	1.98
Mountain	*13.6*	*7.8*	*56.9*	*1.08*	*2.83*
Arizona	2.5	1.4	54.5	1.46	3.03
Colorado	3.2	1.6	51.2	0.73	3.03
Idaho	3.3	2.2	67.9	0.71	1.48
Montana	1.7	0.7	42.5	0.83	2.59
Nevada	0.2	0.1	37.3	4.14	13.04
New Mexico	1.4	0.8	60.9	1.40	2.34
Utah	0.8	0.4	55.1	2.27	5.61
Wyoming	0.6	0.2	35.9	1.49	2.60
Northern Plains	*19.1*	*12.1*	*63.2*	*0.60*	*1.59*
Kansas	5.4	3.2	58.7	0.72	1.91
Nebraska	7.1	4.6	64.2	0.59	1.59
North Dakota	3.2	2.2	67.5	0.50	1.70
South Dakota	3.4	2.1	60.9	0.56	0.96
Southern Plains	*22.7*	*14.4*	*63.2*	*1.14*	*2.78*
Arkansas	4.4	3.5	78.4	0.96	2.12
Louisiana	1.3	0.9	66.1	2.29	7.32
Mississippi	2.7	2.2	79.1	1.70	3.71
Oklahoma	3.2	1.6	50.5	1.08	2.85
Texas	11.0	5.6	50.4	0.87	2.24
Central	*50.0*	*28.7*	*57.4*	*0.64*	*2.24*
Illinois	8.0	4.5	55.8	0.39	1.65
Indiana	4.6	2.6	56.2	0.68	2.35
Iowa	11.8	6.9	59.0	0.34	1.40
Michigan	3.5	2.2	61.3	1.70	4.50
Minnesota	8.4	5.5	65.1	0.58	1.82
Missouri	4.1	1.9	46.9	0.88	2.67
Ohio	4.0	2.1	52.5	0.90	3.07
Wisconsin	5.5	2.9	52.4	0.90	3.04
Southeast	*27.2*	*18.2*	*67.0*	*1.71*	*3.88*
Alabama	2.9	2.1	72.7	1.72	2.80
Florida	6.1	3.7	59.8	1.62	3.24
Georgia	4.2	3.2	76.3	1.49	3.93
Kentucky	2.3	0.9	36.8	1.29	4.11
North Carolina	6.2	4.5	73.2	1.50	2.88
South Carolina	1.3	0.9	70.7	2.09	4.65
Tennessee	2.0	1.0	49.4	1.72	4.76
Virginia	1.9	1.0	51.3	2.71	5.72
West Virginia	0.3	0.2	53.4	5.08	23.83

(continued)

Appendix Table 12-3 (continued)

State	Total Value of Agricultural Output in 2002	2002 Output Value Attributable to Productivity Growth since 1949		Agricultural Research and Extension Intensity	
		Value	Share of Total	1975	2002
	billions of dollars		*percent*	*percent*	
Northeast	*10.8*	*6.3*	*58.0*	*2.17*	*5.15*
Connecticut	0.4	0.2	52.2	3.42	9.10
Delaware	0.7	0.5	70.9	1.33	2.23
Maine	0.4	0.2	58.8	1.48	6.57
Maryland	1.3	0.8	65.1	1.64	4.40
Massachusetts	0.3	0.2	51.7	3.88	8.53
New Hampshire	0.1	0.1	53.9	4.40	14.80
New Jersey	0.6	0.3	41.9	6.06	7.07
New York	2.7	1.4	49.9	2.51	7.92
Pennsylvania	3.9	2.4	62.2	1.23	2.74
Rhode Island	0.1	0.0	53.8	11.70	12.30
Vermont	0.4	0.2	53.4	1.84	2.88

Sources: Developed by the authors.

Appendix Table 12-4 Simple Approximate Average Benefit-Cost Ratios, Benefits over 54 Years, 1949–2002, by State

	Research Costs Accumulated over the Years						
	1949–02	1910–02	1939–92	1929–82	1939–92	1929–82	1929–82
	Benefits 100% Attributable to Public R&D $r = 0.03$				Benefits 50% Attributable to Public R&D $r = 0.03$		$r = 0.05$
State or Region	(1)	(2)	(3)	(4)	(5)	(6)	(7)
Pacific	*32.1*	*25.8*	*35.6*	*41.1*	*17.8*	*20.5*	*14.3*
California	36.9	30.2	41.3	48.5	20.7	24.2	17.0
Oregon	14.4	11.0	15.5	17.1	7.7	8.6	6.0
Washington	28.4	22.4	31.3	35.8	15.6	17.9	12.0
Mountain	*25.1*	*18.5*	*27.5*	*30.5*	*13.8*	*15.3*	*10.5*
Arizona	20.3	16.1	23.8	28.5	11.9	14.2	10.5
Colorado	22.4	17.7	25.9	31.7	12.9	15.8	10.2
Idaho	48.6	36.0	53.1	57.5	26.6	28.8	19.5
Montana	34.2	22.7	34.6	35.0	17.3	17.5	12.7
Nevada	4.4	3.2	5.1	5.4	2.5	2.7	1.9
New Mexico	15.6	11.4	16.5	18.0	8.2	9.0	5.2
Utah	14.0	10.1	15.3	16.9	7.7	8.4	6.1
Wyoming	17.5	11.6	17.1	17.0	8.5	8.5	6.1
Northern Plains	*54.1*	*39.5*	*58.1*	*63.6*	*29.0*	*31.8*	*22.2*
Kansas	41.0	30.2	43.4	47.5	21.7	23.8	16.4
Nebraska	57.8	43.9	64.5	73.0	32.2	36.5	25.6
North Dakota	54.7	38.1	58.6	64.0	29.3	32.0	22.2
South Dakota	74.7	51.7	76.0	77.7	38.0	38.8	27.6
Southern Plains	*23.7*	*17.6*	*24.9*	*27.3*	*12.4*	*13.6*	*8.4*
Arkansas	48.7	35.7	51.4	55.3	25.7	27.6	18.6
Louisiana	14.9	11.7	15.7	17.5	7.8	8.7	6.3
Mississippi	31.6	23.1	32.4	34.9	16.2	17.4	12.6
Oklahoma	17.6	12.6	18.0	19.0	9.0	9.5	5.4
Texas	13.2	9.8	14.1	15.9	7.1	7.9	3.0
Central	*35.3*	*25.2*	*37.7*	*40.6*	*18.8*	*20.3*	*13.7*
Illinois	47.5	31.6	48.8	49.4	24.4	24.7	16.3
Indiana	30.2	20.5	31.1	32.8	15.5	16.4	11.0
Iowa	53.3	37.5	57.9	62.1	28.9	31.0	20.4
Michigan	18.2	13.9	19.9	21.8	9.9	10.9	7.3
Minnesota	44.2	31.8	49.1	55.6	24.6	27.8	19.0
Missouri	28.2	21.5	30.2	33.6	15.1	16.8	11.9
Ohio	24.5	16.2	25.2	25.7	12.6	12.8	8.3
Wisconsin	27.3	21.0	29.9	33.6	14.9	16.8	11.8
Southeast	*23.6*	*18.1*	*25.3*	*28.6*	*12.6*	*14.3*	*10.1*
Alabama	26.2	19.4	26.7	28.6	13.4	14.3	9.9
Florida	21.6	18.2	24.8	30.7	12.4	15.3	10.9
Georgia	30.7	24.6	34.0	40.6	17.0	20.3	14.9
Kentucky	19.5	13.6	20.4	21.6	10.2	10.8	7.3
North Carolina	28.7	23.0	31.3	36.5	15.6	18.2	13.1
South Carolina	19.3	13.8	19.8	21.6	9.9	10.8	7.6
Tennessee	17.0	12.7	17.9	19.6	8.9	9.8	6.8
Virginia	11.9	9.3	12.7	14.7	6.3	7.3	5.3
West Virginia	7.9	4.8	7.4	7.0	3.7	3.5	2.5

(continued)

Appendix Table 12-4 (continued)

	Research Costs Accumulated over the Years						
	1949–02	1910–02	1939–92	1929–82	1939–92	1929–82	1929–82
	Benefits 100% Attributable to Public R&D				Benefits 50% Attributable to Public R&D		
	$r = 0.03$				$r = 0.03$		$r = 0.05$
State or Region	(1)	(2)	(3)	(4)	(5)	(6)	(7)
Northeast	*17.6*	*11.8*	*17.9*	*18.1*	*8.9*	*9.0*	*6.3*
Connecticut	13.0	7.7	12.5	11.3	6.2	5.7	4.2
Delaware	34.8	24.0	35.7	37.6	17.9	18.8	12.8
Maine	27.2	18.0	27.2	27.8	13.6	13.9	10.4
Maryland	21.6	15.9	23.0	25.3	11.5	12.6	8.8
Massachusetts	13.9	7.9	13.0	11.9	6.5	6.0	4.3
New Hampshire	12.3	7.3	12.1	11.2	6.1	5.6	4.2
New Jersey	8.6	5.6	8.5	8.0	4.2	4.0	3.1
New York	11.7	8.1	12.1	12.6	6.0	6.3	4.5
Pennsylvania	30.4	21.7	31.9	33.6	15.9	16.8	11.3
Rhode Island	5.9	3.9	5.7	5.6	2.9	2.8	2.1
Vermont	25.5	15.6	24.7	23.6	12.3	11.8	8.1

Sources: Developed by the authors.

Appendix Table 12-5 Benefit-Cost Ratios—Econometric Estimates versus Approximations, by State

	Logarithmic Model, Marginal BCR		Approximate Average BCR Costs 1929–1982, Benefits 1949–2002	
State or Region	State R&E "Private" (1)	State R&E "Social" (2)	100% Attribution (3)	50% Attribution (4)
Pacific	*21.8*	*32.9*	*41.1*	*20.5*
California	33.3	43.4	48.5	24.2
Oregon	11.3	24.1	17.1	8.6
Washington	20.9	31.2	35.8	17.9
Mountain	*20.0*	*31.6*	*30.5*	*15.3*
Arizona	26.6	36.9	28.5	14.2
Colorado	31.1	43.8	31.7	15.8
Idaho	34.0	44.8	57.5	28.8
Montana	22.0	32.2	35.0	17.5
Nevada	7.3	19.2	5.4	2.7
New Mexico	15.6	28.2	18.0	9.0
Utah	11.0	24.5	16.9	8.4
Wyoming	12.7	23.6	17.0	8.5
Northern Plains	*42.4*	*54.5*	*63.6*	*31.8*
Kansas	33.6	45.3	47.5	23.8
Nebraska	51.3	64.9	73.0	36.5
North Dakota	37.3	46.0	64.0	32.0
South Dakota	47.4	61.7	77.7	38.8
Southern Plains	*20.2*	*31.0*	*27.3*	*13.6*
Arkansas	26.8	35.7	55.3	27.6
Louisiana	12.2	23.0	17.5	8.7
Mississippi	15.1	25.3	34.9	17.4
Oklahoma	19.0	31.4	19.0	9.5
Texas	28.2	39.4	15.9	7.9
Central	*33.7*	*46.8*	*40.6*	*20.3*
Illinois	43.0	53.8	49.4	24.7
Indiana	27.1	39.4	32.8	16.4
Iowa	57.8	69.2	62.1	31.0
Michigan	17.1	31.5	21.8	10.9
Minnesota	40.6	55.4	55.6	27.8
Missouri	34.7	49.9	33.6	16.8
Ohio	22.4	37.0	25.7	12.8
Wisconsin	26.7	38.3	33.6	16.8
Southeast	*15.1*	*26.7*	*28.6*	*14.3*
Alabama	13.4	24.8	28.6	14.3
Florida	21.6	28.2	30.7	15.3
Georgia	20.5	31.0	40.6	20.3
Kentucky	18.5	30.5	21.6	10.8
North Carolina	19.9	27.5	36.5	18.2
South Carolina	11.2	23.1	21.6	10.8
Tennessee	15.7	31.3	19.6	9.8
Virginia	11.8	26.3	14.7	7.3
West Virginia	3.8	17.6	7.0	3.5

(continued)

Appendix Table 12-5 (continued)

	Logarithmic Model, Marginal BCR		Approximate Average BCR Costs 1929–1982, Benefits 1949–2002	
State or Region	State R&E "Private" (1)	State R&E "Social" (2)	100% Attribution (3)	50% Attribution (4)
Northeast	*9.4*	*18.4*	*18.1*	*9.0*
Connecticut	5.4	14.2	11.3	5.7
Delaware	15.8	21.5	37.6	18.8
Maine	13.5	20.1	27.8	13.9
Maryland	14.1	26.1	25.3	12.6
Massachusetts	4.7	13.3	11.9	6.0
New Hampshire	4.4	14.0	11.2	5.6
New Jersey	4.7	13.7	8.0	4.0
New York	8.3	18.1	12.6	6.3
Pennsylvania	18.0	30.3	33.6	16.8
Rhode Island	2.4	9.9	5.6	2.8
Vermont	12.4	21.5	23.6	11.8

Sources: Developed by the authors.

Appendix Table 12-6 Spillover Potentials, 2002 Expenditures by States on Research and Extension

	Based on Output Mix			Based on USDA Regions		
State or Region	**Spillins**	**Spillouts**	**Ratio**	**Spillins**	**Spillouts**	**Ratio**
	millions of dollars (2000 prices)			*millions of dollars (2000 prices)*		
United States total	*125,767*	*97,186*	*1.29*	*71,217*	*27,973*	*2.55*
Pacific						
California	2,611	8,808	0.30	1,083	747	1.45
Oregon	2,977	2,409	1.24	1,363	187	7.28
Washington	2,484	1,903	1.31	1,368	177	7.71
Mountain						
Arizona	2,431	1,395	1.74	1,199	507	2.37
Colorado	2,876	2,216	1.30	1,179	645	1.83
Idaho	2,585	1,031	2.51	1,224	327	3.74
Montana	2,308	812	2.84	1,229	293	4.19
Nevada	2,739	671	4.08	1,242	207	6.01
New Mexico	2,937	738	3.98	1,240	217	5.71
Utah	3,204	1,110	2.89	1,230	290	4.24
Wyoming	2,475	303	8.17	1,256	104	12.04
Northern Plains						
Kansas	2,668	2,172	1.23	1,093	296	3.69
Nebraska	2,989	2,516	1.19	1,083	325	3.33
North Dakota	1,994	867	2.30	1,139	157	7.27
South Dakota	3,192	784	4.07	1,160	94	12.31
Southern Plains						
Arkansas	2,095	1,494	1.40	1,418	358	3.96
Louisiana	2,465	1,806	1.37	1,414	373	3.79
Mississippi	2,351	1,805	1.30	1,410	389	3.63
Oklahoma	2,855	2,125	1.34	1,419	354	4.01
Texas	2,710	5,545	0.49	1,269	951	1.33
Central						
Illinois	2,428	2,217	1.10	1,848	887	2.08
Indiana	2,634	1,976	1.33	1,871	723	2.59
Iowa	2,618	3,064	0.85	1,817	1,104	1.65
Michigan	3,293	4,078	0.81	1,822	1,068	1.71
Minnesota	3,299	3,798	0.87	1,827	1,032	1.77
Missouri	3,336	2,727	1.22	1,869	736	2.54
Ohio	3,227	2,964	1.09	1,856	832	2.23
Wisconsin	2,855	3,836	0.74	1,813	1,134	1.60
Southeast						
Alabama	2,654	1,660	1.60	1,836	617	2.98
Florida	1,658	2,672	0.62	1,723	1,522	1.13
Georgia	2,405	3,158	0.76	1,755	1,266	1.39
Kentucky	2,750	2,000	1.37	1,821	737	2.47
North Carolina	1,845	2,577	0.72	1,743	1,363	1.28
South Carolina	2,724	1,264	2.15	1,853	477	3.88
Tennessee	3,573	2,543	1.40	1,824	714	2.55
Virginia	3,376	2,944	1.15	1,807	846	2.14
West Virginia	3,239	1,878	1.72	1,844	555	3.32

(continued)

Appendix Table 12-6 (continued)

	Based on Output Mix			Based on USDA Regions		
State or Region	**Spillins**	**Spillouts**	**Ratio**	**Spillins**	**Spillouts**	**Ratio**
Northeast	*millions of dollars (2000 prices)*			*millions of dollars (2000 prices)*		
Connecticut	2,285	602	3.80	1,406	309	4.55
Delaware	1,351	157	8.61	1,422	145	9.79
Maine	1,724	347	4.97	1,414	231	6.13
Maryland	2,846	1,270	2.24	1,382	548	2.52
Massachusetts	2,203	467	4.72	1,412	250	5.65
New Hampshire	2,491	382	6.53	1,419	181	7.83
New Jersey	2,209	800	2.76	1,394	433	3.22
New York	2,444	4,407	0.55	1,231	2,064	0.60
Pennsylvania	3,023	2,558	1.18	1,335	1,021	1.31
Rhode Island	1,939	102	18.93	1,431	62	23.09
Vermont	2,388	228	10.46	1,425	118	12.06
Simple Average	*2,620*	*2,025*	*2.69*	*1,484*	*583*	*4.46*

Sources: Developed by the authors.

Appendix Table 12-7 Spillover Potentials, 1949–2002 Expenditures by States on Research and Extension

	Based on Output Mix			Based on USDA Regions		
State or Region	Spillins	Spillouts	Ratio	Spillins	Spillouts	Ratio
	millions of dollars (2000 prices)			*millions of dollars (2000 prices)*		
United States total	*7,783,624*	*5,558,130*	*1.40*	*4,996,437*	*1,629,201*	*3.07*
Pacific						
California	162,851	448,576	0.36	80,580	38,066	2.12
Oregon	183,231	135,072	1.36	94,364	10,496	8.99
Washington	152,633	111,120	1.37	94,432	10,362	9.11
Mountain						
Arizona	149,681	61,715	2.43	85,992	22,411	3.84
Colorado	178,056	103,497	1.72	84,888	30,138	2.82
Idaho	158,689	53,087	2.99	86,787	16,845	5.15
Montana	142,067	48,689	2.92	86,682	17,581	4.93
Nevada	168,128	26,960	6.24	88,006	8,311	10.59
New Mexico	179,745	46,244	3.89	87,248	13,616	6.41
Utah	196,559	55,674	3.53	87,113	14,562	5.98
Wyoming	151,203	28,562	5.29	87,788	9,833	8.93
Northern Plains						
Kansas	164,590	141,011	1.17	81,349	19,229	4.23
Nebraska	186,346	132,323	1.41	82,057	17,103	4.80
North Dakota	123,354	51,632	2.39	84,647	9,334	9.07
South Dakota	196,967	59,536	3.31	85,373	7,156	11.93
Southern Plains						
Arkansas	131,305	86,826	1.51	100,651	20,811	4.84
Louisiana	151,918	127,937	1.19	99,244	26,439	3.75
Mississippi	146,286	112,171	1.30	99,816	24,151	4.13
Oklahoma	176,196	119,783	1.47	100,866	19,953	5.06
Texas	168,411	299,979	0.56	92,989	51,458	1.81
Central						
Illinois	152,848	129,438	1.18	121,750	51,793	2.35
Indiana	164,513	131,656	1.25	122,265	48,188	2.54
Iowa	165,621	151,617	1.09	121,347	54,615	2.22
Michigan	204,864	203,815	1.01	121,525	53,368	2.28
Minnesota	206,218	194,546	1.06	121,599	52,852	2.30
Missouri	207,581	164,485	1.26	122,812	44,361	2.77
Ohio	201,159	175,862	1.14	122,098	49,357	2.47
Wisconsin	176,678	197,694	0.89	120,799	58,452	2.07
Southeast						
Alabama	163,588	133,213	1.23	123,856	49,492	2.50
Florida	102,741	137,068	0.75	120,284	78,071	1.54
Georgia	151,209	174,214	0.87	121,312	69,844	1.74
Kentucky	171,281	122,726	1.40	124,394	45,192	2.75
North Carolina	116,205	157,901	0.74	119,607	83,490	1.43
South Carolina	169,593	92,942	1.82	125,657	35,087	3.58
Tennessee	221,717	156,267	1.42	124,558	43,877	2.84
Virginia	208,575	196,500	1.06	122,983	56,481	2.18
West Virginia	201,564	59,553	3.38	127,843	17,602	7.26

(continued)

Appendix Table 12-7 (continued)

	Based on Output Mix			Based on USDA Regions		
State or Region	**Spillins**	**Spillouts**	**Ratio**	**Spillins**	**Spillouts**	**Ratio**
Northeast	*millions of dollars (2000 prices)*			*millions of dollars (2000 prices)*		
Connecticut	140,614	38,402	3.66	103,101	19,719	5.23
Delaware	84,856	10,625	7.99	104,089	9,837	10.58
Maine	105,462	23,973	4.40	103,480	15,928	6.50
Maryland	176,650	78,438	2.25	101,691	33,817	3.01
Massachusetts	134,710	41,045	3.28	102,877	21,957	4.69
New Hampshire	152,564	20,575	7.42	104,096	9,765	10.66
New Jersey	135,181	69,611	1.94	101,307	37,663	2.69
New York	149,557	262,383	0.57	92,787	122,857	0.76
Pennsylvania	185,790	152,845	1.22	98,971	61,019	1.62
Rhode Island	118,793	10,932	10.87	104,412	6,613	15.79
Vermont	145,277	19,411	7.48	104,068	10,047	10.36
Simple average	*162,159*	*115,794*	*2.48*	*104,092*	*33,942*	*4.90*

Sources: Developed by the authors.

CHAPTER 13

Synthesis

The history of American agriculture is one of continuing growth and constant change. During the first three hundred years, beginning with the settlement at Jamestown in 1607, growth and development in U.S. agriculture was achieved by doing more with more, at the extensive margin. As the frontier expanded and more land was brought into production by more people, the number of farms and farmers grew. Over time, these farms became more productive through the development and adoption of a host of biological and mechanical innovations, mainly developed without much government involvement. Some of the earlier innovations are visibly evident today—such as barbed wire and steel plows. But many of the crop variety innovations were to counter co-evolving pest and disease pressures or to adapt varieties to new environments, and their impacts are not revealed in aggregate yields that grew very slowly before 1935.

The beginning of the 20th Century saw the beginnings of a new era of growth and development in U.S. agriculture. The frontier had closed and the period of land clearing and homesteading was coming to an end—although total land in farms did not peak until the 1940s. Agriculture entered a period of doing more with less through intensification of production on a constant and then shrinking land base while shedding labor through labor-saving innovations, reducing the number of farms and concomitantly increasing farm size (Schultz 1951). The closing of the frontier coincided with the opening of the era of organized agricultural science, a public and private enterprise that gained traction in the late-1800s and grew geometrically through most of the 20th Century. The consequences of that investment for U.S. agriculture are difficult to decipher and distinguish from other vectors of change; but there can be little doubt that the consequences were profound.

We have described the development of agriculture (Chapters 2 through 5) and documented the public investments in agricultural R&D in the United

J.M. Alston et al., *Persistence Pays: U.S. Agricultural Productivity Growth and the Benefits from Public R&D Spending*, Natural Resource Management and Policy 34, DOI 10.1007/978-1-4419-0658-8_13, © Springer Science + Business Media, LLC 2010

States over the past 100 years (Chapters 6 and 7); modeled and measured the consequences of those investments for agricultural production and productivity over the second half of the 20th Century (Chapters 8 through 10); expressed those consequences as benefit-cost ratios, interpreted those results, and explained their implications (Chapters 11 and 12). This chapter offers a summary and synthesis of the main findings, highlighting key points that distinguish the work in this book from previous work or that have particular implications for policy. The discussion here presents ideas and findings roughly in the order in which they were presented in the previous chapters, but some issues cross those boundaries. One such issue is presented next.

13.1 Factology

Studies of the relationship between research and productivity rely on the painstaking and demanding work of statisticians and economists who create the data on inputs and outputs required to analyze production relationships. In his Waugh Lecture to the American Agricultural Economics Association, Bruce Gardner discussed the importance of both the activity of creating data and of the point that econometricians and other data users should know how the data they use were created.

> Agricultural economists and other social scientists tend to take data as facts. . . . The problem is the data are not facts. Facts are what is really there. Data are quantitative representation of facts, which statistical workers and economists concoct (Gardner 1992, p. 1074).

> I call the study of how primary statistical information is made into economic data "factology." The neglect of factology risks scientific ruin (Gardner 1992, p. 1067).

Gardner drew specific attention to the measurement of agricultural inputs (especially capital), outputs, and productivity as instances where a lot of effort and judgment goes into the creation of the "data," such that the data themselves are very much transformed from the raw material used to make them, and consequently areas where factology matters more than most.

In his Presidential Address to the American Economic Association, Zvi Griliches made some similar points:

> We ourselves do not put enough emphasis on the value of data and data collection in our training of graduate students and in the reward structure of our profession. It is the preparation skill of the econometric chef that catches the professional eye, not the quality of

> the raw materials in the meal, or the effort that went into procuring them (Griliches, 1994, p. 14).
>
> [We] often misinterpret the available data because of inadequate attention to how they are produced and that same inattention by us to the sources of our data helps explain why progress [in understanding the sources of productivity growth] is so slow … . Great advances have been made in theory and in econometric techniques, but these will be wasted unless they are applied to the right data (Griliches, 1994, p. 2).

Unfortunately, too few practitioners have embraced the lessons from Gardner's Lecture and Griliches' Address. However, some progress has been made with developing and documenting improved measures of agricultural inputs, outputs, and productivity, and agricultural research investments, which are the raw materials for many studies of returns to agricultural R&D. In developing this book we spent a lot of effort on creating the data and documenting sources in the spirit of Gardner, and on understanding the data and matching them to the task at hand, in the spirit of Griliches.

Inputs, Outputs and Productivity

In Chapters 3, 4, and 5 we reported a variety of measures of quantities of inputs, outputs and productivity. In many cases these measures rest on an invisible raft of assumptions and methodological choices made by the unsung "statistical workers" to whom Gardner and Griliches referred in pointing out that both the effort to make the data, and the data-making decisions and their implications, deserve more acknowledgment than they typically receive.

In our attempt to discern what happened to inputs, outputs, and productivity in U.S. agriculture, among states and over time, and why, we paid a lot of attention to the the role of the data. In addition to dealing with widely-recognized problems in forming price and quantity indexes, we also grappled with a range of less-widely recognized aspects. These include the adjustment of prices and quantities to address changes in quality of inputs and outputs, the use of local rather than national prices, and myriad other choices that went into constructing the InSTePP data series. We analyzed how these types of data decisions, along with differences in underlying data sources and aggregation procedures, could account for the substantial unexplained differences between our InSTePP productivity indexes and their counterparts published by the USDA ERS (2008c).

Public and Private Agricultural R&D

Over the past century and a half, public participation in U.S. agricultural research and extension developed hand in hand with the private sector, and in concert with broader public science policy and spending decisions. The extent and form of that participation changed markedly over time. By 2007 the enterprise had grown to the point where an estimated $9.4 billion was spent on food and agricultural R&D performed in the United States.

Over time, along with the overall growth we saw an evolution in the balance of sources of funds and performing agencies, between intramural USDA research, research conducted by state agencies (i.e., the SAESs and other cooperating agencies), and research by the private sector. Beginning in the middle of the 19th Century, public spending on agricultural R&D grew rapidly, especially during the first three quarters of the 20th Century. Real public spending increased by an average of 4.99 percent per year from 1900 to 1970, growing faster than the real value of agricultural output. Since then, growth in public agricultural R&D spending has generally slowed; to 1.74 per year for the period 1970–1990, and 0.99 percent per year for the period 1990–2007. Prior to World War II, about half of public agricultural R&D was performed in federal government laboratories. The intramural share of public agricultural research peaked at 53 percent in 1941, and has trended downward since. In 2007, 33 percent of public agricultural research was conducted in federal laboratories and the remaining 67 percent was conducted in SAES facilities. Public-private shares have also changed, influenced by intellectual property policies and practices that expanded to encompass new forms of protection for plant and animal genetic innovations in the 1970s and 1980s. In 1960, the public share was 60 percent of the public- and private-sector total. Since then, the public-sector gave some ground, shrinking to just over 50 percent of the agricultural R&D total in 2006.

A distinguishing attribute of much agricultural R&D is its site-specificity, and so the conduct of agricultural R&D is geographically dispersed. Every state continues to support an agricultural experiment station. On average, the SAESs spent $67.8 million per state in 2007, but there was a large variation around that average (from $330.0 million in California to just $5.8 million in New Hampshire). The pattern of funding of agricultural research by the SAESs is not especially congruent with the distribution of the value of agricultural production among the states. Smaller agricultural states generally invested more intensively in agricultural research. For example, in 2003–05, the intensities ranged from $6.83 on public agricultural R&D per dollar of gross value of agricultural production for Rhode Island to $1.05 for California (and $0.67 for Iowa and $0.47 for South Dakota, the lowest intensities among states). Overall, the commodity orientation of public agricultural R&D has changed little. Crops research has constituted a fairly constant 40 to 44 percent of total research over the past several decades, with research on specialty crops being a fairly constant share of crop-specific research (about 35 percent). Around 26 percent of total agricultural R&D has been directed to livestock, with the balance (between 27–34 percent) going to "other," including non-commodity-specific, R&D. A notable development documented in this volume is the longer-run decline in the share of SAES research dedicated to maintaining or enhancing farm productivity (an estimated 66 percent of SAES research in 1975, down to 57 percent in 2007).

13.2 A Systematic Slowdown?

The data presented in Chapter 6 show an ever-shifting balance in the sources of funding for agricultural research and extension and in the performers of research and extension across the states and over time. While the long history has been one of strong growth in total spending on agricultural R&D, the more-recent picture is one of slowing growth, shifting of funding emphasis away from sources that support the traditional agenda, and a shifting of spending emphasis away from farm-productivity oriented R&D.

Changes in the path of research spending, beginning in the late 1970s, might have contributed to a slowdown in U.S. agricultural productivity growth beginning in the 1990s. In Chapter 5 we presented a comprehensive analysis of state-specific agricultural productivity patterns that indicates a very substantial, statistically significant slowdown in productivity growth. Specifically, across the 48 states for the period 1949–1990 multi-factor productivity grew at an average annual rate of 2.02 percent. Subsequently, across the 48 states for the period 1990–2002 multi-factor productivity grew at an average annual rate of 0.97 percent.

A similar slowdown is apparent in partial factor productivity measures that express an index of total output relative to use of land or labor rather than all inputs, and in crop yields. Less complete but otherwise similar evidence is available for some other more-developed countries, suggesting that we are experiencing a global slowdown in agricultural productivity growth, with China as a notable exception (Alston, Beddow and Pardey 2009). It remains to be seen how much of the U.S. agricultural productivity slowdown is temporary, perhaps as a result of a run of bad seasons, and how much of it will endure. The answer will depend on the importance of the past slowdown in spending on farm-productivity-oriented R&D as a contributing factor, which is difficult to identify with confidence and precision until more data become available.

13.3 Attribution

A host of attribution problems bedevil attempts to model the relationship between agricultural R&D and productivity, as discussed in Chapters 8 and 9. In applied economics generally it is difficult to attribute effect to cause in passively generated data; hence the current enthusiasm among economists for so-called "natural experiments" in which the causal variables of interest are subject to substantial exogenous shifts while other factors are relatively constant.

Unfortunately we are constrained to work on a problem for which the data were not generated by a convenient natural experiment, where the agricultural research and extension investments undertaken by individual U.S. states and the federal government have grown together, with very substantial common trends—albeit with some independent variation. We have much less-complete data on private agricultural research spending in the United States, and private and public research spending in other countries and international agencies. However, the limited data that are available suggest that these investments also have some common trends with U.S. public agricultural research and extension investments. Thus, we have common trends among included and omitted variables, potentially giving rise to multicollinearity among the included variables and omitted variables bias in the measured effects. In Chapters 10 and 11, we explore the implications of these data limitations for econometric estimates and benefit-cost ratios.

Counterfactuals

Alston and Pardey (2001, p. 142) phrased the "attribution problem" as follows: "We want to be able to say which research, conducted (or paid for) by whom, and, in particular, when, was responsible for a particular productivity improvement." This phrasing presupposes that it was research, and not something else, that caused the productivity growth in question. In developing our measures of productivity we took care to account for other possible sources of measured productivity growth, but we may not have completely succeeded. In particular the kinds of disorganized activities that were the main source of agricultural innovations for the first three hundred years of U.S. agriculture might have continued to contribute to productivity growth in the most recent hundred years. In addition weather patterns might involve cycles or trends that have implications for measured changes in productivity, especially over shorter intervals. In evaluating and interpreting our measures of benefits, in Chapter 12, we were conscious of these possibilities.

These aspects of the attribution problem relate to the more general problem of defining the relevant counterfactual alternative. Is it reasonable to conduct a benefit-cost analysis that assumes that the U.S. federal government investment in agricultural R&D would have been the same even if all of the states had invested nothing? The answer is almost surely no given the direct and indirect linkages between federal and state spending. Similarly, and perhaps more importantly in the present context, is it reasonable to assume that, in the absence of any agricultural research spending in the United States, agricultural yields and productivity would have remained constant? The answer is a resounding no. A substantial share of the total annual investment in agricultural R&D is "maintenance" research. This is particularly apparent for crop varieties, which are continually adapted and replaced to sustain yield gains in the face of coevolving pests and diseases that would otherwise cause yields to fall. Indeed, in the future, maintenance research may have to increase as a share of total agricultural research as more effort will be required to adapt varieties in the face of changes in climate and competing demands for water and other resources (Ruttan 1982, p. 60).

Research Lags

Much of our discussion of models in Chapters 8 through 10 was concerned with two other, perhaps related, elements of the attribution problem: namely, the specification of R&D lags (the temporal aspect) and the representation of spillovers (the spatial aspect). Agricultural research takes a long time to affect productivity and then it affects productivity for a long time. It is difficult, econometrically, to identify this lag relationship with the available data. Our econometric results in Chapter 10 support a model in which agricultural research affects subsequent productivity for up to 50 years, although in most of the cases we considered the main impacts were exhausted within 35 years. Our examination of technology timelines and evidence on the adoption processes for a range of agricultural technologies reinforces the view that the overall R&D lag must be much longer than allowed by many studies, and that lags in the range of 35–50 years are certainly plausible. The choice of lag model affects findings concerning the returns to research, and the relative importance of own-state investments versus spillover impacts from research undertaken in other states or by the federal government.

Spillovers

Technology spillovers arise when benefits from R&D are not confined to those who fund the research. The biological nature of agricultural production processes means that agricultural technologies tend to be specific to particular agroecological zones. Agroecological boundaries that define the economic potential of particular agricultural technologies do not match up to geopolitical boundaries that define the basis for decisions about which research to fund. The mismatching between the boundaries that are relevant to those who fund research, and the boundaries that define who benefits, introduces a spatial dimension to market failures in agricultural R&D. Individual state governments can address spatial spillovers within their own jurisdictions, but to address spillovers across states requires either a mechanism for cooperation among state governments or a higher level of government that encompasses the affected regions. A complicating factor both for managing and modeling spatial agricultural R&D spillovers is that there is not always a strong connection between spatial proximity and agroecological similarity. For instance, California has greater spillover potential with regions of other countries that have a Mediterranean climate, and with far distant states like Florida that also produce a lot of fruit and vegetables, than with adjacent states.

Our results in Chapters 10 through 12 show that spatial technology spillovers are a critical element of the picture in U.S. public agricultural R&D. In every state the own-state benefits from SAES research are less than the national benefits, and in some states, much less. Consequently, even if every state invested the amount that would maximize its own-state benefits from agricultural R&D, the result would be an underinvestment from a national perspective. Federal support for SAES research can be justified on these grounds. Our results indicate that even with substantial support from the federal government, most states substantially underinvest in agricultural R&D, in the sense that both the in-state and national returns well exceed the costs of additional investments in agricultural R&D. Spatial technology spillovers provide a justification for both federal support of SAES research and for intramural research conducted by the USDA—in some cases where technology might apply in many individual states, it makes economic sense to conduct the research nationally rather than to try to coordinate and stimulate the research activities of the states that have a common interest.

13.4 Research Returns

Our principal findings can be summarized as follows. First, using our preferred logarithmic model, of the agricultural productivity growth in the period 1949–2002 attributable to public research and extension (averaging 1.87 percent per year across the 48 states), 57 percent is accounted for by own-state research and extension. The remaining 43 percent is accounted for by research and extension conducted by other states (30 percent) or by USDA intramural research (13 percent). The amount of productivity growth accounted for by interstate spillovers and USDA intramural research combined is relatively constant across states (ranging from 0.79 to 0.82 percent per year). It is more variable as a share of total state-specific productivity growth attributable to research and extension, which varied from 1.38 to 2.42 percent per year. These findings mean that there are important differences between state-specific ("private") and national ("social") benefits from SAES research, and studies that do not account for spillovers are likely to suffer from econometric biases and lead to ill-founded policy prescriptions.

Second, our estimated marginal benefit-cost ratios reflect these spillover relationships, combined with the patterns of agricultural production and research spending across the states. The benefit-cost ratios vary substantially across states but there are some consistent patterns. Using a real discount rate of 3 percent per year, we estimated that federal intramural research yielded a national social benefit of $18 per dollar of additional research (from a small simulated increase in 1950) while for state-specific SAES research and extension, the national benefits ranged from $10 to $69 across the states, with an average of $32.[1] The total national benefits from SAES research include own-state benefits and spillover benefits combined. Every state had a benefit-cost ratio from own-SAES research and extension substantially greater than $1 per dollar of spending (the "private" own state benefit-cost ratios ranged from $2 to $58), and the average across the states was $21. These estimates of national own-state benefit-cost ratios (and the corresponding internal rates of return) are at the low end of the range compared with previous published results, reflecting our effort to minimize misattribution bias and other specification errors. Nevertheless, our results mean that from a national perspective, USDA intramural research and SAES research and extension in every state yielded high returns; i.e., that the nation has underinvested in these activities.

Our specific results obtained in this study have been conditioned by a host of assumptions that were imposed in the analysis. Some such assumptions were necessary to reduce the dimensions of the empirical problem, especially in relation to the nature of the research lag distribution, as has been long recognized in studies of returns to R&D. For instance, Griliches (1979) suggested that:

> ...it is probably best *to assume* a functional form for the lag distribution on the basis of prior knowledge and general considerations and not to expect the data to answer such fine questions. That is, a "solution" to the multicollinearity problem is a moderation of our demands on the data—our desires have to be kept within the bounds of our means (Griliches 1979, p. 106, emphasis in original).

In our particular setting, the potential problems of multicollinearity and identification were many times greater than in the typical study using a single time series; recall, we allowed for federal research plus research and extension in 48 states with interstate spillovers in every direction. Consequently, we imposed a great deal of structure on the estimates, and these impositions might have had significant implications for the particular results. While we examined the sensitivity of estimation results to some of the dimensions of the specification, and took comfort from the apparent robustness, we would suggest that any specific results ought to be used with caution, paying attention to the context in which they may be applicable.

Nevertheless we have presented compelling evidence that agricultural R&D conducted either federally or by individual states yields large benefits relative to

1 The corresponding national ("social") internal rates of return are 18.7 percent per year for USDA intramural research; for extension and SAES research they range from 15.3 to 29.1 percent per year, with an average across the states of 22.7 percent per year. The own-state ("private") SAES research range from 7.4 to 27.6 percent per year, with an average of 18.9 percent per year.

costs and that interstate spillovers (or multistate impacts more generally) are a very important element of the picture. In particular, as we showed in Chapter 12, the findings of high returns to agricultural R&D are driven primarily by fundamental factors. Specifically, agricultural productivity growth is very valuable relative to public agricultural R&D spending. Consequently, if the growth in value is attributable to that spending, it is inevitable that the measured benefit-cost ratio will be very large.

13.5 Prospects

Our observation of a productivity slowdown raises questions about the future. We projected productivity growth forward using our estimated econometric model under alternative assumptions about growth in spending on R&D. Importantly, given the long lags, it takes a long time for a change in spending to work through and engender a change in the productivity path. Even under optimistic assumptions about a restoration of growth in support for R&D oriented toward farm productivity enhancement, the projected path of productivity growth over the coming decades is much slower than the two percent per year that characterized the last half of the 20th Century. Sustaining even a rate of one percent per year, as during the most recent period of our data, may require a restoration of growth in funding that does not seem likely to be forthcoming in the present policy environment, given recent policy patterns and the prevailing general economic conditions.

In some senses, current concerns about a slowdown in agricultural productivity and a national underinvestment in agricultural R&D are like the current concerns about global climate change and polices to reduce atmospheric carbon. It is easy to deny the evidence or dismiss claims about the impacts as being overstated given that the linkages are difficult to prove unequivocally. Clearly, not everyone agrees about climate change or what to do about it; the same is true for agricultural R&D and productivity. In both cases, even if we are confident of net national benefits, the time lags between policy action and realizing benefits are long and uncertain, and we cannot be sure who, precisely, will reap those benefits. To many it may seem reasonable to say we can afford to wait until we have more information or a return to better economic times before we act to address this problem, which is really a problem for a future generation.

In the case of climate change, the public discourse and government policy have been shifting in a direction of consensus that the problem exists and the time to act to address it is now, though the extent of actual policy change has been small so far. In the case of agricultural R&D and productivity growth we are a long way from any consensus; even among agricultural economists, many seem to take for granted a continuation of past productivity growth. If that complacent confidence is not borne out, over the coming decades persistently slower productivity growth will have cumulative effects on the path of agricultural productivity, and thus on the production of food, the demand for resources to produce food, and the global supply and demand balance. The ultimate consequences will include faster rates of depletion of natural resource stocks and, nevertheless, higher rates of human suffering from poverty and malnutrition. These negative effects of a slower path of productivity growth will be significant, cumulative, pervasive, and difficult to reverse.

References

Abramovitz, M. 1956. "Resource and Output Trends in the United States since 1870." *American Economic Review* 46(2):5-23.

Acquaye, A.K. 2000. "Parametric and Nonparametric Measures of State-Level Productivity Growth and Technical Change in U.S. Agriculture: 1949-91." Unpublished PhD Dissertation, University of California, Davis.

Acquaye, A.K.A., J.M. Alston, and P.G. Pardey. 2002. "A Disaggregated Perspective on Post-War Productivity Growth in U.S. Agriculture: Isn't that Spatial?" Chapter 3 in V.E. Ball and G.W. Norton, eds., *Agricultural Productivity: Measurement and Sources of Growth.* Boston: Kluwer Academic Publishers.

Acquaye, A.K., J.M. Alston and P.G. Pardey. 2003. "Post-War Productivity Patterns in U.S. Agriculture: Influences of Aggregation Procedures in a State-Level Analysis." *American Journal of Agricultural Economics* 85(1):59-80.

Acquaye, A.K.A., J.M. Alston and P.G. Pardey. 2006. "Agricultural Productivity." Tables in S.B. Carter, S.S. Gartner, M.R. Haines, A.L. Olmstead, R. Sutch and G. Wright, eds., *Historical Statistics of the United States, Earliest Times to the Present: Millennial Edition, Volume 4, Part D, Economic Sectors.* Cambridge: Cambridge University Press.

Adams, J.D. 1990. "Fundamental Stocks of Knowledge and Productivity Growth." *Journal of Political Economy* 98(4):673-702.

Adusei, E.O. and G.W. Norton. 1990. "The Magnitude of Agricultural Maintenance Research in the USA." *Journal of Production Agriculture* 3(1):1-6.

Alston, J.M. 2002. "Spillovers." *Australian Journal of Agricultural and Resource Economics* 46(3):315-346.

Alston, J.M. 2007. "Benefits and Beneficiaries from U.S. Farm Subsidies." Working Paper developed for the AEI Project *Agricultural Policy for 2007 Farm Bill and Beyond.* Washington, DC: American Enterprise Institute for Public Policy. Available at http://aic.ucdavis.edu/research/farmbill07/aeibriefs/20070515_alstonSubsidiesfinal.pdf.

Alston, J.M., B.A. Babcock and P.G. Pardey. 2009 (forthcoming). *The Shifting Patterns of Agricultural Production and Productivity Worldwide.* Ames: MATRIC Electronic Book. Available at http://www.matric.iastate.edu/publications.aspx.

Alston, J.M., J.M. Beddow and P.G. Pardey. 2009 (forthcoming). "Mendel versus Malthus: Research, Productivity and Food Prices in the Long Run." Department of Applied Economics Staff Paper. St. Paul: University of Minnesota.

Alston, J.M., C. Chan-Kang, M.C. Marra, P.G. Pardey and T.J. Wyatt. 2000a. *A Meta Analysis of Rates of Return to Agricultural R&D: Ex Pede Herculem?* IFPRI Research Report No. 113. Washington, DC: International Food Policy Research Institute.

Alston, J.M., B.J. Craig and P.G. Pardey. 1998. "Dynamics in the Creation and Depreciation of Knowledge, and the Returns to Research." EPTD Discussion Paper No. 35. Washington, DC: International Food Policy Research Institute.

Alston, J.M., M.C. Marra, P.G. Pardey and T.J. Wyatt. 2000b. "Research Returns Redux: A Meta-Analysis of The Returns to Agricultural R&D." *Australian Journal of Agricultural and Resource Economics* 44(2):185-215.

Alston, J.M., G.W. Norton and P.G. Pardey. 1995. *Science under Scarcity: Principles and Practice for Agricultural Research Evaluation and Priority Setting.* Ithaca: Cornell University Press (re-printed in soft cover by CAB International 1998).

Alston, J.M. and P.G. Pardey. 1996. *Making Science Pay: Economics of Agricultural R&D Policy.* Washington, DC: American Enterprise Institute for Public Policy.

Alston, J.M. and P.G. Pardey. 1999. "The Economics of Agricultural R&D Policy." Chapter 2 in J.M. Alston, P.G. Pardey and V.H. Smith, eds., *Paying for Agricultural Productivity.* Baltimore: Johns Hopkins University Press.

Alston, J.M. and P.G. Pardey. 2001. "Attribution and Other Problems in Assessing the Returns to Agricultural R&D." *Agricultural Economics* 25(2-3):141-152.

Alston, J.M. and P.G. Pardey. 2006a. "Agricultural Productivity." Essay in S.B. Carter, S.S. Gartner, M.R. Haines, A.L. Olmstead, R. Sutch and G. Wright, eds., *Historical Statistics of the United States, Earliest Times to the Present: Millennial Edition, Volume 4, Part D, Economic Sectors.* Cambridge: Cambridge University Press.

Alston, J.M. and P.G. Pardey. 2006b. "Productivity and Investments." In S.B. Carter, S.S. Gartner, M.R. Haines, A.L. Olmstead, R. Sutch and G. Wright, eds., *Historical Statistics of the United States, Earliest Times to the Present: Millennial Edition, Volume 4, Part D, Economic Sectors.* Cambridge: Cambridge University Press.

Alston, J.M. and P.G. Pardey. 2008. "Public Funding for Research into Specialty Crops." *Hort-Science* 43(5):1461-1470.

Alston, J.M., P.G. Pardey and H.O. Carter, eds. 1994. *Valuing UC Agricultural Research and Extension.* Davis: University of California, Agricultural Issues Center.

Alston, J.M., P.G. Pardey and V.W. Ruttan. 2008. "Research Lags Revisited: Concepts and Evidence from U.S. Agriculture." Department of Applied Economics Staff Paper P08-14. St. Paul: University of Minnesota.

Alston, J.M., P.G. Pardey, S. Wood and L. You. 2009 (forthcoming). "Projecting Agricultural R&D Potentials." Chapter in P.G. Pardey, S. Wood and R. Hertford, eds., *Research Futures: Projecting Agricultural R&D Potentials for Latin America and the Caribbean.* Washington, DC and St. Paul: Inter-American Development Bank with the Regional Fund for Agricultural Technology, International Food Policy Research Institute and International Science and Technology Practice and Policy Center, University of Minnesota.

Alston, J.M. and R.J. Venner. 2002. "The Effects of the US Plant Variety Protection Act on Wheat Genetic Improvement." *Research Policy* 31(4):527-542.

Andersen, M.A. 2005. "Pro-Cyclical Productivity Patterns in U.S. Agriculture." Unpublished PhD Dissertation, University of California, Davis.

Andersen, M.A, J.M. Alston and P.G. Pardey. 2007. "Capital Use Intensity and Productivity Biases." Department of Applied Economics Staff Paper No. P07-06. St. Paul: University of Minnesota.

Andersen, M.A., J.M. Alston and P.G. Pardey. 2009. "Capital Service Flows: Concepts and Comparisons of Alternative Measures in U.S. Agriculture." Department of Applied Economics Staff Paper No. P09-8. St. Paul: University of Minnesota.

Araji, A.A., F.C. White and J.F. Guenthner. 1995. "Spillovers and the Returns to Agricultural Research for Potatoes." *Journal of Agricultural and Resource Economics* 20(2):263-276.

Atwater, W.O. 1891. "Report of the Director of the Office of Experiment Stations for 1890." In *Report of the Secretary of Agriculture for 1890.* United States Department of Agriculture. Washington: Government Printing Office.

Baker, G.L., W.D. Rasmussen, V. Wiser and J.M. Porter. 1963. *Century of Service: The First 100 Years of the United States Department of Agriculture.* Washington, DC: Government Printing Office.

Ball, V.E. 1984. "Measuring Agricultural Productivity: A New Look." USDA Economic Research Service Staff Report AGES 840330. Washington, DC: United States Department of Agriculture.

Ball, V.E. 1985. "Output, Input, and Productivity Measurement in U.S. Agriculture: 1948-79." *American Journal of Agricultural Economics* 67(3):475-486.

Ball, V.E., J.C. Bureau, R. Nehring and A. Somwaru. 1997. "Agricultural Productivity Revisited." *American Journal of Agricultural Economics* 79(4):1045-1063.

Ball, V.E., J.-P. Butault, and R. Nehring. 2001. *U.S. Agriculture, 1960-96: A Multilateral Comparison of Total Factor Productivity.* USDA Technical Bulletin No. 1895. Washington, DC: United States Department of Agriculture.

Ball, V.E., F.M. Gollop, A. Kelly-Hawke and G.P. Swinand. 1999. "Patterns of State Productivity Growth in the U.S. Farm Sector: Linking State and Aggregate Models." *American Journal of Agricultural Economics* 81(1):164-179.

Ball, V.E., C.A.K. Lovell, H. Luu and R. Nehring. 2004. "Incorporating Environmental Impacts in the Measurement of Agricultural Productivity Growth." *Journal of Agricultural and Resource Economics* 29(3):436-460.

Ball, V.E. and G.W. Norton. 2002. *Agricultural Productivity: Measurement and Sources of Growth.* Boston: Kluwer Academic Publishers.

Ballester, M., M. Garcia-Ayuso and J. Livnat. 2003. "The Economic Value of the R&D Intangible Asset." *European Accounting Review* 12(4):605-633.

Barfield, C.E., ed. 1997. *Science for the 21st Century: The Bush Report Revisited.* Washington, DC: American Enterprise Institute.

Barton, G.T. and M.R. Cooper. 1948. "Relation of Agricultural Production to Inputs." *Review of Economics and Statistics* 30(2):117-126.

Barton, G.T and D.D. Durost. 1960. "The New USDA Index of Inputs." *Journal of Farm Economics* 42(5):1398-1410.

Baum, T.E.L. and S.L. Clement. 1958. "The Changing Structure of the Fertilizer Industry in the United States." *Journal of Farm Economics* 40(5):1186-1198.

Bayoumi, T., D.T. Coe and E. Helpman. 1999. "R&D Spillovers and Global Growth." *Journal of International Economics* 47(2):399-428.

BEA (Bureau of Economic Analysis). 2007a. "National Income and Product Accounts (NIPA) Tables." Washington, DC: United States Department of Commerce. Obtained August 2007 from http://www.bea.gov/national/nipaweb.

BEA (Bureau of Economic Analysis). 2007b. "Current Dollar and Real Gross Domestic Product." Washington, DC: United States Department of Commerce. Obtained March 2007 from http://www.bea.gov/national/xls/gdplev.xls.

BEA (Bureau of Economic Analysis). 2007c. "Gross-Domestic-Product-by-Industry Accounts." Washington, DC: United States Department of Commerce. Obtained August 2007 from http://www.bea.gov/industry/gpotables/gpo_action.cfm.

BEA (Bureau of Economic Analysis). 2008a. *A Guide to the National Income and Product Accounts.* Washington, DC: United States Department of Commerce. Obtained May 2008 from http://www.bea.gov/national/pdf/nipaguid.pdf.

BEA (Bureau of Economic Analysis). 2008b. "National Income and Product Accounts (NIPA) Table: Table 1.1.9. Implicit Price Deflators for Gross Domestic Product." Washington, DC: United States Department of Commerce. Obtained December 2008 from http://www.bea.gov/national/nipaweb/selecttable.asp.

Beddow, J.M., P.G. Pardey and T.M. Hurley. 2009. "Space, Time and Crop Yield Variability: An Economic Perspective." Paper presented at the 53rd Annual Conference of the Australian Agricultural and Resource Economics Society (AARES), Cairns, Queensland, February.

Benedict, M.R. 1953. *Farm Policies of the United States, 1790-1950: A Study of the Origins and Developments.* New York: Twentieth Century Fund.

Bernstein, J.I. 1989. "The Structure of Canadian Inter-Industry R&D Spillovers, and the Rates of Return to R&D." *Journal of Industrial Economics* 37(3):315-328.

Bernstein, J.I. and T.P. Mamuneas. 2006. "R&D Depreciation, Stocks, User Costs and Productivity Growth for US R&D Intensive Industries." *Structural Change and Economic Dynamics* 17(1):70-98.

Bernstein, J.I. and M.I. Nadiri. 1988. "Interindustry R&D Spillovers, Rates of Return, and Production in High-Tech Industries." *American Economic Review* 78(2):429-434.

Bernstein, J.I. and M.I. Nadiri. 1989. "Research and Development and Intra-Industry Spillovers: An Empirical Application of Dynamic Duality." *Review of Economic Studies* 56(2):249-267.

Binswanger, H.P. 1974a. "A Microeconomic Approach to Induced Innovation." *Economic Journal* 84(336):940-958.

Binswanger, H.P. 1974b. "The Measurement of Technical Change Biases with Many Factors of Production." *American Economic Review* 64(6):964-976.

Binswanger, H.P. 1974c. "A Cost Function Approach to the Measurement of Elasticities of Factor Demand and Elasticities of Substitution." *American Journal of Agricultural Economics* 56(2):377-386.

BLS (Bureau of Labor Statistics). 1989. *The Impact of Research and Development on Productivity Growth.* Bulletin No. 2331. Washington, DC: United States Department of Labor.

BLS (Bureau of Labor Statistics). 1992. Unpublished Computer Run on U.S. Agricultural Multifactor Productivity, 1948-90. United States Department of Labor, Washington, DC.

Bonnen, J.T. 1986. "A Century of Science in Agriculture: Lessons for Science Policy." *American Journal of Agricultural Economics* 68(5):1065-1080.

Borlaug, N. 1982. "Feeding Mankind in the 1980s: The Role of International Agricultural Research." Session II in T.J. Davis, ed., *Increasing Agricultural Productivity.* Proceedings of the Third Annual Agricultural Sector Symposium. World Bank Technical Paper No. 1. Washington, DC: World Bank.

Bouchet, F., D. Orden and G.W. Norton. 1989. "Sources of Growth in French Agriculture." *American Journal of Agricultural Economics* 71(2):280-293.

Boulding, K.E. 1966. "The Economics of Knowledge and the Knowledge of Economics." *American Economic Review* 56(1/2):1-13.

Brandt, J.A., and B.C. French. 1981. *An Analysis of Economic Relationships and Projected Adjustments in the U.S. Processing Tomato Industry.* Giannini Foundation Research Report No. 331. Davis: University of California.

Bredahl, M.E., W.K. Bryant and V.W. Ruttan. 1980. "Behavior and Productivity Implications of Institutional and Project Funding of Research." *American Journal of Agricultural Economics* 62(3):599-602.

Brennan, J.P. 2007. "Beyond Semi-Dwarf Wheat Yield Increases: Impacts on the Australian Wheat Industry of On-Going Spillovers from the International Maize and Wheat Improvement Center." *Australian Journal of Agricultural and Resource Economics* 51(4):385-401.

Brennan, J.P. and M.C.S. Bantilan. 1999. *Impact of ICRISAT Research on Australian Agriculture.* Report prepared for Australian Centre for International Agricultural Research. Economic Research Report No. 1. Wagga Wagga, Australia: New South Wales Department of Agriculture.

Brennan, J.P. and P.N. Fox. 1995. *Impact of CIMMYT Wheats in Australia: Evidence of International Research Spillovers.* Economics Research Report No. 1/95. Wagga Wagga, Australia: New South Wales Department of Agriculture.

Brennan, J.P., I.P. Singh and L.G. Lewin. 1997. "Identifying International Rice Research Spillovers in New South Wales." *Agricultural Economics* 17(1):35-44.

Breusch, T.S. and A.R. Pagan. 1980. "The Lagrange Multiplier Test and its Applications to Model Specification in Econometrics." *Review of Economic Studies* 47(1):239-253.

Brodell, A.P. and A.R. Kendell. 1950. *Life of Farm Tractors.* Bureau of Agricultural Economics FM Report No. 80. Washington, DC: United States Department of Agriculture.

Brown, M. and A. Conrad. 1967. "The Influence of Research on CES Production Relations." Chapter in M. Brown, ed., *The Theory and Empirical Analysis of Production: Studies in Income and Wealth, Volume 3.* New York: Columbia University Press for National Bureau of Economic Research.

Brown, R.S. 1978. "Productivity, Returns and the Structure of Production in U.S. Agriculture, 1947-74." Unpublished PhD Dissertation, University of Wisconsin, Madison.

Butler, L.J. and B.W. Marion. 1985. *The Impacts of Patent Protection on the US Seed Industry and Private Breeding.* North Central Research Publication 304, North Central Project No. 117, Monograph 16. Madison: University of Wisconsin.

Caballero, R.J. and A.B. Jaffe. 1993. "How High are the Giants' Shoulders: An Empirical Assessment of Knowledge Spillovers and Creative Destruction in a Model of Economic Growth." Chapter in O. Blanchard and S. Fischer, eds., *National Bureau of Economic Research Macroeconomics Annual, Volume 8.* Cambridge: MIT Press.

Calderini, D.F. and G.A. Slafer. 1998. "Changes in Yield and Yield Stability in Wheat during the 20th Century." *Field Crops Research* 57:335-347.

Capalbo, S.M. 1988. "A Comparison of Econometric Models of U.S. Agricultural Productivity and Aggregate Technology." Chapter in S.M. Capalbo, and J.M. Antle, eds., *Agricultural Productivity: Measurement and Explanation.* Washington DC: Resources for the Future.

Capalbo, S.M. and M. Denny. 1986. "Testing Long-Run Productivity Models for the Canadian and U.S. Agricultural Sectors." *American Journal of Agricultural Economics* 68(3):615-625.

Capalbo, S.M, and T.T. Vo. 1988. "A Review of the Evidence on Agricultural Productivity and Aggregate Technology." Chapter 3 in S.M. Capalbo, and J.M. Antle, eds., *Agricultural Productivity: Measurement and Explanation.* Washington, DC: Resources for the Future.

Carson, C.S., B.T. Grimm and C.E. Moylan. 1994. "A Satellite Account for Research and Development." *Survey of Current Business, Bureau of Economic Analysis.* Washington, DC: United States Department of Commerce, pp. 37-71.

Chan-Kang, C. and P.G. Pardey. 2009 (in preparation). "A Century of Wheat Varietal Innovation in the United States: an Empirical Assessment." Department of Applied Economics Staff Paper. St. Paul: University of Minnesota.

Chavas, J.-P. and T.L. Cox. 1992. "A Nonparametric Analysis of the Influence of Research on Agricultural Productivity." *American Journal of Agricultural Economics* 74(3):583-591.

Clifton, R.T. 1970. *Barbs, Prongs, Points, Prickers, and Stickers: A Complete and Illustrated Catalogue of Antique Barb Wire.* Norman: University of Oklahoma Press.

Cochrane, W.W. 1958. *Farm Prices: Myth and Reality.* Minneapolis: University of Minnesota Press.

Cochrane, W.W. 1993. *The Development of American Agriculture: A Historical Analysis.* Second edition. Minneapolis: University of Minnesota Press.

Coe, D.T. and E. Helpman. 1995. "International R&D Spillovers." *European Economic Review* 39(5):859-887.

Coe, D.T., E. Helpman and A.W. Hoffmaister. 1997. "North-South R&D Spillovers." *Economic Journal* 107(440):134-149.

Cooke, K.J. 2002. "Expertise, Book Farming, and Government Agriculture: The Origins of Agricultural Seed Certification in the United States." *Agricultural History* 76(3):524-545.

Cooper, M.R., G.T. Barton and A.P. Brodell. 1947. *Progress of Farm Mechanization.* Miscellaneous Publication No. 630. Washington, DC: United States Department of Agriculture.

Cox, T.L. and J.P Chavas. 1990 "A Non-Parametric Analysis of Productivity: The Case of U.S. Agriculture." *European Review of Agricultural Economics* 17(4)449-464.

Craig, B.J. and P.G. Pardey. 1990. "Multidimensional Output Indices." Department of Applied Economics Staff Paper. St. Paul: University of Minnesota.

Craig, B.J. and P.G. Pardey. 1996a. "Inputs, Outputs, and Productivity Developments in U.S. Agriculture." Contributed Paper in *Proceedings of the Conference on Global Agricultural Science Policy for the Twenty-First Century,* Melbourne, Australia.

Craig, B.J. and P.G. Pardey. 1996b. "Productivity Measurement in the Presence of Quality Change." *American Journal of Agricultural Economics* 78(5):1349-1354.

Daberkow, S. and W. Huang. 2006. "Nutrient Management." Chapter 4.4 in K. Wiebe and N. Gollehon, eds., *Agricultural Resources and Environmental Indicators, 2006 Edition.* Economic Information Bulletin No. 16. Washington, DC: United States Department of Agriculture, Economic Research Service. Obtained December 2008 from http://www.ers.usda.gov/publications/arei/eib16/.

Dalrymple, D.G. 2004. "Biological Research and Agricultural Productivity: The Timeless Wisdom of the Red Queen." Paper presented at All-University of California Twenty Fifth Anniversary Conference on Economic History, Davis.

Davey, M.E. 1994. *Research and Funding, Fiscal Year 1995.* CRS Issue Brief. Washington, DC: Library of Congress, Congressional Research Service.

David, P.A. 1966. "The Mechanization of Reaping in the Ante-Bellum Midwest." Chapter in H. Rosovsky, ed., *Industrialization in Two Systems: Essays in Honor of Alexander Gerschenkron.* New York: Wiley and Sons.

Davis, J.S. 1980. "A Note on the Use of Alternative Lag Structures for Research Expenditure in Aggregate Production Function Models." *Canadian Journal of Agricultural Economics* 28(2):72-76.

Day-Rubenstein, K. and K.O. Fuglie. 2000. "The CRADA Model for Public-Private Research and Technology Transfer in Agriculture." Chapter 8 in K.O. Fuglie and D.E. Schimmelpfennig, eds., *Public-Private Collaboration in Agricultural Research: New Institutional Arrangements and Economic Implications.* Ames: Iowa State University Press.

Day-Rubenstein, K, P.W. Heisey, C. Klotz-Ingram and G.B. Frisvold. 2000. "Competitive Grants and the Funding of Agricultural Research in the U.S." Paper presented at American Agricultural Economics Association annual meetings, Tampa.

Dehmer, S. and P.G. Pardey. 2010 (in preparation). "Private Agricultural R&D in the United States, 1950-2006." Department of Applied Economics Staff Paper. St. Paul: University of Minnesota.

Dimitri, C., A. Effland, and N. Conklin. 2005. *The 20th Century Transformation of U.S. Agriculture and Farm Policy.* Economic Information Bulletin No. 3. Washington, DC: United States Department of Agriculture, Economic Research Service.

Dixon, R. 1980. "Hybrid Corn Revisited." *Econometrica* 48(6):1451-1461.

DOD (Department of Defense). 2008. *Fiscal Year 2008: Agency Financial Report.* Washington, DC: Department of Defense. Obtained May 2009 from http://www.defenselink.mil/comptroller/afr.

Doll, J.P. 1967. "An Analytical Technique for Estimating Weather Indexes from Meteorological Measurements." *Journal of Farm Economics* 49(1):79-88.

Dorfman, J.H. and K.A. Foster. 1991. "Estimating Productivity Changes with Flexible Coefficients." *Western Journal of Agricultural Economics* 16(2):280-290.

Durost, D.D and G.T. Barton. 1960. *Changing Sources of Farm Output.* Production Research Report No. 36. Washington, DC: United States Department of Agriculture.

Dutfield, G. 2002. "Trade, Intellectual Property and Biogenetic Resources: A Guide to the International Regulatory Framework." Background paper for *Multi-Stakeholder Dialogue on Trade, Intellectual Property and Biological and Genetic Resources in Asia.* Geneva: International Centre for Trade and Sustainable Development.

Duvick, D.N. 2001. "Biotechnology in the 1930s: The Development of Hybrid Maize." *Nature Reviews-Genetics* 2:69-74.

Emmons III, W.M. 1993. "Franklin D. Roosevelt, Electric Utilities, and the Power of Competition." *Journal of Economic History* 53(4):880-907.

Englander, A.S., R.E. Evenson and M. Hanazaki. 1988. "R&D, Innovation and the Total Factor Productivity Slowdown." *OECD Economic Studies* 11:7-42.

Evans, L.T. 1993. "Increases in Yield: Trends and Limits." Chapter in L.T. Evans, ed., *Crop Evolution, Adaptation and Yield.* Cambridge: Cambridge University Press.

Evenson, R.E. 1967. "The Contribution of Agricultural Research to Production." *Journal of Farm Economics* 49(5):1415-1425.

Evenson, R.E. 1988. "Research, Extension, and U.S. Agricultural Productivity: A Statistical Decomposition Analysis." Chapter 10 in S.M. Capalbo and J.M. Antle, eds., *Agricultural Productivity Measurement and Explanation.* Washington, DC: Resources for the Future.

Evenson, R.E. 1989. "Spillover Benefits of Agricultural Research: Evidence from US Experience." *American Journal of Agricultural Economics* 71(2):447-452.

Evenson, R.E. 1996. "Two Blades of Grass: Research for U.S. Agriculture." Chapter 11 in J.M. Antle and D.A. Sumner, eds., *The Economics of Agriculture, Volume 2, Papers in Honor of D. Gale Johnson.* Chicago: University of Chicago Press.

Evenson, R.E. 2002. "Economic Impacts of Agricultural Research and Extension." Chapter 11 in B.L. Gardner and G.C. Rausser, eds., *Handbook of Agricultural Economics, Volume 1A: Agricultural Production.* New York: Elsevier.

Evenson, R.E. and Y. Kislev. 1973. "Research and Productivity in Wheat and Maize." *Journal of Political Economy* 81(6):1309-1329.

Evenson, R.E. and Y. Kislev. 1975. *Agricultural Research and Productivity.* New Haven: Yale University Press.

FAO (Food and Agriculture Organization of the United Nations). 2008. FAOSTAT database. Rome: Food and Agriculture Organization. Obtained October 2008 from http://faostat.fao.org.

FAO (Food and Agriculture Organization of the United Nations). 2009. FAOSTAT database. Rome: Food and Agriculture Organization. Obtained August 2009 from http://faostat.fao.org.

Feder, G. and G.T. O'Mara. 1982. "On Information and Innovation Diffusion: A Bayesian Approach." *American Journal of Agricultural Economics* 64(1):145-147.

Foley, J.A., R. DeFries, G.P. Asner, C. Barford, G. Bonan, S.R. Carpenter, F.S. Chapin, M.T. Coe, G.C. Daily, H.K. Gibbs, J.H. Helkowski, T. Holloway, E.A. Howard, C.J. Kucharik, C. Monfreda, J.A. Patz, I.C. Prentice, N. Ramankutty and P.K. Snyder. 2005. "Global Consequences of Land Use." *Science* 309(5734):570-574.

Fowler, C. 1994. *Unnatural Selection: Technology, Politics, and Plant Evolution.* Yverdon, Switzerland: Gordon and Breach.

Fox, A.S. 1966. *Demand for Farm Tractors in the United States: A Regression Analysis*. Agricultural Economic Report No. 103. Washington, DC: United States Department of Agriculture, Economic Research Service.

Fuglie, K., N. Ballenger, K. Day, C. Klotz, M. Ollinger, J. Reilly, U. Vasavada and J. Yee. 1996. *Agricultural Research and Development: Public and Private Investments Under Alternative Markets and Institutions.* Agricultural Economic Report No. 735. Washington, DC: United States Department of Agriculture, Economic Research Service.

Fuglie, K.O. and P.W. Heisey. 2007. *Economic Returns to Public Agricultural Research.* Economic Brief No. 10. Washington, DC: United States Department of Agriculture, Economic Research Service.

Fuglie, K.O., J.M. MacDonald and E. Ball 2007. *Productivity Growth in U.S. Agriculture.* Economic Brief No. 9. Washington, DC: United States Department of Agriculture, Economic Research Service.

Gardner, B.L. 1992. "How the Data We Make Can Unmake Us: Annals of Factology." *American Journal of Agricultural Economics* 74(5):1066-1075.

Gardner, B.L. 2000. "Economic Growth and Low Incomes in Agriculture." *American Journal of Agricultural Economics* 82(5):1059-1074.

Gardner, B.L. 2002. *American Agriculture in the Twentieth Century: How It Flourished and What It Cost.* Cambridge: Harvard University Press.

Goldin, C. 2006. "Years of School Completed, by Sex, Race, and Ethnicity: 1940-1997." Table Bc 737-792 in S.B. Carter, S.S. Gartner, M.R. Haines, A.L. Olmstead, R. Sutch and G. Wright, eds., *Historical Statistics of the United States, Earliest Times to the Present: Millennial Edition.* New York: Cambridge University Press.

Goldin, H.H. 1947. "Governmental Policy and the Domestic Telegraph Industry." *Journal of Economic History* 7(1):53-68.

Greene, W.H. 2000. *Econometric Analysis, 4th Edition.* New Jersey: Prentice Hall.

Griliches, Z. 1957a. "Hybrid Corn: An Exploration in the Economics of Technological Change." *Econometrica* 25(4):501-522.

Griliches, Z. 1957b. "Specification Bias in Estimates of Production Functions." *Journal of Farm Economics* 39(1):8-20.

Griliches, Z. 1958. "The Demand for Fertilizer: An Economic Interpretation of a Technical Change." *Journal of Farm Economics* 40(3):591-606.

Griliches, Z. 1960a. "Estimates of the Aggregate U.S. Farm Supply Function." *Journal of Farm Economics* 42(2):282-293.

Griliches, Z. 1960b. "Measuring Inputs in Agriculture: A Critical Survey." *Journal of Farm Economics* 42(5):1411-1427.

Griliches, Z. 1960c. "The Demand for a Durable Input: Farm Tractors in the United States, 1921-57." Chapter in A.C. Harberger, ed., *The Demand for Durable Goods.* Chicago: University of Chicago Press.

Griliches, Z. 1961. "Comment" on D. Creamer "An Appraisal of Long-Term Capital Estimates: Some Reference Notes." In The Conference on Research in Income and Wealth, *Output, Input and Productivity Measurement: Studies in Income and Wealth, Volume 25.* Princeton: Princeton University Press for National Bureau of Economic Research.

Griliches, Z. 1963. "The Sources of Measured Productivity Growth: United States Agriculture, 1940-60." *Journal of Political Economy* 71(4):331-346.

Griliches, Z. 1964. "Research Expenditures, Education and the Aggregate Agricultural Production Function." *American Economic Review* 54(6):961-974.

Griliches, Z. 1979. "Issues in Assessing the Contribution of R&D to Productivity Growth." *Bell Journal of Economics* 10(1):92-116.

Griliches, Z. 1980a. "Hybrid Corn Revisited: Reply." *Econometrica* 48(6):1463-1465.

Griliches, Z. 1980b. "Returns to Research and Development Expenditures in the Private Sector." Chapter 8 in J. Kendrick and B. Vaccara, eds., *New Developments in Productivity Measurement and Analysis.* Chicago: University of Chicago Press for the National Bureau of Economic Research.

Griliches, Z. 1986. "Productivity, R&D, and Basic Research at the Firm Level in the 1970s." *American Economic Review* 76(1):141-154.

Griliches, Z. 1992. "The Search for R&D Spillovers." *Scandinavian Journal of Economics* 94(supplement):S29-S47.

Griliches, Z. 1994. "Productivity, R&D, and the Data Constraint." *American Economic Review* 84(1):1-23.

Griliches, Z. 1996. "R&D and Productivity: The Unfinished Business." Chapter in Z. Griliches, *R&D and Productivity: The Econometric Evidence.* Chicago: Chicago University Press.

Griliches, Z. 2001. "Issues in Agricultural Productivity Measurement." Chapter 3 in J.M. Alston, P.G. Pardey and M.J. Taylor, eds., *Agricultural Science Policy: Changing Global Agendas.* Baltimore: Johns Hopkins University Press.

Gutierrez, C.N., C.A. Glassman, J.S. Landefeld and R.D. Marcuss. 2007. *An Introduction to the National Income and Product Accounts.* Washington, DC: United States Department of Commerce. Obtained May 2008 from http://www.bea.gov/scb/pdf/national/nipa/methpap/mpi1_0907.pdf.

Haines, M.R. 2006. "Population, by Age: 1900-2000 [Annual estimates]." Table Aa 125-144 in S.B. Carter, S.S. Gartner, M.R. Haines, A.L. Olmstead, R. Sutch and G. Wright, eds., *Historical Statistics of the United States, Earliest Times to the Present: Millennial Edition.* New York: Cambridge University Press.

Haines, M.R. and R. Sutch. 2006. "Population: 1790-2000 [Annual estimates]." Table Aa 6-8 in S.B. Carter, S.S. Gartner, M.R. Haines, A.L. Olmstead, R. Sutch and G. Wright, eds., *Historical Statistics of the United States, Earliest Times to the Present: Millennial Edition.* New York: Cambridge University Press.

Hall, B.H. 2006. "R&D, Productivity and Market Value." IFS Working Papers W06/23. London: Institute for Fiscal Studies.

Hall, B.H. 2007. "Measuring the Returns to R&D: The Depreciation Problem." NBER Working Paper 13473. Washington, DC: National Bureau of Economic Research.

Hall, B.H. and J. Mairesse. 1995. "Exploring the Relationship between R&D and Productivity in French Manufacturing Firms." *Journal of Econometrics* 65(1):263-293.

Hall, J. and G.M. Scobie. 2006. "The Role of R&D in Productivity Growth: The Case of Agriculture in New Zealand: 1927 to 2001." New Zealand Treasury Working Paper 06/01. Wellington, New Zealand: The Treasury.

Hall, R. 1994. "It's Done—And Now We're Starting to Implement our Reorganization." *USDA News* 53(5). Washington, DC: United States Department of Agriculture, Office of Communications.

Hanson, R. and S. Highlander. 2004. "Protecting Plant Inventions." Chapter in A. Hopkins, Z.Y. Wang, R. Mian, M. Sledge and R.E. Barker, eds., *Molecular Breeding of Forage and Turf.* Dordrecht: Kluwer Academic Publishers.

Hardman, L.L. and D.L. Hansen. 2006. *Genetics to Genomics: Landmark Discoveries from the Minnesota Agricultural Experiment Station.* St. Paul: University of Minnesota.

Harris, A.W. 1892 and 1893. "Report of the Director of the Office of Experiment Stations for [1891 and 1892]." In *Report of the Secretary of Agriculture for [1891 and 1892].* United States Department of Agriculture. Washington: Government Printing Office.

Hathaway, D.E. 1959. "Agriculture in an Unstable Economy Revisited." *Journal of Farm Economics* 41(3):487-499.

Hausman, J.A. 1978. "Specification Tests in Econometrics." *Econometrica* 46(6):1251-1271.

Hayami, Y. 1969. "Resource Endowments and Technological Change in Agriculture: U.S. and Japanese Experiences in International Perspective." *American Journal of Agricultural Economics* 51(5):1293-1303.

Hayami, Y. and V.W. Ruttan. 1970. "Factor Prices and Technical Change in Agricultural Development: The United States and Japan: 1880-1960." *Journal of Political Economy* 78(5):1115-1141.

Hayami, Y. and V.W. Ruttan. 1971. *Agricultural Development: An International Perspective.* Baltimore: Johns Hopkins University Press. (reprinted 1985).

Heim, M.N. and L.L. Blakeslee. 1986. "Biological Adaptation and Research Impacts on Wheat Yields in Washington." Paper presented at American Agricultural Economics Association annual meetings, Reno.

Homer, C., J. Dewitz, J. Fry, M. Coan, N. Hossain, C. Larson, N. Herold, A. McKerrow, J.N. Van Driel and J. Wickham. 2007. "Completion of the 2001 National Land Cover Database for the Conterminous United States." *Photogrammetric Engineering and Remote Sensing* 73:337-341.

Hoppe, R.A., ed. 2001. *Structural and Financial Characteristics of U.S. Farms: 2001 Family Farm Report.* AIB-768. Washington, DC: United States Department of Agriculture, Economic Research Service.

Hoppe, R.A. and P. Korb. 2006. *Understanding U.S. Farm Exits.* Economic Research Report No. 21. Washington, DC: United States Department of Agriculture, Economic Research Service.

Hoppe, R.A., P. Korb, E.J. O'Donoghue and D.E. Banker. 2007. *Structure and Finances of U.S. Farms: Family Farm Report, 2007 Edition.* Economic Information Bulletin No. 24. Washington, DC: United States Department of Agriculture, Economic Research Service.

Houck, J.P. and P.W. Gallagher. 1976. "The Price Responsiveness of U.S. Corn Yields." *American Journal of Agricultural Economics* 58(4, Part 1):731-734.

Huang, N. and E. Diewert. 2007. "Estimation of R&D Depreciation Rates for the U.S. Manufacturing Sector and Four Knowledge Intensive Industries." Paper prepared for Sixth Annual Ottawa Productivity Workshop, Bank of Canada.

Huffman, W.E. 2009. "Measuring Public Agricultural Research Capital and Its Contribution to State Agricultural Productivity." Unpublished Manuscript, Department of Economics, Iowa State University.

Huffman, W.E. and R.E. Evenson. 1989. "Supply and Demand Functions for Multiproduct U.S. Cash Grain Farms: Biases Caused by Research and other Policies." *American Journal of Agricultural Economics* 71(3):761-773.

Huffman, W.E. and R.E. Evenson. 1992. "Contributions of Public and Private Science and Technology to U.S. Agricultural Productivity."*American Journal of Agricultural Economics* 74(3):751-756.

Huffman, W.E. and R.E. Evenson. 1993. *Science for Agriculture: A Long-Term Perspective.* Ames: Iowa State University Press.

Huffman, W.E. and R.E. Evenson. 2000. *The Development of U.S. Agricultural Research and Education: An Economic Perspective.* Ames: Iowa State University, Department of Economics. (first published 1993).

Huffman, W.E. and R.E. Evenson. 2001. "Structural and Productivity Change in US Agriculture, 1950-1982." *Agricultural Economics* 24(2):127-147.

Huffman, W.E. and R.E. Evenson. 2006a. *Science for Agriculture: A Long-Term Perspective.* Second edition. Ames: Iowa State University Press. (first published 1993).

Huffman, W.E. and R.E. Evenson. 2006b. "Do Formula or Competitive Grant Funds have Greater Impacts on State Agricultural Productivity." *American Journal of Agricultural Economics* 88(4):783-798.

Huffman, W.E. and R.E. Just. 1994. "Funding, Structure, and Management of Public Agricultural Research in the United States." *American Journal of Agricultural Economics* 76(4):744-759.

Huffman, W.E. and R.E. Just. 1999. "Agricultural Research: Benefits and Beneficiaries of Alternative Funding Mechanisms." *Review of Agricultural Economics* 21(1):2-18.

Huffman, W.E. and R.E. Just. 2000. "Setting Efficient Incentives for Agricultural Research: Lessons from Principal-Agent Theory." *American Journal of Agricultural Economics* 82(4):828-841.

Huffman, W.E., G. Norton, G. Traxler, G. Frisvold and J. Foltz. 2006. "Winners and Losers: Formula versus Competitive Funding of Agricultural Research." *Choices* 21(4):269-274.

Hurst, W.M. 1933. *Power and Machinery in Agriculture.* Miscellaneous Publication No. 157. Washington, DC: United States Department of Agriculture.

Jaffe, A.B. 1986. "Technological Opportunity and Spillovers of R&D: Evidence from Firm's Patents, Profits, and Market Value." *American Economic Review* 76(5):984-1001.

Jaffe, A.B. 1988. "Demand and Supply Influences in R&D Intensity and Productivity Growth." *Review of Economics and Statistics* 70(3):431-437.

Jaffe, A.B. 1989. "Characterizing the 'Technological Position' of Firms, with Application to Quantifying Technological Opportunity and Research Spillovers." *Research Policy* 18(2):87-97.

Jaffe, A.B. 2000. "The U.S. Patent System in Transition: Policy Innovation and the Innovation Process." *Research Policy* 29(4-5):531-557.

James, J.S., P.G. Pardey and J.M. Alston. 2008. "Agricultural R&D Policy: A Tragedy of the International Commons." Department of Applied Economics Staff Paper P08-08. St. Paul: University of Minnesota.

Janis, M.D. and J.P. Kesan. 2002. "U.S. Plant Variety Protection: Sound and Fury...?" *Houston Law Review* 39(3):727-778.

Jasny, N. 1935. "Tractor Versus Horse as a Source of Farm Power." *American Economic Review* 25(4):708-723.

Jin, S., S. Rozelle, J.M. Alston and J. Huang. 2005. "Economies of Scale and Scope and the Economic Efficiency of China's Agricultural Research System." *International Economic Review* 46(3):1033-1057.

Johnson, D.C. 1990. *Floriculture and Environmental Horticulture Products: A Production and Marketing Statistical Review, 1960-88.* Statistical Bulletin No. 817. Washington: United States Department of Agriculture, Economic Research Service.

Johnson, D.K.N. 1999. "150 Years of American Invention: Methodology and a First Geographical Application." Wellesley College Working Paper 99-01. Wellesley: Department of Economics.

Johnson, D.K.N. 2006. "Patents Granted, by Sector of Use: 1840–1996." Table Cg 69-107 in S.B. Carter, S.S. Gartner, M.R. Haines, A.L. Olmstead, R. Sutch and G. Wright, eds., *Historical Statistics of the United States, Earliest Times to the Present: Millennial Edition.* Cambridge: Cambridge University Press.

Johnson, G.L. 1952. *Burley Tobacco Control Programs: Their Over-all Effect on Production and Prices, 1933-50.* Kentucky Agricultural Experiment Station Bulletin No. 580. Lexington: University of Kentucky.

Johnson, N.L. and V.W. Ruttan. 1997. "The Diffusion of Livestock Breeding Technology in the U.S.: Observations on the Relationship Between Technical Change and Industry Structure." *Journal of Agribusiness* 15(1):19-35.

Johnson, P.R. 1977. "The Elasticity of Foreign Demand for U.S. Agricultural Products." *American Journal of Agricultural Economics* 54(4):735-736.

Jones, C.A., H. El-Osta, and R. Green. 2006. *Economic Well-Being of Farm Households.* Economic Brief No. 7. Washington, DC: United States Department of Agriculture, Economic Research Service.

Jorgenson, D. 1990. "Productivity and Economic Growth." Chapter in E. Berndt and J. Triplett, eds., *Fifty Years of Economic Measurement: The Jubilee Conference on Research in Income and Wealth.* Chicago: University of Chicago Press.

Jorgenson, D.W. and F.M. Gollop. 1992. "Productivity Growth in U.S. Agriculture: A Postwar Perspective." *American Journal of Agricultural Economics* 74(3):745-750.

Juma, C. 1989. *The Gene Hunters: Biotechnology and Scramble for Seeds.* Princeton: Princeton University Press.

Just, R.E., J.M. Alston and D. Zilberman, eds. 2006. *Regulating Agricultural Biotechnology: Economics and Policy.* New York: Springer-Verlag.

Just, R.E. and W.E. Huffman. 1992. "Economic Principals and Incentives: Structure, Management and Funding of Agricultural Research in the United States." *American Journal of Agricultural Economics* 74(5):1101-1108.

Kalaitzandonakes, N., J.M. Alston and K.J. Bradford. 2006. "Compliance Costs for Regulatory Approval of New Biotech Crops." Chapter 3 in R.E. Just, J.M. Alston and D. Zilberman, eds., *Regulating Agricultural Biotechnology: Economics and Policy.* New York: Springer-Verlag.

Karagiannis G. and G.J. Mergos. 2000. "Total Factor Productivity and Technical Change in a Profit Function Framework." *Journal of Productivity Analysis* 14(1):31-51.

Kaylen, M.S., J.W. Wade, and D.B. Frank. 1992. "Stochastic Trend, Weather and U.S. Corn Yield Variability." *Applied Economics* 24(5):513-518.

Kealey, T. 1996. *The Economic Laws of Scientific Research.* New York: St. Martin's Press.

Keller, W. 2001. "Knowledge Spillover at the World's Technol.ogy Frontier." CEPR Discussion Paper No. 2815. London: Center for Economic Policy Research.

Kendrick, J.W. 1983. *Inter-Industry Differences in Productivity Growth.* Washington, DC: American Enterprise Institute.

Kennedy, R.M. 1990. "Title XVI—Research." Chapter in S.L. Pollack and L. Lynch, eds., *Provisions of the Food, Agriculture, Conservation, and Trade Act of 1990.* Agricultural Information Bulletin No. 624. Agriculture and Trade Analysis Division, Economic Research Service. Washington, DC: United States Department of Agriculture.

Kerr, N.A. 1987. *The Legacy: A Centennial History of the State Agricultural Experiment Stations, 1887-1987.* Columbia: Missouri Agricultural Experiment Station.

Key, N. and W. McBride. 2007. *The Changing Economics of U.S. Hog Production.* Economic Research Report No. 52. Washington, DC: United States Department of Agriculture, Economic Research Service.

Key, N. and M.J. Roberts. 2007. "Measures of Trends in Farm Size Tell Differing Stories." In *Amber Waves.* Washington, DC: United States Department of Agriculture, Economic Research Service. Available on line at http://www.ers.usda.gov/AmberWaves/November07/DataFeature/.

Kevles, D.J. 1990. "Principles and Politics in Federal R&D Policy, 1945-1990: An Appreciation of the Bush Report." Preface to the 40th Anniversary Edition, V. Bush, *Science the Endless Frontier.* Arlington: National Science Foundation, pp. ix-xxv. (reprinted in *Nonlinear Science Today* 2(1):14-24).

Khanna, J., W.E. Huffman and T. Sandler. 1994. "Agricultural Research Expenditures in the United States: A Public Goods Perspective." *Review of Economics and Statistics* 76(2):267-277.

King, J.K. and D. Schimmelpfennig. 2005. "Mergers, Acquisitions, and Stocks of Agricultural Biotechnology Intellectual Property." *AgBioForum* 8(2/3):83-88.

King, J.L. 2001. *Concentration and Technology in Agricultural Input Industries.* Agricultural Information Bulletin No. 763. Washington, DC: United States Department of Agriculture, Economic Research Service.

Kislev, Y. and W. Peterson. 1982. "Prices, Technology and Farm Size." *Journal of Political Economy* 90(3):578-595.

Klotz, C., K. Fuglie and C. Pray. 1995. *Private Sector Agricultural Research Expenditures in the United States 1960-92.* ERS Staff Paper No. 9525. Washington, DC: United States Department of Agriculture, Economic Research Service.

Knudson, M. and C.E. Pray. 1991. "Plant Variety Protection, Private Funding, and Public Sector Research Priorities." *American Journal of Agricultural Economics* 73(3):882-886.

Kokic, P., A. Davidson and V. Boero Rodriguez. 2006. "Australia's Grains Industries: Factors Influencing Productivity Growth." *Australian Commodities* 13(4):705-712.

Kolady, D.E. and W. Lesser. 2009. "But are they Meritorious? Genetic Productivity Gains under Plant Intellectual Property Rights." *Journal of Agricultural Economics* 60(1):62-79.

Koo, B., P.G. Pardey, J. Drew and C. Nottenburg. 2009 (in preparation). "The Evolving Intellectual Property Landscape for Plant Varieties in the United States, 1930-2008." Department of Applied Economics Staff Paper. St. Paul: University of Minnesota.

Krell, A. 2003. *The Devils Roe: A Cultural History of Barb Wire.* London: Reaktion Books.

Landes, W.M. and R.A. Posner. 2003. *The Economic Structure of Intellectual Property Law.* Cambridge: Belknap Press.

Law, M.T., J.M. Tonon and G.J. Miller. 2008. "Earmarked: The Political Economy of Agricultural Research Appropriations." *Review of Agricultural Economics* 30(2):194-213.

Leavitt, C.T. 1933. "Attempts to Improve Cattle Breeds in the United States, 1790-1860." *Agricultural History* 7(2):51-67.

Leiby, J.D. and G.D. Adams. 1991. "The Returns to Agricultural Research in Maine: The Case of a Small Northeastern Experiment Station." *Northeastern Journal of Agricultural and Resource Economics* 20(1):1-14.

Lev, B. and T. Sougiannis. 1996. "The Capitalization, Amortization, and Value-Relevance of R&D." *Journal of Accounting and Economics* 21(1):107-138.

Lichtenberg, F.R. and B. van Pottelsberghe de al Pottierie. 1998. "International R&D Spillovers: A Comment." *European Economic Review* 42(8):1483-1491.

Lindner, R.K., A. Fisher and P.G. Pardey. 1979. "The Time to Early Adoption." *Economics Letters* 2(2):187-190.

Loomis, R.A. and G.T. Barton. 1961. *Productivity of Agriculture: United States, 1870-1958.* Technical Bulletin No. 1238. Washington, DC: United States Department of Agriculture.

Lopez, R.A. and H.H. Ramos. 1998. "Supply Response and Demand for Basic Grains in El Salvador." *Agribusiness* 14(6):475-481.

Lubowski, N.K., M. Vesterby, S. Bucholz, A. Baez and M.J. Roberts. 2002. *Major Uses of Land in the United States, 2002.* Economic Information Bulletin No. 14. Washington, DC: United States Department of Agriculture, Economic Research Service.

Luh, Y.H. and S.E. Stefanou. 1991. "Productivity Growth in U.S. Agriculture Under Dynamic Adjustment." *American Journal of Agricultural Economics* 73(4):1116-1125.

MacDonald, J. 2008. *The Economic Organization of U.S. Broiler Production.* Economic Information Bulletin No. 38. Washington, DC: United States Department of Agriculture, Economic Research Service.

MacDonald, J., R. Hoppe and D. Banker. 2006. *Growing Farm Size and the Distribution of Farm Payments.* Economic Brief No. 6. Washington, DC: United States Department of Agriculture, Economic Research Service.

Manuelli, R.E. and A. Seshadri. 2003. "Frictionless Technology Diffusion: The Case of Tractors." NBER Working Paper No. 9604. Washington, DC: National Bureau of Economic Research.

Maredia, M.K., R. Ward and D. Byerlee. 1996. "Econometric Estimation of a Global Spillover Matrix for Wheat Varietal Technology." *Agricultural Economics* 14:159-173.

Martin, P.L. and A.L Olmstead. 1985. "The Agricultural Mechanization Controversy." *Science* 227(8):601-606.

Martini, D.D. and E. Silberberg. 2006. "The Diffusion of Tractor Technology." *Journal of Economic History* 66(2):354-389.

McCunn, A. and W.E. Huffman. 2000. "Convergence in Productivity Growth for Agriculture: Implications of Interstate Research Spillovers for Funding Agricultural Research." *American Journal of Agricultural Economics* 82(2):370-388.

Mead, C.I. 2007. *R&D Depreciation Rates in the 2007 R&D Satellite Account.* BEA Report. Washington, DC: Bureau of Economic Analysis.

Minasian, J.R. 1962. "The Economics of Research and Development." Chapter in R. Nelson, ed., *The Rate and Direction of Inventive Activity: Social and Economic Factors.* Princeton: Princeton University Press for National Bureau of Economic Research.

Minasian, J.R. 1969. "Research and Development, Production Functions and Rates of Return." *American Economic Review* 59(2):80-85.

Mohnen, P. and N. Lepine. 1991. "R&D, R&D Spillovers and Payments for Technology: Canadian Evidence." *Structural Change and Economic Dynamics* 2(1):213-228.

Moschini, G. and H. Lapan. 1997. "Intellectual Property Rights and the Welfare Effects of Agricultural R&D." *American Journal of Agricultural Economics* 79(4):1229-1242.

Mowery, D.C., R.R. Nelson, B.N. Sampat and A.A. Ziedonis. 2001. "The Growth of Patenting and Licensing by U.S. Universities: An Assessment of the Effects of the Bayh-Dole Act of 1980." *Research Policy* 30(1):99-119.

Mullen, J.D. 2007. "Productivity Growth and the Returns from Public Investment in R&D in Australian Broadacre Agriculture." *Australian Journal of Agricultural and Resource Economics* 51(4):359-384.

Myers, R.J. and T. Jayne. 1997. "Regime Shifts and Technology Diffusion in Crop Yield Growth Paths with an Application to Maize Yields in Zimbabwe." *Australian Journal of Agricultural and Resource Economics* 41(3):285-303.

Nadiri, M.I. and I.R. Prucha. 1996. "Estimation of the Depreciation Rate of Physical and R&D Capital in the U.S. Total Manufacturing Sector." *Economic Inquiry* 34(1):43-56.

NAS (National Academy of Sciences). 1992. *The Government Role in Civilian Technology: Building a New Alliance.* Washington, DC: National Academy Press.

Naylor, R., W. Falcon and E. Zavaleta. 1997. "Variability and Growth in Grain Yields, 1950-94: Does the Record Point to Greater Instability?" *Population and Development Review* 23(1):41-58.

NIH (National Institutes of Health). 2008. "NIH Competing and Non-Competing Awards by Fiscal Year and Funding Mechanism." Washington, DC: NIH Research Portfolio Online Reporting Tool (RePORT). Obtained July 2008 from http://report.nih.gov/award/awardtr.cfm.

NIH (National Institutes of Health). 2009. "A Short History of the National Institutes of Health." Bethesda: National Institutes of Health. Obtained March 2009 from http://history.nih.gov/exhibits/history/index.html.

Nordhaus, W.D. 2004. "Retrospective on the 1970s Productivity Slowdown." NBER Working Paper No. 10950. Washington, DC: National Bureau of Economic Research.

Norton, G.W. and J. Ortiz. 1992. "Reaping the Returns to Research." *Journal of Production Agriculture* 5(2):203-209.

NRC (National Research Council). 1972. *Report of the Committee on Research Advisory to the U.S. Department of Agriculture.* Board on Agriculture. Washington, DC: National Academy Press.

NRC (National Research Council). 1989. *Investing in Research: A Proposal to Strengthen the Agricultural, Food and Environmental System.* Board on Agriculture. Washington, DC: National Academy Press.

NRC (National Research Council). 1994. *Investing in the National Research Initiative: An Update of the Competitive Grants Program in the U.S. Department of Agriculture.* Board on Agriculture. Washington, DC: National Academy Press.

NRC (National Research Council). 1995. *Colleges of Agriculture at the Land Grant Universities: A Profile.* Committee on the Future of Colleges of Agriculture in the Land Grant System, Board on Agriculture. Washington, DC: National Academy Press.

NRC (National Research Council). 2000. *National Research Initiative: A Vital Competitive Grants Program in Food, Fiber, and Natural Resources Research.* Board on Agriculture and Natural Resources. Washington, DC: National Academy Press.

NRI (National Research Initiative). 2009. "Program Synopsis: National Research Initiative (NRI) Competitive Grants Program." Washington, DC: United States Department of Agriculture. Obtained March 2009 from http://www.csrees.usda.gov/funding/nri/nri_about.html.

NSB (National Science Board). 1993. *Science and Engineering Indicators 1993.* NSB 93-1. Arlington: Government Printing Office.

NSB (National Science Board). 2008. *Science and Engineering Indicators 2008, Volumes 1 and 2.* Arlington: National Science Foundation.

NSF (National Science Foundation). 2007. "NSF Survey of R&D Expenditures at Universities and Colleges." WebCaspar database. Arlington: National Science Foundation. Obtained August 2007 from http://webcaspar.nsf.gov.

NSF (National Science Foundation). 2008a. "National Patterns of R&D Resources: 2007 Data Update." NSF 08-318. Arlington: National Science Foundation, Division of Science Resources Statistics. Obtained March 2008 from http://www.nsf.gov/statistics/nsf08318/.

NSF (National Science Foundation). 2008b. "NSF Survey of R&D Expenditures at Universities and Colleges." WebCaspar database. Arlington: National Science Foundation. Obtained July 2008 from http://webcaspar.nsf.gov.

NSF (National Science Foundation). 2008c. "NSF Survey of Federal Funds for Research and Development." WebCaspar database. Arlington: National Science Foundation. Obtained July 2008 from http://webcaspar.nsf.gov/.

NSF (National Science Foundation). 2009a. "A Timeline of NSF History." Arlington: National Science Foundation. Obtained March 2009 from http://www.nsf.gov/about/history/overview-50.jsp.

NSF (National Science Foundation). 2009b. "NSF Survey of Federal Funds for Research and Development," WebCaspar database. Arlington: National Science Foundation. Obtained March 2009 from http://webcaspar.nsf.gov/.

OECD (Organisation for Economic Co-operation and Development). 2002. *Frascati Manual: Proposed Standard Practice for Surveys on Research and Experimental Development.* Paris: Organisation for Economic Co-operation and Development.

OECD (Organisation for Economic Co-operation and Development). 2008. "Main Science and Technology Indicators Volume 2008 Release 02, Source OECD Science and Technology Statistics Database." Paris: Organisation for Economic Co-operation and Development. Obtained March 2009 from http://www.sourceoecd.org.

Offutt, S. 1993. "The National Research Initiative: Competing at the Margin." Chapter in R.D. Weaver, ed., *U.S. Agricultural Research: Strategic Challenges and Options.* Bethesda: Agricultural Research Institute.

Olmstead, A.L. 1975. "The Mechanization of Reaping and Mowing in American Agriculture, 1833-1870." *Journal of Economic History* 35(2):327-352.

Olmstead, A.L. and P.W. Rhode. 1993. "Induced Innovation in American Agriculture: A Reconsideration." *Journal of Political Economy* 101:100-118.

Olmstead, A.L. and P.W. Rhode. 1994. "The Agricultural Mechanization Controversy of the Interwar Years." *Agricultural History* 68(3):35-53.

Olmstead, A.L. and P. W. Rhode. 1998. "Induced Innovation in American Agriculture: An Econometric Analysis." *Research in Economic History* 18:103-119.

Olmstead, A.L. and P.W. Rhode. 2000. "The Transformation of Northern Agriculture from 1910 to 1990." In S.L. Engerman and R.E. Gallman, eds., *Cambridge Economic History of the United States, Volume III, The Twentieth Century.* New York: Cambridge University Press, pp. 693-742.

Olmstead, A.L. and P.W. Rhode. 2001. "Reshaping the Landscape: The Impact and Diffusion of the Tractor in American Agriculture, 1910-1960." *Journal of Economic History* 61(3):663-698.

Olmstead, A.L. and P.W. Rhode. 2002. "The Red Queen and the Hard Reds: Productivity Growth in American Wheat, 1800-1940." *Journal of Economic History* 62(4):929-966.

Olmstead, A.L. and P.W. Rhode. 2006. "Farms and Farm Structure." In S.B. Carter, S.S. Gartner, M.R. Haines, A.L. Olmstead, R. Sutch and G. Wright, eds., *Historical Statistics of the United States, Earliest Times to the Present: Millennial Edition.* Cambridge: Cambridge University Press.

Olmstead, A.L. and P.W. Rhode. 2008. *Creating Abundance: Biological Innovation and American Agricultural Development.* New York: Cambridge University Press.

OMB (Office of Management and Budget). 2008. *Budget of the United States Government: Historical Tables.* Executive Office of the President of the United States. Washington, DC: Government Printing Office.

Orland, B. 2004. "Turbo-Cows: Producing a Competitive Animal in the Nineteenth and Early Twentieth Centuries." Chapter in S.R. Schrepfer and P. Scranton, eds., *Industrializing Organisms: Introducing Evolutionary History.* New York: Routledge.

OTA (Office of Technology Assessment). 1977. *Organizing and Financing Basic Research to Increase Food Production.* Washington, DC: Government Printing Office.

Oury, B. 1965. "Allowing for Weather in Crop Production Model Building." *Journal of Farm Economics* 47(2):270-283.

Pakes, A. 1978. "Economic Incentives in the Production and Transmission of Knowledge: An Empirical Analysis." Unpublished PhD Dissertation, Harvard University, Cambridge.

Pakes, A. and M. Shankerman. 1987. "The Rate of Obsolescence of Patents, Research Gestation Lags, and the Private Rate of Return to Research Resources." Chapter 4 in Zvi Griliches, ed., *R&D, Patents, and Productivity.* Chicago: University of Chicago Press for National Bureau of Economic Research.

Pardey, P.G., J.M. Alston, J.E. Christian and S. Fan. 1996. *Hidden Harvest: U.S. Benefits from International Research Aid.* Food Policy Report. Washington, DC: International Food Policy Research Institute.

Pardey, P.G., J.M. Alston and R.R. Piggott, eds. 2006. *Agricultural R&D in the Developing World: Too Little, Too Late?* Washington, DC: International Food Policy Research Institute.

Pardey, P.G., J.M. Alston and V.W. Ruttan. 2010 (forthcoming). "The Economics of Innovation and Technical Change in Agriculture." Chapter in B.H. Hall and N. Rosenberg, eds., *Handbook of Economics of Technical Change.* Amsterdam: Elsevier.

Pardey, P.G., M.A. Andersen and J.M. Alston. 2009 (forthcoming). "A Long-Run Price Index and the Real Cost of U.S. Agricultural Research." Department of Applied Economics Staff Paper. St. Paul: University of Minnesota.

Pardey, P.G., M.A. Andersen, B.J. Craig, and J.M. Alston. 2009a (forthcoming). "InSTePP U.S. Production Accounts—Primary Data Documentation of Agricultural Input, Output and Productivity Series, 1949–2002, Version 5." Department of Applied Economics Staff Paper. St. Paul: University of Minnesota.

Pardey, P.G. and N.M. Beintema. 2001. *Slow Magic: Agricultural R&D a Century After Mendel.* IFPRI Food Policy Report. Washington, DC: International Food Policy Research Institute.

Pardey, P.G., N.M. Beintema, S. Dehmer and S. Wood. 2006. *Agricultural Research: A Growing Global Divide?* IFPRI Food Policy Report. Washington, DC: International Food Policy Research Institute.

Pardey, P.G. and B.J Craig. 1989. "Causal Relationships Between Public Sector Agricultural Research Expenditures and Output." *American Journal of Agricultural Economics* 71(1):9-19.

Pardey, P.G., B.J. Craig, M.A. Andersen and J.M. Alston. 2009b (forthcoming). "Measuring Capital Inputs Using the Physical Inventory Method with Application to U.S. Agriculture." Department of Applied Economics Staff Paper. St. Paul: University of Minnesota.

Pardey, P.G. and S. Dehmer. 2010 (forthcoming). "Science Spending—A Changing World Order?" Department of Applied Economics Staff Paper. St. Paul: University of Minnesota.

Pardey, P.G., J.S. James, J.M. Alston, S. Wood, B. Koo, E. Binenbaum, T.M. Hurley and P. Glewwe. 2007. "Science, Technology and Skills." Background Paper for World Bank's *World Development Report 2008.* St. Paul, Rome and Washington, DC: University of Minnesota, CGIAR Science Council and World Bank.

Pardey, P.G., B. Koo and C. Nottenburg. 2004. "Creating, Protecting, and Using Crop Biotechnologies Worldwide in an Era of Intellectual Property." *Minnesota Journal of Law, Science & Technology* 6(1):213-252.

Pardey, P.G., J. Roseboom and B.J. Craig. 1992. "A Yardstick for International Comparisons: An Application to National Agricultural Research Expenditures." *Economic Development and Cultural Change* 40(2):333-349.

Park, W.G. 1995. "International R&D Spillovers and OECD Economic Growth." *Economic Inquiry* 33(4):571-591.

Pasour, Jr. E.C. and M.A. Johnson. 1982. "Bureaucratic Productivity: The Case of Agricultural Research Revisited." *Public Choice* 39(2):301-317.

Perrin, R.K., K.A. Kunnings and L.A. Ihnen. 1983. *Some Effects of the US Plant Variety Act of 1970.* Economics Research Report No. 46. Raleigh: North Carolina State University.

Peterson, W.L. 1969. "Return to Poultry Research in the United States." *Journal of Farm Economics* 49(3):656-669.

Peterson, W.L. 1992. "Is the Demand for Experiment Station Personnel Declining?" *Review of Agricultural Economics* 14(1):55-64.

Phillips, P.W.B. and G.G. Khachatourians. 2001. *The Biotechnology Revolution in Global Agriculture: Innovation, Invention, and Investment in the Canola Industry.* Wallingford: CAB International.

Pollack, S.L. and L. Lynch, eds. 1991. *Provisions of the Food, Agriculture, Conservation, and Trade Act of 1990.* Agriculture and Trade Analysis Division, Economic Research Service, Agriculture Information Bulletin No. 624. Washington, DC: United States Department of Agriculture.

Pray, C.E. and C. Neumeyer. 1989. "Trends and Composition of Private Food and Agricultural R&D Expenditures in the United States." Department of Agricultural Economics Working Paper. New Brunswick: Rutgers University.

Productivity Commission. 2007. *Public Support for Science and Innovation.* Research Report. Canberra: Australian Government Productivity Commission.

Raines, F.Q. 1968. "The Impact of Applied Research and Development on Productivity." Department of Economic Working Paper No. 6814. St Louis: Washington University.

Rasmussen, W.D. and G.L. Baker. 1972. *The Department of Agriculture.* New York: Praeger Publishers.

Ravenscraft, D. and F.M. Scherer. 1982. "The Lag Structure of Returns to Research and Development." *Applied Economics* 14(6):603-620.

Rawson, J.M. 1997. *Agricultural Research, Education, Extension and Economics Programs: A Primer.* CRS Report No. 97-325. Washington, DC: Congressional Reporting Service. Obtained March 2009 from http://ncseonline.org/NLE/CRSreports/Agriculture/ag-73.cfm.

Ray, S.C. 1982. "A Translog Cost Function Analysis of U.S. Agriculture 1939-77." *American Journal of Agricultural Economics* 64(3):490-498.

Richter, M.K. 1966. "Invariance Axioms and Economic Indexes." *Econometrica* 34(4):739-755.

Robbins, C.A. and C.E. Moylan. 2007. "Research and Development Satellite Account Update: Estimates for 1959-2004." *Survey of Current Business, Bureau of Economic Analysis* 87(10):49-64.

Robson, M., J. Townsend and K. Pavitt. 1988. "Sectoral Patterns of Production and Use of Innovations in the U.K.: 1945-83." *Research Policy* 17(1):1-14.

Rossiter, M.W. 1975. *The Emergence of Agricultural Sciences: Justus Liebig and the Americans, 1840-1880.* New Haven: Yale University Press.

Russell, E.J. 1966. *A History of Agricultural Science in Great Britain 1620-1954.* London: George Allen & Unwin Ltd.

Ruttan, V.W. 1956. "The Contribution of Technological Progress to Farm Output: 1950-1975." *Review of Economics and Statistics* 38(1):61-69.

Ruttan, V.W. 1980. "Bureaucratic Productivity: The Case of Agricultural Research." *Public Choice* 35(5):529-547.

Ruttan, V.W. 1982. *Agricultural Research Policy.* Minneapolis: University of Minnesota Press.

Ruttan, V.W. 1983. "Agricultural Research Policy Issues." *Horticultural Science* 18(6):809-818.

Ryan, T.J. 1977. "Supply Response to Risk: The Case of U.S. Pinto Beans." *Western Journal of Agricultural Economics* 2:35-43.

Ryerson, K.A. 1933. "History and Significance of the Foreign Plant Introduction Work of the United States Department of Agriculture." *Agricultural History* 7(3):110-128.

Salmon, S.C. and A.A. Hanson. 1964. *The Principles and Practice of Agricultural Research.* London: Leonard Hill.

Schaible, G. and M. Aillery. 2006. "Irrigation Water Management." Chapter 4.6 in K. Wiebe and N. Gollehon, eds., *Agricultural Resources and Environmental Indicators, 2006 Edition.* Economic Information Bulletin No. 16. Washington, DC: United States Department of Agriculture, Economic Research Service. Obtained December 2008 from http://www.ers.usda.gov/publications/arei/eib16/.

Schankerman, M. 1979. "Essays on the Economics of Technical Change: The Determinants, Rate of Return and Productivity Impact of Research and Development." Unpublished PhD Dissertation, Harvard University, Cambridge.

Scherer, F.M. 1982. "Inter-Industry Technology Flows and Productivity Growth." *Review of Economics and Statistics* 64(4):627-634.

Scherer, F.M. 1984. "Using Linked Patent and R&D Data to Measure Interindustry Technology Flows." Chapter 20 in Z. Griliches, ed., *R&D, Patents, and Productivity.* Chicago: University of Chicago Press.

Scheuring, A.F., C.O. McCorkle and J. Lyons. 1995. *Science and Service: A History of the Land Grant University and Agriculture in California.* Oakland: University of California, Division of Agriculture and Natural Resources.

Schillinger, W.F. and R.I. Papendick. 2008. "Then and Now: 125 Years of Dryland Wheat Farming in the Inland Pacific Northwest." *Agronomy Journal Supplement* 100(3):S166-S182.

Schimmelpfennig, D. and P. Heisey. 2009. *U.S. Public Agricultural Research: Changes in Funding Sources and Shifts in Emphasis, 1980-2005.* Economic Information Bulletin No. 45. Washington, DC: United States Department of Agriculture, Economic Research Service.

Schimmelpfennig, D. and C.Thirtle. 1999. "The Internationalization of Agricultural Technology: Patents, R&D Spillovers and their Effects on Productivity in the European Union and the United States." *Contemporary Economic Policy* 17(4):457-468.

Schmitz, A. and D. Seckler. 1970. "Mechanized Agriculture and Social Welfare: The Case of the Tomato Harvester." *American Journal of Agricultural Economics* 52(4):569-577.

Schultz, T.W. 1953. *The Economic Organization of Agriculture.* New York: McGraw-Hill.

Schultz, T.W. 1956. "Reflections on Agricultural Production Output and Supply." *Journal of Farm Economics* 38(3):748-762.

Senauer, B., E. Asp and J. Kinsey. 1991. *Food Trends and the Changing Consumer.* St. Paul: Eagan Press.

Sexton, R.J. 1990. "Imperfect Competition in Agricultural Markets and the Role of Cooperatives: A Spatial Analysis." *American Journal of Agricultural Economics* 72(3):709-720.

Shanks, S. and S. Zheng. 2006. "Econometric Modelling of R&D and Australia's Productivity." Staff Working Paper. Canberra: Productivity Commission.

Shaw, L.H. 1964. "The Effect of Weather on Agricultural Output: A Look at Methodology." *Journal of Farm Economics* 46(1):218-230.

Short, S. 1987. "Measuring Agricultural Labor: Hours and the Rate of Return to Equity in Farm Assets." Appendix in National Economics Division, Economic Research Service, *Economic Indicators of the Farm Sector: Production and Efficiency Statistics, 1985.* ECIFS 5-5. Washington, DC: United States Department of Agriculture.

Shumway, C.R. and A.A. Chang. 1980. "Supply Response of Texas Field Crops: An Evaluation of the CET Linear Supply Model." *Western Journal of Agricultural Economics* 5(2):149-164.

Sliker, B.K. 2007. "2007 R&D Satellite Account Methodologies: R&D Capital Stocks and Net Rates of Return." Bureau of Economic Analysis Report. Washington, DC: United States Department of Commerce.

Smith, C.W., J. Betrán and E.C.A. Runge. 2004. *Corn: Origin, History, Technology and Production.* Hoboken: John Wiley and Sons.

Sparger, J.A. 2009. "Is the Share of Agricultural Maintenance Research Rising?: Implications for Future Productivity Growth in U.S. Agriculture." Unpublished MSc Dissertation, Department of Agricultural and Applied Economics, Virginia Polytechnic Institute and State University, Blacksburg.

Stallings, J.L. 1960. "Weather Indexes." *Journal of Farm Economics* 42:180-186.

Stallings, J.L. 1961. "A Measure of the Influence of Weather on Crop Production." *Journal of Farm Economics* 43(5):1153-1160.

Star, S. 1974. "Accounting for the Growth of Output." *American Economic Review* 64(1):123-135.

Sterlacchini, A. 1989. "R&D, Innovations, and Total Factor Productivity Growth in British Manufacturing." *Applied Economics* 21(11):1549-1562.

Strickler, P.E. and C.A. Hines. 1960. *Numbers of Selected Machines and Equipment on Farms with Related Data.* Agricultural Research Service Statistical Bulletin No. 258. Washington, DC: United States Department of Agriculture.

Stumpf, P.K. 1992. "The Competitive Research Program of the USDA: Past, Present, and Future." *Plant Cell* 4:116-118.

Sullivan, P., D. Hellerstein, L. Hansen, R. Johansson, S. Koenig, R. Lubowski, W. McBride, D. McGranahan, M. Roberts, S. Vogel and S. Bucholtz. 2004. *The Conservation Reserve Program: Economic Implications for Rural America.* Economic Research Service Agricultural Economic Report No. 834. Washington, DC: United States Department of Agriculture.

Sumner, D.A. 1985. "Farm Programs and Structural Issues." Chapter in B.L. Gardner, ed., *U.S. Agricultural Policy: The 1985 Farm Legislation.* Washington, DC: American Enterprise Institute.

Sumner, D.A. 1986. *Structural Consequences of Agricultural Commodity Programs.* AEI Occasional Paper. Washington, DC: American Enterprise Institute.

Sutch, R. 2006. "Aggregate Measures and Long-Term Gross Domestic Product Series." In S.B. Carter, S.S. Gartner, M.R. Haines, A.L. Olmstead, R. Sutch and G. Wright, eds., *Historical Statistics of the United States, Earliest Times to the Present: Millennial Edition.* Cambridge: Cambridge University Press.

Sutch, R.C. 2008. "Henry Agard Wallace, the Iowa Corn Yield Tests, and the Adoption of Hybrid Corn." Working Paper 14141. Cambridge: National Bureau of Economic Research.

Swallow, B.M., G.W. Norton, T.B. Brumback and G.R. Buss. 1985. *Agricultural Depreciation and the Importance of Maintenance Research.* Department of Agricultural Economics Research Report No. 56. Blacksburg: Virginia Polytechnic Institute and State University.

Syme, J.R. 1970. "A High-Yielding Mexican Semi-Dwarf Wheat and the Relationship of Yield to Harvest Index and Other Varietal Characteristics." *Australian Journal of Experimental Agriculture and Animal Husbandry* 10(44):350-353.

Terleckyj, N. 1974. *Effects of R&D on the Productivity Growth of Industries: An Exploratory Study.* Washington, DC: National Planning Association.

Thirtle, C.G. and P. Bottomley. 1988. "Is Publicly Funded Agricultural Research Excessive?" *Journal of Agricultural Economics* 31:99-111.

Thirtle, C., L. Lin, J. Holding, L. Jenkins and J. Piesse. 2004. "Explaining the Decline in UK Agricultural Productivity Growth." *Journal of Agricultural Economics* 55(2):343-366.

Thirtle, C., J. Piesse, and D. Schimmelpfennig. 2008. "Modeling the Length and Shape of the R&D Lag: An Application to UK Agricultural Productivity." *Agricultural Economics* 39(1):73-85.

Traxler, G. and D. Byerlee. 2001. "Linking Technical Change to Research Effort: An Examination of Aggregation and Spillovers Effects." *Agricultural Economics* 24(3):235-246.

True, A.C. 1894. "Report of the Director of the Office of Experiment Stations for 1983." In *Report of the Secretary of Agriculture for 1983.* United States Department of Agriculture. Washington: Government Printing Office.

True, A.C. 1895. "Education and Research in Agriculture in the United States." In *U.S. Department of Agriculture Yearbook 1894.* Washington, DC: United States Department of Agriculture.

True, A.C. 1898-1901. *A Report on the Work and Expenditures of the Agricultural Experiment Stations for the Year Ended June 30, [1897-1900].* United States Department of Agriculture, Office of Experiment Stations. Washington, DC: Government Printing Office.

True, A.C. 1900. "Agricultural Experiment Stations in the United States." In *U.S. Department of Agriculture Yearbook 1899.* Washington, DC: United States Department of Agriculture.

True, A.C. 1928. *A History of Agricultural Extension Work in the United States, 1785-1923.* Miscellaneous Publication No. 15. Washington, DC: United States Department of Agriculture.

True, A.C. 1937. *A History of Agricultural Experimentation and Research in the United States, 1607-1925.* Miscellaneous Publication No. 251. Washington, DC: United States Department of Agriculture.

Tweeten, L. 1967. "The Demand for United States Farm Output." *Food Research Institute Studies* 7:343-369.

Tweeten, L. 1977. "The Elasticity of Foreign Demand for U.S. Agricultural Products: Comment." *American Journal of Agricultural Economics* 54(4):737-738.

U.S. Bureau of the Census. (various years). *Census of the United States: Agriculture.* U.S. Department of Commerce. Washington, DC: Government Printing Office.

U.S. Bureau of the Census. 1922. *Fourteenth Census of the United States taken in 1920: Agriculture.* U.S. Department of Commerce. Washington, DC: Government Printing Office.

U.S. Bureau of the Census. 1956-1991. "Census of Horticultural Specialties [1954-1988]." *United States Census of Agriculture.* U.S. Department of Commerce. Washington, DC: Government Printing Office.

U.S. Bureau of the Census. 1975. *Historical Statistics of the United States: Colonial Times to 1970.* U.S. Department of Commerce. Washington, DC: Government Printing Office.

U.S. Bureau of the Census. 2007. "Annual Population Estimates 2000 to 2006." *Population Estimates: National and State Population Estimates.* U.S. Department of Commerce. Washington, DC. Obtained August 2007 from http://www.census.gov/popest/states/NST-ann-est.html.

U.S. Census Bureau. 2009. "International Database: Total Midyear Population for the World: 1950-2050." U.S. Department of Commerce. Washington, DC: Obtained March 2009 from http://www.census.gov/ipc/www/idb/worldpop.php.

U.S. Congress. 1968. *Department of Agriculture and Related Agencies Appropriation Bill, 1969.* Senate Report No. 1138, 90th Congress, 2nd session. Washington, DC: Government Printing Office.

U.S. Congress. 1993. *Conference Report to Accompany H.R. 5847, Agriculture, Rural Development, Food and Drug Administration, and Related Agencies Appropriation Bill, 1993.* Washington, DC: Government Printing Office.

USDA. (various years). *Agricultural Statistics.* Washington, DC: United States Department of Agriculture.

USDA. 1890. "Report of the Director of the Office of Experiment Stations for the Year 1889." In *Annual Report of the Department of Agriculture for the Year 1889.* Secretary of Agriculture. Washington: United States Department of Agriculture.

USDA. 1915. *Farmers' Institutes Work in the United States in 1914, and Notes on Agricultural Extension Work in Foreign Countries.* Bulletin No. 269. Washington, DC: Government Printing Office.

USDA. 1917. *Report of Cooperative Extension Work in Agriculture and Home Economics. Part II of Report on Experiment Stations and Extension Work in the United States.* Washington, DC: Government Printing Office.

USDA. 1918-1922 and 1925. *Cooperative Extension Work.* Office of Cooperative Extension Work. Washington, DC: Government Printing Office.

USDA. 1941-1949 and 1953. *Report of Cooperative Extension Work in Agriculture and Home Economics.* Washington, DC: Government Printing Office.

USDA. 1957. *Yearbook of Agriculture.* Washington, DC: Government Printing Office.

USDA. 1962. *Agricultural Statistics.* "Table 539: Horses and Mules: Number on Farms, Values and Classes, Jan.1, United States, 1920-61." Washington, DC: United States Department of Agriculture.

USDA. 1996. "U.S. Department of Agriculture—Reorganizing the People's Department." Chapter 5 in *USDA Fact Book 1996.* Washington, DC: United States Department of Agriculture, Office of Communication. Obtained March 2008 from http://www.usda.gov/news/pubs/factbook/contents.htm.

USDA. 1998. Economics, Statistics and Market Information System (ESMIS) and Albert R. Mann Library, Cornell University. Obtained March 1998 from http://usda.mannlib.cornell.edu/MannUsda/homepage.do.

USDA. 2004. *Farm Numbers and Land in Farms.* SB-991. Washington, DC: United States Department of Agriculture.

USDA. 2005. *Plant Variety Protection Act and Regulations and Rules of Practice.* Washington, DC: United States Department of Agriculture, Agricultural Marketing Service.

USDA ARS (Agricultural Research Service). 1955-1960. *Report on the Agricultural Experiment Stations, [1954-1959].* Washington: Government Printing Office.

USDA ARS (Agricultural Research Service). 1961. *Funds for Research at State Agricultural Experiment Stations, 1960.* Washington: Government Printing Office.

USDA CRIS (Current Research Information System). (various years). Unpublished annual data files, 1970 to 2007. United States Department of Agriculture, Washington, DC.

USDA CRIS (Current Research Information System). 1993. *Manual of Classification of Agricultural and Forestry Research: Revision V.* Washington, DC: United States Department of Agriculture, Cooperative State Research Service.

USDA CRIS (Current Research Information System). 1998. *Manual of Classification of Agricultural and Forestry Research: Revision VI.* Washington, DC: United States Department of Agriculture, Cooperative State Research Service.

USDA CRIS (Current Research Information System). 2005. *Manual of Classification of Agricultural and Forestry Research: Revision VII.* Washington, DC: United States Department of Agriculture, Cooperative State Research Service.

USDA CRIS (Current Research Information System). 2008. "Selected CRIS Funding Summaries: Access by Fiscal Year 2007." *Reports.* United States Department of Agriculture, Washington, DC. Obtained August 2009 from http://cris.csrees.usda.gov/fsummaries.html.

USDA CSESS (Cooperative State Experiment Station Service). (1962 and 1963). *Funds for Research at State Agricultural Experiment Stations, (1961 and 1962).* Washington: Government Printing Office.

USDA CSREES (Cooperative State Research, Education and Extension Service). 1995-1998. *Inventory of Agricultural Research, Fiscal Years [1994-1997].* Washington, DC: United States Department of Agriculture.

USDA CSREES (Cooperative State Research, Education and Extension Service). 1980-2006. "Sources of Funds Allocated for Cooperative Extension Work." Unpublished annual data files, Cooperative State Research, Education and Extension Service, Washington, DC.

USDA CSREES (Cooperative State Research, Education and Extension Service). 2008. Data Tables. Unpublished, Cooperative State Research, Education and Extension Service Budget Office, Washington, DC. Obtained April 2008.

USDA CSRS (Cooperative State Research Service). 1964. *Funds for Research at State Agricultural Experiment Stations, 1963.* Washington, DC: Government Printing Office.

USDA CSRS (Cooperative State Research Service). 1965-1974. *Funds for Research at State Agricultural Experiment Stations and Other State Institutions, [1964-1973].* Washington, DC: Government Printing Office.

USDA CSRS (Cooperative State Research Service). 1972-1977. *Inventory of Agricultural Research FY [1971-1976].* Washington, DC: United States Department of Agriculture.

USDA CSRS (Cooperative State Research Service). 1975 and 1976. *Funds for Research at State Agricultural Experiment Stations and Other Cooperating Institutions, [1974 and 1975].* Washington, DC: Government Printing Office.

USDA CSRS (Cooperative State Research Service). 1977. *Inventory of Agricultural Research FY 1976 and Transition Quarter.* CSRS-3B-77, Volume II. Washington, DC: United States Department of Agriculture.

USDA CSRS (Cooperative State Research Service). 1982-1994. *Inventory of Agricultural Research FY [1979-1993].* Washington, DC: United States Department of Agriculture.

USDA CSRS (Cooperative State Research Service). 1993. "1993 Budget Explanatory Notes (prepared for Appropriations Committee hearings)." Unpublished annual reports, United States Department of Agriculture, Washington, DC.

USDA ERS (Economic Research Service). 1984. *Economic Indicators of the Farm Sector: Production and Efficiency Statistics, 1981.* ECIFS 2-5. Washington, DC: United States Department of Agriculture.

USDA ERS (Economic Research Service). 1986. *Economic Indicators of the Farm Sector: Production and Efficiency Statistics, 1984.* ECIFS 4-4. Washington, DC: United States Department of Agriculture.

USDA ERS (Economic Research Service). 1991. *Economic Indicators of the Farm Sector: Production and Efficiency Statistics, 1989.* ECIFS 9-4. Washington, DC: United States Department of Agriculture.

USDA ERS (Economic Research Service). 1992. *Economic Indicators of the Farm Sector: Production and Efficiency Statistics, 1990.* ECIFS 10-3. Washington, DC: United States Department of Agriculture.

USDA ERS (Economic Research Service). 2006. "Farm Business and Household Survey Data: Customized Data Summaries from ARMS, Farm and Operator Households: Structure and Finance." Washington, DC: United States Department of Agriculture. Obtained December 2006 from http://www.ers.usda.gov/Data/ARMS/app/Farm.aspx.

USDA ERS (Economic Research Service). 2007. "Farm Income." *Data Sets.* Washington, DC: United States Department of Agriculture. Obtained November 2007 from http://www.ers.usda.gov/Data/FarmIncome.

USDA ERS (Economic Research Service). 2008a. "Agricultural Resource Management Survey." Unpublished data files, United States Department of Agriculture, Washington, DC. Extraction provided by R. Green.

USDA ERS (Economic Research Service). 2008b. "U.S. Production Agriculture Expenses, All Categories, 1910-2007." *Data Sets: Farm Income: Income and Production Expenses.* Washington, DC: United States Department of Agriculture. Obtained December 2008 from http://www.ers.usda.gov/Data/farmincome/FinfidmuXls.htm.

USDA ERS (Economic Research Service). 2008c. "Agricultural Productivity in the United States." *Data Sets.* Washington, DC: United States Department of Agriculture. Obtained November 2008 from http://www.ers.usda.gov/Data/AgProductivity/.

USDA ERS (Economic Research Service). 2009a. "Agricultural Productivity in the United States." *Data Sets.* Washington, DC: U.S. Department of Agriculture. Obtained September 2009 from http://www.ers.usda.gov/Data/AgProductivity/.

USDA ERS (Economic Research Service). 2009b. "Income and Production Expenses." *Data Sets.* Washington, DC: United States Department of Agriculture. Obtained May 2009 from http://www.ers.usda.gov/Data/farmincome/FinfidmuXls.htm.

USDA NASS (National Agricultural Statistical Service). (various years). *Farms, Land in Farms, and Livestock Operations.* Statistical Bulletins. Washington, DC: United States Department of Agriculture. Obtained January 2008 from http://usda.mannlib.cornell.edu/MannUsda/viewDocumentInfo.do?documentID=1259.

USDA NASS (National Agricultural Statistical Service). 1999. *1997 Census of Agriculture.* Washington, DC: United States Department of Agriculture.

USDA NASS (National Agricultural Statistical Service). 2000-2009. "Census of Horticultural Specialties [1998-2007]." *United States Census of Agriculture.* Washington, DC: United States Department of Agriculture.

USDA NASS (National Agricultural Statistical Service). 2004. *2002 Census of Agriculture, United States Summary and State Data. Volume 1, Geographic Area Series Part 51, Table 55.* Washington, DC: United States Department of Agriculture.

USDA NASS (National Agricultural Statistical Service). 2009. *Quick Stats* (Agricultural Statistics Database). Washington, DC: United States Department of Agriculture. Obtained June 2009 from http://www.nass.usda.gov/Data_and_Statistics/index.asp.

USDA Office of Experiment Stations. 1895. *Statistics of Agricultural Colleges and Experiment Stations, 1894.* Circular No. 27. Washington: United States Department of Agriculture.

USDA Office of Experiment Stations. 1897. *Statistics of Land-Grant Colleges and Agricultural Experiment Stations, 1896.* Circular No. 35. Washington: United States Department of Agriculture.

USDA Office of Experiment Stations. 1902-1915. *Annual Report of the Office of Experiment Stations for the Year Ended June 30, [1901-1914].* Washington: Government Printing Office.

USDA Office of Experiment Stations. 1916. *Report on Agricultural Experiment Stations and Cooperative Agricultural Extension Work in the United States for the Year Ended June 30, 1915.* Washington: Government Printing Office.

USDA Office of Experiment Stations. 1918-1926. *Work and Expenditures of the Agricultural Experiment Stations, [1916-1924].* Washington: Government Printing Office.

USDA Office of Experiment Stations. 1926-1954. *Report on the Agricultural Experiment Stations, [1925-1953].* Washington: Government Printing Office.

USDA RPDES (Research Program Development and Evaluation Staff). 1967-1969. *An Inventory of Agricultural Research FY (1966-1968).* Washington: United States Department of Agriculture.

USDA SEA (Science and Education Administration). 1979-1981. *Inventory of Agricultural Research FY (1977-1978).* Volume II. Washington: Government Printing Office.

USDA SEA (Science and Education Administration). 1981. "1981 Budget Explanatory Notes (prepared for Appropriations Committee hearings)." Unpublished annual reports, United States Department of Agriculture, Washington, DC.

USDA SES (Science and Education Staff). 1970-1972. *Inventory of Agricultural Research FY (1969-1970).* Washington: United States Department of Agriculture.

U.S. Department of Commerce. 1950. "Characteristics of the Population," *Census of Population.* Washington, DC: United States Department of Commerce.

U.S. Department of Commerce. 1980. "Earnings by Occupation and Education." Unpublished subject summary data files of Census of Population, United States Department of Commerce, Washington, DC.

U.S. Department of Commerce. 1990. "Earnings by Occupation and Education." Unpublished subject summary data files of Census of Population. United States Department of Commerce, Washington, DC.

U.S. Department of the Treasury. 1889 and 1890. *An Account of the Receipts and Expenditures of The United States for the Fiscal Year Ending June 30.* Washington, DC: Government Printing Office.

U.S. Department of the Treasury. 1894-1907. "A Combined Statement of the Receipts and Expenditures of the Government for the Fiscal Year Ended June 30." In *Letter from the Secretary of the Treasury.* Washington, DC: Government Printing Office.

U.S. Department of the Treasury. 1908-1911. "A Combined Statement of the Receipts and Disbursements of the Government for the Fiscal Year Ended June 30." In *Letter from the Secretary of the Treasury.* Washington, DC: Government Printing Office.

U.S. Department of the Treasury. 1912-1926. "A Combined Statement of the Receipts and Disbursements Balances, etc., of the Government for the Fiscal Year Ended June 30." In *Letter from the Secretary of the Treasury.* Washington, DC: Government Printing Office.

U.S. Department of the Treasury. 1927-1939. "Combined Statement of the Receipts and Expenditures Balances, etc., of the Government for the Fiscal Year Ended June 30." In *Letter from the Secretary of the Treasury.* Washington, DC: Government Printing Office.

U.S. Department of the Treasury. 1940-1975. *Combined Statement of Receipts, Expenditures and Balances of the United States Government for the Fiscal Year Ended June 30.* Washington, DC: Government Printing Office.

U.S. Department of the Treasury. 1976-1983. *Combined Statement of Receipts, Expenditures and Balances of the United States Government for the Fiscal Year Ending September 30.* Washington, DC: Government Printing Office.

U.S. Department of the Treasury. 1984-2000. *United States Annual Report. USDA Appendix. Fiscal Year Ending September 30.* Washington, DC: Treasury Department Financial Management Service.

U.S. House of Representatives. 1925-1929. *Agricultural Appropriation Bill. Hearings before the Subcommittee of the Committee on Appropriations.* Washington, DC: Government Printing Office.

U.S. House of Representatives. 1930-1941. *Agricultural Department Appropriation Bill. Hearings before the Subcommittee of the Committee on Appropriations.* Washington, DC: Government Printing Office.

U.S. House of Representatives. 1952 and 1954-1984. *Department of Agriculture Appropriations. Hearings before the Subcommittee of the Committee on Appropriations.* Washington, DC: Government Printing Office.

Van Halen, L. 1973. "A New Evolutionary Law." *Evolutionary Theory* 1:1-30.

Veeman, T., J. Unterschultz and B. Stewart. 2007. "Canadian and Prairie Agricultural Productivity: Measurement, Causes, and Policy Implications." Rural Economy, University of Alberta, Edmonton, Alberta, Canada. Presented at AES Conference *Food and Fuel: The Implications for Agricultural Research Policy,* Saskatoon, Saskatchewan, Canada.

Waggoner, P.E. 1976. "Research and Education in American Agriculture." *Agricultural History* 50(1):230-247.

Wallace, E. 1920. "Mathematical Inquiry into the Effect of Weather on Corn Yield in the Eight Corn Belt States." *Monthly Weather Review* 48(8):439-446.

Wallace, H.A. and W.L. Brown. 1988. *Corn and Its Early Fathers.* Revised edition. Ames: Iowa State University Press.

Wells, O.V. 1937. "The Depression of 1873-79." *Journal of Farm Economics* 19(2):621-633.

Wetherill, C.M. 1862. *Chemical Analysis of Grapes.* USDA Report. Washington, DC: Government Printing Office.

White, F.C. and J. Havlicek, Jr. 1982. "Optimal Expenditures for Agricultural Research and Extension: Implications of Underfunding." *American Journal of Agricultural Economics* 64(1):47-55.

Wilcox, W.W. 1947. *The Farmer in the Second World War.* Ames: Iowa State College Press.

Wooldridge, J.M. 2002. *Econometric Analysis of Cross Section and Panel Data.* Cambridge: MIT Press.

World Bank. 2007. *World Development Indicators 2007 CD-ROM, First edition.* Washington, DC: World Bank.

World Bank. 2008. "International Comparison Program, 2005 edition." Washington, DC: World Bank. Obtained May 2008 from http://web.worldbank.org/WBSITE/EXTERNAL/DATASTATISTICS/ICPEXT/0,,menuPK:1973757~pagePK:62002243~piPK:62002387~theSitePK:270065,00.html.

World Bank. 2009. *Statistical Manual: Growth Rates.* Washington, DC: World Bank. Obtained January 2009 from http://web.worldbank.org/WBSITE/EXTERNAL/DATASTATISTICS/EXTDECSTAMAN/0,,contentMDK:20878490~isCURL:Y~menuPK:2648208~pagePK:64168445~piPK:64168309~theSitePK:2077967,00.html.

Wright, B.D. 1983. "The Economics of Invention Incentives: Patents, Prizes, and Research Contracts." *American Economic Review* 73(4):691-707.

Wright, B.D. and P.G. Pardey. 2006. "The Evolving Rights to Intellectual Property Protection in the Agricultural Biosciences." *International Journal for Technology and Globalization* 2(1/2):12-29.

Wright, B.D., P.G. Pardey, C. Nottenburg and B. Koo. 2007. "Agricultural Innovation: Economic Incentives and Institutions." Chapter in R.E. Evenson and P. Pingali, eds., *Handbook of Agricultural Economics: Volume 3.* Amsterdam: Elsevier.

Yee, J. and W.E. Huffman. 2001. "Rates of Return to Public Agricultural Research in the Presence of Research Spillovers." Paper presented at American Agricultural Economics Association annual meetings, Chicago.

Young, E. 2008. *The 2002 Farm Bill: Provisions and Economic Implications.* Washington, DC: United States Department of Agriculture, Economic Research Service. Obtained December 2008 from http://www.ers.usda.gov/Publications/AP/AP022/.

Zhao, S., K. Nossal, P. Kokic and L. Elliston. 2008. "Productivity Growth: Australian Broadacre and Dairy Industries." *Australian Commodities* 15(1):236-242.

Index

LaVergne, TN USA
18 December 2009

167405LV00002B/1/P

9 781441 906571